THE APPLAUSE ACTING SERIES

DUO!

THE BEST SCENES FOR THE 90'S
SCENES FOR TWO

Edited by John Horvath,
Lavonne Mueller
and
Jack Temchin

Introduction by Michael Howard

D0063304

APPLAUSE
NEW YORK • LONDON

Duo! The Best Scenes for the 90's
Scenes for Two
Edited by John Horvath, Lavonne Mueller, and Jack Temchin
Introduction by Michael Howard
Copyright © 1995 Applause Books

An extension of this copyright notice, together with CAUTION and performance rights information, will be found in the "Acknowledgements" section at the end of the book.

Library of Congress Cataloguing-in-Publication Data

Duo! : the best scenes for the 90's / edited by John Horvath and Lavonne Mueller

   p.   cm.
  ISBN 1-55783-030-4 : $12.95

  1. Acting. 2. Dialogues, English. 3. English drama--20th century. I. Horvath, John. II. Mueller, Lavonne.
PN2080.D86   1994
792'.028--dc20
          90-30113
          CIP

British Library Catalog in Publication Data
A Catalogue Record of this book is available from the British Library

Applause Books
211 West 71st Street
New York, NY 10023
Phone (212) 496-7511
Fax: (212) 721-2856
Front cover photos © Gerry Goodstein

406 Vale Road
Tonbridge Kent TN9 1XR
Phone 073 235-7755
Fax 073 207-7219

CONTENTS

MAN/WOMAN SCENES (Guide to Genre/Age Range)

SCENES FOR TWO WOMEN

SCENES FOR TWO MEN

✤ Introduction

●●●●●●●●●●●●●●●●●●●●●●●●●●●MICHAEL HOWARD

If you are standing in a book store searching for a scene that will perfectly suit you, wondering whether to buy this book — pause and consider. There is danger here.

If it is possible that you might be seduced into rehearsing a scene without reading the play, close this book and go directly to the play section. You will save yourself from an embarrassing confrontation. What if the auditioner or teacher likes the material but is unfamiliar with it, and begins to ask you about it? And worse, what if he or she *is* familiar with it and begins to question you because parts of the relationship or situation have been unrealized? Perhaps, as important, you will have deprived yourself of the pleasure and stimulation of the play.

But you knew that, of course. Once you have chosen your scene, you intended to read the play — and not just once, but two or three times. Excellent. Then march directly to the cash register and buy this book. You will find it is like a Mexican pinata — crack it open and all kinds of gifts and surprises pour out. New writers, new plays, contemporary situations, fresh voices, newly explored subjects. You will find somewhere in this volume a writer who speaks directly, intimately to you, who expresses your conflicts and dilemmas perfectly. The editors have done splendid work in putting together new writers first produced in the 1980's, along with more established writers and their new and lesser known work.

Given this smorgasbord, this lavish selection of appetizers, how do you choose? What should you be asking yourself, looking for, as you read through these scenes? Briefly then:

Choose something you like, about which you can say "oh *yes*, I *know* about that." Choose a scene that explores a subject close to you, by a writer who speaks in your rhythms — a scene that in some miraculous way is about a part of you and your life, even though the plot may differ. Do not doubt for a moment that such a scene exists, or even that you will be able to find two or three in this book. It is here. Look for it. For some of you, David Mamet will seem to speak in your personal tongue, and for others he will be speaking in a foreign language. Do not feel you "ought" to be able to understand and play every writer equally — no actor can. And do not choose a scene you think "they" will like. When you have found "your" scene, you will search out the play with anticipation and excitement. If, finally, you fall somewhat short of this goal, the effort will have brought you closer to the potential for doing your best work.

Here are a few other things to consider as you search for a scene.

• Choose a scene in which your character drives and moves the scene.

• Choose a scene in which you could be cast. Do not do "Lear" if you are 25 years old. Even if you can do it magnificently, do not trust the imagination of the auditioner.

• Certainly choose a scene that you feel confident and capable of accomplishing. Notice I did not suggest one in which you will feel comfortable. Better a scene that makes your heart race a little, in which there is some danger — a chance of failing or of succeeding brilliantly. "He's OK", or "that was nice" are not the kinds of comments that will get you work. You must find material that challenges and stimulates you, that demands courage, that has the potential to take people by surprise.

Hopefully you have not just rushed into the bookstore because you have an audition tomorrow. If you are sensible, you are preparing one or perhaps two monologues and a scene, so that you will be ready before you get the call. Then all you will need to a brush up.

Some thought on auditioning: If you have chosen well, are connected to the material, and are well rehearsed, what you must do now is find a way to sent the message, "I'm glad to be here, I'm delighted that you want to see my work, I like to act, so just sit back and relax." This non-verbal message can best be sent when your preparation for the audition includes a way of putting yourself in a creative place, one that makes you want to act. For example, I know an actor who listens to music on his walkman while he is in the waiting room, because that particular music not only raises his spirits, but leads him into wanting to live in the imaginary reality. The auditioners have spent their day trying to stay concentrated, drinking lots of black coffee, and attempting to make nervous actors more relaxed. Imagine the impact when you come in, communicating in attitude and action the message "I'm fine, this is what I love to do."

Choose the best actor you can find to be your partner (and enjoy the fact that, for once, you are the casting director). A good actor will challenge you, will give you more, will force you to fight for your point of view — all of which will help you act better.

Finally, remember that clever business will not get you work. The auditioners are looking for the way in which the actor/character stands revealed.

I have been talking only about auditioning. In fact, some of you are looking for material for an acting class. (Are you still standing there in the book stalls wondering whether to buy this book?) Classes differ a great deal from each other and much depends upon the nature of the class and its specific emphasis. However . . .

• As in choosing audition material, after you choose the scene, read the entire play. Read it more than once. Read other plays by the same author. For the same reasons.

• Do not be concerned with type — not even gender. Your acting teacher is not a casting director, so use whatever will be useful to you. For example, if an actor is developing Shaw's Joan of Arc, she might find it extremely useful to work on the St. Crispins Day speech in Shakespeare's *Henry V.*

• Choose a scene that will challenge and stretch you and your acting teacher. (I confess, there are some scenes — I won't tell you which — that, when they are announced, a small, hopefully inaudible sigh escapes: "Oh dear," I think, "not again.") Happily, this book presents you with many possibilities that you will respond to, and which your teacher may not have seen.

In many ways this book was revelation for me. It has sent me to the book stores. It is exciting to see such good and various writing, so much of it unfamiliar, and all of it relatively recent.

Among other things, it bodes well for the 1990's.

✤ Editors' Note

●●●●●●●●JOHN HORVATH, LAVONNE MUELLER, JACK TEMCHIN

The scenes contained in this volume are presented exactly as written by the playwrights, with no internal deletions. Our introductions to each scene follow the headings "Characters" and "Setting"; the playwrights' stage directions are contained in parentheses. If any two-character scene is interrupted by a third character, some external business, or an event which would be difficult to reproduce in a classroom or audition situation, we have enclosed the section in brackets as a suggested cut.

We suggest that you always read and study the entire play before working on a particular scene. When trying to locate a play, check the "Source" listing at the conclusion of each scene. If there is no listing, the play was only available in manuscript form at the time this book was published. Many of the plays excerpted herein may soon be available in acting or trade editions, so check with your local bookstore or the major play publishers. If a play is not yet published, a copy of the manuscript may be available directly from the author or agent listed in the acknowledgement pages.

We would like to thank Bryna Wortman, Chris Ryan, Katherine Longtin, Tom Dobrocky, Ken Benson, Stephanie Sobel, Roy Seiler, Helene Davis and the staff of Applause Theatre Books for their help and support in assembling this volume.

Man-Woman Scenes

✢ American Notes

•••••••••••••••••••••••••••••••LEN JENKIN

CHARACTERS: FABER *(40's)*, PAULINE *(19)*
SETTING: *A motel office in the Midwest, the present.*

FABER, *a traveling salesman, can't sleep so he talks to* PAULINE, *a college student, who works in the motel office at night. This motel is one of many along the highway in middle America, and* FABER *and* PAULINE *are two lonely people with fears and dreams.*

FABER: Pauline, would you . . . could you sing me a song?
PAULINE *(Laughs)*:   I can't sing.
FABER: That's a lie, Pauline.
PAULINE: O.K. I *won't.* You wouldn't want to hear it, Mr. Faber, believe me.
FABER: You're wrong there, Pauline. I'd like it.
PAULINE: I don't know any songs.
FABER: You must know *one* song, Pauline, the one you learned in the third grade, where everybody stood in a row. Sing it, and I'll be sitting here much happier, I think.
PAULINE: I'm not responsible for your happiness, Mr. Faber.
FABER: Yes you are, Pauline, and I'm responsible for yours. *(A silence)*
PAULINE: We didn't stand in a row. We sat in a circle.
   (FABER *reaches over and turns off the radio.* PAULINE *sings, very quietly and simply)*
   Down in the valley, valley so low
   Late in the evening, hear the train blow
   Roses love sunshine, violets love dew
   Angels in heaven, know I love you
   Down in the meadow, down on my knees
   Praying to heaven, give my heart ease

Give my heart ease, love, give my heart ease
Praying to heaven, give my heart ease . . .
That's all I know.
(FABER *applauds solemnly*)
Are you making fun of me?

FABER: I am extremely serious here, Pauline.

PAULINE: Good, 'cause I'd like you to consider something, Mr. Faber. This conversation is not just your conversation with me. This is *our* conversation, Mr. Faber, and now it's your turn. Sing.

FABER: I can't sing, Pauline.

PAULINE: That's what I said, Mr. Faber.

(FABER , *with much hesitancy, begins to sing some romantic ballad — [Actor's choice] — poorly. He stops*)

FABER (*Sings much louder, and begins to bang on the chair in rhythm*):
Let's twist again, like we did last summer
Yeah, let's twist again, like we did last year
Do you remember when, we were really humming
C'mon, let's twist again, twisting time is here . . . *

PAULINE: Shhhh . . . You'll wake everybody up.

FABER: All the customers are wide awake, Pauline. One is upstairs walking the floor, and the other one is me. (FABER *stands, and twists, along with very loud singing*)
Round and round and up and down we goooooo again
Baby let me know, you love me so, and then . . .
Let's twist again, like we . . .

PAULINE: STOP! (FABER *stops singing abruptly*)

FABER: What kind of lipstick is that you got on, Pauline? Flamingo pink? Tangerine blush?

PAULINE: I'm not wearing any lipstick.

FABER: What kind of perfume you wearing? Lily of the Valley? Tiger Musk? Orange Blossom Special?

PAULINE: I'm not wearing any perfume.

FABER: I smell something, Pauline.

PAULINE: Maybe it's my shampoo.

FABER: Answer me something, Pauline. What kind of shampoo?

PAULINE: Apple something . . . with keratin, whatever that is. Why are you interested in . . .

FABER: That's private stuff I'm asking about, Pauline. You buy it in the supermarket, but you rub it right on your body. Have a drink. (*Takes out bottle*)

PAULINE: I think I've had enough.

FABER: The last one . . .

(PAULINE *still refuses.* FABER *refills his own. The bottle is empty*)
We got a dead soldier here. (*He drops the bottle in the trash*)

PAULINE: You know, Mr. Faber, I've been thinking about what you said, about me sort of . . . doing more. Maybe moving away to a bigger place or something. I mean, if my Mom is . . .

FABER: Don't blame me, Pauline.

PAULINE: Blame you?

FABER: One day ten years from now you're lying face down on a cot in some furnished room, crying into your pillow — and you remember. It was me told you to leave the bosom of your home and family. You hurry down to Woolworth's and buy one of those fat black magic markers and you go out to the graveyard and write insulting remarks all over my lilywhite headstone.

PAULINE: That's an ugly story. And it's a lie. You won't be dead in ten years, and I won't be in a room somewhere, crying.

FABER: You know the future, Pauline? Should hang a sign on your desk, LIFE READING, TEN BUCKS. You got gypsy blood?

PAULINE: I don't know. May be.

FABER: Maybe you do. (*Silence*) You know, Pauline, I am convinced that for miles around, at this moment, we are the only creatures with their eyes open. The little raccoons and squirrels and stuff in the woods, they're all sleeping, and the people too, all snug in their beds, whole sky over the town is thick with dreams . . .

PAULINE (*Looks at her watch*): Mr. Mason opens the Snack Shop by the Trailways stop by six, so he's probably up now. And Dexter. He drew the graveyard shift this month, so he's . . .

FABER: Pauline? I'd like to mention something here. It doesn't matter who the fuck is actually awake, or asleep, or dead, I'm talking about a feeling.

PAULINE: I'm talking about the facts.

FABER: You getting a little sarcastic here, Pauline?

PAULINE: Yes. You've been confusing me, Mr. Faber. And scaring me . . . a little.

FABER: I don't want to do that. I didn't mean to do that. (*A silence*) We're a bunch of poor bastards here, Pauline. Roam the planet like starving dogs, and never get it right. Find any little scrap of something in this world and it's thank God and step careful, cause you're likely to lose that too. You spend a lot of nights talking to the itinerant sleepers, Pauline. The sleepwalkers. Whatta they have to say on the subject?

PAULINE: You're the only one who ever . . .

FABER: Maybe you don't hear them cause your pretty head falls over and you sleep at the desk, and all the storytellers can't bear to wake you, so they keep it to themselves and tiptoe by.

PAULINE: I don't think so, Mr. Faber. Sometimes I do get sleepy, but I always wake myself, 'cause what if a car pulls in, and I'm sleeping with my head on the desk, like this. (*Does so*) How does that look, to someone coming in, I mean?

FABER: I don't know. Looks all right to me.

PAULINE (*Sitting up*): It does not. I do all kinds of things to keep awake. Homework, the radio . . . You know, sometimes I just think about what might happen to me . . . if I'll ever get married, or even finish college and find some kind of interesting job. I think about my Mom, and start feeling sad for her and all. Then sometimes I go outside and sit in one of those lawn chairs in front of the office and just wait for it to get light. It happens real slow, so you have to slow yourself down to it or you get bored, cause it takes a few hours. When the first edge of the sun is up, I go back inside and make coffee. It can get real cold out there. Once I did that in the snow. I just kept shaking it off me, and walking around to get warm. I couldn't really tell when the sun came up. The snow was dirty gray in the dark and became white. The sky just got lighter and lighter — till it was light.

Source: Dramatists Play Service, Inc.

✤ Apocalyptic Butterflies

•••••••••••••••••••••••••••••WENDY MACLEOD

CHARACTERS: HANK *(20's-30's)*, TRUDI *(20's-30's)*
SETTING: *Fryeburg, Maine, the present.*

HANK, *a shoe salesman, and his wife, Muriel, have a tempestuous relationship. Muriel is disgusted with* HANK's *insensitivity.* HANK *is frustrated my Muriel's fastidiousness around the house and by her inability to make love since their baby's birth seven months ago.* HANK *has stormed out of the house to meet* TRUDI, *a pretty, free-spirited woman he has been seeing on the side. As this scene begins, they have just finished making love in a cheap motel room.*

TRUDI: Hank? That reality thing is happening again.
HANK: Aren't you sleepy?
TRUDI: Women don't go to sleep right after. It's different for women. It gets them stirred up.
HANK: Didn't you come?
TRUDI: That's not the issue, Hank. Trust me. The issue is I'm in bed with a man doesn't love me. How am I supposed to feel about that?
HANK: How do you know I don't love you?
TRUDI: I felt it when you kissed me.
HANK: I kissed you wrong.
TRUDI: When a man loves me he kisses me so tender I feel like crying.
HANK: I was too rough. I was too rough with you.
TRUDI: Sometimes when a man loves you he can be rough. It's like he can't forgive your body for being separate from his so he bashes up against you like the collision could help the situation. But what I can't figure out is why some men adore you and others can take you or leave you. Or take you and leave you.
HANK: Or how somebody can love you and then stop loving you.
TRUDI: She ain't stopped loving you, Hank. It just got buried. She probably don't feel nothing for nobody right now. When a person's unhappy their heart goes dead.
HANK: She loves that baby.
TRUDI: Sure she loves the baby, a baby that young doesn't count as

another person. It's like taking care of your arm, it's instinct. It's instinctual.

HANK: You have beautiful breasts.

TRUDI: Yeah.

HANK: You have beautiful skin.

TRUDI: Yeah.

HANK: Soft.

TRUDI: Yeah.

HANK: These are compliments. You're not supposed to say yeah to your own compliments.

TRUDI: Guys have said that stuff to me before so I'm used to it. Always they're talking about how soft my skin is so I figure it's true.

HANK: I love your teeth.

TRUDI: Come on.

HANK: I do.

TRUDI: They're crooked. I adopted a melancholy attitude to get out of smiling.

HANK: They make me want to run my tongue over them.

TRUDI: Yeah?

HANK: Anyone ever tell you that before?

TRUDI: No.

HANK: When I see your teeth suddenly I want to get bitten. I want you to bite me.

TRUDI: Bite you where?

HANK: On my ear.

   (TRUDI *suddenly sits up*)

TRUDI: Hank. It's that reality thing. For a second you were my highschool boyfriend. You were Scotty and I was 16 and you loved me. Scotty loved me. He stole money from the cash register at Gifford's ice cream parlor to buy me diamond earrings. He was a criminal for me, that's how much he loved me.

HANK: I wish I'd known you when you were 16.

TRUDI: I wish I was 16.

HANK: No you don't.

TRUDI: I do. I do.

HANK: What happened to Scotty?

TRUDI: I broke up with him. I broke up with him for another guy. Then I broke up with that guy for another guy and each time I thought I was getting closer to something I wanted but I was getting farther and farther away. Scotty wanted me to marry him but I said no way even though I was pregnant and could have used the assistance. I had an abortion and after that I associated him with feeling so scared and doing something so bad.

HANK: You didn't do anything wrong, Trudi.

TRUDI: I did everything wrong. I did everything so wrong I got nobody to talk to but some stranger.

HANK: I'm not some stranger.

TRUDI: No?

HANK: No. I'm not a stranger and I'm not going anyplace. I'm gonna watch over you while you sleep. I'll be like an angel. Like your guardian angel.

TRUDI: Why don't she love you, Hank? If you were mine I'd love you.

HANK: She used to love me. But then something happened.

TRUDI: What happened? What?

HANK: She overheard me tell this joke. It was down at the shoe outlet. She said it was a woman-hating joke and when the guys laughed it was evil man laughter. She said a man who loved a woman couldn't tell a joke like that. She said my love for her should carry over into my life with men.

TRUDI: What was the joke?

HANK: I don't want to tell you, it's not funny no more. It was a dirty joke, you know. There's been other stuff too. Like she's tired all the time with the baby and wants me to clean the house.

TRUDI: Do you?

HANK: I been meaning to, but like I don't know which stuff you use where. Like whether to use Top Job, Ajax, whatever. I used Lysol on the tub. She said that was incorrect so the hell with her.

TRUDI: Yeah, a tub needs an abrasive like Comet or Ajax, like that.

HANK: See? I don't know that stuff.

TRUDI: You could learn that stuff.

HANK: Look at it from my perspective. I work 40 to 50 hours a week at the outlet. I'm doing my part.

TRUDI: But she doesn't feel you're doing your part.

HANK: No.

TRUDI: So you gotta respect her perspective.

HANK: What about my perspective? I gotta perspective too. Nobody respects my perspective.

TRUDI: Give and take, you know.

HANK: When a woman says give and take, she means give and give and give some more. I know. I've heard that give and take stuff.

TRUDI: What about your sex life?

HANK: I can't discuss my sex life with you.

TRUDI: Why not? I'm part of it.

HANK: She says the doctor says no sex for 8 weeks after the baby's born. You believe that?

TRUDI: Sure I do. But if you're wondering about it, call the doctor. Say Muriel couldn't remember exactly what he said.

HANK: I can't do that. Let's say she's telling the truth.

TRUDI: Okay.

HANK: And the doctor said that to her.

TRUDI: Okay.

HANK: I think she's happy about it.

TRUDI: Oh.

Source: Dramatists Play Service, Inc.

✤ Away

•••••••••••••••••••••••••••••••MICHAEL GOW

CHARACTERS: MEG *(20's)*, TOM *(20's)*
SETTING: *Backstage of a theatre. England, 1967.*

MEG *and* TOM *have just been in a performance of* A Midsummer Night's Dream. *It is Christmas 1967 and time for* MEG *and* TOM *to go off for a holiday. Both* MEG *and* TOM *feel a nostalgic sadness about leaving the play.*

TOM: You going away tomorrow?
MEG: We're leaving really early.
TOM: Well . . . have a good time.
MEG: Where are you going?
TOM: Up the coast. Some beach.
MEG: Have a good time.
TOM: Bound to.
MEG: See you.
TOM: Yeah . . . see you in pictures.
MEG: You too.
TOM: No thanks.
MEG: You were really good in the play.
TOM: Bull.
MEG: You were!
TOM: Cut it out. I'll get a fat head.
MEG: My olds are waiting.
TOM: Anyway, I got this for you. As a memento of the play.
MEG: Thanks.
TOM: It was a real laugh being in the play with you.
MEG: No-o . . .
TOM: It was! So I got you something as a token of my appreciation.
MEG: What is it?
TOM: If you open it up you might find out. It's a piece of junk, actually. Actually I nicked it. But it's the thought that counts.
MEG: You nicked it?
TOM: Actually, I got a night job and slogged me guts out for ten years to pay for it.
MEG: A brooch.
TOM: A mere bauble.
MEG: It's really nice. That's really nice of you.

TOM: Oh, stop before you start sobbing.

MEG: I really like it.

TOM: It's from the bottom of my heart, actually.

MEG: I wish I'd got you something

TOM: I have some beautiful memories.

MEG: Oh, yuck.

TOM: Sick, eh?

MEG: It was good fun, though. Pity it was only for one night. Fancy doing it night after night like in America. Plays go on for years there. London too. Wouldn't you get sick of it?

TOM: Depends who else was in it. Be great if you hated everyone's guts.

MEG: But then it'd only be the same as a proper job.

TOM: What are you going to be when you grow up?

MEG: An engine driver. You?

TOM: I'll wait and see.

MEG: I'd better be going. Thanks for the brooch.

TOM: It matches your eyes.

MEG: Yellow?

TOM: Joke.

MEG: Ha ha.

TOM: Sorry.

MEG: Well . . .

TOM: The olds.

MEG: Have a good Christmas.

TOM: Don't go yet.

MEG: Why?

TOM: This is fun.

MEG: What is?

TOM: Trying to think of things to say.

MEG: We haven't done the weather yet.

TOM: Do you really like the brooch?

MEG: Yep.

TOM: Good.

MEG: I really like it.

TOM: It was either jewelry or perfume. But it's hard to buy perfume for someone you don't know very well. You need to know their personal chemical make up. I could have got something on spec and it mightn't have worked on you and you'd have to put it on and stunk like a dead dog. You wouldn't have been able to wash it off, either. You have to wait till something like that fades. You wouldn't be so nice about me in the play then, eh? My name'd

be mud. That's why I went for jewelry. Safer. Better bet. Actually
I asked around a few places. Got a bit of advice. Shop girls and
that.

MEG: And they said jewelry?

TOM: Most of them. They said I should opt for the jewelry. A few
suggested some perfume. Very subtle stuff. Couldn't actually
smell it. One of them tried some on and I was halfway down her
neck before any smell registered. Pointless.

MEG: Well . . . I still wish I'd got you something.

TOM: Bottle of gin would've been nice.

MEG: Oh.

TOM: Or a Harley Davidson.

MEG: Is he a poet?

TOM: It's a bike.

MEG: I knew that.

TOM: Poet! Why would I want a poet?

MEG: Maybe you read poetry.

TOM: Me? Come one! Me?

MEG: You might. You're pretty . . .

TOM: Deep?

MEG: You're pretty quiet.

TOM: Soulful?

MEG: Still waters run deep. My father's always saying that.

TOM: Still waters stink.

Source: Currency Press

✣ Beirut

•••••••••••••••••••••••••••••••••ALAN BOWNE

CHARACTERS: TORCH *(male, 20's)*, BLUE *(female, 20's)*
SETTING: *A shabby basement apartment in an abandoned building on the Lower East Side of Manhattan, the near future.*

TORCH *has tested positive for the AIDS virus and has been quarantined with other "positives" in the Lower East Side, which is patrolled by guards and fenced off from the rest of the city.* TORCH *has been tattooed with a decal proclaiming his status as a "positive."* BLUE *is in love with him and sneaks past the guards to visit him. To escape detection, she has had a false decal pasted to her body so that she will appear to be a "positive," too.*

TORCH: What if you die from it, Blue? And I gotta live with that?

BLUE: Come over here.

TORCH: Answer me!

BLUE: Come over here and I'll tell you.

TORCH: Tell me from there! I wanna hear this. How I. Can sit here. And watch those nice little tits of yours? Shrivel up like raisins. Sit here and watch you lose like 50 pounds in 24 hours. While your *head!* Puffs up! To twice its size! And that *I* done it to you. This I wanna hear.

(Beat)

BLUE: You want pizza? You got pizza. With this decal I can sneak out and sneak in. You want stickball? You got it. Wanna get drunk? Wanna nice t-shirt? It's all yours. And if one of us starts to die? Then a light meal, a glass of wine, and four grams of seconal.

(Beat, as he stares at her)

BLUE: Two grams apiece. We could go to sleep in each other's arms. Naked. So the guard should get off on it.

TORCH *(Staring)*: You gonna get serious? Or what?

(BLUE stretches out and smiles)

BLUE: I *am* serious. You really like my tits? I never thought you did. My ass maybe, but —

TORCH: I could really see this. Oh sure. You and me playin house in here. On Sundays we take a little stroll inna park. You seen Tomkins Square lately? It's where they pile the bodies. And burn 'em on Sundays. We could walk around, sniffin the fresh air. We could watch the people who can't control themselves? Squattin in the gutters wit' the shit runnin outa them like rusty tap water. Or! We could go to the laundromat on Avenue A? And watch people tryin to unglue the t-shirts from their sores to wash 'em. And then! Come back home and *fuck*! Wit' two water glasses and a killer dose of reds in this little *altar* next to the bed! (*Nods madly*) It's the American Dream!

BLUE: I usta think that too.

TORCH: *Think what*?

BLUE: That life was over here, and death was way over there. That they don't mix. But *now*? They're joined at the hip.

TORCH: What we need here! Is some adult maturity!

BLUE: It's a lovely thing you're feelin for me. How you don't wanna infect me and all? But stick it up your ass, *all right*?

TORCH: I ain't lissenin no more!

BLUE: Because I got two choices. First, I can live without risk and feel dead. Or second? I can risk death and feel alive. *I would not be the bitch that fell for a prick like you if I would choose the first*!

TORCH: *I never liked your tits*! Very seldom. Do you find a decent pair of tits.

BLUE: Yeah? Well, *testicles*? Are a turn-off!

TORCH: Either they got cow udders or pimples!

BLUE: And I bet that *you*! Got the kinna testes that flap against a girl's ass when you fuck her! Whap! Whap! Whap!

TORCH: Tits that are nice and firm and just the right size — ?

BLUE: It drives you crazy! Cold wet dog balls beatin time on your ass —

TORCH: *Suicide*! Is a sin! It's anti-nature. Un-Italian! And non-American!

(*He crosses to sink, grips it, not looking at her. During following, she rises from mattress and approaches him; finally, she begins caressing his back*)

BLUE: You had a choice about gettin this disease? Or you had *one* word to say about *one* thing that has happened to you in your whole life, including you got born? No. It was always other people or god or some shit that made your choices. You ain't owned *one* minute of your life, Torch. But that moment you die? You can choose it. You can choose when, you can choose how. You *own* it, Torch. You don't wanna give me a baby? O.K. Then give me that moment. That moment when we die. It will belong to us, Torch, and to nobody else.

(*Beat, as he feels her body on his back. He breaks away, crossing to radio*)

TORCH: You wanna lissen to some music? (*Twirls dial*) Popular? Classical? Jazz?

BLUE: All I'm sayin, is it don't have to be a sin!

TORCH (*Abandoning radio*):   You end up in hell!

BLUE: Oh my god! (*Looking about in mock-terror at sleazy room*) How will we *handle* it?

TORCH: Shut up! (*Grab sheet, covers himself with it*) And go home. (*Huddles on bed under sheet*)

BLUE (*Sitting on mattress*):   So. That's settled. I'm gonna get curtains for in here. And as for that guard? I know what to do about *him*. Got the idea from this TV program they showed the other night, NBC, coast to coast, about plagues like in Europe hundreds of years ago? This was supposed to make us. Feel *better*? I dunno. Anyway, they told how the people who got the Black Death? A more Christian disease than what we got now, I mean you died in a matter of mere days. How these people who caught it got very pissed off about the ones who didn't catch it. So the sick ones would sit by their front windows until well persons passed by on the street? And then suddenly reach out! Grab them! And *breathe* into their faces! People. Never. Change. (*Beat; chuckling*) So that's what I'll do to that guard. When he's good and hot, I'll ask him to come closer. And then *breathe* on him!

TORCH (*Under sheet*):   This thing here is not airborne! It's a fluid transmission only!

BLUE: Thank you, doctor. *So I'll spit on him!* We can always scare him off, scare him so bad he'll stop bothering us. There's power in being sick, Torch.

(*Beat*)

TORCH: Blue?

BLUE: Yeah?

TORCH: I got a hard-on.

(*Beat*)

BLUE: Me too.

TORCH: But the thing is, you can't have it.

BLUE: Come out from under there. I want you to look. In the candlelight? There's these little specks floatin in the air. Little animals just waiting. To kill off the things that get weak. They float and turn and dance in the light. Come on. Look.

TORCH (*Still under sheet*):   No.

BLUE: O.K., so here comes a microbe!

(*She gets under sheet with him; we see only their forms under it, rolling about*)

TORCH: Stop it!

BLUE: I'm a germ! I'm gonna kill you!

TORCH: You can't *do* this!

BLUE: Call out the National Guard!

TORCH: You gonna haveta do this, Blue, all by yourself. (*Big, emphatic*) It ain't. My. *Responsibility*!

(*Beat, as their forms freeze beneath sheet*)

BLUE: You dickless dink. Of a cop-out.

TORCH: Huh?

(BLUE *whips away the sheet and stands up over him, enraged*)

BLUE: I bet you been tellin that to girls. *Your whole life*!

TORCH (*Sitting up*):   The fuck is that suppose to mean?

BLUE: Men? Are *pussies*!

TORCH: Who?

BLUE: Always like — (*Sarcastic macho mimicry*) She *begged* me for it! Wadn't *my* fault if she got hurt! The stupid cooz!

(TORCH *grabs her and pulls her down onto mattress; rolls her onto her back; into her face:*)

TORCH: Hey. Bitch! You wanna get lucky, or what???

BLUE (*Struggling beneath him*):   I can just see you! If I come down with this? You gonna be crawlin around here goin. It wadn't *me*. *She* asked for it. I was just this. Innocent bystander!

TORCH: Jesus, I never met such a fuckhead! So we won't do it! So get outa here!

(*She flips him over; into his face:*)

BLUE: You say it.

TORCH: Say what?

BLUE: That you wanna be *inside* me! (*Beat*) That what you feel, I gotta feel. That what I gotta face, you gotta face.

(*Beat*)

TORCH: You are some kinna fazool. Some kinna magazine. Like *Modern Romance*, like *Teenage Love*, like — How'd I ever fall in love wit' you? In the middle! Of a disease???

BLUE: Piss on this love you got! I don't want excuses here, Torch.

TORCH: So what *do* you want?

BLUE: I want you to climb inside me. And never leave.

(*Beat*)

TORCH: I get it. You want my soul, right?

BLUE: That's right.

TORCH: Typical bitch.

BLUE: That's right.

TORCH: Eight inches of dick ain't enough for you, hey?

BLUE: (*Contemptuously*) *What* eight inches?

TORCH: Give or take a centimeter!

BLUE: Good-bye. (*She angrily rummages in debris for her dress*)

TORCH: Fuckin how can this be? You love somebody and don't wanna give 'em a disease? And that makes you this. *Sonofabitch*?

BLUE (*Pulling dress over her head*):   Pre-plague? You woulda said, Hey you! Wit' the face! You gettin all hung-up and hurt here? So it's your *own* fuckin fault, you chee-chee[1]!

TORCH: It's not the same!

BLUE (*Smoothing dress; grabbing up purse; rummaging in it*):   It's the same.

TORCH: Bitches in a plague? Are sows in shit!

BLUE (*Throwing packs of cigarettes at him*):   Here's some extra cigarettes. (*Again rummages in purse*) And somewhere. In here. I brung you a Mars bar.

TORCH: Under your thumb, that's where you want us. In a fuckin cage which only you got the key! Well, lemme tell you, wit' a guy? It's different! He wants a good time, a nice fuck, a few laughs, and then. He wants. To go out. *And play some pool*!
(*Beat, as she pauses, looking at him*)

BLUE: What. Are you talking about?

TORCH: We'd be trapped here! Lookin for spots on each other alla time. I can't live inside of you, Blue, in some kinna romantic magazine. Even if I forget and drink outa the same glass as you? Much less fuck you? I would hate myself.

BLUE: Guys always do.

TORCH: Do *what*?

BLUE: Hate themselves after fucking. You guys can have this 4th of July experience up a woman's vage and still feel like total shit afterwards. Why is that?

TORCH: You keep changin! The subject!

BLUE: The subject! Is you got no *balls*!

TORCH: Fuckin *what*? I don't wanna *murder* you! Is that O.K.?

BLUE: No, I won't eat that.

TORCH: It's the truth!

BLUE: I gotta go.

TORCH: What, I'm some kinna limp! wimp! Cause I don't wanna fill you fulla parvoviroids[2]?

BLUE: *Shit on this virus mumbo*! What you don't want. Is *me*. A human being on your hands who might feel pain. Or make a demand. Or need you in her guts when there's nothing left. (*Beat*)

TORCH: That! Is totally. And complete. *Bullshit!*

BLUE: Torch, I didn't risk my life to come here for a *visit!* I came to live with you, maybe even to die with you. I didn't know what I'd find. Would your skin be smooth and white, like before, or would you be covered with sores? I didn't know. And I didn't care. (*Beat*)

TORCH (*Pleading*): Blue —

BLUE: I know. It's like I said. (*Turns to ascend stairs to entrance door*) You're a pussy.

TORCH (*Springing to his feet*): You eat that!

BLUE: Die alone.

(*He crosses quickly and grabs her. A significant beat as he looks into her face, makes his decision, then flings her back onto mattress*)

TORCH: All right. Take off your dress.

BLUE: You take it off.

(*He rips the dress from her body and grabs her between the legs*)

TORCH: You talk pretty hot for such a dry hole!

BLUE: You man enough to get it wet?

TORCH: Maybe I don't *care* if it's wet.

BLUE: Hey! Use the *palm* of your hand! What am I, a video game?

TORCH: Oh, so *now* you're gonna tell me how to give satisfaction!

BLUE: You gotta tell men everything!

TORCH: There ain't gonna be no love in this, Blue!

BLUE: *Love?* You hide behind it, anyway.

TORCH: I'm a loaded gun, Blue!

BLUE: So shoot me!

TORCH: I got poison fangs, Blue!

BLUE: So bite me!

TORCH: There's *death* in this, Blue!

(*Beat, as they stare into each other's eyes. She grasps him by the back of the neck and draws him down to her for a long, deep kiss. They begin making love as the lights dim. Curtain*)

Source: Broadway Play Publishing, Inc.

---

[1]Slang for cheap girl.
[2]Pronounced as written.

✤ A Betrothal

••••••••••••••••••••••••••••LANFORD WILSON

CHARACTERS: WASSERMAN (*50's-60's*), JOSLYN (*40's-50's*)
SETTING: *The corner of a large tent at a flower show.*

Two lonely, asocial flower breeders meet at a flower show where they each have entered their prize creations. JOSLYN *is bitterly indignant because her "Little Soldier" has been neglected by the judges.* WASSERMAN *is dejected because his "Tanya" has also been passed over. As they seek shelter from the rain and the hordes of flower enthusiasts, the mismatched couple begin to discover they have some things in common.*

WASSERMAN (*Looking at her with amazement*): I know you. How extraordinary. I don't know anyone. I've seen you.
JOSLYN: Sing me none of your seens.
WASSERMAN: You're a teacher.
JOSLYN: I beg your pardon, I am not.
WASSERMAN: You most certainly are.
JOSLYN: I am not, I know what I am.
WASSERMAN: You teach.
JOSLYN: I do not.
WASSERMAN: You did, you must have.
JOSLYN (*A beat*): I have my pursuits, thank you. What I do and what I've done are not for the ears of idle strangers.
WASSERMAN: Last year you taught!
JOSLYN: I did not!
WASSERMAN: You came to the gate!
JOSLYN: I came to no gate of yours, you can be sure. I peer through no gates, thank you.
WASSERMAN: You came just inside, and there you stood. Looking just as you do now.
JOSLYN: I did not. I come in gates only when I'm invited in, and I'm invited in only where I ask to be and I did not ask, thank you.
WASSERMAN: You came to Castle Crampton. I saw you at the gate. Believe me, I certainly didn't intend to see you, I don't see any of them, they sometimes see me, it can't be helped, they ask their questions, they talk on and on, some of them, it's all very . . . and the children pour in on their field trips, the musicians, you know

they have hundreds of them for the chamber orchestras, the quartets, and they're so talky, I'm afraid. You were a chaperone to one of the children's classes.

JOSLYN: I beg your pardon, I have no class.

WASSERMAN: And in they poured and there you stood. Just inside the gate.

JOSLYN: In the line of one's employment one is sometimes called upon, quite against one's will, to fulfill the place of those who are irresponsible enough to become ill.

WASSERMAN: I would never insist, of course, you know where you did and didn't go. I must say I don't at all feel comfortable around children. They don't seem to watch where they're going, they tend to step on me. But if you're the principal and went along in place of one of the . . .

JOSLYN: I am certainly not a principal.

WASSERMAN: Or an assistant principal with the duty of replacing some . . .

JOSLYN: I am certainly no assistant principal.

WASSERMAN: Or the librarian and were asked to fill in for . . .

JOSLYN: I am not a librarian for any of your . . .

WASSERMAN: Or the assistant librarian.

JOSLYN: I have my pursuits. You, of course, might be interested in the likes of Castle Crampton Gardens, I assure you I would not be.

WASSERMAN: Oh, my goodness, no.

JOSLYN: I disdained to step one foot into such a place. One look was all I needed to understand the whole of Castle Crampton completely. Tacky little bedded-out beds, looking as though they belonged in front of a gas station.

WASSERMAN (*Loving it*): Oh, my goodness!

JOSLYN: Municipal gardening, indeed. Worse here than abroad if you can believe it, and Crampton worst of all.

WASSERMAN: Oh, yes!

JOSLYN: I know the philosophy. Rows of wax begonias, never was a plant so aptly named. Your cup of tea, well, you can have it. No doubt little Tanya would blend in well . . .

WASSERMAN: Oh, dear, no. I'm afraid even Tanya couldn't save the place.

JOSLYN: All your geometrical beds, squares and circles and triangles. Yellow marigolds, surrounded by a cunning little ring of blue *Ageratum houstonianum*, surrounded by a nice contrasting lipstick red of, maybe, *Salvia splendens* "Harbinger." "Castle Crampton" spelled out in petunias and lobelia. They might as well use spray paint. A Spanish castle, a Venetian court, a ballroom lawn, no doubt, with German statuary.

WASSERMAN: Yes, yes, yes . . . all of it.

JOSLYN: Tulips by the hundreds, I'm sure, in the spring.

WASSERMAN: By the thousands! I plant them, they buy them by the truckloads, ripped out the day they're shot and replaced by marigolds, not even stock.

JOSLYN: You plant them? You? Not just an innocent tourist, but responsible for that mess?

WASSERMAN: Oh, Lord no, responsible, never, I wouldn't presume. I wouldn't made a decision myself, what if someone saw it? Oh, I'm terribly sorry, I know you and you don't know me, what am I thinking . . . I'm not in the habit of meeting . . . allow me to introduce . . . uh, Ms. J. H. Joslyn, this is Mr. Kermit Wasserman; Mr. Wasserman, Ms. Joslyn. How do you do? It is my misfortune to be one of the assistant gardeners at Crampton.

JOSLYN: How do you do? I was just going.

WASSERMAN: Oh, my yes, I'm afraid you'd better, because if you're going to be wicked about Crampton, I couldn't tear myself away and I shouldn't hear it. My own garden, of course, very small, is a cottage, Englishy sort of thing, very modest, but enough for me and my iris. And yours?

JOSLYN: Sing me no yourses, my garden's my garden. Certainly not English cottage. I farm, I don't decorate. I breed. I grow eggplant and squash, kale and kohlrabi. And I breed intermediate iris for strength and substance. I'm none of your watercolorists.

WASSERMAN: You're not, by any chance, colorblind?

JOSLYN: I beg your pardon?

WASSERMAN: I'm terribly sorry, I don't know what came over me. It's just that one who has created such a lovely texture and, as you say, substance, and neglected so completely . . .

JOSLYN: Rolls right off my back. There's no reason for me to stay, what did I expect? I don't know how some people call themselves scientists.

WASSERMAN: Ms. Joslyn, I may be vain, I may have expected too much, but you cannot . . .

JOSLYN: How could you have overlooked so basic a thing as stalk?

WASSERMAN: I could say the same for you, you know, were I the sort who . . .

JOSLYN: The color may be striking but there's nothing under it!

WASSERMAN: You have created a castle without a flag!

JOSLYN: I care for more than flashy headgear, thank you!

WASSERMAN: And you might as well be breeding galoshes!

JOSLYN: I am a great breeder, sir!

WASSERMAN: And, madam, so am I!

JOSLYN: I've toiled in the fields, sir, for thirty years!

WASSERMAN: And so have I!

JOSLYN: And you've nothing to show for it.

WASSERMAN: No one wants your Little Soldier!

JOSLYN: No one needs your Tanya!

WASSERMAN: If my Tanya had the texture of your Little Soldier!

JOSLYN: If my Soldier had the color of Tanya . . . !

(*There is a dead pause. It extends. Their words hang in the air. They think for a moment. They consider, each with their own thoughts. They picture it. She sits*)

WASSERMAN (*Imagining it*): Oh, my . . .

JOSLYN: Hummm . . .

WASSERMAN: Oh, my, that would be something . . .

JOSLYN: Hummmmmm . . .

WASSERMAN: In four years . . . maybe five. Six at the outside . . . Can you see it?

JOSLYN (*Musing*): Just never mind, I see what I see . . .

WASSERMAN: I've never seen anything like it.

JOSLYN: There's never been anything like it.

WASSERMAN: Not to push, and I don't think it's vanity, but Best of Show would be in the bag.

JOSLYN: In a jerkwater show like this? I wouldn't waste our time.

WASSERMAN: One might easily interest the nurseries in such a . . . uh . . .

JOSLYN: Oh, my good man, beating them away with our umbrellas.

WASSERMAN: The Sass Award is not at all out of the question.

JOSLYN: Sing me no Sass Awards, we're talking the cover of the Royal Horticultural Society's Garden Magazine.

WASSERMAN: Perhaps you had better be listed as breeder, I wouldn't be able to tolerate the limelight. Fame has always . . .

JOSLYN (*Musing*): Sing me no limelight, read me no fame; we're talking fortune.

WASSERMAN: Indeed. Not be crass, but . . . ?

JOSLYN: Thousands. Tens of thousands.

WASSERMAN: A better income, I would think, than assisting at a school library.

JOSLYN: Fuck the school library.

WASSERMAN: Indeed.

JOSLYN: Fuck Castle Crampton.

WASSERMAN: Oh, indeed.

(*A long pause, they dream. Then delicately turn to particulars. She clears her throat*)

JOSLYN (*Inquiring lightly*):   Ah . . . how are . . . her . . . uh . . . rhizomes?

WASSERMAN: Well, actually, now that you ask, very strong indeed, really quite remarkable.

JOSLYN: Are they?

WASSERMAN: And . . . uh . . . his?

JOSLYN: Well, uh . . . adequate certainly . . . uh . . . perhaps not absolutely . . . the . . . uh . . .

WASSERMAN: Only that?

JOSLYN: I've probably seen better increase.

WASSERMAN: Tanya increases like a weed.

JOSLYN: *Does* she? The little devil.

WASSERMAN: And, uh, his . . . seed pod?

JOSLYN: Oh, marvelous, of course, with all that upper strength. Unfailing.

WASSERMAN: I thought so. I must tell you, Tanya has been known to disappoint me there.

JOSLYN: Well, she's terribly delicate, it would be uncaring to expect . . .

WASSERMAN: I'm afraid, though, we'd much better have your Little Soldier as the seed parent.

JOSLYN: Absolutely. He won't mind playing the girl. Not for Little Tanya. Of the Golden Hair! I assume the bud-count, actually . . .?

WASSERMAN: Oh, yes, two. And she has been known to have two branches.

JOSLYN: Oh, I'm glad to hear it. That might make it much easier. Though we have to get some starch in her. Strengthen those limbs. Not stout — just strong. He'll do wonders for that.

WASSERMAN: And as for color, I'm glad to say, there, Tanya is very dominant.

JOSLYN: The little vixen! He's not very sure of himself there, I'm glad to say.

WASSERMAN: Oh, she'll take care of him nicely.

JOSLYN: My, my, my . . .

WASSERMAN: I must say . . .

JOSLYN: So convenient that you live so close.

WASSERMAN: Isn't it?

JOSLYN: Lovely Mahopac. (*Pause*) You understand, I think this should be exclusive. I don't want to see her red hair pussyfooting around with . . .

WASSERMAN: Madam! You overreach yourself. Tanya's fidelity, I assure you is irreproachable. You had much better be concerned about your Little Soldier.

JOSLYN: You have his word.

WASSERMAN: Well . . . one hears stories . . .

JOSLYN: Would you agree to begin with my seed bed? I make all my own soil, pure compost. A good grade of builders sand.

WASSERMAN: That's quite fine by me . . . You won't mind if I visit the site first, just to . . .

JOSLYN: Oh, by all means. I think we should begin first thing in the morning. I'll drive over to your place . . .

WASSERMAN: Oh, excellent, excellent . . . We can collect her lovely pollen at the crack of dawn . . .

JOSLYN: I have a divine set of sable brushes — never been touched. So exorbitant, but I couldn't help myself.

WASSERMAN: How impulsive!

JOSLYN: Oh, I know. I've been waiting for the right occasion . . . I knew it'd come.

WASSERMAN: Intuition . . . I don't expect to sleep a wink.

JOSLYN: Nor I.

WASSERMAN: Well. I must say. (*He gets up, walks a few steps, a new dignity*) They're all drifting back, the judging must be over. Ha! If they only knew.

JOSLYN: Look at them. Do you watch the presentation of the ribbons? And all their giggling little squeals when they win?

WASSERMAN: Not usually, I'm afraid. Crowds, you know, with nothing to look at . . . except people, of course . . . but perhaps this year . . . just to see how it's done. Just to get into practice.

JOSLYN: Might as well get in the habit of being notable. I must say, Mr. Wasserman, you're looking like a championship breeder.

WASSERMAN: And you, Ms. Joslyn.

JOSLYN: Ah! The sun's come out. And look whose golden hair is flashing in the light. She must be a hundred yards away.

WASSERMAN: She has reason to be excited tonight.

JOSLYN: I'm as nervous as a schoolgirl.

WASSERMAN: I think you're blushing.

JOSLYN: So are you.

WASSERMAN: Well, let us sit here, then, and wait for the onslaught of the unsuspecting crowd. (*They sit*)

JOSLYN: I must say it has been a very good show this year.

(*They open their programs and begin to study them*)

Source: *Best Short Plays 1987*, Applause Theatre Books

✥ Beyond Your Command

●●●●●●●●●●●●●●●●●●●●●●●●●●●●●●●●●RALPH PAPE

CHARACTERS: DANNY (17), DIANE (17)
SETTING: *The Johnson Home, South Plainfield, New Jersey, August 1963.*

Nick, a vacuum cleaner salesman, has taken on DANNY *as an assistant for the summer. They have come to the home of the Johnsons, a black family, to try to make a sale. The March on Washington is taking place and the television set is turned on. While Nick and Mrs. Johnson go off to inspect her old vacuum cleaner,* DIANE *, the Johnson daughter, arrives home from work. Knowing that her family cannot afford a new vacuum cleaner,* DIANE *is wary of* DANNY's *sales pitch.*

(DIANE *re-enters living room.* DANNY *is smiling at her*)
DANNY: We meet again.
(DIANE *just stares at him*)
So. Hot enough for you?
(DIANE *looks around the living room, at the equipment on the floor*)
Oh, by the way, my name is Danny.
DIANE (*Abruptly*):   Did my mother tell you that my father just went back to work after a three month layoff?
DANNY: No. She didn't.
DIANE: Would it *mean* anything to you if she had?
DANNY: Whoa, take it easy. What are you trying to say?
DIANE: I'm trying to say that I'd hate to see my mother spending money which we don't have on something we have absolutely no use for. *That's* what I'm trying to say.
DANNY (*Confidentially*):   Your mother made it *real* clear to us before that she doesn't need a new machine. O.K.?
DIANE: Then why are you trying to sell her one?
DANNY: Whoa, whoa! *He* does the selling, I just do the lugging. (*Beat*) Look, the only reason we're even here is that a Mrs. Baker over on, uh, Pine Street gave us your mother's name as a lead —
DIANE: *Alice* Baker? You mean that crazy Alice Baker sent you over here?!
DANNY (*Pleasantly*):   Well, I don't know if she's *crazy* or not. I never actually met the lady. (*Confidentially*) Anyway, just between us, I

told Nick he's only wasting his time here.

DIANE: You told him that, did you?

DANNY: That's right.

DIANE: I don't believe you.

DANNY: You don't?

DIANE: No, I don't. But unfortunately, my *mother* has this thing for trusting people. Sometimes, the *wrong kind* of people.
(DANNY *is crushed when he realizes she means him*)
I have to go to the store. Now, I *don't* want to come back here and discover that you and your friend have unloaded one of these *things* on my mother —

DANNY: Hey, wait a minute —

DIANE: Do you hear what I'm telling you? Yes or no?

DANNY: No. I mean — wait a minute, huh? He's *not* my friend, he's my old man's friend and I told you, I just work for the guy — and only for another week at that —

DIANE: Then what? You going into business for yourself?

DANNY: You got to be kidding! (*To himself*) God, how I hate this job! (*To her — he needs to know*) You mean . . . I *really* come across like that?

DIANE (*Starting to believe him*): Well . . .

DANNY: I'm starting college, all right? Wow! You really think *this* is what I want to do for a living?

DIANE: Well . . .

DANNY: Gimme a break, huh!
(*Beat*)

DIANE: Look . . . if I'm guilty of having made a false assumption about you —

DANNY: Yeah?

DIANE: — I apologize.

DANNY: Yeah, well . . . (*Beat*) Hey, that's cool. Forget it.
(*An awkward pause as they look at each other.* DIANE *shifts her attention to the TV. At some point, they sit down on the couch*)

DIANE: Did . . . uh . . . Bob Dylan come on yet?

DANNY: Who? Oh, you mean the folk singer? That new guy?

DIANE: Yes. Bob Dylan. The *poet*.

DANNY: I didn't see him. He's supposed to be at this thing, huh?

DIANE: In there somewhere, they say.

DANNY: Well, I'm sure I would've spotted him. I mean, with that nose and all.

DIANE: He's a poet. The size of his nose isn't important.

DANNY: If you say so.

DIANE:　You don't think he's a poet?

DANNY:　I don't know very much about poetry.

DIANE:　Well . . . I think he's quite good.

DANNY:　Hey, no offense, but really, I mean the guy can't sing, you know?

DIANE:　It's the words that count.

DANNY:　Yeah, the words are O.K., I guess. (*Beat*) I like Otis Redding.

DIANE:　He's very good.

DANNY:　Very good? Hey — he's *great*.

DIANE:　What are you, an authority?

DANNY:　I know what I feel. I trust my feelings.

DIANE:　Well . . . so does Bob Dylan.

DANNY:　Well — (*Flustered*) Well, good for him then — (*Another awkward pause*)

DIANE (*More friendly*):　Where are you gong to college?

DANNY:　Rutgers. I wanted to go out of state, but — hell, I actually applied to Yale.

DIANE:　You did?

DANNY:　I wasn't good enough. Big surprise.

DIANE:　Doesn't hurt to try.

DANNY:　I was hoping somebody up there'd make a mistake and I'd sort of slip in by accident.

DIANE:　Can that happen?

DANNY:　It was a long shot, I got to admit. (*Beat*) One good thing. At least I'll be out of that house. Living on the campus.

DIANE:　I wish *I* were going to be living away from home —

DANNY:　Believe me, boy, I know what you mean.

DIANE:　I'm going to be going right next door to you at Douglass. Only, we can't afford the rates for the dorms, so —

DANNY:　Really? No kidding? This semester?

DIANE:　Uh-huh.

DANNY:　Hey Diane, that's fantastic. (*Explains*) Uh . . . I overheard your mother say your name in there — (*Beat*) So — you excited?

DIANE:　Very much.

DANNY:　Yeah, I know. College, right?

DIANE:　Right.

DANNY:　What are you taking?

DIANE:　Political science.

DANNY:　I don't know what I'm going to take. Just a basic Liberal Arts background — check things out. (*Beat*) I don't know anybody who's ever been to college.

DIANE: Me either.

DANNY: So — does that make you nervous?

DIANE: No. Does it make *you* nervous?

DANNY: Well, the thing is . . . oh boy, even talking about this makes me nervous —

DIANE: That's O.K. I have to go now, anyway.

DANNY: The thing is, see, I'm not . . . um . . . all that . . . you know . . . smart.

DIANE: Yes, I know.

DANNY: You do?

DIANE: I'm teasing you, I'm teasing you.

DANNY (*Serious*): Yeah, well. I hope you'll pardon me for not laughing.

DIANE: I was just teasing you. *God.* (*She starts to leave, but Danny's words stop her*)

DANNY: Let me tell you something. There's certain things you shouldn't kid people about, and one of them is their IQ.

DIANE: What *is* your IQ?

DANNY: I'm serious. What I said.

DIANE (*Heading for front door*): I have to go now. (*Stops*) Please. I meant what I said before. I don't want to come back here and find out that my mother —

DANNY: I'll take care of everything. Don't worry. (DIANE *again heads for the door*) Guess we'll probably be bumping into each other from time to time —

DIANE (*Opening screen door*): Bye, now.

DANNY: Hey — uh, Diane?

DIANE: Now what?

DANNY: Just out of curiosity. Do you know what your IQ is?

DIANE: One hundred and thirty-five.

DANNY: That much?

DIANE: Oh, that's no so high. I mean, it *is* considered very good, but —

DANNY: Sure, sure. Rub it in.

(*Beat.* DIANE *just stares at him*)

DIANE: You are a very comical person,you know that ? (*She exits*)

Source: Dramatists Play Service, Inc.

✥ Big Time

•••••••••••••••••••••••••••••••KEITH REDDIN

CHARACTERS: PETER (20's-30's), FRAN (20's-30's)
SETTING: *New York City, the present.*

This play is a fugue for a group of upwardly-mobile young business exec-
utives who are trying to score points and make their mark. Paul, a financier,
is sleeping with FRAN, *an executive, who is sleeping with* PETER, *a photo-*
journalist. When Paul finds out about FRAN *and* PETER, *he proposes to*
FRAN, *who holds him off. While Paul is out of town on business,* FRAN *is*
spending time with PETER. PETER *is holding a magazine.*

PETER: These pictures.
FRAN: Yeah.
PETER: You see how these were cropped?
FRAN: Uh huh.
PETER: I did not do this.
FRAN: No?
PETER: That was not what I intended.
FRAN: What did you intend?
PETER: Not this. (*Hits magazine*)
FRAN: It looks okay.
PETER: Yeah, it look okay, but it's not what I wanted, if I wanted
   this, I would of taken the picture like this.
FRAN: But you didn't.
PETER: No. These people . . .
FRAN: Where?
PETER: The people at *People.*
FRAN: The magazine *People.*
PETER: These guys . . .
FRAN: The *People* people . . .
PETER: Fran, I'm explaining something here . . .
FRAN: Sure.
PETER: It pisses me off.
FRAN: It looks fine.
PETER: They fuck around with my stuff, these fucking graphic
   people, what the fuck do they know . . .
FRAN: Peter, I do graphics, I know what I'm doing.

PETER: I'm not talking about you Fran.

FRAN: Then what are we talking about?

PETER: We're talking about other people . . . people who have no . . . no artistic sense, you know, these people, they see these pictures as something to fill up space, to offset copy, and . . . I mean, you crop something . . .

FRAN: Peter, I do this for a living, and it doesn't look like shit, I saw the picture before, I saw what you took, and I'm looking at the thing now, and it doesn't look that bad, believe me.

PETER: It doesn't.

FRAN: No.

PETER: That is your opinion.

FRAN: Yes.

PETER: Well, fabulous. I've got your opinion on this.

FRAN: What the fuck is that supposed to mean?

PETER: What?

FRAN: That I've got your opinion, sarcastic thing.

PETER: I wasn't being sarcastic.

FRAN: No?

PETER: No, you gave me your opinion, and I . . .

FRAN: You think I don't know what I'm talking about?

PETER: No, Fran . . .

FRAN: You think I just look at pictures that you or somebody else takes, and I don't know anything? You think I like doing pastup, that layout is all I'm capable of . . .

PETER: No, why am I defending myself all of a sudden?

FRAN: The picture here, the one you're showing me, the one you took, it's a picture of Molly Ringwald at some fucking party.

PETER: I know.

FRAN: So my point is, who cares?

PETER: What?

FRAN: Who really cares if you take a great shot of Molly Ringwald eating shrimp salad?

PETER: It was a good picture, Fran, the point . . .

FRAN: Who cares?

PETER: I care.

FRAN: What happened to pictures of bodies lying in a ditch in Central America . . .

PETER: Fran, come on . . .

FRAN: No, there is a difference here . . .

PETER: Of course, I know this.

FRAN: So, where . . . I can't believe I am getting so upset about this . . .

PETER: I don't know why either.
FRAN: I just . . . I mean I know what a good picture is and what's shit, I do . . . but you say these things about, you know, what I do, my job, and you have this attitude . . . Jesus, I want to go out for a while.
PETER: Where do you want to go?
FRAN: I don't know.
PETER: Listen, let me get my coat.
FRAN: Let me go out for a while.
PETER: Okay.
FRAN: I just want to go out by myself for . . . you know?
PETER: Oh. Okay.
FRAN: I'm just . . . I'm sorry I got mad, I don't know what's . . .
PETER: Look . . .
FRAN: I'm . . .
PETER: I didn't mean anything about you, Fran.
FRAN: Let's drop it, okay?
PETER: Sure.
FRAN: It's just, you act like I don't know anything. You're just like everybody else.
PETER: Look, I wasn't talking about you.
FRAN: You're just like everybody else, like Paul and like Jeremy and sometimes I think it's very important for you to keep me in place . . . like you stay over there . . .
PETER: That's not . . . I was talking about a picture that I . . . it was a good picture.
FRAN: No, you can go here and here and here, and Paul goes here and here, but you, Fran, you have to stay there, you have to be there when I get back, you have to be where I left you, you should be there when I come through the door, don't you understand I don't like my job, I've said it enough times, I've said I'm bored and I'm wasting my time . . .
PETER: It's not a waste . . .
FRAN: I am wasting my time, and you don't even hear me, I am wasting my time Paul, I am . . .
PETER: I'm Peter, Fran.
FRAN: That's what I said.
PETER: No, you called me Paul.
    (*Pause*)
FRAN: No, I . . .
    (*Pause*)

PETER: Fran . . .

FRAN: I'm just gonna go . . .

PETER: Where are you going, Fran. Sit down. Take off your coat.

FRAN: No.

PETER: Take it off, sit down.

FRAN: No.

PETER: Fran, take it easy.

FRAN: No, I will not. No. You can take it easy. You should sit down. Sit down, Peter.

(*Peter sits*)

I don't want you to call me.

PETER: Okay.

FRAN: You call me, I'll hang up. I'll just hang up on you.

Source: Broadway Play Publishing, Inc.

✤ Borderline

●●●●●●●●●●●●●●●●●●●●●●●●●●●●●●●●JOHN BISHOP

CHARACTERS: CHARLES (30's), KAREN (30's)
SETTING: A large city, the present.

CHARLES is a marketing executive whose life has become a series of mean-
ingless, often violent encounters with the women in his life: his wife, his secretary, and KAREN, a very attractive colleague. The women swirl fluidly in
and out of scenes with CHARLES, blurring the borders of his life, and the set-
tings are left purposely vague, allowing for freedom in staging. Here,
CHARLES has a "meeting" with KAREN.

KAREN: Do another hit.
    (She hands CHARLES a spoon of cocaine. He snorts it)
CHARLES: This is why your mind is weird, right?
KAREN: Only on special occasions.
CHARLES: You mean like Tuesdays, Wednesdays, Thursdays . . .
KAREN: Like now.
CHARLES: You mean I'm a special occasion?
KAREN: We are.
CHARLES: Yeah. We are. (Beat) Put on something else.
KAREN: What?
CHARLES: Anything. Something else.
    (She crosses and mimes changing cassette on stereo)
    I love watchin' you walk. It is, actually, my hobby.
KAREN: Your hobby.
CHARLES: And it's my job. "Your job, should you choose to take it
    . . . " Hey, did he ever choose not to take one of those jobs?
KAREN: Who?
CHARLES: The guy. "Mission Impossible." "Your job, should you
    choose . . . No I choose not to, fuck it."
KAREN: Can I tell you something . . . serious.
CHARLES: Okay.
KAREN: You got some problems at work.
CHARLES: Babe, I got problems with work.
KAREN: McKee thinks you aren't doing enough on the brand.
CHARLES: Fuck him.
KAREN: Wrong.

CHARLES: Know something? You can only do certain jobs so good. You can't do them better, because there is no better. You got this thing . . . this product and you market it. You do it good, which is, on a scale of one to ten, as against a painting, say, well it's a two . . . maybe a two. A good painting being a ten. A hook shot from the key is an eight. But I can't paint and they don't pay me for hook shots. So I do my job good . . . and that's it. But it's only a two.

KAREN: See, there's another game goin' on. It's called "upper management comfort factor". They gotta think you're dedicated.

CHARLES: I am. I am committed to pursuing quality excellence.

KAREN (*Laughs*): You're dangerous.

CHARLES: You bring me up here to shape me up? That it? I was wonderin' why . . .

KAREN: Oh fuck off. I brought you here . . . no I didn't *bring* you here . . . I *asked* you here because I wanted to. 'Cause I think you're bright . . . and funny . . . and you're the best at marketing I've ever seen. I think you could, if you wanted to, go right to the top in this company.

CHARLES: Do you . . . also, think I'm sexy? That is, I warn you, a trick question.

KAREN (*Beat, then matter of factly*): Yeah, you're sexy.

CHARLES: So are you. (*Pause*) So . . . what do we do about it?

KAREN: Nothin', you're married.

CHARLES: Yes, I am. I am also heavily into sin.

KAREN: Another hobby?

CHARLES: Hobbies are it with me. 'Cause the fuckin' work is nowhere, Karen. Admit it Karen, it's nowhere. You care about it?

KAREN: Yes.

CHARLES: Enough to kill your wife?

KAREN: What?

CHARLES: Nothin'.

KAREN: Want another hit?

CHARLES: Want to dance?

KAREN: Okay.

(*They stand. He moves toward her*)

CHARLES: You got cocaine on your nose.

KAREN: Tacky.

(*She reaches to rub it off. He stops her*)

CHARLES: I'll do it.

(*He brushes it with his finger. Puts his finger on her lips. She licks it. He puts his hand gently over her mouth. She kisses it. He puts both*

hands on her face)
You are so goddamn beautiful.
(*He kisses her. He puts his arms around her waist, pulling her closer. He puts his hand under her blouse at the back. He puts another hand on her butt. She starts to pull back a bit*)
Please don't stop me. Please don't stop me.
(CHARLES *and* KAREN *continue to kiss . . . growing more passionate*)

Source: Dramatists Play Service, Inc.

✤ The Boys Next Door

•••••••••••••••••••••••••••••TOM GRIFFIN

CHARACTERS: NORMAN *(40's)*, SHEILA *(20's)*
SETTING: *The apartment, the present.*

NORMAN *and* SHEILA *are mentally handicapped.* SHEILA *has come to visit* NORMAN *at his apartment for the first time.* SHEILA *wears her best outfit and carries a bouquet of wildflowers.*

NORMAN: Hi, Sheila.
SHEILA: Hi, Norman.
NORMAN: Hi, Sheila.
SHEILA: Hi, Norman.
NORMAN: Hi, Sheila. My name is Norman Bulansky. Welcome to my home. Won't you take a seat?
   (SHEILA *enters. She stands with the flowers and looks about*)
SHEILA: This is nice, Norman. It's cozy.
NORMAN: It used to be better when we had those little rugs. Arnold's got them hid.
SHEILA: Arnold, ick! He's not here, is he?
NORMAN: Oh boy, that's all we need. Oh boy!
SHEILA: Arnold, ick!
NORMAN: Oh boy! *(Pause)* Can I manage your coat?
SHEILA: I don't have one.
NORMAN: Oh boy!
SHEILA: I got to leave at nine. The bus comes then. It's seven-thirty now.
NORMAN *(With a kitchen timer):*   See this? It's a timer. It times things. Eggs and . . . eggs, and things. I'll just set it and then you won't be late.
SHEILA: It's seven-thirty now. I got to leave at nine.
NORMAN: All I do is set it like this. On the nine. See? Don't worry. This works like a butler or somebody. *(Carefully placing it down)* My name is Norman Bulansky. Won't you take a seat?
SHEILA: I got these for you. I picked them.
NORMAN *(Taking the flowers, pleased):*   You're welcome very much. They're pretty. You're welcome, thank you. Thank you.
SHEILA: I picked them in that lot near the Getty station. You know

that lot?

NORMAN: Getty gas. That's good gas. Would you please like a doughnut?

SHEILA: You got a jar or something to put them in?

NORMAN (*Studying the doughnuts, mystified*): I got them on plates. In piles. See. They won't fit in a jar.

SHEILA: Gee, Norman, you're silly. I mean the flowers.

NORMAN: The flowers? Oh boy, I thought you wanted a jar for the doughnuts. Oh boy, I'm sure silly. You ain't kiddin', oh boy!
(*They both laugh. Pause*)
Would you please like a doughnut?

SHEILA: I got to go at nine. The bus comes then.

NORMAN: Maybe I'll have one, thank you. (*Takes one, chomps*) They call this one honey-dipped. But you know what? It's not real honey. I told Arnold that and he said we should picket.

SHEILA: Maybe we should put them in a jar or something.

NORMAN: I'll get a jar or something. (NORMAN *places the flowers on the couch, then starts for the kitchen, but is distracted*)

SHEILA: This is nice, Norman. Real cozy. We don't have stuff on the wall in our home. We used to, but Helen with the tic eats paper sometime. It's awful.

NORMAN: Oh boy, you bet.

SHEILA: She ate a picture of God one day. God and His friends eating. She just ate it. We still got the frame, but God's all eaten up.

NORMAN: God? She ate a picture of God? Oh boy!

SHEILA: One time, Helen ate a roll of toilet paper.

NORMAN: Want to see the bathroom? We got a nice bathroom.

SHEILA: No thank you. I went before.

NORMAN (*One last shot*): We got swans in there.

SHEILA (*After a pause*): This is nice, Norman. It's cozy.

NORMAN: We used to have this poster with kitties on it, but Jack said it was too baby. I kind of liked it though. Would you please like a doughnut? (NORMAN *sits on the couch, crushing the flowers. He realizes what he has done. A very nervous pause. To himself*) Oh-oh. Oh boy, oh-oh. Oh-oh . . . (*An agonized moment*) Sheila, are the flowers under me? Do you remember?

SHEILA: I got them in that lot near the Getty station.

NORMAN: That's good gas. Getty gas. (*Gets up, sees the flowers*) Sheila, I think somebody sat on these. I think I'm very sorry but I was just sitting down to have a doughnut and for us to talk.

SHEILA (*Unconcerned*): That's okay, Norman.

NORMAN: But they're all broken.

SHEILA: Flowers grow right back.

NORMAN (*Stuffing the flowers in his pocket*): I feel awful bad about them, Sheila.

SHEILA: That's okay, Norman, flowers break a lot. That's how come you get them free.

NORMAN (*His pockets stuffed*): Would you please like a doughnut?

SHEILA: I had spaghetti for supper.

(*Pause. Suddenly* NORMAN *gets an idea and rushes to the refrigerator. He opens the freezer and pulls out a present: a doughnut box with maybe thirty stick-on bows attached. He gives it to her*)

NORMAN: Sheila, I got you this. It's a present. Can I have the bows?

SHEILA: No. They're pretty. I want them.

NORMAN: Open it.

SHEILA (*Opening it*): Oh, Norman, I feel all jumpy.

NORMAN: Me too. Can I have the bows?

SHEILA: No. (*Pulls out a large clump of newspaper packing*) I know what's in it. Let me guess. A frog.

NORMAN: Nope. Oh boy, a frog'd be hard to wrap.

SHEILA: Gee, Norman, you're funny.

NORMAN: I am? Oh boy, you ain't kiddin', oh boy!

SHEILA (*Giggling*): You are, Norman. You're funny.

NORMAN: Oh boy!

(SHEILA *unwraps a set of keys, smaller, but similar to his*)

SHEILA: Oh, Norman. Keys. You got me keys. Oh, Norman . . .

(SHEILA, *very affected, is at a loss.* NORMAN *beams*)

NORMAN: They're nice, huh? Try them on. Oh boy, I can't wait to see them on.

SHEILA: Norman, this is the best present I ever got.

NORMAN: Try them on. Put them on your belt. They'll fit good.

SHEILA (*Looping the keys on her belt*): What side?

NORMAN: Whatever makes you feel more balanced. Jack, he got me the ring. It's made of metal. And Arnold got me all the keys. He says that the movie theatre has all keys around that nobody uses too much. And Lucien, he gave me that little bitty key. It's from this diary he got, but he can't write so who cares?

SHEILA (*Stunned with her good fortune*): They're the most beautiful keys I ever saw.

NORMAN: They should be. They're right from the movies.

(*The kitchen timer rings. Panic strikes them both.* NORMAN *shuts it off*)

NORMAN: Oh boy! Did that go fast! Oh boy!

SHEILA: I got to go. I got to go for the bus at nine.

NORMAN   Seven-thirty and nine are too soon together, oh boy!

SHEILA (*Gathering the bows and the box and the crumpled newspaper*):   I got to go, Norman.

NORMAN: A butler couldn't tell you better time. Would you please like a doughnut?

SHEILA: The bus goes at nine. It don't wait.

NORMAN: My name is Norman Bulansky. Welcome to my home. Thank you for visiting with me. (*Pulling the flowers from his pockets*) I'm sorry I broke your flowers. Come again.

SHEILA (*Kissing him on the cheek*):   Norman, this is the most best beautiful present I ever got.

NORMAN (*Overwhelmed*):   Welcome to Norman Bulansky. Come again.

Source: Dramatists Play Service, Inc.

✤ Brilliant Traces

●●●●●●●●●●●●●●●●●●●●●●●●●●●CINDY LOU JOHNSON

CHARACTERS: HENRY (20's), ROSANNAH (20's)

SETTING: HENRY's *home in Alaska, in the middle of nowhere, the present.*

HENRY *is a recluse who lives in a secluded shack in Alaska. He works as a cook on an oil rig and hibernates during his time off. One night during a blizzard, a very distraught girl in a wet, tattered wedding gown bursts through his door, and asks him for shelter, passing out on the floor.* HENRY *gently removes her wet clothing, cleans her up and puts her to bed; she sleeps for two days. When she wakes up,* ROSANNAH *is still distraught and confused, and* HENRY, *unaccustomed to having his lair invaded by strangers, does his best to comfort her.*

HENRY (*Putting a spoon, bread, and butter, etc. on the table*):   Why don't you eat?

ROSANNAH: Oh OK. (*She doesn't move. Instead she stares at* HENRY)

HENRY (*Pointing to the table*):   Over here.

ROSANNAH (*Still staring*):   Have we met?

HENRY: When?

ROSANNAH: Earlier.

HENRY: Well, no. I mean the other night we . . . we didn't exactly meet but . . .

ROSANNAH: What?

HENRY: Well, you *arrived.*

ROSANNAH (*Re-stating this, trying to get information*):   I arrived.

HENRY: Yes, and then, shortly thereafter, you . . . well you went to sleep . . . suddenly.

ROSANNAH: I went to sleep? I just lay down and went to sleep?

HENRY: Yes. Well, no. You kind of . . . fainted.

ROSANNAH: Fainted?

HENRY: Uhhunh. I think the soup's cooled off now. Why don't you try it?

ROSANNAH: I don't remember fainting.

HENRY: I do. I remember.

ROSANNAH: I just fell down onto the floor?

HENRY: You sort of sank. Very gently.

ROSANNAH (*Trying to visualize this*):   Oh. I sank. (*Beat*) Then how did I . . . ? (*Looking at the bed*) I mean, I woke up in that bed.

HENRY: Oh. Well, I put you there.
(ROSANNAH *looks up at him, startled*)
I mean you were on the floor. So I put you there.

ROSANNAH: Oh.

HENRY: That's all.

ROSANNAH: Oh . . . And then I just slept like that — in that bed — for two days? Not moving?

HENRY: Yes. (*Pauses*) Well, one time — I think it was the first night — You sort of rose up.

ROSANNAH: I rose up?

HENRY: Yes. I mean in the bed. You kind of rose up, but I don't really think you were awake. I think you were dreaming.

ROSANNAH: I just rose, dreaming?

HENRY: Yes.

ROSANNAH: I just . . . What do you mean, I "rose up"?

HENRY: Well, you sat up very slowly and you sort of spoke. But you didn't seem conscious. It was like you were dreaming. You didn't seem awake at all.

ROSANNAH: What did I say?

HENRY: You just . . . I don't know . . . you were just . . . you know — dreaming. Mumbling. You were probably just talking in your sleep. Are you hungry? You must be starving.

ROSANNAH: Could you understand anything I said?

HENRY: When?

ROSANNAH: When I rose up and spoke. Could you understand anything I said?

HENRY: (*Reluctantly*) Unhunh.

ROSANNAH: What was it? What did I say?

HENRY: Well, you said . . . (*He stops for a moment, then looks directly at* ROSANNAH) You said you were the prettiest girl I'd ever seen. (ROSANNAH *is startled. She stares at* HENRY *for a moment, and then looks away*)

ROSANNAH: Oh . . . Well . . . That's strange. That's very odd.

HENRY: Why don't you sit down?
(ROSANNAH *doesn't move*)
Here. Really. Why don't you sit —
(*Seeing* ROSANNAH *is too dazed and lost to move* HENRY *finally takes her to the chair. He seats her*)
Here. I think if you just sit here and have some soup.
(*He moves the bowl in front of her. She smiles weakly, but then flies*

back into herself, disturbed. She glances briefly at the bowl but takes no action. Finally he takes her spoon)
Here.
(Feeding her)
There.
(He feeds her one spoonful after the next. She takes three or four bites slowly, in this way, then jumps up, abruptly, grabbing the spoon from his hand)
ROSANNAH: What are you doing?
HENRY: What?
ROSANNAH: I can feed myself! I don't need anybody to feed me. Who do you think I am? Somebody who *needs* someone to feed her?
HENRY *(Backing up)*:   No . . . I . . . No.
(ROSANNAH puts the spoon down. She sits back down)
ROSANNAH *(Embarrassed by the outburst)*:   Excuse me.
HENRY: That's all right.
ROSANNAH: I'm terribly sorry. I don't know what's wrong with me. *(Beat)* I don't quite know.
(She eats. HENRY watches)
HENRY *(After a pause)*:   I'm really *very* sorry I cooked your shoes.
ROSANNAH: Oh . . . Well . . . Anyway . . .
HENRY: I would have been more careful if I'd realized their value.
ROSANNAH: Yes . . . No, that's all right. The soup's good.
HENRY: Oh.
ROSANNAH: Very tasty. *(She jumps up abruptly)* I'd better go.
HENRY: What?
ROSANNAH: Do you know exactly where I am?
HENRY: What do you mean?
ROSANNAH *(Vaguely)*:   I have to call the people.
HENRY: What people?
ROSANNAH: Those men who fix things . . . you know . . . because my car . . . I'm very dizzy.
HENRY: Here. Sit down. *(He sits her down)* You don't have much color. I think you really need to eat. I mean, I really think you need to eat *a lot!*
ROSANNAH: No. I'd better — *(She almost tries to stand back up)*
HENRY: I think you're depleted. You look depleted.
ROSANNAH *(Panicked)*:   Where am I? What is this place?
HENRY: *Here?*
ROSANNAH: Yes.
HENRY: This is my home.
ROSANNAH: Oh. *(She glances around)* It's very nice.

HENRY: Thank you. Here. (*Handing her a spoon*) I think you're weaker than you realize.

ROSANNAH: No. I realize I'm weak. I'm fully aware of it. I'm a very weak person.

HENRY: I wasn't saying you were a weak person. I'm sure you're not a weak person. I'm sure you're just —

ROSANNAH: It's because I'm so limited. I'm terribly limited.

HENRY: What?

ROSANNAH: I am. I wish I weren't. I wish I were — *expansive* — you know. But I'm not. I'm limited. Terribly terribly limited.

HENRY: I think you need some more soup.

ROSANNAH: And I don't know how I got this way. Somehow my perspective has been narrowed — I think I am living in the clutches of a very narrow perspective. And I don't think that's fair. I think if you're in the clutches of a very narrow perspective, you shouldn't *know* about it. You'd be satisfied, but *knowing*, being fully aware — I mean —

HENRY (*Handing her the spoon again*):   I think you're just hungry.

ROSANNAH (*Stopping and focusing on him*):   Oh. (*She looks down into her bowl. She eats. She eats it all*) There. I ate it all. I feel better. Thank you.

HENRY: You're welcome.

ROSANNAH: I feel — nourished.

HENRY: Good.

ROSANNAH: I was just a bit confused back there. For good reason. I've been traveling a long time, and then there was that storm and all, and then sleeping for two days. You can imagine that would confuse anyone. Don't you think?

HENRY: Yes I do. I think it would. Why don't you eat your bread?

ROSANNAH: What?

HENRY (*Buttering it*):   Here. There. It's all buttered.

(ROSANNAH *stops, surprised*)

HENRY (*Suddenly looking up*):   I'm sorry. I didn't mean to butter it. I am sure you can butter your own bread. I am sure you're the kind of person who can butter her own bread. Here's another piece. (*He slices another piece*) You butter it. This one's for me. (*He takes a bite of the one he's buttered*) That's yours. (*He points to the other one*)

ROSANNAH: No, thank you.

HENRY: It's really good bread.

ROSANNAH: I'm pretty full.

HENRY: Please. (*Beat*) I made it myself. You could just try it.

ROSANNAH (*Pauses and then takes a bite*):   It's good.

HENRY: Don't you want some butter on it?

ROSANNAH (*Examining him*):   You're the kind of person who takes care of people, aren't you?

HENRY: What?

ROSANNAH: I see that you're the kind of person who takes care of people — watches out for them. Feels responsible.

HENRY: No. I'm not. I don't.

ROSANNAH: Well, you certainly come across as the kind of person who —

HENRY (*Cutting her off*):   I'm not that kind of person.

ROSANNAH: Oh. (*Eating her bread*) Do you live here alone?

HENRY: Yes.

ROSANNAH: No family? No —

HENRY (*Cutting her off*):   You done?

ROSANNAH: Yes.

(*He roughly clears the table.* ROSANNAH *watches him for several moments.*)

My name's Rosannah DeLuce.

HENRY (*Not turning around*):   Henry Harry.

ROSANNAH: What?

HENRY: I'm Henry Harry.

ROSANNAH: Oh. (*Beat*) You've been very kind . . . I mean, thank you for —

HENRY (*Cutting her off*):   You were almost frozen to death. I didn't do anything you wouldn't do for a sick dog.

ROSANNAH: Oh.

HENRY: Someone comes banging into your home, you don't have to be any particular kind of person to *feed* them.

ROSANNAH: No. I wasn't implying —

HENRY: You'd have to be pretty far gone if you didn't even feed them.

ROSANNAH: That's true. I was just making an observation — I mean it just crossed my mind that —

HENRY: Any one human being on this earth would feed another if he was sitting right in front of him and so hungry he couldn't even think straight.

ROSANNAH (*Gently but firmly*):   I can think straight. I thought we had established that I was feeling a little disoriented, like any *normal* human being would if they'd been driving for many many days and then been sleeping for two. I can think very straight.

(*She pauses, but* HENRY *does not respond*)

Yes . . . well I guess I'd better see about my car. (*She heads to the door*)

HENRY (*Turning*):   Where are you going?

ROSANNAH: I'm going to see about my car.

HENRY: It's still snowing like crazy out there.

ROSANNAH: Well, I'll just see why it died.

HENRY: See why it died? You won't even see your car.

ROSANNAH: I'll do my best. (*She turns back to the door*)

HENRY: Sit down.

ROSANNAH (*Startled*):   What?

HENRY: SIT BACK DOWN!

ROSANNAH: Excuse me, but if I want to go look at my car —

HENRY: You walk ten feet out there everything'll just look white and you'll be lost and frozen.

ROSANNAH: I can find my way to my car.

(*She opens the door. Suddenly, and with force,* HENRY *is in front of her. He slams the door closed*)

What are you doing?

HENRY: Didn't you *hear* me?

ROSANNAH: You're not going to let me out?

HENRY: You'll freeze to death!

ROSANNAH: I will not!

(*She grabs the door. He grabs her arm*)

OW! Let go!

HENRY: You want me to just let you go out there and freeze to death?

ROSANNAH: Let go!

HENRY: No.

ROSANNAH (*Struggling*):   Let me go!

HENRY: No!

(ROSANNAH *suddenly punches him. He is taken off guard and falls. She runs to the door. He gets up and catches her. They struggle. Finally he gets her pinned against the wall*)

I'm not going to let you go out there. For Christ's sake. I *washed* you!

(ROSANNAH *is stunned.* HENRY *lets her go. She sits down. He is badly shaken*)

I'm sorry.

(ROSANNAH *sees how broken up he is. She examines him from a distance. He does not see this*)

ROSANNAH: I can look at my car later.

(HENRY *nods, beaten*)

Source: Dramatists Play Service, Inc.

✤ Burn This

•••••••••••••••••••••••••••LANFORD WILSON

CHARACTERS: PALE (*30's*), ANNA (*30's*)
SETTING: *A loft in Lower Manhattan, the present.*

ANNA *is a vibrant, creative, but frustrated dancer-turned-choreographer. Her loft apartment is shared with Larry, a gay advertising executive and, until his recent death in a boating accident, Robbie, a close friend and fellow dancer. A month after the funeral,* ANNA *is aroused late one night by the frenetic arrival of* PALE, *Robbie's volatile older brother, who has come to collect Robbie's belongings.* ANNA *is appalled, amused and attracted to* PALE, *who is drunk and high on cocaine. Since he must spend the night,* ANNA *is a captive audience for* PALE's *ravings and his rampantly sexual advances.*

ANNA: Do you read music?
PALE: What for? Nobody does that shit. I get going some symphony, these like giant themes come to me, these like world-shaking changes in tempo and these great huge melodies, these incredible variations, man. Get like the whole fuckin' war in it. (*He stops, bends over*) My heart's killing me. My throat's hurtin', burnin', man. What a fuckin' night. Bust up my hand on that fucker's tooth. (*He looks out the window. Pause*) Half my fuckin' adult life, I swear to Christ, has been spent looking for a place to park. (*Beat. He look at her*) What are you wearin' that thing?
ANNA: I keep hoping I'll have a chance to go back to bed and get my rest.
PALE: Sure. Don't worry about rest, we'll all get our rest. Whatta you call that thing?
ANNA: It's called a Hapi coat.
PALE: That's somethin' to wear, you do your Hapi? The Indians wear that, the Hopis?
ANNA: I got it in Japan.
PALE: Those Orientals are short, it might give them better cover.
ANNA: I just grabbed something.
  (*Pause. He looks at her, looks around the room. Back to her*)
PALE: So the three of you lived here. You and the two faggots.
ANNA (*A long stunned pause*): We were all very good friends.
PALE: Tellin' Mom and Aunt Ida and all the neighborhood bitches

how you and Robbie did things, horseback, and the races and shit. Said everything except your little boy was a real hot fuck.

ANNA (*Pause*):   It was very humiliating. They didn't know; it wasn't my place to tell them.

PALE: They know, they just don't know.

ANNA: Well, whatever. I didn't feel it was my place.

PALE (*Banging on the sofa*):   Fuckin' fruit. Fuck! Fuck! Fuck! Fuck! Fuck! Bastard! Taking his fuckin' little Greek boyfriend out to the island, talking about him in the paper, on that TV thing. "You dance real good." "Well, I get a lot of help from my friend Dominic." Suckin' my dick for me, whatever the fuck they do.

ANNA: Don't you know? I thought you'd know. They have anal intercourse, take turns having oral —

PALE: HEY! HEY! People don't *see* those programs! On TV, Channel Q, whatever, don't matter. People see that. People say, I saw your queer brother on the TV with his boyfriend. People the family works for. That crap. He live here, too? Dominic?

ANNA: He spent about half the time here. We'd been trying to get him to move in, there's plenty of room. Dom was great, you'd have liked him. It's very different here without them.

PALE: I'm just trying to get a picture —

ANNA: Well, don't bother if you didn't give a damn for him; it's a little late to cry now.

PALE: — Robbie cookin', Dominic serving wine, you lighting candles. The fruit in there running around without his clothes on. *What do you know what I feel?* I got my hand bleeding again. Fuckin' myself into little pieces here. I got to wear this look like a fuckin' bum. (*He bends over, starts to cry, stifles it*) Shit, man; shit, man. Awww shit. (*Taking off his pants*) I can't get fucked up; you go get your rest, you're worried about rest. I can't fuckin' stand up; I sit down, I'm gonna cry. Come undone. I got to wear these tomorrow — (*Presses them on table*) I can't fuck myself.

ANNA (*Overlapping*):   Jimmy, for godsake. Jimmy. If you're worried, I can press them in the morning. Seven o'clock we can go down to the basement. Listen, if you're very quiet, we can sneak down now. We'll take the stairs, 'cause the elevator — Jimmy. Jimmy.

(*He has crawled onto the sofa and completely covered himself with an afghan, head and all. His body is racked with crying.* ANNA *looks at him for a moment. She finishes the last of her coffee. What the hell , finishes his brandy as well*)

I know. I miss him like hell. I go to the studio, I think I see him ten times a day. Someone dressed like him, or walking like him.

Then I remember he's gone, and it's all that loss all over again. I know.

PALE (*He has poked his head from the afghan*):   He was always . . . very . . . (*Gestures light*)

ANNA: I know. He worked harder than anyone I've ever known.

PALE (*Looks around*):   Where's my . . .

ANNA: I drank it.

PALE: I'm gonna have to have another.

(*She gets up*)

I'll get it.

ANNA: That's okay, you got the last one.

PALE: I'll send you a fuckin' case.

ANNA: It's fine, Jimmy. Just — what? Cool it, okay?

PALE: Jimmy you're callin' me. I like that. Nobody calls me that. Fuckin' place, man. Fuckin' haunted.

ANNA: Yes, it is. So's the studio. So's the streets around the neighborhood. (*Sitting on the sofa*) So's the whole island of Manhattan.

PALE: So's Jersey. (*Pause*) I'm gonna be sick here.

ANNA: The brandy doesn't help.

PALE: No, it's good for it. You don't do nothing to your hair? It's just like that?

ANNA: It costs a fortune. (*Pause*) Oh, God.

PALE: You're done in, huh?

ANNA: No, I'm up. I'm an early riser, anyway. Not usually this early, but . . . No, I'm just . . . blue. Remember that? When people used to feel blue? I'm feeling blue.

PALE: Me too. (*Not looking at her breasts or touching them*) You almost got no tits at all, you know?

ANNA: I know. Thanks.

PALE: No, that's beautiful. That's very provocative. Guy wants to look, see just how much there is. Tits are very deceptive things.

(*Pause. Rubs his chin on the top of her head. Sings very softly, very slowly*)

"I'd . . . rather . . . be . . . blue . . . thinking of you . . . "

ANNA: You're burning up.

PALE (*Sings, same*):   "Oh . . . oh . . . oh . . . I'm on fire . . . " That's just the toaster oven. Always like that.

ANNA: You're not sick, you don't have a fever?

PALE: Normal temperature about a hundred and ten. Aww, man, I'm so fucked. My gut aches, my balls are hurtin', they're gonna take stitches on my heart; I'm fuckin' *grievin'* here and you're givin' me a hard-on. Come on, don't go away from me — everybody's fuckin' flyin' South, man . . . like I was the . . . aw shit, man. I'm gonna cry all over your hair.

(*He does cry in her hair*)

ANNA: What, Jimmy?

PALE: Come on, don't look at me.

ANNA: Jimmy, stop. Enough already, don't; you're gonna hurt yourself or something.

PALE: Good. Good. Don't look.

ANNA: I was very angry at the funeral. I thought I hadn't had a chance to have a moment, but Larry and I went back to the cemetery a couple of days after and we cried the whole day; but don't break your heart. You know? (*Kisses him lightly*) Jimmy?

PALE: You went back?

ANNA: Larry and I.

PALE: Come on. You make me upset.

ANNA: You're making yourself upset.

PALE: No, the other way. I'm getting all riled here. I got no place for it. I got like a traffic jam here. (*Kisses her lightly*) You okay?

ANNA: I'm fine.

PALE: I'm like fallin' outta the airplane here. (*Pause*) You always smell like that?

ANNA: Shampoo.

PALE: My shampoo don't make me smell like that. Let's just start up the engines real slow here . . . maybe go halfway to the city and stop for somethin' to eat . . . You talk to me, okay? . . . You're gonna find out there's times . . . I'm a real good listener.

Source: Hill and Wang/FSG

✤ The Cocktail Hour

•••••••••••••••••••••••••••••••••A.R. GURNEY

CHARACTERS: JOHN (40's), NINA (40's)
SETTING: *The living room of Bradley and Ann's home in upstate New York, the mid-1970's.*

Two of Bradley and Ann's children, JOHN and NINA, have come home for a visit. Before dinner, they must endure the cocktail hour, a family tradition of sitting in the living room with drinks and pleasantly conversing. Brother Jigger, Bradley's favorite, has been unable to attend this little family reunion. JOHN, a moderately successful playwright, has written an autobiographical play which threatens to "spill the beans" about the entire family. Bradley has offered his son twenty thousand dollars to shelve the play, since it promises to be an embarrassment if it is produced. Dinner has been delayed by the inexperienced maid. Bradley and Ann are off talking long distance to Jigger, and JOHN and NINA are waiting for dinner to be served.

(JOHN *is sitting on the couch. His glass is now empty.* NINA *comes in with a plate of carrot sticks and celery*)

NINA: Here are more munchies. It might be a little while before we eat.

JOHN: What's new with Jigger?

NINA: I don't know. I just had a chance to say hello. But I know how these things work. Mother will get on the phone in their bedroom, and Pop will be on the extension in the guest room, and everyone will talk at once. (*She finds her glass*) Don't you want to get in on the act?

JOHN: I'll wait till things settle down.

NINA: We're lucky that whoosie out there in the kitchen messed up on the meat. I told her we'll be a minimum of twenty minutes, during which time she can at least *think* about making gravy.

JOHN: You know. I just thought: isn't this familiar?

NINA: What?

JOHN: This. You and me. Sitting here. Stomachs growling. Waiting to eat.

NINA: Because of the cocktail hour . . .

JOHN: Because of Jigger.

NINA: It wasn't always Jigger.

JOHN: Most of the time it was. I was the good little boy, remember? I'd dash home, do my homework, wash my hands, brush my hair, sit here all during cocktails, and then just as we were about to eat, Jigger would call to say that he was still at some game or something.

NINA: Sometimes.

JOHN: All the time. So you'd dig into another one of your Albert Payson Terhune dog books, and Mother and Pop would have another drink and talk about their day, and I'd just sit here stewing.

NINA: That's your problem.

JOHN: Well, it was the maid's problem, too, remember? All those maids, over the years, coming to the doorway in their rustly, starchy uniforms and saying, "Dinner is served, Missus," and Mother would say, "Give us five more minutes, Mabel, or Jean, or Agnes, or whatever your name is this month," but it wouldn't be five, it would be fifteen, it would be half an *hour*, before Jigger got home and our parents would rise from the couch and stagger into the dining room to eat.

NINA: They never staggered, John.

JOHN: No, you're right. They held it beautifully. The cook held dinner beautifully. And the maid kept the plates warm. The cocktail hour kept all of life in an amazing state of suspended animation.

NINA: But oh those meals! Remember those *meals*? Three courses. Soup, a roast, home-made rolls, a home-made dessert! Floating Island, Brown Betty, Pineapple Upside Down Cake . . .

JOHN: Stewed prunes . . .

NINA: Only occasionally. And even that was good!

JOHN: Maybe. But how did those poor souls put up with us night after night? Well, of course, they didn't. They lasted a month or two and then quit, one after the other. We were lucky that one of them didn't appear in the doorway some night with a machine gun and mow us all down!

NINA: Oh, honestly, John. We were good to everyone who worked for us. We'd always go out in the kitchen and make a huge fuss.

JOHN: Oh sure, and cadge an extra cookie while the poor things were trying frantically to clean up. Oh God, Nina, what shits we were about maids!

NINA: We drove them to church, we paid their medical bills . . . (*She takes her shoes off and sprawls on the couch*)

JOHN: We were shits! When Grandmother died, she left five hundred dollars to each of the three maids that had served her all her life, and the Packard to the chauffeur.

NINA: Mother made it up to them.

JOHN: Oh sure. She tried. And they tried to make it up to themselves all along the way. Remember the one who stole all that liquor? Or the one who started the fire, smoking in the cedar closet? Or the one who went stark raving mad at breakfast and chased Mother around with a butter knife? Oh they had their moments of revenge. But we still built our life on their backs. Has it ever occurred to you that every dinner party, every cocktail hour, good Lord, every civilized endeavor in this world is based on exploiting the labor of the poor Cheryl Maries toiling away offstage.

NINA: Her name is Shirley Marie. (*Pause*) I think. (*Pause*) And she's exploiting *us*. She's probably getting fifty bucks for three hours work, when Mother and I did most of it anyway.

JOHN: There you go. Now we're exploiting each other. Pop always carries on about the importance of civilized life, but think of what it costs to achieve it. Between what Freud tells us we do to ourselves, and what Marx tells us we do to each other, it's a wonder we don't crawl up our own assholes.

NINA: Nicely put, John. All I know is, according to your good wife Ellen, whenever you and she give a party in New York, you're the first one to want to hire some poor out-of-work actor to serve the soup.

JOHN: Yeah, I know. It's a shitty system, but I can't think of a better one.

NINA (*Getting up, making another drink*): I think *you're* a shit, John. I'll say that much.

JOHN: What else is new?

NINA: No, I mean now. Tonight. For this.

JOHN: For this?

NINA: Coming up here. Stirring things up. With your play.

JOHN: This is probably one of the most decent things I've ever done.

NINA: Badgering two old people? Threatening them with some ghastly kind of exposure in the last years of their lives?

JOHN: I came here to get their permission.

NINA: You came here to stir things *up*, John. You came here to cause trouble. That's what you've done since the day you were born, and that's what you'll do till you die. You cannot let people alone, can you? A rainy day, a Sunday afternoon, every evening when you finished your homework, off you'd go on your appointed rounds, wandering from room to room in this house, teasing, causing an argument, starting a fight, leaving a trail of upset and unhappy people behind you. And when you finished with all of us, you'd go down in the kitchen and start on the cook. And when the cook left, you'd tease your teachers at school. And now that you're writing plays, you tease the critics! Anyone in authority comes under your guns. Why don't you at least be constructive about it, and tease the Mafia or the C.I.A. for God's sake. (*She sits in a chair opposite him*)

JOHN: Because I'm not a political person.

NINA: Then what kind of person *are* you, John? Why are you so passionately concerned with disturbing the peace? I mean, here we are, the family at least partially together for the first time in several years, and possibly the last time in our lives, and what happens: you torment us with this play, you accuse us of running a slave market in the kitchen, you make us all feel thoroughly uncomfortable. Have you ever thought about this, John? Has it ever come to mind that this is what you do?

JOHN: Yes.

NINA: Good. I'm so glad. Why do you suppose you do it?

JOHN (*Moving around the room*):   Because there's a hell of a lot of horseshit around, and I think I've known it from the beginning.

NINA: Would you care to cite chapter and verse?

JOHN: Sure. Horseshit begins at home.

NINA: He's a wonderful man.

JOHN: He's a hypocrite, kiddo! He's a fake!

NINA: Sssh!

JOHN: Talk about civilization. All that jazz about manners and class and social obligation. He's a poor boy who married a rich girl and doesn't want to be called on it.

NINA: That is a lie! He was only poor after his father died!

JOHN (*With increasing passion*):   Yes, well, all that crap about hard work and nose to the grindstone and burning the midnight oil. What is all that crap? Have you ever seen it in operation? Whenever I tried to call him at the office, he was out playing golf. Have you ever *seen* him *work*? Has he ever brought any work *home*? Have you ever heard him even talk on the *telephone* about work? Have you ever seen him spade the garden or rake a leaf or change a light bulb? I remember one time when I wrote that paper defending the New Deal, he gave me along lecture about how nobody wants to work in this country, and all the while he was practicing his putting on the back lawn!

NINA: He's done extremely well in business. He sent us to private schools and first-rate colleges.

JOHN: Oh, I know he's done well — on charm, affability, and Mother's money — and a little help from his friends. His friends have carried him all his life. They're the ones who have thrown the deals his way. You ask him a financial question, he'll say, "Wait a minute, I'll call Bill or Bob or Ted."

NINA: Because that's *life*, John! That's what business *is*! The golf course, the backgammon table at the Mid-Day Club, the Saturn Club grille at six — that's where he *works*, you jerk!

JOHN: Well then that's where his family is, not here! Did he ever show you how to throw a ball or dive into a pool? Not him. Mother did all that, while he was off chumming it up with his pals. All he ever taught me was how to hold a fork or answer an invitation or cut in on a pretty girl. He's never been my father and I've never been his son, and he and I have known that for a long time.

Source: Dramatists Play Service, Inc.

✢ Coyote Ugly

•••••••••••••••••••••••••••••••••LYNN SIEFERT

CHARACTERS: DOWD (*late 20's*), SCARLET PEWSY (*12*)
SETTING: *A house and its environs in the Southwest, the present.*

SCARLET *is a precocious youngster. She traps animals and repairs them, fishes like a bandit, and can swear like her mother Andreas and her father Red. But she's thrown for a loop when a brother,* DOWD, *returns home with a prospective wife.* SCARLET *was born after* DOWD *left. Here, after going fishing, they get to know each other.*

>   (*Late afternoon of the same day. Outside,* DOWD *and* SCARLET *clean fish near the house. Iridescent scales fly. They work awhile in silence*)

SCARLET: I was named after Scarlet O'Hara.

DOWD: It fits.

SCARLET: Frankly, my dear, I don't give a damn. That's from the book, *Gone With the Wind.*

DOWD: So, you read it.

SCARLET: Read that page. (*Pauses*) You think I'm ugly.

DOWD: Don't be silly.

SCARLET: You never look at me.

DOWD: That's because you're so ugly.

SCARLET: Yeah? Well any kid *you* had would be crazy.

DOWD: Yeah?

SCARLET: And stupid.

DOWD: Yeah?

SCARLET: And mean.

DOWD: Yeah?

SCARLET: AND ugly.

DOWD: Is that so.

SCARLET: Just like you.

DOWD: Is that so.

SCARLET: That's so all right. (*Pause*) Tomorrow I'll take you up to a place where the fish leap right up out of the water right up into your arms scaled clean and ready to eat.

DOWD: You should have taken me there today.

SCARLET: I didn't know if I liked you or not. (*Pause*) These fish? They got no bones neither. Because they're so young.

DOWD: Jellyfish.

SCARLET: Huh-uh. No jellofish in the San Carlos. Mystery fish. They got squirmy no-bone bodies. (*Pause*) Do you remember being born?

DOWD: Nobody remembers being born.

SCARLET: I do.

DOWD: Nobody but you.

(*Drawing with her stick*, SCARLET *illustrates her story in the sand and in the air*)

SCARLET: I blame my whole life on that hide-a-bed. I was produced on it after one night of hot sex. Who knows. Ma tried to get rid of me but I was too serious about living. She took ice showers and sat out late waiting for the chill. She beat me with her fist while I was still inside her and that's why she can't lay a hand on me now. There was this creep had pink hair and one eye name of Danny Dog used to drive Red around before he worked for a living. This one eye of his was glass. Just some old marble he'd stuck in. He didn't have no brakes so he'd pick Red up by punching it from the road, coasting to the house, sliding into a three-sixty, swinging Red into the rear, then gunning it fast back to the road. One day he gunned it so hard his marble eye popped out and he drove up onto the porch. Ma come running out screaming and hollering all pooched out with me inside her. HEY YOU WHAT ARE YOU UP TO YOU GO ON HOME NOW, Ma said. Danny Dog pointed to the eye in the palm of his hand. Ma give the pickup a shove. Danny Dog beat it to the road without a look back. Right then. When she was least expecting me, I popped out like Danny Dog's eyeball. Ma fell down kicking and cussing with me still hooked up to her. I hated her already so I bit her. I bit her and I bit her. She started running. She ran dragging me behind her all the way to Phoenix. You want to know what happened to my neck. She ran and I flew out behind. She felt like nothing by then but she was driven driven driven. She ran up the front steps of a man's house. Man's name was Keeper. Sign on the porch said SCISSORS SHARPENED. Ma rang the bell. I bit her feet. She pulled on the front door. She pulled so hard the whole house came off in her hand. That's all I remember.

DOWD: Mom says you came packed in a box.

SCARLET: That's *her* story. Red says I come naturally deformed to hold a rifle . . . That's his story.

DOWD: What's yours?

SCARLET: I told you. (*Pause*) You think I'm rotten.

DOWD: I don't think you're rotten. I think you're dramatic.

SCARLET: I'd ruther be rotten. When you're rotten you can shove a
fish down somebody's THROAT . . . When you're dramatic you
have to eat it yourself.

DOWD: Is that so.

SCARLET: That's so all right.

DOWD: I'll show you how so that is. (*He picks up a fish head and
attempts to shove it down* SCARLET's *throat*) SO! SO! SO! SO! SO!
(SCARLET *frees herself. She goes after* DOWD *with a fish head in one
hand and a scaling knife in the other*)

SCARLET: I got a whole world inside me wants to be born, Dowd.
Bite it. (*She bites the fish*)

DOWD: That's disgusting.

SCARLET: It's not disgusting. It's dramatic. Bite it. (*She slices the air
with the knife*) Bite it bite it bite it bite it bite it. (*She nicks his face*)

DOWD: HEY!

SCARLET: Scairdy cat! (*She runs out of reach, laughing. Puts her knife in
her belt-pouch. Challenges him*)

DOWD: Me? I'm a coach! Give me the knife before you hurt some-
body.
(*He moves cautiously toward her. She stays just out of reach. He
lunges at her. They fight. Finally,* DOWD *pins her and straddles her.
She giggles.* DOWD *holds on until she seems to give up. He releases her*)
I'm not playing anymore.
(*In one motion,* SCARLET *yanks him back down by the neck of his shirt
and applies the knife to his neck. She laughs*)

SCARLET: I never was.

DOWD: So, put down the knife.

SCARLET: I will. After.

DOWD: After what?

SCARLET: A couple things. Kiss me. Do it.

DOWD: Christ. Okay. (*He pecks her forehead*)

SCARLET: Lips.

DOWD: Okay. (*He pecks her lips*)

SCARLET: Harder. And better.

DOWD: What do you say we call it a day little doggie.

SCARLET: Open your mouth. (*She applies pressure*) Open it. (*He does.*
SCARLET *kisses him thoroughly*)

DOWD: There. Finished? Up we go.

SCARLET: I said a couple things. Take off my shirt.

DOWD: You're a little.

SCARLET: Take off my shirt I said. So. Take off my shirt. Knives bite. Tits don't.

DOWD: Little sis. You don't have any tits.

SCARLET: Got a knife. (*She begins unbuttoning her shirt*) There's a tiny part of you wants to do it The fourth part of you wants to do it.

DOWD: Wouldn't you rather play softball?

SCARLET: Don't give me words. (*Pause*) You think I'm ugly.

DOWD: I think you're a kid.

SCARLET: Is that so.

DOWD: That's so all right.

SCARLET: I'll show you how so that is.

(*She rolls on top of him. She pulls herself away. Pause. He pulls her to him*)

Source: Dramatists Play Service, Inc.

✤ A Critic and His Wife

●●●●●●●●●●●●●●●●●●●●●●●●●●●JOHN FORD NOONAN

CHARACTERS: LEN (*30's*), REBECCA (*30's*)

SETTING: *An apartment with many shelves of books. The Upper East Side of New York City. Four in the morning, the present.*

LEN, *a major theatre critic, has just signed a contract for a novel. He rushes home to tell his wife the good news, but she is too absorbed in reading* Tell Me A Riddle *by Tillie Olsen to listen. She even refuses to join* LEN *at an important opening because she's been "touched" by the book. Nine hours later, she hands* LEN *some typewritten pages.*

LEN: This was typed on my typewriter!

REBECCA: Read.

LEN (*Reading*):   Oh God!

REBECCA: What's wrong?

LEN (*Quoting 'three' times*):   "EVERYTHING AROUND ME USED TO TOUCH ME" . . .

REBECCA: Say it!

LEN: That's a great opening sentence. That opening sentence is even better than my opening sentence. (*Reading on*) Oh, God! The whole first paragraph's great . . . Oh, God! The second paragraph's even better. (*Clutching chest, gesture of relief*) Thank God!

REBECCA: What's wrong

LEN (*Again quoting*):   "EVERYTHING LEAKS BUT NOTHING COMES OUT"? . . . "ANGER IS MY LAST TRUE FRIEND." (*Lets out "YUCK" sound*) The ending falls completely apart. The last two paragraphs are a mess. Phew! That was a close call. Don't keep it a secret. Tell me.

REBECCA: Tell you what?

LEN: Who wrote it?

REBECCA: I did.

LEN: You've never written anything before.

REBECCA: I have now.

LEN: You have no background, no experience, no standards to go by. Rebecca, you're an absolute beginner. Beginners don't just . . . just . . .

REBECCA: What about the title?! (*Pointing, "Quoting"*) TIRED OF

NOT BEING TOUCHED ANYMORE!

LEN: We should wait on the title until after we figure a way to clean up the messy ending. In all my years I've often found the right title by first cleaning up a messy ending.

REBECCA: Why won't you see the miracle?

LEN: What miracle?

REBECCA: *TIRED OF NOT BEING TOUCHED ANYMORE* is why I couldn't stop reading Tillie Olsen all day. It's why I had to call in and cancel. I was moved. I was touched. I cried the first time through and again the twenty-fourth. Len, I didn't pick the title. The title picked me. What you just read had to be written. It didn't matter that I wasn't a writer. I had no choice but to put it down.

LEN: I feel the same way about my review.

REBECCA: Then you do see, don't you?

LEN: But we've still got to clean up your last few paragraphs. This is definitely a publishable piece. Maybe not in an established, reputable daily with a six-figure readership but certainly —

REBECCA: Len, a couple, who's us, married a long time, the same day write down the same thought. Now this couple, who's still us, are both disgusted by shallowness, enraged by mediocrity, yes, . . . Rebecca and Len are half dead with never being touched anymore!

LEN: Don't tell me. Put it into the ending.

REBECCA: But —

LEN: The ending needs it. The ending's just like you. It doesn't add up.

REBECCA: What did you just say?!

LEN: All this wonderful stuff, this incredible promise, Rebecca, goddamn it, you had the Harper & Row job in the bag. Lord God, woman, for once in your life finish something you start!!

(REBECCA *lifts typewriter from desk*)

That's in permanent position.

(REBECCA *crosses to bedroom door*)

I command you to put it back, now.

(REBECCA *enters bedroom, slams door behind her*)

Rebecca, open this door!!

(*Sound of lock being clicked*)

Rebecca, I'm warning you!

(*Suddenly door opens. Out steps* REBECCA)

REBECCA: I think I have it in me to be a real writer.

LEN: You'll only know by —

REBECCA: Do you think I have it in me to be real writer?

LEN: Off of just one piece it's very —

REBECCA: I'm going to stay in here till I find the right ending. The door will be locked. You'll be out here. I'll be in there.

LEN: Hold it. You can't just —

REBECCA: I'm going all the way. I'm desperate. I'm a certain way and perhaps for the first time, I'm fighting for my life. It's war. It's blood, death, dread and all that horror.

LEN: Baby, you're starting to sound a little —

REBECCA: Till then, don't talk to me!

LEN: WHAT?!!

REBECCA: Nothing. No messages. No whispers. No notes under the door.

LEN: Suppose it take days. Weeks —

REBECCA: The fridge is full. You know where everything is.

(REBECCA *kisses* LEN *on cheek*)

See you when I see you. (*Goes back into bedroom. Locks door. Sound of typing*)

Source: John Ford Noonan

❖ Driving Miss Daisy

ALFRED UHRY

CHARACTERS: HOKE (60-85), DAISY (72-97)
SETTING: *Atlanta, Georgia, from 1948 to 1973.*

Miss DAISY's *eyes are failing so her son, Boolie Werthan, has hired* HOKE, *a black man, to drive his mother on errands. When the scene opens, Miss* DAISY *finally gives in and allows* HOKE *to drive her to the store.*

HOKE: Mornin', Miz Daisy.
DAISY: Good morning.
HOKE: Right cool in the night, wadn't it?
DAISY: I wouldn't know. I was asleep.
HOKE: Yassum. What yo' plans today?
DAISY: That's my business.
HOKE: You right about dat. Idella say we runnin' outta coffee and Dutch Cleanser.
DAISY: We?
HOKE: She say we low on silver polish too.
DAISY: Thank you. I will go to the Piggly Wiggly on the trolley this afternoon.
HOKE: Now, Miz Daisy, how come you doan' let me carry you?
DAISY: No, thank you.
HOKE: Ain't that what Mist' Werthan hire me for?
DAISY: That's his problem.
HOKE: All right den. I find something to do. I tend yo' zinnias.
DAISY: Leave my flower bed alone.
HOKE: Yassum. You got a nice place back beyond the garage ain' doin' nothin' but sittin' there. I could put you in some butter beans and some tomatoes and even some Irish potatoes could we get some ones with good eyes.
DAISY: If I want a vegetable garden, I'll plant it for myself.
HOKE: Well, I go out and set in the kitchen then, like I been doin' all week.
DAISY: Don't talk to Idella. She has work to do.
HOKE: Nome. I jes' sit there till five o'clock.
DAISY: That's your affair.
HOKE: Seem a shame, do. That fine Oldsmobile settin' out there in

the garage. Ain't move a inch from when Mist' Werthan rode it over here from Mitchell Motors. Only got nineteen miles on it. Seem like that insurance company give you a whole new car for nothin'.

DAISY: That's your opinion.

HOKE: Yassum. And my other opinion is a fine rich Jewish lady like you doan' b'long draggin' up the steps of no bus, luggin' no grocery-store bags. I come along and carry them fo' you.

DAISY: I don't need you. I don't want you. And I don't like you saying I'm rich.

HOKE: I won' say it then.

DAISY: Is that what you and Idella talk about in the kitchen? Oh, I hate this! I hate being discussed behind my back in my own house! I was born on Forsyth Street and, believe you me, I knew the value of a penny. My brother Manny brought home a white cat one day and Papa said we couldn't keep it because we couldn't afford to feed it. My sisters saved up money so I could go to school and be a teacher. We didn't have anything!

HOKE: Yassum, but look like you doin' all right now.

DAISY: And I've ridden the trolley with groceries plenty of times!

HOKE: Yassum, but I feel bad takin' Mist' Werthan's money for doin' nothin'. You understand?

DAISY: How much does he pay you?

HOKE: That between me and him, Miz Daisy.

DAISY: Anything over seven dollars a week is robbery. Highway robbery!

HOKE: Specially when I doan' do nothin' but set on a stool in the kitchen all day long. Tell you what, while you goin' on the trolley to the Piggly Wiggly, I hose down yo' front steps.
(DAISY *is putting on her hat*)

DAISY: All right.

HOKE: All right I hose yo' steps?

DAISY: All right the Piggly Wiggly. And then home. Nowhere else.

HOKE: Yassum.

DAISY: Wait. You don't know how to run the Oldsmobile!

HOKE: Miz Daisy, a gearshift like a third arm to me. Anyway, thissun automatic. Any fool can run it.

DAISY: Any fool but me, apparently.

HOKE: Ain't no need to be so hard on yo'seff now. You cain' drive but you probably do alotta things I cain' do.

DAISY: The idea!

HOKE: It all work out.

DAISY (*Calling offstage*):   I'm gone to the market, Idella.

HOKE (*Also calling*):   And I right behind her!

(HOKE *puts on his cap and helps* DAISY *into the car. He sits at the wheel and backs the car down the driveway.* DAISY, *in the rear, is in full bristle*)

I love a new car smell. Doan' you?

(DAISY *slides over to the other side of the seat*)

DAISY: I'm nobody's fool, Hoke.

HOKE: Nome.

DAISY: I can see the speedometer as well as you can.

HOKE: I see dat.

DAISY: My husband taught me how to run a car.

HOKE: Yassum.

DAISY: I still remember everything he said. So don't you even think for a second that you can — wait! You're speeding! I see it!

HOKE: We ain't goin' but nineteen miles an hour.

DAISY: I like to go under the speed limit.

HOKE: Speed limit thirty-five here.

DAISY: The slower you go, the more you save on gas. My husband told me that.

HOKE: We barely movin'. Might as well walk to the Piggly Wiggly.

DAISY: Is this your car?

HOKE: Nome.

DAISY: Do you pay for the gas?

HOKE: Nome.

DAISY: All right then. My fine son may think I'm losing my abilities, but I am still in control of what goes on in my car. Where are you going?

HOKE: To the grocery store.

DAISY: Then why didn't you turn on Highland Avenue?

HOKE: Piggly Wiggly ain' on Highland Avenue. It on Euclid, down there near —

DAISY: I know where it is and I want to go to it the way I always go. On Highland Avenue.

HOKE: That three blocks out of the way, Miz Daisy.

DAISY: Go back! Go back this minute!

HOKE: We in the wrong lane! I cain' jes' —

DAISY: Go back I said! If you don't, I'll get out of this car and walk!

HOKE: We movin'! You cain' open the do'!

DAISY: This is wrong! Where are you taking me?

HOKE: The sto'.

DAISY: This is wrong. You have to go back to Highland Avenue!

HOKE: Mmmm-hmmmm.

DAISY: I've been driving to the Piggly Wiggly since the day they put it up and opened it for business. This isn't the way! Go back! Go back this minute!

HOKE: Yonder the Piggly Wiggly.

DAISY: Get ready to turn now.

HOKE: Yassum.

DAISY: Look out! There's a little boy behind that shopping cart!

HOKE: I see dat.

DAISY: Pull in next to the blue car.

HOKE: We closer to the do' right here.

DAISY: Next to the blue car! I don't park in the sun! It fades the upholstery.

HOKE: Yassum.

(*He pulls in, and gets out as* DAISY *springs out of the back seat*)

DAISY: Wait a minute. Give me the car keys.

HOKE: Yassum.

DAISY: Stay right here by the car. And you don't have to tell everybody my business.

HOKE: Nome. Doan' forget the Dutch Cleanser now.

(DAISY *fixes him with a look meant to kill and exits.* HOKE *waits by the car for a minute, then hurries to the phone booth at the corner*)

Hello? Miz McClatchey? Hoke Coleburn here. Can I speak to him (*Pause*) Mornin' sir, Mist' Werthan. Guess where I'm at? I'm at dishere phone booth on Euclid Avenue right next to the Piggly Wiggly. I jes' drove yo' mama to the market. (*Pause*) She flap around some on the way. But she all right. She in the store. Uh-oh. Miz Daisy look out the store window and doan' see me, she liable to throw a fit right there by the checkout. (*Pause*) Yassuh, only took six days. Same time it take the Lawd to make the worl'.

Source: Theatre Communications Group

✤ Emerald City

•••••••••••••••••••••••••••DAVID WILLIAMSON

CHARACTERS: COLIN *(30's-40's),* KATE *(30's-40's)*
SETTING: *Colin and Kate's home in Sydney, Australia, the present.*

COLIN, *a successful screenwriter, is intelligent, thoughtful, and sometimes arrogant, especially concerning the philosophical but uncommercial screenplays he writes. His wife,* KATE, *who works in publishing, is attractive, vivacious, and outspoken. They have uprooted their children, Penny, Sam and Hannah, from the more provincial Melbourne and moved to the "Emerald City" of Sydney, where there are more opportunities for projects and for disillusionment and treachery.*

KATE: Penny lied about where she was last weekend.
COLIN: Penny? She's never lied in her life.
KATE: Well, she's just started.
COLIN: Wasn't she here last weekend?
KATE: Colin, as a father you're a joke.
COLIN: As a wife you don't give me many laughs.
KATE: If you ever give another interview in which you claim to do fifty percent of the household chores and put the responsibilities of fatherhood before your work I'll ring the bloody journalist and demand the right of reply.
COLIN: I do the shopping.
KATE: I pin a series of lists headed 'butcher,' 'greengrocer', 'delicatessen' to your jumper which you usually manage to leave at the right shop and which you often remember to collect. I'm the one who does all the thinking.
COLIN: *I'll* do the thinking, *you* spend an hour a day behaving like a fork lift truck. Have you ever had to have a prolonged conversation with Doug the butcher? He's a great guy, but after the weather it can get tricky. Especially when the only reason he can think of as to why I do the shopping at ten every morning and why I don't speak like an outback Queenslander, is that I'm the boyfriend of a Qantas flight director.
KATE: Let him think it.
COLIN: I don't want him to think it. I'm not.
KATE: There's nothing wrong with being gay.

COLIN: Nothing wrong at all, except that I'm not. And while we're on this, will you stop all this nauseating stuff with young Sam about, 'No one knows what one's sexual preferences will be until one grows up, but if one's sexual preferences *do* turn out to be minority preferences, one must *never* be ashamed of it.'

KATE: You're just prejudiced against gays.

COLIN: I am not in the *least* prejudiced against gays. I just want the kid not to feel guilty if by some odd chance he grows up hetero.

KATE: You *are* prejudiced.

COLIN: It took fifteen million years of evolution for my genes to get to me, I'd just like to see them go a bit further. Where *was* Penny?

KATE: At a disco called 'Downmarket.' She was supposed to be studying at her friend's place.

COLIN: Disco? When she was in Melbourne the only thing she'd listen to was Mozart.

KATE: I'd be surprised if 'Downmarket' is noted for its Mozart.

COLIN: How did you find out?

KATE: A twenty-three-year-old German tourist turned up on our doorstep looking for our daughter.

COLIN: What did he want?

KATE: It wasn't Mozart. Apparently he felt an offer had been made on the dance floor.

COLIN (*Shocked*):   That's terrible. She's only thirteen.

KATE: Fifteen, but it's still a worry.

COLIN: Those discos are where the pushers operate.

KATE: Our daughter says it isn't a problem. If you stay out on the dance floor they soon stop bothering you.

COLIN: We'll have to do something.

KATE: I've stopped this week's pocket money.

COLIN (*Agitated*):   That'll really strike terror into her.

KATE: What do you want me to do? Lock her in a dark cupboard for a month?

COLIN: This is serious. She's rubbing shoulders — and God knows what else — with pushers and pimps. What's made her interested in discos, for God's sake?

KATE: This is a very cosmopolitan city.

COLIN: Discos aren't cosmopolitan, they're tawdry.

KATE: I was going to say tawdry, but I didn't want to be rude about your chosen city.

COLIN: Don't sit there being smug. This is serious. We've got to take firm action.

KATE: What do you suggest?

COLIN: If we let her keep on going like this she'll end up in William Street hopping into passing Jaguars.

KATE: If you're so worried, you take over the problem. And you can handle Sam and Hannah as well.

COLIN: What's wrong with Sam and Hannah?

KATE: Sam's apparently running a protection racket in his sixth grade —

COLIN *(Interrupting)*:   Protection racket? In Melbourne we couldn't get him away from his computer.

KATE: New city, new skills. And Hannah's teachers say she's depressed.

COLIN: Who wouldn't be in this family?

KATE: How about taking some of the blame for that yourself? You can go to the schools and hear the bad news next time! I'm sick to death of organizing this menagerie. I've got problems of my own.

COLIN: Such as?

KATE: Such as going quietly crazy because my idiot boss refuses to publish the first manuscript in years that's got me excited.

COLIN: That black woman's novel?

KATE: I wish you wouldn't keep call her, 'that black woman.'

COLIN: What am I expected to call her? 'That woman whose complexion is not as ours?'

KATE: Call her by her *name*.

COLIN: I forget it.

KATE: Take the trouble to *learn*.You've heard it often enough. Her name is Kath Mitchell and her book is called —

COLIN *(Interrupting)*:   I know the name of her book. Who could forget it? 'Black Rage.'

KATE: See?

COLIN: See what?

KATE: The tone of contempt.

COLIN: It's a terrible title.

KATE: Just because she's a member of a minority who've been made marginal in a land they owned for forty thousand years, and a member of another minority who've been made marginal by the post agricultural patriarchy for eight thousand years, doesn't entitle you to dismiss *her* or her *work*.

COLIN: I haven't.

KATE: You'd better not. It gives her work a lot of power.

COLIN: Whereas mine, being pale and male, is limp?

KATE: Your work hasn't got her power. No.

COLIN (*Hurt*):   Thank you.

KATE (*Attempting tact, which she's not very good at*):   But yours has got certain qualities her hasn't.

COLIN: Of course. It's more frivolous, less passionate, less committed. You know, I've got a certain sympathy for your boss. Why *shouldn't* he publish stuff people want to read, instead of yet another frothing-mouthed cry of rage from yet another disadvantaged minority? I *hated* those bleak Melbourne bookshops full of surly pinched-faced zealots shuffling down corridors stacked with envy, anger and hate.

KATE: You prefer Sydney bookshops? Filled with cookbooks?

COLIN: If people want cookbooks, let them have cookbooks.

KATE: I'm not devoting my life to improving the North Shore souffle!

COLIN: Of course not. You're going to keep trying to publish stuff that nobody wants to read.

KATE: I'm going to keep trying to publish books which prick the consciences of a few thousand people out there and make them aware that under the gloss of affluence there is *real* suffering. Did you know that rents are so high in this sub-tropical lotus land that all the women's hostels are overflowing and five hundred women and their kids are being turned away every week? Families are out there sleeping on golf courses and in car wrecks?

COLIN: What do you want me to do? Go to my nearest golf course and redirect them here? What do your two thousand pricked consciences actually go and *do* when they've put down the book?

KATE: Eventually they change the consciousness of this nation. They make it a fairer place for everyone.

COLIN: Kate, the country isn't going to become fair because someone in a book says it should be. The unpalatable truth is that we're an egocentric species who care a lot about ourselves and our children, a little bit for our tribe, and not much at all for anyone else.

KATE: Where did you pick up that right-wing drivel?

COLIN: Kate, can you be honest with yourself for a change without *posing*? Whenever one of those ads comes on urging us to save starving children, we're shocked by the images of the emaciated kids, we look at each other and murmur 'Must do something', but we don't even *note down the number*. But if our young Sam so much as whimpers in the night, we're instantly awake, bolt upright, staring at each other with fear in our eyes. Face up to this awful equation: one cut finger of Sam's equals more anguish than a thousand deaths in Ethiopia!

(*The logic hits home*)

KATE: All right. Most of us *are* selfish. We're taught to be.

COLIN: We aren't taught! No parent is *taught* to care more about their child than someone else's!

KATE: All right. We *are* selfish, but we can be taught to change. We can be taught to *care* about others. Sometimes the process is slow and you don't think it's happening at all, but it is. We don't have eight-year-olds working in mine pits any more. Perhaps you hadn't noticed?

COLIN (*Suddenly reflective*): No, we don't.

KATE: Things *can* change for the better, but I'm sure you're not convinced.

COLIN: I want to be convinced. I *hate* the thought that humanity is grasping and egocentric, but the evidence often seems overwhelming, and some of it comes from pretty close to home.

KATE: You mean me?

COLIN: No, I mean *me*.

(*Pause*)

KATE: I *am* getting tired of organizing this family, Colin. You're too self-obsessed to ever do your share and I'm starting to feel very, very trapped. (KATE *exits*)

Source: Applause Theatre Books

✤ For Whom the Southern Belle Tolls

•••••••••••••••••••••CHRISTOPHER DURANG

CHARACTERS: LAWRENCE *(20's)* GINNY *(20's)*
SETTING: LAWRENCE's *apartment, St. Louis, the present.*

In this delightful sendup of THE GLASS MENAGERIE, TOM, *at his mother's request, has brought home a co-worker from the factory: a possible romantic interest for his difficult brother* LAWRENCE. *The romantic interest —a young woman named* GINNY *proves to have her own interests and may not be exactly what her mother had in mind. But a rapport between Ginny and Lawrence does spring up.*

(LAWRENCE *stands still, uncomfortably.* GINNY *looks at him pleasantly. Lawrence is a sensitive young man, dressed in his nightshirt. He is a hypochondriac, and has many psychosomatic ailments, including a pronounced limp. Ginny is a "regular guy" kind of girl and works at the factory with Lawrence's brother. She is hale and hearty, and also hard of hearing. She doesn't think she's hard of hearing, however. She thinks she hears fine. Also, she talks rather loudly —both out of enthusiasm and out of her hearing problem. Slight silence at the beginning.)*

GINNY: Hi!
LAWRENCE: Hi. *(pause)* I'd gone to bed.
GINNY: I never eat bread. It's too fattening. I have to watch my figure if I want to get ahead in the world. Why are you wearing that nightshirt?
LAWRENCE: I'd gone to bed. I wasn't feeling well. My leg hurts, and I have a headache, and I have palpitations of the heart.
GINNY: I don't know. Hum a few bars, and I'll see.

(LAWRENCE *looks at her oddly, decides to ignore her mishearing.)*
LAWRENCE: We've met before, you know.
GINNY: *(not able to hear him)* Uh huh.

LAWRENCE: We were in high school together. You were voted Girl Most Likely to Succeed. We sat next to one another in glee club.

GINNY: I'm sorry, I really can't hear you. You're talking too softly.

LAWRENCE: (*louder*) You used to call me BLUE ROSES.

GINNY: Blue roses? Oh yes, I remember, sort of. Why did I do that?

LAWRENCE: I had been absent from school for a several months, and when I came back, you asked me where I'd been, and I said I'd been sick with viral pneumonia, but you thought I said "blue roses".

GINNY: I didn't get much of that, but I remember you now. You used to make a spectacle of yourself every day in glee class, clumping up the aisle with this great big noisy leg brace on your leg. God, you made a racket.

LAWRENCE: I was always so afraid people were looking at me, and pointins. But then eventually mama wouldn't let me wear the leg brace anymore. She gave it to the salvation army.

GINNY: I've never been in the army. How long were you in for?

LAWRENCE: I've never been in the army. I have asthma.

GINNY: You do? May I see

LAWRENCE: (*confused*) See it?

GINNY: Well, sure, unless you don't want to.

LAWRENCE: Maybe you want to see my collection of glass cocktail stirrers.(*He limps to the table that contains his cherished collecion of glass cocktail stirrers.* GINNY *follows him amiably. but having no idea what he's talking about.*)

LAWRENCE: (*holds up a swizzle stick*) I call this one Stringbean, because it's long and thin.

GINNY: Thank you. (*puts it in her glass and stirs it*)

LAWRENCE: (*fairly appalled*) They're not for use. (*takes it back from her*) They're a collection.

GINNY: Well I guess I stirred it enough.

LAWRENCE: They're my favorite thing in the world.(*holds up another one*) I call this one Q-tip, because I realized it looks like a Q-tip, except it's made out of glass and doesn't have little cotton swabs at the end of it. (GINNY *looks blank.*) Q-TIP.

GINNY: Really? (*takes it and puts it in her ear*)

LAWRENCE: No! Don't put it in your ear. (*takes it back*) Now it's disgusting.

GINNY: Well, I didn't think it was a Q-tip, but that's what you said it was.

LAWRENCE: I call it that. I think I'm going to throw it out now. (*holds up another one*) I call this one Pinocchio because if you hold it perpendicular to your nose it makes your nose look long.

(*holds it to his nose*)

GINNY: Uh huh.

LAWRENCE: And I call this one Henry Kissinger, because he wears glasses and it's made of glass.

GINNY: Uh huh. (*takes it and stirs her drink again*)

LAWRENCE: They're just for looking, not for stirring.(*calls off-stage*) she's making a mess with my collection.

GINNY: You know what I take your trouble to be, Lawrence?

LAWRENCE: Mama says I'm retarded.

GINNY: I know you're tired, I figured that's why you put on the nightshirt, but this won't take long. I judge you to be lacking in self-confidence. Am I right?

LAWRENCE: Well, I am afraid of people and things, and I have a lot of ailments.

GINNY: But that makes you special, Lawrence.

LAWRENCE: What does?

GINNY: I don't know. Whatever you said. And that's why you should present yourself with more confidence. Throw back your shoulders, and say, "HI! HOW YA DOIN'?" Now you try it.

LAWRENCE: (*unenthusiastically, softly*) Hello. How are you?

GINNY: (*looking at watch, in response to his supposed question*) I don't know, it's about 8:30, but this won't take long and then you can go to bed. Alright, now try it. (booming) "HI! HOW YA DOIN'?"

LAWRENCE: Hi. How ya doin'?

GINNY: Now swagger a bit. (*kinda butch*) HI. HOW YA DOIN'?

LAWRENCE: (*imitates her fairly successfully*) HI. HOW YA DOIN'?

GINNY: Good, Lawrence. That's much better. Again. HI! HOW YA DOIN'?

LAWRENCE: HI! HOW YA DOIN'?

GINNY: THE BRAVES PLAYED A HELLUVA GAME, DON'TCHA THINK?

LAWRENCE: THE BRAVES PLAYED A HELLUVA GAME, DON'TCHA THINK?

GINNY: HI, MRS. WINGVALLEY. YOUR SON LAWRENCE AND I ARE GETTING ON JUST FINE, AREN'T WE. LAWRENCE?

Source: *Best American Short Plays 1993-1994*, Applause Theatre Books

✤ Frankie and Johnny in the Clair de Lune

•••••••••••••••••••••••••TERRENCE MCNALLY

CHARACTERS: JOHNNY (*late 30's, 40's*), FRANKIE (*30's*)
SETTING: FRANKIE's *one-room apartment in New York's West 50's,
the present.*

FRANKIE *is a waitress in a restaurant where* JOHNNY *is the new short-order
cook. They have just made love for the first time. While they both have had a
great time,* JOHNNY *is more forthright about expressing it and he's very
direct in general.* FRANKIE *is more hesitant and wary. Now, she's made him
a meat loaf sandwich and insists he must leave when he's finished eating it.
It's turning into a long good-night snack.*

JOHNNY: Your meat loaf is directly from Mount Olympus. Your
father was a very lucky guy.
FRANKIE: It's his recipe. He taught me.
JOHNNY: Yeah? My old man was a great cook, too.
FRANKIE: Mine didn't have much choice.
JOHNNY: How do you mean?
FRANKIE: My mother left us when I was seven.
JOHNNY: I don't believe it! My mother left us when I was seven.
FRANKIE: Oh come on!
JOHNNY: Boy, you really, really, really and truly don't know me.
Just about the last thing in the entire world I would joke about is
a mother who wasn't there. I don't think mothers are sacred. I
just don't think they're especially funny.
FRANKIE: Me and my big mouth! I don't think you realize how seri-
ous I am about wanting you to leave now.
JOHNNY: I don't think you realize how serious I am about us.
FRANKIE: What us? There is no us.
JOHNNY: I'm working on it. Frankie and Johnny! We're already a
couple.
FRANKIE: Going out with someone just because his name is Johnny
and yours is Frankie is not enough of a reason.
JOHNNY: I think it's an extraordinary one. It's fate. You also said
you thought I had sexy wrists.
FRANKIE: One of the biggest mistakes in my entire life!

JOHNNY: It's gotta begin somewhere. A name, a wrist, a toe.

FRANKIE: Didn't they end up killing each other?

JOHNNY: She killed him. The odds are in your favor. Besides, we're not talking about ending up. I'm just trying to continue what's been begun.

FRANKIE: If he was anything like you, no wonder she shot him.

JOHNNY: It was a crime of passion. They were the last of the red hot lovers. We're the next.

FRANKIE: You're not from Brooklyn.

JOHNNY: Brooklyn Heights.

FRANKIE: I knew you were gonna say that! You're from outer space.

JOHNNY: Allentown, Pennsylvania, actually.

FRANKIE: Very funny, very funny.

JOHNNY: You've never been to Allentown.

FRANKIE: Who told you? Viv? Martin? I know, Molly the Mouth!

JOHNNY: Now who's from outer space? What the pardon-my-French fuck are you talking about?

FRANKIE: One of them told you I was from Allentown so now you're pretending you are so you can continue with this coincidence theory.

JOHNNY: You're from Allentown? I was born in Allentown.

FRANKIE: Very funny. Very funny.

JOHNNY: St. Stephen's Hospital. We lived on Martell St.

FRANKIE: I suppose you went to Moody High School, too.

JOHNNY: No, we moved when I was eight. I started out at Park Lane Elementary though. Did you go to Park Lane? This is incredible! This is better than anything in Shirley MacLaine.

FRANKIE: It's a small world and Allentown's a big city.

JOHNNY: Not that small and not that big.

FRANKIE: I still don't believe you.

JOHNNY: Of course you don't. It's one big pardon-my-French again fucking miracle and you don't believe in them.

FRANKIE: I'll tell you one thing: I could never, not in a million years, be seriously involved with a man who said "Pardon my French" all the time.

JOHNNY: Done. Finished. You got it.

FRANKIE: I mean, where do you pick up an expression like that?

JOHNNY: Out of respect for a person. A woman in this case.

FRANKIE: The first time you said it tonight I practically told you I had a headache and had to go home.

JOHNNY: That's so scary to me! That three little words, "Pardon my French," could separate two people from saying the three little words that make them connect!

FRANKIE: What three little words?

JOHNNY: I love you.

FRANKIE: Oh. Them. I should've guessed.

JOHNNY: Did you ever say them to anyone?

FRANKIE: Say them or mean them? My father, my first true love and a couple of thousand men since. That's about it.

JOHNNY: I'm not counting.

FRANKIE: You're really from Allentown?

(JOHNNY *nods, takes a bite out of his sandwich and makes a "Cross-MyHeart" sign over his chest. Then he pushes his empty milk glass towards* FRANKIE *meaning he would like a refill, which she will get*) How did you get so lucky to get out of there at eight?

JOHNNY (*Talking and eating*): My mother. She ran off with somebody she'd met at an A.A. meeting. My father took us to Baltimore. He had a sister. She couldn't cope with us. We ended up in foster homes. Could I have a little salt? I bounced all over the place. Washington, D.C. was the best. You go through that Smithsonian Institute they got there and there ain't nothing they're gonna teach you in college! That place is a gold mine. Portland, Maine, is nice, too. Cold though.

FRANKIE: You didn't miss much not staying in Allentown . . . My big highlight was . . .

JOHNNY: What?

FRANKIE: Nothing. It's stupid.

JOHNNY: I've told you stupid things.

FRANKIE: Not this stupid.

JOHNNY: No fair.

FRANKIE: All right! I played Fiona in our high school production of *Brigadoon*.

JOHNNY: What's stupid about that? I bet you were wonderful.

FRANKIE: It's hardly like winning a scholarship to Harvard or being the class valedictorian. It's an event; it shouldn't be a highlight.

JOHNNY: So you're an actress!

FRANKIE: You mean at this very moment in time?

JOHNNY: I said to myself "She's not just a waitress."

FRANKIE: Yeah, she's an unsuccessful actress! What are you really?

JOHNNY: I'm really a cook.

FRANKIE: Oh. When you put it like that, I'm really a waitress. I haven't tried to get an acting job since the day I decided I never was gonna get one. Somebody told me you gotta have balls to be a great actress. I got balls, I told 'em. No, Frankie you got a big mouth!

JOHNNY: Would you . . . ? You know . . . ?

FRANKIE: What?

JOHNNY: Act something for me.

FRANKIE: What are you? Nuts? You think actors go around acting for people just like that? Like we do requests?

JOHNNY: I'm sorry. I didn't know.

FRANKIE: Acting is an art. It's a responsibility. It's a privilege.

JOHNNY: And I bet you're good at it.

FRANKIE: And it looks like I'll die with my secret. Anyway, what happened to your mother?

JOHNNY: I tracked her down when I was eighteen. They were still together, living in Philadelphia and both drinking again. They say Philadelphia will do that to you.

FRANKIE: So you saw her again? You see, I never did.

JOHNNY: But how this potbellied, balding, gin-breathed stranger could have been the object of anyone's desire but especially my mother's! She was still so beautiful, even through the booze, but he was one hundred percent turkey.

FRANKIE: Mine was killed in a car wreck about three, no, four years ago. She was with her turkey. He go it, too. I didn't hear about it for almost a month.

JOHNNY: What people see in one another! It's a total mystery. Shakespeare said it best: "There are more things in heaven and on earth than are dreamt of in your philosophy, Horatio." Something like that. I'm pretty close. Did you ever read *Hamlet*?

FRANKIE: Probably.

JOHNNY: I like him. I've only read a couple of his things. They're not easy. Lots of old words. Archaic, know? Then all of a sudden he puts it all together and comes up with something clear and simple and it's real nice and you feel you've learned something. This Horatio was Hamlet's best friend. He thought he had it all figured out, so Hamlet set him straight. Do you have a best friend?

FRANKIE: Not really.

JOHNNY: That's okay. I'll be your best friend.

FRANKIE: You think a lot of yourself, don't you?

JOHNNY: Look, I'm going all over the place with you. I might as well come right out with it: I love you. I'm in love with you. I personally think we should get married and I definitely want us to have kids, three or four. There! That wasn't so difficult. You don't have to say anything. I just wanted to get it out on the table. Talk about a load off!

Source: Dramatists Play Service, Inc.

✤ Fresh Horses

•••••••••••••••••••••••••••••••LARRY KETRON

CHARACTERS: LARKIN (20's), JEWEL (16)
SETTING: *An abandoned railroad station in the rural south.*

LARKIN, *a temporary college drop-out, begins to be lured back to the coed joys of campus life when a party of female ex-classmates drops by for some soul-searching fun. The party fizzles when* JEWEL, LARKIN's *new nubile girlfriend, enters with her most recent saga of life on the other side of the tracks.*

JEWEL: Then you don't even want to give me a chance to explain?
LARKIN: I gave you a chance, too many chances. This whole five months I've known you has been *me* going slowly down into a hole. Because you don't have brain one or any social grace and nobody wanted to be around us except others of the same type like Jean McBaine and her daughter Laurel. And you have a bad temper, I think you even scare people. And you haven't even finished high school so you have this pervasive dumbness which follows you around like a dog. And hitting the bottom of the hole was finding out you were married. But I even tried to work *that* out somehow. Then you break up a night I'm having, you take my car for a few minutes, and I sit here all night long! Bullshit! I've had it. I had fun here last night for the first time in a long time.
JEWEL (*Sarcastically*):   No, you never had *fun* with me.
LARKIN: I had fun with you. But not like last night. Last night was *fun*. It was loose. There was . . . happiness in it. That group that was here, we were all on the same plane.
JEWEL: What am I, on Mars?
LARKIN: Yes. As a matter of fact, you're on fucking Mars. Those kids and me, we have things in common to talk about. We have school in common. They were refreshing. Fucking wasn't the *only* thing I wanted to do with them.
JEWEL: That's *all* you want to do with me.
LARKIN: It's all we *do*! There's nothing else *to* do! We can't *talk*. I can't, for example, discuss with you, the, the, the . . . or when's the last time we were together somebody had an *idea*? Never.

JEWEL: I can't talk good to you. You get me all nervous inside with butterflies. But those girls that were here? I told them a whole story I heard over at Jean's about a little girl fell into the river and this guy tried to save her but couldn't —

LARKIN: Over at Jean's. We try to talk and the only thing you can say is something you heard somebody *else* say over at Jean's.

JEWEL: I don't hear you no brilliant conversation!

LARKIN: Don't argue with me! You shouldn't have left me alone all night, Jewel. After I had such a good time with those people here, I started getting more and more angry at you until I popped. Then I settled down. And I sat here all night. And I realized what a good time I had had earlier before you showed up to spoil everything.

JEWEL: Yeah, everywhere I go.

LARKIN: Whose fault is that?

JEWEL: I hate those girls who were here.

LARKIN: Of course you do, that's you!

JEWEL: Life is handed to them. Life is not handed to me. I got no advantages. Everything's always been against me.

LARKIN: Who wants to listen to that? I want to listen to somebody who wants to *help* herself, not somebody who all she can do is twist your guts out.

JEWEL: No you don't! You don't know what it was like growing up like I did with that —

LARKIN: Don't start!

JEWEL: — with this *body*! Looking seventeen when I was fourteen, looking nineteen at sixteen. I never fit in with anybody.

LARKIN: Don't do this to my sympathy, not anymore!

JEWEL: You don't even care what happened to me last night. You're as cruel and awful as everybody else I ever met.

LARKIN: I'm not going to listen to something from you that may or may not be true.

JEWEL: You think I wouldn't have got back here quick if I could?

LARKIN: I don't know. That's the thing, I do not know. Okay, why couldn't you?

JEWEL: I drove out and met Green at the back of the Blue Devil Drive-In Restaurant.

LARKIN: See, that you would even *go* to a hangout like the Blue Devil! It's just a hangout for thugs.

JEWEL: That's where he told me to meet him! I had to if I wanted him to go along with the annulment.

LARKIN: Why didn't you tell me you were going to meet him *there*,

I wouldn't have let you go or I would have gone with you.

JEWEL: You didn't ask me. (*Pause*) I parked in the back where he was with some other guys.

LARKIN: Thugs. Hoodlums.

JEWEL: And he come over to my car.

LARKIN: To *my* car! And he *came* over. He didn't *come* over, he *came* over, he *came* over, it's past tense, it's already happened, Jewel.

JEWEL: Don't correct my English!

LARKIN: Did he ask you where you got the car?!

JEWEL: He knew it was somebody else's car. And he made me get in the back seat with him. He said just to talk. I give him the paper this lawyer give me for him to sign it. And he did sign it. But by then a bunch of these other guys had started gathering around and some of them got in with us.

LARKIN: Got in the car?

JEWEL: Some of em in the front seat and some in the back. One of them was Green's old man, he was there. He's even more awful than my stepfather ever was. Everybody's drinkin cans of beer and I was so a-scared I could have died. I didn't know what they were going to do.

LARKIN: Well what did they do, Jewel!

JEWEL: They all started grabbing me and touching me. Or tryin to cause I was strugglin. Then Green made them stop and I thought he was gonna protect me but I should of known better. He was only keeping them off a me till they paid him.

LARKIN: Paid him what?

JEWEL: Till they gave him money. Cause he had told them he would show me off for money from them.

LARKIN: What?!

JEWEL: So they started paying him. And one would hold me and he would pull up my shirt and bra and show me off to one or two of them, then others would pay and he'd show me off to *them*. Then one or two would get out of the car and others would get in and the same thing. And the windows were all fogged up and I was getting dizzy and shaken and bruised and I couldn't even struggle any more or think straight. Then I know people paid *more* money and Green pulled my pants down and my under-wear down and every one of them was laughing and slappin each other around and crawling over each other to get a better view of me and drinkin beer and passin liquor around and then some would get in and some would get out and Green with his whole fist full of money. I was in shock, swear I was.

LARKIN (*His hand is on her shoulder*):   Jewel . . . Jewel, did they rape you? Are you telling me you were raped in the back of my car?

JEWEL: I don't know!

LARKIN: Of course you know!

JEWEL: I was in shock, I said! I said it was awful and I am only clear about it as much as I've told you!

LARKIN: How long did this go on, Jewel?

JEWEL: I don't know, I don't know! It seemed like a long time. At one point they held my nose and made me drink liquor.

LARKIN: You were assaulted! If you were raped, too, that's — we'll have to get the cops!

JEWEL: No! Just, no! I want to be done with it and forget about it. I went through it and it's over. I passed out, I must have passed out. I woke up this morning in the back seat with my clothes every-which-a-way. I straightened myself up and come right here.

LARKIN: Did you recognize any the others besides Green and his old man?

JEWEL: One. That friend of Tipton's was one of them.

LARKIN: Who?!

JEWEL: Sproles. That guy Sproles.

LARKIN: Sproles!?

JEWEL: He was one of them. He paid his money to see me. I swear it.

(*Pause.* LARKIN *is blown away*)

LARKIN: I can't go out and, I don't know, avenge this for you.

JEWEL: Who asked you to?

LARKIN: Because everybody's going to have a different story, aren't they, Jewel? Everybody's going to have a different tale to tell. (*Then*) Will you let me take you to a *doctor*?

JEWEL: NO! JUST SHUT UP ABOUT IT! (*Pause*) Now that I've said my piece, I'll leave. Now that I've lost any chance I had of having you, I'll just leave. I know you don't want me now, I'm used, I'm worn-out as far as you're concerned. I'm bad goods. Ya can't trust me. I'll get your money back to you somehow. I don't *know* how. But if it takes ten years, I'll do it. (*Pause*) You deserve one of those college girls. Somebody new. Somebody really up there. One of those you can be proud of to take around with you places. You think I'm a dope. But deep down I've always been smart enough to know it wouldn't last.

LARKIN: Everything you told me about last night, was it true?

JEWEL: You're not going to believe me if you don't want to.

LARKIN: See . . . even the way you *reply* to me, I feel like I'm being manipulated. Even the way you reply. I can't let somebody manipulate me.

JEWEL: What does that mean?

LARKIN: Draw stupid emotions out of me by telling me stories of bad luck all the time and manipulating me.

JEWEL: Bad luck, yeah . . .

LARKIN: Whatever it is, then, whatever it is! But they're horror stories one right after the other and you've used them to suck me in and suck me in deeper. It's got to stop. I even feel it right now, Jesus Christ, I feel it right this second! I don't have any damn respect for myself. I don't feel like I'm making decisions based on anything but sex and sympathy, it's stupid. I'm sleepwalking with a hard-on.

JEWEL (*Sarcasm and anger*):   Then why don't you just wake up?

LARKIN: That's the plan.

JEWEL (*Softer*):   I'm going to walk over the hill. And if I never see you again ever, don't worry about it. I'm used to it. I'm going over to Jean's house and get as drunk as I can.

LARKIN: Good, you go on.

JEWEL: I will. (*As she starts out*)

LARKIN: Jewel!?

JEWEL: What?

LARKIN (*A beat, then*):   Please don't go over to Jean's.

JEWEL: Ha . . . (*She walks out the door and disappears*)

Source: Dramatists Play Service, Inc.

✤ The Girl Next Door

•••••••••••••••••••••••••••LAURENCE KLAVAN

CHARACTERS: BILL BAILEY (20's), JILL DAILEY (20's)
SETTING: *A house in a Long Island suburb, the present.*

In the conservative suburb of Leveltown, Long Island, JILL DAILEY, *a free-loving, foul-mouthed bohemian, has rankled her neighbors with her wild ways. Her next-door neighbor,* BILL BAILEY, *a TV censor with repressed yearnings for* JILL, *has come to set her straight.*

JILL: What do *you* want?
BILL: Well, I just —
   (*She turns from him, starts into her house. He helplessly follows. They enter the debris-strewn house. Music stifles normal talk*)
BILL (*Yells*):   I WAS JUST WONDERING IF YOU COULDN'T — TURN IT DOWN?
JILL: On? Turn what on?
BILL: OFF! TURN IT OFF!
   (JILL *turns off the radio. She is clearly drunk*)
JILL: Sorry, I couldn't hear you, the music was too loud. Now, what did you want?
BILL: Nothing. Nothing. As long as everything stays the way it is.
JILL: But I thought that's what you *never* want. For things to stay the way they are.
BILL: Not exactly. But close.
JILL: Right. *That's* how you like them to be — not exactly, but close.
   (*Beat*)
BILL: Well, you've been keeping up with your neighbors. Good for you.
   (*He turns to go. She stops him with —*)
JILL: But some things can't *be* that way, right? They're either what they are or they're nothing. Like my radio. I've had it rigged. So it's always at this volume. See?
   (*She turns it on; it's painfully loud*)
BILL: PLEASE! —
   (*She turns it off*)
BILL: I thought you came here to be quiet.

JILL: Well, I've tried, but I can't *be* quiet! (*Calms*) In case you haven't noticed.

BILL: Well, maybe you and your radio should go back to the city then. Amidst all the police sirens, tires screeching and blood-curdling screams, you might fit right in. But in Leveltown, you stand out.

(*Beat*)

JILL: You know, your wife's a pretty good ventriloquist. She can throw her voice all the way from next door.

(BILL *starts at this*)

BILL: That's a filthy thing to say. But maybe I shouldn't be surprised. Look at your house.

JILL: Oh, and what's it like?

BILL: Well, it *could* be the way it used to be, the way the other houses are. There used to be such light and space, distance between a bureau and a divan. There's great potential here. But you just throw it away. Which is apparently the only thing you do. I wonder where you and Roland found the room to —

JILL: There was an ottoman free. You and your wife, Paragraph, ought to try it sometime.

(*Beat*. BILL *ignores that*)

BILL: There are possibilities here. In terms of alterations, I mean.

JILL: Well, go ahead — what are you waiting for? Alter away. Cut off my wing, knock out my skylight, fill in my cesspool, bulldoze my badminton court. Set your sights and reduce me to rubble. Who's stopping you?

(BILL *is made uncomfortable by this*)

BILL: You're not my — responsibility.

JILL: Why not? I'm a dirty word to you, right?

BILL: I only came to stop the — music.

JILL: No, you didn't. The music wasn't too loud, it was a siren song to you. You came because I reek between the legs, I could bathe all day. Because I can't cook for shit, sometimes I think of little boys naked, and I haven't read anything better than the Cable Guide in years. Because I'm not careful with cash — there are dollar bills like dustballs on my floor and dustballs the size of tumble weeds. Because I use kleenex for tampons and kleenex for napkins. Because I don't use kleenex; I pick my nose so much I get nose bleeds. Because I shoplift shoelaces from stores. Because sometimes, I like to be buttfucked. (*Beat*) Because you're crazy about me.

BILL (*Shocked*):   What? But that's — ridiculous! —

JILL: I knew it the first moment you looked at me. It's like on TV: Channel 25 is the preacher, Channel 23 is the porn. We're so much alike: Bill and Jill, Bailey and Dailey, numbers 23 and 25, two letters, two numbers, apart.

(BILL *stands back, deeply affronted*)

BILL: You're — insane! —

JILL: I was only having Marvin what'shisname because I wasn't having you.

BILL: His name is Roland — and be quiet!

(BILL *snaps her radio back on, full blast. Then he runs out.* JILL *just stands there, watching him go, smiling to herself*)

Source: The Tantleff Office

✤ The Girl Next Door

•••••••••••••••••••••••••••LAURENCE KLAVAN

CHARACTERS: BILL BAILEY (20's), PAGE BAILEY (20's)
SETTING: *A house in a Long Island suburb, the present.*

The house inhabited by Jill Dailey, the slut of conservative suburb Leveltown, Long Island, has just been found to be polluted with radon. Young matron PAGE BAILEY *discusses the event with her TV censor husband,* BILL BAILEY . . . *and discovers he may harbor secret desires for Jill.*

(PAGE *turns to* BILL. *He shakes his head, with disbelief*)
PAGE: It *is* horrible, isn't it, Bill.
BILL: Yes. It came under her house. Like a — curse.
PAGE (*Encouraged*):   Exactly. Exactly like that.
BILL: Well, we can't just — watch it happen.
PAGE: No. We can't.
BILL: We have to *do* something.
PAGE: I agree.
BILL: She *is* a human being.
      (PAGE *turns to look, slowly, at him*)
PAGE: What do you mean, Bill?
BILL: Well, just what I said.
PAGE: But . . . what happened to the man who went out in the cold in his pajamas, just to shush her?
BILL: Well, yes, she *is* loud and profane —
PAGE: And everything you hate —
BILL: And everything I hate. But she's also a human being, being thrown out into the cold. Maybe even contaminated into the cold. We can't just turn our backs. Can we?
      (*Beat.* PAGE *turns away from him*)
PAGE: *I'm* just glad they're demolishing her house *after* the TV comes.
      (BILL *is quietly stunned*)
BILL: And you call yourself a Christian.
PAGE: I'm a Christian, not a saint. And neither, from the sound of this discussion, are you, Bill Bailey.
BILL: I deeply resent that, Page.

PAGE: I thought you'd be so *glad* she was gone. Just imagine, the quiet again!

BILL: That wouldn't have been a problem. I bought her a Walkman.

PAGE: You — what?

BILL: I bought her a little . . . well, it's just a little — they used to be expensive, Page, you're thinking four or five years ago, but now you can get them on the street for as little as — (*Sternly*) . . . I did it for us, Page.

PAGE: Did you get her any *tapes* to go with it?

BILL: Oh, no, she has plenty of those. (*Chuckles*) Though, frankly, her taste in music is pretty —

PAGE: Did you give her flowers, too? Or maybe a nice house plant? Or just a packet of seed? Or maybe — some of your *own*, Bill? (PAGE *turns away, livid*)

BILL: I'm blushing for you, Page. That's all I can say.

PAGE: I think you're already blushing, and you're just saying it's for me. Except you wouldn't do anything for me — you're just doing a little something for yourself! What's happened to you, Bill? (PAGE *collects herself*) This goes beyond the media coverage or even our marriage, Bill. This involves Leveltown. This involves America. Do you think that — stuff — grew under her house by accident? Do you think it'll stop there as long as she's alive?

BILL: What are you saying?

PAGE: These things really happen. I heard it from people who know. Isn't it a little *odd* Radon didn't come here until she did? And what's going to keep her from spreading it to the rest of us?

BILL: I don't want to hear any more! (*He turns away from her, to the window*)

PAGE: Think about it, Bill. Then think about us. Think about the world. But, for goodness' sake, don't think about *her* —

Source: The Tantleff Office

✛ Going In

•••••••••••••••••••••••••••••DAVID KRANES

CHARACTERS: JONAS (40's), MEG (40's)
SETTING: JONAS's den. Bookcases crammed mostly with medical books and journals.

MEG and JONAS entertain Polly and her husband. JONAS gets drunk and Polly taunts him about trying to stay young by buying jukeboxes from his childhood. JONAS accuses Polly of staying young by wearing revealing clothes. Polly throws a drink in JONAS's face and leaves with her husband. MEG, who does not witness the drink-throwing scene but knows her husband is troubled, now enters the den to talk to JONAS about his state of mind.

MEG: Why are you acting this way? (*He doesn't turn*) Why are you being so irritating and mean?

JONAS (*He turns in to her*): Excellent questions.

MEG: I'm very serious.

JONAS: I know . . . I know.

MEG: Are you going to tell me?
   (JONAS *moves inside himself*)
   . . . Would you ever have an affair with Polly? Do you find her attractive?

JONAS (*Brought out*): Where does that question come from?

MEG: From my watching the way she tries to play with you. She teases you. She gets very coy.

JONAS: There is a *word* for her.

MEG: Which is?

JONAS (*Near overlap*): Not one which you would like hearing, I think.

MEG: Why are you acting the way you are?

JONAS (*Smile*): I'm just an irrepressible guy.
   (MEG *moves to make herself a light drink*)
   I'm *not* an irrepressible guy. I was *once* an irrepressible guy. Somewhere in the weave of all that . . . is a probable truth — I'm not a genius any more. I'm not a hero. Neither god nor king! So we have the initial stages of adjustment to . . . It will be a brief but mean-spirited transition period in my life. I will my to keep

it mildly tolerable, but, given the dimensions of my particular
history, it may get out of bounds.

MEG: . . . That was a devastating thing you did to Carter.

JONAS: Which?

MEG: Today.

JONAS: Specifically.

MEG: Not going.

JONAS: How do you know?

MEG: It would be a devastating thing for any young man . . . to
have a moment of triumph and have his father choose not to be
present!

JONAS: . . . And you've talked with him?

MEG: No. Well, actually . . . No, he . . .

JONAS: He what?

MEG: He called. There were a series of parties. Victory parties. Cel-
ebrations. He said he didn't know, really, when he'd . . .

JONAS: And he said, "Why didn't Dad come? I'm devastated."?

MEG: Oh, for God's . . . !

JONAS: Well, did he *say* he was crushed?

MEG: Stop being such a bloody scientist!

JONAS: "I yam . . . who I yam!"
   (*Pause*)

MEG: *Are* you having an affair with Polly?

JONAS: I love it! . . . No.

MEG: *Have* you had one?

JONAS: No.

MEG: Would you *like* to have one?

JONAS: No.

MEG: Would you like to have one with *anybody*?

JONAS: I choose . . . Ann Margaret or Marie Curie! (*A beat*) or
Loretta Lynn. (*A beat*) Or . . . if I can't have Loretta Lynn, I choose
Sissy Spacek . . . Or . . .

MEG: Let's go to bed. We can pick up in the morning.

JONAS: Go ahead.

MEG: Jonas, please . . . !

JONAS: No.

MEG: Are you waiting for Car? (*No response*) Are you? Are you
going to apologize to him?

JONAS: Go to bed. You can pick up in the morning.

MEG: I hate you when you're like this.

JONAS: Thank God, it's so seldom.

MEG: I'm not sure.

JONAS: Take my word for it.
   (MEG *glares at him*)
   (*Direct*) Take my word for it.
MEG: People used to say you were charming. (JONAS *nods*) You
   don't have any response to that?
JONAS: Which people were they? And how long ago did they stop
   saying that?
MEG: . . . I'm going.
JONAS: To?
MEG: Bed.
JONAS: Good.
   (*A beat. She leaves*)
   (*After her*) Meg?
MEG (*Appearing, leaning back in the door*):   Yes?
JONAS: Why can't you just *love* me through this? Not make a multi-
   ple-choice test out of it. Just . . . ride quietly with me through?
MEG: Youre being "quiet"?
JONAS: No. But why can't you?
MEG: Because I think it's a cliché. "Middle-age Crisis." Because eve-
   rybody's read all about it in Sheila whats-her-name's book.
JONAS: *Passages.*
MEG: Yes. And because you're very bright . . .
JONAS: Thank you.
MEG: . . . And you should just see it for what it is, the cliché that it
   is, and be above it.
JONAS: Meg?
MEG: Jonas?
JONAS: Why can't you just *love* me through this cliché? Take the
   ride quietly?
MEG (*Leaving*):   Good night!
JONAS: . . . Good night. (JONAS *sits in the chair a moment. He gestures
   with his hands — as though he's having a discussion, a very REA-
   SONABLE discussion, with himself . . . or* MEG *. . . or someone. He
   gets up, meanders, starts up one or two of the jukes, freshens his drink,
   turns the lights off so that the only lights in the room are the jukes. Still
   standing*) You don't radiate! Why would you radiate?! How long
   do you think a person can radiate?! You radiate and that's the
   end of you; it's all you can *do*; radiate, radiate, radiate. So, you go
   in. You take the sword in your bloody, fucking hand, and you go
   . . . !
MEG (*From a distant room*):   Jonas . . . ?!
   (JONAS *stops*)

. . . Jonas . . . ?!

JONAS: Yes?!

MEG: Is Car home?!

JONAS: No!

MEG: . . . Are you talking to yourself?!

JONAS: Yes!

(*Silence*)

(*To himself*) You go in. "Mistah Kurtz — he daid" In and *in*! You use a . . . And you use a . . . You watch the flotsam. You watch the foreign bodies floating on any of the visible channels. Fitzer has *fish* in his brain!

(*Sound of a car outside, pulling up the driveway and into the garage.* JONAS *turns the lights back on. He takes a book from the shelf*)

(*Self conversation*) "To whom should one attribute the theory of *innate heat*?" "Galen!" "Wrong. Aristotle!" "Wrong. Hippocrates!" "Who's right here?!" "What *is* the theory of *innate heat*?" "Pneuma!" "'Pneuma'! A *word* can't be a theory!" Then: "That's what distinguishes the living from the dead in any organism . . .": *Innate heat.* "Good! Good, Doctor! Yours is not the ordinary mind!" "Well, all my life, I have striven to be . . ." "Excellent! Strive!" "Thank you."

Source: *Best Short Plays 1988,* Applause Theatre Books

✤ Handy Dandy

•••••••••••••••••••••••••••••WILLIAM GIBSON

CHARACTERS: HENRY PULASKI (57), MOLLY (72)
SETTING: *A courtroom.*

MOLLY, *a Catholic nun, appears before Judge* HENRY PULASKI *without the benefit of a lawyer. This is* MOLLY'*s fourth appearance in court for trespassing on Skidmore Laboratory. She is protesting the making of nuclear weapons.*

PULASKI: Now the Commonwealth anticipates that in your trial you'll attempt to introduce evidence as to your reasons for trespassing.
MOLLY: Oh, I just might, yes.
PULASKI: Which is what I'm to rule on today. In a trespass case an admissible defense would be consent of the owner, say. Or justification, if your reason constitutes legal justification I would of course allow it in. If it doesn't it's not relevant.
MOLLY: May I ask two questions, Your Excellency?
PULASKI: Honor, go ahead.
MOLLY: What's legal justification?
PULASKI: Oh, if my child for instance runs onto your lawn and I chase after him, there's no intent to trespass, just to retrieve the child.
MOLLY: What's illegal justification?
PULASKI: It doesn't exist.
MOLLY: Why not?
PULASKI: Because I throw it out.
MOLLY: Do you have a child, Henry?
PULASKI: I sometimes wonder. That's four questions.
MOLLY: If I had a child now I would think, when I saw the missiles zooming in, did I do anything to keep it from happening?
PULASKI: And that's your defense?
MOLLY: Yes, I don't see that it differs from snatching a child away on the lawn from somebody with a power mower. I'd say there's oh a billion power mowers in Cambridge at that one laboratory —
PULASKI: I will ask one question. And you're not obliged to answer today —

MOLLY: I don't mind.

PULASKI: Did anyone at Skidmore Laboratory ask you to leave?

MOLLY: Not ask. Shouted. Get out of here with them doves!

PULASKI: What doves?

MOLLY: We each had a lovely white dove. As a gift to Mr. Skidmore —

PULASKI: And who shouted?

MOLLY: The captain of security. Secure them doves! he said. Because once he grabbed us they were flying everywhere, a beautiful sight. It was a dove that descended from heaven of course —

PULASKI: Ahuh.

MOLLY: — and a voice said, This is my beloved Son, it didn't say, This is Skidmore Lab, where they make the little tin brains for Frankenstein monsters —

PULASKI: I know what they make there.

MOLLY: — first-strike weapons, missiles —

PULASKI: I know what they make there.

MOLLY: — and lasers, particle beam weapons —

PULASKI: They don't make power mowers! — and your private feelings about it are of no relevance to the law of trespass.

MOLLY: Of no —

PULASKI: The moment the owner through an authorized agent said to get out, whatever consent of justification may have existed ab initio terminated.

MOLLY: And what are *your* private feelings about it?

PULASKI: Also irrelevant, I've taken an oath to uphold the law as it stands. You'll have an opportunity at your trial to take the witness stand and testify, but not about Skidmore's contents, the Pope's encyclicals, or athlete's foot in Bangladesh.

MOLLY: So the jury must find whether I'm guilty of trespassing with no idea why?

PULASKI: That's correct.

MOLLY: I don't believe this world.

PULASKI: You can't make a speech to the jury, Sister, and any attempt to do so would be contemptuous of an order of this court.

MOLLY: Why?

PULASKI: Because I'm now ruling it not relevant.

MOLLY: Henry, you run a court where everything that's most relevant isn't relevant.

PULASKI: Unhappily this court doesn't make the law. I call the balls and strikes, and it's not for me to change the law; it's up to others.

MOLLY: Well, I'm trying.

PULASKI: Try a different branch of government, the legislative. Now —

MOLLY: Doesn't it ever happen you uphold the law and justice guggles down the drain?

PULASKI: It happens every day. Every day.

MOLLY: What a sorrowful job you have, Henry.

Source: Dramatists Play Service, Inc.

✣ The Heidi Chronicles

•••••••••••••••••••••••••WENDY WASSERSTEIN

CHARACTERS: SCOOP (20's), HEIDI (20's)
SETTING: *At the Eugene McCarthy for President Rally, 1967.*

HEIDI, *in a skirt and shawl, is standing alone by the food table.* SCOOP, *slightly intense but charismatic in blue jeans and workshirt, comes over to her.*

SCOOP: Are you guarding the chips?
HEIDI: No.
SCOOP: Then you're being very difficult.
HEIDI: Please, help yourself.
SCOOP: Where are you going?
HEIDI: I'm trying to listen to the music.
SCOOP: Janis Joplin and Big Brother and the Holding Company. "A-" singer. "C+" band. Far less innovative than the Kinks. You know, you really have one hell of an inferiority complex.
HEIDI: I do?
SCOOP: Sure. I have no right to say you're difficult. Don't you believe in human dignity? I mean, you're obviously a liberal or you wouldn't be here.
HEIDI: I came with a friend.
SCOOP: You came to Manchester, New Hampshire in a blizzard to ring doorbells for Gene McCarthy because of a friend? Why the fuck didn't you go skiing instead?
HEIDI: I don't ski.
   (SCOOP *offers* HEIDI *a potato chip*)
SCOOP: "B-" texture. "C+" crunch. You go to one of those Seven Sister schools?
HEIDI: How did you know?
SCOOP: You're all concerned citizens.
HEIDI: I told you, I came because of a friend.
SCOOP: That's bullshit. Be real. You're neat and clean for Eugene. You think if you go door to door and ring bells, this sucker will become President and we'll all be good people and wars in places you've never heard of before will end, and everyone will have enough to eat and send their daughters to Vassar. Like I

said, neat and clean for Eugene.

HEIDI: Would you excuse me?

(SCOOP *smiles and extends his hand to her*)

SCOOP: It's been lovely chatting with me.

HEIDI: A pleasure.

SCOOP: What's your name?

HEIDI: Susan.

SCOOP: Susan what?

HEIDI: Susan Johnston. See ya.

SCOOP: Hey, Susan Johnston, wouldn't you like to know who I am?

HEIDI: Uh . . .

SCOOP: C'mon, nice girl like you isn't going to look a man in the eye and tell him, "I have absolutely no interest in you. You've been incredibly obnoxious and your looks are 'B-'."

HEIDI: Why do you grade everything?

SCOOP: I used to be a very good student.

HEIDI: Used to?

SCOOP: I dropped out of Princeton. The Woodrow Wilson School of International Bullshit.

HEIDI: So what do you do now?

SCOOP: This and that. Here and there.

HEIDI: You work for McCarthy? Well, you are at a McCarthy dance.

SCOOP: I came with a friend. Susan, don't you know this is just the tip of the iceberg? McCarthy is irrelevant. He's a "C+" Adlai Stevenson. The changes in this country could be enormous. Beyond anything your sister mind can imagine.

HEIDI: Are you a weatherperson?

SCOOP: You mean, am I a real life radical? Do I make bombs in my parents' West Hartford basement? Susan, how could I be a radical? I played lacrosse at Exeter and I'm a Jew whose first name is Scoop. You're not very good at nuance. And you're too eager to categorize. I'm a journalist. I'm just here to have a look around.

HEIDI: Do you work for a paper?

SCOOP: Did they teach you at Vassar to ask so many inane questions in order to keep a conversation going?

HEIDI: Well, like I said. I have to meet my friend.

SCOOP: Me, too. I have to meet Paul Newman.

HEIDI: Please tell him Susan says "hi".

SCOOP: You don't believe I have to meet Paul Newman.

HEIDI: I'm sure you do.

SCOOP: I'm picking him up at the airport and taking him and Mr.

McCarthy to a press conference. Paul's a great guy. Why don't you come drinking with us? We can rap over a few brews.

HEIDI: I'm sorry. I can't.

SCOOP: Why not?

HEIDI: I just can't.

SCOOP: Susan, let me get this straight. You would rather drive back to Poughkeepsie with five virgins in a Volkswagen discussing Norman Mailer and birth control on dangerous frozen roads than go drinking with Eugene McCarthy, Paul Newman and Scoop Rosenbaum? You're cute, Susan. Very cute.

HEIDI: And you are really irritating!!

SCOOP: That's the first honest thing you've said all night! Lady, you better learn to stand up for yourself. I'll let you in on a scoop from Scoop.

HEIDI: Did they teach you construction like that at Princeton?

SCOOP: I dig you, Susan. I dig you a lot.

HEIDI: Can we say "like" instead of "dig"? I mean, while I'm standing up for myself . . .

SCOOP: I like you, Susan. You're prissy, but I like you a lot.

HEIDI: Well, I don't know if like you.

SCOOP: Why should you like me? I'm arrogant and difficult. But I'm very smart. So you'll put up with me. What?

HEIDI: What what?

SCOOP: You're thinking something.

HEIDI: Actually, I was wondering what mothers teach their sons that they never bother to tell their daughters.

SCOOP: What do you mean?

HEIDI: I mean, why the fuck are you so confident?

SCOOP: Ten points for Susan.

HEIDI: Have we moved on to points from letter grades?

SCOOP: There's hope for you. You're going to be quite the little politico.

HEIDI: I'm planning to be an art historian.

SCOOP: Please don't say that. That's really suburban.

HEIDI: I'm interested in the individual expression of the human soul. Content over form.

SCOOP: But I thought the point of contemporary art is that the form becomes the content. Look at Albers' "Homage to A Square." Three superimposed squares and we're talking perception, integration, isolation. Just three squares and they reflect the gross inadequacies of our society. Therefore, your argument is inconclusive.

HEIDI: Don't give me a Marxist interpretation of Albers.

SCOOP: You really are one fuck of a liberal! Next thing you'll tell me is how much Herbert Marcuse means to you. What?

HEIDI: Nothing.

SCOOP: I don't fuckin' believe it! You've never read Marcuse!

HEIDI: Isn't Paul Newman waiting for you, Scoop?

SCOOP: Isn't your friend waiting for you, *Heidi*? (SCOOP *jumps up*) Basket, Rosenbaum, 30 points. The score is 30 to 10.

HEIDI: How did you know my name?

SCOOP: I told you I'm a journalist. Do you really think anything gets by *The Liberated Earth News*?

HEIDI: That's your paper?

SCOOP: Editor-in-chief. Circulation 362 and growing. Okay. Truth. I know your name is Heidi because it says so (*He points to her breast*) right there on your name tag. Heidi. H-E-I-D-I.

HEIDI: Oh!

SCOOP: Oh!!!!

HEIDI: Oh well . . . (*She begins to pull the tag off*)

SCOOP: You don't have to look at the floor.

HEIDI: I'm not.

SCOOP: I've got nothing on you so far. Why are you so afraid to speak up?

HEIDI: I'm not afraid to speak up.

SCOOP: Heidi, you don't understand. You're the one this is all going to affect. You're the one whose life this will all change significantly. Has to. You're a very serious person. In fact, you're the unfortunate contradiction in terms — a serious good person. And I envy you that.

HEIDI: Thank you. I guess.

SCOOP: Yup. You'll be one of those true believers who didn't understand it was just a phase. The Trotskyite during Lenin's New Economic policy. The worshipper of fallen images in Christian Judae.

HEIDI: And you?

SCOOP: Me? I told you. I'm just here to have a look around.

HEIDI: What if you get left behind?

SCOOP: You mean if after all the politics you girls decide to go "hog wild", demanding equal pay, equal rights, equal orgasms?

HEIDI: All people deserve to fulfill their potential.

SCOOP: Absolutely.

HEIDI: I mean, why should some well-educated woman waste her life making you and your children tuna fish sandwiches?

SCOOP: She shouldn't. And for that matter, neither should a badly educated woman. Heidella, I'm on your side.

HEIDI: Don't call me "Heidella". It's diminutive.

SCOOP: You mean "demeaning", and it's not. It's endearing.

HEIDI: You're deliberately eluding my train of thought.

SCOOP: No, I'm subtly asking you to go to bed with me . . . before I go meet Paul Newman. (*Covered pause*)

HEIDI: Oh.

SCOOP: You have every right to say no. I can't guarantee absolute equality of experience.

HEIDI: I can take care of myself, thanks.

SCOOP: You've already got the lingo down, kiddo. Pretty soon you'll be burning bras.

HEIDI: Maybe I'll go "hog wild".

SCOOP: I hope so. Are you a virgin?

HEIDI: Excuse me?

SCOOP: If you choose to accept this mission, I'll find out one way or the other.

HEIDI (*Embarrassed*): That's okay.

SCOOP: Why do you cover your mouth when you talk about sex?

HEIDI: Hygiene.

(*She laughs nervously.* SCOOP *takes her hand away from her mouth*)

SCOOP: I told you. You're a serious good person. And I'm honored. Maybe you'll think fondly of all this in some Proustian haze when you're thirty-five and picking your daughter up from The Ethical Culture School to escort her to cello class before dinner with Dad, the noted psychiatrist and Miro poster collector.

HEIDI: No. I'll be busy torching lingerie.

SCOOP: Maybe I'll remember it one day when I'm thirty-five and watching my son's performance as Johnny Appleseed. Maybe I'll look at my wife who puts up with me and flash on when I was editor of a crackpot liberal newspaper and thought I could fall in love with Heidi Holland, the canvassing art historian, that first snowy night in Manchester, New Hampshire, 1967.

HEIDI: Are you guarding the chips?

SCOOP: No. I trust them. (*He kisses her*)

Source: *The Heidi Chronicles & Other Plays*, Vintage Books

✦ Hunting Cockroaches

•••••••••••••••••••••••••••JANUSZ GLOWACKI

CHARACTERS: HE (*30's*), SHE (*30's*)
SETTING: *A squalid, shabby room serving as a living room, bedroom and kitchen. New York, the present.*

SHE *(Anka) is a Polish actress in New York who can't get any parts due to her accent.* HE *(Janek) is her husband, a writer, famous in Poland, who teaches at Staten Island College for little pay. They are both having trouble sleeping, worrying about their green cards and expired visas.*

HE (*Waking or pretending to wake up*): What time it is?
SHE (*Rapidly walks to the window, looks out into the street at the large clock on the corner*): One hour later than usual. Lately you are asking me what time it is at 3 in the morning — now it's 4 in the morning.
HE: You are screaming again . . . Lately you scream in your sleep all the time.
SHE: Do I?
HE: You sit up in the bed and scream. (*Imitates her scream*)
SHE: You'll wake up everybody in the building.
HE: Then you go back to sleep immediately.
SHE: Immediately.
HE: Immediately. But then I can't fall asleep.
SHE: Yes, I know, in the morning you have your lecture at Staten Island Community College. Where they pay you nothing, but help us with our application for the green card. And you hate your classes, because: "How can you teach Franz Kafka to students who drive to school in sport cars?" . . . All right, let's go to sleep.
(HE *turns light out. They pull the blanket over their heads. Moment of silence*)
Oh my God! (SHE *turns light on*)
HE: What are you dreaming about?
SHE: I'm not dreaming about anything.
HE: You weren't dreaming about anything?
SHE: No. I wasn't even asleep.
HE: But why do you start screaming?
SHE: Because I felt like it.

HE: Maybe you were dreaming that we were back in Poland.

SHE: No.

HE: Or that somebody broke into the apartment through the window.

SHE: We have heavy iron bars on all the windows. No one can get through those bars.

HE: No harm checking. (*At the window, shakes the bars*) No, with those bars there, it would be impossible for anyone to get through that window. Your dreams are absolutely moronic.

SHE (*A look of disgust on her face, whacks the floor hard with her shoe, then whacks it again*):   It ran under the floorboard.

HE: Cut it out. That old bag under us will call the super. He's been waiting for a chance to get rid of us. Do you know how much he'd get for an apartment like this? Nowadays, in neighborhood like this? On the Lower East Side?

SHE: Oh, it's a terrific neighborhood all right. Some apartment. Constantly broken into, fifth floor without an elevator, cold in winter, hot in summer, and you can't put an air-conditioner in because the fuses will be blown . . .

HE: We can't afford an air-conditioner.

SHE: Muggers, rapers . . .

HE: It's a neighborhood for artists.

SHE: For cockroaches.

HE: What do you have against cockroaches? New York is full of cockroaches. They're everywhere. Even in millionaires' houses.

SHE: How do you know? Have you ever been in a millionaire's house?

HE: Cockroaches don't spread infection and they eat only garbage. Remember Gregor?

SHE: Gregor who?

HE: The hero of Kafka's *Metamorphosis*. The one who was transformed into a cockroach. His sister used to bring him fresh rolls, cheese and milk . . . he wouldn't even spit on it. The only thing he'd touch was garbage.

SHE: I've seen them touch our caviar.

HE: Even if they did, how much food could a cockroach eat?

SHE: Then it's the rats who eat up our food.

HE: The mice.

SHE: The rats.

HE: They're big mice. Anyhow, the mice eat the cockroaches.

SHE: How do you know?

HE: I watched them.

SHE: I heard that rats eat children.

HE: We don't have any children.
SHE: Aha . . .
HE: For God's sake, don't start that about having a baby. That's all we'd need. A baby. I want to know where we'd put it?
SHE: Over there. (*Points*)
HE: And what about us?
SHE: Over here.
HE: And what about me? Where'd I do my writing?
SHE: You're not doing any writing.
HE: I have nothing to write about.
SHE: Have you ever thought about writing nursery rhymes?
HE: Enough about baby.
SHE: That would change everything. You'd start writing. You wouldn't have any other way out.
HE: I'd always have one way out. Through the window.
SHE: With those iron bars?
HE: Let's go to sleep.
SHE: Let's.
(*Humming a lullaby, "Aa, kotki dwa, szare, bure obydwa . . . "[Aa, pussycats two, both of them are black, both of them are blue . . .] with the heavy movements of a woman in the last stages of pregnancy,* SHE *climbs into bed and turns light out. The phone rings and wakes them up. With a start they both jump out of bed. In the process the pillow slips out from under her nightgown*)
HE: What time it is?
SHE: Ten past four.
HE: Who could be calling at this time of night? (HE *turns light on*)
SHE: I have no idea.
HE: Burglars? Maybe they're checking to see if we're in?
(*The phone keeps ringing*)
SHE: Well, answer it if you're so curious.
HE: Maybe it's the super. I told you not to pound on the floor. Maybe it's . . . (*Starts to whistle*)
SHE: Stop that whistling.
(HE *keeps on whistling*)
You always whistle when you're afraid of something. I can't stand it any longer. Maybe it's who?
HE: KGB?
SHE: KGB?
HE: To scare me.
SHE: But why would they want to scare you?
HE: Because they know I hate them. Because I'm a writer, an emigré writer and I could write something.

SHE: But you're not writing anything.

HE: But I could start writing at any time.

SHE: Then start.

HE: But I don't have anything to write about.

SHE: Why would they want to scare you? You're already scared of them. Maybe it's the Immigration Office.

HE: What for?

SHE: I don't know. Maybe someone squealed on us.

HE: Squealed about what?

SHE: That our visas expired.

HE: But they promised we'd get green cards.

SHE: But we didn't get them yet. We've still got to go for another interrogation.

HE: It's not an interrogation, it's an interview. The fact that we got the notice to go means that everything's fine. Millions of people in New York are just waiting for that.

SHE: To go for an interrogation?

HE: To go for an interview.
    (*The phone keeps ringing*)

SHE: Maybe someone's calling from Europe? The time's different there. What time it is in Europe now?

HE: What time it is here?

SHE: Quarter past four.

HE: Then in Europe it must be . . .

SHE: In the morning?

HE: Yes.

SHE: Then it has to be someone from Europe.

HE: Andrzej is in France. Maybe he's calling. But just what do you think he wants from us? Oh, I know, of course. He is jealous.

SHE: Jealous? Of what?

HE: What do you mean of what? He emigrated only to Paris, and I am in New York, and I made it here.

SHE: But you didn't make it.

HE: But he doesn't know it. Maybe we should answer the phone.

SHE: Maybe we should.
    (*Bending over the telephone, they wordlessly encourage each other to pick up the receiver. Just at the moment* HE *reaches for it, the phone stops ringing*)

HE: Damn it, why did you tell me not to answer it? Now it's too late.

Source: Samuel French, Inc.

✤ Ice Cream

•••••••••••••••••••••••••••CARYL CHURCHILL

CHARACTERS: PHIL (20's), VERA (40)
SETTING: *A London flat, the present.*

VERA, *an American, is on a tour of England with her husband Lance, who is researching his family tree. They meet* PHIL *and his sister Jaq, who are English.* PHIL, *they determine, is a cousin of Lance. Which makes what happens between* VERA *and* PHIL *indefensible and irresistible. In the previous scene in a pub,* PHIL *has seen a man he says he hates.*

        (VERA *and* PHIL *kiss*)
VERA: This is a mistake.
PHIL: OK.
VERA: It didn't happen.
PHIL: No problem.
VERA: Some people do this, I don't, I never did do this, not just because of Aids, even when I was young and it was practically compulsory I was never particularly . . . it's been a relief to me that monogamy is fashionable because it was always my secret / preference.
PHIL: Secret vice?
VERA: No that's right, chastity, fidelity was my secret vice, I thought it meant I was frigid / or anyway rigid —
PHIL: I don't think you are.
VERA: well I'm not, but I thought I didn't have an appetite for life and adventure or I was insecure, I guess I may be insecure but then some of the most flamboyantly sexual people I've known have also been the most flamboyantly insecure so I don't know. I must be insecure right now or I wouldn't be talking so much.
PHIL: It wouldn't be fair to Lance.
VERA: It wouldn't — look I'm not even remotely considering. Lance adores you like I don't know I'd say like a son but the age difference is hardly, like a brother maybe, a long lost / brother, well yes cousin is it after all, kissing
PHIL: Cousin.
VERA: cousins, but Lance just is crazy about you and so am I which is all that was. I guess you feel drawn to your own flesh and

blood which is after all why the incest taboo, you don't taboo things nobody wants to do, you don't taboo kissing the furniture. Not that the relationship is within the proscribed whatsits. And anyway you're not my flesh and blood only Lance's which is kind of the same thing but of course it's not. When I think of my European ancestors I see this long row of women picking cabbages.

PHIL: Is that what they did?

VERA: I've no idea, it's a cliché, I guess I think in clichés all the time. It's depressing but then I think hell, clichés are just what's true, what millions of people have already realized is true. Like proverbs are true. A stitch in time does in fact save nine.

PHIL: Too many cooks do spoil the broth.

VERA: The early bird does catch the worm.

PHIL: Many hands do make light work. Many cooks do make light broth.

(*They laugh*)

PHIL: Two is company and three is a crowd.

VERA: There you are.

PHIL: I think you're very nice.

VERA: Good. I hope that's good?

PHIL: It is good. I'm not at all nice. I get angry.

VERA: You have good reason.

PHIL: I didn't say without reason. I have bloody good reason, don't worry.

VERA: That man sounds just horrible.

PHIL: I'll probably kill him.

VERA: Don't talk like that.

PHIL: Don't talk, all right I won't *talk.*

VERA: You're angry now. Don't be angry with me.

PHIL: The trouble with relations is they're irritating. Nothing personal. They are irritating.

VERA: Irritating does feel personal.

PHIL: Not *you, Vera,* but being related.

VERA: I kind of like it.

PHIL: That must be nice for you.

(*Pause*)

VERA: Well, there we are.

(*Pause*)

PHIL: I like your ears. People will have mentioned your eyes.

(*Pause*)

VERA: I love you. I just want to say that. I don't mean anything by it. Lance loves you too, I know he does. That's one more reason why I couldn't possibly, so it's all right to say it. You won't feel it's an overture. People feel being loved is a pressure, they like it better if you don't care, I used to notice that in the days when I felt I had to and one of the reasons I didn't take to it was I always did care when I shouldn't have. But this is quite different. Lance and I both love you. And Jaq too, we love Jaq. But somehow we particularly . . . I just wanted to get that out of the way.

PHIL: I need you.

VERA: We would do anything for you. I would die. Do I speak in clichés? I *would* die.

Source: Samuel French, Inc.

✤ In a Pig's Valise

●●●●●●●●●●●●●●●●●●●●●●●●●●●●●●●ERIC OVERMYER

CHARACTERS: TAXI (30's), DOLORES (20's)
SETTING: *At* TAXI's *office and at the Heartbreak Hotel at Neon and*
Lonely, the present.

DOLORES CON LECHE *wants* TAXI *to find out who is stealing her dreams.*

TAXI: The voice at the other end of the line had had an Hispanic
accent that was sweet as sucre and resonated like dollar signs in
my ears. I won't perjure myself and tell you that the prospect of
meeting that voice in person wasn't better than a poke in the eye
with a sharp forty-five. I needed the job.
(*The phone rings.* TAXI *answers it*)
TAXI: Nice pair of lungs, Miss —
DOLORES: Con Leche.
TAXI: Con Leche. What you've told me so far is close enough for
Cliff Notes. Why don't we get together? You can fill in the fine
print.
DOLORES: Your place or mine?
TAXI: Let's face off at center ice.
DOLORES: Know the Heartbreak?
TAXI: Hotel for mutants?
DOLORES: That's the one. Meet me tonight at the Heartbreak, Mr.
Taxi. After midnight. You can catch my act.
TAXI: I'm running a fever already.
DOLORES: It's an eye-opener.
(*She hangs up as lights and music dissolve.* TAXI *hangs up. He burps
delicately*)
TAXI: Those dissolves always make me motion sick. Whoever she
was, she gave great phone. After I hung up the horn, I closed the
office for the afternoon. I gave my faithful amanuensis, "Legs"
Lichtenstein, the rest of the week off. She'd earned it. I hadn't
paid her since fiscal '57. Legs. What a word jockey. But that's
another story. I sauntered over to my local gin joint and tossed
down a couple of muscles. For you rookies out there, a muscle is
standard-issue detective drink: Kahlua and Maalox. Then I
grabbed some shut-eye in the back of my Chevy. (*Beat*) Con
Leche's voice haunted my dreams like guava jelly. Spread sweet

and smooth. I was stuck on that voice. Like enamel on a molar. (*Shivers*) If I come down with something. Neon and Lonely. The Heartbreak Hotel at Neon and Lonely. Love it.

(*A throbbing bass line is heard.* TAXI *snuffs his cigarette and turns up his collar*)

Something funky this way comes.

(DOLORES *steps out of the shadows*)

DOLORES: Nice pair of — lungs, Mr. Taxi.

TAXI (*In the VO*): I had eggroll all over my kisser. An Hispanic hallucination was hovering nearby like heat on a desert highway.

DOLORES: You talking to me? And why the past tense, pal?

TAXI: It's a convention, sweetheart. You ain't supposed to hear, dig? It's for them. (*Indicates audience*) The Big VO. Keeps 'em au courant.

DOLORES: Is a VO anything like an MO?

TAXI (*Warily*): Maybe. Who wants to know? Let's just say I'm cogitating a capella.

DOLORES: It's a free country.

TAXI: Don't kid yourself. Say, you got a Dramamine, sister? I got a case of dissolve sickness. I feel like a side o' slaw strewn on a soggy paper plate.

DOLORES: Those hard-boiled similes get pretty thin. As thin as the skin on a cup of hot cocoa.

TAXI: As thin as the crust on an East Coast pizza pie.

DOLORES: Neon and Lonely. Great spot for a rendezvous.

TAXI: This corner is seedier than a strawberry.

DOLORES: And darker than a landlord's heart. Thanks for showing up, Mr. Taxi.

TAXI: My pleasure, Miss Con Leche. Sleep is out of style this season. Let's get down to the storyline. What's the drumbeat, baby?

DOLORES: I want you to locate something for me.

TAXI: Is it yours?

DOLORES: Yeah.

TAXI: Sounds legal. Maybe we can do business. I have irresistible charm. Once you meet me, you never want to let me go.

DOLORES: I find that difficult to swallow. Although I can believe the vice squad feels that way.

TAXI: They refer you?

DOLORES: As a matter of fact, Mr. Taxi, I picked you at random from the yellow pages. I was trying to call a cab.

TAXI: I've heard that one. If I had a thousand bucks for every time I've heard that one, I wouldn't be here now.

DOLORES: I just assumed that all private dicks were alike —

TAXI & DOLORES (*In unison, more or less*):   In the dark.

TAXI: Let's eight-six the bright banter, shall we? And enough with the dick jokes. I hear enough dick jokes in the course of a day —

TAXI & DOLORES (*In unison, more or less*):   To choke a horse.

TAXI: Okay, Con Leche. Lay it on me with a trowel. This missing something — stolen?

DOLORES: Repeatedly.

TAXI: Once rabid, twice shy. Valuable?

DOLORES: Priceless.

TAXI: Sure, sure, they all say that. I'm not your insurance company, lady.

DOLORES: Uninsurable.

TAXI: No kidding. Description.

DOLORES: Dreams.

TAXI (*Sighs*):   Could we be specific, Miss Con Leche? What are we talking about here?

DOLORES: Dreams. Someone is stealing my dreams.

TAXI: Dreams.

DOLORES: Stolen? Lifted. Light-fingered. Long gone.

TAXI: Let's get literal, Miss Con Leche.

DOLORES (*Touching herself*):   This is as literal as I get, Mr. Taxi.

TAXI: Metaphor is for poets, kid. We hard-boiled guys go for palpable factology. We like simile. Like or as. Like a dream. As if in a dream. But not a dream dream. I don't believe in dreams. Except the kind that exist out there in the zeitgeist. You can put your meathooks on 'em.

DOLORES: Zeitgeist?

TAXI: Like, my dream is a pair of center-court season tickets. My dream is a condo in the clouds. My dream is a garnet-colored Jag with custom plates.

DOLORES: You're slow, Taxi. I'm hablando-ing straight. Someone is stealing my dreams. My brain's being boosted. Look.
    (*Flashback music*)

DOLORES: It all began a month ago. I answered an ad —

TAXI (*Detecting ferociously*):   What ad? Where?

DOLORES: Cool your jets. This ad for folk dancers. Ethnic folk dancers. That's my profession. They were hiring ethnic folk dancers down at The Heartbreak Hotel.

TAXI: Flashback me back, baby, and don't edit the tape. Sure you don't have a Dramamine?

DOLORES: Watch my tracks, hard guy.

Source: *Seven Different Plays*, Broadway Play Publishing, Inc.

✤ Italian American Reconcilation

•••••••••••••••••••••JOHN PATRICK SHANLEY

CHARACTERS: ALDO (30's), JANICE (30's)
SETTING: *The rear of* JANICE's *house in Little Italy, New York, the present.*

ALDO, *an intense Italian guy, wants to help his pal, Huey, who has been an emotional wreck ever since his divorce from* JANICE *three years ago. Huey's plan is to break up with Teresa, his present girlfriend, and try to win back* JANICE. *He calls upon* ALDO *to pave the way for him with* JANICE, *who is extremely volatile. Just before the divorce,* JANICE *had killed Huey's dog with a zip gun and had taken a shot at Huey.* ALDO *decides that it would be in Huey's best interest* not *to reconcile with* JANICE, *and to insure Huey's failure, plans to seduce* JANICE *himself.*

> (JANICE *steps out onto her balcony. She is an angular, patrician Roman with strawberry blond hair and austere good looks. She's wearing a soft white nightgown which makes her look like a young girl. In her arms she cradles six fat roses. She looks at the sky, full of emotion. One by one she tosses the flowers to the ground below. The last bloom she starts to smell, changes her her mind suddenly, and throws it down as well. She looks down at the flowers, and bleakly says, "What for?" Then she goes back inside.* ALDO, *in a sharp jacket and tie, appears at the garden gate. He tries to open it, fails, and climbs over. He sees the flowers lying on the ground. He calls in a loud whisper)*

ALDO: Janice. Janice. Janice.
> (JANICE *reemerges. She's tying a black velvet robe with padded shoulders. The effect is striking but more adult and severe)*

JANICE: Who's that?
ALDO: It's Aldo. Scalicki.
JANICE: What are you doing in my backyard?
ALDO: I rang the bell about fifty times, but nobody answered.
JANICE: It's broken.
ALDO: You should have it fixed.
JANICE: Why?
ALDO: So it rings.
JANICE: What do I care if it rings? I don't see anybody.

ALDO: Well, you still might get a delivery or something. Flowers or something. Somebody send you flowers?

JANICE: Yes.

ALDO: Very nice.

JANICE: They're from Huey.

ALDO: How you know that?

JANICE: I know.

ALDO: Well, then, you shouldn't be so confident. You're wrong. I sent the flowers.

JANICE: You? Why would you send me flowers?

ALDO: I sent them for Huey.

JANICE: Can't even manage to send his own flowers.

ALDO: What d'you mean?

JANICE: He's hapless. He's a buffoon.

ALDO: He's my best friend.

JANICE: That's your problem.

ALDO: Anyway, it's a shame you destroyed them like this.

JANICE: They were dead anyway.

ALDO: Maybe they were dead, but they were expensive. (*He starts to gather them*) They're not really destroyed. (*He lays them on the table*)

JANICE: Why are you here?

ALDO: Beautiful night.

JANICE: I wish it would rain.

ALDO: Beautiful stars.

JANICE: Stars make me think of death.

ALDO: I can smell the greenness of the leaves.

JANICE: It smells like a cemetery. What are you doing here?

ALDO: Huey asked me to come.

JANICE: Why?

ALDO: He wants to patch it up with you.

JANICE: Patch up what?

ALDO: What d'you think? The marriage.

(JANICE *chuckles dryly*)

What's so funny?

JANICE: Think about it.

ALDO: You wanna come down?

JANICE: No.

(*A pause*)

ALDO: Janice, Janice, Janice.

JANICE: What?

ALDO: We've seen some stuff, huh?

JANICE: What are you talking about?

ALDO: 'Member when we were kids? I'd play Julius Caesar and you'd stab me with the rubber knife and yell Die! Die!

JANICE: I remember.

ALDO: You were some nutty little girl.

JANICE: You were a jerk.

ALDO: I was very innocent.

JANICE: You were a jerk.

ALDO: I was a little kid. I was supposed to be a jerk.

JANICE: You did it perfectly.

(A pause)

ALDO: Janice, Janice, Janice.

JANICE: Why do you keep saying that?

ALDO: We've been around the block a few times.

JANICE: Aldo. You are still the same hammerheaded clown you always were. Are you trying to be smooth? You come here outta no place. You send flowers. You say, Janice, Janice, Janice. Am I supposed to be getting the idea? How 'bout just spitting it out?

ALDO: Huey wants to make it up with you.

JANICE: Why are you saying this? Where's Huey?

ALDO: He sent me first.

JANICE: Oh, I get it. He always was a coward.

ALDO: Huey is not a coward.

JANICE: Huey always was a coward, and you always were a stooge. If he wasn't a coward he'd be standing here in his own shoes speaking his own words. If you weren't a stooge, you wouldn't be a standing in somebody else's love scene. Ain't you got no girl of your own?

ALDO: I got girls comin' out my ears.

JANICE: What a picture.

ALDO: I didn't come here to talk about me.

JANICE: That's 'cause you're a stooge.

ALDO: Stop callin' me that! You can be a very difficult woman to talk to, Janice.

JANICE: Really?

ALDO: Yes. I mean, if I was here on my own . . . I mean, if I was the specific guy who was tryin' to romance you, I gotta tell you I wouldn't even know where to begin. You are so . . . nasty.

JANICE: I am?

ALDO: Yeah, you're like a fiend. Your eyes look like vampire vulture monster fiend eyes.

JANICE: They do?

ALDO: Yes, they do. And you always smile only for the wrong, the most horriblest reason. Sometimes when you smile I expect to see like fangs fall down over your lower lip. I've had the experience when you smile where I wanted to run away down the street 'cause I was afraid you were gonna bite me.

JANICE: Really?

ALDO: You're not angry?

JANICE: Why would I be?

ALDO: I thought 'cause I was telling you the truth that I might be insulting.

JANICE: I'm not insulted.

ALDO: Well, good. 'Cause it feels much more relaxing for me to tell the truth. I expected to have to do a lot of lying tonight.

JANICE: Why?

ALDO: You know.

JANICE: No, I don't.

ALDO: You know. Romance. Lies.

JANICE: I like the truth.

ALDO: So do I. You know, sometimes when I catch sight a you unexpected, my balls jump up in a bunch like I dropped 'em inna glass a ice water
(JANICE *laughs heartily*)
You think that's funny?

JANICE: Yeah. Don't you?

ALDO: Yeah, but I thought you'd be like the last person in the world to get the joke.

JANICE: You don't know me, Aldo.

ALDO: I guess not.

JANICE: You always amazed me. Why'd you let me stab you and bury you and treat you like a dog?

ALDO: I don't know.

JANICE: You oughta think about these things.

ALDO: I have thought about 'em, and I still don't know.

JANICE: I did all that stuff to you to see how much you'd take. I thought, Maybe if I kick him one more time, he'll stand up and take my shoes away.

ALDO: Take your shoes? Why would I take your shoes?

JANICE: To take charge of me like a man.

ALDO: What are you saying?

JANICE: You still don't get it, do you? I was flirting with you.

ALDO: That was flirting?

JANICE: Sure.

ALDO: No, that wasn't flirting. You may have felt flirting, but you weren't doing flirting. You were treating me like I was the snake in the apple tree.

JANICE: You just didn't get it.

ALDO: I woulda gotten it if you did it right.

JANICE: You would have gotten it if you weren't so stupid.

ALDO: All right. Anyway, thanks.

JANICE: For what?

ALDO: I don't know. For feeling like flirting with me, even if I didn't get it. Listen, I wanna apologize for what I said before. I don't think you're nasty.

JANICE: I am, though.

ALDO: No. It's like this what we were just talking about. I've just misunderstood you, so I was afraid of you.

JANICE: You've understood me well enough. I've never asked to be understood any better.

ALDO: But you're not this monster I made you out. You don't have evil eyes. You don't have big teeth and you're not gonna bite me.

JANICE: I might.

ALDO: Listen, Janice, I think you're okay. You've had your problems just like the rest of us and who am I to pass judgement on you? No matter what I said, you and I go back to the beginning and under everything I'm always gonna have a warm spot for you. The final ultimate drift is I know you're a nice person and I'm gonna make a real effort to remember that from now on.

JANICE: Don't bother on my account.

ALDO: I am, though. I'll tell you something. I'm very titillated that you was flirting with me, even in those ancient days. Have you ever . . . felt like that . . . since?

JANICE: Never.

ALDO: You must have your romantic fantasies here, livin' by yourself. Like you're that princess trapped in that castle surrounded by thorny bushes. Waiting for Prince Valiant to happen by. You must have thoughts like that. On occasion.

JANICE: Never.

ALDO: The thought of you has crossed my mind from time to time. In an unterrifying way. I have a fantasy life, you know.

JANICE: Do you?

ALDO: Oh yes. I have a very full and real fantasy life, and from time to time, you appear there.

JANICE: Aldo, are you hitting on me?

ALDO: Maybe I am.

JANICE: This is too delicious.

ALDO: What d'you mean?

JANICE: You're supposed to be here for Huey.

ALDO: So. Maybe I'm not the stooge you thought. Maybe I got my own agenda of feelings. Janice, I'm gonna be out there with you. I've been thinking about you. The thought of your face and your figure has been eating me up lately. How 'bout it?

JANICE: How 'bout what?

ALDO: How 'bout I come upstairs and we rip up the bed a little bit?

JANICE: Just like that.

ALDO: That's right. Impulsive.

JANICE: All right. What the hell.

ALDO: Really?

JANICE: I'll come down an open the door. (JANICE *goes in*)

ALDO (*To himself*): That was easy.

(JANICE *comes back on the terrace with a zip gun.* ALDO *has his back to her*)

JANICE: Aldo.

(ALDO *turns around and sees the gun*)

ALDO: Holy Moly!

(JANICE *fires. The gun, defective, blows up. It burns her fingers. She drops it.* ALDO, *meanwhile, dives under the table*)

JANICE: You dunce! You oaf! You slimy sewer rat. Damn it. Look at that. I burned my finger. What do you take me for, you comical boob? Am I not supposed to see through you? You're like cellophane! Let's rip up the bed a little bit. God!

ALDO: Don't shoot me!

JANICE: I can't. My gun broke.

ALDO (*Comes out from under the table*): You shot a gun at me.

JANICE: Don't be obvious.

ALDO: You tried to kill me!

JANICE: I burned my finger. That's what I get for usin' zip guns. Next time it's Smith and Wesson.

Source: Dramatists Play Service, Inc.

✤ June 8, 1968

●●●●●●●●●●●●●●●●●●●●●ANNA THERESA CASCIO

CHARACTERS: COOKIE (*30*), BEDRA (*15*)
SETTING: *A railroad track in Elizabeth, New Jersey. June 8, 1968.*

BEDRA *is very 60's, wearing a peace sign, political buttons, and beaded high-top moccasins.* COOKIE *is a handsome, lanky man. As Bobby Kennedy's death train rumbles close to a marsh in New Jersey,* COOKIE *and* BEDRA *meet.* COOKIE, *a faded rock star turned CIA man, has been sent to dupe* BEDRA *into giving him proof she holds of the assassination.*

COOKIE: Look, if I make you uncomfortable, I'll leave. (*Gathers his things*)
BEDRA: I'm alone most of the time. I practice speaking to guys in my room. I rehearse witty repartee so that if I ever get to go to college I'll be socially competent.
COOKIE: With shoes like that, you'll attract boys, no problem.
BEDRA: Are you making fun?
COOKIE: Hell no. I saw Grace Slick wearing those same shoes during her concert last week.
BEDRA: Far out.
COOKIE: They look better on you.
BEDRA: Oh sure.
COOKIE: You remind me of her a little.
BEDRA: You can stay until the train passes, I guess.
COOKIE: Well, thanks, babe. How about we cook up these frog legs?
BEDRA: I simply adore frog legs, thank you.
COOKIE: I have a can of Sterno. I'll do the cooking. (*Sets up a can of Sterno on the train tracks*)
BEDRA: I brought some Pop Tarts. The newest in prepackaged snacks. (*Overturns contents of her bag, looking for Pop Tarts*) If you're looking for the tapes they're not in here.
(*Looks at* COOKIE; *he looks back*)
COOKIE: Tapes of what? Of me?
BEDRA: Ah, here. (*Has Pop Tarts*) Ever had one?
COOKIE: Not yet.
BEDRA: They're made from old album covers.

COOKIE: Whose?

BEDRA: Yours.

COOKIE: At least they're good for something.

BEDRA: And the Monkees.

COOKIE: Oh, below the belt.

BEDRA: Hit Parade thinks Art Garfunkel sounds just like you used to.

COOKIE: I tried to convince CBS records to start the rumor that I had died and Garfunkel was really me reincarnated but they didn't buy it. They think he's really Connie Francis. Garfunkel copied my style. Without shame and verbatim, stole from me right and left.

BEDRA: Same sort of insipid falsetto. Same darting pudenda-like tongue used in a feigned swoon of sensuality. Same lack of razor stubble and same artistic pretension.

COOKIE: You grew up into an avant-garde kind o' gal, didn't you?

BEDRA: I'm going to be a radical when I get a little older. Maybe sooner. I know something no one else knows.

COOKIE: Now there's a puerile notion if I ever heard one.

BEDRA: Don't you want to know what it is?

COOKIE: Everybody thinks they know something special.

BEDRA: That's so cynical, are you a radical?

COOKIE: Not yet. I'm going to work inside the system to accomplish something. Right now, though, I have to carefully edit all of my opinions. They're giving me my own variety show next fall. On prime time.

BEDRA: What sort of Faustian dickering did you have to do to arrange that?

COOKIE: How can you ask that?

BEDRA: You mean some TV people just appeared at your door and offered you a show after all these years of lying fallow?

COOKIE: Is that so hard to believe?

BEDRA: Yes.

COOKIE: You're right. Meeting you is one of the terms of my agreement.

BEDRA: Bullshit. You're a jerk. Even when I was a member of your fan club I thought you were vapid. Go away.

COOKIE: Why are you so mad at me?

BEDRA: This is my spot. I don't know what you're doing here.

COOKIE: You are really paranoid. It so happens that I frequently hunt frogs here. I thought I discovered this oasis.

BEDRA: I thought you lived in Kentucky or someplace.

COOKIE: What, I can't move? I moved back to New York to begin preproduction for my television show.

BEDRA: That makes sense, I suppose.

COOKIE: Maybe I'll write a song about us waiting here for the train.

BEDRA: I don't need you to make me famous. You might need me, though. I am the key player in revealing a monumental conspiracy and it's not inconceivable that they'll do a movie about me with Jill St. John or maybe Katherine Ross playing me. I think Katherine Ross has a more intelligent look so, naturally, she's my first choice. I'll get you an audition but I can't make any promises because, personally, I think it's too late for you to make another start in show business.

COOKIE: Does the gun frighten you?

BEDRA: Should it?

COOKIE: Yes.

BEDRA: I've been around guns all my life. (*Takes gun from him*)

COOKIE: There's such a trend these days for kids to reveal that they've lived tough and sordid lives. They think it makes them just fascinating.

BEDRA: It does. I became a migrant worker when I was twelve. Picking lettuce for a dollar a day in California before Cesar Chavez came along and organized us.

COOKIE: All manner of guns and violence involved in that kind o' life, I'd imagine. So how'd you get here from California?

BEDRA: What, I can't move? On my fifteenth birthday last year Bobby Kennedy visited the farm where I worked. I was fraught with disease — I had carbuncles and my tongue was turning black for no apparent reason. I was sticking to this mattress in the bus — we lived in an old bus, propped up on some cinderblocks, three families and me, a total of eighteen people. The mattress was thick with smegma and crusty with squashed bugs. It had that dead bug smell. That smell that comes from a jar full of lightning bugs that you leave on the window sill all night. I had running sores and festering wounds which are one in the same thing but that's what I had. When I met Bobby Kennedy. He took my sticky, fetid body in his arms and he cried for me. He gave me some iced tea from a thermos. It was the best thing I have ever tasted. The owner of the farm came with a gun and said to Bobby, "You're just a do-gooder trying to make some headlines." Bobby said, "You are something out of the 19th century. I wouldn't let an animal live in this bus." And the farmer, our boss, said, "They like it. It's like camping out."

COOKIE: So, migrant worker girls have a lot of time to listen to the radio and belong to my fan club?

BEDRA: What's it to you?

COOKIE: I'm just finding the dichotomy of you rather hard to believe. I thought you might be someone else, that's all.

BEDRA: Oh yeah, who? (*Shoots a frog; there isn't anything left of it*)

COOKIE: Great Captain Scott, you obliterated it.

BEDRA: You're supposed to use rabbit shot, not a damn 357. Jeez.

COOKIE: Where is your sportsmanship, darlin'? It's more of a challenge this way. To aim so perfectly you destroy only the heads and keep the legs completely intact.

BEDRA: Something about frogs reminds me of men who work for the FBI.

COOKIE: Really? They remind me of Mafia men. Try again. You'll improve.

BEDRA: The day after Bobby Kennedy visited the farm, the farm owner flew east to New Jersey, just a few miles from here. He was going to his goddaughter's fifteenth birthday soirée. The farmer was best friends with a Mafia boss and was an American godfather to the Mafioso's shy and uncomely daughter. To show his respect he gives his goddaughter a thoroughbred pony for her birthday. A pony and a book of Alexander Pope's writing. (*Shoots another frog. A better aim this time*)

COOKIE (*Picks it up and hangs it with the rest*):
   "Who sees with equal eye, as God of all,
   A hero perish or a sparrow fall,
   Atoms or systems into ruin hurled,
   And now a bubble burst, and now a world."

BEDRA: You're so versed in Alexander Pope, name the piece that's from.

COOKIE: It's from Epistle I of Alexander Pope's *An Essay on Man*.

BEDRA: Verse?

COOKIE: Pardon?

BEDRA: What verse?

COOKIE: 87.

BEDRA: You know Verse 309? It's my favorite.

COOKIE: Start it for me. It's been since high school.

BEDRA: No one studies this stuff in high school. You were sent here to chat me up, weren't you? They taught you all these things about me, didn't they? So you'd gain my confidence and make me divulge my secret. Oh my God, I'm living a movie.

COOKIE: I've always liked Alexander Pope. Verse 309 was my wife's favorite. Let's see . . . "Yet let me flap this bug with gilded wings,/This painted child of dirt that stinks and stings" —

BEDRA: "Whose buzz the witty and the fair annoys,/Yet wit never tastes and beauty never enjoys." It's my favorite verse too.

COOKIE: How do you know so much Alexander Pope? Being a migrant worker and all.

BEDRA: The farmer I worked for made me wrap the book for his goddaughter. I memorized a lot. I'm a quick study. He tells his goddaughter's father about Bobby visiting. The Mafia guy hates Bobby because of the organized crime hullabaloo in 1963 and accepts the farmer's contribution to the "Assassination of Bobby Kennedy Fund." And, get this, when I was a migrant worker on that ranch I found out that Lee Harvey Oswald worked there in the fifties and Sirhan Sirhan visited there on several occasions.

COOKIE: Who are you?

BEDRA: Michelle Phillips.

COOKIE: You don't want to be her, do you? A piece of Muzak fluff with a group like the Mamas and the Papas on the fast fade off the charts.

BEDRA: She isn't a virtuoso singer, I know that. But she has skin like Formica. I have pores the size of dimes. I use nail polish remover to clear up my skin. I'm an orphan, you know.

COOKIE: No you're not.

BEDRA: What do you mean, no you're not. A statement like I'm an orphan is not a statement a person can dispute.

COOKIE: I'm an orphan.

BEDRA: How very Dickensian. Who's the patron saint of orphans?

COOKIE: St. Jerome Iliani.

BEDRA: How did you know that?

COOKIE: I'm from the CIA. I know everything I'm supposed to know.

Source: International Creative Management

✤ Laughing Wild

•••••••••••••••••••••••CHRISTOPHER DURANG

CHARACTERS: MAN (20's-40's), WOMAN (20's-40's)
SETTING: *A television talk show, the present.*

Since this is a self-contained scene, let Christopher Durang explain it all for you:

> (*Enter the* MAN *dressed as the Infant of Prague. Now what do I mean by this? The Infant of Prague is a 17th-Century artist's invention of what the Christ Child, triumphant, might look like. Catholics are familiar with the look of this — usually in Infant of Prague statues — found in their churches, or sometimes on dashboards. Non-Catholics usually have not heard of the Infant of Prague, but some may recognize the "look". The "look". is this: a golden-haired child (of about ten to twelve maybe), dressed ornately. The most common look has white robes, embroidered with pearls and jewels, covered with a bright red cape, with white ruffles at the neck and wrists. On the top of the child's golden curls is a great big whopping crown, of gold and red, not unlike the crown in Imperial Margarine commercials on TV. [That is, it's big and has the "ball-like" red thing at the top of it.] The Infant in his left hand always carries a large orb [usually blue, and with a gold cross on top of it], and always has his right hand raised, with his first two fingers held upright, and his thumb and other two fingers folded in on one another. Since the Infant of Prague is usually a statue or sometimes a large doll whose silhouette often spreads out like an inverted "Y" due to the fullness of his robes, the New York designer chose to make the costume resemble a statue rather than a person. The robes spread out very wide to the side [on a kind of inner tubing] so that as costumed the Infant looked rather like an enormous, walking chess piece. When the audience saw underneath the Infant's robes, they saw a smooth, stretched white covering out of which two slippered feet protruded — again, looking very much like the bottom of a statue, and not that of a human being. Anyway, that, in words, is what the Infant of Prague looks like. And that is how the* MAN *is dressed on his entrance. The Infant's personality, by the way, as played by the* MAN, *is sunny and beatifically unflappable*)

WOMAN (*To herself*):   Why am I dreaming about the Infant of Prague? I don't even know what that is.

MAN (*To audience; not in character as the Infant, and perhaps lowering his upraised right hand*): I dreamt I was the Infant of Prague appearing on the Sally Jesse Raphael show, though I've never even heard of her. (*The* MAN *raises his right hand, with its two upraised fingers, and resumes being the Infant*)

WOMAN: Infant of Prague, won't you sit down?

MAN: Thank you, Sally, I only stand.

WOMAN: I'm not Sally. Sally is dead.

MAN (*With sympathy*): Oh. And is she in heaven with my father?

WOMAN: I really don't know. Enough chitchat. Tell me — "Infant of Prague" — is that your first name?

MAN: My name is the Infant of Prague, and I am a representation of the Christ Child.

WOMAN: Really. Where do you live?

MAN: I am housed in the Church of Our Lady of Victory in Prague, capital of Czechoslovakia.

WOMAN (*A penetrating question*): Where is Prague exactly?

MAN: It's in Czechoslovakia.

WOMAN: And where is Czechoslovakia?

MAN (*Confused*): It's in Prague.

WOMAN: Ahahahahahahaha! (*To Infant*) That's my signature. Do you like my glasses? They're red. That way you can't tell if roving street gangs beat me up or not.

MAN: What?

WOMAN: Never mind. Tell us, Infant, a little bit about yourself.
(*The Infant addresses a lot of his comments directly and happily to the audience because he is a born teacher, and because he is divine*)

MAN: A statue of me was given to the Discalced Carmelites in Prague in 1628 by princess Polyxena Lobkowitz.

WOMAN: Polly who Lobka-what?

MAN: The statue was a gift from her mother, Maria Mariquez de Lara, who had brought the statue with her to Bohemia when she married the Czech nobleman, Vratsilav of Pernstyn.

WOMAN: Princeton? Princeton, New Jersey?

MAN: No, not Princeton. *Pern*-styn.

WOMAN: Uh huh. I wonder if I have any other guests that could come on. (*Calls off-stage*) Oh, Ed? Is there anybody back there? (*To herself*) Who's Ed? I don't know any Ed. Oh never mind (*To Infant*) Tell us, Infant, a little about what you're wearing. (*To audience*) That's pretty wild, isn't it troops?

MAN: I'm glad you asked me that, Sally.

WOMAN: I'm not Sally. Sally's dead.

MAN: Then she's in heaven with my father. My inner garments are similar to the priest's alb, and are made of white linen and of lace. (*Proudly shows a bit of his undergarments, or beneath a ruffle*)

WOMAN: Ooooh, this is getting racy.

MAN: Please don't make sacrilegious remarks or I'll have to leave.

WOMAN: I always get the difficult guests. First Eartha Kitt, and now a tea cozy.

MAN (*Turning as in a fashion show*):   Covering my inner garments is a miniature liturgical cope, made of heavy damask, richly woven with gold and embroidered with pearls. (*In the New York production, the* WOMAN *actually went out into the audience to ask her questions, rather as Phil Donahue and Sally Jesse Raphael often do*)

WOMAN: Wow, you could really feed a lot of starving people with that outfit, there, couldn't you, Infant?

MAN (*Firmly*):   Most people do not eat gold and pearls, Sally.

WOMAN: Sally's dead, how many times do I have to tell you that!

MAN: Three times, representing the Blessed Trinity. Father, Son and Holy Spirit.

WOMAN (*Referring to the orb*):   What's that little paperweight in your hand?

MAN: This is not a paperweight. It is a miniature globe, signifying the world-wide kingship of the Christ Child.

WOMAN: Uh huh. Well, fine, let's move on, shall we? (*A glint in her eye*) Let's talk about condoms for a bit. Your church isn't very big on condoms, is it?

MAN: When people ask me, the Infant of Prague, for advice on sexuality, I sometimes think to myself, what do I know about sex? — I'm an infant. What's more, I'm the Infant of Prague; I can't sit down, let alone have sex. (*Laughs goodnaturedly at his quip*) But what people don't realize sometimes is that God my father has a holy and blessed purpose to the mystery of sexuality, and that purpose is to create other little infants like myself to glorify God and creation. That is why condoms are wrong because anything that intercepts — or *contra*-cepts — this process is deeply wrong.

WOMAN: Now let's get real here for a second, Infant. People are always going to have sex, and now we have this deadly disease AIDS which is killing people, and one of the ways to protect oneself is to use a condom. Now don't you think we better get *practical* here, and get people to use condoms? Whaddya say, Infant of Prague???

MAN: We must instruct the people at risk to abstain from sex.

WOMAN: Oh, well, fine. And we can tell the waterfall to stop falling, but is that practical?

MAN: Moses parted the Red Sea. (*Smiles at the audience, having made an unassailable point*)

WOMAN: Uh huh. So let's get this straight — you would prefer that adolescents die from AIDS rather than tell them about condoms?

MAN: I do not prefer this at all, Sally. Yes, I know, Sally is dead. Sorry, I keep forgetting. Sally, I would tell all the teenagers of the world to be like me, an infant without sexual urges, until they were much, much older and ready to commit to one person for life, and to glory in the sacramental beauty of sex, within marriage, where during the actual act of intercourse all you can think about is "Procreation! Procreation! I am going to have a little baby, a little infant to glorify God!"

WOMAN: Well, the teenagers in New Jersey are gonna love that answer. *Come on, Infant.* Don't you think you're a *little* impractical?

MAN: The Divine *is* impractical, that's why it's divine.

(*The Infant smiles delightedly, another unassailable point. The* WOMAN *would like to kill him*)

WOMAN (*To audience*): We have to take a little break here but we'll be right back with more of the Infant of Prague.

(*ON-THE-AIR sign goes off; and theme music starts. Off the air, the* WOMAN *unleashes her pent-up fury and begins to pummel the Infant*) YOU JERK, YOU STUBBORN SHIT, YOU EFFEMINATE EUNUCH, YOU MAKE ME WANT TO VOMIT WITH YOUR HOLIER THAN THOU ATTITUDE! WHY SHOULD WE LISTEN TO YOU ABOUT SEX??? YOU'RE AFRAID OF SEX, YOUR IDEAS ON SEX ARE RIGID AND INSANE, AND SOMEONE SHOULD HAVE YOU KILLED! I WANT YOU *DEAD*! DIE, DIE, DIE!

(*The Infant looks startled and alarmed during this outburst. Towards the end of her outburst, one of her hits makes him fall over backwards, and the* WOMAN *dives on top of him, continuing her pummelling. The ON-THE-AIR sign comes back on, as does the theme music. The* WOMAN *looks out, caught in the act of straddling and beating up her guest. She gets off of him and talks to the camera. The Infant remains on the ground, unable to stand up due to the weight of his clothes and crown. He struggles from time to time, moving his slippered feet about pathetically*)

Well, we're back on the air now. Ahahahahaha. Let's *talk* about "air," and the ozone layer, shall we? (*Notices the Infant's strug-gling; explains to the camera*) He fell down during the commercial.

MAN: Would you help me stand up, please?

WOMAN: Wait a minute. Give me your opinion on the destruction of the ozone layer.

MAN: I am opposed to the destruction of the ozone layer, Sally.

WOMAN: Who did we tell you was dead?

MAN: Sally.

WOMAN: Right answer. All right, I'll help you up now.

(*The* WOMAN *helps the Infant stand up. He look disoriented for a moment*)

Okay. Let's go for the "gold". What about homosexuality — is it disgusting or is it delightful?

MAN: It is a grievous sin. But I love homosexuals, I just want them to be celibate until they die.

WOMAN: Who booked this jerk on here anyway??? (*Calls off-stage again*) Ed, I'm talking to you!

MAN: Where is Sally?

WOMAN: Who is Ed?

MAN: I don't want to be interviewed by you anymore. (*Starts to wander toward off-stage and to call out*) Sally? Sally!

WOMAN (*Takes out a gun and aims it at him*):   I killed Sally Jesse Raphael, and I can kill you! (*Shoots him several times*)

MAN: It is not possible to kill the Infant of Prague.

(*He exits happily. She is enraged*)

WOMAN (*Calling off after him*):   I hate you, I hate you, you Infant of Prague! (*To audience*) I hate religious bigots. And I hate people who think they know what's right. And I hate people who are filled with hate. And I hate people who are filled with love. I wish my mother had had me killed when I was a fetus. That's the kind of person I am. Do you get it? Ahahahahahaha!

WOMAN'S VOICE (*On tape*):   My next guest today is Rama Sham Rama.

WOMAN: I don't want no fucking next guest! (*Shoots her gun off-stage, apparently stopping Rama Sham Rama; then calls off in the other direction*) Ed!! You're fired! (*Shoots her gun off in Ed's direction*)

Source: Dramatists Play Service, Inc.

✥ Lend Me a Tenor

••••••••••••••••••••••••••••••••KEN LUDWIG

CHARACTERS: MAX *(30's)*, MAGGIE *(20's)*
SETTING: *An elegant suite in an old-world hotel in Cleveland, Ohio, 1934.*

MAGGIE *is* MAX's *girlfriend.* MAX *loves* MAGGIE *very much, but she is currently in awe of Tito Merelli, a world-famous tenor who is coming to Cleveland to perform.* MAX *fancies himself a good tenor, but nobody takes him seriously. In this scene* MAGGIE *isn't even taking* MAX's *love seriously.*

MAX: ... Sir? ... Sir? (MAX *hangs up*) He's gonna kill me.
MAGGIE: He will not. He'd have nobody to yell at. At least nobody who takes it the way you do.
MAX: Maggie, the man is two hours late! The rehearsal starts in *ten minutes*!!
MAGGIE: He'll be here, Max. This is Tito Merelli. He's a genius. They just don't think like other people.
MAX: So what are you saying? He's a grown man and he can't tell time?
MAGGIE: I'm just not worried, OK? (*Pause*) Oh, Max, just think of it. Tonight. The curtain rises and he walks onstage. And suddenly there's nothing else in the world but that ... that *voice.* (*Pause*)
MAX: I can sing too, you know.
MAGGIE: Oh, Max — (*She laughs out loud*)
MAX: I can! What are you — "Oh, Max."
MAGGIE: You don't sing like Tito Merelli.
MAX: Not yet. OK?
MAGGIE: You don't.
MAX: In your opinion. It's a matter of taste.
MAGGIE: It is not! I wish you wouldn't fool yourself. He's a star, Max. He sings all over the world. He's in *Life* magazine!
MAX: So is Rin Tin Tin.
MAGGIE: And he's very sensitive.
MAX: How do you know that?
   (*Beat. She realizes she's caught*)
MAGGIE (*Casually*):   Because I met him. Last year.

MAX: . . . You did? You never told me that.

MAGGIE: It was no big thing. When I was in Italy with Daddy, we went to La Scala and he was in *Aïda*. Then afterwards we went backstage and . . . well, there he was, all by himself, behind the curtain. He was wearing a sort of . . . loincloth and his whole body was pouring with sweat. Anyway, he looked up and saw us and do you know what he did, Max? He kissed my palms.

MAX: Yeah? So what?

MAGGIE: It was romantic.

MAX: He's Italian! They kiss everything!

MAGGIE: Fine, forget it.

MAX: If it moves they kiss it.

MAGGIE: Max!

MAX: So what else happened?

MAGGIE: Nothing. (*Pause*) Of any importance.

MAX: . . . Something else happened?

MAGGIE: Not really.

MAX: Something sort of happened.

MAGGIE: It wasn't important.

MAX: What happened!

MAGGIE: It was nothing! Oh — ! (*Reluctantly; embarrassed*). . . . I fainted.

MAX: You fainted?

MAGGIE: It must have been the heat and all the excitement. I remember thinking suddenly, my God, it's like an oven back here. And we were talking and he sort of . . . stared right at me, and then I . . . blacked out.

MAX: Oh, great. I mean this is terrific. My fiancée meets this — this sweaty Italian guy and she keels over.

MAGGIE: From the heat! . . . And I'm not your fiancée, Max.

MAX: Wait a minute. Did I ask you to marry me or not? Huh? Remember that? What did you — you black out during the proposal?

MAGGIE: I heard it, Max, and I said no.

MAX: You said you'd think about it.

MAGGIE (*Taking his hand*):   Max. I'm just not ready yet. I want something special first. Something wonderful and romantic.

MAX: I'm not romantic? I don't believe this. What do you call a rowboat at three A.M., huh? Moonlight shimmering on the water. Nobody for miles.

MAGGIE: You lost the oars.

MAX: But it was fun! It turned out fun!

MAGGIE: We spent thirty hours in a rowboat, Max.

MAX: That's not the point!

MAGGIE: I haven't had any flings, Max.

MAX: Flings?

MAGGIE: Flings.

MAX: I've been asking you to fling with me for three years! I begged you!

MAGGIE: I don't mean that! I just feel that I need some . . . wider experience.

MAX: Oh. Sure. I get it. You mean like Diana.

MAGGIE: Diana?

MAX: Desdemona. Soprano.

MAGGIE: Oh, her.

MAX: She's flinging her way through the whole cast. All the men are getting flung out. You should see the guy who plays Iago. He's supposed to be evil. He can hardly walk.

MAGGIE: Max —

MAX: He's limping now —

MAGGIE: Max, listen. Let's be honest. When you kiss me, do you hear anything? Special?

MAX: Like what?

MAGGIE: Like . . . bells.

MAX: You wanna hear bells?

MAGGIE: I guess it sounds stupid, doesn't it?

MAX: Yeah. It does.

MAGGIE: Just forget it.

Source: Samuel French, Inc.

✤ A Lie of the Mind

•••••••••••••••••••••••••••••••SAM SHEPARD

CHARACTERS: BETH (20's-30's), FRANKIE (20's-30's)
SETTING: BETH's *parents' house in Montana, the present.*

FRANKIE *and* BETH *are both recuperating: he from a gunshot wound in the leg accidentally inflicted by* BETH's *father, and she from a near-fatal beating inflicted by her husband, Jake,* FRANKIE's *older brother.* FRANKIE *has come to visit* BETH, *hoping that Jake has not killed her. A simple, sensitive young man,* FRANKIE *is devoted to Jake and alarmed by* BETH's *sexual advances.* BETH, *a sensual amateur actress, is confused from her brain injury and her speech is slurred. She is still in love with Jake and substitutes* FRANKIE *for Jake in her mind.*

(*Lights remain up on stage-left set with* FRANKIE *on his back stretched out on sofa, head upstage, and* BETH *on her knees beside him, wrapping Baylor's shirt around his injured leg*)

FRANKIE: Uh — look — Beth — don't you think you oughta put your shirt back on?

BETH: You need it.

FRANKIE: I don't. Really. I don't. It's stopped bleeding. It hasn't bled for a long time now.

BETH: It could start again.

FRANKIE: It just aches a little. It's not bleeding anymore.

BETH: It's going up your leg now.

FRANKIE (*Sits up fast*):   What is?

BETH: Black line. That's bad.

FRANKIE: What's that mean? A black line. (FRANKIE *pulls his pant leg up. Looks at his leg*)

BETH: It's bad. Poison.

FRANKIE (*Pushing his pant leg down again*):   Look — please, just leave it alone and put your shirt back on. Your dad might come back in here.

BETH: He's asleep.

FRANKIE: Well, then your mother or your brother could come. Somebody could come in here.

BETH: Doesn't matter.

FRANKIE: It does matter! I'm on thin ground as it is without them seeing you on your knees with your shirt off. What're they gonna think if they walk in here and find you rubbing my leg with no shirt on? Please stop rubbing my leg now!

BETH: Don't you like it?

FRANKIE: Just stand up. Stand up on your feet and put your shirt back on. Please, Beth. Just act like we're having a conversation or something.

BETH: You don't have to be afraid of them. They're afraid of you.

FRANKIE: How do you figure that?

BETH: They tell it in their voice.

FRANKIE: They want to kill me.

BETH: Only Mike. But he won't.

FRANKIE: What makes you so sure about that?

BETH (*Quick*):   Because only half of him believes you're what he hates. The other half knows it's not true.

(*Pause.* FRANKIE *stares at her*)

FRANKIE: I though you couldn't uh —

BETH: What?

FRANKIE (*Lies back down*):   I don't know. I thought you couldn't talk right or something. You sound okay to me.

BETH: I do?

FRANKIE: Yeah. Your dad said there was — I mean you were having some kind of trouble.

BETH: Oh. There was that time. I don't know. I get them mixed. I get the thought. Mixed. It dangles. Sometimes the thought just hangs with no words there.

FRANKIE: But you can speak all right?

BETH: It speaks. Speeches. Speaking. In me. Comes and goes. Again. I don't know why. You hear me? Now?

FRANKIE: Yes. You sound all right. I mean it sounds like you're doing pretty good.

BETH: Sound like it.

FRANKIE: Yeah.

BETH: You can speak? Speech.

FRANKIE: Me, yeah, sure.

BETH: But you can't walk.

FRANKIE: No. Not right now.

BETH: I would rather walk than talk.

FRANKIE: Yeah — do you — would you mind getting up off the floor, please, and putting your shirt back on?

BETH: Maybe they'll have to cut your leg off.

FRANKIE (*Sits up fast again*):   What? Who do you mean?

BETH: Maybe cut. Like me. Cut me. Cut you out. Like me. See?

(*She bends her head forward and pulls the hair up on the back of her neck to show* FRANKIE *a nonexistent scar.* FRANKIE *looks at the place on her head that she's showing him*)

BETH (*Showing* FRANKIE *back of her head*):   See? Tracks. Knife tracks.

FRANKIE (*Looking at her head*):   What? There's nothing there. There's no scar there.

BETH (*Straightens her head again*):   No brain. Cut me out. Cut. Brain. Cut.

FRANKIE: No, Beth, look — they didn't — they didn't operate did they? Nobody said anything about that.

BETH: They don't say. Secret. Like my old Mom. Old. My Grand Mom. Old. They cut her. Out. Disappeared. They don't say her name now. She's gone. Vanish. (*She makes a "whooshing" sound like wind*) My Father sent her someplace. Had her gone.

FRANKIE: They wouldn't just go in there and operate without your consent. They can't do that. It's a law. They need written consent or something. Somebody has to sign something.

BETH: Mike.

FRANKIE: What?

BETH: Mike did.

FRANKIE: No, Beth. I don't think you've got this right. Mike wouldn't do something like that.

BETH: He wants me out.

FRANKIE: He's your brother. He loves you.

BETH (*Stands, moves away from* FRANKIE):   You don't know him!

FRANKIE: Well, there's no scar there, Beth. (*Unwraps the shirt from his leg and offers it out to her*) Here, take this shirt back. Please. Come and take it.

(*Pause. Slowly* BETH *bends down and takes shirt. She stands with it and holds it out away from herself. She giggles to herself*)

BETH (*Holding shirt out*):   Look how big a man is. So big. He scares himself. His shirt scares him. He puts his scary shirt on so it won't scare himself. He can't see it when it's on him. Now he thinks it's him.

(*She giggles and puts the shirt back on. Buttons it up.* FRANKIE *watches her, still sitting on sofa*)

Jake was scared of shirts. You too?

FRANKIE: No. I'm only scared of people.

(BETH *starts moving in circles, pulling the front of the shirt out away from herself and looking at the buttons and fabric*)

BETH (*Referring to shirt*):   This is like a custom. Big. Too big. Like a custom.

FRANKIE: A what?

BETH: Custom. Like a custom.

FRANKIE: A custom?

BETH: For play. Acting.

FRANKIE: Oh. You mean a "costume"?

BETH: Costume.

FRANKIE: Yeah. A "costume". I get what you mean.

BETH: Pretend.

FRANKIE: You were in a play, right? I mean you were acting.

BETH (*Moving, playing with shirt*): Pretend is more better.

FRANKIE: What do you mean?

BETH: Pretend. Because it fills me. Pretending fills. Not empty. Other. Ordinary. Is no good. Empty. Ordinary is empty. Now, I'm like the man. (*Pumps her chest up, closes her fists, sticks her chin out and struts in the shirt*) Just feel like the man. Shirt brings me a man. I am a shirt man. Can you see? Like father. You see me? Like brother. (*She laughs*)

FRANKIE: Yeah. You liked acting, huh?

(BETH *keeps moving, finding variations off the shirt to play with.* FRANKIE *sits on sofa watching her*)

BETH: Pretend to be. Like you. Between us we can make a life. You could be the woman. You be.

FRANKIE: What was the play you were in? Do you remember?

BETH (*Moving toward* FRANKIE): You could pretend to be in love with me. With my shirt. You love my shirt. This shirt is a man to you. You are my beautiful woman. You lie down.

(BETH *moves in to* FRANKIE *and tries to push him down on the sofa by the shoulders.* FRANKIE *resists*)

FRANKIE: Now, wait a second, Beth. Wait, wait. Come on.

(BETH *keeps trying to push* FRANKIE *back down on sofa but* FRANKIE *stays sitting*)

BETH (*Giggling, pushing* FRANKIE): You fight but all the time you want my smell. You want my shirt in your mouth. You dream of it. Always. You want me on your face.

(FRANKIE *pushes her away hard, then sits on edge of sofa.* BETH *stands away from him*)

FRANKIE (*Pushing her away*): Now cut it out!

(*Pause as* BETH *stares at him from a distance*)

Now, look — I can't hang around here. I didn't come here to fool around. I've gotta get back home and talk to Jake about this. That's the whole reason I came here. He's gonna think something went wrong.

BETH: Jake.

FRANKIE: Yeah. He's gonna think somethin' happened to me.

BETH: Your other one. You have his same voice. Maybe you could be him. Pretend. Maybe. Just him. Just like him. But soft. With me. Gentle. Like a woman-man.
(BETH *starts moving slowly toward* FRANKIE. FRANKIE *stands awkwardly, supporting himself by the sofa, on his bad leg*)

FRANKIE: I need to find some transportation outa here! I need to find my car! I can't hang around here, Beth.

BETH (*Moving toward* FRANKIE):   You could be better. Better man. Maybe. Without hate. You could be my sweet man. You could. Pretend to be. Try. My sweetest man.
(*As* BETH *gets closer,* FRANKIE *starts to move around the sofa, hopping on his bad leg and trying to keep the sofa between him and* BETH)

FRANKIE (*Hopping away from her*):   No, Beth. This is not something I want to do right now. It's not good for my leg. I should be resting it. I have to be getting out of here now.

BETH (*Moving after him slowly*):   You could pretend so much that you start thinking this is me. You could really fall in love with me. How would that be ? In a love we never knew.

FRANKIE: You're Jake's wife. We've got no business messing around like this! Now it's time for me to go. I have to go now. I have to find my car.

BETH: It's buried.

FRANKIE: What?

BETH: There's a blizzard. It's buried. We have to stay together now. Us. That's funny how we wind up. (*Laughs*)

FRANKIE: A blizzard? What're you talking about, a blizzard. How long was I asleep?

BETH (*Moving toward porch, pointing out*):   See? Look. Out there. Everything's white.

FRANKIE (*Trying to move away from sofa, toward porch*):   When did that happen?

BETH: We have to stay alone. Together. Here. Us.
(FRANKIE *takes a couple of hopping steps and falls to the floor.* BETH *moves to him*)

FRANKIE (*On floor*):   Goddamnit!
(FRANKIE *clutches his leg in pain.* BETH *kneels beside him and starts to take her shirt off again.* FRANKIE *stops her, reaches out and grabs her wrists*)
No! Look — don't take your shirt off again! Don't do it. The shirt is not gonna do my leg any good. It's useless. Understand? The shirt is no help. So just leave it on. Okay? Just leave the shirt on, Beth.
(*He lets go of her wrists. She stops trying to take the shirt off*)

BETH: Maybe they'll cut. Cut.

FRANKIE: Stop saying that! I don't like the sound of it. It's not as bad as all that. Amputation is not the answer here. Is there any way you could make a phone call for me?

(BETH *stands, moves to sofa and sits. She watches* FRANKIE *on the floor*)

BETH (*Sitting on sofa*): You can only think of far away? Only thoughts of where you came from? Nothing here? Nothing right here? Now.

FRANKIE: I'm in a situation here that I didn't expect to be in. You understand me? I didn't expect to be stuck here.

BETH: Stuck. Like me. Stuck.

FRANKIE: This is your home. You live here. I don't.

BETH: But you have brain.

FRANKIE: What?

BETH: Brain. In you. Thinking.

FRANKIE: So do you!

BETH: No. Mike took it. My father told him to.

(*She gets up from sofa and crosses past* FRANKIE *to porch. She looks out.* FRANKIE *on floor behind her*)

FRANKIE: Beth, that's just not true. That's not true. I don't know where you got that idea from. You'd be dead if you didn't have a brain. You can't live without one.

BETH (*Looking out over porch*): Then why is this so empty? So empty now. Everything. Gone. A hole.

(*Sound of* MIKE *breathing heavily offstage*)

FRANKIE: What's that? Beth? What's that sound? Is someone out there? Beth.

(BETH *continues looking out over porch*)

Help me get back on the couch now. There's somebody coming.

Source: New American Library

✤ Life Under Water

•••••••••••••••••••••••RICHARD GREENBERG

CHARACTERS: KIP (20's), JINX (40's)
SETTING: A beach house on Long Island, the present.

KIP, *an intelligent, restless young man, is spending the summer alone with his mother,* JINX. KIP *feels that* JINX *is morally lax because, since her husband left, she has been dating Hank, a married man. As* JINX *prepares for a date with Hank, she and* KIP *square off for a verbal sparring match.*

(KIP *alone in his room lying on his bed. His mother's voice offstage*)

JINX: Kip? . . . Kip! Telephone! . . . It's your father. He's calling from Indianapolis . . . It's long distance so take your time. Bleed him dry . . . Kip! . . . (*She enters, putting on her earrings, perhaps barefoot — she's getting ready for the evening*) Are you or aren't you?
(*He doesn't respond*)
Do you want to talk about it?

KIP: There's a call from Indianapolis. Shouldn't you be on the line?

JINX: You're more important.

KIP: You just want to frustrate my father. You want him to lose his patience and his money.

JINX: He can afford it. The man is not a pauper.

KIP: Why don't you talk?

JINX: Do you know what he netted last year? *Netted*?

KIP: I'm not interested.

JINX: Of course, if he's got any of it left, it's a miracle, with that blushing young bride of his.

KIP: I don't care.

JINX: Twenty-three years old, well, I don't want to talk about it, it's too sickening . . .

KIP: What time is it in Indianapolis, anyway?

JINX: And have you heard the latest? Did I tell you? In deference to the new Barbie doll, he's having — it's *too* funny — plastic surgery. Could you . . . ?
(*She might exit here to get her shoes, deliver her next line offstage, re-enter, sit, put on shoes, etc. The scene should have that kind of activity, that slight distractedness on* JINX's *part*)

KIP: I think they're central time, aren't they? Isn't that the time they go by . . . ?

JINX: The middle-aged man's recipe for rejuvenation — a nip and a tuck and a youngish fuck.

KIP: Mother!

JINX: Oh, I'm sorry. I've forgotten your sensibility. An entire generation and I'm stuck with the one member who has a *sensibility*. In any case, he's dead to me now. Talk to him. Get it over with.

KIP: No.

JINX: Why not?

KIP: He's a phony.

JINX: I should never have let you read *Catcher in the Rye*. Phony. Your concerns are hopeless.

KIP (*Sitting up, readying himself for the evening*): I need fifty.

JINX: I don't think so.

KIP: For tonight. Look, I'll pay you back. I'll mow a lawn or something.

JINX: It won't be necessary.

KIP: It's a gift then?

JINX: The fifty won't be necessary.

KIP: Oh? How do you figure?

JINX: You're staying in tonight.

KIP: I don't think so.

JINX: I'm going out so you're staying in.

KIP: You're going out so I'm staying in? What is that, physics?

JINX: Common sense. I don't want the house to be left alone.

KIP: It's a big house, Mother. It can take care of itself, What's the matter? Don't you trust me?

JINX: Not since you were sixteen and had that affair with that rock singer . . .

KIP: Folk singer.

JINX: Whatever. She had gonorrhea.

KIP: Pyorrhea! Pyorrhea! When will you learn? Her gums were infected, not her sex organs. She was a virgin.

JINX: Many times over. Listen, I don't want to argue. Your father's on the phone. Sound prosperous and well-adjusted and happy that he's gone. There's money in it for you. And merchandise. Maybe a Porsche.

KIP: I don't want to talk to him.

JINX: That's the spirit. Try to convey that during the conversation if you can. I hate that shirt.

KIP: It's tailor-made from England.

JINX: Don't lie to me. I know where it's from. And it's all frowsy around the elbows.

KIP: Overseas shipping.

JINX: Why do you lie the way you do? I mean, I can understand lying in the abstract. For a purpose. But you tell people you summer in Newport instead of the Hamptons. That your father is in steel instead of oil. That's lateral mobility. What does it get you?

KIP: It feels more real.

JINX (*Fed up*):   You're such a *problem child*! Change the shirt.

KIP: Have I offended you? Did I say something to offend you? What? Tell me.

JINX: Kip, please.

KIP: I didn't mean to offend you. I never do. It just happens. If you'd just make a list — just make a list — of acceptable things to say and unacceptable things to say, I'd be grateful, I would. I'd study it.

JINX: Now, Kip . . .

KIP: Because, Mother, I really *don't* mean to offend. I just say what's on my mind sometimes.

JINX: I'm leaving. Do what you want about the phone.

KIP: Where are you going?

JINX: Out.

KIP: Who with?

JINX: Is that a *significant* question?

KIP: Only if it leads to a significant answer.

JINX: Hank Renshaw.

KIP: It's a significant question.

JINX: You over-interpret.

KIP: He's *married*.

JINX: Drinks, that's all. Maybe a late supper.

KIP: Maybe an early breakfast. I can't stand it. It's disgusting to me.

JINX: Kip!

KIP: Did I do it again? I'm sorry. I didn't mean to offend you.

JINX: Don't wait up.

KIP: Mother, I'm too old for this. I can't have curfews any more. I can't have my life run by you. What will I do with my night?

JINX: I leave you to your own devices.

KIP: No you don't. You strip me of my devices. I need human society.

JINX: I don't know why. You're not very good in it.

KIP: I'm improving.

JINX: Read something. Drink something.
  (*She kisses his forehead*)
  Good night.

KIP: You make me so lonely.

JINX: Good night. (*She exits*)

Source: *Best Short Plays 1987*, Applause Theatre Books

✤ Lips Together, Teeth Apart

•••••••••••••••••••••••••TERRENCE MCNALLY

CHARACTERS: SAM TRUMAN (30's), CHLOE HADDOCK (late 30's)
SETTING: *A summer beach house in Long Island, with a swimming pool, a Fourth of July weekend.*

SAM *and* CHLOE *are brother and sister, spending the holiday with their mates, Sally and John.* SAM *is a self-employed businessman.* CHLOE *loves musical comedy and is always performing in community shows. She has a daughter named Megan. There's been tension among the four friends and we are about to find out why as* SAM *is toweling off in the half-door shower on the deck of the pool.*

(CHLOE *walks over to the shower*)
CHLOE: I'm so glad to see you two getting along — or should I be waiting for the other shoe to drop?
SAM: Your husband turns on a dime. Prick, nice, prick, nice. I wish he'd make up his mind.
(CHLOE *starts the cassette player. We hear clumsy piano playing*)
What the hell is that music?
CHLOE: It's Megan playing the chords to my number. I know it doesn't sound like much.
SAM: Jesus!
CHLOE: It's just chords, for Christ's sake. Give the kid a break. Vladimir Horo-what's-his-hoosie couldn't do much with just chords.
SAM: What are you doing?
CHLOE: I want to see your dick.
SAM: What? No! Are you nuts?
CHLOE: Oh, come on, I'm your big sister. Let me see it.
SAM: No.
CHLOE: I let you see my thing when I was in high school and you were still some little squirt in the fifth grade. You and your friend Claude Barbizon came into my bedroom. I didn't make *you* beg.
SAM: What drugs do you take? What cult have you joined?
CHLOE: When did you become such a prude?

SAM: I'm not a prude and I resent you saying that. I resent it very much.

CHLOE: It's not like I asked to see your bank balance.

SAM: I don't believe this.

CHLOE: Come on, let me see it. For old time's sake. I'll never ask you again. It's a onetime proposition.

SAM: There. Are you satisfied?

CHLOE: It's very nice.

SAM: Thank you.

CHLOE: I'm impressed.

SAM: Thank you.

CHLOE: And I'll tell you something. It's much bigger than you-know-who's, certainly in that state of flaccidity. Is that a word? I think I just made it up. You tell him I said that and I'll deny every word of it. My compliments to our parents.

(*We see* JOHN *and* SALLY *laughing and talking within the house*)

SAM: What are they doing in there?

CHLOE: Talking.

SAM: I hear laughing.

CHLOE: All right, they're laughing.

SAM: Would you please see what your husband is doing with my wife?

CHLOE: Right now it looks like he's got her legs over her head in some *Kama Sutra* position we learned at Club Med.

(SAM *emerges from the shower with a towel around his waist and crosses to* CHLOE)

SAM: That's not funny.

CHLOE: I know.

SAM: Then you know?

CHLOE: I only know what I read in the paper.

SAM: He's fucking her.

CHLOE: He fucked her. It's over.

SAM: How do you know?

CHLOE: He told me.

SAM: And you believe him?

CHLOE: Yes.

SAM: Why?

CHLOE: I want to.

SAM: That's a wonderful reason.

CHLOE: You got a better one?

SAM: The truth.

CHLOE: That word has gotten more people into more trouble than all the lies that were ever told. Fuck the truth. It's more trouble than it's worth. (*She goes back to her cassette and rewinds it to the beginning*) If I don't believe the son of a bitch, I've only got one option as I see it.

SAM: What's that?

CHLOE: Wait till he's sound asleep, take a hammer, and bludgeon him to death.

(SAM *moves away and stubs his foot on the deck*)

SAM: Ow!

CHLOE: What's the matter?

SAM: I got a splinter. Sally! Sally!

Source: Plume

✤ A Little Like Drowning

•••••••••••••••••••••••••ANTHONY MINGHELLA

CHARACTERS: ALFREDO (20's), LEONORA (20's)
SETTING: *Outside their house in England and then the beach, 1929.*

LEONORA *and* ALFREDO MARE *were married three years earlier in Italy.* ALFREDO *had spent much time in England and lost a lot of his Italian heritage. But* LEONORA *had never left Italy before they married. Then, they were passionately in love; now, a child later with another on the way, the marriage is going sour.*

(ALFREDO *leads* LEONORA, *pregnant, down the steps. She is blindfolded with a bright handkerchief*)

LEONORA: Can I look?

ALFREDO: Not yet.

LEONORA: We're outside! Why have you brought me outside?

ALFREDO: Don't be so impatient.

LEONORA: The baby. Alfredo!

ALFREDO: Don't worry. I've got you. I won't let you fall.

LEONORA: Not this baby stupid. Theresa. What if she wakes up and we're both outside?

ALFREDO: A minute. She'll be all right. Anyway, shut up, we're here. Now, I'm going to take off your blindfold but don't open your eyes until I say. (*Does so*) Right. Now, ready?

LEONORA: Yes. Can I open my eyes?

ALFREDO: Yes!

(*She does so*)

LEONORA: It's dark. It's night. What am I supposed to be looking at?

ALFREDO: This!

LEONORA: What's this?

ALFREDO: The car, mamma! The car!

LEONORA: What car? This car?

ALFREDO (*Waving his arms in a flapping gesture of impatience*): Aiee! Which car, which car! Questa macchina qui! Questa stupenda favolosa Alfa Romeo! Which car!

LEONORA: Ah that car! The one you drive home in. And? (*She pinches his cheek teasingly*)

ALFREDO: How did you know?

LEONORA: I told you. I saw you drive home in it.

ALFREDO: How did you know to look?

LEONORA: Because you were late. Because I stood in the window waiting for you to come. Because I miss you.

ALFREDO: Okay.

LEONORA: Because you're always late home these days.

ALFREDO: Okay, okay. You can smell the leather, Leonora. So soft.

LEONORA: It's a beautiful car.

ALFREDO (*Grunts irritated*): I knew you would be like this.

LEONORA: Like what?

ALFREDO: Criticizing me. You can never let me enjoy anything. I work and I struggle. And I mean why do you think I'm late home?

LEONORA: I don't know. Remind me.

ALFREDO: And what does that mean I'd like to know?

LEONORA: It means good you've got a new car.

ALFREDO: We've! We've!

LEONORA: Yes — we've got a new car. And I'm pleased we can afford it because I'm sure I don't know where the money came from to pay for it. Anyway, yes, good, fine. I have to go in now. Your daughter's crying.

ALFREDO: I can't hear anything.

LEONORA: No. You never can. (*She turns to go back in*)

ALFREDO: Aiee. Leonora. Leonora!

(*She comes back*)

LEONORA: What?

ALFREDO: Mamma. Let's go for a ride, huh? Scusi, eh? Come on. We can put Theresa in the carry cradle.

LEONORA: It's too late. It's too dark.

ALFREDO: Come on.

LEONORA: It's too cold.

ALFREDO: This car has heating. It's an oven with the heater on.

LEONORA: Then it'll be too hot.

ALFREDO: Da mi pazienza!

LEONORA (*Relenting*): Okay. (*Laughs suddenly*) Hey, your face!

ALFREDO (*Sulkily*): What's wrong with my face?

LEONORA (*Putting her finger to his mouth*): I'll sit the baby on your lip.

ALFREDO: It's important for me to have a good car. Who's impressed — in this country — gl'inglesi — who's impressed with a man comes to do business with you driving a jalopy? Now I'm a serious proposition.

LEONORA: OK, Mr. Serious Proposition, take us for a ride and don't spare the horses.

ALFREDO: OK, wife.

LEONORA: OK, husband. (*She turns to go back in*)

ALFREDO: I'll take you up on the hill and show you the city at night. Eh Leonora, che meraviglia! Hundreds of tiny lights, each one a house.

LEONORA: Oh no. We want to go to the seaside. And don't say it's too dark —

ALFREDO: But that's miles.

LEONORA: And this car can't go for miles or what? I want to walk on a beach with you. Like when we were courting.

ALFREDO: Right. We'll go to the beach. What the hell!

LEONORA: I'll get Theresa.

ALFREDO: And get a coat! For me, too. We'll freeze to death.

(*Shakes his head, then looks admiringly at the car. Walks its length proudly, breathing in the smell of paint and leather.* LEONORA *puts on a coat or shawl or both.* ALFREDO *puts on a trenchcoat*)

(*The beach. They walk for a bit, arms round each other,* LEONORA *pulls them to one side suddenly, mischievously*)

ALFREDO: Eh! What are you doing?

LEONORA: I want to get my dress wet again! Do you remember?

ALFREDO: I remember. Lunatic!

LEONORA: I remember standing — this is afterwards — standing in your bedroom, in your dressing-gown — pinned up to the throat, ha!, with you pressing my dress, getting the creases out, that terrible old iron, and you telling me to stop howling.

ALFREDO: Which you didn't.

LEONORA: Imagine you ironing now!

ALFREDO: It had flowers along the bottom.

LEONORA: Yes.

ALFREDO: Tiny embroidered flowers. Lovely.

LEONORA: How do you remember that?

ALFREDO: Kissing the hem of your dress. I remember that vividly.

LEONORA: Getting home late thinking my mother would notice.

ALFREDO: Why? Nothing had happened.

(*He tries to kiss her legs as he holds the hem of her dress. She, embarrassed, shrugs him off. He looks distressed, hurt. A familiar rebuff. She moves away. She stands, looking out to sea, she's happy. Unaware of his frustration*)

LEONORA (*Delighted*):   I want to come here every night! The air! It's beautiful. The sea! I feel alive. As if someone slapped my face. Suddenly awake.

(ALFREDO's *quiet*)

Hey Alfredo. Fredo!

ALFREDO: Si, si vengo. (*He goes to her, puts his feet under hers and walks along the shore daring the waves*) Attenzione! Attenzione! (*This is a happy sing-song voice. But the moment passes and they are left silent*)

ALFREDO: My ears are cold.

LEONORA: I'll kiss them. (*She does so*)

ALFREDO: Mmm. That's nice. But they're still cold.

LEONORA: I'll rub them. (*She does so*)

ALFREDO (*Distant suddenly*): Listen, what about Theresa?

LEONORA: Oh, she's fast asleep. She'll be fine in your new car. It's so warm! Anyway come on I want to play!

ALFREDO: Now what? Play what?

LEONORA: Hopscotch!

ALFREDO: Madonna! It's dark . . . Leonora . . . how can we play hopscotch?

LEONORA: Easy. Anyway. You can cheat and I won't know. Wonderful. Here's a stone. That's yours.

ALFREDO: Aiee! I don't want to.

LEONORA: Because you don't know the rules.

ALFREDO: Because I don't know the rules.

LEONORA: I'll teach you.

ALFREDO: You're crazy.

LEONORA: Yes.

ALFREDO: And your stomach?

LEONORA: My stomach's fine. We'll have a gymnast. (*She marks out a hopscotch pitch*)

ALFREDO: I want him to be a singer. Or a footballer.

LEONORA: Him!

ALFREDO: OK. Or her.

LEONORA: I'll start. Watch me! (*She throws a pebble*)

Source: *Whale Music & Other Plays*, Methuen Inc.

✤ The Loman Family Picnic

•••••••••••••••••••••••DONALD MARGULIES

CHARACTERS: HERBIE (40), DORIS (38)
SETTING: *Their apartment in Coney Island, Brooklyn, around 1965.*

DORIS *and* HERBIE LOMAN *have a marriage of misunderstanding and frustration.* HERBIE *works as a lamp salesman while* DORIS *plans for her son's Bar Mitzvah. They're so bored with each other that they fantasize about each other's death.* HERBIE *is eating a late dinner while* DORIS *watches him.*

HERBIE: It was around eleven one night.
DORIS: Yeah . . . ?
HERBIE: We were in bed, watching the news. You got up to go to the john; I dozed off; you came back. The toilet was still running. And then you shook, like.
DORIS: Hm.
HERBIE: The kind of shake you do when you're in a dream, falling?
DORIS: Uh huh . . . ?
HERBIE: Well, your shake woke me up and I looked at you and you looked funny to me.
DORIS: Uh-oh.
HERBIE: Very white; and I touched you and you felt funny.
DORIS: Uy.
HERBIE: I shookyou: Doris, Doris. Itwas like you passed out, only worse.
DORIS: Uy uy uy.
HERBIE: 9-1-1 I called. I held your cold foot and told you, we're gonna get you some oxygen, Doris, everything's gonna be okay. And the sirens came soon, red lights flashed 'round the windows, and the buzzer buzzed and I buzzed 'em in. They're on their way up, Doris, don't worry, any minute . . . The bell. I let 'em in, I was still in my shorts and didn't even care, didn't even think to put on my pants. And they came in, noisy with oxygen, stretcher; they zetzed some furniture on the way in.
DORIS: Not my *furniture* . . .
HERBIE: Easy, I said, and led 'em to the bedroom, and I sat up in bed watching them work on you. Boy, they hit you hard.

DORIS: They did?

HERBIE: Don't hurt her, you got to do that so hard? They pumped on you, your pajama top was open, and I wasn't even embarrassed 'cause these guys are professionals, I thought, they do this all the time. Remember the time the car died on that bad part of Ocean Avenue and the Triple-A guys started her right up?

DORIS: Yeah. . . ?

HERBIE: That's what I thought: Come on, guys, start her up.

DORIS (*Laughs affectionately*): Oh, Herbie . . .

HERBIE: Let's go. One more press, two more, come on Doris, three more, come on, okay this time, *this* time, come on baby. You were gonna snap out of it like when you think in the movies somebody drowned but they cough up water and they're fine. Cough, Doris. Come on, cough. And then you were gonna sit up and turn pink again and say what the hell happened, Herbie?

DORIS: Of course.

HERBIE: I waited. (*A beat*) What the hell happened you were supposed to say. (*Pause;* DORIS *is shaking her head*)

DORIS (*After a beat*): Well, *you*. You took forever.

HERBIE: Yeah . . . ?

DORIS: Talk about milking it: longest deathbed scene in history.

HERBIE: You're kidding.

DORIS: The waiting. The drama. The boredom. What a character; couldn't let go. (HERBIE *laughs*) I thought I myself would die of exposure to weeks of fluorescent lighting and hospital food.

HERBIE: You're funny.

DORIS: Every day was something else. Good news one minute, talk about safe-deposit boxes the next. You did not know what hit you, my darling.

HERBIE: Is that so.

DORIS: You looked at me with a look: what is going on? Your lungs went, then your kidneys conked out and the whites of your eyes went yellow and you blew up like Buddha.

HERBIE: Geez . . .

DORIS: You were all tubes and bags of plasma and shit, bubeleh, and your big belly trembled with the air the machine fed you. Do you want to die?, I asked you on Day 12, and you shook your head yes.

HERBIE: I did?

DORIS: Yes, and then something remarkable happened to your face:

HERBIE: What.

DORIS: It lost all the tensed-up lines in your forehead and round your mouth. And your features looked young and smooth, like when you were a G.I. You were Claude Rains turning visible again, for the last time, before my very eyes. The old Herbie came back, the *young* Herbie, the Herbie before *everything, my* Herbie, smooth of brow and cute of nose . . . The face of my oldest of friends came into focus out of the fog of machines and sour odors . . . I got you back for a second, Herbie, so letting you go wasn't so bad.

(HERBIE *holds her hand. They look at one another for a beat. He remembers something*)

HERBIE: Oh, and the part I thought you'd love:

DORIS: What.

HERBIE: While they were pumping away at you?

DORIS: Uh huh . . . ?

HERBIE: The doorbell rang. The schmuck from downstairs.

DORIS: Friedberg?

HERBIE: The schmuck, right?

DORIS: Yeah. What did *he* want?

HERBIE: Wait. "What the hell kind of racket's going on up here," he says, "you know what time it is?!!" Look, I said, my wife just passed away.

DORIS (*Amused*):   Uy vey.

HERBIE: "Oh yeah?," the schmuck says, "Oh yeah? Well you should hear what it sounds like downstairs!"

(DORIS *and* HERBIE *laugh hysterically*)

Source: Dramatists Play Service, Inc.

✤ Lost

••••••••••••••••••••••••••••ROBERT HOLMAN

CHARACTERS: GEOFFREY (30's), MAY (60's)
SETTING: MAY's *home in Redcar, Cleveland, England. June, 1982.*

GEOFFREY, *a naval lieutenant, has come to inform* MAY *that her son, Ian,* GEOFFREY's *friend and fellow navy man, has been killed in the line of duty.*

> (MAY APPLETON *is sitting knitting. She is listening to a radio play.* MAY *is a small, plumpish woman of sixty-one. She has a round face and her hair is newly set. She is wearing her best summer dress with her best shoes.* GEOFFREY CHURCH *is standing behind her in the open doorway.* GEOFFREY *is a tall, slender man of thirty-one. He is wearing his lieutenant's naval uniform)*

GEOFFREY: Mrs. Appleton.

> (MAY *jumps with a start. She turns)*

I'm so sorry, the door was open.

MAY (*Standing up with her knitting*):   I'm busy givin' the house a blow through before our Gillian comes round. Jim an' 'is tobacco seem t'get everywhere these days.

GEOFFREY: I'm Geoffrey Church. I'm a friend of Ian's.

MAY: A friend of our Ian's?

GEOFFREY: Yes. May I come in?

MAY: Gillian is comin' with the kiddies at any moment.

GEOFFREY: May I, please?

MAY: Yer'd better come in then.

> (GEOFFREY *enters the room.* MAY *puts her knitting on the chair and turns the radio off)*

If yer've come t'see Jim he's down at the Legion playin' 'is snooker. Gillian's comin' with the kiddies f'tea. It's the little one's birthday.

GEOFFREY: Have you not heard from Portsmouth, Mrs. Appleton?

MAY: We haven't heard anythin'.

GEOFFREY: Someone should have been in touch with you.

MAY: It's our Ian?

GEOFFREY: I'm so sorry no one's told you.

MAY: Yer'd better sit herself down.

> (GEOFFREY *sit in the other chair)*

GEOFFREY: Why don't you sit down, Mrs. Appleton.

(MAY *sits. Silence, except for the ticking of the clock*)

MAY: D'yer want to wait for Jim? D'yer want a cup of tea? (*A slight pause*) We haven't heard from Ian for over five years, yer know.

GEOFFREY: He was on *Glamorgan*, Mrs. Appleton.

MAY: Has he been killed?

GEOFFREY: Yes.

(*A slight pause*)

MAY: The last time we heard anythin' from 'im he was on that aircraft-carrier the *Hermes*.

GEOFFREY: He transferred to *Glamorgan* eighteen months ago.

MAY: We thought he must be there, or thereabouts.

GEOFFREY: I'm so very sorry.

(*A slight pause*)

MAY: It's the television given Jim the snooker. It has a lot of men, hasn't it?

GEOFFREY: Yes.

MAY: Those with time on their hands. We don't rent. (*A slight pause*) I've been livin' with the television on, an' the radio. We thought with 'im bein' on the *Hermes*, we thought well, it's an important boat, they won't want that to be hit. The littler ones don't matter so much, do they?

GEOFFREY: No.

MAY: Ian wanted to get on in the Navy, he had to move about. Go to the ships 'e was told.

GEOFFREY: Yes.

MAY: Before the *Hermes* he was on the *Bronington*. That was with the Prince of Wales, yer know, with Prince Charles?

GEOFFREY: Yes.

MAY: Ian was a midshipman, or some such thing. He talked all about Prince Charles. We laughed about it. (*A slight pause*) I felt proud in my own way. Just a little thing like that. It led you to imagine things, didn't it?

GEOFFREY: I was on *Bronington*, too.

MAY (*Pleased*): Were you?

GEOFFREY: Yes, with Ian.

MAY: Were your mum an' dad pleased for you?

GEOFFREY: Very much so.

MAY (*Confidentially*): It's not a secret — I had never felt so proud before. I know Ian thought we were bein' silly makin' the fuss we did. But yer children matter to you, don't they?

GEOFFREY: Yes.

MAY: Ian wasn't good in that way — lettin' other people get enjoyment from what he was doin'. Yer'd've thought 'is parents, wouldn't you?

GEOFFREY: Yes.

MAY: He must've thought it was a lot to ask. I don't know why. (*A slight pause*) No, I don't know why. Something in his make-up. (*A slight pause*) Have you come a long way to come an' see us?

GEOFFREY: My family live in the Peak District, Mrs. Appleton. I travelled there yesterday, and came away after an early lunch.

MAY: Are you hungry?

GEOFFREY: No.

MAY: I have some sandwiches cut. Or a pastry. You'd be most welcome.

GEOFFREY: No, really, thank you.

(*A slight pause*)

MAY: It's Alexander's birthday. He's three. Katharine is seven. They're shooting up. (*A slight pause*) Are you from a Navy family?

GEOFFREY: Yes, I am, very much so.

MAY: I know that's true a lot of the time in the Navy, with all its customs.

GEOFFREY: My father was Vice-admiral.

MAY: That's very high up, isn't it?

GEOFFREY (*Nervously*): Yes. (GEOFFREY *plays with his fingers*) It's a hard act to follow. I feel it very often.

MAY: It is a pressure for you, isn't it? I can imagine.

GEOFFREY: Yes. (GEOFFREY *plays with his fingers*) My grandfather was Admiral of the Fleet.

MAY: Was that during the war?

GEOFFREY: Yes.

MAY: Jim was in the Air Force. On the ground. That's where we met up. (*A slight pause*) I always think it must be rotten on family life, being high up in anything. That's what I imagine.

GEOFFREY: It is indeed so. I have a family now, with two little girls. One must make very positive decisions. The Navy is not terribly understanding of family life. (*A slight pause*) You are right, Mrs. Appleton. Just last evening I was arguing with my father. He does not comprehend my mother's feelings, let alone my wife's. (*A slight pause*) Though my mother is silent on the issue. (*A slight pause*) I've just been appointed to Chatham on the Flag Officer's staff. It's a shore job in the supply department. He says all I'm doing is dishing out Mars Bars — which up to a point is true. (*A slight pause*) My father's a stranger to me. I love my children. (*A slight pause*) I don't know how much Ian talked to you about the Navy?

MAY: Did 'e talk t'you?

GEOFFREY: Considerably at times, yes. We were very close. He loved the life in a way I never shall.

MAY: You know more than me.

(*They are looking at one another*)

Yer can't upset us any more about Ian. He wasn't the son we wanted.

GEOFFREY: I think you're being very hard on him.

MAY: Not as hard as he was on us. He's destroyed his father. (*A slight pause*) Some things women cope with better than men. I'd say 'e'd only hurt me very deeply. (*A slight pause*) Because he's so hurt his father over the last few years. And he's really hurt me as well. (*A slight pause*) It's not fair what Ian's gone an' done. (MAY *hides a tear*) He's been good-riddance-to-bad-rubbish for so long. (*Silence, except for the ticking of the clock.* MAY *looks up. She has a single tear in her eye*) He was my son.

Source: Methuen London Ltd.

✤ Love Is Not a Water Solution

●●●●●●●●●●●●●●●●●●●●●●●●●●●●●●●LEONARD MELFI

CHARACTERS: LYRIC (30's), FERN (20's)
SETTING: *Manhattan, the present.*

This is an 'encounter' — LYRIC *is a rich young yuppie whose young wife has recently died of cancer . . .* FERN *is also rather well-off; she is unmarried and pregnant and the father of the baby is her older brother, all by mutual consent.*

(*Curtain up. Lights up. Hazy traffic sounds. We are in an outdoor side-walk café on Columbus Avenue. The sun is shining brightly.* LYRIC *is sitting by himself; he is drinking champagne.* FERN *is also sitting alone, at a table next to his; she is drinking white wine.* LYRIC *wants to talk to her; it is quite obvious. But* FERN *is into her own daydreaming world at the moment*)

LYRIC (*Finally*): Listen: would it be all right with you if I tell you something?

(FERN *doesn't really hear him*)

I'm sorry . . . (LYRIC *lights up a cigarette; he takes a big sip of his champagne, and then he pours more from the bottle in the ice bucket. Finally, again*) What I wanted to tell you . . . is that I really think it's a beautiful day today . . . and that you match the beauty of the day!

(FERN *stirs a bit*)

Did you hear me, Miss? You're a beautiful woman, who is as beautiful as this day is beautiful! (*Louder*) Did you hear me?!

FERN: Yes . . .

LYRIC: Aw, good! You really did hear me?!

FERN: Yes . . . I did.

LYRIC (*A pause*): Do you want me to leave you alone?

FERN: Yes.

LYRIC: I gotcha then. Sorry.

FERN: I'm not feeling good.

LYRIC: Oh? Well, to be perfectly honest with you: I'm not feeling too good either.

FERN (*A pause*): Thanks for the compliment anyway.

LYRIC: You're welcome.

FERN: Listen . . . I . . . ?

LYRIC: Yes, go on.
FERN: Well, I don't mind the way you look either.
LYRIC: Hey, thanks!
FERN: You're welcome.
LYRIC: Do you live here?
FERN: Around the corner.
LYRIC: I live here too.
FERN: Where?
LYRIC: On Central Park West. I live in a hotel. The Hotel May-flower.
FERN: How come?
LYRIC: How come what?
FERN: How come a hotel?
LYRIC: I just moved here a few weeks ago. I'm not settled down yet. I'm having a hard time. I keep trying out new hotels. I've moved in and out of four of them already in the last couple of weeks. I'm really restless. I've got anxiety inside of me that you wouldn't believe. I know it sounds crazy, but I've been in The Plaza, The Waldorf, The New York Hilton, and The Roosevelt was my last. The Mayflower is my fifth one.
FERN: You must have money.
LYRIC: I do.
FERN: So you don't have to worry. You can do what you want.
LYRIC: What about you?
FERN: You mean do I have money or not?
LYRIC: Yeah.
FERN: My parents take care of me right now.
LYRIC: That's a good deal.
FERN: No, not really.
LYRIC: You want some of my champagne?
FERN: No . . .
LYRIC: I'll get the waiter to bring another glass.
FERN: I don't like champagne. It always gives me a headache. I think it's the bubbles. They don't agree with me at all. I like beer a lot. But it's fattening. So I sip cold white wine very slowly. But I like mixed drinks too: mainly when the weather is colder. I really feel sick! And I don't mean physically, either! I mean mentally! I've been trying to fight depression for the last two weeks now. You've been moving in and out of hotels for the last two weeks, while I've been trying to prevent myself from having a nervous breakdown! (FERN *drinks her wine nervously*)

Source: Glenn Young c/o Applause Theatre Books

✤ Millenium Approaches

•••••••••••••••••••••••••••••••TONY KUSHNER

CHARACTERS: JOSEPH PORTER PITT (20's, early 30's), HARPER
AMATY PITT (20's, early 30's)
SETTING: Their home, New York City, the present.

JOE and HARPER are Mormons. JOE is a chief clerk for a Justice on the
Federal Court of Appeals. He has been offered a job in Washington by Roy
Cohn, legendary power lawyer and political fixer extraordinaire. But he has
begun questioning his sexuality and his marriage. HARPER is his intense
wife, now hooked on valium, who is asking herself questions she never dared
to ask before. And JOE.

(That night. HARPER and JOE at home)
HARPER: Where were you?
JOE: Out.
HARPER: Where?
JOE: Just out. Thinking.
HARPER: It's late.
JOE: I had a lot to think about.
HARPER: I burned dinner.
JOE: Sorry.
HARPER: Not my dinner. My dinner was fine. Your dinner. I put it
back in the oven and turned everything up as high as it could go
and I watched till it burned black. It's still hot. Very hot. Want it?
JOE: You didn't have to do that.
HARPER: I know. It just seemed like the kind of thing a mentally
deranged sex-starved pill-popping housewife would do.
JOE: Uh huh.
HARPER: So I did it. Who knows anymore what I have to do?
JOE: How many pills?
HARPER: A bunch. Don't change the subject.
JOE: I won't talk to you when you . . .
HARPER: No. No. Don't do that! I'm . . . I'm fine, pills are not the
problem, not our problem, I WANT TO KNOW WHERE
YOU'VE BEEN! I WANT TO KNOW WHAT'S GOING ON!
JOE: Going on with what? The job?
HARPER: Not the job.

JOE: I said I need more time.

HARPER: Not the job!

JOE: Mr. Cohn, I talked to him on the phone, he said I had to hurry . . .

HARPER: Not the . . .

JOE: But I can't get you to talk sensibly about anything so . . .

HARPER: SHUT UP!

JOE: Then what?

HARPER: Stick to the subject.

JOE: I don't know what that is. You have something you want to ask me? Ask me. Go.

HARPER: I . . . can't. I'm scared of you.

JOE: I'm tired, I'm going to bed.

HARPER: Tell me without making me ask. Please.

JOE: This is crazy, I'm not . . .

HARPER: When you come through the door at night your face is never exactly the way I remembered it. I get surprised by something . . . mean and hard about the way you look. Even the weight of you in the bed at night, the way you breathe in your sleep seems unfamiliar. You terrify me.

JOE (*Cold*):   I know who you are.

HARPER: Yes. I'm the enemy. That's easy. That doesn't change. You think you're the only one who hates sex; I do; I hate it with you; I do. I dream that you batter away at me till all my joints come apart, like wax, and I fall into pieces. It's like a punishment. It was wrong of me to marry you. I knew you . . . (*She stops herself*) It's a sin, and it's killing us both.

JOE: I can always tell when you've taken pills because it makes you red-faced and sweaty and frankly that's very often why I don't want to . . .

HARPER: Because . . .

JOE: Well, you aren't pretty. Not like this.

HARPER: I have something to ask you.

JOE: Then ASK! ASK! What in hell are you . . .

HARPER: Are you a homo? (*Pause*) Are you? If you try to walk out right now I'll put your dinner back in the oven and turn it up so high the whole building will fill with smoke and everyone in it will asphyxiate. So help me God I will. Now answer the question.

JOE: What if I . . .
      (*Small pause*)

HARPER: Then tell me, please. And we'll see.

JOE: No. I'm not. I don't see what difference it makes. I think we ought to pray. Ask God for help. Ask him together . . .

HARPER: God won't talk to me. I have to make up people to talk to me.

JOE: You have to keep asking.

HARPER: I forgot the question. Oh yeah. God, is my husband a . . .

JOE (*Scary*): Stop it. Stop it. I'm warning you. Does it make any difference? That I might be one thing deep within, no matter how wrong or ugly that thing is, so long as I have fought, with everything I have, to kill it. What do you want from me? What do you want from me, Harper? More than that? For God's sake, there's nothing left, I'm a shell. There's nothing left to kill. As long as my behavior is what I know it has to be. Decent. Correct. That alone in the eyes of God.

HARPER: No, no, not that, that's Utah talk, Mormon talk, I hate it, Joe, tell me, say it . . .

JOE: All I will say is that I am a very good man who has worked very hard to become good and you want to destroy that. You want to destroy me, but I am not going to let you do that.

HARPER: I'm going to have a baby.

JOE: Liar.

HARPER: You liar. A baby born addicted to pills. A baby who does not dream but who hallucinates, who stares up at us with big mirror eyes and who does not know who we are.

(*Pause*)

JOE: Are you really . . .

HARPER: No. Yes. No. Yes. Get away from me. Now we both have a secret.

Source: Theatre Communications Group

✤ Mollie Bailey's Traveling Family Circus: Featuring Scenes from the Life of Mother Jones

•••••••••••••••••••••••••••••MEGAN TERRY

CHARACTERS: GUS (20's), MOLLIE (14)
SETTING: 1800's.

This play consists of imagined and possible events in the lives of MOLLIE BAILEY *and Mother Jones. The playwright gives us a circus history of two mothers working every night and every day for motherhood, sisterhood, and brotherhood. Just before this scene begins,* MOLLIE, *as a young girl, tells her father she wants to marry. Her father feels* GUS *is a cheap musician unworthy of her affection. But* MOLLIE *is determined in her love.*

MOLLIE: He was standing in lantern light playing his violin.
(*Violin music*)
His own mother had introduced him, and the light was turning his red-blond hair into the Loving-light of Angels that always fly around the Holy Mother to love and protect her. And my heart began to shake, Mother. This light was lighting the head of my beloved. And his eyes were closed as he played. And the sight of his hair and the sweet lightness of his fiddle made my own heart burst open and fly to his head and enclose him. — At that moment — at that very moment, he opened his eyes, still playing such sweet sound on his violin. When I saw the light in his eyes, I left my seat and walked toward him. I was in a trance of divine love, Mother, of such energy and purity the likes of which I have never known. The entire audience seemed to feel as I did — there was a hush —
(*Violin stops*)
— an awesome hush — and then the applause didn't quit. I was at his feet by this time, and as he bowed to the applause, I told him, "I loved your music with all my heart and soul."
(*She has been walking to* GUS *as she has been saying this while he plays in a spot. He bows, puts away his violin, takes her hand and kisses it*)
GUS: Will you walk with me to feel the moonlight?

(*Adoringly, she nods*)

GUS (*As they walk in a fallow spot*):   Look at the horse tracks here. Want to follow them?

MOLLIE: We don't know where they go.

GUS: That's right.

MOLLIE: If you'll hold my hand, I won't be frightened.

GUS: What's your name?

MOLLIE: Mollie.

GUS: Mollie, you like music?

MOLLIE: I love *your* music.

GUS (*Tripping*):   WhoooooHa.

MOLLIE (*Catches him*):   I've got you.

GUS: *I* was supposed to take care of *you*.

MOLLIE (*Holding him*):   You're strong.

GUS (*Feeling her*):   So are you. How'd you get so strong?

MOLLIE: Playing piano, playing organ, building treehouses —

GUS: These horse tracks are leading us right up into the moonlight, and it seems to begin, the moonlight does, at the corners of your mouth — they're always smiling, even if you're not. You're the prettiest, strongest girl I ever met. (*Kisses her chin*)

MOLLIE: Sir! You kissed my chin.

GUS: I'm gonna do it again, I can't stop.

MOLLIE: But we're not married. It might be a sin?

GUS: Tastes so good, I can't stop, so you'll have to marry me. I'll have to marry you, and everyone will be happy. Would you be happy to have me kissing you like this, and this . . . all night and all day? We won't have to stop if we're married.

MOLLIE: But how would you have the time to play your violin?

GUS: That's why I love you so. You feel as warm and strong and cozy and vibrant as my fiddle. But you can kiss me back. Do it again, oh kiss me, kiss me again.

MOLLIE: I can't.

GUS: Why not?

MOLLIE: I can't breathe. I can't get my breath.

GUS: Kiss me and let it go into my mouth.

MOLLIE (*Shocked*):   What? But sir!

GUS: Gus. Call me Gus. Your breath will come again. It's love you're in. And that's passion took your breath away. Sink into my arms. There, I've got you. Let it win. Ah, there, there, there, see how good we feel? Hold me hard, again, Again. Oh, my God, I've prayed to meet you. At last, a woman strong as me! (*He pulls her down, and puts his head against her breast*) Rock me. Hold me like you're never gonna see me again.

MOLLIE: I won't. You're leaving town with your family tonight.

GUS: That's right. Dear Mollie, if we get married, you'll come too.

MOLLIE: My folks?

GUS: We'll run away.

MOLLIE: Your folks?

GUS: If you can hold me like this, we can be each other's folks.

MOLLIE: Sir, what am I doing to you that you love so much?

GUS: Through your touch I can feel the deep warm woman strength that comes from your bones to mine. Our hearts are keeping perfect time.

Source: Broadway Play Publishing, Inc.

✤ Music from a Locked Room

•••••••••••••••••••••••••••••••JOHN LOGAN

CHARACTERS: CLINTON (30's), AMELIA (30's)
SETTING: *The balcony of* CLINTON's *elegant townhouse, London, 1939.*

CLINTON, *a charming, foolishly romantic upper-class gentleman, is hosting a cocktail dance along with Dolores, his sensible, practical wife.* AMELIA, *one of the party guests, is* CLINTON's *old friend and lover. She is a beautiful, intelligent, adventurous woman with whom* CLINTON *is still in love.*

AMELIA: I haven't eaten so much in years. I'm bloated.
CLINTON: You look splendid.
AMELIA: It's the tan.
CLINTON: It's you. (*Beat*)
AMELIA: Everyone is deeply tanned in Spain. It's very near to North Africa, of course. They say that at one time the continents were joined . . .
CLINTON: Your eyes, your skin . . .
AMELIA: Long ago, they say, there was the tiniest strip of land stretching from Cadiz to Tangier. It's only about twenty miles. One can easily see them as having been joined . . . at one time . . . No Strait of Gibraltar . . . can you imagine?
CLINTON: You haven't changed a jot.(*Pause*)
AMELIA: Dolores is lovely.
CLINTON: Yes, she is. She's a wonderful woman.
AMELIA: You must love her very much.
CLINTON: I do. (*Beat*)
AMELIA: I'd make a horrible wife.
CLINTON: You would. (*She laughs*) Same old laugh.
AMELIA: Clinton, I can't see how you thought I'd be so terribly changed.
CLINTON: I wasn't sure. I was terrified that we would have nothing to say to each other.
AMELIA: Silly old Clinton.
CLINTON: I thought it would be so difficult to see you. So alien and difficult. But it's not, of course. It's so perfectly comfortable. "Silly old Clinton" you call me. And you laugh. And I look at you like this. Like then.

AMELIA: Ah, but so much has happened.

CLINTON: Nothing has happened.

AMELIA: You have a lovely wife and a beautiful home. You have a proper life here. A secure life. The life you always wanted.

CLINTON: Mm. (*Beat*) Dolores wants to have a child.

AMELIA: You should, you'd make a splendid father.

CLINTON: You think so?

AMELIA: Of course.

CLINTON: I don't know what to think. The thought of having a child seems so . . . mature.

AMELIA: It's a commitment.

CLINTON (*Laughs*): Yes, it is rather. (*Beat*)

AMELIA: And you'll send your son to Eton and then Cambridge. The proper education for the proper young gentleman. And he'll be just like you at school, wide -eyed and innocent.

CLINTON: Was I really so innocent?

AMELIA (*Smiles*): Yes, Clinton, you were.

CLINTON: And what about you? That first evening at the dance? You were hardly Mata Hari!

AMELIA: I distinctly remember it was I who asked you to dance.

CLINTON: God, I was petrified.

AMELIA: I know.

CLINTON: But then the music started up— what was it?

AMELIA: "What'll I Do."

CLINTON: That's right, and all the while I'm wondering who is this forward creature?

AMELIA: And I thinking: well, he certainly can dance. And so slim-hipped.

CLINTON: And you, dripping carnality and thinking yourself quite the seductress. And I thought, "Well, this is really it, I suppose. How smashing."(*Beat*) I could've conquered the world.

AMELIA: We could've. That evening.(*Pause*)

CLINTON: I long for that again. I long for you again, Amelia.

AMELIA: Darling, you know me. Can't stay put. I'm too rebellious for this life.

CLINTON: There are other lives.

AMELIA: Not for you. You didn't come to Africa.

CLINTON: Perhaps I would now. (*Pause*) Do you love Gustavo?

AMELIA: No.

CLINTON: But you love me?

AMELIA: I do.(Beat) I didn't expect this.

CLINTON: What did you expect then?

AMELIA: I don't know — I didn't expect to feel like this. I haven't . . . felt like this . . . in years. And you. I expected to find you a stranger. Marked by the years apart, somehow.

CLINTON: Two hours ago I was. You wouldn't have known me. You would have passed me on the street without knowing me-- just another gray man on his way to the City. But then just seeing you come through the door — like always — and playing all the old games together, just the same. And laughing. Do you remember how happy we were?

AMELIA: Do you remember how different we are?

CLINTON: I miss our old volatility.

AMELIA: It drove you to distraction.

CLINTON: It inspired me!

AMELIA: You're an old romantic fool, you know.

CLINTON: I am. I'm devastated by you. Always was. I don't think I was ever so happy, you know. I feel . . . incomplete without you.

AMELIA: Laughing again. I'd forgotten what that's really like. Not much laughter in Spain.

CLINTON: I remember that most of all. More than anything.

AMELIA: What?

CLINTON: Being so happy. This way. Because I haven't been like this for so long. (Beat) For me it's all just . . . slipping away, Amelia, little by little, and I can't seem to grasp it. Get it back.

AMELIA: Get what back?

CLINTON: Everything. Anything. My life is . . .it's just all evening out — no more pain and no more elation anymore. Just . . . *incomplete*. And I can't live like this anymore. I can't. And Dolores deserves more than this. I want her to be happy, you see? And how can she be with this? With me like this? All so . . . *hollow*.

AMELIA: You can't think that of yourself.

CLINTON: Amelia, you don't know. You don't know what my life's been like. Don't tell me I'm wrong when every morning I wake up aching. *Aching* . . .

AMELIA: God, Clinton . . .

CLINTON: I want to have what I had then. What we had then. Both of us. Both the laughter and the pain — but *something*!

AMELIA: We can't go back, darling. You know that.

CLINTON: *I don't know that.*

AMELIA: Everything changes, Clinton.

CLINTON: No, nothing changes, Amelia. Not if we don't let it.

AMELIA:　We can't stop it.

CLINTON:　We Can! As long as we have music we can try to dance.

AMELIA:　Darling, we can't dance today. Not now.

CLINTON:　We're both here. And we have the music.

AMELIA:　And you take my hand . . .

CLINTON:　And the world is ours to conquer again.

AMELIA:　Still the same lad — with the same wide, wondering eyes. In this moonlight it seems the years have never passed.

CLINTON:　They haven't, Amelia. They haven't. (*Pause*)

AMELIA:　No, Clinton. For the sun will rise tomorrow and our moonlight will be gone. Just another lovely lingering memory.

Source: James J. Bagley

✤ Other People's Money

●●●●●●●●●●●●●●●●●●●●●●●●●●●●●●●JERRY STERNER

CHARACTERS: LAWRENCE GARFINKLE (40's), KATE SULLIVAN (35)
SETTING: GARFINKLE's *office in New York, the present.*

GARFINKLE *is an obese but elegant New York take-over artist with a penchant for donuts who has made a move on the staid and very Yankee New England Wire and Cable company. So far, he has had his way with the financial machinations, but the company's lawyer,* KATE SULLIVAN, *has stopped him cold with an injunction to stop buying up shares. She has a family attachment to New England Wire and Cable and she's a Wall Street lawyer who nevertheless hates bullies. That's the situation but the truth is that she and* GARFINKLE *will fall in love in this most Shavian comedy.*

(*Lights up in* GARFINKLE's *office as he screams at his unseen staff.* KATE *looks on in amusement*)

GARFINKLE: Seventeen lawyers on my payroll. Three goddamned law firms on retainer. And all of you together ain't worth some broad wet behind the ears. Some crew — you managed to work it out so in a free market in a free country I can't buy some shit-ass stock that every other asshole can buy. Congratulations. You know what? You — all of you — are destroying the capitalist system. And you know what happens when capitalism is destroyed? The Communists take over. And you know the one good thing that happens when the Commies take over? The first thing they do is kill all the lawyers!! And if they miss any of you — I'll do it myself.

(KATE, *moving into his office, applauds*)

You liked it?

KATE: Loved it.

GARFINKLE: The Wall Street version of "Let's win one for the Gipper."

KATE: It was wonderful. It's a shame Judge Pollard couldn't hear you.

GARFINKLE: Stop gloating. It doesn't become you. What do you want?

KATE: A donut.

GARFINKLE (*Mimicking her*):   It's too early to be hungry.

KATE (*Mimicking him*):   You have to be hungry to have a donut?

GARFINKLE (*Tossing her a donut*):   I see gloating is good for the appetite.

KATE: Who would know better than you?

GARFINKLE: My luck. I meet a broad . . . sweet, nice, Irish. In two weeks she turns into Don Rickles.

(KATE *laughs*)

I like it when you laugh. You laugh nice.

KATE: You have the most incredible sense of humor. You make me laugh.

GARFINKLE: Uh-oh. Here it comes. I'm in trouble.

KATE (*Flirtatious*):   Let's be friends. Let's work it out. Let's settle.

GARFINKLE: You've been eating too many donuts.

KATE: You only settle when you're in trouble. I thought I heard, "I'm in trouble."

GARFINKLE: Only with you. You're wet behind the ears. I want you wet between your legs.

(KATE *chokes on her donut*)

Aha — gotcha.

(*She nods, still choking*)

Nice to see a girl blush nowadays.

(*He moves behind her, gently and awkwardly patting her back as one would a child*)

KATE: . . . Not blushing . . . choking.

GARFINKLE: . . . Are you all right?

(*She nods*)

Good. I don't want you to sue Dunkin' Donuts. The only thing better than their donuts is their stock.

KATE: Now that you almost killed me, can we talk?

GARFINKLE: Talk. I'm listening. Just don't die on me.

KATE: What do you want to go away?

GARFINKLE: . . . What do you mean?

KATE: What number do we buy you out at?

(GARFINKLE, *feigning horror, pretends to draw drapes, check for bugs, etc.*)

What are you doing?

GARFINKLE: Greenmail! Are you offering me greenmail?

KATE: Will you stop it?

GARFINKLE: Are you?

KATE: Stop acting like it's new to you. You've done it three times in the past.

GARFINKLE: I've done shit in the past. I don't play that way. It was never my idea. (*Talking into her briefcase*) And I want the record to show it's not in this case either.

KATE: Why are you so uptight about it? It's not illegal.

GARFINKLE: No, it's not. It's immoral. That distinction has no relevance for you lawyers — but it matters to me.

KATE: For someone who has nothing nice to say about lawyers you certainly have enough of them around.

GARFINKLE: You have to. They're like nuclear warheads. They have theirs so you need yours — but once you use them they fuck everything up. They're only good in their silos.

KATE (*Laughs*):   I'll have to remember that.

GARFINKLE: Let me ask you something. You have authorization to offer me greenmail? . . . Bet your ass you don't. The others didn't either. It only comes from the lawyers. It's a lawyer's scheme. Everybody walks out happy. I get paid off. You get paid off. Yorgy keeps his company. Billy boy keeps his inheritance. The employees keep their jobs. Everybody comes out.

KATE: Sounds pretty good to me.

GARFINKLE: Except the stuckholders. Their stock falls out of bed. They won't know what hit them.

KATE: I don't believe this. We better stop hanging out together. I turn into Don Rickdes and you turn into Albert Schweitzer.

GARFINKLE: Not Albert Schweitzer — Robin Hood. I'm a modern-day Robin Hood. I take from the rich and give to the middle class. Well . . . upper middle class.

KATE: Can we be serious now?

GARFINKLE: I am serious. I really believe that . . . So what's your number?

KATE: The stock is eighteen. We'll buy it back at eighteen.

GARFINKLE: First you laugh at me and then you insult me.

KATE: Why? Who else you know would buy a million shares of New England Wire and Cable at eighteen?

GARFINKLE: Me. I'll pay twenty for them.

KATE: You can't. You got trouble.

GARFINKLE: No trouble. Just delay.

KATE: I could maybe . . . get them to stretch to twenty.

GARFINKLE: Now, why would I sell you something at the same price I was willing to pay for it?

KATE: Your average cost was thirteen. Thirteen from twenty, times a million, isn't a bad day's pay on one little deal.

GARFINKLE: I'm not interested in seven million. I'm interested in value. The value here is no secret. I spelled it out for them. I was being conservative.

KATE: Spell it out for me. What's the number?

GARFINKLE: Twenty-five.

KATE: Impossible.

GARFINKLE: What's impossible — It's worth it or they'll pay it?

KATE: Both. That stock hasn't seen twenty-five in ten years.

GARFINKLE: You want history? That stock was once sixty. I was once skinny . . . Well, skinnier.

KATE: Take twenty.

GARFINKLE: Take a walk. Twenty-five is my number. And that's a favor.

KATE: I can't deliver that.

GARFINKLE: I know. Let's talk about something nice. Let's talk about your eyes.

KATE (*Getting up to leave*):   I really thought we could work something out.

GARFINKLE: We can't. You're too far away.

KATE: You could lose it all.

GARFINKLE: I could. That's why so few of us have the balls to play the game.

KATE: Thanks for the donut.

GARFINKLE: Don't be depressed. You're in a tough place. Go fight your fight. It's not personal — it's principle. Hey, no matter what — it's better than working at the post office.

KATE (*Softly*):   Oh yeah . . . It's better than the post office.

Source: Applause Theatre Books

✤ The Perfect Party

●●●●●●●●●●●●●●●●●●●●●●●●●●●●●●●●●●A.R. GURNEY

CHARACTERS: TOD (30's-40's), LOIS (30's-40's)
SETTING: *The library of Tony and Sally's home, the present.*

Tony has become obsessed with throwing the most perfect party in recorded history. He thinks that this will help to improve his status and his self-worth. He has quit his job and has planned the party for months, causing his wife, Sally, to question his sanity. When LOIS, *a powerful, snobbish society reporter arrives to review the party for a major newspaper, Tony realizes that she can make or break him with her review. In desperation, Tony poses as* TOD, *his imaginary, evil twin brother. He plans to seduce* LOIS *and thereby earn a favorable review.*

> *(After a moment,* TOD *comes in. He wears a tuxedo, and looks just like Tony, except that he has a black mustache, slicked-back hair and a pronounced limp.* LOIS *watches him the mirror as he closes the study door behind him. The party sounds die out)*

TOD (*Speaking throughout in a corny Italian accent*):   You Lois?
LOIS: I try to be, at least during daylight hours.
TOD: How about at night?
LOIS: Oh well, then I'm the Queen of Rumania.
> (TOD *comes farther into the room; he drags his foot behind him in an exaggerated limp. He might sing Italian words seductively "Spaghetti"* ... *"Spumoni"* ... *"Scongili"* ... *etc. Finally:*)
TOD: Would you like to see my cock?
LOIS: I beg your pardon?
TOD: I said I've been drinking since seven o'clock.
LOIS: I hope you're still in control of all your faculties.
TOD: Goddam right, you stupid mother.
LOIS: What?
TOD: I said I thought I might have another. (*He limps to the bar*) May I mix you one?
LOIS: I don't think so, thank you.
TOD: It would do you good, you silly snatch.
LOIS: Excuse me?
TOD: I can easily mix you up a special batch.
LOIS: No thank you. No. Thank you.

TOD (*Beginning to circle around her*):   Tell me about yourself, Lois.

LOIS: Where do I begin?

TOD: Do you like to fuck?

LOIS: Only when I laugh.

TOD: You're make it hard for me.

LOIS: Don't hold it against me.

TOD: You're turning me on. I have a weakness for repressed women.

LOIS: What makes you think I'm repressed?

TOD: I can tell. You're all bottled up.

LOIS: You think so?

TOD: Oh yes. Luckily, I like to open bottles. Particularly with my teeth.

LOIS: You're wasting your time.

TOD: Am I?

LOIS: Oh yes. I'm much more at home with the twist-off top. (TOD *sits down beside her on the couch*)

TOD: You've got all the right answers, don't you, Lois?

LOIS: That's because I'm on to you. I know all about you.

TOD: What do you know? Be specific. Be concrete. (*He adjusts his stiff leg*)

LOIS: I know, for example, that you've been out there wandering around from person to person, group to group, sowing seeds of dissension. I know you're here to systematically destroy your own brother's party.

TOD: Well you're wrong on that, Lois. I'm here to salvage it.

LOIS: Ha, ha. That's good one. Ha, ha, ha. How, pray tell?

TOD: By giving you such a fucking good time in bed, Lois, that you'll stagger bowlegged back to your word processor and write an out-and-out rave!

LOIS: Ha, ha. And how do you propose to get me into that bed, Tod?

TOD: Well first, of course, I plan to give you a good, stiff drink. (*He gets up and goes to the bar again*)

LOIS: I don't want a drink, Tod. I believe I've already indicated as much.

TOD: You'll want one, Lois, after you see what I'm making. (*He begins mixing a concoction in a silver cocktail shaker*)

LOIS: Does it have a local habitation and a name?

TOD: I call it a Cardinal Sin.

LOIS: Then I won't like it. I have strong reservations about the Catholic hierarchy, coming as I do from New York.

TOD: I think you'll love this one, Lois. I think you'll lap it up. (*He works on the drink*)

LOIS: Suppose I take a sip of this drink. Suppose I even chug-a-lug it. What happens next?

TOD: Well, of course, by then I'd be sitting beside you. And what I'd do is put my arm around you, and slowly caress your left breast until your nipple was firm and erect.

LOIS: But I wouldn't allow that, Tod. I'd take your hand and remove it with my own.

TOD: You wouldn't be able to, Lois. Both your hands would be thoroughly preoccupied.

LOIS: Preoccupied?

TOD: Yes. One would be holding the Cardinal Sin.

LOIS: All right. I'll grant that. But the other?

TOD: The other would be perched, like a frightened bird, on my throbbing loins.

LOIS: Hmmm.

TOD: You see. You get the picture? (*He continues to concoct the drink*)

LOIS: I'm afraid I don't, Tod. I mean here we are in the middle of a party. People are bursting through that door every other minute.

TOD: That's why I'd maneuver you immediately to the master bedroom, under the pretext of showing you pictures of children and dogs.

LOIS: But still, people would come in and out. Visiting the bathroom. Combing their hair. Getting their coasts, if the party continues to degenerate.

TOD: We'd solve that problem with Vaseline.

LOIS: Vaseline? Don't be foolish. Vaseline solves many problems, but not that one.

TOD: We'll put it on the doorknob, Lois, rendering it virtually unturnable. (*He moves toward her again*)

LOIS: You have an answer for everything, don't you?

TOD: I believe I do. Yes.

LOIS: Well I'm still not sure I'd like such a situation, with people banging on the door and rattling the doorknob. I think I'd be distracted.

TOD (*Sitting behind her, on the back of the couch*): You wouldn't hear a thing, Lois. And I'll tell you why. Because by that time you would be writhing naked on the bed, among the furs and Burburys, emitting a series of wild exuberant love cries, ending in a veritable Vesuvian eruption of delight. People will be running for cover, Lois. You'll be scattering red hot lava over a relatively

large area. And then, while you're still smouldering, maybe smoking occasionally but temporarily inactive, I'm going to take you into the bathroom, and give you a bath, and anoint your erogenous zones with Oil of Olay. And then dial your editor in New York, and hand you the telephone, and you're going to say into that phone, "Truly this was a perfect party, and I'm mighty glad I came."
(Pause)

LOIS: You think I can be bought, don't you?

TOD: Yes I do.

LOIS: Know what I think, Tod?

TOD: No. What do you think, Lois?

LOIS: I think you've said those things hoping I'll be shocked. I think you want me to reject that drink, repulse your advance, and run from this room. I think you want me to pan this poor party in no uncertain terms.

TOD: You think that?

LOIS: Yes I do. But it won't happen, Tod. Bring me that drink immediately.
    (He hobbles back to the bar to get the drink. He might sing a few more Italian words as he goes. He brings the drink; it is a weird, bubbling, bright red potion, emitting smoke. She takes it, looks at it, and smiles) A Cardinal Sin, eh?

TOD: That's what it's called in *The Story of O*, Lois.

LOIS: Down the hatch, with a one-two-three. *(She slugs it down, then slams the glass on the coffee table)* There. I intend to take you on and top you, Tod, point by point, game by game. The bets aren't in yet, and the match isn't over. *(She stands up)* So show me that master bedroom. Let's strip for action, and commence firing. And when everything's said and done, I want you to know that I still intend to assess this evening with a clear unjaundiced eye!
    (He grabs her and kisses her)

Source: Dramatists Play Service, Inc.

✤ Personals

•••••••••••••DAVID CRANE, SEITH FRIEDMAN, MARTA KAUFFMAN

CHARACTERS: SAM (30's), CLAIRE (30's)
SETTING: CLAIRE's apartment.

CLAIRE and SAM accidentally meet each other at a bar. They have an awkward conversation and he spills a drink on her skirt and then they decide they might as well have dinner together. As this scene opens, they have become lovers.

SAM: Hi. How long you been up?

CLAIRE: I never went to sleep.

SAM: You've been out here all night?

CLAIRE: Mmm hm.

SAM: Why?

CLAIRE: I knew that if I went to sleep, when I woke up it'd be tomorrow. And I didn't want to lose what was left of today. So I stayed up.

SAM: You should have woke me.

CLAIRE (With a smile): I tried.

SAM: Sorry. (SAM leans down and they kiss. He begins to put his shirt on)

CLAIRE: You leaving?

SAM: No. I'm freezing. Do you want me to leave?

CLAIRE: No.

SAM: Then I'm not.

CLAIRE: Okay. So, how does it feel to be dating the girl next door?

SAM (Gently teasing): It has been great. No rushing across town at six a.m. to get changed for work. No heavy decision about "your place or mine". And whenever we want to see each other, we can just bang on the wall or yell through the vent in the kitchen. What do you think?

CLAIRE: What happens if we have a fight?

SAM: I guess we bang harder and yell louder. What's wrong? I'm having a great time with you, and I could keep having a great time, but if I'm the only one having a great time, sooner or later I'm gonna feel pretty dumb. So . . .

CLAIRE (*Turning to him*):   You know how when you really fall for someone, how you get this . . . this feeling inside you like . . . like you've got a . . . little bird in here and it's trying to fly out? Well, Sam, you give me birds.

SAM: Thank you.

CLAIRE: And that's why I don't think we should see each other anymore.

SAM: Whoa, go back.

CLAIRE: We live next door to each other. After we break up I won't want to see you bringing someone else home and hear the two of you singing in the shower or even ride down in the elevator with you and have nothing to say. And, Sam, this building is going co-op and I don't want to have to move.

SAM: Wait a minute. Why are we breaking up?

CLAIRE: Have you ever been involved with someone where you didn't break up?

SAM (*Thinks*):   No.

CLAIRE: So let's walk away while it's still wonderful. Let's call it quits before things start to go wrong. Before it starts to not work out. Before all I've got left are a lot of dead birds.

SAM: Claire, what makes you think it's gonna be any easier breaking it off now? I'm still gonna want you every time I see you in the compactor room tying up your old newspapers into those neat little bundles. Am I crazy? This is good, right?

CLAIRE: Right, but —

SAM: No "buts". Good is good. I've spent an awful long time waiting for "good". I like it. You like it?

CLAIRE: So far.

SAM: Good. Then I'm sorry, but I'm not going anywhere.

CLAIRE: Good.

SAM: We're just going to have to wait and see.

CLAIRE: I hate "wait and see". I hate "giving it time" and "trusting it".

SAM: It's gonna be all right.

CLAIRE: I hate that too.

SAM: Come on. What do you say? (*He kisses her*) Hey, you wanna go feed the birds?

(*They kiss again*)

Source: Samuel French, Inc.

✤ Psycho Beach Party

•••••••••••••••••••••••••••••••CHARLES BUSCH

CHARACTERS: KANAKA (*late teens*), CHICKLET (*15*)
SETTING: *Malibu Beach, 1962.*

In this satire of 60's beach movies, guys want to skip school and their jobs and girls want to be the reason they skip . . . Except for CHICKLET. *(NB: Charles Busch himself played this part but he says that a girl will do just fine.)*

(CHICKLET, *a perky, fifteen-year-old girl skips on*)

CHICKLET (*To the audience*):   Hi folks, welcome to Malibu Beach. I hope you brought your suntan lotion cause here it's what you call endless summer. My name's Chicklet. Sort of a kooky name and believe me, it has nothing to do with chewing gum. You see, I've always been so darn skinny, a stick, a shrimp, so when other girls turned into gorgeous chicks, I became a chicklet. Can't say I've always been thrilled with that particular nomenclature but it sure beats the heck out of my real name, Florence. I'm supposed to meet my girlfriends, Marvel Ann and Berdine here at the beach. Marvel Ann calls it a "man hunt". I don't know what's wrong with me. I like boys, but not when they get all icky and unglued over you. All that kissy kissy stuff just sticks in my craw. I don't know, maybe I need some hormone shots. I do have a deep, all-consuming passion. The mere thought fills me with tingles and ecstasy. It's for surfing. I'm absolutely flaked out about riding the waves. Of course, I don't know how to do it, not yet, but I'm scouting around for a teacher and when I do, look out world. You'll be seeing old Chicklet flying over those waves like a comet.

(KANAKA, *the macho king of the surfers, enters, drinking from a coffee mug*)

CHICKLET: I can't believe it. You're the great Kanaka, aren't you?

KANAKA: Yes, I am the party to whom you are genuflecting.

CHICKLET: Oh gosh, I'm just like your biggest fan. I was standing down front during the surfing competition —

KANAKA: Hey, cool down. Pour some water on that carburetor.

CHICKLET: I haven't even introduced myself, I'm Chicklet Forrest.

You're like a living legend. Did you really ride the killer wave off the coast of Bali?

KANAKA: In handcuffs. So how come you know so much about surfing?

CHICKLET: I don't but I'm dying to learn.

KANAKA: A girl surfer? That's like a bad joke.

CHICKLET: Why? Couldn't you teach me? I'm a great swimmer.

KANAKA: You're a tadpole. You're not meant to hit the high waves. It's like a mystical calling. Sorry, babe, sign up with the YMCA.

CHICKLET: But Kanaka . . .

KANAKA: Hey, little girl. I'm drinking my morning java, my grey cells are still dozing, in other words, angel, buzz off.

BERDINE (*Offstage*):   Chicklet! Come on!

CHICKLET: Well, you haven't heard the last of me. You'll see, I'm going to be your greatest student if it kills you. Tootles. (*She exits*)

Source: Samuel French, Inc.

✣ Road

•••••••••••••••••••••••••••JIM CARTWRIGHT

CHARACTERS: JOEY (17), CLARE (17)
SETTING: *A small Lancashire town, the present.*

This play looks at the denizens of a depressed British neighborhood and their dead-end lives. JOEY, a young man who lives at home with his parents, is disgusted with his life and his surroundings. He has starved himself and remained in bed for the past four days. His girlfriend, CLARE, has come to visit him to try to talk him out of his depression, and has ended up in bed with him.

(*Lights come up and it's night. JOEY and CLARE are sitting up in bed*)
JOEY: I said go home.
CLARE: No, I'm staying with you. Anything you can do, I can do better.
JOEY (*He's pleased, he yodels*):   OOOOOOOOOOOHHHHhhhhhhh !
CLARE: Are we protesting?
JOEY: I don't know, love.
CLARE: We might die then?
JOEY: Aye.
CLARE: Why we doing it, Joe?
JOEY: Why are you here, anyway?
CLARE: I don't know. I suppose I don't know what else to do. Every day's the same now. You were my only hobby really, now you're out of it, seems mad to carry on, all me ambition's gone. I filled in a *Honey* quiz last week. 'Have you got driving force?' I got top marks all round. But where can I drive it, Joe? I lost my lovely little job. My office job. I bloody loved going in there you know. Well you do know, I told you about it every night. I felt so sweet and neat in there. Making order out of things. Being skillful. Tackling an awkward situation here and there. The boss smiling at me, telling me I was a good worker. Feeling the lovely light touch of morning when I went out to work. To have a destination. The bus stop, then the office, then the work on the desk, the day's tiny challenge. I mean tiny compared to proper big company work. But I loved it. Exercise to my body, my imagination,

my general knowledge. Learning life's little steps. Now I'm saggy from tip to toe. Every day's like swimming in ache. I can't stand wearing the same clothes again and again. Re-hemming, stitching, I'm sick with it, Joe. I'm the bottom of the barrel. I must be. How many letters have I writ? A bloody book's worth, and only ten replies, each the same really. Seven bleeding photo-bleeding-copied. I heard my mum cry again last night. My room's cold. I can't buy my favorite shampoo. Everybody's poor and sickly-white. Oh Joe! Joe! Joe!

JOEY (*Comforts her*):   Never mind lovey. Never mind.

CLARE: Oh Joe I want to understand. Are we protesting?

JOEY: No we're just . . .

CLARE: Eh?

JOEY: Seeing what will take place in our heads.

CLARE: But we might die.

JOEY: We might not. We might have some secret revealed to us.

CLARE: Oh, Joe.

MOTHER'S VOICE (*From outside*):   Your mum's on the phone, Clare. She's worried, when are you going home? (*No reply*) Clare.

CLARE: Tell her I'm on an adventure and not to worry!

JOEY: (*Pleased*) Oh yes! (*Yodels*) OOOOOOOOOOOOHhhhhhhhhhhh-hhh. (*Kisses her*)

MOTHER'S VOICE: Oh Clare. Oh.

(*She goes away. The sound of her going down the steps. Pause*)

CLARE: I've never been so happy as the day we met, you know.

JOEY: Go on. It was good though, wun't it? I remember you pulled your T-shirt down a bit to show me your tan.

CLARE: Oh yeah, I did.

JOEY: You were a right flirt then wun't you?

CLARE: No! That was the first time I'd ever done owt so brave.

JOEY: Yeah maybe, but you'd had it before 'an't you?

CLARE: Only once. With Gary Stones. On his couch when his mum was ill upstairs. I didn't like it much.

JOEY: I'm not surprised.

CLARE: What do you mean?

JOEY: He's like bad beef that bloke, he's enough to turn a woman gay, him.

CLARE: Is he heck.

JOEY: Oh well go and have a pigging scene with him then.

CLARE: Oh. (*Silence*) What about you, then? You've had more than a few sexual whatsisnames before me, sexual adventures shall we say. According to what I've heard anyroad. What about her then,

Jackie Snook. She's no starlet is she, more like a fartlet. Looks like God give her an extra armpit to use as a mouth . . .

JOEY: Shut it.

CLARE: Uh. (*Silence*) Eh Joe, serious though, tell me about your first sex. You never have.

JOEY: Why?

CLARE: I told you. (*No reply*) Now we're together in this we should bring everything out to view. The muck with the jewels. Put what's inside on exhibit. Let's get everything right out.

JOEY: Well this is what I'm trying to do, get everything out.

CLARE: Come on then.

JOEY: Yeah. Right then. Okay, I was . . . I thought I'd told you this.

CLARE: No.

JOEY: Okay. Me and Steve Carlisle went to the Nevada in Bolton, roller skating, Thursday night, 'The brothel on wheels'. I was about fourteen then. We was pretending to be French, talking to birds in the accent. This girl was next to me an' I said 'Ello you are verrrry beootiful.' She said 'You're not French, you.' I said 'I ham, I ham.' Anyway I kept it up for about fifteen minutes, then admitted it wun't true, took her over the park and fucked her up against a bulldozer wheel.

CLARE: Oh. And what was it like?

JOEY: Very muddy.

CLARE: Uh.

JOEY: Are you jealous now?

CLARE: Am I heck.

(JOEY *gives a gentle laugh. Pause*)

(*A thought has just struck her*) Joe?

JOEY: Yeah.

CLARE: This what we're doing, is it owt to do with Phil Bott? Phil the commie. Because he's bonkers. He talks so fast I've never understood word he's said yet. He's not somewhere behind this is he Joe? Tell me no.

JOEY: No. (*Pause*) I tried all that for a bit. I went with Phil to his meetings in Liverpool. Lots of shouting and cheeks shaking with passion. A lot a big slow dockers all sad, kept on murmuring to the speech bits that called for revolution. Vanessa Redgrave was there, she's tall. I couldn't properly understand what was going on. But I kept going along, and reading, till I did, to an extent. My brain was like a pin cushion by the end, the ideas were so sharp. Like nasty glass they tore into that lump of brain. I cun' stand it. I cun' decide who to attack. Looking at the world, every-

one believed in what they was doing, I cun' attack for that, it's
what everyone does. I decided there's not one person to blame,
it's been going on too long. There's not just good and bad, everything's deeper. But I can't get down there to dig out the answer. I
try. I try me bestest. I keep plunging meself in me mind but I
return empty-handed. I'm unhappy. So fucked off! And every
bastard I meet is just the same.

(*Silence.* CLARE *tries to kiss him. He resists. Pause*)

CLARE: Joe, I'm getting hungry. (*Pause*) Joe.

(*He pulls the sheet back hard*)

JOEY: Go!

CLARE: No, Joe. No.

JOEY: Get out!

CLARE: No. (*She pulls the covers back up*)

JOEY: Well don't start, then.

(*Pause*)

CLARE: Why we doing this, Joe?

JOEY: I'm after something.

CLARE: What?

JOEY: How should I know? If I knew it I wun't be piggin' after it,
would I?

CLARE: I don't understand you.

JOEY: Look there's summat missing. LIfe can't be just this, can it?
What everybody's doing.

CLARE: That way madness lies.

JOEY: Eh?

CLARE: That's what my mum says. Any time there's any of that.
Any clever talk on the telly or in a play, she says it to us. She
says just get on with it. Live your life and that's all there is to it.

JOEY: Oh?

CLARE: Well what does that mean?

JOEY: Does she do it then?

CLARE: Well, I, how . . .

JOEY: Piss off.

CLARE: Eh?

JOEY: You're not serious. You're not even a joke. You're just like all
the rest of them. Frightened to sniff the wind for fear it'll blow
your brain upside down and then you'll (*He puts on a pathetic
voice*) 'Have to do something different'. Wasting your whole
lives. Work, work, work, work, work. Small wages, small wages,
small wages. Gettin' by with a smile. Gettin' by without a smile.
Work, work work, work. Small wages. Then death with the big

'D'. Not even a smell left over from it all. If you're lucky, a see-through memory, slowly dissolving like 'Steradent'.

CLARE: Don't insult my mum you!

JOEY: OH FOR FUCK'S SAKE, IS THAT ALL YOU CAN SAY?

CLARE (*Seeing he's out of control, trying to cool him*): Oh Joe. Come on. Bloody hell, I didn't mean nowt.

JOEY: EH!

CLARE (*Trying again*): I'm sorry, Joe. Okay. Bloody hell. I mean bloody hell. Come on Joe. I didn't mean nowt when I said it. I mean this is not like you Joe.

JOEY (*Anger rising again*): UH.

CLARE: Now don't start, Joe. What I mean is you must admit you've not shown me this face before. I had no idea.

JOEY (*Coming round, a bit embarrassed*): Ay well, try having an idea now and again, eh. It don't hurt you know. Try, try it.

CLARE (*Faked laugh*): Eh, come on now. (*Pause. Silence. A bit afraid, quiet*) When did you start thinking like this, Joe?

JOEY (*Quietly*): When did I start? When did I stop's more like it! What the fuck's it all about Clare?! That's the one, that's the boy, that's putting the head butt on my heart. You don't get the chance to find out. They rush you from the cradle to the grave. But now we've come to a standstill, no job, no hope, you've got to ask the question. You've got to ask. And it does you fucking good, too.

CLARE: It don't look like it's done you much good. Lying here, half-dead.

JOEY: Come on love. What the fuck else is worth doing? (*He shoves his face violently at hers*) EH?!!
(*She screams. Loud knocking starts on the door. He pulls her to him and kisses her with love. Blackout*)

Source: Methuen Inc.

✣ Shivaree

•••••••••••••••••WILLIAM MASTROSIMONE

CHARACTERS: CHANDLER (20's-30's), LAURA (20's-30's)
SETTING: *An apartment in the South, the present.*

CHANDLER *is a hemophiliac confined to his room in the family house tended by his mother, who is a cab driver. He has commissioned Scagg, a low-life boarder in the house, to bring him a prostitute, for which he has been saving loose change for the past year.* LAURA *is a "working girl" who has been around the block a few times, but is warm and friendly.*

CHANDLER: How do you do?
LAURA: Hi.
CHANDLER: Won't you sit down?
LAURA: I am.
CHANDLER: At the table?
LAURA: Oh, you like it on the table?
CHANDLER: No. No. I mean . . .
LAURA: Look, I understand. I do a guy who's into closets.
CHANDLER: No, I mean for a drink of wine or tea or . . . that's all I have. Scagg brought this wine. Not having drunk it, I can't testify as to its merits.
LAURA: What's the matter?
CHANDLER: I don't remember where I hid it. I didn't want my . . . well, actually I wanted to put it where it wouldn't get broken.
LAURA: Scagg said it's goodnight if you get cut.
CHANDLER: That's not true.
LAURA: I had a client do a massive coronary on me once. Thing was, I didn't know and kept going.
CHANDLER: I wish I could remember . . . I was here and . . .
LAURA: That's ok. I don't need any wine.
CHANDLER: Do you like music?
LAURA: I'd gut my dog if I thought it'd make a good sound.
CHANDLER: What would you like to hear?
LAURA: Whatever brings ya to a head, sweetheart. (CHANDLER *puts on a tape*) You read all these books?
CHANDLER: Yes.
LAURA: I like brains.
CHANDLER: Pardon?

LAURA: Brains, I like em.

CHANDLER: I'm a bibliophile.

LAURA: O, I'm sorry.

(*The music comes on. It's Johnny Mathis singing "Misty".* LAURA *bursts out laughing*)

CHANDLER: Would you prefer something else?

LAURA: No, love, it's fabulous. Relax.

CHANDLER: I am.

LAURA: No you're not. Really. Let yourself go.

CHANDLER: Thank you.

LAURA: Let's sit on the bed and talk about it.

CHANDLER: Momentarily.

LAURA: It's alright, love, 'least you don't want t'pour teryaki sauce all over me.

CHANDLER: Pardon?

LAURA: Nothin'. You still looking for that wine?

CHANDLER: Yes.

LAURA: Wouldn't you rather undress me?

CHANDLER: I would really like to have some wine first.

LAURA: You wanna do this some other time?

CHANDLER: Would that be inconvenient?

LAURA: I'm booked all week what with the A.M.A. and Shriners conventions.

CHANDLER: No. Now. Tonight.

LAURA: So we gotta rise to the occasion 'cause I got other people to see.

CHANDLER: O.

LAURA: You thought I'd stay all night?

CHANDLER: Well, yes.

LAURA: It's a hundred big ones for all night, babe.

CHANDLER: I didn't know.

LAURA: Otherwise, it's thirty-five a throw.

CHANDLER: Thirty-five?

LAURA: For a straight jump.

CHANDLER: What else's, you know, available?

LAURA: Well, there's straight, half and half, doggie-doggie, 'round the world.

CHANDLER: Fine.

LAURA: You want the works?

CHANDLER: Sure.

LAURA: Whoa, wild man, — that's two hundred and fifty plus mucho stamina.

CHANDLER: O. O, I see. Let's . . . just regular.

LAURA: Well, let's get the fish in the pan here, babe.

CHANDLER: I'm not quite ready.

LAURA: Want me to talk filthy?

CHANDLER: No. Thank you.

LAURA: Wis un accent, eh, amor?

CHANDLER: Thank you just the same.

LAURA: Wanna just shoot the breeze awhile?

CHANDLER: Would that be possible?

LAURA: Walter used to have to talk first.

CHANDLER: Walter?

LAURA: Philosophy Proff, Tuesday nights.

CHANDLER: Really? What'd he talk about?

LAURA: Talked about them Greek boys an diabolical materialism. Hooked up a garden hose to the exhaust pipe, sat in the back seat, and there went my education. — So what should we talk about?

CHANDLER: Why did he kill himself?

LAURA: The man had a thing about, you know, reality . . . all that about — I can think therefore I'm here.

CHANDLER: "I think therefore I am."

LAURA: They changed it?

CHANDLER: No. It's still the same.

LAURA: So, let's talk about the planets. — What's that?

CHANDLER: That's an artist's conception of the origin of our universe. It's called the BIG BANG THEORY.

LAURA: I know that theory. Feel better? Good. Let's go.

CHANDLER: Please! — Please don't squeeze my wrist so hard.

LAURA: What'd I do.

CHANDLER: I bruise quite easily.

LAURA: Jesus. What is this thing you've got?

CHANDLER: Blood disorder. Not contagious. Inherited. Actually it's the lack of a protein the blood plasma which regulates the time it takes for blood to clot.

LAURA: That's a real bitch. Can I undress you?

CHANDLER (*Pause*): Yes.

(*She begins to undress him*)

LAURA: What a fine ascot. Silk? Relax. Your neck's so tight. Let your arms just hang down. Sure. Yes. Yes. Relax. Touch me. Not there. Somewheres else. Close your eyes. Close 'em. Shh! Don't talk. Touch my belly. Yes. That's where it all is. You are such a lovely man.

[(MARY's *voice interrupts over c.b.*)
MARY (*On c.b.*):   Mobile to Home Base, copy?
LAURA: Police!
CHANDLER: Don't move! Please! Don't make a sound!
LAURA: I'm on probation. You got a back door here? (*Grabbing her belongings in a rush*)
CHANDLER: Please! It's my mom!
MARY: Mobile to Home Base, c'mon!
LAURA: Home Base to Mobile, copy?
CHANDLER: Wall to wall, treetop tall. Sorry to wake you sugar, but I'm taking some oil people over the the Palm Room and I won't be home till very late, so don't you worry none, k?
CHANDLER: OK.
MARY: Sugar? You brush your teeth?
CHANDLER: Yes, Ma'm.
MARY: Dental Floss?
CHANDLER: Yes, Ma'm.
MARY: Brush 'em again, honeybabe.
CHANDLER: Yes, ma'm.
MARY: Night, night, lovy. Over.
CHANDLER: Good night. Over.
LAURA: Your mama loves ya.
CHANDLER: I really need some wine.
LAURA: You don't need wine. You need to come over here.
CHANDLER: I know it's right here! Somewhere!
LAURA: And after wine you'll wanna brush your teeth and floss! Bonzo's gonna think I'm moonlighting.]
CHANDLER: What are you doing?
LAURA: Seducing you.
CHANDLER: O.
LAURA: C'mon now, lay your sweet head down on your nice white pillow.
CHANDLER: Pillow! (*He springs up for the pillow, finds the wine under it*) Eureka! Would you like some?
LAURA: Just a swig.
CHANDLER: Caps so tight.
LAURA: You have to break the metal band first.
CHANDLER: I can't seem to . . .
LAURA: Here.
CHANDLER: Oh, God.
LAURA: You cut?
CHANDLER: On the cap.

LAURA: Oh, shit, you gonna die now?
CHANDLER: My life is not that exciting.
LAURA: Please don't die on me, cupcake.
CHANDLER: I'm fine.
LAURA: Let me call an ambulance.
CHANDLER: No. I'm fine.
LAURA: You faintin'?
CHANDLER: No.
LAURA: Sure?
CHANDLER: Yes.
LAURA: You look pale.
CHANDLER: I'm Caucasian. Thank you.
LAURA: You're so cold.
CHANDLER: I have to rest now.
LAURA: You ain't checkin out, are ya.
CHANDLER: No. Please go!
LAURA: I'll come back some other time.
CHANDLER: Yes.
   (CHANDLER *gets into bed.* LAURA *covers him*)
LAURA: And we can talk about the stars and all.
CHANDLER: Yes.
LAURA: And maybe you'd like to take Walter's Tuesday night slot.
CHANDLER: Please go.
LAURA: Sweetie babe? I need the money.
CHANDLER: But nothing happened.
LAURA: You pay for the time, not the ride, babe.
CHANDLER: I gave it to Scagg.
LAURA: Scagg? He don't take the squirt, boy. I need some paper t'
   account my time t' Bonzo.
CHANDLER: Scagg's got it.
LAURA (*Grabbing his face*):   If you lie, me and Bonzo's coming back.
   (*Exit* LAURA)

Source: Samuel French, Inc.

✥ Sight Unseen

•••••••••••••••••••••••••DONALD MARGULIES

CHARACTERS: NICK (40's), PATRICIA (40's)
SETTING: *A cold farmhouse in Norfolk, England, the present.*

NICK *and* PATRICIA *are a married couple living in England.* PATRICIA *is an American while* NICK, *who is an archaeologist, is English.* PATRICIA *has invited a long-ago boyfriend she knew in America to stay with them while he's in England for an exhibit of his celebrated paintings.*

> (PATRICIA *is sweeping the floor.* NICK *watches while preparing tea for the two of them*)

PATRICIA: We'll give him our bed. (*He doesn't respond*) Nick?
NICK: Yes?
PATRICIA: We'll give him our bed. (*A beat*) Alright?
NICK: Fine.
>   (*Pause*)
PATRICIA: I'll *offer* it. How's that? I'll *offer* him the bedroom. It'll be up to him. Alright?
NICK: Alright.
PATRICIA: We can sleep on the futon down here. Don't you think?
>   (NICK *shrugs. A beat*)
>   Don't you think it would be easier?
NICK: Fine.
PATRICIA: *Do* you? Do you think it would be easier?
NICK (*Over "would be easier?"*): Fine. Whatever.
PATRICIA: *Tell* me.
NICK: Yes, I think it would be easier.
>   (*Pause*)
PATRICIA: God, I should change the sheets. Don't you think?
NICK: Patricia . . .
PATRICIA: I really just changed them, should I bother to change them?
NICK: For one night?
PATRICIA: That's what *I* thought: it's only one night. No, I'm not going to change them.
NICK: Don't.
PATRICIA: We can get away with it. He doesn't have to know.

NICK: No.

PATRICIA: They're clean. Tomorrow I'll change them. When he leaves. In the morning.

NICK: Yes. Bright and early. When he leaves. In fifteen hours, eight of which will be spent sleeping. Come have tea.

(*Pause. She continues sweeping*)

Patricia, come have your tea.

PATRICIA: Do you mind about the bed?

NICK: What do you mean?

PATRICIA: Do you mind about us giving him the bed?

NICK: Mind?

PATRICIA: I mean, don't you think it would be more comfortable? It's warmer in the bedroom. He'll be cold. Americans are always cold. (*Pause*) Nick? Do you mind about the bed.

NICK: I have your tea.

PATRICIA: *Do* you? Tell me.

(*Pause*)

NICK: It's only for one night. (*A beat. He reminds her*) Tea.

(*She continues puttering*)

We'll be fine downstairs. We'll light a fire. Warm it up. We've spent nights downstairs in front of the fire before. Right? Haven't we?

PATRICIA: What am I going to do with him?

NICK: What do you *mean* what are you going to do with him? You should have thought about that before.

PATRICIA (*Over "You should have . . . "*): I mean it's been fifteen years. What am I going to *do* with him? What do I say?

NICK: Patricia. Really.

PATRICIA: This is foolish. Stupid. Let's go and leave a note.

NICK: Alright, love. Let's.

PATRICIA: "Called away suddenly."

NICK: Yes. Okay. "Dramatic findings in Cotswolds require our presence."

PATRICIA (*Laughs, then*): What time is it?

NICK: Nearly half past four.

PATRICIA: Damn. I've got to get to the butcher.

NICK: I have your tea. He's not bloody royalty, you know.

(*She puts on her coat*)

Where are you going?

PATRICIA: To get a lamb roast.

NICK: Why don't I come *with* you?

PATRICIA: Someone has to be here.

NICK: You don't expect *me* to . . .

PATRICIA: I'll be right back.

NICK: *I* shouldn't be the one who . . .

PATRICIA: Please, Nick. Please.

NICK: Wait for him to get here.

PATRICIA: Nick . . .

NICK: No, take him with you. Show him the town. He'll be here any time.

PATRICIA: The butcher will be closed.

NICK: *I'll* go to the butcher, you stay.

PATRICIA: You won't know what to get.

NICK: A lamb roast, you said. Let *me* go. You can be here when he arrives. He's *your* friend.

PATRICIA: You're mad about the bed.

NICK: I am not mad about the bloody bed!

PATRICIA (*Over "the bloody bed."*):   If you don't want him to have our bed, *tell* me! *Tell* me you don't want him to!
(*Pause*)

NICK (*Simply*):   He has it already.
(*Pause*)

PATRICIA: Why didn't you tell me not to invite him?

NICK: Me? Tell you? What do you mean?

PATRICIA (*Over "What do you mean?"*):   Why didn't you forbid me from seeing him again?

NICK: Forbid you? How, Patricia? How could I forbid you? *Why* would I? I wouldn't presume to forbid you to do anything.

PATRICIA: *Why? Why* wouldn't you?
(*They look at one another. Pause. She starts to exit. He calls*)

NICK: Patricia. (*She stops and turns. Pause*) Come home soon?

Source: Dramatists Play Service, Inc.

✤ Spoils of War

MICHAEL WELLER

CHARACTERS: MARTIN (*16*), ELISE (*40's*)
SETTING: ELISE's *Greenwich Village apartment, the mid-1950's.*

MARTIN *has come to visit his mother,* ELISE, *for a week between the end of school and the start of his summer job.* ELISE *has been on her own since her husband, Andrew, left her.*

(MARTIN *enters, sets down the valise and begins straightening up, folding bed away, etc. He is just sixteen, his face still boyish and open, but with a veiled, secretive quality which shows itself from time to time. He rarely looks people in the eye. Noting the darkness of the room, he approaches the window to pull open the curtains. As he does so,* ELISE *enters and the room fills with light.* MARTIN *turns and sees her*)

MARTIN: Mom!

ELISE: Angel! (ELISE, *breathless, sets down sketch case and shopping bag full of magazines*) Sorry I'm late, they put us on double overtime again, have you been here long, god my feet are killing me, those stairs, let me look at you! Just as I thought, the handsomest man in the universe. Welcome home, angel!

(*As they embrace, what sounds like Mexican bullfight music begins to play from next door, festive and bright.* ELISE *is in her early forties, with a gypsylike beauty and a playful, seductive manner that is unconscious and natural. But there are also a poise and reserve about her that suggest a person who has learned to put a brave face on her loneliness. She is dressed for a wilting hot day in the early summer, something handmade that, like all her clothing, shows her own unique sense of flair and style. At their embrace, the music swells from next door*)

ELISE: Now then, first things first — how was the train ride down?

MARTIN: Just a train ride. Why is it so hot in here?

ELISE: It's nearly summer, that's why: cold in winter, hot in summer, any complaints see the man in the moon. (*Through the following,* ELISE *sits, removes shoes, massages feet, checks frayed hem, then pulls magazines from shopping bag and sorts them into piles on the table*)

MARTIN: I'll open the window.

ELISE: The noise will drown out Mrs. Salvatore's music. She put her speakers right up against the wall especially for me, lovely neighbor, a gypsy, like your mother.

MARTIN: I'll turn on the fan . . .

ELISE: Stupid thing, two days after I had it repaired, kaput, a waste of money. Speaking of which, I'm the tiniest bit short till payday, so a major decision has to be made about this evening — dinner or a movie, you choose.

MARTIN: I'm seeing some friends from school.

ELISE: On your first night home?

MARTIN: It was kind of last minute, on the train ride.

ELISE: What am I running here, a halfway house for transient teens?

MARTIN: My summer job doesn't start till next Monday and there's an early train upstate, we have the whole week together . . . (*He exits with his suitcase*)

ELISE: May I then expect the pleasure of his company on his last, if not his first night home?

MARTIN (*Reenters*): Absolutely.

ELISE: Sunday night, make a note.

MARTIN (*Smiles*): "Note".

ELISE: Now tell me all about Parent's Day. Did you read your essay out loud? In front of the entire school? Did they applaud, and anyone who didn't their name and address, I'll deal with them personally.

MARTIN: It went fine, Mom.

ELISE: "It went fine, Mom." Now doesn't that conjure a vivid picture, yes, I see it all . . .

MARTIN: I'll tell you while we eat, okay?

ELISE: Excellent! Raid the icebox, whatever you find, that's dinner. (*Plops down some magazines conspicuously*)

MARTIN: Why the magazines?

ELISE (*Reads titles*): *Construction Quarterly* — *Contractor's Annual* — *Perspectives in Extruded Plastic*. These titles are sheer poetry.

MARTIN (*On the way out*): Changing careers again? (*Exits*)

ELISE: Don't be such a Smart Smerdley, your mother has had the inspiration of a lifetime.

MARTIN (*Off*): Not another one!

ELISE (*Loud*): We are about to possess a home of our own. I mean a *real* home, what do you say to that?

MARTIN (*Off*): The others weren't real?

ELISE (*Loud*): They weren't *ours*. (*Quieter*) The husband owns title, don't ask me why. Hus-*bands*. When love goes wrong, we don't stoop to payoffs — I don't, anyway. Pride. Tant pis pour moi.

MARTIN (*Off*): I can't hear you.

(ELISE *flips through magazines, circling an item, dog-earing a page, etc.*)

ELISE: Aren't you sick of all this moving around? Wouldn't it be lovely to live somewhere spacious and light and permanent where I could get back to my poetry and you had your own room for . . . well, whatever. What are you up to out there, plotting the Revolution?

MARTIN (*Off*):   Of course, what else?

ELISE (*Smiles*):   You see, it's all to do with these new materials they developed for the war. Now they're looking like mad for peacetime markets, like housebuilding — only contractors won't use anything new until it's proven, and how can you prove it till you use it. And *that*, my dear, is where we come in . . .

MARTIN (*Reenters with milk bottle, half-full*):   This is all I could find.

ELISE: Milk! What luck, my absolutely favorite meal. You can live for years on nothing else, did you know that?

MARTIN: It's warm.

ELISE: As nature intended. Did you ever hear of a refrigerated cow?

MARTIN: Is the icebox broken, too?

ELISE: No, angel, there is nothing wrong with the icebox. Or the fan, for that matter. It's the electric company, I don't know what is the matter with those people . . .

MARTIN (*Flipping wall switch*):   The power's been disconnected?

ELISE: It was that or the phone. And since nothing exciting ever entered my life through the icebox, I paid the phone bill.

MARTIN: Mom, what do you live on?

ELISE (*Snippy*):   On the fact that I'm putting you through school and you'll have opportunities I never had. What a shame my Little Lord Fauntleroy missed the Depression, or he wouldn't be so quick to judge his own flesh and blood . . .

MARTIN: Okay, take it easy, all I meant . . . never mind.

ELISE: What, angel? You're such a Moody Morris. I thought my little ambassador would come home glowing with triumph.

MARTIN: I guess I'm just tired. It's a long train ride down. Tell me your idea, I'll get the glasses for dinner.

(ELISE *watches his exit to the kitchen. Something is up*)

ELISE: I'm approaching all the manufacturers with a proposition: they contribute their most controversial products from which I'll offer to build The Home of The Future. They get a free showcase, we get a free house, and free enterprise triumphs once again.

MARTIN (*Reenters, holding two mismatched glasses to the light to check for dirt*):   What do we build his house on?

ELISE: On a piece of land, silly head, what else?

MARTIN: And where do we get this piece of land?

ELISE: In the fullness of time, all will be revealed: Sunday night.

MARTIN: What's the big deal about Sunday, just tell me.

ELISE (*Teasing*): Curiosity killed the cat.

MARTIN: Mom, it's just another pipe dream.

ELISE: *Pipe dream?* Where on earth do you pick up these curious expressions?

MARTIN: You know what it means.

ELISE: Une rêve du pipe? Is that, for instance, when you send your son to one of the best progressive schools in the East and he's failing nearly every subject at midyear? (*Teasingly*) Plus caught drinking in the science lab? And taking the school jeep on a midnight joyride over very dangerous logging trails which nearly got him expelled, not to mention killed — and I hope you know how much I'd save having you at a public school here in the city — but no, the mother pesters and pleads till the headmaster gives him one last chance, all because she has this *pipe dream* he'll end up with an A-minus average, write a brilliant essay and be chosen as the school's first exchange student ever . . . is that what you mean by a pipe dream?

MARTIN: Why *did* you leave me up there? How come you didn't just bring me home?

ELISE: I feel innuendo peeking through the window. What are you trying to say, angel mine?

MARTIN: I'm not *trying* to say anything. I asked a question, you obviously don't want to answer, and that's the end of that.

ELISE: Mais quelle force! Quelle finalité. Je suis desolé. (*Smiles*) Did you understand?

MARTIN: Why should I?

ELISE: Darling, you're not off to Switzerland as a tourist, you represent a school, an entire nation, you must be fluent in the language.

MARTIN: That was French, Mom. The Swiss speak German.

ELISE (*Snaps*): Don't lecture me about the Swiss. I knew a dwarf from Zurich once. He spoke French. To me, anyway.

MARTIN: Why do you say these stupid things when you don't know what you're talking about . . . !

ELISE (*Grandly*): Switzerland is a mountainous country full of very clean people who stayed neuter in the war. They eat lots of chocolate and always know what time it is. If they want to speak German, that's their problem.

MARTIN: Neutral, Mom. They were *neutral* in the war.

ELISE: That's what I said.

MARTIN: You said neuter.

ELISE: A pedant, no less
(MARTIN *start out*)

MARTIN: Where do you think you're going?

ELISE: I have to get ready.

MARTIN: Darling, I only have you for one short week. Let's both try
hard to make the most of our time together. Sit.
(MARTIN *obeys*. ELISE *joins him and mimes that his head is a box with a
lid she can unlock and open. An old game*)

ELISE: Now then:
Turn the key
Open the lid
Look where all
The secret are hid . . . !

MARTIN (*Brushing her hand aside*): Don't.

ELISE: Do you want me to say I'm sorry? Is that really necessary?
You know I wanted to be at Parents' Day. Imagine how I felt
missing my son's finest hour, but we were weeks behind on the
autumn line and they asked us to volunteer for overtime —
which does not mean *volunteer*, it means which of you is truly
dedicated to Maison de Maurice Continental Fashions. If I'd
taken time off . . . you know how hard I've worked all year for
promotion . . .

MARTIN: Are we ever going to see Andrew?

ELISE: Ah. So *that's* what this is all about.

MARTIN: We've been back in the city for almost a year.

ELISE: Shouldn't you be getting ready for your friends?

MARTIN: You always do this.

ELISE: Do what?

MARTIN: I bring up his name and, bang, you change the subject.

ELISE: There's nothing to say. He's not interested in us, *finis*.

MARTIN: How do you know?

ELISE: After ten years out West we return to his city and nothing,
not a peep — (*Stops herself*) No, I swore I would never do this. I
will not poison the well. I'm sure he has his reasons.

MARTIN: Was he the one who left?

ELISE: There was a war . . .

MARTIN: I mean after.

ELISE: Oh, who left who, what difference could it possibly make
now? People change. He went away, he came back . . . different.

MARTIN: Why? What was he like before the war?

ELISE (*Beat*): Before the war . . . was a whole other world. Into the sunset, red flags waving, artists and workers of the world united.

MARTIN (*Trying to get it straight*): And I was . . . *after* that?

ELISE: You were never not there, my angel, my blessing.

MARTIN: Mom, I'm serious . . .

ELISE: Darling, I've had a long day. Tomorrow. We'll have a nice talk tomorrow, all right?

MARTIN: What if he did want to see us?

ELISE: What if the moon was green cheese. He could have seen you on his own at Parents' Day if it's me he's afraid of.

MARTIN: He didn't know you wouldn't be there.

ELISE: That's hardly the point . . . what do you mean "he didn't know."

MARTIN: How could he, we haven't been in touch.

ELISE: You said he *didn't* know . . .

MARTIN: I said . . .

ELISE: Martin, look at me, I heard you.

MARTIN: You heard wrong.

ELISE (*Agitated*): Have you been in touch with him, has he called you at school, was he at Parents' Day?

MARTIN: Of course, not. How could you even think something like that?

ELISE: I'm sorry, darling. You'd have told me, wouldn't you.

MARTIN: Cross my heart and hope to die, okay?

ELISE: No secrets. Not between the two of us.

MARTIN: It's only 'cause you said we'd all be together when we got back East . . .

ELISE: Never . . .

MARTIN: You did, Mom, when we left New Mexico, that first night in the motel . . .

ELISE: I said no such thing.

(*Tired of this*, MARTIN *goes off to wash.* ELISE *is puzzled by his behavior. As she explains herself, we can see an edginess in her manner. First, she glances around to make sure he is gone; then, talking, she removes a flask from her handbag, pours a slug of bourbon into her milk, sips, and replaces flask in bag*)

ELISE: I may have touched on the possibility of an evening together — something along those lines. I don't consider it extravagant of me to assume, after ten years, he might be just the least bit curious about . . . us. (*Quieter*) Who'd have thought he'd still be so terrified of contact.

MARTIN (*Breezes in combing hair*): Can I use your toothbrush? I left mine at school.

ELISE: What a handsome young man. You'll break some poor woman's heart one day. Not that one . . . !!!

(MARTIN *has lifted the wrong glass of milk. Pause. He brings it to his nose and smells, then sets it down*)

ELISE: It's been a funny old year, darling. You see, I finally understand something, and it hasn't been easy. No one is going to help us. (*Brighter*) But when you return from Europe, we'll have our very own home, that's a promise. And we'll burn electricity till the wires hum hallelujah!

MARTIN: Mom.

ELISE (*Distant*): I thought I could leave this damn city behind.

MARTIN: Mom.

ELISE: What is it, angel?

MARTIN: I think the house is a great idea.

ELISE (*Beams*): In that case, I'm sure *some* people in Switzerland speak German. Prosit! (*Raises glass*) Now then, a warm bath, then slide between the sheets with a nice, fat Russian novel while my little genius slips into the night, with his mysterious friends from school. Undo me.

(MARTIN *hesitates, then unfastens his mother's dress down the back*)

ELISE (*Sings*):

I dreamed I saw Joe Hill last night
Alive as you or me
Says I, but Joe, you're ten years dead

MARTIN:

I never died, says he
I never died, says he . . .

Source: Samuel French, Inc.

✤ The Talented Tenth

•••••••••••••••••••••••••••RICHARD WESLEY

CHARACTERS: BERNARD (*Black, 30's*), TANYA (*Black, 20's*)
SETTING: TANYA's *apartment, the present.*

BERNARD *has a wife, children and a mistress, named* TANYA. *He is trying to raise money to buy a black radio station. Throughout the play, he is trying to figure out how he misplaced his youthful idealism. He occasionally remembers his student lover, a woman who went to Angola and died. Here, he tries to leave* TANYA, *who won't make it easy for him.*

(TANYA's *apartment, as she massages* BERNARD's *temples*)
TANYA: You've got too much pressure on you, honey. You need to relax.
BERNARD: I don't want to relax. I just want some peace and quiet.
TANYA: Isn't that the same thing?
BERNARD (*Continuing*): I'm gonna take a couple days away, I think. I got some "crazy" money stashed. Maybe I'll fly out to the Coast and "chill" for a "minute".
TANYA: Can I go with you?
BERNARD: No.
TANYA: Is *she* going?
BERNARD: No.
TANYA: Then why can't I go?
BERNARD: I want to go alone.
TANYA: I see.
BERNARD: Don't start with me, Tanya.
TANYA: I'm not starting anything. You want to go alone. Fine.
BERNARD: Got some things I want to work out.
TANYA: What things?
BERNARD: Let me worry about that.
TANYA: Am I involved?
BERNARD: Tanya . . .
TANYA: Alright, I'll shut up.
BERNARD: I'm sorry I didn't make that party with you.
TANYA: Me, too. You could have at least called.
BERNARD: I just couldn't.
TANYA: Your wife?

BERNARD: I was afraid I'd run into someone who knows me. Or worse, someone who knows Pam.

TANYA: That's bound to happen sooner or later, Bernard.

BERNARD: Why let it happen at all?

TANYA: You know, I'm getting a little tired of being your best-kept secret.

BERNARD: You have to expect it when you become a man's mistress, Tanya.

TANYA: Don't you ever say anything like that to me again. I'm not your mistress.

(TANYA *gets up and moves away from him*)

BERNARD: I'm sorry. I didn't know I was hurting your feelings.

TANYA: I don't know how much longer I can keep this up.

BERNARD: Look, I told you if you wanted to call it quits, it was fine with me. I mean, you're too young and beautiful to be stuck up under a married man.

TANYA: I'm not stuck up under you. I love you.

BERNARD: Why?

TANYA: What's this: Feeling sorry for yourself and seeking absolution?

BERNARD: I'm looking for answers. I don't even know how I got here anymore.

TANYA: Where?

BERNARD: Here. This point in my life. I'm scared and I'm angry because I want to change my life and do some things I've never had a chance to do. But if I do, then I hurt my wife and my children and everyone who depends on me, so I stay where I am and I dream. But I don't dare *act*. And yet I *want* to act . . . before it's too late.

TANYA (*Looks at him before speaking*):   You know, you can talk and philosophize all you want to; you can even pretend that this anxiety you're feeling is some sort of mid-life crisis, but I know what you're really saying: You want to leave Pam.

BERNARD: I've tried to leave her. I can't.

TANYA: I know. You're loyal to her. That's what attracted me to you.

BERNARD: It's more than loyalty. She's a part of me.

TANYA: You love her.

BERNARD: That's what I tell myself.

TANYA: Don't you know?

BERNARD: We've been together fifteen years.

TANYA: You're sick.

BERNARD: Sick?

TANYA: No, not sick. Selfish.

BERNARD: Because I don't know my own feelings?

TANYA: You know your feelings, alright. You like the idea that you can be married to one woman and have an affair with another, and then expect both of them to be forgiving of you because you refuse to choose. Why should you choose? You're having the best of both worlds. Meanwhile, your wife and I are miserable.

BERNARD: Then why do you stay with me?

TANYA: Because I love you.

BERNARD: It's not enough. Take it from one who knows.

TANYA: I don't know anything deeper than love. I haven't lived that long.

BERNARD: You ever been to Angola?

TANYA: Angola?

BERNARD: You want to go?

TANYA: What? What are you talking about?

BERNARD: It's a place I dream about sometimes.

TANYA: What's in Angola?

BERNARD: Forget it. Forget I mentioned it.

TANYA: You want it to end between us, don't you?

BERNARD: If you had seen the way I went off on Pam —

TANYA: Please, I don't care about Pam. Don't tell me a damn thing about you and her. I only care about us. Let's talk about us. You want to end it?

BERNARD: We should. I can't carry all this around with me any longer.

TANYA: It hasn't been easy for me, either, Bernard.

BERNARD: Yeah, baby. I know.

TANYA: Just like that, huh? I should have seen it coming. This is so predictable.

BERNARD: Yeah . . .

TANYA: You know, it'll be eighteen months for us tomorrow.

BERNARD: A year and a half . . .

TANYA: Will I ever see you again?

BERNARD: Maybe here and there . . . I don't know, Tanya.

TANYA: I was never happier with anyone than I am with you.

BERNARD: I better go . . .

TANYA: Bernard! Look me in the face. Tell me you don't love me anymore. Tell me you don't want to be around me anymore.
(BERNARD *comes face to face with her.* TANYA *stares at him. He looks at her*)

BERNARD: I don't love you.

TANYA: Just like that.

BERNARD: What other choice do I have? I won't leave my wife and children, and I can't ask you to wait for me forever. Let's just stop it, now.

TANYA: I know you're right. I know there's no other way.

BERNARD: I'm sorry. It's my fault. I've been a fool.

TANYA: Maybe we've both been fools.

BERNARD: Yes.

TANYA: Goodbye.

BERNARD: Goodbye.

(BERNARD *turns away from* TANYA. *Just as suddenly, he turns back to her and grabs her about the waist and pulls her close to him. She throws her arms around him and they kiss passionately, falling to the floor and making love*)

Source: The Gersh Agency

✤ To Gillian On Her 37th Birthday

●●●●●●●●●●●●●●●●●●●●●●●●●●●●●MICHAEL BRADY

CHARACTERS: DAVID *(30's)*, GILLIAN *(30's)*
SETTING: *A small island off the coast of New England, the present.*

DAVID *is a college professor of English, temporarily retired because he is mourning the death of his wife two years ago. It is the eve of* GILLIAN, *his wife's, birthday and* DAVID *has been making life miserable for his daughter Kate and his in-laws who are trying to set him up with a young woman named Kevin. Here,* GILLIAN, *as a ghost, appears to* DAVID — *something they are both used to.*

(*Evening. The lapping of the tide and the sound of wind passing through the rigging of boats is just barely audible*)
DAVID: What's life? What's it cost? No . . . Who took the cookie from the cookie jar? (*Pause*) I said who took the cookie from the cookie jar? Damn it, who took the cookie from the cookie jar?
GILLIAN: You.
(GILLIAN *enters abruptly. She is in her middle thirties, dressed for the beach. Both stare at the water for a time, not looking at each other*)
DAVID: Not me.
GILLIAN: Yes, you.
DAVID: Not you?
GILLIAN: Umm-hmmm. (*No*)
DAVID: Then who?
GILLIAN: Why, you!
DAVID: Me?
GILLIAN: Yes, you! You took the cookie from the cookie jar.
(*Pause*)
DAVID: What's life?
GILLIAN: A magazine.
DAVID: What's it cost?
GILLIAN: Ten cents.
DAVID: That's cheap.
GILLIAN: That's life.
DAVID: What's life. Don't answer that.
GILLIAN: How's your dog?

DAVID: Ready for a romp.

GILLIAN: The correct response to "How's your dog?" is "Good, how's your dog?"

DAVID: I was always a bit slow.

GILLIAN: That part I liked.

(DAVID *moves toward her.* GILLIAN *steps away*)

The waves are singing tonight.

DAVID: What do they say?

GILLIAN: That's a secret.

DAVID: You can tell me.

GILLIAN: They're singing life goes on.

DAVID: That's it?

GILLIAN: Life goes on and on.

DAVID: Profound, those waves.

GILLIAN: Mr. Cynic, Mr. Simple truths are never enough for you, Mr. Literature, Mr. Symbolism, . . .

DAVID: Enough.

GILLIAN: Mr. Book of the Month, Mr. PBS, Mr. S.A.T., Mr. . . .

DAVID: Enough! Enough. (*Pause*) Let the games begin.

GILLIAN: No games tonight.

DAVID: How about Great Apes and Baboons, always one of your favorites.

GILLIAN: No.

DAVID: Our little primate friends, come on.

GILLIAN: Read my lips. (*Mouthing 'n' 'o'*)

DAVID: How about an orangoutang?

GILLIAN: Maybe an orangoutang.

DAVID: Give us a young one, seeking acceptance into tribe.

GILLIAN (*Imitates a young orangutan, picking at her clothes, cheeks puffed out*):   I prefer the young ones.

DAVID: Don't we all?

GILLIAN: You dirty filthy goat.

DAVID: I'm not a goat. I'm just a poor fisher boy lost on the shore.

GILLIAN: Oh, God, not this one again.

DAVID: If you could only help me, Ma'm, I'd be so grateful.

GILLIAN: How grateful?

DAVID: Oh, I'd do anything you might ask.

GILLIAN: Anything, my wild stallion?

DAVID: Stop it.

GILLIAN: You want Sister Theresa of the Little Flowers, or a real woman, with real passions?

DAVID: I think Sister Theresa might be quite relaxing.

GILLIAN: You get the whole package, my avenger, my little tug boat of love.

DAVID: Tug boat of love?

GILLIAN: Excuse me, Mr. Boundless wit. You need discipline, boy.

DAVID: Oh?

GILLIAN: We've been very moody lately, haven't we?

DAVID: What do we mean?

GILLIAN: We mean, snap at your own daughter like that, snap at *our* daughter.

DAVID: That was pretty bad. (*Pause*) Maybe we should have had another child. For balance. (*Pause*) Well, there was a lot happening back then. We both had careers. We couldn't . . .

GILLIAN: What do you mean "we", white man?

DAVID: We couldn't or we didn't want . . .

GILLIAN: One of us wanted another child.

DAVID: Yes.

GILLIAN: And one of us did not. (*Pause.* GILLIAN *points toward the sky*) Northern sky, late summer, 47th latitude. What constellation? Can you take it, State University?

DAVID (*Making buzzer sound*): Cygnus, the swan.

GILLIAN: Correct. (*Imitating a swan, arms spread backward*) Give that man . . . peace of mind.

DAVID: Yeah.

GILLIAN: That's your job, isn't it? (*Examining the house*) She's a nice little house.

DAVID: Where we shall retire.

GILLIAN: That would have been nice.
(*Long pause*)

DAVID (*Staring at the house*): The insurance covered everything, purchase price, points, buy back, even money in the bank. You were most thorough.

GILLIAN: I could build a quilt with all your guilt . . .

DAVID (*Singing*): "Said Barnacle Bill the sailor . . ."

GILLIAN: You need toughening up, boy. All this misshapen, misapplied an-goo-ish!

DAVID (*French*): "*C'est moi, c'est moi*, I'm forced to admit."

GILLIAN: Mr. Victim, Mr. Suffer-too-much! You need . . . (*Gesturing*) an infusion of zee life force!

DAVID: Not the life force.

GILLIAN (*Looking in the direction where* KEVIN *exited*): She's very . . . how shall I say? . . . very . . .

DAVID: . . . very ten years younger?

GILLIAN: That about covers it. I'm going to give you some pearls of wisdom, Bucky.

DAVID: Ah, pearls.

GILLIAN: Sex . . . You remember sex?

DAVID: How did it go again? Connect part 'A' to part 'B' . . .

GILLIAN: Sex is a normal, may I repeat n-o-r-m-a-l function of the adult primate, any primate. She seems quite nice.

DAVID: So you think . . .

GILLIAN: I just said what I think. (*Pause*) And watch your step with young Cynthia.

DAVID: What?

GILLIAN: The sap she's a-running in those veins.

DAVID: So?

GILLIAN: So? (*Pause*) And ease up on Rachel.

DAVID: Message received.

GILLIAN: Since when do you need me to . . .

DAVID: I said, message received. (*Pause*) What's life?

GILLIAN: I asks myself but I get no answers. (*Pause*) Gonna let you in on a secret, Bucky, just you and me.

DAVID: I like secrets.

GILLIAN: You may not like this one.

DAVID: Tell me anyway.

GILLIAN: The secret is, Bucky, I'm dead. Very . . . very . . . very dead. (*Long pause. Lights begin to fade around* GILLIAN). Got to go, Mr. Man . . .

DAVID: Don't go. What's life? What's it cost?

GILLIAN (*Softly*):   Ten cents.

DAVID: That's cheap.

(*The lights fade around* GILLIAN *as she exits*)

Source: Broadway Play Publishing, Inc.

❖ The Value of Names

●●●●●●●●●●●●●●●●●●●●●●●●●●●●●●●●●JEFFREY SWEET

CHARACTERS: BENNY *(60's)*, NORMA *(early 20's)*
SETTING: *A patio in the Hollywood Hills, the present.*

NORMA, *who is about to change her name, discusses the consequences of this act with her father.*

BENNY: Does it sound too Jewish?
NORMA *(To audience)*:   No, hold on. First, a couple of things you should know: A patio up in the Hollywood Hills. Over there, the Pacific Ocean. Next to me, my father. On the whole, I have less trouble with the Pacific.
BENNY *(As in "Are you finished?")*:   OK?
NORMA: Sure. Go ahead.
BENNY: Does it sound too Jewish?
NORMA: Pop . . .
BENNY: You're changing your name. Stands to reason there's something about the one you've got you don't like. Or maybe find inconvenient.
NORMA *(To audience)*:   I should have known he'd take it like this.
BENNY: Could put you at a disadvantage. A name like Silverman. Some parts — the casting directors won't even look at you. I know. Say, for instance, they do a new version of *The Bells of St. Mary's.* Casting people see the name Norma Silverman, what are they going to say? "Nope, don't call her. A person obviously without nun potential. Get me an O'Hara or a Kelly. Get away with this Silverman." And there goes your chance to play Ingrid Bergman. Of course, Bergman, too, is a name that's a little suspect.
NORMA: Pop . . .
BENNY: But then, one look at her, that question's laid to rest. Even if she did play Golda Meir once. One look at that nose of hers. That was not a Jewish nose. But then — thanks to the magic of science — who can tell from a nose?
NORMA: Of course.
BENNY: I could show you Horowitzes and Steins and Margulieses with noses on them look like they belong to Smiths. Very funny seeing a Smith nose on a Horowitz. Or a Horowitz nose on a

Smith, although this is rarer.

NORMA: They don't transplant noses.

BENNY: You want to know why?

NORMA (*With a side-long look to the audience*): OK, why?

BENNY: Run the risk of the body rejecting. Sure, it's a big problem. Heart transplant, kidney transplant — the body sometimes says, "No, thank you. Take it away." A case like that, all that happens is maybe someone dies. But a nose transplant — could you imagine the humiliation if that happened? Walking down the street, maybe you hiccup, a slight tearing sensation, and suddenly there's a draft in the middle of your face. You look down on the pavement, see two dainty nostrils staring up at Heaven.

NORMA: Are you finished?

BENNY: Are you?

NORMA: With what?

BENNY: This nonsense. This changing your name nonsense.

NORMA: It's not nonsense. I'm going to do it.

BENNY: Fine. So do it. So what do you want from me?

NORMA: I don't want from you. I just thought I should tell you.

BENNY: OK, you've told me. So what do you want me to say? You want me to say congratulations? Like you're having a baby — congratulations? You're having a new name — how wonderful! And who's the father of this new name? I know who the father of the old name is. I see him sometimes on the Late Show.

NORMA: OK, Pop.

BENNY: It's not OK. But never mind, we won't talk about it.

NORMA: Fat chance.

BENNY: So what else is new? A sex change?

NORMA: It doesn't have anything to do with Jewish or not Jewish.

BENNY: What *has* it to do with?

NORMA: You.

BENNY: Oh. *I'm* the "to-do-with"?

NORMA: Here we go.

BENNY: *I'm* the reason you're changing your name?

NORMA: Do you want me to explain now? Or shall I give you a little more room for a tirade?

BENNY: What tirade?

NORMA: The tirade you're gearing up for.

BENNY: Who, me?

NORMA: Oh, great, now we get a double feature of innocent *and* cute. I wish you'd understand.

BENNY: What's to understand? You're changing your name. You're changing your name because it's my name. This makes me feel instantly terrific and wonderful. It makes me feel how glad I am to have my daughter's love and respect. How fulfilling it is to be a parent. How worth it all it's all been. Would you like a little coffee?

NORMA: Look, every time I've done anything, every time I've been reviewed, they always put in that I'm your daughter. My name is not Norma Silverman. My name is Norma Silverman, Benny Silverman's daughter.

BENNY: So what are you trying to do — convince people you're the product of a virgin birth?

NORMA: I'm very proud of being your daughter. But I would like, for once, when I get on a stage, for them to see me. Not just see you in me.

BENNY: Don't talk dirty.

NORMA: There's a comparison implied there. "Is she as good as?"

BENNY: Aren't you?

NORMA: I don't think I should have to fight that. You really don't want to understand, do you?

BENNY: Sure, you want to be you. New all we've got to do is set it to music and Sammy Davis will sing it. Who put you up to this?

NORMA: What?

BENNY: This is your mother's idea, isn't it?

NORMA: No.

BENNY: I recognize the style.

NORMA: What do you mean?

BENNY: Right after the divorce, she got her driver's license changed back to her maiden name. Sarah Teitel. And her checking account and her magazine subscriptions and all the rest. Sarah Teitel. Didn't want to be known by her married name any more, thank you very much. Oh no. Said she wouldn't use it ever again. You know what I did? I made the alimony checks out to "Mrs. Benny Silverman." Would have loved to see her face when she had to endorse them.

NORMA: She didn't have anything to do with this.

BENNY: Maybe not, but she didn't tell you no.

NORMA: Actually, she told me you'd probably scream your head off, but she understood.

BENNY: That's generous of her.

NORMA: She respected my decision. Because that's what it was, Pop — my decision. She didn't enter into it. It's something I decided to do by myself, for myself. It's what I wanted.

BENNY: Fine — you wanted, you got.

NORMA: You know something — if you look at in the right way, it's a compliment.

BENNY: It is?

NORMA: If you look at it the right way.

BENNY: Let's hear this right way.

NORMA: Never mind.

BENNY: No compliment?

NORMA: Help.

BENNY: First it's out with the name, then it's goodbye compliment. Beats me why I should give you a cup of coffee.

NORMA: I don't want a cup of coffee.

BENNY: I can understand that. If I were you, I'd have enough trouble sleeping at night.

Source: Dramatists Play Service, Inc.

✣ Wrong Turn at Lungfish

●●●●●●●●●●LOWELL GANZ, GARRY MARSHALL

CHARACTERS: DOMINIC DE CAESAR (20's), ANITA MERENDINO
(20's)
SETTING: A New York City hospital room, the present.

ANITA, a tough street young woman, with a bad inferiority complex, has
been reading to a blind professor named Peter Ravenswaal. Over a period of
days, they have become friends. But ANITA's tough boyfriend, DOMINIC,
wants her to get money from the old man because he's on the run from
police and gangsters. Ravenswaal has gotten overexcited pointing out to her
that DOMINIC is a goon. The fact that her arm is in a sling from DOMINIC's
persuasion bears him out. Ravenswaal now lies unconscious in bed on life
support. DOMINIC has been hiding in the bathroom.

(DOMINIC comes out of the bathroom. He's unhappy)
ANITA: I'm sorry.
DOMINIC: Sorry? I come sneaking back up here to take you out of
this place and start on our wonderful trip together and I almost
walk right in the middle of a circus. Doctors, nurses, people
screaming — I could've been caught.
ANITA (Placating him): Okay, it's all calmed down now.
DOMINIC: Did you at least talk to him?
ANITA: I couldn't. He was like all out of his head.
DOMINIC: Then forget it.
ANITA: Okay.
DOMINIC: Let's get out of here before something else happens.
ANITA (Sits in chair): I'm just gonna wait for him to wake up so we
can have a nice goodbye. Then we'll be going.
DOMINIC: What did they give you here? Stupid pills? This guy
could never wake up. I heard the nurse. That's a trained person.
Sometimes they stay like this a hundred years. You're gonna sit
here all that time? 'Cause if you are, you're gonna do it alone. In
fact, if you're here another two seconds, you're gonna be alone.
'Cause I'm leaving. Now. With or without one Miss Merendino.
ANITA (Frightened): Please, Dommy —
DOMINIC: What, "Please, Dommy"? I got no time for "Please,

Dommy." People are looking for me.

ANITA:　Look, if I just wait for one hour . . .

DOMINIC:　Watch this hand. (*She flinches*) Don't flinch. Just watch the hand. Watch what it's doing. (DOMINIC *starts to wave goodbye*) It's waving "bye- bye."

ANITA (*Breaking down, she stands*):　Dommy, no.

DOMINIC (*Taunting*):　Bye-bye.

ANITA:　All right, I'll get my stuff. I'll get my things in my room.

DOMINIC:　Too late. You pissed me off. I'm going alone. I'll find somebody who don't give me so much trouble.

ANITA:　I won't give you no trouble. I swear to God. Please take me. Please, Dommy, don't leave me behind. (*She's begging*) I don't want to be alone. I hate being alone. I'll leave right this second. Please.

(*Pause*)

DOMINIC:　Go get your stuff.

(*She hugs him and runs out of room*)

I'm a marshmallow.

Source: Samuel French, Inc.

Woman-Woman Scenes

✤ Across Oka

•••••••••••••••••••••••••••ROBERT HOLMAN

CHARACTERS: EILEEN (70), TESSA (46)

SETTING: *The cobbled backyard of a small terraced house in England. A warm July afternoon, the present.*

Shortly after the demise of TESSA's *father and* EILEEN's *husband, mother and daughter seek to find comfort in each other's grief.* EILEEN *saw her husband as a dreamer who resented his rigid life of husband and father.*

TESSA: Mum, I think your own doctor should write a death certificate. I'm not certain I can. Don't you worry about it. I'll ring him.

EILEEN: Will you?

TESSA: Yes.

EILEEN: Don't listen ti 'im if 'e goes on about yer dad. It'll be stuff and nonsense.

TESSA: Dad came to me about his incontinence. It's very, very common. There's nothing to be ashamed of.

EILEEN: I didn't know that?

TESSA: He didn't want you worried.

EILEEN: I was worried.

TESSA: I know you were.

EILEEN: Then why didn't you tell me?

TESSA: He asked me not to.

EILEEN: Did he ring you?

TESSA: Yes. He came to the hospital. We looked at him properly.

EILEEN: I didn't know any of this, Tess.
    (*A slight pause*)

TESSA: I asked him to tell you, but he wouldn't.

EILEEN: Why?

TESSA: I don't know, Mum.

EILEEN: He was getting his own back, wasn't he?

TESSA: That's very silly.

EILEEN: Is it?

TESSA: You must know it is.

EILEEN: I don't. (*A slight pause*) Jolly was very bitter, you know. He thought life had let him down.

TESSA: Did he?

EILEEN: He was very bitter. I'd be a fool if I didn't know that I was his life.

TESSA: I think you're twisting things, Mum.

EILEEN: Twisting what?

TESSA: Twisting your memories. (*A slight pause*) When I was seven, Jolly was working. You've nothing to feel guilty about.

EILEEN: He wanted to study, you know. He always did. We couldn't afford it. All my life that's what I've said. When you went off to university, he shone like the sun. He said: I wanted Stephen to be the doctor, but now it's our Tess. (*A slight pause*) I just worried you'd fall into bad company.

TESSA: I didn't, did I?

EILEEN: No, you've made your life very good. He was proud of you. (*A slight pause*) He could always meet you, Tess. D'you know what I mean?

TESSA: Not really, I don't.

EILEEN: In intelligence, up here. (EILEEN *taps her head*) I've wanted to say this for a long time. Not way, so much as admit. For most of my life I've been a very jealous woman.

TESSA: Mum —

EILEEN: If yer dad had been on his own — this is true, Tess — you'd have come home much more often. I've seen yer dad broken because you didn't come home.

(TESSA *looks down, and then she looks back up*)

TESSA: Why don't we wait before we say these things?

EILEEN: I want you to understand that I do know what I'm like.

TESSA: Mum —

EILEEN: Jolly used to say that you make time for the things you really want to do. You didn't come home because of me. That is the truth, isn't it?

TESSA: I've had my career. And Matty. I've wanted him to grow up responsibly and strong.

EILEEN: Yes.

TESSA: It isn't you. Now isn't the time. Not for recrimination.

EILEEN: I'm worried there never will be a time. Yer dad used to say:

our Tess has outgrown us, Eileen. I used to say: she's flown the nest, pet. (*A slight pause*) He was such a dreamer. It was me who made the ends meet. I was busy running the family. (*A slight pause*) I used to think: we'll not have a family if I let him dream — we'll be out on the streets — we'll be begging. Isn't that stupid? I'm sorry, Tess.

TESSA: It isn't stupid, Mum.

EILEEN: It is, you know. (*A slight pause*) I suppose the one thing I've learnt — is that somehow you do get by. That must be true, because we did.

TESSA: Yes.

EILEEN: I am sorry.

TESSA: You've nothing to be sorry for.

EILEEN: I have, you know.

Source: Methuen London Ltd.

✤ Aunt Dan & Lemon

●●●●●●●●●●●●●●●●●●●●●●●●●●●●WALLACE SHAWN

CHARACTERS: AUNT DAN (40's), MOTHER (40's)
SETTING: *A dark room, 1960.*

AUNT DAN *is an eccentric, passionate professor whose stories and seductive opinions enthrall both Lemon and her mother. In this scene,* MOTHER *and* AUNT DAN *explore the ease with which good and bad become reconciled in the human mind.* MOTHER *has previously confessed to* AUNT DAN *that Kissinger believes what he's doing is right — that he can't avoid war.*

AUNT DAN (*To* MOTHER):   Susie, he is not a private individual like you and me — he works for the *government*! I mean, you're talking here as if you were trying to tell me that you and I are so nice every day and why can't our governments be just like us! I can't believe you're saying that! Don't you understand that you and I are only able to be nice because our governments — our governments are *not* nice? Why do you think we've set these things up? I mean, a state, policemen, politicians — what's it all for? The point is so we don't all have to spend our lives in some ditch by the side of the road fighting like animals about every little thing. The whole purpose of government is to use force. So we don't have to. So if I move into your house and refuse to leave, you don't have to kick me or punch me, you don't have to go find some acid to throw in my face — you just nicely have to pick up the phone and call the police! And if some other country attacks our friends in Southeast Asia, you and I don't have to go over there and fight them with rifles — we just get Kissinger to fight them for us.

MOTHER: But Dan —

AUNT DAN: These *other* people use force, so we can sit here in this garden and be incredibly nice. Otherwise we'd be going around covered with scars and bruises and our hair all torn out, like stray cats.

MOTHER: But are you saying that governments can do anything, or Kissinger can do anything, and somehow it's never proper for us to say, Well we don't like this, we think this is wrong? Do you mean to say that we don't have the right to criticize this person's decisions? That no one has the right to criticize them?

AUNT DAN: No, I don't say that. Go right ahead. Criticize his deci-sions all you like. I don't know. Go ahead and criticize every-thing he does.

MOTHER: I don't —

AUNT DAN: Particularly if you have no idea what you would do in his place.

MOTHER: Dan, I'm not . . .

(*Silence*)

AUNT DAN: Susie, I'm simply saying that it's terribly easy for us to criticize. It's terribly easy for us to sit here and give our opinions on the day's events. And while we sit here in the sunshine and have our discussions about what we've read in the morning papers, there are these certain *other* people, like Kissinger, who happen to have the very bad luck to be society's leaders. And while we sit here chatting, they have to do what has to be done. And so *we* chat, but *they* do what they *have* to do. *They* do what they *have* to do. And if they have to do something, they're pre-pared to do it. Because I'm very sorry, if you're in a position of responsibility, that means you're responsible for doing whatever it is that has to be done. If you're on the outside, you can wail and complain about what society's leaders are doing. Go ahead. That's fine. That's your right. That's your privileged position. But if you are the one who's in power, if you're responsible, if you're a leader, you don't have that privilege. It's your job to do it. Just to do it. Do it. Do it. Don't complain, don't agonize, don't moan, don't wail. Just do it. Everyone will hate you. Fine. That's their right. But you have to do it. Of course, you're defending *those very people*. *They're* the ones you're defending. But do you expect to be *understood*? You must be nuts! You must be crazy! — insane! All day long you're defending *them* — defending, defending, defending — and your reward is, they'll spit in your face! All right — so be it. That's the way it is. The joy of lead-ership. But you can bet that what Kissinger says when he goes to bed at night is, Dear God, I wish I were nothing. Dear God, I wish I were a little child. I wish I were a bird or a fish or a deer living quietly in the woods. I wish I were anything but what I am. I am a slave, but they see me as a master. I am sacrificing my life for them, but they think I'm scrambling for power for myself. For myself! Myself! *None* of it is for myself. I *have* no self. I am a leader — that means I am a slave, I am less than dirt. *They* think of themselves. *I* don't. They think, what would *I* like? What would be nice for *me*? I think, what has to be done? What is the thing I *must* do? I don't think, what would be nice for *me* to do?

No. No. Never. Never. Never that. Only, what is the thing I *must* do? What is the thing I *must* do. (*Silence*) And then these filthy, slimy worms, the little journalists, come along, and it is so far beyond their comprehension — and in a way it's so unacceptable to them — that anyone could possibly be motivated by dreams that are loftier than their own pitiful hopes for a bigger byline, or a bigger car, a a girlfriend with a bigger bust, or a house with a bigger game-room in the basement, that, far from feeling gratitude to this man who has taken the responsibility for making the most horrible, shattering decisions, they feel they can't rest till they make it impossible for him to continue! They're out to stop him! Defying the father figure, the big daddy! Worms! Worms! How *dare* they attack him for killing peasants? What decisions did *they* make to day? What did *they* have to decide, the little journalists? What did *they* have to decide? Did they decide whether to write one very long column or two tiny little columns? Did they decide whether to have dinner at their favorite French restaurant or to save a little money by going to their second-favorite French restaurant instead? Cowards! Cowards! If anyone brought them a decision that involved human life, where people would die whatever they decided, they would run just as fast as their little legs would carry them. But they're not afraid to trying to stop *him*, of making people have contempt for *him*, of stirring up a storm of loathing for *him*, of keeping him so busy fending off their attacks that he can't breathe, he can't escape, he just has to collapse or resign! I would love to see these cowards face up to some of the consequences of their murder of our leaders! I would love to see them face some of the little experiences our leaderless soldiers face when they suddenly meet the North Vietnamese in the middle of the jungle. That might make the little journalists understand what they were doing, the little cowards. Have they ever felt a bayonet go right through their chests? Have they ever felt a knife rip right through their guts? Would they be sneering then, would they be thinking up clever ways to mock our leaders? No, they'd be squealing like pigs, they'd be begging, begging, "Please save me! Please help me!" I would love to be hiding behind a tree watching the little cowards screaming and bleeding and shitting in their pants! I would love to be watching! Those slimy cowards. So let's see them try to make some decisions. Let's see them decide that people have to die. They wouldn't have the faintest idea what to do. But they just sit in their offices and toss them off. Well, do you think Kissinger is just sitting in *his* office casually making this *decisions*?

Do you think he makes those decisions lightly? What do you think? Do you think he just sits in his office and tosses them off? Do you think he just makes them in two minutes between bites of a sandwich?

(*A long silence*)

MOTHER: Dan, I'm sure he makes his decisions thoughtfully. And I'm sure he believes himself to be justified. But I was asking, is he *actually* justified, as far as *I* am concerned? I'm sure he's weighed those lives in the balance against . . . some large objective. But I was asking, has he weighed them, actually, at — at what I would consider their correct measure? (*A silence*) Does he have a heart which is capable of weighing them correctly?

AUNT DAN: What? What? I don't believe this! I don't believe what I'm hearing from you! Look, I'm sorry, Susie, but all I can say to you is that if he sat at his desk weeping and sobbing all day, I don't think he'd be able to do his job. That's all I can say. He has just as much of a heart as anyone else, you can be sure of that, but the point is that the heart by itself cannot tell you what to do in a situation like that. The heart just responds to the present moment — it just sees these people in a village who've been hit by a bomb, and they're wounded and dying, and it's terribly sad. But the mind — the mind sees the story through to the end. It sees that yes, there are people who are wounded and dying in that village. But if we *hadn't* bombed it, some of those same people would have been marching tomorrow toward the *next* village with the grenades and machine guns they'd stored in that pretty little church we blew up, and when they *got* to the village, they would have burned it to the ground and raped the woman and tortured the men and killed whole families — mothers and children. Of course, those things aren't actually happening now, so the heart doesn't care about them. But the things that will happen tomorrow are real too. When it *is* tomorrow, they'll be just as real as the things that are happening now. So I'm asking you, Susie, here is Kissinger. Here is the man who must make the decisions. What do you want this man to do? I am only asking what you want him to do. What is it that you want him to do?

MOTHER (*After a long pause*):   Well, I suppose I want him to assess the threat he is facing . . . with scrupulous honesty . . . and then I want him to think about those people. Yes, I suppose I do want him to weep and sob at his desk. Yes. Then let him makes his decisions.

Source: Grove Press

✤ Blind Date

●●●●●●●●●●●●●●●●●●●●●●●●●●●●●●●●HORTON FOOTE

CHARACTERS: DOLORES (30's), SARAH NANCY (16)
SETTING: *Living room in a house in a small Texas town, 1920's.*

DOLORES *is concerned that boys are not dating her niece,* SARAH NANCY, *who is visiting for the summer.* DOLORES *has prepared a little fundamental romantic advice based on her own experience. A blind date is about to arrive as the art of conversation is being explained.*

DOLORES: Now where were we. Oh, yes. I was going over my list of things to talk about. (DOLORES *picks up her list and begins reading*) One: Who is going to win the football game next Friday? Two: Do you think we have had enough rain for the cotton yet? Three: I hear you were a football player in high school. What position did you play? Do you miss football? Four: I hear you are an insurance salesman. What kind of insurance do you sell? Five: What is the best car on the market today to you think? Six: What church do you belong to? Seven: Do you enjoy dancing? Eight: Do you enjoy bridge? (*She puts the list down*) All right, that will do for a start. Now, let's practice. I'll be Felix. Now. Hello, Sarah Nancy.
(*A pause,* SARAH NANCY *looks at her like she thinks she's crazy*)
Now, what do you say, Sarah Nancy.

SARAH NANCY: About what?

DOLORES: About what? About what you say when someone says hello to you, Sarah Nancy. Now, let's start again. Hello, Sarah Nancy.

SARAH NANCY: Hello.

DOLORES: Honey, don't just say hello and above all don't scowl and say hello. Smile. Hello, how very nice to see you. Let me feel your warmth. Now, will you remember that? Of course you will. All right, let's start on our questions. Begin with your first question. (*A pause*) I'm waiting, honey.

SARAH NANCY: I forget.

DOLORES: Well, don't be discouraged. I'll go over the list carefully and slowly again. One: Who is going to win the football game next Friday? Two: Do you think we have enough rain for the cot-

HELEN (*Straightening up*):   For the moment.

AMY: They say it helps to eat molasses.

HELEN (*Looks at* AMY, *pauses*):   Ahhhhhhh — (*She leans over the wagon*)

AMY: I'm not seasick. Isn't that wonderful! (HELEN *straightens up and looks at* AMY *dubiously*) Maybe . . . it's 'cause . . . when I was a child and we visited Grandma, you used to let me climb the rigging of the old whalers on the wharf.

HELEN: Those whalers I let you climb . . . were not roaring . . . kicking . . . plunging. Ahhhhhhh . . . (HELEN *leans over the wagon and is sick again*)

AMY: Maybe Mr. Schoolcraft will stop the train and let us rest.

HELEN: Never sail under a captain who knows your folks at home. (*The wagon slows in its rocking and then stops*)

HELEN: Oh Lord, at last. No movement. At last. (AMY *helps her mother from the wagon and they sit on the ground*) I never knew . . . how wonderful it was . . . just . . . to . . . be . . . still.

AMY: The earth's moving all the time.

HELEN: Oh, Amy. (*She holds her stomach*)

AMY: Our clothes are scattered on the floor . . . and the molasses keg fell. It's oozed all over our dresses. Mrs. Schoolcraft told us not to put our things in barrels — he said the wagon would shake the barrels to pieces. (AMY *takes off her shoes and holds them up. She walks in her stocking feet*) Our clothes are ruined.

HELEN: They're not . . . ruined.

AMY: Where can I get pretty clothes out here?

HELEN: You don't need them.

AMY: I'm not making this whole trip looking like an old hag.

HELEN (*Building up to a laugh*):   So . . . you'll wear that dress over there . . . and, mile by mile, lick it clean . . . like an old cow.

AMY: It's not funny.

HELEN (*Giggling*):   Being an old cow is better than being an old nag.

AMY (*Looking directly at her mother*):   I said . . . *hag.*

HELEN (*Stops laughing*):   Is that directed to me? (*They stare at each other coldly*)

AMY: I was expecting my mother to know how to keep my clothes properly.

HELEN: You're fourteen years old. Keep them "properly" yourself. (AMY *turns away from her mother, sulking*)

AMY: What do you expect . . . from . . . (*Mumbles*)

HELEN: What was that? (*Silence*) I asked you, what did you say?

AMY: What do you expect . . . from a spoiled officer's wife?

ton yet? Three: I hear you were a football player in high school. What position did you play? Do you miss football? Four: I hear you are an insurance salesman. What kind of insurance do you sell? Five: What is the best car on the market today, do you think? Six: What church do you belong to? Seven: Do you enjoy dancing? Eight: Do you enjoy bridge? Now, we won't be rigid about the questions, of course. You can ask the last question first if you want to.

SARAH NANCY: What's the last question again?

DOLORES: Do you enjoy bridge?

SARAH NANCY: I hate bridge.

DOLORES: Well, then, sweetness, just substitute another question. Say, do you enjoy dancing?

SARAH NANCY: I hate dancing.

DOLORES: Now, you don't hate dancing. You couldn't hate dancing. It is in your blood. Your mother and daddy are both beautiful dancers. You just need to practice is all. Now . . .

SARAH NANCY: Why didn't you get me a date with Arch Leon? I think he's the cute one.

DOLORES: He's going steady, honey, I explained that.

SARAH NANCY: Who is he going steady with?

DOLORES: Alberta Jackson.

SARAH NANCY: Is she cute?

DOLORES: I think she's right cute, a little common looking and acting for my taste.

SARAH NANCY: He sure is cute.

DOLORES: Well, Felix Robertson is a lovely boy.

SARAH NANCY: I think he's about a cute as a warthog.

DOLORES: Sarah Nancy.

SARAH NANCY: I think he looks just like a warthog.

DOLORES: Sarah Nancy, precious . . .

SARAH NANCY: That's the question I'd like to ask him. How is the hog pen, warthog?

DOLORES: Precious, precious.

SARAH NANCY: Anyway, they are all stupid.

DOLORES: Who, honey?

SARAH NANCY: Boys.

DOLORES: Precious, darling.

SARAH NANCY: Dumb and stupid. (*She starts away*)

DOLORES: Sarah Nancy, where in the world are you gong?

SARAH NANCY: I'm going to bed.

DOLORES: Sarah Nancy, what is possessing you to say a thing like that. You're just trying to tease me.

SARAH NANCY: Oh, no, I'm not. (*She starts away*)

DOLORES: Sarah Nancy, you can't go to bed. You have a young man coming to call on you at any moment. You have to be gracious . . .

SARAH NANCY: I don't feel like being gracious. I'm sleepy. I'm going to bed.

DOLORES: Sarah Nancy, you can't. Do you want to put me in my grave? The son of one of your mother's dearest friends will be here at any moment to call on you, and you cannot be so rude as to go to bed and refuse to receive him. Sarah Nancy, I beg you. I implore you.

SARAH NANCY: Oh, all right. (*She sits down*) Ask me some questions.

DOLORES: No, dear. You ask me some questions.

SARAH NANCY: What church do you attend?

DOLORES: That's lovely. That's a lovely question to begin with. Now I'll answer as Felix will. Methodist.

SARAH NANCY: That's a dumb church.

DOLORES: Sarah Nancy.

SARAH NANCY: I think it's a dumb church. It's got no style. We used to be Methodist but we left for the Episcopal. They don't rant and rave in the Episcopal Church.

DOLORES: And they don't rant and rave in the Methodist Church either, honey. Not here. Not in Harrison.

SARAH NANCY: Last time I was here they did.

DOLORES: Well, things have changed. Anyway, you're not supposed to comment when he answers the questions, you're just supposed to sit back and listen to the answers as if you're fascinated and find it all very interesting.

SARAH NANCY: Why?

DOLORES: Because that's how you entertain young men, graciously. You make them feel you are interested in whatever they have to say.

SARAH NANCY: Suppose I'm not.

DOLORES: Well, it is not important if you are or not, you are supposed to make them think you are.

Source: *Best Short Plays 1988*, Applause Theatre Books

✛ Breaking the Prairie Wolf Code

●●●●●●●●●●●●●●●●●●●●●●●●●●●●●LAVONNE MUELLER

CHARACTERS: HELEN (*30's*), AMY (*14*)
SETTING: *The Overland Trail to California, 1886.*

HELEN, *a widow, and her daughter,* AMY, *are making the westward crossing to California.* HELEN, *once married to an officer in the East, is used to having orderlies wait on her. Now she is experiencing the deep West and struggling with a young daughter and a harsh life. As the scene opens,* AMY *and* HELEN *are riding in a bouncing wagon.*

HELEN: Are you holding on, Amy?

AMY: Yes, Mama.

HELEN: My fingers are bleeding.

AMY: Maybe Mr. Schoolcraft will help us.

HELEN: Never sail under a captain who knows your folks at home.

AMY: We should have been whalers.

HELEN: I think we are.

AMY: I didn't know a wagon train would be like this.

HELEN: The noise.

AMY: The dust.

HELEN: Everybody's swearing. Each person on his own. And one general chorus.

AMY: I can't tell the officers from the stevedores.

HELEN: Isn't that Mr. Bluster riding along the side?

AMY: He's the fourth and last officer.

HELEN: Bluster's the last officer?

AMY: Yes, Mama.

HELEN: It's a relief to know the exact number of men entitled to yell at us.
(*The wagon rocks and* HELEN *and* AMY *deal with this motion*)
Sometimes . . . it's almost beautiful. All these wagons in a line . . . rolling . . . their gigantic arcs in the lazy swell of the wind . . . rolling . . . rolling in our little trough . . . holding on. (*Long pause*) I . . . I think I'm seasick. Are you?

AMY: No.

HELEN: Oh, no! (*She leans over the rocking wagon, ill*)

AMY: Are you all right, Mama?

HELEN: Don't you say that to me!

AMY: It's true. Everybody says so.

HELEN: I'm doing the best I can. Do you hear me . . . you little ungrateful twit. (*She starts to shake* AMY) I'm a widow. No colonel husband, no more orderlies, no more money. (*Pause*) I'm alone! (HELEN *pushes* AMY *angrily to the floor. After a pause,* AMY *plucks at the dress she is wearing as she sits in the molasses.* HELEN *looks at* AMY, *then starts to giggle.* AMY *slowly begins to giggle, too.* HELEN *sits down next to* AMY, *puts one arm around her, and uses the other arm to play in the molasses. They both begin to flap playfully in the molasses*) Like fly paper.

AMY (*Sings*):   We're two little flies, trying to fly —

HELEN (*Sings*):   We're two little flies —

AMY (*Sings*):   . . . who can't go high.
(*They giggle*)

HELEN: We'll have to wash everything up.

AMY: I'll do it.

HELEN (*Standing*):   I can do it, as long as there's no . . . pitching and rolling. Oh, why did I have to say that? (*She lies down beside the wagon*)

AMY: We could sleep in the wagon.

HELEN: I like it outside.

AMY: Me, too.

HELEN: We'll keep things as normal as possible. We'll have tea. every night before bed.

AMY: Like always.
(HELEN *pulls her little teapot by the fire. She has two little cups. She puts out a glass candelabra with a candle in it. She pours them a cup of tea*)
Tell me about your first kiss.

HELEN: I was fifteen.

AMY: Daddy?

HELEN: Yes.

AMY: What was it like?

HELEN: We were sitting on a bench . . . in the park.

AMY: What's it like?

HELEN: It's like . . . ice skating for the first time. He was on one side of the bench, leaning toward me . . . and I had to . . . move smoothly across that patch of land between two faces . . . wanting to glide . . . wanting to . . . just run. Run on skates. Then I moved . . . carefully . . . close. I was skating! His cheek was next to mine. I was there. I . . . got to the other side without falling. I wasn't on the ice anymore . . . but in the air. In a strange weightless place that held me and filled me with wonder.

(*Pause*)

AMY: Will that happen to me?

HELEN: Your grandmother says the officers stationed at Fort Mackinaw near our new house are very handsome . . . and very romantic.

AMY: I only get to meet officers?

HELEN: In California, who else is educated . . . and refined?

AMY: Mother!

HELEN: I want a prince for you. I want a poet . . . a hero.

AMY: That's a lot, Mama.

(AMY *laughs, but* HELEN *is serious. They put down their cups and look up at the sky*)

HELEN: It's so beautiful — look, Amy. If the stars had arms, they'd hold us.

AMY: They're the same stars in New York.

(*Wolves are heard*)

What's that terrible sound?

(*They listen*)

Hear?

HELEN: Yes.

AMY: What is it?

HELEN: The cries of prairie wolves.

AMY: It's . . . so terrible.

(*Pause as they listen*)

What do you think they're doing?

HELEN: Oh . . . just ordinary animal things. Remember our old cat, Benny?

AMY: Yes.

HELEN: Well, they're most likely doing what she always did.

AMY: What's that?

HELEN: Playing batt-paws . . . and other ancestral games.

AMY: You think so?

HELEN: Sure.

AMY: Why are they . . . howling like that?

HELEN: Those wolves are telling secrets. That's all. (*She listens*) And before the journey is over, we'll break the code.

AMY: Really?

(*They listen to the wolves*)

Mama . . . can I crawl in beside you?

HELEN: Come on, honey.

(AMY *crawls on the blanket next to her mother. Her mother puts an arms around her*)

AMY: What's . . . that noise?

HELEN: Just the wind . . . on the water bucket under the wagon. The wind on the spokes and brake rigging. (*Pause*) I think about your daddy all the time . . . and you know something, I think we can make ourselves dream. About the dead. After all, he's just waiting in the dark. Waiting for us to close our eyes to his dark.

AMY: Remember when you told me maple leaves . . . were falling stars.

HELEN: You kept a jar of them by your bed.

AMY: Daddy said that whenever apple trees don't grow apples for the Indians, and just as they start to chop it down, one Indian shouts: "Don't kill it! The tree promises to bear fruit!"

HELEN: They frighten the tree fertile.

AMY: Daddy said it always worked.

HELEN: We'll frighten ourselves brave. (*Pause. Calls*) Prairie . . . don't cut us down!

AMY (*Calling*): We promise to live out West!

AMY/HELEN (*Together*): Forever.

(*Pause*)

HELEN: Every apple tree makes me think of my husband . . . my soldier.

AMY: Makes me think of my daddy.

(*Wolves are heard. They listen*)

I miss the East. Homey smells of scorched paper lamp shades. I . . . pine for sidewalks . . . after a summer shower. Remember how the city smells like a hot dish towel. How the smell sticks.

HELEN: Oh, honey, we've got a new home on the trail. A gypsy home. Instead of our old room back home, we've got clouds like tobacco leaves . . . coming home to roost right on top of us. We can chase them away when the stars come out. Amy, out here we can walk barefoot in the sky.

Source: Dramatists Play Service, Inc.

✤ Candy and Shelley Go To The Desert

●●●●●●●●●●●●●●●●●●●●●●●●●●●●●PAULA CIZMAR

CHARACTERS: CANDY (20's), SHELLEY (20's)
SETTING: *The desert in Nevada.*

CANDY *and* SHELLEY, *childhood friends, are making a journey through the desert just for the fun of it. Their car becomes overheated and breaks down. They get out and wait in the clay soil and lifeless-rock landscape of "nowhere".*

CANDY (*Overlapping*):   Oh I can get such a good tan out here. Even. All over. Sun just everywhere, just reflecting off everything. No shadows. Mmmm, this is nice.

SHELLEY (*Sneezes; overlapping*):   Listen to me. I'm allergic. There's no pollution. None of the bacteria I'm used to. I could die out here. You know, when the early explorers visited native tribes in the Americas, the Indians started keeling over left and right from foreign flu bugs.

CANDY: Mm-hmm. You better take off your sandals or you'll have tan lines on your toes.

SHELLEY: You can't survive without your own bacteria. You can't take a fish out of water.

CANDY: Water. What a good idea. Maybe there's an oasis out there.

SHELLEY: No, there would have to be coconut trees. Gee, a macaroon would be good. I'm starved.

CANDY: If you would have let me buy that ice chest at the K-Mart in Ohio you could eat right now.

SHELLEY: Macaroons don't need an ice chest. Oooh, a cinnamon roll with raisins. Hot from the oven. A steak. Blood red.

CANDY: You're a vegetarian.

SHELLEY: A steak. And nachos. A pepperoncini salad. Onion soup with melted cheese. Fried eggs. A hot pastrami sandwich with sauerkraut. And lasagna. That's what I want. Scratch that. Scratch all of that. Watermelon. Yeah.

(SHELLEY *sighs, then sneezes.* CANDY *holds her arms and legs at weird angles to catch the rays*)

CANDY: Mm. I know what I want. Yeah. I want hot sex. Hot hot sex.

SHELLEY: In this heat?

CANDY: Hot desert sands, a hot desert breeze, vapors, and a hot hot hot young man.

SHELLEY (*Sneezing*): Got any cough syrup?

CANDY: A biker, maybe.

SHELLEY: Even a Kleenex?

CANDY: Biker, mmmm, yeah.

SHELLEY: I need medicine. (*She starts checking pockets, purse, knapsack, for something to take. As she searches, she discovers another minicorpse*) No! No! Here's another one! It's a lizard graveyard. What are they doing? What are they doing?

CANDY: One hot hot biker.

SHELLEY: You know, probably if we got in the car and took off, I'd feel a lot better.

CANDY: Or a lot of them. Hubba hubba.

SHELLEY (*Sneezing; starts packing up their things*): Well, now that you've had a little rest from driving,we should get going.

CANDY: Yeah. He'd pull up on his hot hot machine. Or they would.

SHELLEY: I promise to follow the map better this time — we'll just drive uptown until we hit I-80, then turn right. That's east, got it? Uh, like taking the FDR up to the 59th Street Bridge. See?

CANDY: Ooooh. Bikers like those guys with the shrunken heads on their helmets that we saw at that last Foster's Freeze. Oooooo-eee Vrrummm, rrummm. Rummmm. (*She sits up, grasps "handlebars" and "kicks the bike into gear" — as if she were really on a chopper*)

SHELLEY: Uh, Candy, catch my drift there? Like, we'll go home.

CANDY: You wanted to see the Pacific Ocean. Rrrummmm, RRRRummm.

SHELLEY: I'm sure it looks just like the Atlantic. Just the same except it's on the wrong side when you look at it.

CANDY: Never saw a biker eat a vanilla cone with sprinkles before.

SHELLEY: Candy. Look. It's about time we admitted that this so-called get-away-from-it-all experience is not working out.

CANDY: All those sprinkles, he kind of closed his eyes and . . . oh.

SHELLEY: Maybe the Bahamas this fall — a nice condo on the water, I think.

CANDY: Mmm. And then that one teeny drip of icy . . . white . . . frozen . . . custard . . . cream, just one drip on his chest, kind of melting down over his —

SHELLEY: Candy, let's go.

CANDY: Mmm. He had a real good tan and a lot of terrific blonde hair on his chest, did you notice that?

SHELLEY: Yeah, but he was peeling. Let's go. We've gotta get somewhere civilized before dark.

CANDY: I'd lick it off.

SHELLEY (*Sneezing*): I'm sick.

CANDY: Come on, think of it. A steamy biker boy. Spikes on his cap. Thighs all swathed in leather.

SHELLEY: In this heat?

CANDY: Relax. They've got us where they want us. We're at their mercy now. They're just waiting till we get a little weaker, then they'll swoop in for the kill. (*Beat*) Hear their bikes. Rrrummm, rrrummm.

SHELLEY: Please. We've had enough. I'll be good I swear it. I'm sorry I made you stop at that Union 76 trucker place in Iowa. I know you didn't want to.

CANDY: Oooh. I am ready for you, Mr. Desert Man.

SHELLEY (*Trying to drag* CANDY *to the car*): You've got to take me home now.

CANDY (*Singing the Little Eva song*): Chains! My baby's got me locked up in chains . . . and it ain't the kind . . . that you can see . . .

SHELLEY: So . . . here's the plan. I'll go to the car. I'll get in and sit down and you'll come over there in a second or two and we'll drive off. Simple. I'm sorry you have to drive all the way. I'll . . . I'll pay for all the motels going back. Okay? Look, it's just that I never learned to drive stick shift, that's all. Hey . . . we'll drive along and I'll really learn this time. You work the pedals, and I'll shift. Right?

(CANDY *continues humming the song, while deliberately and sensuously basking in the sun*)

Candy. Listen to me. This is the kind of place where lunatics bury hundreds of sunburned tourists in the sand after they chop them into little pieces and set fire to their baby oil. People carry axes out here.

CANDY: Mmmmm, motor boy.

SHELLEY: Candy, cut it out. Now look —

CANDY: Ohh ohh take me.

SHELLEY: Candy —

(CANDY *continues humming, then stops abruptly. There are sounds of bikers off in the distance*)

Oh God.

CANDY: Wow.

SHELLEY: Snap out of it. This is serious now.

CANDY: Wow I didn't really think they would really —

SHELLEY: We've gotta get out of here.

(*The sounds of the motorcycles grow louder and louder*)

CANDY: Wow. Dozens of little specks, all heading this way.

SHELLEY: Oh no.

CANDY: Gee. And there's more behind them.

SHELLEY: Candy!

CANDY: Wow. Like an ant farm.

(SHELLEY's *anxiety is escalating — in fact, she's in a full-scale panic*)

Source: Dramatists Play Service, Inc.

♣ The Early Girl

•••••••••••••••••••••••••••••CAROLINE KAVA

CHARACTERS: JEAN (25), LILY (17)
SETTING: *A house of prostitution in a mining town out west, 1938.*

JEAN *and* LILY *are two of the girls employed by Lana, the strict owner of a bordello.* JEAN *is witty, intense, and has a college education.* LILY, *the youngest and newest girl, is very beautiful, spirited and innocent. The previous evening,* LILY *was in a fight with George, one of the other girls, because she kissed Eric, a client with whom George is in love. George also accused* JEAN *and* LILY *of being lesbians.* LILY *now holds a cold compress over her eye.*

JEAN: Mornin' Bright Eyes. (*She takes down her mug, fills it with water*)
LILY: (Ha. Ha. Ha.) . . . Laurel just talked to me.
JEAN: Yeah? What was that like? (*She takes her pill*)
LILY: . . . You're the Early Girl today, you know.
JEAN: You mean this isn't the prom?
LILY: Lana's taking me to the doctor. I don't think there's anything really wrong with it, do you?
JEAN: I can't say.
LILY: I mean, the swelling's gone down, don't you think?
JEAN: I don't know anything about medicine. I know a little about embalming. If you were a corpse, I could give you a pretty accurate prognosis.
LILY: It's not funny. It hurts.
JEAN: I'm sure.
LILY: And it looks like hell.
JEAN: You're right.
LILY: Really?
JEAN: It suits you.
LILY: Thanks a lot.
JEAN: What do yo want me to say? I don't feel sorry for you, Lily. You deserved to be hit.
LILY: . . . I thought we were friends.
    (*Pause.* JEAN *starts to leave*)
    . . . Where are you going?

JEAN: If anyone needs me, I'll be in my castle.

LILY: I need you!

JEAN (*Overlap*): In my little room! (*She exits*)

LILY: I gotta talk to you! Jean!

JEAN (*Re-entering*): Okay, what? . . . I'm here.

LILY: . . . It's about last night . . .

JEAN: Yeah?

LILY: What George said.

JEAN: What was that? . . . I don't remember anything George said, Lily, all I remember is sounds.

LILY: You don't care, do you? You don't care about anything.

JEAN: That came through loud and clear.

LILY: Well, I'm plutonic.

JEAN: What?

LILY: *We* are. Just friends. That's all.

JEAN: *Pla*tonic, not *plu*tonic. Although, you may be right.

LILY: I'm not in love with you.

JEAN: Did George give you a concussion?

LILY: My pupils aren't dilated.

JEAN: That's too bad.

(*Beat*)

LILY: I'm gonna have to start using you for an extra.

JEAN: Because we're just friends?

LILY: To show we're not involved.

JEAN: And performing a sex act together should make that perfectly clear to everyone. I'm not in love with you either, by the way.

LILY: I didn't think you were.

JEAN: Thank you.

LILY: But George thinks —

JEAN: What do you care what George thinks? George is fired.

LILY: Laid off.

JEAN: But you won't be here when she gets back. So what are you so worried about?

LILY: I just don't want people thinking that, okay?

JEAN: People?

LILY: You know.

JEAN: Not George?

LILY: Clients.

JEAN: Oh.

LILY: If they think that you and I can't have sex together with them, well, they may think that you and I are having sex together.

JEAN: Alone?

LILY: By ourselves.

JEAN: You've obviously given them a lot of thought.

LILY: Well, that's what I'm here for.

JEAN: Can I ask you a question?

LILY: Sure. I'm really glad we're talking.

JEAN: So am I. Are clients the only people that matter to you, Lily?

LILY: No, there's Dolly —

JEAN: Aren't we people too?

LILY: I guess — yeah — Look, Lana will be down any minute —

JEAN: You guess?

LILY: Oh, fuck you, Jean! You pick apart every little word I say! I don't talk as good as you! I'm not a dropout! I talk like a regular person!

JEAN: You talk like a whore!

LILY: What did you call me?

JEAN: You've never heard the expression?

LILY: I'm not a whore.

JEAN: What about the rest of us?

LILY: I'm not a —

JEAN: What about George, and me, and Pat, and Laurel? Exclude Lana, it makes it easier.

LILY: I can't talk to you —

JEAN: This is my best English — *What the fuck do you think we are anyway?* . . . I'm waiting, Lily Lang.

LILY: We're . . .

JEAN: We're what? I'm dying to hear this.

LILY: Working girls.

JEAN: And that's all?

LILY: Forget it.

JEAN: Great. (*She starts to leave*)

LILY: Wait a minute!

JEAN: Got a fin? I'm only a working girl —

LILY: We can't be just whores!

JEAN: Oh, yes we can . . . Eric is not a trick to George. You knew that, you knew that from Day One. Whatever your interest, whatever your opinion, George has real feelings for that creep. Jesus Christ! When feelings manage to go on here, Lily, we respect them! They're precious. They're damn precious few.

LILY: I fucked up. I fucked up. All right?

JEAN: This is not the Lounge at your Holiday Inn, Lily. It's not even the basement. It's much lower than that. It's filthy, and demeaning, and we're up to our necks in slop. But we're still people, goddamit, all of us, people! If you let yourself forget that, for one minute, you're nothing but a whore!

LILY: . . . I'm sorry.

JEAN: Don't let it happen again.

(*Doorbell rings*)

JEAN: I mean it . . . (*Taking off robe, putting on shoes*) I'm not saying it's easy, Lily. 'Cause it isn't. It's hard, real hard. It takes work. That's what makes us "working girls." . . . We can call ourselves that —

(*Doorbell rings*)

JEAN: . . . including you.

[LANA (*Off*): Parlor One, Jean!

JEAN: (Okay, okay.) (*She exits*)]

Source: Samuel French, Inc.

✛ Emily

•••••••••••••••••••••••••••STEPHEN METCALFE

CHARACTERS: HALLIE (20), EMILY (20)
SETTING: *A health club in New York City, the present.*

HALLIE *and* EMILY, *best friends, are struggling to do a Jane Fonda-like exercise regimen.* HALLIE *is a New Yorker by way of Texas.* EMILY *is a native New Yorker; she has yet to exercise the emotion of love.*

EMILY: God, I love weights. I love Nautilus equipment. Look around this place. Look at all these girls, Hallie, in their Spandex and Lycra and leg warmers and headbands. Look at them. Sweating. Straining. Lifting. Stretching. Killing themselves. Beating their beautiful bodies into shape.

HALLIE: Sluts. Let me get this straight. You break off the relationship but you want the man to think it's his idea?

EMILY: Yup.

HALLIE: An' so you ask them to marry you, hopin' they'll say no?

EMILY: Knowing they will. It saves their feelings, Hallie. This way they think they're hurting my feelings. And they're not. Nobody's feelings are hurt. Everybody is happy.

HALLIE: I think it's weird. Ugh. (*Rising, looking towards a mirror*) Business lunches are turnin' me into a Pillsbury dough girl. I order salad and end up eatin' a pound a' blue cheese dressing. (*Looking around*) I loathe every woman here. Hold my legs while I do some sit ups.

EMILY: I've never been in love, Hallie. Maybe it's because I don't trust love. Love doesn't last. What is love? Love is biology. Love is enzymes. Love is crazy chemicals in the blood stream. Love is secretions. Is an intelligent woman supposed to trust secretions? No.

HALLIE: How many's that?

EMILY: Three. Let's go take a sauna, I'm exhausted.

HALLIE: Emily! I've got to do at least ten!

EMILY: Men are so fragile. I hesitate to get close to a man because I'm afraid I'll hurt him.

HALLIE: Or maybe he'll hurt you.

EMILY: Hallie, please. A woman's heart is as tough as nails.

HALLIE: Right. Ugh! I can't make it.

EMILY: A woman is as tough as nails.

HALLIE: How many's that?

EMILY: Five, let's go take a shower.

HALLIE: Two more.

EMILY: Hearts break. There are harsh words. Tears. Men don't like to cry and so they end up hating you.

HALLIE: Emily, if the right guy came along, you'd kill for him.

EMILY: That's ridiculous.

HALLIE: You wouldn't be able to help yourself.

EMILY: Hallie, a woman can always help herself.

HALLIE: One more. Jesus. Why am I killin' myself like this? The only thing that's losin' weight is my boobs. (*She tries to sit up. She can't*)

EMILY: Space. A woman needs space. A woman needs room to move. A man should give you room.

HALLIE (*Collapsing; pause*): Men have always given me a lot of room. (*Rising*) Gotta run.

EMILY: I thought we were having dinner.

HALLIE: Can't. I! Have got a date!

EMILY: He any good?

HALLIE: He walks, he talks, he breathes. He doesn't make as much money as I do but he's flesh and blood.

EMILY: Is he straight?

HALLIE: Oh, God . . . please! (*Exiting*) Talk to you!

EMILY (*Calling after her*): Stay in charge!

Source: Samuel French, Inc.

✜ Gertrude Stein and a Companion

•••••••••••••••••••••••••••••••••••WIN WELLS

CHARACTERS: GERTRUDE (*50's*), ALICE (*40's*)
SETTING: *Paris, 1930's.*

GERTRUDE STEIN *is robust, over-powering, positive and warm.* ALICE *is quiet and reserved. As the scene opens, we are introduced to the love story of these two women. This scene is not an intellectual exercise but a personal story about two people who care deeply about one another.*

(ALICE *is at her desk with* GERTRUDE *standing over her*)
GERTRUDE: Alice, what are you doing?
ALICE: I'm nearly finished.
GERTRUDE: Yes. But with what?
ALICE: I've written everyone to tell them about Basket.
GERTRUDE: Ah . . . yes . . . dear Basket . . . poor dog.
ALICE: He was a dear animal, even being so famous . . . I had come to depend on his depending on me. There is no one to depend on me any longer and I do need dependented.
GERTRUDE: You need what?
ALICE: Depen-dented.
GERTRUDE: Depen-dented.
ALICE: Dependented.
GERTRUDE: Where did you get such a word?
ALICE: It *seems* a good word. Is it not a good word?
GERTRUDE: I don't know if it is *good* or not. It is certainly delicious. Depen-dented . . . indeed. Oh, I like that. Dependent-ed-in-deed.
ALICE: I have made a decision. Sort of a decision. Well . . . not really a decision, because I am not certain I have decided . . . but . . . I think I have decided that I want to go to heaven.
GERTRUDE: Alice, are you mad — ?
ALICE: . . . Because you, I think, *will* be there.
GERTRUDE: . . . that I will be in heaven?
ALICE: I think that what you are in now is a sort of limbo. Bernard Fay thinks that eventually you will be released from . . . well . . . limbo and go to heaven . . . eventually. Bernard has been converted, he is Christian now, and suggests I should become . . . if *eventually* I'd go where you *will* go.

GERTRUDE: Go? Eventually? No doubt you see it like a train's journey across the Pyrenees.

ALICE: Oh no . . . not a train. I had to sit in the aisle on my luggage from Nice to Paris. No. Not a train.

GERTRUDE: Then, as we were in the Ford during the first war?

ALICE: Oh, yes, that would be charming. You sitting high in the driver's position and me beside you . . .

GERTRUDE: Issuing injunctions and commands?

ALICE: You had no sense of direction.

GERTRUDE: And yours has certainly gone peculiar now. Perhaps you are going senile.

ALICE: No, to heaven.

GERTRUDE: You are getting older.

ALICE: Yes. Yes, I am. I am old. I have been asked to do an article, a survey of haute couture of Paris for a magazine . . . so I know I am old.

GERTRUDE: And with that there is a connection?

ALICE: Yes. They are to call the article, "Fifty Years of French Fashion".

GERTRUDE: And?

ALICE: Do you suppose there isn't anyone else *alive* whose memory goes back so far? I am old.

GERTRUDE: In eighteen hundred and ninety-four . . .

ALICE: Oh, God. Eighteen hundred ninety-four? So long. So long ago.

GERTRUDE: I was a student at the Harvard Annex.

ALICE: Radcliffe, dear. Its name was changed *years* ago.

GERTRUDE: And I wrote then and it is true now, "Sometimes I fiercely and defiantly declare that I won't believe either in the now or in the future." And I do not. I do not believe in heaven!!!

ALICE: Nevertheless, I intend that we shall . . . both of us . . . go there.

GERTRUDE: Where are you going *now*?

ALICE: To Rome. Well — anyway — to make arrangements to go to Rome.

GERTRUDE: To Rome?

ALICE: To see if I can see if the Pope will see me.

GERTRUDE: The *Pope*?

ALICE: Arrangements must be made . . . for Rome . . . *and* heaven. In that order, I'd suppose. (*Exits*)

Source: Samuel French, Inc.

✤ Ghost on Fire

•••••••••••••••••••••••••••••MICHAEL WELLER

CHARACTERS: MICHELLE-MARIE (20's), JULIA (30's)
SETTING: JULIA's *living room. New York City, the present.*

JULIA *and her husband, Dan, worked together in college days making films.
A third member of their team, Neil, is dying of a brain tumor. Neil, who
makes crass commercial films, urges* JULIA's *husband, Dan, to go off on the
road with him and find a story for his last chance at making an artistic film.
As the scene opens, Neil's wife,* MICHELLE-MARIE, *expresses her concerns
about her dying husband to* JULIA.

MICHELLE-MARIE: I don't believe they're doing this. What happens
if Neil needs attention when they're miles from a doctor?
JULIA: I know.
MICHELLE-MARIE: You want them to go, don't you?
JULIA: What I want right now doesn't really matter.
MICHELLE-MARIE: Look, I know you think I'm a little, what, like
ignorant or uneducated or something, not quite in your league?
Well, fine, but I am his wife, and I don't want him running off to
the drop-end of nowhere. It's suicide, Julia, and suicide is a sin
in my religion. (*Takes pills out*)
JULIA: Want some water for those?
MICHELLE-MARIE: See that — like I couldn't get myself a glass of
water if I wanted one. I was a waitress, you know; I served the
public.
JULIA: This isn't easy for you, I know that. But it's not easy for me,
either.
MICHELLE-MARIE (*Beat*): So it's true, then. You still love him.
JULIA: Neil? Are you serious?
MICHELLE-MARIE: It's cool. I'm not the jealous type. We could be
friends, you know.
JULIA: What nonsense has Neil been feeding you?
MICHELLE-MARIE: For your information, Julia, Neil is not the first
college guy I's ever with, not by a long, long shot. I am very
familiar with the college situation including the Big Man On
Campus, in't that what you call it, B.M.O.C.? So, okay, Danny's
suddenly the Bit Man Hotshot Film Director and Neils' just li'l

ol' Number Two. Hell, I'd 'a probably dumped Neil for someone like him too; it's human nature.

JULIA: I hate to burst your bubble, Michelle, but none of us was ever an "item" in school. We made films together. We were a team.

MICHELLE-MARIE: Neil said you were in love with him.

JULIA: Love! We had one date, all of which we spent talking about Danny.

MICHELLE-MARIE (Beat): He is so full of shit, isn't he? Why does he always have to go and tell stories like that, it's so darn juvenile.

JULIA (Beat): Danny back then . . . he was blessed. Like he couldn't get over just being in the world. It was so infectious. Me . . . I was the assistant. The idea he'd ever take me seriously . . . in that way. In any way. Except Neil, he knew all along, 'cause it was him, after school I mean, when the two of them moved to L.A., he was the one who called. Danny was feeling down and Neil thought maybe I could cheer him up if I flew out. I thought he was nuts. But of course I went. And Danny . . . he just lit up. Amazing. 'Cause of me. And for a while, it was so good. Was was was. Jesus, listen to me — sounds like a funeral oration.

MICHELLE-MARIE: Neil loves my breasts.

JULIA: Pardon me?

MICHELLE-MARIE: "Super-titties", he calls 'em. You gotta admit, they ain't bad for three kids. I nursed 'em all, you know.

JULIA: They'll thank you one day, I'm sure.

MICHELLE-MARIE: Boy is it nice to have a regular old conversation with someone. That's what I miss here. Friends. Just drop on by for a jaw, a cup of coffee, like in the commercials. What's the one — "Here's to good friends, tonight . . . " — no, wait, that's beer; what's the coffee one? I love the commercials. They put an awful lot of thought into some of them.

JULIA (Coffee cup): Help yourself. Only moments ago that cup was held between the lips of Brad Starkey himself.

MICHELLE-MARIE: I love the kind of humor you have. (Moves to JULIA) The three of you are really close, aren't you. That must be nice.

JULIA: Feeling better?

MICHELLE-MARIE: I want him home with me, Julia. Isn't that normal? I'm awake all night thinking and thinking what's the right thing to do. I wish there was a switch to turn your damn brain off.

JULIA: In the end, I think it has to be up to Neil how he chooses to live the time he has left.

MICHELLE-MARIE: It's up to God, Julia, that's the only one it's up to, and I'm not about to let Neil commit the worst sin of his life and get sent straight to hell for it. Please help me. Just swear how he asked Dan for poison. It's the truth, so you won't be giving false testimony. The lawyer told me contemplated suicide is grounds to have him declared mentally incompetent, and then he'd have to come home in my custody. You just keep 'em busy when they get back and I'll call the police —

JULIA: Isn't that going a little far?

MICHELLE-MARIE: What all else can I do? He's the only good thing ever happened in my life. Just tell me how to get him back.

JULIA: You poor kid.

(MICHELLE-MARIE *leans helpless against* JULIA)

MICHELLE-MARIE: He can't stand to be near me anymore. I try to be nice as pie but it only makes him angrier. If I'm not what he wanted, why didn't he just go away after the first night like the rest of 'em? What kind of perfume is that you're wearing?

JULIA (*Beat*):   Givenchy.

MICHELLE-MARIE: It's nice. You have such beautiful hands. May I do one little thing, Julia. (*Kisses her hand*) Do you mind?

JULIA (*Rising*):   I'll put on some fresh coffee.

(MICHELLE-MARIE *holds her tight and kisses her on the lips*)
Stop it, Michelle, what's the matter with you?

MICHELLE-MARIE: I can be wild too, see? You three aren't the only ones. Doesn't that qualify me for membership in this little deal y'all got going here?

JULIA: You're crazy!

MICHELLE-MARIE: And you're full of shit, all of you. The way Neil carried on, I thought I'd be meeting Jesus on the Throne of Glory. What's Danny got that Neil hasn't got — look at this place, you don't even own a dishwasher.

JULIA (*Furious*):   Neil is nothing without my husband. He's a server and that's all he'll ever be because he doesn't know how to rise above the people around him. I'm sorry, Michelle, but you asked for this!

MICHELLE-MARIE: God help me if I ever have to die among people like you.

Source: Grove Press

✤ A Girl's Guide to Chaos

•••••••••••••••••••••••••••••CYNTHIA HEIMEL

CHARACTERS: CLEO (30's), RITA (30's)
SETTING: *New York, the present.*

CLEO *and* RITA *are concerned about the "great boyfriend crunch". How do you steal a girl's boyfriend and still observe etiquette?*

CLEO: Oh, I don't know, I don't know. What am I going to do? I'm just not the type. I mean, the minute a friend gets involved with a man, I no longer see him as available, ever. I would never go out with a girl's boyfriend. It's not done. It deserves the death penalty.

RITA: Okay, sugar, which girl's boyfriend are you going to steal?

CLEO: Oh my God, oh my God. Cynthia's.

RITA: Now, Cleo. Look at me. Listen to what I'm saying very, very carefully. Are you paying attention? Good. Don't do it. Don't even think about doing it. Girl, you do value your face don't you? She'll rip it off your head. Hon, she'll shoot you in the foot. Not only that, but I'll kill you myself.

CLEO: Listen, it's not my idea. He just keeps calling and calling. He stutters when he asks me out. It's so cute.

RITA: And where is Cynthia when he's making all these calls?

CLEO: Home, I guess. Playing house with the baby Kiwi.

RITA: Are we in the movie *Gaslight*?

CLEO: *Gaslight*? Was that with Joseph Cotten?

RITA: Cleo, you're driving me mental. You said you were going after Cynthia's boyfriend. The Kiwi is her boyfriend.

CLEO: No, no, no, I mean Jake, of course. What do you think I am, suicidal? Her ex-boyfriend. I have a little trouble with the space-time continuum.

RITA: Well, Jesus, Jake. That's a relief. But I see what you mean. It'll still be weird.

CLEO: She'll hate it. She'll just hate it. I'll have nothing more to do with him. What could I have been thinking?

Source: Fireside Books/Simon Schuster

✤ Greenland

•••••••••••••••••••••••••••HOWARD BRENTON

CHARACTERS: JUDY (33), BETTY (50's)
SETTING: BETTY's garden outside her house.

BETTY, concerned about the morality of the present times, argues with her daughter JUDY about the climate of England during the present Thatcher years.

(JUDY comes on. She carries a pair of garden shears. Her arms are full of cut and mutilated flowers. She strews the flowers about the floor, lethargic gestures. She stands, looking out, the shears dangling from her hand. BETTY comes on. She stops)

BETTY: Judy. Thank God you got back home, dear.

(Nothing from JUDY. BETTY gushes)

Oh I'm dead on my feet. First the BBC wanted me on Newsnight Special, then they didn't. Was I furious! I made a scene they won't forget. And thank the good Lord, it looks like Mrs. Thatcher is back in. It's wonderful to think that God is working his purpose out, through an English Prime Minister. (She realizes. She lifts her glasses and looks around the floor)

(JUDY lets the shears fall from her hand. They clatter on the stage)

What have you done? The garden.

(She pauses. Then she rushes off. She comes back onto the back of the stage, as if out to a garden. She has a flashlight. She flits it about her in bewilderment)

JUDY (Aside): Why do I hate her so? Because everything I do, is what she does. She is a fundamentalist, I am a fundamentalist. She to one extreme, I to another. I can only be what she is, the other way round. I know the way she thinks, I feel it in my own thoughts. I hear the edge of her voice in my voice. When I am her age, I know my body will be just like hers.

(BETTY at the back, rushing about, 'in the garden')

BETTY: How could you . . . how could you! (She stops. The flashlight on a particular spot) Oh look. My lilies too. Little madam! Give her a good thwack on the backside! Her father . . . But her father is in America. With a harlot from Chicago . . . Oh please! (Flitting the flashlight 'around the garden') Don't tell the media that! So many humiliations. I know I am, to many, a laughing-stock. But that about Hugh, I could not bear . . . Someone there? *Express, Sun, Star*? They don't throw Christians to the lions now, they throw them to mockery. Which is worse? No! (*Closes her eyes*) Is a wrecked garden in Wimbledon to be my Gethsemane? (*She trembles, mouth open. Wet lower lip*) When I was a little girl, nine years old, I read John Bunyan's *Pilgrim's Progress*. Under the bedclothes, at night, with a torch. There were fearsome pictures. The Slough of Despond. The Castle of Giant Despair. I wanted to scream. Oh Lord, this world is a terrible place. (*She composes herself. She goes back 'into the kitchen'*) Well you ungrateful little madam . . .

JUDY: Don't start Mum . . .

BETTY: Arrested, naked in the street for all to see! And what are the police going to do?

JUDY: No charges. You know there'll be no charges! You rang the station! And got me out, because of who you are!

BETTY: For which I get no thanks?

(*They glare at each other. A pause*)

Look at the state of your life . . .

JUDY: I was chucked out of my flat, that's all . . .

BETTY: No money, thirty-three, having to come begging to me for a roof over your head . . .

JUDY: You said you'd love me at home . . .

BETTY: But you've been here six months! Sleeping 'til midday, out to heaven knows when. You would think, with all I do for people, the Lord would give me a daughter . . . but no.

JUDY: Mother, has it never struck you that we both want the same thing?

BETTY: Never!

JUDY: You and your Christian lunatics, your anti-porners, your clean-up TV campaigners, in your gospel halls? I and my friends, street-theatre clowns, squatters, in our resource centres in shabby shops? We all want a new world. That has . . . Light. That's human, and decent, and . . . Clean? We both want . . . A new Jerusalem?

BETTY: Clean? You say the word 'clean'? Wash your mouth out, girl. What was that thing I found in your room?

JUDY: Thing?

BETTY: On top of the wardrobe!

JUDY: You've searched my room?

BETTY: That wicked, filthy thing!

JUDY: You mean my vibrator? (*She smirks*) Try it Mum. Next time you feel a prayer coming on.

(*From* BETTY *a deep sound*)

BETTY: Ooooh, ooooh.

JUDY: We must . . . Oh I hate talking like this . . . Mum, we must find out real selves.

BETTY: We must find God.

JUDY: Have you seen how people are living out there? On the estates? Their only chance is to save themselves.

BETTY: Salvation is Heaven's gift. It is certainly not the gift of a Lesbian theatre company performing in the nude. 'Find your real self'? Will you do that with some battery operated, plastic carrot, that you stick up your private parts?

JUDY: Sometimes I think it's you that's got the dirty mind.

BETTY: Nothing shocks me, girl. When you campaign against immorality, you learn the worst. None of it shocks me. (*A pause*) It just makes me fall to my knees and pray.

JUDY: I'm not going to kneel down and close my eyes with you Mum. I've done that so often, just not to have this argument . . .

BETTY: Just a little one.

JUDY: No.

BETTY: A quick word with Him . . .

JUDY: No!

BETTY: 'Jerusalem' . . . Ooooh . . . I can see your 'holy city' my girl. The city of perpetual indulgence. Your only church a VD clinic. Abuse of the body, slavery to all that's base.

JUDY: I can see your 'Jerusalem'. A police state. All human desires, censored. 'Hallelujahs' broadcast on megaphones at each street corner. And lovers torn apart by cops at night.

(*A pause. They look at each other, appalled*)

BETTY: Don't have anything more to do with those people, Judy. Those . . . 'women'. Please.

JUDY: Do you want to meet my lover? She is very sweet. You'd like her.

BETTY: Ooooh. I . . .

JUDY: Mum.

BETTY: Don't touch me!

(*They are looking at each other.* BETTY, *mouth open, wet lower lip. Then she rushes off*)

JUDY (*Aside*):   Just one crack. In the lines of a famous face. Just one glimpse that you may be wrong, Mum. (JUDY *looks about her. She picks up the garden shears. She opens and shuts them a couple of times,*

despondent) Well come on, you stupid cow. Come back and tell me Jesus forgives. We'll have a cup of cocoa, then I'll kneel down with you in tears. For a bit of peace and quiet. I . . .
(*The sound of a car starting*)
Mum? Mum?
(*Car lights pass across the back wall of the stage*)
Mum! (JUDY *rushes off and back on at the back of the stage*) Where's she gone? (*Aside*) How strong is she? Not that much, after all? (*A look of horror, very like* BETTY's *wet lip look*) I should know. I do know. Oh God, what have I done? (*She rushes off*)

Source: *Plays: Two*, Methuen Drama

✤ Lettice and Lovage

•••••••••••••••••••••••••••••PETER SHAFFER

CHARACTERS: LOTTE (40's), LETTICE (40's)

SETTING: *An imposing Tudor staircase in the grand hall of Fustian House.*

LETTICE *is a guide appointed by the Preservation Trust to show people around this gloomy old house. Behind her stands a motley group of tourists. To one side stands* LOTTE, *a severe looking woman.* LOTTE *likes unvarnished facts and is sent to spy on* LETTICE. LETTICE *has been taking liberties with the truth.*

LOTTE: This is intolerable.

LETTICE: I beg your pardon.

LOTTE: I find this absolutely intolerable!

LETTICE: I'm sorry? I don't understand.

LOTTE: Miss Douffet, is it not?

LETTICE: That is my name, yes.

LOTTE: Yes! Well I would like to speak to you at once, please — in private.

LETTICE: On what subject?

LOTTE: I said private, please.

LETTICE: I find this extremely odd. I am not used to having my tours interrupted with uncivil demands.

LOTTE (*To the* PUBLIC): Would you please excuse us now? It is most urgent that I speak to this lady alone. The tour is at an end at this point anyway, I believe.

LETTICE: It is. But its conclusion is a graceful adieu, not an abrupt dismissal. And it is spoken by me.

LOTTE: I'm sorry but I really have to insist. (*To the* PUBLIC) Please forgive me, but I do have the most imperative business with this lady. (*She looks at them hard, and her look is very intimidating*) Please.

[(*They stir uneasily*)]

LETTICE (*To the* PUBLIC): Well — it seems I have to let you go — regrettably without ceremony. What can be so urgent as to preclude manners I cannot imagine! I do hope you have all enjoyed yourselves.

[(*Murmurs of enthusiastic assent: 'Oh yes!' . . . 'Thank you! . . .'*)]

The way out is over there. You will find placed by the exit a small saucer into which, if you care to, you may deposit such tokens of appreciation as you feel inclined to give. Thank you and goodbye.

[THE PUBLIC: Goodbye, Miss . . . Goodbye . . . Thank you . . .

(They go out, bewildered and extremely curious, looking back at the TWO LADIES. *As the* LAST ONE *disappears,* LOTTE's *manner becomes even colder)*]

LOTTE: You are not permitted to receive tips, I believe.

LETTICE: I do not regard them as that.

LOTTE: What then?

LETTICE: What I called them. Some people are appreciative in this world. They warm to the thrilling and romantic aspect of our great History.

LOTTE: Others, however, warm to accuracy, Miss Douffet. And others again — a few — are empowered to see that they receive it.

LETTICE: I don't understand you.

LOTTE: Myself, for example. My name is Miss Schoen, and I work for the Preservation Trust. In the personnel department.

(A pause)

LETTICE: Oh.

LOTTE: Reports have been coming steadily for some time of bizarre inaccuracies in your tour here. Gross departures from fact and truth. I have myself today heard with my own ears a generous sample of what you have been giving the public, and every one of those reports falls far short of what you are actually doing. I can hardly think of one statement you made in my presence that is correct.

LETTICE: The gastronomic references for a start. They are all correct. I would like you to know I am an expert in Elizabethan cuisine.

LOTTE *(Crisply)*: I am not talking about the gastronomic references — which in any case form no part of your official recital. Today I listened to a farrago of rubbish unparalleled, I should say, by anything every delivered by one of our employees. The whole story of John Fustian's leap upstairs, for example, concluding with his actually feeding fried hedgehogs into Queen Elizabeth's mouth directly from his fingers. As for the tale of Arabella Fustian — that is virtually fabrication from beginning to end. The girl was crippled by a fall, certainly, but it is not known how she fell. Her engagement was broken off but it is not known why, or who broke it. And so far from staying in her room singing thereafter, she lived to become a respected figure in the vicinity, noted for her work among the poor. The composer Henry Purcell was not, to my knowledge, involved in her life in any way. (*A long pause*) Well! ... What do you have to say?

LETTICE: I'm sorry — but I cannot myself get beyond your own behaviour.

LOTTE: Mine?

LETTICE: What you have just done.

LOTTE: I don't understand.

LETTICE: What you have done here, Miss Schoen, today. I don't mean your rudeness in interrupting my talk, unpleasant as that was. I mean coming here at all in the way you have . . . Pretending to join my group as a simple member of the public. I find that quite despicable.

LOTTE: I beg your pardon?

LETTICE: Deceitful and despicable. It is the behaviour, actually, of a spy.

LOTTE: Well, that is what I am. I came here with that specific intention. To observe unnoticed what you were doing.

LETTICE: To spy.

LOTTE: To do my duty.

LETTICE: Duty?!

LOTTE: Precisely. My duty . . . The precise and appropriate word.

LETTICE: To embarrass your employees — that is your duty? To creep about the Kingdom with a look of false interest, guidebook in hand — and then pounce on them before the people in their charge? . . . Is that how you conceive your duty — to humiliate subordinates?

LOTTE: This is a sidetrack.

LETTICE: It is not. It really is not!

LOTTE: A total sidetrack and you know it! My behaviour is not the issue here. Yours — *yours* is what we are discussing! It is that which needs explaining! You will report tomorrow afternoon at my office in London. I believe you know the address. 14 Architrave Place. Three o'clock, if you please.

LETTICE (*Alarmed*):   Report? . . . For what? Report? . . . I don't understand. What do you mean?
(*Pause*)

LOTTE (*Coldly*):   I suggest you now attend to the next group of tourists awaiting you. And that you confine yourself strictly to the information provided by the Trust. I will see you at three tomorrow. Good afternoon.

(*She goes out.* LETTICE *stands, appalled*)

LETTICE (*Calling after her, in rising panic*): I . . . I'm to be tried, then?
. . . I'm to be judged? . . . Haled to Judgement?
(*A pause.* MISS SCHOEN *has gone*)
(*In dismay*) Oh dear.
(*A grim music*)

Source: Samuel French, Inc.

✤ Loon Woman

●●●●●●●●●●●●●●●●●●●●●●●●●●●●●●●MARGARET HUNT

CHARACTERS: MAGGIE (30's), ABBY (15)
SETTING: *A hospital lounge, New York, the present.*

A nervous breakdown forces Joan to the hospital for treatment. The next day, her younger sister, MAGGIE, *and her daughter,* ABBY, *aren't feeling terribly stable themselves.*

MAGGIE: (Off): In O.T.? God! She's making ashtrays! (MAGGIE *enters with a heavy shopping bag.* ABBY *appears in doorway to patients' wing.* MAGGIE *doesn't want to see her.* MAGGIE *sings a few bars of "Ding dong the witch is dead," then sees herself in a mirror.)*

MAGGIE: Hi, Joan, how are you? You look. . .crazy as a LOON! *(Laughs)* Stop. Stop it! Hi, Joan. How's the food here? Did you tell the cooks how to cook yet? Did they tell you they don't cook with nuts? *(Laughs wildly)* Cut it OUT!. . . Hi, Joan, you look great. I brought all the stuff you asked for (Quavering) your gigantic Rolodex, fifty pounds of wacko files, and--(*She explodes with laughter and falls on the floor*)

MAGGIE: Oh, God, it's contagious. she goes crazy and I catch it. *(Laughs)* The one time in my life I get the upper hand and I lose my mind. *(Laughs through next sentence)* Hi, Joan, well, I'm sure glad to see you . . . locked up! Oh God. *(Collapses in giggles)*
(ABBY *appears in bedroom doorway)*

ABBY: What's the matter with you?
(MAGGIE *screams and drops the shopping bag)*

MAGGIE: AH! Oh. Nothing, honey, nothing. I'm — AH — a little upset, that's all.

ABBY: You're laughing at her, aren't you? You're laughing at my mom being sick. That's disgusting. You're her sister, you're supposed to love her. She loves you, that's for sure.

MAGGIE (*Hysterical*):   I was just laughing from the tension, from the relief she's finally been (*Quavers*) taken off (*Builds to laugh*) my hands. (*Continues laughing*) I'm sorry. I'm sorry. I'm sorry. This is hysteria. Somewhere, down below, in like the fourth sub-basement, there's a subclinic. They take the crazy people into the hospital up here, and they have this little room downstairs where they put the relatives who have gone insane from living with them — oh, honey, don't cry. I'm sorry, I'm sorry. (MAGGIE

goes to ABBY *and embraces her*) I was just talking about myself. I . . .
I didn't mean you were insane —
ABBY: I know.
MAGGIE: I'm sorry . . . I didn't know you were here . . .I just got
carried away . . . Why are you here, anyway?
ABBY: I came to see my mom, but they said I can't see her without
her permission—and they won't tell me where she is. I looked
everywhere up here—(*Pause*) Maggie, do you think my mom's
. . . gonna be . . . better? Do you think she's gonna get well?
MAGGIE: Abby, she doesn't want you to see her like this. (*Pause*)
ABBY: (*Hoarsely*): I miss her, you know.
MAGGIE (*Nervously*):   Yes! Definitely. Of course. Honey, this isn't . . .
this isn't like . . . you know . . . uh . . . Hell, I don't know what it
isn't, but it's better than you think.
ABBY: I was thinking about Mrs. Rochester, you know, Mrs. Rochester in *Jane Eyre*? She went crazy, and she never got any better.
They had to lock her up in the . . . attic. Remember?
MAGGIE: Oooh, that was a wonderful book, wasn't it? God, I loved
that book when I was a kid! But, Abby, your mother isn't like
Mrs. Rochester. Mrs. Rochester was completely different. She
was a homicidal maniac, for one thing, and Mr. Rochester said
she was unchaste and a drunkard — of course, men say a lot of
things when the honeymoon is over —
ABBY: But why couldn't they *make* Mrs. Rochester better? Why did
they have to lock her up for the rest of her life?
MAGGIE (*Racing*):   Well, uh, well, because Mrs. Rochester lived a
hundred years ago. More, in fact. Back then, they didn't know
beans about mental illness. They didn't have all the drugs and
tranquil — they didn't have Freud. Yeah! Mrs. Rochester came
before Freud. That was why everybody just kind of washed their
hands and put her in the attic. But see, Freud found out that people can change, people who have certain kinds of problems, uh,
can work them out if their problems aren't too wacky — well,
most people, maybe not schizophrenics — but your mom isn't a
schizophrenic. And Mrs. Rochester probably *was*. Hell, I'm not
explaining this too well. But, say if mental illness were like baseball, then Mrs. Rochester was in the major leagues and your
mom is barely in the minors, like not even double-A ball, you
know?
ABBY: I think baseball is really boring.
    (ABBY *starts to cry.* MAGGIE *runs over and puts her arms around*
ABBY)

MAGGIE: Honey, please don't cry. Your mom's going to be all right, really. It's not like Mrs. Rochester, honest.

(ABBY *pulls away*)

I know you're mad — angry — at me about that song. I'm sorry. I guess I'm a little edgy. I spent so many hours with her I feel a little crazy — myself. Why don't we do something fun? Go someplace nice . . . someplace *you* think is nice, where they play the kind of music you like — you know . . . loud.

ABBY: Heavy metal.

MAGGIE: Heavy metal, right! Would you like that? We could ask your dad to come with us.

(*Pause*)

ABBY: Okay. Sure, that'd be all right . . . yeah. I'll call my dad. (ABBY *heads toward phone, then stops, turns to* MAGGIE) Maggie, do you hate my mom?

MAGGIE: Of course not! I love her . . . I've . . . always loved her

ABBY: Then why were you laughing about her being in the hospital? Why were you singing about the witch being dead?

MAGGIE: (*Intense*)   Because I love her like a sister. You're an only child. You don't know about sisters. It's different from the way you love your friends.

ABBY: How is it different?

MAGGIE: There's a lot of ground glass in it . . . That's not true. Look, can we talk about this in ten years?

ABBY: I hate when you do that, Maggie. You don't have to tell me, but don't patronize me, okay? I'm not dumb.

MAGGIE: You're still a kid. And I'm not a mother. I don't know what you're supposed to tell kids about anything — my mother told me nothing, just to be on the safe side.

ABBY: Do you hate my mom because she's —

MAGGIE: STOP SAYING THAT! I do not *hate her*! But for as long as I can remember, she's told me what to do. From telling me how to wash dishes when I was six to telling me how to make perfect rice yesterday. You say you don't like to be patronized? Well, neither do I. And when someone has patronized you for 30 years, you don't feel lovey-dovey about her. You get tired of hearing about how to make perfect rice. You get tired of all her perfections because she makes you feel like dirt. You think she's so arrogant that the world has got to kick the shit out of her, okay? And when it does, you laugh! I'm glad she's locked up in the psycho ward because I think it means that her arrogance broke down. I hope that when she comes out of that place that she won't go back to telling me how to live my life because she'll know better. I'm glad she cracked up because I hope I'll be able to like her — love her — again. That's why I was singing and laughing. Because for the first time in 30 years I feel completely free. (*Pause*) And I'm ashamed of myself for it.

ABBY: I don't think I have time for dinner. I don't feel like it. My dad —

MAGGIE: Maybe we could go to a bar and tie one on.

ABBY: I just don't feel like it, that's all . . . (ABBY *pulls envelope from her pocket*) Will you give my mom this? She'll be lonely tonight. I think she's afraid of the dark. Will you take it?

MAGGIE (*Taking envelope*): Sure.

ABBY: Call me at my dad's, okay? Tell me how she liked it.

MAGGIE: I can't. She's in occupational therapy. I was just gonna leave it at the desk with all this--

ABBY: It's a poem! I want to know what she reall thinks of it. You have to watch her read it.

MAGGIE: (Desperate to please): I'll wait for her. Watch her like a goddamn hawk. I'll take notes. I just wish I hada camera--

ABBY: Don't get crazy.

MAGGIE: I'm trying, I'm trying. (MAGGIE *picks up her purse, heads toward door, looks into mirror on way out*) You're gonna burn in hell for that damn song. If you could one time pass up the opportunity to look at yourself, none of this would have happened. (*She turns mirror to wall*) (*Black out*)

Source: Silverman and Shulman

✤ Mama Drama

•• LESLIE AYVAZIAN, DONNA DALEY, CHRIS-
TINE FARRELL, MARIANNA HOUSTON,
RITA NACHTMANN, ANNE O'SULLIVAN,
ANN SACHS

CHARACTERS: SANDI (16), MERRY (20's)
SETTING: MERRY's *apartment.*

MERRY *provides* SANDI *with all the comforts of home during the teenager's
pregnancy. The only price for* MERRY's *unstinted generosity is* SANDI's
*child when it is born. The appointed time grows nearer and the deal threat-
ens to come apart.*

MERRY: Oh, Sandi — you shouldn't be in here with these paint
fumes.

SANDI: You're not my mother.

MERRY: Let's open a window. It's a beautiful day. Maybe we can go
for a walk together. Get some exercise? You always come to this
room. Don't you like the den with the pull-out? The reception is
better down there.

SANDI: I like this room the way it is. You shouldn't have painted it
that piss yellow. What else are you going to do to ruin it? You
putting up those uh . . .

MERRY: Rainbows.

SANDI: Rainbows are for jerks.

MERRY: They're for babies.

SANDI: So the baby gets the rainbow and I get the shaft.

MERRY: You get your whole life . . .

SANDI: Blah, blah, blah, you going out or not?

MERRY: No.

SANDI: You said we could walk together so why can't you just
walk yourself and while you're out there get me some Kent 100s
— menthols.

MERRY: Don't start that, Sandi. You promised you wouldn't smoke.

SANDI: Now I'm promising I will.

MERRY: Smoking is very bad for you.

SANDI: For me? You're just afraid I'm going to mess up your precious little baby.

MERRY: I'd like to see you do something productive.

SANDI: This isn't productive enough for you? My Grandpa says to tell you don't look a gift horse in the mouth.

MERRY: A gift horse — I give you plenty — you have a very nice set-up here.

SANDI: Did I forget to thank you today and kiss your toes?

MERRY: I want you to be happy while you're here.

SANDI: Will you care if I smoke till my lungs blow up the day after I hand it over? I'd just like to live here a little while afterward just to see — but I hate it here. I'm glad it's only three more shit-filled weeks.

MERRY: Two more.

SANDI: You hope it's tonight.

MERRY: No I don't.

SANDI: I bet you wouldn't care if I pumped poison inside of myself after it's yours — you probably hope I do.

MERRY: That isn't true.

SANDI: Bye, Sandi — good riddance — go die, please. I need some cigarettes.

MERRY: Well I'm not going to get them.

SANDI: I want a six pack — you got one?

MERRY: Not this again.

SANDI: I'm a fucking prisoner. What if it dies?

MERRY: Stop.

SANDI: It'd be better off. I pity the poor fucking kid living with you.

MERRY: I'm helping you. I'm helping you as much as you're helping me. What would you have done with a baby? Moved on the street?

SANDI: Given it to someone better.

MERRY: WHERE WOULD YOU HAVE LIVED? YOU'RE NOT SUCH A PRIZE. YOUR OWN PARENTS KICKED YOU OUT AND I WOULD HAVE DONE THE SAME . . . ONLY SOONER. YOU MAKE ME CRAZY . . . SOMETIMES I JUST WANT TO TAKE YOU . . . AND . . . YOU MAKE ME SO ANGRY . . . It's almost over . . . I shouldn't have said any of that . . . I'm so sorry, sweetheart. (*She takes* SANDI *in her arms and rocks her*) . . . It's almost over . . . I shouldn't have said that . . . I'm so sorry sweetheart. I'm so sorry.

SANDI: You know what I hope? I hope this kid turns out just like me. I bet you'd be so pissed.

MERRY: You're lovely. You're a good girl. I wouldn't be pissed. I'm actually going to miss you — I swear that's the absolute truth.

SANDI: And you called me sweetheart. I'm very helpful around the house.

MERRY: You are.

SANDI: Jeannie says you and me look alike.

MERRY: Sandi —

SANDI: I babysit real good.

MERRY: Sandi —

SANDI: Do you think we look alike?

MERRY: You still can't come back here after the baby's born.

SANDI (*Turns up TV*):   Shhh . . . this is the best part.

MERRY (*Turns volume on TV down*):   Sandi, you can't visit here ever again — you do know that. The agreement is still the same.

SANDI: Can I turn it back up please?

MERRY: Did you hear me?

SANDI: Don't get a rash. (*She reaches into her pocket and lights a cigarette*)

MERRY: You can not under any circumstances come here ever again once the baby's mine.

SANDI: Don't work up a sweat, Merry, alright? Some people work up too much sweat over nothing.

(SANDI *focuses on television smoking cigarette. Sound of soap opera. Lights fade*)

Source: Samuel French, Inc.

✤ The Miss Firecracker Contest

•••••••••••••••••••••••••••••BETH HENLEY

CHARACTERS: TESSY (23), CARNELLE (24)
SETTING: *Area behind a large carnival tent.*

After all the other contestants have arrived, CARNELLE *makes a somewhat hurried entrance.* TESSY, *the beauty contest coordinator, offers last minute encouragement.*

TESSY (*As she enters the dressing room carrying only the tap shoes*): It's over here. It's this way. It's this way, here!
CARNELLE'S VOICE: Oh. Oh, I see. I see!
TESSY: Can you make it?
CARNELLE (*Making her way into the dressing room*): Yeah. I got it. Here, I got it. (*Dropping her belongings where she can*) Wheew! Brother. Thanks very much for the help.
TESSY: Sure. It's what I'm here for.
CARNELLE: Oh, look! Is this my dressing room? Is this mine?
TESSY (*Picking up her clipboard and taking a pencil from behind her ear*): Uh huh. It's the only one left. The good ones have all been taken. (*Looking at her watch*) You're running late, you know.
CARNELLE (*Struggling with her belongings*): Yes, I know. I was sewing on my dress. Things aren't going smoothly at all today. Oh, look! Now my hair piece is falling out. I worked all morning on that. So, is your sister nervous?
TESSY: Not really. I guess she knows she doesn't have a chance.
CARNELLE (*As she straightens up her things*): What makes you say that?
TESSY: Well, she's not at all attractive. I'm amazed she ever got in the contest. I'm sure it's just cause the judges think she's some sort of concert pianist. But she just knows that one opus by Johann Sebastian Bach. I swear that's all she knows.
CARNELLE: Hmm, I suppose that talent part of the contest will count quite a bit.
TESSY: Well, she looks like a tank in her swim suit.
CARNELLE: She does?
TESSY: She's hump shouldered from practicing that one Johann Sebastian Bach opus on our piano all day long.

CARNELLE: What a shame.

TESSY: This is strictly confidential, but the word is out that the only real contenders for the Miss Firecracker crown are you and Caroline Jeffers.

CARNELLE (*Overcome*):   Oh, gosh, I don't know —

TESSY: It's the truth. Everyone's saying it. We're all agreed.

CARNELLE: Of course Caroline's really a lovely girl . . .

TESSY: Yeah, except for those yellow teeth.

CARNELLE: Well, I hear she took medicine for seizures that she had as a child and it scraped off most of her tooth enamel.

TESSY: I heard that too, but it doesn't matter.

CARNELLE: It doesn't?

TESSY: I really don't think the judges are interested in sentimentality — just the teeth themselves. (*Referring to the red dress*) That's such a beautiful red dress. It's really very fine.

CARNELLE: Yes, it's beautiful. I'm just a little worried though. It just arrived from Natchez yesterday and, well, it didn't seem to fit me exactly right.

TESSY: What's wrong with that?

CARNELLE: Well, the waist was a little snug. But I worked on it this morning and added in this extra bit of material. (*She shows that a large strip of pink material has been awkwardly added to the bodice of the red dress*)

TESSY (*Disdainfully*):   Oh. Well.

CARNELLE: Course, I know it's not the exact matching color. Actually, my cousin, Elain's gone to get me seamstress, Popeye Jackson, and see what she can do. We couldn't find her last night. She'll fix it right up. This is just temporary.

TESSY: Well, I hope so. It looks a little funny.

CARNELLE (*Looking outside*):   Oh, I know Elain'll bring Popeye; she promised she would. She's never let me down in her life. Gosh, I think I'm starting t'sweat. My make up is melting right down my face. (*She starts fixing her face*)

TESSY (*Looking at her watch*):   Hmm. Actually, you don't have much time. It's only twenty-eight minutes till the opening Parade of Firecrackers. (TESSY *blows her whistle*)

CARNELLE: Oh, my word! Well, I'm ready except for my dress. I mean, my head is ready.

TESSY (*Removing schedule from her clipboard*):   Well, anyway, here's your schedule.

CARNELLE: Thanks.

TESSY: Oh and have you seen the Grand Float they've made for

Miss Firecracker to ride at the head of the Independence Day Parade?

CARNELLE: Oh, yes, I saw it — it's . . . beautiful.

TESSY: Why, yes, it's very fine. Well, I'd better go let Miss Blue know you're checked in. (*After glancing at herself in the mirror*) Oh. Mind if I borrow some of your hairspray?

CARNELLE: No, go ahead.

TESSY: Thanks. (*As she sprays her already rock hard hair*) I, ah, hear your cousin Delmount's back in town.

CARNELLE: Yes, he's back.

TESSY (*Still spraying*): Well, you can tell him for me that I've forgiven him. I understand now that some men just don't have any self control. Just none at all. Think that'll hold?

CARNELLE: Uh huh.

TESSY: Anyway, tell him my Uncle Ferd's given us a new litter of siamese kittens if he wants to drop by and see them. I know he always enjoyed animals.

CARNELLE: I'll tell him.

TESSY: Well, good luck. I'll be standing by backstage running the contest. Let me know if any emergencies arrive.

CARNELLE: Alright.

TESSY: Give em H.

Source: Dramatists Play Service, Inc.

♣ Mrs. Klein

•••••••••••••••••••••••••NICHOLAS WRIGHT

CHARACTERS: PAULA (30's), MELITTA (30's)
SETTING: London, Mrs. Klein's apartment.

PAULA, Mrs. Klein's assistant and MELITTA, Mrs. Klein's daughter, have occasion for their first heart-to-heart chat. At the same time that barriers come down, their competition for Mrs. Klein's affection heats up.

PAULA: I bought a whisky once in a public house. In Bethnal Green. But it was such a noisy an disgusting place I couldn't enjoy it. This is different. This is homelike.
(*Pause*)
MELITTA: Do you have those dreams where something absolutely vital has been hidden away? In some familiar place? You search and search. But the handles keep on coming off the doors. Or empty rooms are suddenly crowded. Or the railway-ticket's missing from your handbag, or the platform's vanished. And you can't admit whatever it is you're doing. Because it's shameful. Do you?
PAULA: Not the same but —. Yes.
MELITTA: It's not just me then.
PAULA: They're anxiety dreams. Everyone has them.
MELITTA: I feel I'm in one all the time.
PAULA: I dream I've killed a child. I told my analyst. She interpreted that I'd felt deserted by her over the Easter break. I said I doubted that was much to do with it, I'd been having this dream for thirty years. She said 'Ah ha, and my consulting-room is number 30.'
MELITTA: Are we like that?
PAULA: I hope not. What about yours?
MELITTA: She wasn't giving satisfaction so I sacked her.
PAULA: What went wrong?
MELITTA: I thought she was my mother. And I couldn't work through it. Couldn't stop thinking, 'damn the bitch', or 'does she love me?'. So she thought, and I agreed, that I was stuck in the transference. I'm a sucker for transference. Can't resist it. Do it to anyone. Dentist. Window-cleaner. Nanki Poo. So on we slogged. For years and years. And nothing changed. Except that bit by bit

I realized that to all intents and purposes she *was* my mother. It was my mother put me on to her. She reads my mother's books, she quotes them word for word and once a month she meets her for tea at Whiteleys. And I couldn't bear it, darling.

PAULA: Who've you gone to now?

MELITTA: Never you mind.

PAULA: I'd like to change my analyst.

MELITTA: Who do you have your eye on?

PAULA: Well it's more a question would she take me.

(MELITTA *spills her whisky. Composes herself. Marks a level on the glass with one finger*)

MELITTA: Be a good girl and fill it up to *here* this time.

(PAULA *does. She looks at the bottle*)

PAULA: It's seven years old. She must be quite a connoisseur.

MELITTA: She is. We drove through France two years ago and just as we were getting on quite well she went in for a claret tasting competition and won first prize. They'd never had a woman champion. Now the mayor sends her a postcard every Christmas. She's a local hero.

(PAULA *smiles*)

It isn't funny, being her daughter. Try it. Perhaps you have.

PAULA: I don't know what you mean.

MELITTA: You've changed.

PAULA: How's that?

MELITTA: You're like some stubborn, slow amoeba making its gains by stealth.

(PAULA *goes to the pin-box and rummages for her five shillings*)

Just what do you think you're doing?

PAULA: I'm getting a taxi.

MELITTA: Put that back.

PAULA: It's in my expenses.

MELITTA: Well you might have told me you had taxi-money.

PAULA: I forgot.

MELITTA: Forgot. You didn't want to leave. You're burrowing in.

(PAULA *throws the box on the ground. It opens and the money falls out*)

PAULA: I have a mother of my own. I don't need yours. If that's the undercurrent. Why do you think I'd want to hurt you? Why? You're like a sister to me. You've been kind and good and generous to me. Nobody else from home has helped me. Not till now. Until your mother, true. Who seems neurotically attached to me for some strange reason. Or some obvious reason. I can't help it.

And I'm under no illusions. And I don't care tuppence for your boring little Oedipal tangles. I have other problems thank you. I've a daughter in Berlin, I have consulting-rooms in Bethnal Green.

MELITTA: Who put you there?

PAULA: No her.

MELITTA: They all did. At the Institute. Committee level. Refugees not wanted. Not in Hampstead. Too much healthy competition. That's why they've dumped you all in these extraordinary places. And she's right behind it.

PAULA: You don't surprise me. Analysts are only human. If you threaten our professional livelihoods you'll get some very primitive responses. That was grubby of you.

MELITTA: Did she tell you how he died?

PAULA: She said a climbing accident.

MELITTA: He killed himself.

(*Pause*)

PAULA: How do you know?

MELITTA: I rang my aunt. Aunt Jolan. Mrs. Vago. Talks for ever, cost a fortune. I could tell at once that she was hiding something. So I asked her very obliquely. Where he went that morning. What he wore. All the little details that I needed to complete the picture. She resisted. Started howling. Then she banged the phone down. But I'd got my answers. I've got good material. And I've worked it through. I've reached the only possible interpretation.

PAULA: Did he leave a note?

MELITTA: No note. That's what he was like. He used to disappear for hours. She'd shake him. 'Where've you been? I thought the cart had run you over!' He'd say: 'Nowhere.' Never let on. Though he might give her a clue. But no confessions. So he'd hardly leave a suicide-note. He wouldn't want to give her the satisfaction.

PAULA: Does your mother know?

MELITTA: Well that depends on whether or not she read my letter.

PAULA: Oh Melitta. She'll be —.

MELITTA: Yes I know.

PAULA: You told her?

MELITTA: Yes!

PAULA: It's horrible.

MELITTA: Yes I know.

PAULA: How could you?

MELITTA: Well I think I must be barmy.
   (*Another drink for both*)
MELITTA: When you saw it, where was it left exactly?
PAULA: There. (*The desk*) It's gone now.
MELITTA: Yes I looked.
   (*Pause*)
PAULA: I'm starving.
MELITTA: Likewise.
   (*Pause*)
PAULA: Was the letter very — ?
MELITTA: Very detailed. Very convincing. Very persecutorily sadistic.
PAULA: Oh my God.
MELITTA: Exactly. (*Pause*) I was sitting in the Wigmore Hall tonight. And they were playing Schubert. So divine. And all that horrible hatred seeped away. I felt that I was looking at it from high up. From somewhere in the ceiling. It was like a pile of rotting clothes. Far distant. From my dizzy height of rational thinking. I felt utterly sane. So I came round here to get my letter back. It seemed so simple. Now all I can imagine is my mother in her first class Pullman, looking for some further reading, putting down her copy of the Psychoanalytic Quarterly —. (*She laughs*)
PAULA: No, Melitta —
MELITTA: No. Or maybe her Country Life —
PAULA: Or Vogue!
   (*They both giggle*)
MELITTA: Or Lilliput!
   (*Both giggle hysterically*)
MELITTA: She'll climb into bed —
PAULA: No, berth!
MELITTA: What?
PAULA: Berth, you know, the —.
MELITTA: Berth, that's right, she'll take her corsets off —
   (*Both giggle furiously*) —
   then up she climbs and —
PAULA: — does her nightie up to her chin —
   (*Both collapse with laughter*)
MELITTA: And then she reads — she reads —
PAULA: 'You cow, you murderess —'
MELITTA: No no no — it's worse than that —.
PAULA: 'Bitch, you killed him —!'
   (*They slowly stop giggling. Then one of them starts giggling again,*

and both collapse with laughter but this time with a sense of guilt. They stop. Pause. They share a handkerchief, wipe their eyes)
Maybe she won't believe it.

MELITTA: She's not stupid.

PAULA: No.

MELITTA: It'll kill her.

PAULA: Yes it very likely will.

MELITTA: Except she could have left it here. It could be in this room.

(They gaze round the room)

PAULA: What was the book you thought I'd moved?

MELITTA: 'The Interpretation of Dreams'.

(PAULA stands up)

PAULA: That seems significant. *(Goes to the bookshelf. Removes the book and takes the keys out)* I thought so. Catch.

(She throws them across the room. MELITTA catches them)
Have a look.

(MELITTA open the filing cabinet)

MELITTA: You keep watch.

PAULA: Who for?

MELITTA: Parental super-egos, darling. Do it. *(She unlocks the filing cabinet)*

PAULA *(Whispers)*:   Go on.

Source: Nick Hern Books

❖ My Mother Said I Never Should

●●●●●●●●●●●●●●●●●●●●●●●●●CHARLOTTE KEATLEY

CHARACTERS: JACKIE (32), MARGARET (54)
SETTING: *London,* MARGARET'*s office. Early April, the present.*

Exuberant yuppie, JACKIE, *returns fifteen year old Rosie safe and sound to their mother's care after the sisters' holiday together. Also intact for now is the fifteen year secret that Rosie is really* JACKIE'*s daughter, a relationship sacrificed for the benefit of* JACKIE'*s career.*

JACKIE (*Enters the office*): Mum! I'm sorry. Didn't you get the message? The delay was twelve hours in the end, airport like an oven.

MARGARET: Rosie's hopelessly overexcited.

JACKIE: I know Mummy, I couldn't get her to sleep. But she's been so good all week, you don't need to worry. She's very sensible for fifteen. Wouldn't let me swim too far out.

MARGARET: She'll be tired for the first day of term now.

JACKIE: That's three days away!

MARGARET: There's all her clothes to wash.

JACKIE: I'd to it, but I've . . .

MARGARET: Got to go back to Manchester for a meeting.

JACKIE (*Pause*): Rosie can wash her own things. She did all our clothes one evening, fixed up a line on the balcony.

MARGARET: It's an adventure with you. (*Pause*) You should see her bedroom, it's like a junkyard — clothes, glue, paint.

JACKIE: She's very creative. Kept writing poetry in the restaurant.

MARGARET: She's full of crazy ideas. (*Testing* JACKIE)

JACKIE (*Pause. Cautious*): Is she?

(*No reply from* MARGARET)
It's just her energy, isn't it?

MARGARET: Well of course, with you . . .

JACKIE: She talks about you a lot.

MARGARET: What about?

JACKIE: Oh, I only mean about your job. She wanted to show me all round where you work.

MARGARET: Did she?

JACKIE: You didn't tell me you were promoted last year. (*Looks over*

MARGARET's *shoulder at the letters she is opening*)

MARGARET: It's nothing glamorous.

JACKIE: You know I'd be useless at this. My typing's awful . . . Do you have to reply to all these?

MARGARET: Mr. Reece dictates, I spend the rest of the morning unravelling his grammar, otherwise British Microwaves would never have any export trade. These young graduates.

JACKIE: I hope they pay you the right scale. You're the one who does all the work.

MARGARET: I'm only his personal assistant.

JACKIE: Don't say 'only'.

MARGARET: Oh I was lucky. My typing speeds are very ordinary. It's only that I've got Pitman's Classic and most of the girls don't learn shorthand these days.

JACKIE: I'm sure it's other qualities got you this job, Mummy.

MARGARET (*Pause. Pleased*):   It's funny, hearing 'Mummy' in this place. You do a job, people treat you differently.

JACKIE: It's only how you treat yourself.

MARGARET (*Pause*):   You look radiant dear.

JACKIE: Swimming and sea air. (*Quiet*) Bit of sun, Mummy. Do you good, too.

MARGARET (*Quiet*):   Sat in the garden this weekend. Been very . . . Been a relief, you having Rosie for this week.

JACKIE (*Pause*):   I hope you kept the appointment? She's a nice woman, isn't she?

MARGARET: It was a very expensive looking waiting room.

JACKIE: Mummy, I asked you to see the specialist, not the wall-paper. What did she say?

MARGARET: Oh — Nothing much.

JACKIE: Did she do some tests?

MARGARET: No.

JACKIE: No?

MARGARET: Says I'm fine. Just menopause, probably.

JACKIE (*Pause*):   Honestly?

MARGARET (*Pause*):   What do you mean?

JACKIE: Well — (*Pause*) — That's such a relief! (*Laughs*) Oh Mummy. We even got a taxi all the way here!

MARGARET (*Pause*):   Now you can go and catch your train to Manchester, can't you.

JACKIE: Mum . . . May Bank Holiday, come and stay with me. Just you, and we'll . . .

MARGARET: Fly kites.

JACKIE (*Laughs, holds out the kite*):   Oh yes, Rosie and I bought you a kite. She says Daddy will show you how to fly it, but I said you're an expert. Do you remember, how you took me flying kites in Richmond Park, and once it got stuck in a chestnut tree, and all the conkers came down?

MARGARET: I thought you'd wiped out that little girl.

JACKIE: So did I. Rosie won't. She'll have kites in her office, or whatever. (*Pause*) I used to wear suits, when I first started my job. (*Puts the kite on the desk. Knocks the photo frame off the desk*)

JACKIE: Oh sorry. (*Bends and picks up the photo frame. Laughs*) Rosie and me in Hulme! God, what a pit. Don't I look awful? Cheese-cloth and flares and eyes like an owl!

MARGARET: All those broken nights.

JACKIE: Don't remind me. And this is Cornwall? Is this Rosie? Oh isn't she sweet! Can I have a copy of this one?

MARGARET (*Pause*):   Rosie's told me, Jackie.

JACKIE (*Terrified*):   I wasn't going to —

MARGARET: No, I expect you had another date planned when you were going to tell me that you'd like Rosie back. Or perhaps you were just going to tell me over the phone.

JACKIE: . . . You need time, to decide . . . in the summer —

MARGARET: It's not my decision. It's Rosie's. And she's made her mind up. (*Pause*) I knew she'd say it one day. Like one of those fairytales.

JACKIE: You haven't told her!

MARGARET: Of course not. She still thinks you're big sister, that's why it's so magical to her.

JACKIE: We were running along this dazzling beach. I thought, is this what I've missed?

MARGARET: Years and years and years you've lost, Jackie. Birthdays and first snowman and learning to ride a bicycle and new front teeth. You can't pull them back.

JACKIE: I can make up for it — somehow —

MARGARET: You can't. Those are my years.

JACKIE: She must remember — I visited!

MARGARET: Treats, she's had with you. A day here and there. That never fooled her. But I let it fool you. I'm the woman who sat up all night with the sick child, who didn't mind all her best crockery getting broken over the years.

JACKIE: Mummy...

MARGARET (*Long pause. Cool*):   What time's your train?

JACKIE: 9:45 — no — I could get the 10:45.

MARGARET: You mustn't miss your meeting.

JACKIE: It would give us another hour. I wish we weren't in your office! (*Panics*) Where's Rosie gone?

MARGARET: Are you going to catch that train, or stay here? You can't do both.

(*Pause.* JACKIE *agonizes.*)

I'll phone you a taxi. (MARGARET *dials, waits, the line is engaged*)

JACKIE (*Quietly*):   You know Mum, the Gallery and everything, I couldn't have done it without you. You can't be a mother and then cancel Christmas to be in New York.

MARGARET (*Telephone connects*):   Taxi to Euston please, immediately. British Microwaves, front entrance. (*Puts receiver down*)

JACKIE: Come and stay, show me how you do things, how Rosie would like her room decorated.

MARGARET: No Jackie, I shall just put a label around Rosie's neck, and send her Red Star.

Source: Methuen London Ltd.

✤ A Narrow Bed

•••••••••••••••••••••••••ELLEN MCLAUGHLIN

CHARACTERS: LUCY (30's), MEGAN (30's)
SETTING: *Corridor outside a hospital room, the present.*

LUCY *and* MEGAN *are the last two members of a rural commune founded in the 60's.* MEGAN's *husband was killed in Vietnam, and he is constantly in her thoughts. Willie,* LUCY's *husband, lies dying inside from relentless alcohol consumption.*

(*The corridor outside Willie's room. A bench.* LUCY *stands.* MEGAN *approaches, carrying two paper cups of coffee*)

LUCY: How about we just sit out here and talk? He's sleeping.

MEGAN: Fine. (*Hands her a cup*) I guess these things always leak, huh?

LUCY: Always. (*They sit*) Thanks for coming.

MEGAN: No big deal. (*About the coffee*) God, this is awful.

LUCY: Isn't it? I practically live on it though. I get a kind of constant ringing in my ears by the end of the day if I work on it. Gives me something to do.

(*Pause*)

MEGAN: So it's definite.

LUCY: What?

MEGAN: The diagnosis.

LUCY: Oh, who knows. Today it's definite, tomorrow maybe they'll think of something else. The problem with this one is that he should be getting better and he's not.

MEGAN: How do you say it? Pancreitis?

LUCY: Pancreatitis. I think. Inflammation of the pancreas. The way they explained it to me this morning, it sounds like what's happening is that the pancreas is actually digesting itself.

MEGAN: Jesus.

LUCY: Yeah. Sounds pretty gothic. But we're supposed to be happy that it's non-surgical, and that they can give him pain-killers, whereas with something else, they couldn't dope him up at all. He's still hurting an awful lot if you ask me. I don't know what to do.

MEGAN: I think you're doing it.

LUCY: Rearranging flowers? Plumping pillows?

MEGAN: Well.

LUCY: I imagine . . . I have this image of myself doing something worthwhile, something heroic, something with a knife in my teeth.

MEGAN: Swinging on ropes.

LUCY: That sort of thing.

MEGAN: I'd like that. I can just see you — chasing nurses down corridors with a saber.

LUCY: Would be fun.

MEGAN: What do you think of the new guy?

LUCY: Oh, I don't know, Megan. It's like talking to a used car salesman. You stop listening to the words after a while and just begin relying on instinct — not the words but the inflection, the tone. Trying to read him.

MEGAN: Do you trust him?

LUCY: So far. He has a scar on his cheek. Sort of an attractive scar, actually, sickle-shaped, under the eye. Apparently his older sister pushed him out of a treehouse. He said she didn't mean to. That's what I'm going on, you understand.

MEGAN: Sounds O.K. to me.

LUCY: You think so?

MEGAN: Sure.

LUCY: Oh, I'd like to believe this guy, Megan, I really would. but I can't help feeling that something is really wrong. I'm much more worried than they lead me to believe I should be. See, he's supposed to be getting better and he's not. That's all I know. The whole message is, you know, a little bedrest, getting him off alcohol and so forth and he'll be fine. But I mean he feels like he's, he feels like he's dying — and they say, oh well, of course, withdrawal, right? But it seems, I just keep thinking they're missing something.

MEGAN: So do you want to move him to Albany?

LUCY: The guy said give him five days, so I'm going to give him five days. He's so sure of himself, this guy. Oh, maybe I'm just totally flipped-out and paranoid. But I just sit there all day and go quietly nutso. I convince myself that they don't know what they're doing, that the diagnosis is wrong — But you know I'm being ridiculous, it's only been a few days, what do I expect, I mean — he'll be fine, he'll be fine.

(*Pause*)

MEGAN: So what about you?

LUCY: What about me?

MEGAN: How are you getting by?
LUCY: Oh, I just aim for stupidity. I try not to think too much. You know. Cigarettes, coffee . . .
MEGAN: Hot baths?
LUCY: To a certain extent. They tend to promote thought though. You know, you sit in the water and the steam rises and all of a sudden you find yourself thinking. They can be dangerous.
MEGAN: Well, everyone on the floor is crazy about Willie. The nurses just light up when I tell them who I'm coming to see.
LUCY: Oh, yeah. Everyone loves him. Everyone's always loved him. Which is just the way he likes it.
MEGAN (*Confused*): Well, he's a wonderful man.
LUCY: And no dummy either. I was actually surprised when they told me the diagnosis this morning, surprised that he'd ruined his pancreas by drinking, that's how good he is. And when I think about it, you know, he wasn't always everyone's darling, that's something he'd had to cultivate over the last ten years because he's needed that many accomplices. And now, he's practically managed to kill himself with a little help from his friends, who just looked the other way and let him go on being drunk, because, after all, he's such a charming drunk . . . Megan, I'm so angry. The gallons of liquor he's tipped back while I've just watched, because he was amusing, because I thought loving him meant not interfering. And now, to sit there and look at him all day and see what that kind of love has allowed him to do. Of course I'm also so . . . so mad at *him*, I guess. Willie. (*Not wanting to cry*) Oh, I don't know, it just seems like such a stupid thing to do to yourself.
MEGAN: It's not that black-and-white.
LUCY (*Dismissing the placation*): I know, Megan, I know. I've read all the brochures from AA, buddy. I realize that it's a disease. But what makes me crazy is this feeling that it's *me* keeping him alive — I think he's letting go, wanting death. It's me, sitting here, holding on to him, talking in my head to his body — 'cause it's his *body* — this animal, all nerves and arteries and veins that he has become all of a sudden — that's what I'm dealing with now — his mind is drifting so much of the time. So I sit there, I look down at his arm, and I guess what I do is I pray, I make deals with his arm, I say, "Keep going, please, for me, keep going." (*Pause*) God, Megan, I'm so exhausted and I've only been doing this for four days. How could you have done this for fifteen years?

MEGAN (*Surprised*):   Well, for one thing I haven't been doing this, what you're doing.

LUCY: But you haven't given up.

MEGAN: How can I? I don't have any choice in this. I can't get any information that says he's alive, but I can't get any that says he's dead. How could I give up?

LUCY: Easy. (MEGAN *shakes her head*) Another person would.

MEGAN: You'd be surprised. It's just different for me. See, I'm in love with a twenty-two-year-old. Even if John's alive, I'm in love with a ghost, someone who doesn't exist any longer. You, you have this person, right in front of you, you can touch him, smell him, hold him, the pain he's going through is something you can see. You don't have to believe anyone else, doctors, nurses, anyone, the truth is right there. I'm just so tired of having to take someone else's word for everything. If I could go there, of course I can't go there — but if I could just *touch* something . . . Well, anyway . . . I didn't mean to, I don't mean to say that what I'm going through . . . what you're going through is in some ways a lot worse . . .

LUCY: I know that. We're not doing comparative suffering here. I know —

MEGAN: I mean, for one thing, you have to deal with the day-to-day struggle of keeping a marriage working, whereas —

LUCY: And you haven't slept with anyone for 15 years.

MEGAN (*Pause*):   You don't know that.

LUCY: What?

MEGAN: You don't know that.

LUCY: Yes, I do. I mean — don't I?

MEGAN: I did.

LUCY: Who? (*Pause*) Of course, you don't have to tell me. (*Pause*) Except that you do . . . have to tell me.

MEGAN (*Laughs*):   All right. All right. There was this guy I saw waiting for a bus. He . . . well, I was really shocked. He looked a lot, I mean a *lot* like John. I saw him from across the street. I was holding all these groceries and I just stood there staring at him like a crazy person. He didn't know I was watching him because he was doing this, well actually, this very *John*-thing, as a matter of fact — he was reading the back of his ticket. That's just what John used to do — he'd read things, the wrappers on candy bars, airplane safety folders, cereal boxes, baggage tickets . . . anyway the guy didn't notice me. But I just couldn't move. I knew it wasn't John but I couldn't seem to convince myself. There was this child in me, this little girl jumping up and down saying "It's him, it's him, he's come back!" Finally I did this thing. I crossed the street and I went up to him. I said, "Excuse me, but I have a sort of unusual request. I'll pay for that ticket, wherever you're going, if you would sit and talk with me for a few minutes." He said, "You'd pay for a ticket to Chicago just to talk?" I said, "You're right, it's not just to talk. You'd have to kiss me." He said something like "What is this?" and then I told him. I showed him a picture of John. He saw the likeness. Anyway . . . anyway, I asked him to come out with me someplace. We turned in the ticket. It was all pretty weird, actually.

LUCY: I bet.

MEGAN: I sort of didn't want to talk, because it would spoil the illusion. But then the illusion wasn't all that pleasant anyway.

LUCY: You made love?

MEGAN: Yeah, got my diaphragm out of the crypt and everything — which meant I had to sneak into the house while he sat in the car. But luckily the whole place was on the Saturday family acid trip and no one noticed.

LUCY: Where did you go?

MEGAN: We took a cabin at the Whispering Pines for about an hour and a half.

LUCY (*Appalled*): Oh my God.

MEGAN: Yeah. It was *beyond* seedy. This bowed mattress on the bed and these incredibly loud springs and the whole place smelling like you were inside an Airwick freshener. Oy. I mean, Lucy. This poor guy. I don't know why he did it — but I'm sure he regretted it as soon as we decided to. And he's trying to deal with *me* and I can't even *look* at him. He probably felt like a stud. A bad stud at that. I kept crying. (*She laughs*)

LUCY (*Horrified but laughing*): That's awful.

MEGAN: I know.

LUCY: Is that the only time?

MEGAN: Well, yeah. I mean, I made out with Woody a couple of times.

LUCY: — Oh, well, who didn't? Woody was . . . Jesus, Megan.

MEGAN: Yeah.

LUCY: Do you masturbate a lot?

MEGAN: You're a nosey son-of-a-bitch, aren't you?

LUCY: Well, I don't know. I just don't know how you do it.

MEGAN: I used to. I still do, it's just . . . I think about John, you know, to get excited and after this long —

LUCY: — You can't remember? —

MEGAN: — No, no, I remember all right. I just feel, it's been so long, I feel like a what-do-you-call-it — necrophiliac. No, that's not what I mean, I feel . . . It makes me sad. It's worse. It makes me crazy. But that's just the way it is.

LUCY: So you still think he's alive.

MEGAN: I don't really want to talk about it again.

LUCY (*Hands up*):   All right, all right.

(*Pause*)

MEGAN: I don't really *think* anything, it's not that sort of thing. At this point, even though he hasn't shown up on any of the lists — he's legally dead. It's completely irrational to think he might still be alive, I know that. (*Pause*) But Lucy, maybe I'm just doing this to myself — you know, some new kind of self-torture, but I . . . Last week I was doing the dishes and, for no reason at all I had this very clear memory — it wasn't a memory, it was a feeling. See, John had this way of pulling on his nose and scratching it at the same time. It was a habitual gesture. He did it when he was confused or when he couldn't think of what to say. So I was standing there at the sink and I suddenly knew, I really *knew* that he had just made that gesture. That he must be alive. I know it sounds —

LUCY: — No it doesn't. I believe you.

MEGAN: You don't think I'm . . .

LUCY: — No I don't.

(*Pause*)

MEGAN: So anyway. That's how I do it.

LUCY: Do what?

MEGAN: You asked how I keep living.

Source: Samuel French, Inc.

✤ Once Removed

•••••••••••••••••••••••••••EDUARDO MACHADO

CHARACTERS: OLGA (34), BARBARA (14)
SETTING: *The living room of a rented house in Haileah, Florida, 1960.*

Living in exile is not the romantic existence OLGA *had imagined for herself and her daughter,* BARBARA. OLGA's *dreams for her daughter retreat in the face of a marginal life in a dirty town next to Miami known only for its dog races.*

OLGA: Lock the doors while I close the windows.
    (BARBARA *goes to door and locks it and* OLGA *closes windows and pulls down the blinds*)
BARBARA: Locked.
OLGA: I'll go lock the kitchen door. Make sure you locked your door right. (OLGA *exits*)
BARBARA: I just did, you just turn the . . .
    (OLGA *re-enters*)
OLGA: It's very important to lock everything in this country. Don't trust the Yankees, remember that. We used to get their upper middle class in Cuba. They're not very nice, believe me.
BARBARA: I don't remember seeing many of them.
OLGA: We took you places where you didn't have to see them. We protected you from North Americans, but . . .
BARBARA: Why?
OLGA: They spit all over the place. They spit at us.
BARBARA: I heard it was more than spit!
OLGA: Don't talk like that in front of your mother. Did you make an appointment for the confession?
BARBARA: I'll just go to confession.
OLGA: No, with the priest from Havana, no, he has so many confessors that he has to make appointments.
BARBARA: I'll go to a regular priest.
OLGA: No.
BARBARA: Jesus is Jesus!
OLGA: No daughter of mine is going to confess to a foreigner.
BARBARA: It's all the same in the eyes of God!
OLGA: Maybe.

BARBARA: I'll make the appointment.

OLGA: Good, I'll go dig it up. Check the door.

BARBARA: The buried treasure?

OLGA: Yes, make sure everything is locked. (OLGA *enters with a small black briefcase*) Here it is. Oh! Home, a little bit of home.

BARBARA: See, you feel better already . . .

OLGA: Yes. Did you make sure it was locked?

BARBARA: Three times. No one knows we have a treasure.

OLGA: They suspect we do.

BARBARA: Why?

OLGA: They know who we are.

BARBARA: No one around here knows we have a past. Believe me, they're either Cubans from Matanzas . . .

OLGA: They know who my father is in Matanzas.

BARBARA: Or Yankees.

OLGA: Yankees like to steal, for them it's a sport.

BARBARA: Don't worry. These are lower class Americans, working class.

OLGA: Don't say working class in front of me.

BARBARA: You might have to become working class.

OLGA: Never. I have a past.

BARBARA: Show them to me. Make me happy.

OLGA: You're right. We must begin before your father finds us. (OLGA *dumps the contents of the briefcase onto the newspaper: diamond rings, bracelets, watches, earrings, jewelry of all kinds.* OLGA *and* BARBARA *fondle the various items*)

BARBARA: Oh.

OLGA: Ay.

BARBARA: Oooohhh.

OLGA: Sweet.

BARBARA: Bright.

OLGA: Yes.

BARBARA: They make me so happy.

OLGA: Our past.

BARBARA: They're so beautiful.

OLGA: Stones. Gold. Solid.

BARBARA: Real.

OLGA: Relics.

BARBARA: Ours.

OLGA: It was worth it?

BARBARA: Yes.

OLGA: All the risks . . .

BARBARA: And you did it for me. I'm so lucky.

OLGA: Your father leaving through the Swiss Embassy . . . My having to eat and then search . . . The ones I stuck inside my girdle . . .

BARBARA: Do you think that when Aunt Rosita gets here she'll want her share back?

OLGA: Of course. Don't get any ideas.

BARBARA: Must be sixty thousand dollars worth.

OLGA: Priceless. And if I die, promise me that you will never sell it.

BARBARA: I promise.

OLGA: Your father is hauling, lifting with his bare hands God knows what for a living. But we promised each other that this, our heritage, will remain the same. Castro may have taken away our business, our home, our church, our nuns and our priests. But the jewelry, we kept.

BARBARA: And on my fifteenth birthday, I'll get to wear some of it, yes?

OLGA: Yes, and we'll introduce you to whatever of our society is left. (*She kisses a bracelet*) My father bought this for me. I miss him.

BARBARA: I miss Grandma. (*She points at two sets of pearl earrings*) She bought me these, right?

OLGA: As soon as you were born, she ran to get your ears pierced. Then she bought two little pearls and two identical but bigger ones for when you come out.

BARBARA: Let me wear the big ones now.

OLGA: When you're fifteen.

BARBARA: It's only eight months away.

OLGA (*Showing her ring*): My engagement ring. It was a decade of jewelry. At fifteen, my coming out diamond ring and matching earrings from my father. At sixteen, my engagement ring from your father. At eighteen, my wedding ring with eighteen diamonds from my father-in-law; he bought it for your father. He wanted the ring to be "featured" in all the wedding pictures. And at nineteen, my mother's gold cross because I had you.

BARBARA: It's a beautiful crucifix.

OLGA: At twenty-one, my cocktail ring with the rubies for my fourth wedding anniversary. Then . . . Then . . . Then, revolution.

BARBARA: How are we having our Spam today?

OLGA: Fried. Fried Spam. But let's not talk about Spam, not until dinner.

BARBARA: You'd think the Catholic Relief would give you something besides Spam, Velveeta Cheese and lima beans.

OLGA: Why do you always have to bring us down to reality? It breaks my heart. I'm thirty-four; I've had my wedding. But that my daughter, my only beautiful daughter, is going to have to come out in America with nothing . . . I raised you to want everything.

Source: International Creative Management

✢ Our Country's Good

••••••••••••••••TIMBERLAKE WERTENBAKER

CHARACTERS: DABBY (20's), MARY (20's)
SETTING: *A convict colony in Australia, 1788.*

A young marine lieutenant is directing rehearsals of the first play ever to be staged in Australia. The cast consists of convicts, many of them illiterate. As this scene opens, two women convicts are attempting to learn their lines.

DABBY: If the latitude of Sydney is 43 degrees, 39 minutes south and Cape York is 10 degrees, 10 degrees, what did they say? 10 degrees, 37 minutes, that's (*She counts on her fingers*) 1,982 minutes, or miles, sail 60 miles a day, 15 on a bad day, due north, keep the coast in sight, 10 weeks, more with adverse winds, then from Cape York another thousand miles, where was I? I'll have to start again!

(MARY BRENHAM *has come on*)

MARY: Are you remembering your lines, Dabby?

DABBY: What lines? No. I was remembering Devon. I was on my way back to Bigbury Bay.

MARY: You promised Lieutenant Clark you'd learn your lines.

DABBY: I want to go back. I want to see a wall of stone. I want to hear the Atlantic breaking into the estuary. I can bring a boat into any harbour, in any weather. I can do it as well as the Governor.

MARY: Dabby, what about your lines?

DABBY: I'm not spending the rest of my life in this flat, brittle burnt-out country. Oh, give me some English rain.

MARY: It rains here.

DABBY: It's not the same. I could recognize English rain anywhere. And Devon rain, Mary, Devon rain is the softest in England. As soft as your breasts, as soft as Lieutenant Clark's dimpled cheeks.

MARY: Dabby, don't!

DABBY: You're wasting time, girl, he's ripe for the plucking. You can always tell with men, they begin to walk sideways. And if you don't —

MARY: Don't start. I listened to you once before.

DABBY: What would you have done without that lanky sailor drooling over you?

MARY: I would have been less of a whore.

DABBY: Listen, my darling,you're only a virgin once. You can't go to a man and say, I'm a virgin except for this one lover I had. After that, it doesn't matter how many men go through you.

MARY: I'll never wash the sin away.

DABBY: If God didn't want women to be whores he shouldn't have created men who would pay for their bodies. While you were with your little sailor there were women in that stinking pit of a hold who had three men on them at once, men with the pox, men with the flux, men biting like dogs.

MARY: But if you don't agree to it, then you're not a whore, you're a martyr.

DABBY: You have to be a virgin to be a martyr, Mary, and you didn't come on that ship a virgin. 'A.H. I love thee to the heart', haha, way up there —

MARY: That was different. That was love.

DABBY: The second difficulty with being a martyr is that you have to be dead to qualify. Well, you didn't die, thanks to me you had three pounds of beef a week instead of two, two extra ounces of cheese.

MARY: Which you were happy to eat!

DABBY: We women have to look after each other. Let's learn the lines.

MARY: You sold me that first day so you and your husband could eat!

DABBY: Do you want me to learn these lines or not?

MARY: How can I play Silvia? She's brave and strong. She couldn't have done what I've done.

DABBY: She didn't spend eight months and one week on a convict ship, did she? Anyway, you can pretend you're her.

MARY: No. I have to be her.

DABBY: Why?

MARY: Because that's acting.

DABBY: No way I'm being Rose, she's an idiot.

MARY: It's not such a big part, it doesn't matter so much.

DABBY: You didn't tell me that before.

MARY: I hadn't read it carefully. Come on, let's do the scene between Silvia and Rose. 'I have rested but indifferently, and I believe my bedfellow was as little pleased; poor Rose! Here she comes' —

DABBY: I could have done something for Rose. Ha! I should play Silvia.

MARY: 'Good morrow, my dear, how d'ye this morning?' Now you say: 'Just as I was last night, neither better nor worse for you.'

DABBY: 'Just as I was last night, neither better nor worse for you.'

Source: Methuen Drama

✤ Paducah

•••••••••••••••••••••••••••••SALLIE BINGHAM

CHARACTERS: SUZI (*late 20's, early 30's*), JULIA (*50's*)
SETTING: *A house in Paducah, Kentucky.*

SUZI *returns home to Paducah, pitching her tent on the family's front lawn, on the day it turns out that her mother is leaving her home and marriage.*

JULIA: You're always so bent on talking —
SUZI: We never have done much of that.
JULIA: Why, your last visit — that was what ruined it, Suzi! You just didn't know when to stop talking — There are some things you can't say in words, Suzi.
SUZI: Like love or hate. That kind of thing?
JULIA: Why, yes. It's just too embarrassing — like looking inside somebody's head and seeing all the thoughts lined up. Haven't you ever NOT said something, Suzi? I sometimes wonder how Donald manages.
SUZI: He doesn't.
JULIA: Is that one of your riddles?
SUZI: Oh, we haven't separated, or anything drastic like that. We've just agreed to let things go —
JULIA: You don't love him anymore.
SUZI: I don't know.
JULIA: You'd know if you didn't!
SUZI: Do you still love Daddy?
JULIA: I'll always love your father. It's in my bones! But I can't live with him anymore.
SUZI: You must have had to talk about that.
JULIA: We know each other so well. It's not really a question of words.
SUZI: You're going to be awfully lonely.
JULIA: Well, I do have some new friends . . .
SUZI: Do you mean . . . boyfriends?
JULIA: There's only one. And he's fullgrown.
SUZI: Somebody I know?
JULIA: I believe you do. I'd rather not discuss it, now. (*Pause*) Where in the world do you think Clete went — flying off the handle like that?

SUZI: It's not somebody young, is it, Mama?

JULIA: Now, I've told you, I don't want to discuss that, not yet! And really we have more important things to consider.

SUZI: Like Clete. What's going to happen to him now?

JULIA: You and Clete — I sometimes used to feel almost jealous.

SUZI: Did you?

JULIA: Why, yes! The two of you were always together —

SUZI: But I would have come to you, any time, Mama, way back then — but you were always upstairs, or out, or talking on the phone —

JULIA: Let's not begin all that.

SUZI: I don't mean it that way! It just never occurred to me you were jealous of Clete —

JULIA: Between Clete and your father, there wasn't much of you left for me.

SUZI: Why, Mama!

JULIA: Let's not make a mountain out of a molehill. That was a long time ago! Water under the bridge! I need to get started.

SUZI: What's left here for me, Mama?

JULIA: Why, Suzi — this is your home. At least, if you don't have one of your own —

SUZI: But you've gone. And Clete's gone! And I don't much like the look of what's left!

JULIA: You still have those sharp little eyes, don't you, Suzi! You see through everything —

SUZI: Don't blame me for that!

JULIA: I'm not blaming you. I just want you to turn those sharp little eyes in a different direction, examine your own future.

SUZI: Right now I don't have one to examine.

JULIA: But you must. You have no choice in the matter! There's the future out there, and it's coming towards you, fast, and if you don't make up your mind, why, it'll come on, anyway, and you'll wake up and find yourself middleaged, and stranded, trying to take care of people when you never did a danged thing for yourself —

SUZI: Why — you used a word —

JULIA: I just said danged.

SUZI: Hallelulia! You CURSED!

JULIA: I don't call "danged" a curse.

SUZI: Are you telling me not to stay.

JULIA: That's your decision, Honey! But if you stay . . . I'm telling you, it's quicksand here! You can sink in up to your chin and not even know it!

SUZI: I'm not going to let that happen.

JULIA: It will, if you don't decide.

SUZI: I've got my pack, out there, and my tent, I can get started in no time.

JULIA: Well, then — what are you waiting for?

SUZI: I've got to take you to town, first.

JULIA: Thank you, Suzi. Just don't ever forget . . . It's warm here, and cozy. Just tuck that into the back of your mind and let it stay there. Warm, and cozy, with good food on the table, and a nice soft bed to sleep in —

SUZI: I won't forget, Mama. I won't let myself forget.

Source: William Goodman

✤ Phantasie

•••••••••••••••••••••••••••••SYBILLE PEARSON

CHARACTERS: D (35), VALERIE (53)
SETTING: VALERIE's *house in Newton, Massachusetts, the present.*

D *has finally tracked down her natural mother,* VALERIE, *after 35 years. As this scene open,* D *and* VALERIE *meet for the first time.*

VALERIE: You can live here if you want.
D: Live here?
VALERIE: If you want. That's cranberry juice.
D: I live in New York. I have a husband. We live in the city. We're having a child.
VALERIE: When?
D: In the spring. A long time.
VALERIE: Kids like spring birthdays. I gave the class parties outside in the spring.
D: You teach?
VALERIE: I started teaching kindergarten. I prefer twelfth.
D: You teach high school.
VALERIE: History. I've just retired. Twenty seven years. I liked it.
      (D *looks over to the laundry bags on the floor.* VALERIE *rises and walks to bags*)
      These are mother's things. She died before the summer. I brought them up here. I should have gotten them over to Goodwill. I was away this summer. (*She goes to desk*) I have lots of pictures of her. Somewhere.
D: Do I look like her?
VALERIE (*Nods*):   You have Mickie's eyes.
D: My father?
VALERIE: Oh, yes, the seed. (*As an apology*) People call me too straight at times. Forgive me. (*She sits*) Please, you want to ask me things.
D: Who was Mickie?
VALERIE: A sophomore at B.C., Catholic and horny. He looked like Heathcliff.
D: The cat?
VALERIE: Cat? Oh, the cartoon cat. (*She laughs*) No. He looked like Brontë's Heathcliff. I wanted literary passion in my life. We were

together one night. His family convinced him that he wasn't
with me that night, and I didn't want a man that didn't want me.

D: I look like him?

VALERIE: From what I remember. It's 35 years.

D: You never saw him again?

VALERIE: It's easy not to see people again, especially if you don't
know them well.

D: Mickie was his real name?

VALERIE: Michael.

D: My husband's name is Michael.

VALERIE: There are a lot of Michaels.

D: Him being Michael feels very weird.

VALERIE: Yes.

D: Did you know my mother? I mean, you know what I mean.

VALERIE: I never met her.

D: Did you know we lived in Newton?

VALERIE: No.

D: Did you teach in Newton?

VALERIE: In Boston. The Boylston School. It's down the street from
the Hotel.

D: Oh.

VALERIE (*Gentle*):   No. I didn't teach you.
(*A cat scratches at door*)
Horace.
(*The scratching stops.* VALERIE *crosses to her cigarettes*)
Smoke?
(D *reaches for a cigarette.* VALERIE, *with her back to* D, *remembers that*
D *doesn't smoke*)
No. That's right you don't.
(D *puts her hand down*)

D: I stopped a while ago.

VALERIE: This bother you?

D: No. (VALERIE *returns cigarette to pack. She sees* D's *uneaten sandwich*)

VALERIE: You don't have to eat what you don't want.

D: I'm waiting for my head to clear.

VALERIE: You've always been allergic?

D: Always.

VALERIE (*Without thinking*):   I don't know what I'd do if I was. I
couldn't live without a cat in the house.
(*A beat of silence.* D *blows her nose for the last time.* VALERIE *walks to
window*)

Rain might be coming back again.

D: Why did you ask about ham?

VALERIE: I gave you to a Jewish Agency.

D: Because you're Jewish.

VALERIE: Because I wanted you to have a good home.

D: Are you Catholic?

VALERIE: No. But my mother was brought up in Europe in a Catholic area, but she was a Protestant who married a Jew, whose family never went to Synagogue, which didn't bother him because he was an atheist. And I end up being baptized at the Second Presbyterian Church where I learned the Highland Fling in Sunday School. But I left the church the day they put the spikes over the front door to impale the pigeons. Which should have been the end of my religious education. But a girl in High School told everybody that my father was Jewish and *I* was anti-semitic since I didn't practise the religion, which sent me to the library where I learned all about Judaism and stayed home on the holidays to the confusion of everyone in my family, including myself.

(*A cat scratches*)

Excuse me.

(*She starts to exit, then crosses back to get her cigarette and exits, closing the door behind her. A spot light on* D. D *speaks to audience. She imitates* VALERIE's *voice*)

D (*In anger*): Easy not to see people, especially if you don't know them well . . . I should have said: If he was the seed and he wasn't responsible. Then who were you? The seed carrier? I mean, shit. Easy not to see people if you don't know them well. And what do I know about you, lady? Nothing. No problem not seeing you again. You're gone! (*She imitates* VALERIE's *gesture*) You went "Whish. Whish. Whish".

Source: Broadway Play Publishing, Inc.

✣ Playing For Time

•••••••••••••••••••••••••••••ARTHUR MILLER

CHARACTERS: ALMA (30's), FANIA (30's)
SETTING: *A concentration camp in Germany, the early 1940's.*

ALMA *is a German Jew and niece of the great composer Gustav Mahler, She has been assigned the duty of conducting an orchestra for the Germans while she is in a concentration camp. Fania is a Jewish woman in the orchestra in the concentration camp, too. As the scene opens, Alma is trying to get Fania to support her rigid demands for the orchestra. Alma feels if the orchestra does not play well, all of them will die.*

ALMA: Talk to me, Fania.
(FANIA *keeps silent, wary of expressing herself*)
There must be strict discipline. As it is, Dr. Mengele can just bear to listen to us. If we fall below a certain level anything is possible . . . He's a violently changeable man.
(FANIA *does not respond, only massages*)
The truth is, if it weren't for my name they'd have burned them up long ago; my father was first violin with the Berlin Opera, his string quartet played all over the world . . .
FANIA: I know, Madame.
ALMA: That I, a Rosé, am conducting here is a . . .
FANIA: I realize that, Madame.
ALMA: Why do you resent me? You are a professional, you know what discipline is required; a conductor must be respected.
FANIA: But I think she can be loved, too.
ALMA: You cannot love what you do not respect. In Germany it is a perfectly traditional thing, when a musician is repeatedly wrong . . .
FANIA: To slap?
ALMA: Yes, of course! Furtwängler did so frequently, and his orchestra idolized him.
(FANIA *keeping her silence, simply nods very slightly*)
I need your support, Fania. I see that they look up to you. You must back up my demands on them. We will have to constantly raise the level of our playing or I . . . I really don't know how long they will tolerate us. Will you? Will you help me?

FANIA: I . . . I will tell you the truth, Madame — I really don't know how long I can bear this. (*She sees resentment in* ALMA's *eyes*) . . . I am trying my best, Madame, and I'll go on trying. But I feel sometimes that pieces of myself are falling away. And believe me, I recognize that your strength is probably what our lives depend on . . .

ALMA: Then why do you resent me?

FANIA: I don't know! I suppose . . . maybe it's simply that . . . one wants to keep *something* in reserve; we can't . . . we can't really and truly wish to please them. I realize how silly it is to say that, but . . .

ALMA: But you *must* wish to please them, and with all your heart. You are an artist, Fania — you can't purposely do less than your best.

FANIA: But when one looks out the window . . .

ALMA: That is why I have told you *not* to! You have me wrong, Fania — you seem to think that I fail to see. But I *refuse* to see. Yes. And *you* must refuse!

FANIA (*Nearly an outcry*): But what . . . (*She fears it will sound accusatory*) . . . what will be left of me, Madame!

ALMA: Why . . . yourself, the artist will be left. And this is not new, is it? — what did it ever matter, the opinions of your audience? — or whether you approved of their characters? You sang because it was in you to do! And more so now, when your life depends on it! Have you ever married?

FANIA: No, Madame.

ALMA: I was sure you hadn't — you married your art. I did marry . . . (ALMA *breaks off. She moves, finds herself glancing out the window, but quickly turns away*) . . . Twice. The first time to that . . . (*She gestures ironically toward her violin case lying on her cot*) The second time to a man, a violinist, who only wanted my father's name to open the doors for him. But it was my fault — I married him because I pitied myself; I had never had a lover, not even a close friend. There is more than a violin locked in that case, there is a life.

FANIA: I couldn't to that, Madame, I need the friendship of a man.

ALMA (*Slight pause*): I understand that, Fania. (*She is moved by an impulse to open up*) Once I very nearly loved a man. We met in Amsterdam. The three good months of my life. He warmed me . . . like a coat. I think . . . I could have loved him.

FANIA: Why didn't you?

ALMA: They arrested me . . . as a Jew. It still astonishes me.

FANIA: Because you are so German?

ALMA: Yes. I am. (*Slight pause*) In this place, Fania, you will have to be an artist and only an artist. You will have to concentrate on one thing only — to create all the beauty you are capable of . . .

FANIA (*Unable to listen further*):   Excuse me, Madame. (*She quickly pulls open the door and escapes into the darkness.*)

Source: The Dramatic Publishing Company

✤ The Possibilities

••••••••••••••••••••••••••••HOWARD BARKER

CHARACTERS: THE OFFICIAL (*30's*), THE WOMAN (*20's*)
SETTING: *An office, the present.*

This is a collection of short and witty plays about power, morality and sex. Sometimes all three. This one is called, "She Sees the Argument But".

(*A* WOMAN OFFICIAL, *seated behind a desk. A* WOMAN *enters, stands before her*)

THE OFFICIAL: We are so glad you could come.

WOMAN: It was — (*She makes a gesture of casualness*)

THE OFFICIAL: So glad. (*Pause*) I can see your ankle. (*Pause*) Do you realize that? (*Pause*) You do realize, of course. (*Pause*) And your eyes are outlined in —

WOMAN: Mascara.

OFFICIAL: Mascara, yes. (*Pause*) Very glad you came because we want to understand and I think you do, too. Terribly want to understand! (*Pause*) You see, all this is, we believe, a positive encouragement to criminality. Speak if you want to. (*Pause*) We feel you aid the social enemy. You put yourself at risk, but also, others. The ankle is — your ankle in particular is — immensely stimulating, as I think you know.

WOMAN: I have good ankles.

OFFICIAL: Good? I don't know about good, do you? In what way good? In a sense they are very bad because they stimulate this feeling I am referring to.

WOMAN: I don't like boiler suits.

OFFICIAL: People call them boiler suits! The word boiler suit is meant to — isn't it — prejudice? I don't think we should have called them boiler suits in the first place. In any case we did not succeed with them. For one thing, girls tightened the seats, or undid buttons far below the needs of ventilation. So, indeed, I share your irritation with the boiler suit. But the ankle. What are you trying to do? (*Pause*) You can speak to me, you know. We only want to understand.

WOMAN (*Pause*):   I wish to — this is a difficult question —

OFFICIAL: Is it? You have drawn attention to your ankle, so presumably you must know why.

(*Pause*)

WOMAN: Not really, no.

OFFICIAL: You don't know why! How bewildering! You go and buy a length of rather fine wool — many weeks of wages for a typist, I suggest — cut, alter and hem it at this specific point, showing the ankle — without knowing why. Is that honestly the case? (*Pause*) I am so glad you came in.

WOMAN (*Pause*):   I wanted men to suffer for me.

OFFICIAL: (*Pause*):   Suffer?

WOMAN: Torment, yes.

OFFICIAL (*Pause*):   I think, don't you, society is so riddled with crisis now, so much healing needs to be done? Crisis after crisis? The food crisis, the health crisis, the newspaper crisis, the suicide epidemic, the lunacy epidemic? So much despair and so much healing to be done? And you say, to all this misery I would add a little more despair, a despair of my own making because it is despair, isn't it? The effect of your ankle on the morning tram, despair?

WOMAN: Yes. Longing and despair.

OFFICIAL: Though of course, among the despairing lurks the criminal. And he, tormented as you wish, will not walk home in silence to his wife, and take his children in his arms with a slightly distant look . . . No, the criminal will own. No city banker has more passion to own. Which is why we stipulated, for a while, the boiler suit. For a long time this damped the criminal statistics. Then they crept up again, thanks to the tightening of the seat and the unnecessary open buttons. You advertise your sexuality.

WOMAN: Yes.

OFFICIAL: I am so glad you came in! (*Pause*) Why don't you marry and show this ankle to your husband?

WOMAN: I am married.

OFFICIAL: You are married! Then why aren't you satisfied to show this ankle in the privacy of your own home?

WOMAN: I don't know.

OFFICIAL: Perhaps you have a secret longing to betray him?

WOMAN: I'm certain of it.

OFFICIAL: You no longer love him?

WOMAN: I love him.

OFFICIAL: You love your husband but you show your ankles to any stranger in the hope of tormenting him, is that correct?

WOMAN: I think so, yes.

OFFICIAL: And where is your responsibility towards the male who cannot contain the lust you stimulate in him?

WOMAN: He should bear his suffering.

OFFICIAL: But you impose it on him!

WOMAN: Yes, and he must bear it. Perhaps I may be seduced. A correct glance or gesture, even a sign of modesty, may do the trick.

OFFICIAL: You are a married woman and you say you may be seduced —

WOMAN: Yes, I am trying to be honest —

OFFICIAL: Bewildering honesty!

WOMAN: Well, do you want me to be honest or not? (*Pause*) I have not yet met this man. But somewhere I have no doubt he does exist.

OFFICIAL: And you are seeking him?

WOMAN (*Pause*): I think so, yes.

OFFICIAL (*Pause*): The world goes on, crises occur, we struggle towards the perfection of democracy, and you, a married woman, dangles her ankle on the bus.

WOMAN (*Pause*): Yes.

OFFICIAL: *You deserve every unwelcome attention that you get.*

WOMAN: Ah . . .

OFFICIAL: And I must say, were some monster brought before me on a charge of violation I should say half-guilty, only half! (*Pause*) My feelings. My real feelings have — soaked through . . .

WOMAN: Good.

OFFICIAL: Don't please, carry your enthusiasm for honesty to such inordinate and —

[(*A* MAN *has entered and sits at the back*)]

WOMAN: Who's he . . . ?

OFFICIAL: The question is, are you mad?

WOMAN: Who's he?

OFFICIAL: I am married, and I have children also, I am capable of love, and have a sexual life, but I do not display myself in public, do I? Perhaps you are mad, have you considered —

WOMAN: Who is he?

OFFICIAL: You see, you cannot see a man without —

WOMAN: I just wanted to —

OFFICIAL: The very locality of a man sets off in you some —

WOMAN: How can I continue to be honest when there is a —

OFFICIAL: *He is a human being just like us.* (*Pause*) Such is the scale of your obsession you refuse to believe he can observe you simply as a person. You think, my ankle will prevent him being a *person* and force him to be a *man*. You continually subvert his right to be a simple person, you *oppress him*. (*Pause*) But he refuses you. He is free. How peaceful he is. He observes you with a wonderful and objective comradeship. Your ankle is simply an exposed and consequently, somewhat absurd, piece of human flesh. Does he show you his? He also has an ankle.

WOMAN (*Pause*):   You are trying to wreck our sanity.

OFFICIAL: Oh, listen, if rational argument is going to be construed as an attempt on your sanity, then your sanity has to be doubted. Is it wrecking your sanity if a man does not suffer your sex?

WOMAN: Perhaps.

OFFICIAL: You define yourself by sexuality?

WOMAN: Yes —

OFFICIAL: You admit your slavery to some arbitrary gendering?

WOMAN: Yes —

OFFICIAL: Bewildering!

WOMAN: I think — this man — this person — frightens me more than a violator would —

OFFICIAL: Oh!

WOMAN: *I am trying to be honest.*

OFFICIAL: *Well, that's not enough!* (*Pause*) That's merely an indulgence. You want us to admire you. But we think you are possibly mad.

WOMAN (*Pause*):   I have to go.

OFFICIAL: The question is, have we the resources to provide a police force whose time and energy are consumed in searching for the violator of women like you? After all, there is a crisis.

(*Pause*)

[(THE WOMAN *goes to* THE MAN)]

WOMAN: You must try to save yourself.

OFFICIAL: Ha!

WOMAN: Yes, you have to try —

OFFICIAL: You look an idiot in those heels —

WOMAN: Look — look at me —

OFFICIAL: He is not moved — he merely suffers the embarrassment any man feels in the presence of a woman who is mad —

WOMAN: Look at me — [(*She slaps him around the face*)

THE MAN: She hit me!]

(*Pause.* THE WOMAN *goes to the table, leans on it*)

WOMAN: You want me to be mad, when it is you who is mad.

OFFICIAL: Am I wearing funny heels? Is my clothing so tight I cannot move naturally? Find a mirror, look in it, and ask yourself who's mad. Look in your eyes, which are ringed with soot, and ask yourself who's mad?

WOMAN (*Pause.* THE WOMAN *is still*):   You make me ashamed . . . of things I should not be ashamed of . . .

OFFICIAL: We only want to understand . . .

(*Pause.* THE WOMAN *leaves the table, goes out. The sound of her heels descending stone stairs*)

Source: Riverrun Press Inc.

✤ Rita, Sue and Bob Too

•••••••••••••••••••••••••••ANDREA DUNBAR

CHARACTERS: RITA (*teens*), SUE (*teens*)
SETTING: RITA's *kitchen. England, the present.*

RITA *and* SUE *are babysitters for Bob's children. They both are having a sexual fling with Bob, and they plan their social life around the times he is available for them. The two friends are sitting at a table.*

RITA: What are we gonna do tonight?
SUE: Fuck knows. There's not much we can do is there?
RITA: So it looks as if we're gonna be just walking around again.
SUE: Well can you come up with any better ideas?
RITA: Roll on Friday.
SUE: Why?
RITA: That's when we see Bob again and won't I be glad.
SUE: I aren't half looking forward to it me.
RITA: Well it's no use sitting here. I'll have to get on with the ironing.
SUE: What you ironing?
RITA (*Getting the ironing board and standing it up*):   Just my jeans and shirt for when we go out.
SUE: Good! You can iron mine while you're at it.
RITA (*Getting iron out of cupboard*):   What's wrong, haven't you got one in your house?
SUE: No.
RITA: Well what do you do for ironing all your clothes?
SUE: Borrow the next door's.
RITA (*Laughing*):   Fucking cheeky aren't you? I'm not your mother you know.
SUE: Well what else can I do?
RITA: Tell your mother to go and buy one. Can't she get one of them clubmen that comes round selling things?
SUE: No. She owes nearly every clubman some money for things she's got and never paid.
RITA (*Rubbing stomach*):   Oh. I've got a right pain. I'll bet I'll come on today.
SUE: Well you'd better bring a rag with you. Just in case.

RITA: I'd better let my mum know.

SUE: What you letting your mother know for, I wouldn't.

RITA: I think she likes to know to make sure I'm not in the club.

SUE: I never even told me mum when I first started my periods.

RITA: Does she know now?

SUE: I should think she does. Well put it this way, if she doesn't some cunt does.

RITA: Why?

SUE: Every time I come on I'll go in the drawer for a rag, but most of the time there never is any. Some twat keeps thieving them.

RITA: It gets like that here sometimes, 'grab the rag while there's some left.' I've even known me and our kid to fight over the last one.

SUE: And what's so good about the last one?

RITA: Ah. Well. The one that doesn't get it has to go to the shop and get some more. And if there's one thing I'm embarrassed about it's walking round a shop with a packet of them in my hands.

SUE: I can remember when I first started. My mum had just come back from that shop. You'll never guess what she did.

RITA: What?

SUE: She threw them on the settee and said 'take them upstairs'. They landed next to my brother, so being nosy he had a look and he burst out laughing.

RITA: All lads are the same. I wonder why they all think being on your periods is funny.

SUE: My brother is a bit of a nutter when he starts cracking out with 'em.

RITA: Why, what does he say?

SUE: Like what you having for tea? — Tampax and chips, or he'll say he packed lunch for Dracula and laugh. When he saw them in the bag, he said hammocks for lazy cunts.

RITA: Oh God.

SUE: What's wrong with you?

RITA: I've just remembered. If I come on I won't be able to go with Bob on Friday.

SUE: Well you can still come and watch.

RITA: Oh no I want to go with him an' all. Do you think he'd mind having a fuck while I'm on?

SUE: I don't bleedin' know. I don't think it would be very nice though, do you?

RITA: Why not a lot of people do it.

SUE: Don't mean to say he will though.

RITA: I don't think he'd notice very much anyway because I'd be ready for finishing.

SUE: Course he'd notice.

RITA: Well I'll have to fuckin' ask him then 'cause I'm not gonna fuckin' miss out. I don't see why I should.

SUE: Well ask him then.

RITA: I might just do that.

SUE (*Passing* RITA's *jeans*): Here's your jeans, are you getting changed in here?

RITA: Might as well.

SUE: I'll just pop my head round the door and tell no-one to come in. (*Goes to door*) Don't come in we're getting changed.

(*Both girls strip down to knickers and bra*)

RITA (*Looking at* SUE): What does that say on your knickers?

SUE: 'Practice makes perfect'.

(*They pull on jeans and shirts while still talking*)

RITA: They don't half put some silly jokes on lasses' knickers now don't they?

SUE: I think some of them are good.

RITA: I don't know why they put them on really. I mean it's not as if you walk about with just knickers on and let everybody see them.

SUE: Yeah, you're right. But you could always show them to your boyfriend.

RITA: You mean Bob?

SUE: Yeah. Oh and I forgot to tell you, you know that lad called David in our class, the one with the blond hair?

RITA: Yes. What about him?

SUE: Well from what I hear, he don't half fancy you.

RITA: That Dave's only sixteen, he's still a kid don't you think? I'll stick to Bob.

SUE: Who wouldn't?

RITA: He's really nice though in't he?

SUE: Yeah. He's the sort of fella I could live with. As long as he isn't doing to me what he's doing to his wife.

RITA: Well you can't expect nowt else can you? If I had a fella like him I'd expect him to do it.

SUE: You wouldn't be bothered if he went with all the lasses he could get?

RITA: 'What you don't know don't hurt you.' Nearly half the fellas, if no more, have a bit on the sly. I bet my mum's having a bit on the sly.

SUE: How do you think that?

RITA: Well she brought a fella home one night and she sent us to bed. She let the fella out of the front door. And when we'd gone to bed, she must of let him in again through the back door.

SUE: How do you know that?

RITA: 'Cause I got out of bed to go to the toilet. And I heard her bed squeaking.

SUE: Well she might have been moving about.

RITA: Are you kidding? With the breathing coming from that bedroom. She was moving all right. But not in her sleep.

SUE: I thought she'd of been past it myself.

RITA: So did I, but we were wrong. I'd love to hide in the bedroom and watch her.

SUE (*Laughing*): Whatever for?

RITA: It's hard to imagine her doing it. I suppose I just want to see how she does it.

SUE (*Laughing*): Like us I think, unless she's doing the sixty-nine.

RITA (*Laughing*): If she was doing the sixty-nine, she won't of had chance to breathe like that.

SUE (*Laughing*): Stop it will you. I'll be peeing myself if you don't shut up.

Source: Methuen, Inc.

✤ The Road To Mecca

•••••••••••••••••••••••••••••ATHOL FUGARD

CHARACTERS: HELEN (60's), ELSA (*late 20's*)
SETTING: *The home of Miss* HELEN *in a small village in the Great Karoo, a semi-desert in the center of South Africa, 1974.*

ELSA *is an independent-thinking young school teacher from Capetown, who has come to see her friend and confidant,* HELEN. *Since the death of her husband fifteen years before,* HELEN *has been making strange but entrancing sculptures of people and animals and indeterminate things out of scrap and headlights and bric a brac. She has filled her yard with these sculptures and calls them her "Mecca". But now she has written a despairing letter to* ELSA *that has caused the young woman to make the arduous journey.*

ELSA: It's time to talk about your last letter, Helen.
HELEN: Do we have to do that now? Can't it wait?
ELSA: No.
HELEN: Please.
ELSA: Sorry, Helen, but we've only got tonight.
HELEN: Then don't spoil it!
ELSA: Helen . . . that letter is the reason for me being here. You do realize that, don't you?
HELEN: Yes. I guessed that was the reason for your visit. But you must make allowances, little Elsie. I wasn't feeling very well when I wrote it.
ELSA: That much is obvious.
HELEN: But I've cheered up ever so much since then. Truly. And now with your visit . . . I just know everything is going to be all right again. I was very depressed you see. I wrote it in a bad depression. But I regretted posting it the moment after I had dropped it into the letter box. I even thought about asking the postmaster if I could have it back.
ELSA: Why didn't you? (*Pause*) Or send me a telegram: "Ignore last letter, Feeling much better." Six words. That would have done it.
HELEN: I didn't think of that.
ELSA: We're wasting precious time. You wrote it, posted it, and I received it.

HELEN: So can't we now, please, just forget it?

ELSA (*Disbelief*): Miss Helen, do you remember what you said in it?

HELEN: Vaguely.

ELSA: That's not good enough. (*She goes to the bedroom alcove and fetches the letter from her briefcase*)

HELEN: What are you going to do?

ELSA: Read it.

HELEN: No! I don't want to hear it.

ELSA: You already have, Miss Helen. You wrote it.

HELEN: But I don't want to talk about it.

ELSA: Yes, you must.

HELEN: Don't bully me, Elsa! You know I don't know how to fight back. Please . . . not tonight. Can't we —

ELSA: No, we can't. For God's sake, Helen! We've only got tonight and maybe a little of tomorrow to talk.

HELEN: But you mustn't take it seriously.

ELSA: Too late, Helen. I already have. I've driven eight hundred miles without a break because of this. And don't lie to me. You meant every word of it. (*Pause*) I'm not trying to punish you for writing it. I've come because I want to try and help. (*She sits down at the table, pulls the candle closer and reads. She struggles a little to decipher words. The handwriting is obviously bad*)
My very own and dearest little Elsie,

Have you finally also deserted me? This is my fourth letter to you and still no reply. Have I done something wrong? This must surely be the darkest night of my soul. I thought I had lived through that fifteen years ago, but I was wrong. This is worse. Infinitely worse. I had nothing to lose that night. Nothing in my life was precious or worth holding on to. Now there is so much and I am losing it all . . . you, the house, my work, my Mecca. I can't fight them alone, little Elsie. I need you. Don't you care about me anymore? It is only through your eyes that I now see my Mecca. I need you, Elsie. My eyesight is so bad that I can barely see the words I am writing. And my hands can hardly hold the pen. Help me, little Elsie. Everything is ending and I am alone in the dark. There is no light left. I would rather do away with myself than carry on like this.
Your ever-loving and anguished
Helen.
(*She carefully folds up the letter and puts it back in the envelope*)
What's all that about losing your house. Who's trying to get you out?

HELEN: I exaggerated a little. They're not really being nasty about it.

ELSA: Who?

HELEN: The Church Council. They say it's for my own good. And I do understand what they mean, it's just that —

ELSA: Slowly, Miss Helen, slowly. I still don't know what you're talking about. Start from the beginning. What has the Church Council got to do with you and the house? I thought it was yours.

HELEN: It is.

ELSA: So?

HELEN: It's not the house, Elsa. It's me. They discussed me . . . my situation . . . at one of their meetings.

ELSA (*Disbelief and anger*):   They *what*?

HELEN: That's how Marius put it. He . . . he said they were worried about me living here alone.

ELSA: *They* are worried about *you*?

HELEN: Yes. It's my health they are worried about.

ELSA (*Shaking her head*):   When it comes to hypocrisy — and blatant hypocrisy at that — you Afrikaners are in a class by yourselves. So tell me, did they also discuss Getruida's situation? And what about Mrs. van Heerden down at the other end of the village? They're about the same age as you and they also live alone.

HELEN: That's what I said. But Marius said it's different with them.

ELSA: In what way?

HELEN: Well, you see, because of my hands and everything else, they don't believe I can look after myself so well anymore.

ELSA: Are they right?

HELEN: No! I'm quite capable of looking after myself.

ELSA: And where are you supposed to go if you leave the village? To a niece, four times removed, in Durban, whom you've only seen a couple of times in your life?

(*Miss* HELEN *goes to a little table at the back and fetches a form, which she hands to* ELSA)

(*Reading*) "Sunshine Home for the Aged". I see. So it's like that, is it? That's the lovely old house on the left when you come into Graaff-Reinet, next to the church. In fact, it's run by the church, isn't it?

HELEN: Yes.

ELSA: That figures. It's got a beautiful garden, Miss Helen. Whenever I drive past on my way up here there are always a few old folk in their "twilight years" sitting around enjoying the sunshine. It's well named. It all looks very restful. So that's what they want to do with you. This is not your handwriting.

HELEN: No. Marius filled it in for me.

ELSA: Very considerate of him.

HELEN: He's coming to fetch it tonight.

ELSA: For an old friend he sounds a little overeager to have you on your way, Miss Helen.

HELEN: It's just that they've got a vacancy at the moment. They're usually completely full. There's a long waiting list. But I haven't signed it yet!

(ELSA *studies Miss* HELEN *in silence for a few moments*)

ELSA: How bad are your hands? Be honest with me.

HELEN: They're not *that* bad. I exaggerated a little in my letter.

ELSA: You could still work with them if you wanted to?

HELEN: Yes.

ELSA: Is there anything you can't do?

HELEN: I can do anything I want to, Elsie . . . if I make the effort.

ELSA: Let me see them.

HELEN: Please don't. I'm ashamed of them.

ELSA: Come on.

(*Miss* HELEN *holds out her hands.* ELSA *examines them*)

And these scabs?

HELEN: They're nothing. A little accident at the stove. I was making prickly-pear syrup for you.

ELSA: There seem to have been a lot of little accidents lately. Better be more careful.

HELEN: I will. I definitely will.

ELSA: Pain?

HELEN: Just a little. (*While* ELSA *studies her hands*) Just that one letter after your last visit, saying you had arrived back safely and would be writing again soon, and then nothing. Three months.

ELSA: I did write, Helen. Two very long letters.

HELEN: I never got them.

ELSA: Because I never posted them.

HELEN: Elsie! Why? They would have made all the difference in the world.

ELSA (*Shaking her head*): No. Muddled, confused, full of self-pity. Knowing now what you were trying to deal with here, they were hardly what you needed in your life.

HELEN: You're very wrong. Anything would have been better than nothing.

ELSA: No, Helen. Believe me nothing was better than those two let-

ters. I've still got them at home. I read them now whenever I
need to count my blessings. They remind me of the mess I was
in.

HELEN: That's why I feel so bad now about the letter I wrote you.
My problems seem so insignificant compared with yours.

ELSA: Don't let's start that, Helen. Sorting our problem priorities
isn't going to get us anywhere. In any case, mine are over and
done with . . . which leaves us with you. So what are you going
to do?

(*Miss* HELEN *doesn't answer.* ELSA *is beginning to lose patience*)

Come *on*, Helen! If I hadn't turned up tonight, what were you
going to say to Dominee Marius Byleveld when he came
around?

HELEN: I was going to ask him to give me a little more time to think
about it.

ELSA: You were going to *ask* him for it, not *tell* him you *wanted* it?
And *do* you need more time to think about it? I thought you
knew what you wanted?

HELEN: Of course I do.

ELSA: Then tell me again. And say it simply. I need to hear it.

HELEN: You know I can't leave here, Elsa!

ELSA: For a moment I wasn't so sure. So then what's the problem?
When he comes around tonight hand this back to him . . .
unsigned . . . and say no. Thank him for his trouble but tell him
you are perfectly happy where you are and quite capable of
looking after yourself.

(*Miss* HELEN *hesitates. A sense of increasing emotional confusion and
uncertainty*)

Helen, you have just said that is what you want.

HELEN: I know. It's just that Marius is such a persuasive talker.

ELSA: Then talk back!

HELEN: I'm not very good at that. Won't you help me, little Elsie,
please, and speak to him as well? You are so much better at
arguing than me.

ELSA: No, I won't! And for God's sake stop behaving like a naughty
child who's been called to the principal's office. I'm sorry, but
the more I bear about your Marius, the worse it gets. If you want
my advice, you'll keep the two of us well away from each other.
I *won't* argue with him on your behalf because there is nothing to
argue about. This is not his house, and it most certainly is not his
life that is being discussed at Church Council meetings. Who the

hell do they think they are? Sitting around a table deciding what is going to happen to you!

HELEN: Marius did say that they were trying to think of what was best for me.

ELSA: No, they're not! God knows what they're thinking about, but it's certainly not that. Dumping you with a lot of old people who've hung on for too long and nobody wants around anymore? You're still living your life, Helen, not drooling it away. The only legal way they can get you out of this house is by having you certified. (*Awkward silence*) We all know you're as mad as a hatter, but it's not quite that bad. (*Another pause*) One little question though, Miss Helen. You haven't been going around talking about doing away with yourself to anyone have you?

HELEN: I told you, Katrina is the only person I really see anymore.

ELSA: And Marius. Don't forget him. Anyway it doesn't matter who it is. All it needs is one person to be able to stand up and testify that they heard you say it.

HELEN: Well, I haven't.

ELSA: Because it would make life a lot easier for them if they ever did try to do something. So no more of that. Okay? Did you hear me, Helen?

HELEN: Yes, I heard you.

ELSA: And while you're about it, add me to your list. I don't want to hear or read any more about it either.

HELEN: I heard you, Elsie! Why do you keep on about it?

ELSA: Because talk like that could be grounds for forcibly committing someone to a "Sunshine Home for the Aged"! I'm sorry, Helen, but what do you expect me to do? Pretend you never said it? Is that what you would have done if our situations had been reversed? If in the middle of my mess I had threatened to do that? God knows, I came near to feeling like it a couple of times. I had a small taste of how bloody pointless everything can seem to be. But if I can hang on, then you most certainly can't throw in the towel — not after all the rounds you've already won against them. So when the dominee comes around, you're going to put on a brave front. Let's get him and his stupid ideas about an old-age home right out of your life. Because you're going to say no, remember? Be as polite and civil as you like — we'll offer him tea and biscuits and discuss the weather and the evils of alcohol — but when the time comes, you're going to thank him for all his trouble and consideration and then hand this back to him with a firm "No, thank you." (*Another idea*) And just to make quite sure he gets the message, you can also mention your trip into Graaff-Reinet next week to see a doctor and an optician.

HELEN: What do you mean?

ELSA: Exactly what I said: appointments with a doctor and an optician.

HELEN: But I haven't got any.

ELSA: You will on Monday. Before I leave tomorrow I'm going to ask Getruida to take you into Graaff-Reinet next week. And this time you're going to go. There must be something they can do about your hands, even if it's just to ease the pain. And a little "regmaker" for your depressions. (*Miss* HELEN *wants to say something*) No arguments! And to hell with your vanity as well. We all know you think you're the prettiest thing in the village, but if you need glasses, you're going to wear them. I'll make the appointments myself and phone through after you've been in to find out what the verdict is. I'm not trying to be funny, Helen. You've got to prove to the village that you are quite capable of looking after yourself. It's the only way to shut them up.

HELEN: You're going too fast for me, Elsa. You're not allowing me to say anything.

ELSA: That's quite right. How many times in the past have we sat down and tried to talk about all of this? And every time the same story: "I'll think about it, Elsa." Your thinking has got us nowhere, Helen. This time you're just going to agree . . . and that includes letting Katrina come in a couple of times each week to do the house.

HELEN: There's nothing for her to do. I can manage by myself.

ELSA: No, you can't. (*She runs her finger over a piece of furniture and holds it up for Miss* HELEN *to see the dust*)

HELEN: Everything would have been spotless if I had known you were coming.

ELSA: It's got to be spotless all the time! To hell with *my* visits and holidays. I don't live here. You do. I'm concerned with *your* life, Helen. And I'm also not blind, you know. I saw you struggling with that large kettle. Yes, let's talk about that. When did you last boil up enough water for a decent bath? Come on, Helen. Can't you remember? Some time ago, right? Is it because of personal neglect that you've stopped caring about yourself or because you aren't able to? Answer me.

HELEN: I can't listen to you anymore, Elsa. (*She makes a move to leave the room*)

ELSA: Don't do that to me Helen! If you leave this room I'm getting into my car and driving back to Cape Town. You wrote that letter. I haven't made it up. All I'm trying to do is deal with it.

HELEN: No, you're not.

ELSA: Then I give up. What in God's name have we been talking about?

HELEN: A pair of spectacles and medicine for my arthritis and Katrina dusting the house —

ELSA: Do you want me to read it again?

HELEN (*Ignoring the interruption*): You're treating that letter like a shopping list. That isn't what I was writing about.

ELSA: Then what was it?

HELEN: Darkness, Elsa! Darkness!

Source: Samuel French, Inc.

✥ A Shayna Maidel

●●●●●●●●●●●●●●●●●●●●●●●●●●●●●●**BARBARA LEBOW**

CHARACTERS: ROSE (*early 20's*), LUSIA (*late 20's*)
SETTING: ROSE's *apartment on the West Side of New York City, 1946.*

ROSA *and* LUSIA *are sisters from pre-World War II Poland, but* ROSE *speaks without an accent. That's because she was separated from her sister and mother when her father took her to America years before. Now, after the war,* LUSIA *has come from Poland, a survivor, the only survivor of their family, except, she hopes, for her husband Duvid.* LUSIA *is about to meet her father for the first time since their separation, and both sister prepare.*

ROSE: Hurry up and let me see!
LUSIA (*Offstage*):   Not right. Is mistake!
ROSE: Well at least let me see!
   (ROSE *sits on the sofa. As she waits impatiently,* LUSIA *is coming into the bedroom very slowly, facing directly toward the audience and looking at herself in the unseen mirror. She is uncomfortable, wearing a modish dress and shoes, which fit well but look out of place on her. She wobbles on the shoes*)
LUSIA: You stay in living room. I come in there. Don't laugh. Is big mistake. Should be wearing this, Ginger Rogers.
   (LUSIA *comes unsteadily into the living room.* ROSE *jumps up, pleased*)
ROSE: Well, call up Fred Astaire! You look great! Turn around. It's perfect. Very American. All we need to do is fix your hair and you'll look like you were born here.
LUSIA: Was born in Poland, like you.
ROSE (*Turning off radio*):   But, don't you want to look like you belong, Lusia?
LUSIA (*Her hand on her chest*):   When feeling here I am home, then I look like belonging more. Before war I have pretty dresses Mama made. I get some again when I can buy myself. No more from you. Everything you want to give me. Already such a present and your bed, even, I sleep in. Yesterday before . . .
ROSE: The day before yesterday.
LUSIA: Yes. You bring me with to movie all day. Ginger Rogers. Cost a lot money. And food, food, food. All the time giving me to eat. And now clothes. No. Is too much. I get it myself.

ROSE: But you have nothing. Everything was taken.

LUSIA: You don't took it! I have suitcase, clothes from the Red Cross. Same what everyone get. Soon one day, I go pick out new something. In store. And it has on it . . . What tell how much . . .

ROSE: A price tag.

LUSIA: A price tag on. No one wore it yet.

(ROSE *looks at* LUSIA *quietly for a while*)

ROSE: At least let me fix your hair, OK? Won't cost a penny. You won't know yourself. (*She sits* LUSIA *on a chair, begins fussing over her hair*) I'm real good at this, I promise. Everyone at work thinks I get it done, but I always do mine myself. And I know you want to look your best for Papa. Now, don't worry, there's plenty of time. After he finishes at the store, he'll have a shave and maybe get his suit pressed, even though it doesn't need it, and get a shoeshine, too. Papa's always turned out like a gentleman. He's getting off early today to come and pick me up so we can meet you at the boat — but not yet. Sit still.

LUSIA (*After a while*): Rayzel, letters coming through front door say for Miss Rose White.

ROSE: I changed it, but not really. It's an exact translation.

LUSIA: Why?

ROSE: Just to sound like everyone else. For instance, you could change your name to Lucy.

LUSIA: What your father thinks to change his name, Weiss to White?

ROSE: His isn't changed. I've never told him I use the other. He probably wouldn't like it.

LUSIA: To change the name don't make you safe, anyway.

ROSE (*Cheerfully brittle*): What do you mean?

LUSIA: Someone knows Rose White is Rayzel Weiss, no matter. A new name don't make no difference.

ROSE: But that's not why —

LUSIA: They come take you when they want.

ROSE: It's just easier this way. I don't have to spell it for people.

LUSIA: Even you should wear a cross around neck, they know who you are. Always with Jewish, they find out the truth.

ROSE (*Shaky, making an effort at being light*): The truth is . . . your hair is all finished. Come and see.

(ROSE *and* LUSIA *go to the bedroom "mirror".* ROSE *stands back as* LUSIA *looks at herself with an expression of surprise, pleasure and bewilderment*)

LUSIA: If I go in street like this —

ROSE: A very attractive young woman.

LUSIA: If Duvid walk near to me, he wouldn't know who I am!

ROSE: But you would know him.

LUSIA: Maybe he different, too. Thin or hair falls out maybe. Or hurt and walks different.

ROSE: But certainly before the war —

LUSIA: Before they take Duvid, already things was bad. Hungry all the time, sickness, everyone frightened. And this was six years ago. I am still a girl your age in little place, not big city. No Ginger Rogers yet. Already I look too much different only from time. I want Duvid should know me, or a friend of him he shows a picture, maybe.

ROSE: I see.

LUSIA: Thank you for pretty dress and shoes and for try to make me look pretty, too. After I find —

(*Doorbell, followed by an impatient knock on the door*)

ROSE: Papa!

(LUSIA *looks about, panicked, runs off into bathroom.* ROSE *stares after her. The bell and knocking continue*)

Just a minute, Papa. I'm coming!

Source: Dramatists Play Service, Inc.

✤ Steel Magnolias

•••••••••••••••••••••••••••••ROBERT HARLING

CHARACTERS: M'LYNN (50's), SHELBY (25)
SETTING: *A beauty shop in the South.*

SHELBY *is the prettiest girl in town and recently married.* M'LYNN *is* SHELBY's *mother and socially a prominent career woman. It is the Saturday before Christmas, and* M'LYNN *is sitting under a hairdryer as* SHELBY *enters the shop.* SHELBY *tells her mother that she is going to have a baby, despite the fact that she's a diabetic.*

M'LYNN: Shelby!
SHELBY: Mama? Where is everybody?
M'LYNN: I thought you weren't coming to town until after lunch.
SHELBY: We got an early start because of the traffic. We wanted to drop in on Jackson's parents on the way down here.
M'LYNN: What a treat!
SHELBY: And you have to catch them early. On Saturdays they leave the house at the crack of dawn to start hunting furry little creatures.
M'LYNN: You must not have visited long.
SHELBY: We didn't. I could tell they were anxious to start killing things. We stopped by the house first. Nobody was there. Where's Truvy?
M'LYNN: She and Annelle are out back sticking pennies in the fuse box. They decorated that little tree and when I plugged it in all the light blew.
SHELBY (*Pointing to a pair of tacky earrings*): What are those things?
M'LYNN: Red plastic poinsettia earrings. They are a gift from Annelle. She has discovered the wonderful world of Arts and Crafts.
SHELBY: Are Tommy and Jonathan home yet?
M'LYNN: Yes. Jonathan got home yesterday morning. He loves his classes. It's all he can talk about. I think the main thing architecture school has taught him is how much he should hate his parents' house. Tommy arrived last night and immediately started terrorizing your father. It's nice having the family home for Christmas.
SHELBY: Some things never change.

M'LYNN: And how are you, honey?

SHELBY: I'm so good, Mama. Just great.

M'LYNN: You're looking well. Is Jackson at the house?

SHELBY: No. You know how twitchy he gets. I sent him to look for stocking stuffers.

M'LYNN: Good thinking.

SHELBY: Uh. Jackson and I have something to tell you. We wanted to tell you when you and Daddy were together, but you're never together, so it's every man for himself. I'm pregnant.

M'LYNN: Shelby?!

SHELBY: I'm going to have a baby.

M'LYNN: I realize that.

SHELBY: Well . . . is that it? Is that all you're going to say?

M'LYNN: I . . . what do you expect me to say?

SHELBY: Something along the lines of congratulations.

M'LYNN: . . . Congratulations.

SHELBY: Would it be too much to ask for a little excitement? Not too much, I wouldn't want you to break a sweat or anything.

M'LYNN: I'm in a state of shock! I didn't think . . .

SHELBY: In June. Oh, Mama. You have to help me plan. We're going to get a new house. Jackson and I are going house hunting next week. Jackson loves to hunt for anything.

M'LYNN: What does Jackson say about this?

SHELBY: Oh. He's very excited. He says he doesn't care whether it's a boy or girl . . . but I know he really wants a son so bad he can taste it. He's so cute about the whole thing. It's all he can talk about . . . Jackson Latcherie Junior.

M'LYNN: But does he ever listen? I mean when doctors and specialists give you advice. I know you never listen, but does he? I guess since he doesn't have to carry the baby, it doesn't really concern him.

SHELBY: Mama. Don't be mad. I couldn't bear it if you were. It's Christmas.

M'LYNN: I'm not mad, Shelby. This is just . . . hard. I thought that . . . I don't know.

SHELBY: Mama. I want a child.

M'LYNN: But what about the adoption proceedings? You have filed so many applications.

SHELBY: Mama. It didn't take us long to see the handwriting on the wall. No judge is going to give a baby to someone with my medical track record. Jackson even put out some feelers about buying one.

M'LYNN: People do it all the time.

SHELBY: Listen to me. I want a child of my own. I think it would help things a lot.

M'LYNN: I see.

SHELBY: Mama. I know. I know. Don't think I haven't thought this through. You can't live a life if all you do is worry. And you worry too much. In some ways it's a comfort to me. I never worry because I know you're worrying enough for the both of us. Jackson and I have given this a lot of thought.

M'LYNN: Has he really? There's a first time for everything.

SHELBY: Don't start on Jackson.

M'LYNN: Shelby. Your poor body has been through so much. Why do you deliberately want to . . .

SHELBY: Mama. Diabetics have healthy babies all the time.

M'LYNN: You are special. There are limits to what you can do.

SHELBY: Mama . . . listen. I have it all planned. I'm going to be very careful. And this time next year, I'm going to be bringing your big healthy grandbaby to the Christmas festival. No one is going to be hurt or disappointed, or even inconvenienced.

M'LYNN: Least of all Jackson, I'm sure.

SHELBY: You are jealous because you no longer have any say-so in what I do. And that drives you up the wall. You're ready to spit nails because you can't call the shots.

M'LYNN: I did not raise my daughter to talk to me this way.

SHELBY: Yes you did. Whenever any of us asked you what you wanted us to be when we grew up, what did you say?

M'LYNN: Shelby, I am not in the mood for games.

SHELBY: What did you say? Just tell me what you said. Answer me.

M'LYNN: I said all I wanted was for you to be happy.

SHELBY: O.K. The thing that would make me happy is to have a baby. If I could adopt one I would, but I can't. I'm going to have a baby. I wish you would be happy, too.

M'LYNN: I wish I . . . I don't know what I wish.

SHELBY: Mama. I don't know why you have to make everything so difficult. I look at having this baby as the opportunity of a lifetime. Sure, there may be some risk involved. That's true for anybody. But you get through it and life goes on. And when it's all said and done there'll be a little piece of immortality with Jackson's looks and my sense of style . . . I hope. Mama, please. I need your support. I would rather have thirty minutes of wonderful than a lifetime of nothing special.

Source: Dramatists Play Service, Inc.

✤ Still Waters

•••••••••••••••••••••••••••••CLAUDIA ALLEN

CHARACTERS: MYRTLE (30's), GERTIE (20's-30's)
SETTING: MYRTLE's *kitchen in rural Michigan, 1945.*

MYRTLE, *an earthy, rural minister woman, presides with a firm but loving hand over her large, live-in family. Her cousin,* GERTIE, *is a sweet woman who hates the thought of sex.* MYRTLE's *brother, Eli, has just left the kitchen with a large squash which he has been lifting like a barbell to build up his arm, injured in the war.*

MYRTLE: Eli, bring back that squash! That's supper!

GERTIE: He's the happiest I've ever seen him.

MYRTLE: You'd never know he's been in a hospital the past eight months. He's just silly.

GERTIE: She's kind of odd. I mean I'm sure she's nice but she's not like most women I know. She's —

MYRTLE: Blunt.

GERTIE (*Nodding*): Uh huh. She is. Don't you think?

MYRTLE: I think it's a good thing for Eli she is. She practically bullied him back into good health. Aunt Charlotte paid my way to go to California to see him when he first got back from the Pacific and I'm telling you he looked like a dead man. He thought he was gonna be a cripple all his life and he didn't want to live. Bernadette would spend hours with him just raising hell —

GERTIE: Myrtle!

MYRTLE: Not literally, Gertie. He had to have surgery five times and she was there when he went to sleep and there when he woke up. And as soon as he was awake she was at him to exercise. She wouldn't let him give up. At night we'd leave there to go find some supper and she'd be white as a sheet, just drained. But Eli never saw that. He just saw her working his fingers hour after hour till they could work as good as anybody's. There was some talk that the Lord worked through me to heal him, but if the Lord was working through anybody in that hospital it was Bernadette.

GERTIE: Tom says a woman shouldn't talk to her man the way Bernadette talks.

MYRTLE: I think how they talk to each other is their own private business. Besides, they're happy. They make each other happy. What's wrong with that?

GERTIE: They are happy. You know, I think that bothers Tom as much as anything.

MYRTLE: Seeing somebody happy?

GERTIE: He always says he's miserable.

MYRTLE: You've never told me that.

GERTIE: Myrtle, it's not something I like to advertise.

MYRTLE: Gert, we've always been more than just cousins. We've always been close, more like sisters.

GERTIE: I know, honey, but there are some things a person just hates to tell. Besides, you're single. And you're a minister.

MYRTLE: That should make me easier to talk to not less.

GERTIE: Myrtle, have you ever . . .

MYRTLE: Ever what?

GERTIE: Had . . . Done . . .

MYRTLE: What? Done what?

GERTIE: You know . . .

MYRTLE (*Still drawing a blank*): Had . . . Done . . . You know? (*Light dawns*) You know. Oh.

GERTIE: Well, have you?

MYRTLE: No. I haven't.

GERTIE: It's awful.

MYRTLE: It's supposed to be so nice, so special.

GERTIE: Well, maybe it is for men.

MYRTLE: It's awful, huh?

GERTIE: It's just like being pounded to death in just the most private place.

MYRTLE: I'm sorry, sweetie. I'm sorry it's that way for you. But to tell the truth, just between us, I have had more than one woman tell me just about the same exact thing. You're not alone.

GERTIE: I hate it. I hate it so much. He's finally given up forcing me, but he's mad about it all the time. He holds it against me. Oh, how can anybody like doing that? It's so — Humiliating. And it hurts.

MYRTLE: How hard for you.

GERTIE: See why I didn't tell you?

MYRTLE: It's nothing to be ashamed of, Gertie. Don't be ashamed.

GERTIE: But I'm supposed to — do it. It says so everywhere. Tom even talked to Reverend Crate about it.

MYRTLE: So what did Cecil have to say?

GERTIE: He said Tom has a right to it whenever he wants. He told him he's got every right to force me.

MYRTLE: That little sonofabitch. (*Catches herself, regains control*) I'm glad Eli didn't hear that. He'd never let me live it down. Go on.

GERTIE: It's just I think they oughta warn you. I was just crazy about Tom when I married him. We had such a nice wedding. You made us such a pretty cake. Daddy was still alive. Tom looked so nice in his suit. I was so happy to marry him. I just had no idea what came with it. I would have stayed single. I would have.

MYRTLE: Your mother never . . . ?

GERTIE: You know how bad her nerves were. I think Daddy used to visit a woman in town.

MYRTLE: Well, maybe that's what Tom oughta do.

GERTIE: Myrtle!

MYRTLE: Well? Oh, I know. Bernadette's not the only person in this house who's a little too blunt at times.

GERTIE: I thought we'd just kiss. Like in the movies.

MYRTLE: Gertie, you grew up on a farm. Didn't you ever come out of the house?

GERTIE: When they'd let the bull out, I'd run to my room and cover my ears. I guess maybe I should've watched.

MYRTLE: Gertie, have you ever considered divorce?

GERTIE: Myrtle!

MYRTLE: Sometimes it is for the best.

GERTIE: It's not Christian.

MYRTLE: My mother divorced my father.

GERTIE: Well — but he was adultering.

MYRTLE: Look, God may not make mistakes but people do. They shouldn't have to suffer their entire lives for a mistake they made when they were young.

GERTIE: Seventeen. I was seventeen. Our wedding night I kept trying to roll away and he kept pulling at my nightgown till he'd torn it. He held my arms down and used his knee to get my legs apart. Then he just did it. And it went on and on and I couldn't breathe. He laid there on top of me and I thought I was going to suffocate. And it went on and on; it felt like it went on forever. He said that means he's good. No matter what I say, that means he's good. There was blood all over and that made him happy. He said he knew he'd be the first. Then he went to sleep, went to sleep in all that. And I had to lay there with his leg across me. I had to lay there till morning when all I wanted in the world was to wash.

MYRTLE: If you can't stand it, you shouldn't have to stand it. And if Tom needs to so bad, he ought to be able to remarry some woman who likes doing it.

GERTIE: How could they?

MYRTLE: Well, I believe some do. Of course, despite what he thinks, he may just not be any good.

GERTIE: Myrtle!

MYRTLE: You know, Gert, there are definite advantages to not having a steady church. I'm just a whole lot freer to say what I really think. And I find that what I really think doesn't always stay within the narrow bounds of thinking in this county. It's your life, Gertie, but don't throw it away if you're only doing it because of what people might think.

GERTIE: I'm worried what God must think.

MYRTLE: I'll ask Him.

GERTIE: You really talk to God?

MYRTLE (*Smiles*): All the time. And he always listens. He may get tired of my point of view, but he always listens.

GERTIE: I couldn't leave Tom.

MYRTLE: Well, honey, suit yourself.

GERTIE: I just wish I liked It.

MYRTLE: I just wish Eli'd bring back that squash.

Source: Victory Gardens Theater

✤ The Talented Tenth

•••••••••••••••••••••••••••••RICHARD WESLEY

CHARACTERS: PAM (*Black, late 30's*), TANYA (*Black, 20's*)
SETTING: TANYA's *apartment, the present.*

Bernard, black and in his forties, is trying to figure out how he lost his youthful idealism, represented for him by his long-ago girlfriend who died in Angola. Now, he has a mistress, TANYA, *who is pressuring him to commit to her, and a wife,* PAM, *who is determined to fight for him.* PAM *visits* TANYA's *home to have a confrontation.*

(*Lights up on* TANYA's *apartment.* PAM *appears at the door and rings the doorbell.* TANYA *answers it and comes face to face with* PAM. *They stare at one another. Then*)

PAM: Tanya Blakely?

TANYA: Look, I don't want any trouble . . .

PAM: Then you know who I am.

TANYA: Yes,

PAM: May I come in?

TANYA: I told you, I don't want any trouble.

PAM: It's a little late to be worrying about causing any trouble, isn't it? May I come in?
(TANYA *steps back and* PAM *enters*)
May I sit down?

TANYA: Oh, you plan to be here that long?

PAM: May I sit down?
(PAM *sits.* TANYA *sits across from her*)

TANYA: Well?

PAM: Looking at you, I see why my husband is so taken with you. I may as well admit it. He's probably in love with you.

TANYA: Yes, he probably is.

PAM: Are you in love with him?

TANYA: Yes.

PAM: Then we have a problem.

TANYA: He's not in love with you, anymore.

PAM: He's told you that?

TANYA: He will.

PAM: You have a lot to learn about men, my dear.

TANYA: How did you find me?

PAM: Sometimes it's necessary to invade your husband's privacy to learn more about him. (TANYA *says nothing*) I want you to know I'm not giving him up.

TANYA: I consider myself warned. Now, if you'll excuse me —

PAM: You and I are not through, yet.

TANYA: Oh, yes we are —

PAM: Sit down.

TANYA: What makes you think you can boss me around in my own house?

PAM: There are rules, Miss Blakely. You know them as well as I do. I'm not the one trying to steal somebody's husband.
(TANYA *sits*)

TANYA: I don't have to steal him. He'll come willingly.

PAM: And how long will he stay? Do you really think he'll give you the same number of years he gave me?

TANYA: The same, and more.

PAM: What are you? Twenty-four? Twenty-five?

TANYA: Why is it relevant?

PAM: I'm thirty-eight. I've seen him through one career crisis after another. I've stood with him at the funerals of both his parents and had him at my side when each of our four children were born. I gave him the money to publish his first book of poetry and flew to Africa with him to attend the funeral of the only woman I think he ever truly loved. I've watched him suffer the indignities of being subordinate to people who didn't have one-tenth his talent or intellect. I've forgotten more about him than you'll ever learn.

TANYA: So?

PAM: I'm here to tell you you're in way over your head.

TANYA: This conversation is useless. I'm not your problem. All I ever had to do was be patient and the man was mine. He's been primed to leave you for years. He was just waiting for the right woman to come along.

PAM: And you think you're that woman?

TANYA: I *know* I'm the right woman. And I'll have babies for him, too. And hold his hands and do everything for him you did, and more.

PAM: I'll bet you would if you had the chance.

TANYA: I will have the chance. Please leave.

PAM (*Rises*): How far will you go for him, Tanya? Tell me that? How much of yourself will you give up? How much pain can you stand? I look at you and I wonder . . .

TANYA: You don't have to wonder about me. Anything you can do, I can do. Anything you know, I know, too. Alright?

PAM: See, that's not even what I'm talking about. I see a strong will, but I don't see character. I see a smooth face — nearly flawless skin. No scars on your knees . . . on your legs . . . your hands. Your parents didn't let you do anything when you were a child, did they? Do you know what pressure is, honey?

TANYA: Go home.

PAM: Disappointment, perhaps? I mean, real disappointment — not a "D" on your term paper, or some puppy love shit. But real disappointment. What do you really know about men besides that sliver of meat that hangs between their legs? Do you know about the torment that burns inside their souls? Can you go into that white heat and cool it down? You'll have to do that a lot with Bernard, you know.

TANYA: Get out, I said.

PAM: I was frightened coming here. I want you to know that. Terribly frightened.

TANYA: I don't give a damn. You need to be frightened.

PAM: Then I saw you and it all came together. I know, now, I don't have to be afraid any longer. You'll send him back to me.

TANYA: All my life, I've had to deal with stuck-up yella bitches like you. Y'all think you're God's gift, with your sense of tradition and your money, and your mixed heritage and all that other shit. I've watched you all get by on nothing more than your looks. What blondes are to brunettes, you bitches are to us. Well, I got your man, honey. Little old black-as-night me and I'm gonna keep him. I don't care how much you know about him, or how many kids y'all got. I don't care if you win every penny in the divorce settlement. I'll still have *him* . . . and whatever he loses I'll build back up for him *double*. And that means twice as much money, twice as many kids and twice as much *woman*!

(PAM *says nothing. She rises and goes to the door. She stops and turns*)

PAM: It's not a new woman he's looking for, Tanya. Ask him about Habiba.

(PAM *turns and goes out.* TANYA *stands watching, puzzled by the comment. She picks up a pillow and throws it with all her might in the direction* PAM *has exited*)

Source: The Gersh Agency

✣ What Mama Don't Know

••••••••••••••••••••••••••••••••JANE MARTIN

CHARACTERS: DILLY (*18*), JENNIFER (*16*)
SETTING: *Montana, 1949.*

Wearing her mother's antique wedding dress, DILLY *and her cousin,* JEN-NIFER, *look into the all-too-familiar future.*

DILLY: There. Oh don't look so shocked. Girls here get bold or go snow crazy. There was some. Young widow down the road took to leaving a red blanket out on a line in the yard after the wash was in two winters back. When the wind was up it would flap and move. She'd see it through the window. Made her feel like there was someone walking around, something alive out there, another person like. Everyday a wind blew she'd put out the red blanket and sit to her window. She told me watching that blanket in the wind was the only thing saved her going crazy. (*Indicating the veil*) Am I on straight?

JENNIFER (*Fixing it*): Will your mother be angry we took it? It's so old.

DILLY: There is nothing to *do*. Besides what people don't know won't hurt 'em. Well? Think anybody will marry me?

JENNIFER: You look very nice.

DILLY: Well, they better. Cairn won't pay for my college.

JENNIFER: Why not?

DILLY: Got the first two nickels he ever made. Tryin' to marry me off to his old dried up, weatherbeaten, masturbatin' rancher friends killed off their first wives makin' 'em mend fence. God, Mama must have been pretty! He knew about Doc he'd fart fire. As if it mattered. That damn Indian just don't know when to quit. Always pretending to be doing something near where I am. It's funny. I got tired of him just like that. (*She snaps her fingers*) If you got married how would you know it wouldn't happen?

JENNIFER: Wouldn't what?

DILLY: Hear a snap like that. (*She snaps her fingers*) Wake up tired of him?

JENNIFER: I don't think most people do.

DILLY: Don't you?

JENNIFER: No.

DILLY (*She snaps her fingers*):   You think Esposito's good looking?

JENNIFER: Good enough.

DILLY: He watches you.

JENNIFER: He watches you.

DILLY: Do you like me? No, do you? (JENNIFER *nods yes*) Would you give me something of yours if I wanted it?

JENNIFER: What thing?

DILLY: Just something.

JENNIFER: Say what?

DILLY: I don't know what. I just mean would you? (*They look at each other.* JENNIFER *doesn't answer*) You look different.

JENNIFER: I've never had on cowboy boots before.

DILLY (*Snaps her fingers*):   Happened to your parents. (JENNIFER *looks down*) I'm sorry.

JENNIFER: Mother calls it a period of adjustment.

DILLY: Shirt has a tear. There's more in the chest.

JENNIFER (*Opens the third drawer by mistake*):   Mother says that because we live and learn there are times when one or the other goes on ahead and then that one must wait or the other must hurry and catch up.

DILLY: Sure. That must be it.

Source: Samuel French, Inc.

✤ Women of Manhattan

•••••••••••••••••••••JOHN PATRICK SHANLEY

CHARACTERS: BILLIE (*30*), RHONDA (*28*)
SETTING: RHONDA's *apartment in Manhattan, the present.*

RHONDA LOUISE *and* BILLIE *sit at the dining room table, each holding a glass of wine.* RHONDA LOUISE *hails from the Deep South and is slightly drunk.* BILLIE *is a native New Yorker who has a dramatic view of life. As the scene opens, both women confront their friendship and an evening without men.*

BILLIE: Don't we look great?

RHONDA: You look beautiful.

BILLIE: You look beautiful! You look like a firefly in a nightclub. What does that mean?

RHONDA: It was your remark.

BILLIE: It was a compliment of some kind, Rhonda Louise. Trust me. But here we are. And I'm stumped, sister, stumped, I really truly am. Cause you are stunning and I am stunning, and this room is just ideal to show how stunning we really are . . .

RHONDA: Like the oysters.

BILLIE: Exactly! But where are the men?

RHONDA: You told me not to invite any men.

BILLIE: I know. I know I did that. But where are the men?

RHONDA: That was the whole point.

BILLIE: I know. But where are they?

RHONDA: The three of us would just deck out and look great for each other and fuck the men.

BILLIE: I know, I know, but don't you feel we're wasting our gorgeousness on each other?

RHONDA: No.

BILLIE: Just a little?

RHONDA: No.

BILLIE: I understand why you're saying that, but come on.

RHONDA: Wait. I know what you're hinting at. That ain't what's going on. Anyway, you're married.

BILLIE: So what?

RHONDA: So you're here without a man cause your husband's out building buildings somewhere.

BILLIE: So what? You're here alone, I mean, without a man, because you threw Jerry out.

RHONDA: Stop. Right there. That's a black lie. I'm here alone tonight cause you knew your husband whadn't gonna be around tonight and you don't cheat so you suggested this girls' night which is fine with me, but don't you then turn around and tell me I don't have a date cause I threw this one guy outta my life. That's just a detail.

BILLIE: Sorry.

RHONDA: If I wanted a guy here tonight there'd be a guy here tonight. I'm dressed up cause you wanted me to dress up. I'll tell you why you're cryin out Where's the men? It's cause we're dressed for men. These clothes evolved outta a situation where observations were made about which kinda garments are effective to wear to attract the male of the species. It's really like female fashion's premier designer is Mister Charles Darwin. The point is these kinds clothes are bait. We're wearin bait. These clothes are just like worms only there's no fish to bite.

BILLIE: Worms!

RHONDA: Bait.

BILLIE: It's weird to think of my clothes as a worm.

RHONDA: And you yourself as a hook.

BILLIE: Especially when I've already landed my fish. Bob. Bob the big-mouthed bass.

RHONDA: Well, that's cause you gotta keep in shape.

BILLIE: What do you mean?

RHONDA: You gotta know, if it came to that extreme, that you could catch another gentleman. My father use to practice fly-fishing in the living room. He'd be casting this fly in and about a sewing hoop to the consternation of my mother. He was practicing outwitting the trout. It's the comparable same thing to happily married women who flirt. They're casting flies in the living room.

BILLIE: Is that what you think of me, Rhonda Louise?

RHONDA: Well. Billie. You are one of the worst flirts I know.

BILLIE: Do you honestly think I flirt to keep in shape in case Bob leaves me?

RHONDA: Yes. Fear! I think that's one of the reasons. But I think you do it too cause you'd like to screw the socks off the lot of 'em.

BILLIE: Is that what . . .

RHONDA: Yes! Horniness! Definitely! And I think you do it too as a sorta check you run to make sure you still exist. That's the most existential reason. I flirt therefore I am. And I think you do it too to . . .

BILLIE: I'M GOING TO TELL YOU WHY I FLIRT.

RHONDA: Why.

BILLIE: Habit.

RHONDA: Oh.

BILLIE: There was probably a dozen reasons why, at one time, but they're all dead now. Still standing up but dead. Like stuffed birds in the Museum of Natural History. Like me. (BILLIE *starts to cry*)

RHONDA: What's the matter, Billie?

BILLIE: I feel dead. I feel dead.

RHONDA: You're not dead, honey.

BILLIE: Yes, I am.

RHONDA: No, you're not. You just feel dead.

BILLIE: The other night, Bob asked me to marry him.

RHONDA: But . . . you are married to him.

BILLIE: He forgot!

RHONDA: He what?

BILLIE: Oh, it was sweet, really. We had this dinner and we drank some champagne and he'd brought me these pink pink roses, and the moment was just so . . . He got carried away and proposed.

RHONDA: But that's just so dear.

BILLIE: Oh, it was precious, it really really was. But it was also just exactly what it is about my marriage that drives me insane. I mean, I could kill!

RHONDA: I don't get it.

BILLIE: It's the courtship. He can't give it up. We can't give it up. It's been three years and we're still on the balcony, if you know what I mean. I thought that marriage was supposed to lead somewhere, not just be some frozen terrific moment. I thought it was supposed to be this great adventure. Like death.

RHONDA: It's hard for me to sympathize, Billie.

BILLIE: Oh, I'm sure it is. Nobody ever sympathizes with me. Their troubles are always worse.

RHONDA: Well. You've always done well that I could see.

BILLIE: And terrible!

RHONDA: You've always had money.

BILLIE: Yes, I have.

RHONDA: And some guy that adored you.

BILLIE: Almost always.

RHONDA: And you're good-looking and you have nice clothes and you've always lived in some place that was great . . .

BILLIE: But it's always been like photographs! And I want to be in a movie! An adventure movie where half my clothes are torn off by a gorilla and I marry the chief and I'm thrown in a volcano but I survive and become a Hollywood star and give it up and become a nun in an insane asylum in France and learn about being silent and unknown, and I invent something . . . useful and good . . . that the government and the corporations want to steal and twist for evil . . .

RHONDA: Billie! Billie! Billie!

BILLIE: What?

RHONDA: What are you talking about?

BILLIE: I just wish that my existence was more . . . picaresque.

RHONDA: And for this you want my sympathy?

BILLIE: No, not for that, Rhonda Louise. I want your sympathy for an ache in me that knows no name.

RHONDA: Alright. For that you have got my sympathy. Ready for dessert?

Source: Dramatists Play Service, Inc.

Man-Man Scenes

✣ Amongst Barbarians

●●●●●●●●●●●●●●●●●●●●●●●●●●●●●MICHAEL WALL

CHARACTERS: RALPH (20's), BRYAN (20)
SETTING: *Prison cell in Penang, Malaysia, the present.*

RALPH *and* BRYAN *face the death sentence for drug-trafficking. As the scene opens, both men contemplate their past life and their grim fate.*

RALPH: I've done a lot of travelling, Bryan.
BRYAN: Well I wish you fucking hadn't. I wish you'd stayed home and sat in front of the telly, instead of . . . Why the fuck couldn't you have left me alone? I was all right.
RALPH: Oh yeah!
BRYAN: I was.
RALPH: Yeah, you were wonderful.
BRYAN: I ain't saying I was wonderful; I'm saying I was all right. I didn't need . . .
RALPH: You needed the money! Well, you *wanted* it. Quit telling yourself lies, why don't you? You did it for the bread. 25,000 and a first-class flight on to Australia — you couldn't resist it. A fortnight in Oz then back home like the fucking Sugar Plum Fairy — Look Ma! You're a victim of your own greed. The new English disease, or haven't you heard . . . ?
BRYAN: Bollocks . . .
RALPH: . . . That's why you were perfect. Or we *thought* you were perfect.
BRYAN: I wasn't perfect, was I?
RALPH: You were not. You were a complete asshole.
BRYAN: You're lucky I haven't broken your fucking neck for you by now.
RALPH: I am?
BRYAN: Fucking lucky. I tell you, they shouldn't've put us in the

same cell together 'cos I'm gonna do for you.

RALPH: Yeah well I sleep with one eye open.

BRYAN: You fucking would.

RALPH: Because that's the only way you'd do it, pal . . .

BRYAN: Stop calling me pal; I ain't your pal . . .

RALPH: You're all talk, like all the English these days . . .

BRYAN: You don't half fucking know a lot about the English considering you don't live there no more . . .

RALPH: . . . They're gonna hang you by the neck until you're fucking dead and then you'll be number one jerk.

BRYAN: Yeah well they're gonna hang you too mate so you're not so bloody smart, are you?

RALPH: You should've gone to Margate for your holidays.

BRYAN: I nearly did. You don't know how true you spoke — I nearly did! 'Cept I won this fucking trip in a raffle. (*Laughs*) Fucking laugh, ennit? That's your sort of humour, ennit? Cunt wins a foreign holiday in a raffle, ends up getting himself topped. You like all that, don't you?

RALPH (*Seriously*): Yeah that's pretty damned funny.

BRYAN: Cunt. I ain't even been abroad before! Har har har!

[(*The* GAOLER *passes by. He's a large Sikh*)

GAOLER: All right boys?

BRYAN: Fuck off, you different-colored bastard.

RALPH: Careful.

GAOLER: Going home soon Bryan. (*He passes on*)

BRYAN: What you mean 'careful'. You mean I might get into trouble?

RALPH: I mean he might come back and knock seven different kinds of shit out of you.

BRYAN: Hilarious.] What is this country anyway? They got Chinks everywhere and they got fucking Pakis running the gaols. Sounds like a pretty fucked-up sort of place to me.

RALPH: Sounds just like home.

BRYAN: What d'*you* know?

RALPH: He's not a Paki.

BRYAN: Well whatever he is.

RALPH: How could he be a Paki?

BRYAN: Well whatever he is.

RALPH: How could he be a Paki?

BRYAN: What are you gonna tell me — he's a fucking Jap or something?

RALPH: He's a Sikh. And it's *not* a surprise to see him here.

Wherever you go in the world you find Sikhs in jobs like this —
they have a reputation for toughness . . .

BRYAN (*Suddenly*): Oh fucking hell though, it ain't fair!

(*He buries his head in his hands.* RALPH *is wearing a Sony Walkman;
he pulls the headphones over his ears and listens to the music*)
Don't put that on! Come on, take it off.

RALPH: Why?

BRYAN: I don't know.

(RALPH *looks at him for a while then takes it off again. Long silence*)
I mean you're carrying on as though this sort of thing is happening to you all the time. I mean don't pretend you couldn't
give a stuff, all right? You gotta be as chewed up about it as I am,
haven't you? Unless you want to fucking die, which I doubt.

(RALPH *says nothing. They look at one another*)

RALPH: Just don't you think of coming up on me when I'm asleep
. . .

BRYAN: No, no, no . . .

RALPH: I mean it — don't even think of it.

BRYAN: All right, no need to threaten me.

RALPH: I just want to make it clear to you, OK?

BRYAN: It's clear, it's clear. Fucking hell, touchy entcha?

RALPH: Yeah. I don't like people coming up on me.

BRYAN: Well you're in the wrong place, son.

(RALPH *looks at him*)
— In here. This is the wrong place for you.

RALPH: Just leave me alone.

BRYAN: Yeah I'll leave you alone. Just like you left me alone.

RALPH: I'm sorry . . .

BRYAN: Oh fucking hell, he's apologizing!

RALPH: ...But you shouldn't win prizes. (RALPH *laughs at him — a
curious, joyless laugh. It's creepy*)

Source: Nick Hern Books

✢ Antigone in New York

•••••••••••••••••••••••••••JANUSZ GLOWACKI

CHARACTERS: SASHA (30's), FLEA (30's)
SETTING: *A pier in the Bronx, the present.*

SASHA *and* FLEA *are homeless people, both emigres from Eastern Europe.
They live in a park.* SASHA *is a Russian Jew;* FLEA *is Polish. He has a
girlfriend in Poland. Right now they are plowing through wooden coffins
loaded and stored for transport. They are looking for a cohort named Paulie
who has died so he can have a decent burial, not in a nameless grave with
other homeless.*

> (*Sounds of the wind howling and a dog barking. Two coffins have been
> pulled aside and opened.* SASHA *and* FLEA *are trying to jimmy open a
> third one*)

SASHA: Shit. It's won't open. Why do they put so many nails in it?
FLEA: Forget that one. Let's do this one. I'm getting some strong
feelings from this one.
> (*They move to another coffin and try to open it, using a knife and a
> piece of metal bar. Suddenly something slips out from inside* FLEA's
> *coat.* FLEA *picks it up and shows it to* SASHA)

FLEA: Look at this.
SASHA: What? Pictures?
FLEA: It's a good one, isn't it? I'm going to send it to Yola. A nice
suit, next to a fancy car.
> (SASHA *is struggling with the coffin lid*)

SASHA: But it's not you.
FLEA: No. I found it.
SASHA: But she'll see that it's not you.
FLEA (*Shakes his head*):   People change.
SASHA: This guy is black.
FLEA: He's not black. (*Examines the picture*) He's just got a heavy
tan.
> (*The two are fighting with the coffin lid*)

FLEA: But he's handsome and about my age. (*Stops working*) He is a
little black, isn't he. I'll have to touch it up with lemon juice. Oh
wait. I have another picture of him in case you want to send one
to your sister in Israel. She'll like it.

(FLEA *hands the second photo to* SASHA. SASHA *takes it to shut* FLEA
up)

SASHA: Come on. Help me with this.

FLEA: Relax. They're watching television. I'm going to send this to
Jola and in three weeks, you'll see . . . (*About the lid*) ah, it's
coming . . . (*Continues his story*) in three weeks a cab will pull up
and stop at the park and Yola will step out of it.

SASHA: There's more nails over here.

FLEA: You know what Jola looks like, don't you?

SASHA: I know. I know.

FLEA: High heels, strong legs, beautifully covered with hair like a
little deer. Her waist is so tiny you can put your hands around it
and an ass like a coach. And teats. You wouldn't believe those
teats. Like boulders.

(*They get the coffin opened.* FLEA *looks inside*)

FLEA: Once she swung around very fast in bed and the right one
chipped my tooth. (*He spits in fond recollection*)

SASHA (*Impatiently waiting for* FLEA *to ID the body*):   So?

FLEA: Just a minute. Let me look. She'll get out of the cab, give the
driver six bucks and ask him to wait. No, it's not him. Do you
think six bucks is enough?

SASHA: Shit. Are you sure?

FLEA: Look for yourself, if you don't trust me.

(SASHA *is trying to fix his ruined glasses. Sound of dog barking*)

FLEA: Why don't you get those damned things fixed?

SASHA: We're lucky that dog is tied up. Throw him some more hot
dogs.

FLEA: I don't have any more.

SASHA: There were two packs there. You ate them both?

FLEA: It's a shame to give such good meat to a lousey dog. Let's
open that one. I have a really strong feeling about that one.

SASHA (*Gives him a dirty look*):   You had a strong feeling about the
last one.

FLEA: Jesus. No matter what I do you don't like it.

(*For a few moments they work on the next coffin in silence*)

FLEA: If she gives him six bucks and asks him to wait but leaves her
suitcase in the trunk do you think he'll steal it? No. Because she's
too smart. She'd take his number and name and she'd get him.

SASHA: Shut up and work.

FLEA: This is the worst one. Look what shit they make these out of.
It's falling apart. She's going to walk through the park and
everyone will stare at her. The cop will salute her. That Jamaican

who busted my ribs will offer her some vodka in a plastic cup. But she won't even spit on him. She'll just walk and search. Then she'll see me.

(*Part of the coffin lid pries open*)

And suddenly she'll run to me and I'll be sitting on the bench like I always am. Maybe I should get up, what do you think, Sasha?

SASHA: Fuck off.

FLEA: Okay. I'll get up and I'll say "welcome to the United States". She'll embrace me. She won't care if I've washed up or not, you know why? Because she's the kind of woman that when she loves a man, she doesn't care about nothing.

SASHA: Listen, Flea . . .

FLEA: Okay. I'm working. I'm doing it. She'll say "I love you, Flea. I came here just to see you." And she'll kiss me, she'll push those two giant boulders up against me and everyone in the park will see that this is true love. And Pixie will bang her head on the bench because she's with that crack dealer with the rat's nest on his head instead of with me. And I'll give Yola those ski boots, she'll try them on and they'll look like they've been made for her. She'll take my hand and we'll walk to the taxi together.

SASHA (*Cuts himself*): Shit.

FLEA: That Indian will fall down and have the worst fit of his life and break the rest of his teeth out. And you, Sasha, you will be weeping with joy because you are my best friend. Even if you were jealous you wouldn't show it because you'll be so miserable that you have to live in that fucking park without your Flea!

(*They get the coffin opened.* FLEA *looks inside*)

FLEA (*Satisfied with his premonition*): See? It's him, just like I said. Look for yourself.

SASHA: Okay. Let's get him out of there.

FLEA: Wait a minute. I feel funny.

SASHA: What do you mean?

FLEA: I better sit down. (*Staggers and almost falls*)

SASHA (*Catches him*): Hey, Flea Flea Flea. Hey. Don't do it. Hold on. (*Shakes him*)

(FLEA *slips out of his hands and falls to the ground in spasms. He's having an epileptic fit.* SASHA *tries to help him. He shoves a wooden stick in his mouth*)

SASHA: Oh my God.

Source: International Creative Management

✤ Beggars in the House of Plenty

•••••••••••••••••••JOHN PATRICK SHANLEY

CHARACTERS: JOHNNY (*18*), JOEY (*20's*)
SETTING: *A house in the Bronx, 1968.*

At the beginning of the second act of this memory play, JOHNNY *is shining a row of shoes and watching TV. He has been the cause of his family's having to move. He set fire to their old house. His older brother,* JOEY, *is outwardly more confident than* JOHNNY *and he's seen the world, largely because he's fought in the war. The brothers are forever sparring verbally and even physically with each other. Here,* JOEY *has just elicited an admission from* JOHNNY *that he's broken up with his girlfriend.*

JOEY: You want me to fix you up with somebody? I gave these girls your picture and they thought you were cute.
JOHNNY: What girls?
JOEY: You want me to introduce you?
JOHNNY: No.
JOEY: You wanna get a drink?
JOHNNY: No. When I'm upset and I drink . . . I hadda unpleasant little episode last night after some gin.
JOEY: What's the matter with you?
JOHNNY: I guess it's the stuff I've seen. I can't get my head around the stuff I've seen.
JOEY: What do you think you've seen?
JOHNNY: I have seen pretty girls ruined. Handsome guys, just like the greatest guys, destroyed. Sometimes I feel like I'm on a force march. I can hear the wind blowin. We all started out together, and then people just started droppin.
JOEY: You haven't seen shit. You should see what I've seen.
JOHNNY: Think what you want.
JOEY: Comon. What are we talkin about? You wanna go someplace and get a drink? It'll do ya good.
JOHNNY: No, it wouldn't. But thanks.
JOEY: That's alright. (*Laughs casually*) So. Have you taken acid?
JOHNNY: Once.
JOEY: I'm tellin Mom.
JOHNNY: What!

JOEY (*Goes and sits*):   I'm tellin Mom! It's information I got, it's a responsibility! You're takin drugs and she don't know it!

JOHNNY: Once!

JOEY: I'm tellin!

JOHNNY: Please don't do that!

JOEY: Why shouldn't I? Huh? Why shouldn't I? Is there some reason I don't know?

JOHNNY: You don't know what I've been through! At least you were in Vietnam! People understand that. They know it was tough. She has these headaches all the time: "Jesus, Mary and Joseph!" Screaming at me. Over nothin! Not that I'm sayin there was never nothin. I admit it. There was a long time when I was doin stuff. Settin fires, breakin windows. And then I was havin all this trouble in school. I was failin everything. They said I had psychological problems, and by the way, fuck them! Showin me inkblots. They said maybe I was retarded, and by the way, fuck them again! And I hadda problem with lyin, I couldn't stop lyin. And I couldn't keep my mouth shut! I stole some records, too, and that turned into a big thing, a regular fuckin witch hunt. I mean, they wanted me DEAD, BROKEN, and RUINED! And if they coulda found a way, these ADULTS—what a fuckin mockery of the word—if they coulda found a way, they woulda EXPUNGED ME. I stole some records from some midget whose life seemed good to me, and these ADULTS, they tried to remount *The Ox Bow Incident*! But I beat their fuckin rap. The school people, the IQ people, the inkblot people, the home people, and by the way, fuck them all! I broke the back of the doomsday squad that was after my ass. If I'm sittin here watchin t.v., with nobody knockin on the door, and Mom quelled, that's a victory. That's fuckin Iwo Jima. I should put my flag up and have a good cry. So yeah, me and Patty broke up, but the good part a that is I'm free. I'm really free. And even though I'm sad, things are a lot better. Even around here. And they're gonna get better yet if I've got anything to say about it.

JOEY: You think so?

JOHNNY: Yeah, I think so. So don't set Mom off with a drug thing. I feel funny sayin it, but the scoop is she's goin through change-a-life. One of the aunts finally told me. You should probably know, too. I thought she was just fuckin crazy.

JOEY: So maybe the last thing she needs is you.

JOHNNY: Or maybe the last thing she needs is YOU. Wavin a fresh red flag in her face. Drugs. I know you've had it hard, Joey. But

I've had it hard, too. Okay?

JOEY: I'm tellin.

(JOHNNY *jumps up*)

JOHNNY: The hell you are! What's the matter with you?

(JOEY *flies out of his chair to confront* JOHNNY)

JOEY: You think you can take me?

JOHNNY: Don't tell her!

JOEY: Do you know how crazy I am, you fuckin little shit! I've ter-rorized people! I could murder you in your sleep tonight, you know that? I could snap your neck and enjoy it!

JOHNNY: And what does that make you but a fuckin animal!

(JOEY *starts strangling* JOHNNY)

JOEY: That's right! I'm a fuckin animal! This is the fuckin jungle!

(*He's got* JOHNNY *on the floor*)

JOHNNY: Go on! Do it, you baboon fuck! You think I give a flier? Do it! DO IT!

(JOEY, *scared, drops him.* JOHNNY *is lying on the rug*)

JOEY: You're crazy.

JOHNNY: I'm crazy? You're the one's gonna get the certificate!

JOEY: I am not!

JOHNNY: Okay, you strangle me and I'm crazy. I invite you to dia-gram that fuckin idea.

JOEY: You just don't understand me.

JOHNNY: I understand you a bit. Dan'el.

(JOHNNY *gets off the floor and sits back down in his chair*)

JOEY: I've got big feelings.

JOHNNY: Congratulations.

JOEY: There's things I wanna do. I fell in love with this girl. Nadine. Garvin. She was a Salvation Army lass. I sent her a dozen red roses every Friday.

JOHNNY: A lass? She was a lass?

JOEY: I'm gonna get a Jaguar XKE.

JOHNNY: We switched, right? We're talking about a car now.

JOEY: I wrote an essay about it. "Why I Want A Jaguar XKE". Fuckin high school.

JOHNNY: You live in a dream world, Joey! I didn't know it now. Just here. But later, man, later I see you clear as you were in this room.

JOEY: What good's it do ya?

JOHNNY: It does me good.

(JOEY *sits down again*)

JOEY: I hear you got thrown outta college.

JOHNNY: Sorta. Yeah. The folks were relieved. It cost them money.

JOEY: So what are you gonna do?

JOHNNY: I'm thinkin about joinin the Marine Corps.

JOEY: I don't see it.

JOHNNY: I didn't ask you to see it.

JOEY: Johnny, you go in the Corps, they'll throw you out.

JOHNNY: They will not.

JOEY: They threw you outta college.

JOHNNY: Not the same.

JOEY: Threw ya outta the Little League, didn't they?

JOHNNY: Yeah.

JOEY: Kindergarten?

JOHNNY: Yeah.

JOEY: Hot lunch program?

JOHNNY: Yeah.

JOEY: High Schools?

JOHNNY: Yeah.

JOEY: Why'd you get thrown outta so many things?

JOHNNY: I don't remember.

JOEY: But you don't think you'll get thrown outta the Corps?

JOHNNY: No.

JOEY: Why not?

JOHNNY: I think I'm changing. I think I've changed.

JOEY: What about your mental health?

JOHNNY: My mental health is better.

JOEY: What was wrong with you anyway?

JOHNNY: I'd start to hear this rhythm, and then everything was in this rhythm.

JOEY: That doesn't sound so bad.

JOHNNY: Well, there was something really bad about it. But I can handle it now.

JOEY: Well, the Drill Instructor's waitin for you, man.

Source: *13 By Shanley*, Applause Theatre Books

✣ Boy's Life

• HOWARD KORDER

CHARACTERS: DON (20's), JACK (20's)
SETTING: DON's apartment, a large city, the present.

Like the scouting magazine of the same name, this play looks into the juvenile pursuits and hobbies of three yuppie college buddies. It is three A.M. and JACK and Phil are hanging out at DON's apartment. DON is sitting on his bed in his underwear, trying to stay awake. JACK has just lit a joint and is trying to keep the party going. Phil is asleep in a chair; his part may be eliminated for a two-man scene.

JACK: Anything on the tube?
DON: There's a guide thing under the clothes there.
JACK: You expect me to touch those?
DON: It's clean, I just haven't folded it yet. Hey, come on, don't start throwing everything around. It's not in the books —
JACK (*Picking up a paperback*): *Clans of the Alphane Moon.* Spaceships, how can you read this stuff?
DON: I like it.
JACK (*Reading off the back*): "A planet of madmen was the key to Earth's survival!"
DON (*Reaching for it*): Come on, Jack, put it down.
JACK (*Opening a page at random*): "His efforts to make a sensible equation out of the situation —"
DON: Jack come on —
JACK: " — out of the situation — "
DON: Jack —
JACK: " — the situation had borne fruit — "
DON: You're *bending* the *cover*!
(*Pause*)
JACK (*Dropping the book*): Nothing personal, Don, but you're one of the most anal slobs I know.
DON: Thank you.
JACK: I mean, it was fine when we lived like this in *college* . . . (*He finds the listings*) Here we are. Let's see, we got, hmm, "Famine '88" . . . "World at War" . . . whoa, tits and car crashes on HBO!
DON: I don't get cable.

JACK: *What*? Are you serious?

DON: I'm not paying to watch TV.

JACK: You gotta get cable, Don. You're showing your age around here.

DON: *Okay*, boss.

[PHIL (*In his sleep*):   It's like your tongue.

(*They both look at* PHIL. *He rolls over.*] *The alarm clock rings.* DON *shuts it off. Pause*)

DON: Time to get up.

JACK: Working the night shift?

DON: Guess I set it wrong.

JACK: Don, let me ask you a question.

DON: Uhm.

JACK: Every time I come here, you're always in your underwear.

DON: So?

JACK: Don't you own any pants?

DON: I like to be prepared.

JACK: For what?

DON: Going to sleep.

JACK: Are we hinting at something?

DON: Forget it.

JACK: Hey, if you want me to go don't just sit there in your shorts in*sin*uating. Just tell me. Look me in the eye and say, Listen here Jack, I'm sorry, it's late, I can *see* you've got *things* on your *mind* but I'd rather go to sleep than sit here in my ratty underwear listening to you. Be honest, Don. Don't get all *ironic* for fuck's sake. Keep me away from irony.

DON: Now listen here, Jack . . .

JACK: Yes?

DON: Have another beer. (*He hands* JACK *a beer*)

JACK: Thank you. (*He opens it but does not drink. Pause*)

DON: So what's on your mind?

JACK: Did I say something was on my mind?

DON: You hinted at it ironically.

JACK: Don, if you knew anything about me at all, you'd know this: Nothing ever bothers me.

DON: You're lucky that way.

JACK: Luck's got nothing to do with it. It's a matter of style. Image. You have a problem, just ask yourself one simple question: What would Ray Charles do in a situation like this? And Ray, I think, hipster that he is —

DON: What problem?

JACK: *The* problem, whatever problem you're *talking* about, I don't know. But Ray, Badass *Ray* —

DON: I don't know, is this my house?

JACK: Fucking myna bird in a sport coat here.

DON: What problems.

JACK: You heard the latest? This girl, he's been seeing her a week, every night he goes to her place, right, they talk about the whales or something, he gets to sleep on the couch. She says she's frigid. He says it doesn't matter. She says her uncle raped her when she was ten. He says I love you. She says maybe you shouldn't come by anymore. He says let's give it time. She says I'm screwing somebody else. He says it's all right, we can work around it. Isn't that so *typical*?

DON: Poor guy.

JACK: Calls me up, he says Jack, listen, I'm scared to be alone tonight —

DON: When?

JACK: This, tonight. What am I gonna do, say no? I mean, a friend's a friend. No matter how you look at it. (*Pause. Lowering his voice*) But I'll tell you something about Phil.

DON: Yeah.

JACK: He's a homo.

DON: What?

JACK: Gay as a coot.

DON: Are you kidding? He told you?

JACK: No he didn't *tell* me, he doesn't even know it.

DON: How do you know it?

JACK: Don, look at the women he goes out with. They eat Kal Kan for breakfast. And *they* all dump *him*. That's not normal.

DON: Is this for real?

JACK: Look at the facts.

(*Pause*)

DON: Well . . . so?

JACK: So?

DON: So he's, you know, so what?

(*Pause*)

JACK: Exactly, so what?

DON: I mean in this day and age . . .

JACK: At this point in time, yes, Don, I know what you're saying, you're right absolutely right. Absolutely.

DON: So what are we *arguing*?

JACK: We're not arguing, we're discussing.

DON: What are we discussing?

JACK: We're not discussing anything.

(*Pause*)

DON: Won't your wife be worried?

JACK: About what?

DON: Where you are.

JACK: Nah. Actually . . . actually she's out of town right now.

DON: Is she?

JACK: Her bank sent her out there, out to, ah, Ohio. Gonna finance another goddamn shopping mall.

DON: She must be doing pretty well, they trust her with that.

JACK: Somebody's gotta put bread on the table.

DON: You guys have a great arrangement.

JACK: I thank Jesus every day.

(*Pause*)

DON: So who's taking care of Jason?

JACK: Well, he's out there with her.

DON: Out there in Ohio.

JACK: It's the kind of place you want to see when you're young.

DON: Sure.

JACK: They'll be back pretty soon.

DON: Yeah.

(*Pause*)

JACK: How's your sex life, Don?

DON: Well, you know.

JACK: I don't know, that's why I'm asking.

DON: It's fine, I'm seeing this girl.

JACK: Well well.

DON: Yeah.

JACK: Well well *well*. What's she like?

DON: She's ah . . . she's sort of . . . I guess she's kind of serious. You know? Very . . . thoughtful. We talk a lot.

JACK: I bet.

DON: No, it's . . . she's always asking me questions. Why do I do this, do I say that . . . we talk about how we feel, about things, and . . . I'm learning to be responsible . . . and, ah . . .

JACK: Tits?

DON: They're okay.

JACK: Hmm. Well, I wish you luck.

(*Pause*)

DON: Actually she may be coming over a little later.

JACK: A *little* later? It's fucking three in the morning.

DON: She's a waitress over by the park, finishes at four.

JACK: Sounds pretty devoted.

DON: Well.

JACK: So why you been keeping her a secret?

DON: She's not a secret, she's . . . you know . . .

JACK: A waitress.

DON: She's really a sculptor.

JACK: Does she get paid for that?

DON: Not yet, no.

JACK: Is she in a *museum*?

DON: She just started . . .

JACK: So she's a dabbler, right? She's a waitress who dabbles, nothing to be ashamed of. Why don't you say that, does it embarrass you?

DON: No . . .

JACK: Really?

(*He rubs his face.* PHIL *mutters in his sleep*)

Hey, you wanna go bowling? That's right, you can't.

DON: What did you mean by that?

JACK: Bowling. Duck pins. Sport of Kings.

DON: About being a waitress.

JACK: Huh? I don't know, that's what she is, right? I didn't mean anything. You wanna go?

DON: It was insulting, Jack.

JACK: I didn't mean it to be.

DON: No, okay, you didn't, but it was. You do that all the time.

JACK: What's this about?

DON: Listen, you could be a little more considerate, all right?

JACK: What am I, your therapist?

DON: Jesus, you're doing it again!

JACK: What?

DON: You're insulting me!

JACK: Oh come on, don't be an asshole.

DON: *Stop* it!

JACK: I'm not doing anything, Don. Why are you getting so excited? Are you under orders? This is not like you. She's a waitress, she's a sculptress, fuck do I care I never even *met* her, tell me —

DON: I feel you really —

JACK: You *feel*, everybody *feels*, *fuck* that. What are you, are you a man? Can't you control yourself? You're *opening up*. You're being *sensitive*. That's a nice *trick*, Don. but don't let it go to your head or you'll wind up getting yanked around by the wiener. (*Pause*) As they say in the vernacular.

DON: I am not getting "yanked around."

JACK: I didn't say you were, I merely —

DON: Then take it back.

JACK: Okay, I hit a sore spot —

DON: Take it back.

JACK: Please, don't *be* this way —

DON: Take it back!

(*Pause*)

JACK: All right, Don. Shhh. All right. This is childish. Be cool. Be *cool*. It's me, remember? Not some lady you're trying to bring home. We *know* each other. We know what we really are. We're men, Don. We do terrible things. Let's admit we like them and start from there. You want to be a different person? Get a hug, all the bad thoughts disappear? I'm sorry, it won't *work* that way. It's not like changing your shirt, we can't *promise* to be better. That's a lie. What do you want, Don? Be honest. Do what you *want*. Please. I beg you. Because if you don't, what kind of ma . . . what are you gonna be then? (DON *says nothing*) I am your friend, Don. I care about you. I really do. Okay? (DON *says nothing*) So you wanna go bowling? Hey, I got some amyl, you wanna do amyl? Don?

DON: All my shoes . . . line 'em up . . .

JACK (*To* DON):   What you want, Don. Just think about it.

(*Pause*)

DON: Yeah.

JACK (*Poking Phil*):   Phil, wake up, we gotta go.

(*Phil rolls over.* JACK *looks at him*)

(*To* DON) Hey, you wanna see something? You'll get a kick out of this, it's up your alley. (*He hands* DON *a piece of notepaper with crayon marking on it*) Jason left that. Go ahead, read it aloud.

DON: "Dear Daddy, Mommy is taking me on jet. We are going to planet light blue. It has a river, and some caves called feeling caves, a waterfall, beds, and slides. There is a city there called 'girls are for you.' I know that is true. I love you but I think I am going to stay here." (*Pause*) Sounds better than Ohio.

JACK: Yeah right. (*Pause*) You know, I read that and I thought . . . what the fuck does this mean? Is he insane? What is going on inside this kid's head? I watch him, right, he's this tiny guy, really, his sneakers are like this big . . . but something's going on in there. Something's going on. (*Pause*) When he was born, did I tell you this? . . . He —

DON (*Handing back the note*):   She's an artist, Jack. Not a waitress. Understand?

(*Pause*)

JACK: Yes, Don. Of course. Thank you. I'm glad we could have this little moment together. Only listen, Don . . . (*Pause*) Don't forget who your friends are.

Source: Dramatists Play Service, Inc.

✥ Cat's-Paw

•••••••••••••••••••WILLIAM MASTROSIMONE

CHARACTERS: VICTOR (20's-30's), DARLING (40's-50's)
SETTING: *A warehouse in Washington, D.C., the present.*

DAVID DARLING, *an offical with the U.S. Government's Environmental Protection Agency, has been held hostage by a radical underground organization known as the People's Guard for thirty-five days. Since the organization's demands for cleaner water have not been met, a car packed with explosives has been detonated near the EPA building, killing twenty-seven people.* VICTOR *is the severe, fanatical head of the organization holding* DARLING *captive.*

> (*Lights up quickly.* VICTOR *is pouring water into a cup.* DARLING *is seated at the table in sweat-pants and a T-shirt.* DARLING's *hands are in his lap, unseen by the audience. He stares at an automatic pistol on the table. A door is ajar. Several televisions on different channels can be heard.* VICTOR *gets a jar of bouillon cubes, removes one*)

DARLING: Excuse me.
> (VICTOR *turns to* DARLING)
Is that beef?
> (VICTOR *shakes his head no*)
If it's all the same to you, might I have beef?
> (VICTOR *considers the question as if it were of profound philosophical moment, pauses, dismisses it, gets a beef cube*)
Thank you.
> (VICTOR *opens and drops the beef cube in the hot water*)
I'm really tired of chicken. Thank you.
> (VICTOR *puts a tray of food on the table.* DARLING *holds his hands up for* VICTOR *to unlock his handcuffs.* DARLING *eats heartily*)
That makes me very uncomfortable.

VICTOR: What does?
DARLING: Leaving that gun there.
VICTOR: Why?
DARLING: Are you testing me?
VICTOR: In what way?
DARLING: To see if I'll pick it up.
VICTOR: Did you want to?

DARLING: No.

VICTOR: Then what's the problem?

DARLING: I just wish you wouldn't . . . leave it . . . out in the open like that.

VICTOR: It tempts you?

DARLING: No . . . I don't know how . . . But I couldn't even if I did . . . Or is it not loaded?

VICTOR: See for yourself.

DARLING: I don't really want to.

VICTOR: Then why give it so much thought?

DARLING: I won't anymore.

VICTOR: Why didn't you shave today?

DARLING: I shaved.

VICTOR: You missed a lot.

DARLING: I'm sorry. It's hard without a mirror.

VICTOR: You'll have to finish eating now.

DARLING: Cathy and Martin usually give me vitamins, too.
(VICTOR *goes to get vitamins*)
And what about my cigarette?

VICTOR: You've had it already.

DARLING: When?

VICTOR: This morning.

DARLING: Did I?

VICTOR: After your first bathroom privilege.

DARLING: Wasn't that yesterday?

VICTOR: No.

DARLING: I'm sure it was.

VICTOR: You're wrong. Finish your broth.

DARLING: Might I have tomorrow's cigarette today?

VICTOR: I should think with the enormity of empty time at your disposal that you'd turn your mind away from these sick habits.

DARLING: It's tough after 25 years.

VICTOR: It's totally devoid of benefits, costs money, ruins health, jeopardizes thinking . . .

DARLING: It's one of the little indulgences I permit myself.

VICTOR: It's irrational behavior, given the knowledge we have . . . Yet you choose to ignore it . . . Don't you see how it carries over into other areas of mental life?

DARLING: I made a little side-deal with life . . . Let me have my little indulgence and I'll give a few useless years off the back end.

VICTOR: If you can't make your own decision, I'll make it for you. No.

DARLING: Does that mean I can't have tomorrow's cigarette today?
VICTOR: That's right.
DARLING: But I can have tomorrow's cigarette tomorrow?
VICTOR: When your pack runs out, that's it.
DARLING: If it's the expense you're concerned about —
VICTOR: The secondary smoke of a cigarette is ten times worse for me than the smoke you inhale. After this pack, no more.
DARLING: Alright. I don't know what the effects will be.
   (VICTOR *gives him a look*)
   But I'll handle it. (*Pause*) I hope. I'm a two packer. Forty a day. Down to one a day.
VICTOR: You tie up two of my people day and night.
DARLING: I read where it's easier to get off heroin than tobacco.
VICTOR: Go on. Fortify your irrationality.
DARLING: I'll manage. (*Pause*) Somehow.
VICTOR: Throw your clothes away. Everything.
DARLING: Alright.
VICTOR: Now would be a good time.
   (DARLING *begins to change*)
DARLING: Am I being released?
   (VICTOR *considers answering the question but doesn't*)
   May I ask what's happening? I haven't seen Cathy or Martin all day. (*Silence*) I don't suppose you'd let me watch the newscast?
VICTOR: No.
DARLING: Alright. I'd be willing to trade one of my bathroom privileges to see it.
VICTOR: You know you don't have that kind of self-control.
   (*Sound of a helicopter passing overhead*)
DARLING: Did something happen?
VICTOR: We have to move along.
DARLING: Hey, my pants are loose! Wait till my wife sees I lost my spare tire! I wish I knew what this was all about.
VICTOR: A reporter might be here.
DARLING: For what?
VICTOR: Interview.
DARLING: Interview me?
VICTOR: Yes.
DARLING: What about my shoes?
VICTOR: They'll shoot from the waist up.
DARLING: Oh, they're bringing cameras? Local or national? Did they give in to your demands? Whatever happens, I just want you to know I appreciate all the little things you've done for me.

The talk. The oranges. I know you must have a lot on your mind.

VICTOR: Shut up.

DARLING: Sorry.

VICTOR: Don't take advantage of my generosity.

DARLING: I'm sorry — I wasn't — that was not my intention.

(VICTOR *waves for him to stop apologizing*)

VICTOR: We have another matter. We're going to administer an injection of scopolamine.

DARLING: What's that?

(VICTOR *fills the syringe*)

VICTOR: A relaxant and truth drug. There are no outstanding effects other than a kind of comfortable tiredness like after a good workout, and for a little while you'll feel light-headed, like after one too many beers. It lasts for about three and a half hours and eventually brings on a deep sleep. (VICTOR *gives* DARLING *a handkerchief*) The only bad thing, it makes you sweat a lot.

DARLING: I don't have anything to hide.

VICTOR: Scopolamine makes you talk a lot, endlessly, but you won't be out of control. You'll just feel like talking, so don't blather and just answer the questions. Understand?

DARLING: Yes, yes, but I don't understand why I have to be under the influence of a drug that might be dangerous.

VICTOR: It's completely safe, Mr. Darling. Roll up your sleeve.

DARLING: If only I understood why.

VICTOR: I want the interview to be especially truthful.

DARLING: I don't know anything that isn't public knowledge.

VICTOR: Is that right?

DARLING: I really think you've got me mixed up with someone else.

VICTOR: Sit down. Please.

DARLING: I mean, my God, to put some foreign substance in my veins —

VICTOR: Did I ever break my word to you?

DARLING: No.

(VICTOR *dabs cotton to alcohol bottle, then to* DARLING's *arm*)

Oh boy oh boy. I haven't had a needle since I don't know when. And I didn't want that one either. Oh boy oh boy.

(VICTOR *injects* DARLING)

Oh boy oh boy oh boy.

VICTOR: Is it working yet?

DARLING: I don't feel any different.

VICTOR: It varies for different chemistries.

DARLING: What's the first thing you feel?
VICTOR: Your head feels clear . . . A sense of well-being . . .
DARLING: I feel it working now.
VICTOR: What's your social security number?
DARLING: 138 42 9834.
VICTOR: Your son Ricky's birthday?
DARLING: July —
VICTOR: July what?
DARLING: I don't even know it without a truth drug.
VICTOR: What does Crystal River mean to you?
DARLING: Crystal River? — Crystal River . . . I handled that project — why do you ask?
VICTOR: When?
DARLING: Oh . . . Years and years.
VICTOR: Don't fight the drug. You'll only hurt yourself.
DARLING: Must be ten years ago . . . I can really feel the effects now . . . What's the drug called?
VICTOR: Scopolamine. Souvenir. (VICTOR *hands* DARLING *the vial*)
DARLING: Why'd you ask me about Crystal River?
(Sound of an industrial bell of a garage door)
VICTOR: Up. In your space. Let's go. Move!
(DARLING *goes up the ladder to the foreman's box.* VICTOR *follows*)
DARLING: Interview's in my room?
VICTOR: No. Up, up.
DARLING: Down here?
VICTOR: Yes. C'mon.
DARLING: Then why am I going up?
VICTOR: Because I said so.
DARLING: I see. Do you suppose I could watch my interview when it's broadcast?
VICTOR: We'll see.
DARLING: Oh boy, that drug gives a pretty good kick.
VICTOR: Let's go.
DARLING: Bye.

Source: Samuel French, Inc.

✣ Chez Rikers

•••••••••••••••••••••••••••CHARLES LEIPART

CHARACTERS: SAM (60's), WAITER (Tom) (20's)
SETTING: A prison cell on Riker's Island, New York, the 1990's.

SAM, a banker, has been removed to a prison cell on Rikers Island, along with his wife and other prominent New Yorkers, after the city has fallen under siege by guerrillas. Thinking they are here for their own protection, they continue to enjoy the vestiges of gracious living supplied by their jailers. But their meal tonight is actually their last, as the Captain, head of the new order, is about to execute them in the morning. SAM's wife has just taken ill, rushes from the cell, leaving SAM alone with the waiter, TOM, a young, idealistic member of the new order. TOM has given SAM two Black Morphies to make the end painless, in exchange for SAM's Rolex watch.

WAITER: Shall I clear, sir?
SAM: I'm sorry — what?
WAITER: Your salad, sir.
SAM: Oh, yes, thank you.
  (WAITER clears SAM's salad to the side trolley)
  What do you want out of all this, Tom?
WAITER: All what, sir?
SAM: This — revolution.
WAITER (Scraping SAM's salad plate on to trolley): Well, sir, after I've served my time, I'd like to take up art.
SAM: Art. I thought about art once myself.
WAITER: Did you? When was that, sir?
SAM: Oh, many years ago. Before I met Mrs. Massey. Before I went into banking. Something I picked up in the service, during the war.
WAITER: Which war was that, sir?
SAM: The Korean.
WAITER: I don't think I know that one. Who won?
SAM: We did. I think. Thomas, please sit down.
WAITER: It's not customary, sir.
SAM: Please. For my sake.
WAITER: All right.
  (SAM helps the WAITER to his chair at table)

Thanks. It's good to take a load off.

SAM: Can I get you anything?

WAITER: No, sir. Resting the old dogs is enough.

SAM: Please.

WAITER: Well — I am a bit hungry. Do you mind, sir, if I finished the rest of your chipped beef?

SAM: Please. Let me serve you.

WAITER: Oh, no, sir, you don't have to serve me.

SAM: I want to. To see how it's done.

WAITER: It's on the second shelf of the trolley, sir. I put the lid on to keep it warm.

   (SAM *goes to trolley, bringing up covered dish*)

SAM: I've got it. Now what?

WAITER: Just bring it over here.

SAM: Right.

WAITER: And a plate.

SAM: Right. (SAM *brings plate and serving dish from trolley*) Like this?

WAITER: From the left, sir.

SAM: Pardon?

WAITER: Serve from the left, clear from the right —
   (SAM *crosses around to the* WAITER'*s left side*)

SAM: — Serve from the left, clear from the right. I see there's a system.

WAITER: Yes, sir.
   (SAM *places plate, serves up food*)
   Thank you.

SAM: Eat hearty, my lad.

WAITER: Don't talk, sir. It disturbs the guest.

SAM: Sorry.
   (*The* WAITER *eats,* SAM *stands over him, watching*)
   There is a certain satisfaction. A certain satisfaction in watching a good meal consumed.

WAITER (*Eating lustily*):   Oh, there is, sir. Half the pleasure is in the watching.

SAM: I can see that. A little gravy on your jacket, son. Allow me —
   (*He dabs at* WAITER'*s jacket with napkin. He pushes Meg's uneaten plate of salad to the* WAITER) You can have Meg's salad, she never touched it, and a bit of bread, son — (*Offering Meg's dinner roll*) — I recommend it for negotiating the gravy.

WAITER: You're hovering, sir.

SAM: Pardon?

WAITER: Hovering. Stand back a bit, sir.

SAM: Oh. Sorry. (*He steps back. Pause*) We appreciate this opportunity.

(WAITER *nods*)

We appreciate this opportunity to serve, Tom, while Mrs. Massey is out of the room. A bit of wine, son?

WAITER: I don't think I should, sir, being on duty —

SAM: We are your last couple tonight, aren't we?

WAITER: Yes, sir, I believe you are.

SAM: Then I don't think one glass would hurt. (SAM *pours wine into glass for* WAITER)

WAITER: Thank you.

SAM (*With a gesture*): To your health, Thomas.

(*Pause. The* WAITER *picks up the glass*)

WAITER: And to yours, sir. (*He drinks*)

SAM: Is there anything I can get you?

WAITER: Please sit down, Mr. Massey. You're making me nervous.

SAM: Sorry. (SAM *sits in Meg's chair, opposite*) It's just so damn good to be useful, son. (*Pause.* SAM *watches the* WAITER)

WAITER: What about your art, sir? You said you had one.

SAM: Yes, I did. A bit of art can be a great solace to the spirit. Especially at midnight, in a strange land, at 40 below, somewhere north of the 38th parallel. Nothing too unusual, actually. It was quite big then. Painting-by-Number.

WAITER: Painting-by-Number?

SAM: Yes. That's where the pattern of what you are to paint, the picture, is already printed on the canvas in very faint blue lines, with dozens and dozens, if not hundreds and hundreds, of little blue numbers inside of them. And you begin to paint. Filling in each little numbered space with the correspondently numbered pigment. It's quite systematic, actually. For an art. I did a very nice Spaniel, I recall, and then a Golden Retriever, 12 by 14, but my favorite was the Masterpiece Series, "Recreate the Experience of the Old Masters in Your Own Home", it said on the box. I did a rather nice BLUE BOY, that's Gainsborough, a very good MONA LISA, and a passable Van Gogh, something with sunflowers, I think — I used up two entire tubes of Cadmium Yellow #17 on that one. Oh, those sunflowers almost did me in. Sometimes I was tempted to cheat, and go outside the blue lines, but I restrained myself. I stuck with it. To the finish. (*Beat*) You need a great deal of patience to pursue Painting-by-Number. And a very steady hand. Not mine tonight. A young man's hand. I recommend it, Tom, because at the end of the road, when you've painted that last number 17, you have a very fine piece of art, your own Van Gogh, done in your own hand. No amount of money can buy that, son.

WAITER: I don't think I have the hands for it. I'd probably smear those paints all outside the lines.

SAM: Let me see.

WAITER: Oh, they're a couple of real meat-hooks, sir.

SAM: Let me be the judge of that. (*He takes the* WAITER'*s hand*) It's a fine hand, Tom. A strong, capable, artistic hand.

WAITER: You think so?

SAM: It reminds me of my grandfather's hand. Do you mind, son?

WAITER: Mind, sir?

SAM: If I hold it.

WAITER: Well, I —

SAM: Just for a moment.
      (*Pause. The* WAITER *gives* SAM *his hand*)
      Grandpa wanted me to go to work in the brickyard.

WAITER: The brickyard?

SAM: That's how he made his fortune. In bricks. Every Sunday he would take me by the hand and walk me over the railroad tracks to the old section of town, to his brickyard. "This is where we make the bricks, Sammy. This is the sand, and this is the clay, and those are the big black ovens where we bake 'em." And then, he would point with pride to stacks of newly-baked bricks, " — and there's the order for the new bread factory going up in colored-town. You and Grandpa make the bricks, the bricks that build the factories, that make the People's bread." (*Pause*) I failed him, Tom.

WAITER: Failed him, sir?

SAM: I went into banking. (*He releases the* WAITER'*s hand*) It was a great loss. A great loss to this nation, son. My Grandpa's capable hands. When I was home last — for his funeral — I got a bit hungry, so I decided to take a walk. Across the railroad tracks, into colored-town, looking for that bread factory. But it was gone. Someone had torn it down, and was putting up a hi-rise. "LUXURY 1 & 2 BEDROOM APTS, NOW RENTING."

WAITER: There were many abuses under the old system, sir. But the Captain promises plenty of bread for everyone.

SAM: Yes. We're all in the captain's capable hands.

WAITER: Yes, sir. (*Pause. The* WAITER *carefully lays his fork and knife across his plate*) I'm finished now, sir, thank you.

SAM: Pardon?

WAITER: You can clear now.

SAM: Oh. Yes. Very good. (SAM *gets up, starts to clear plate from left*)

WAITER: From the right, sir.

SAM: From the right. (*He clears away the* WAITER'*s plates to the service trolley*)

WAITER: Shall I proceed with dessert, sir?

SAM: Do we get dessert?

WAITER: Oh, yes. Mrs. Massey ordered Pedro's Jello Supremo.

SAM: Well, then. Bring it on.

(WAITER *starts out*)

Tom, one moment. I've been hoping to leave you — leave you with some bit of wisdom —

WAITER: Yes, sir?

SAM: But it seems to have gone clear out of my head.

WAITER: That's all right, sir. The Rolex is enough.

SAM: It's been a pleasure serving you.

WAITER: It's been a pleasure serving you. (*Beat*) Is — is there anything I can get you?

SAM: The Black Morphies are much appreciated — (SAM *brings out the two black capsules from his pocket, setting them on the table in front of him*)

WAITER: Shall I order the expressos?

SAM: No. Not just yet. Do you mind, son? Before Mrs. Massey returns, I'd like to be alone.

WAITER: Yes, sir. (WAITER *steps to cell door*)

SAM: Tom —

WAITER: Sir?

SAM: You don't think you could find me a brick, do you?

WAITER: A brick, sir?

SAM: It would be a great comfort. Thank you.

Source: Susan Schulman Literary Agency

✤ Club Hellfire

●●●●●●●●●●●●●●●●●●●●●●●●●●●●●●LEONARD MELFI

CHARACTERS: SLICE (20's), SILKY (20's)

SETTING: *A club in the Village for sex, drugs, music and anything else you can imagine, the present.*

Every matchup of the sexes can be found here, doing any and every sex act. SLICE *is a regular customer who dresses flashily. He gets his name because he's always eating pizza. He's got a wife named Sacrilege who's addicted to the Club.* SILKY *is the club bartender who likes to get into the action. He's also a thief. It's getting late in the night and depression is setting in.* SLICE *is eating a pizza.*

SILKY (*A pause*):   I love you, Slice.
SLICE: What brought that on?
SILKY: I don't know.
SLICE: Well, thanks anyway.
SILKY: Don't mention it.
SLICE: How are things inside?
SILKY: Shitty.
SLICE: What does that mean?
SILKY: I don't know.
SLICE: I never heard you talk that way before. Especially when it had to do with Club Hellfire.
SILKY: I'm beginning to think that Club Hellfire sucks.
SLICE: Aw, c'mon, c'mon!
SILKY: I don't know, I don't know . . .
SLICE: You better do something about it then.
SILKY: Like what, for instance?
SLICE: I don't know. I'm not sure.
SILKY   I'm mixed-up. I'm confused.
SLICE: It's your imagination.
SILKY: I'm not certain about that.
SLICE: What's bringing this on, all of a sudden, like this? It's not you, it's not like you.
SILKY: I know.
SLICE (*A pause*):   Have a slice of pizza. I've had enough.
SILKY: I don't feel like eating right now.
SLICE: You'd better go to a shrink an the morning.

(SILKY *looks at his wrist-watch*)

SILKY: It's gonna be daylight before we know it. (*A pause*) I came out there twice tonight . . . I shot my wad twice out there tonight, with people gathered around me, watching me, looking at me, when I did it: when I splashed all over the place.

SLICE: So?

SILKY: I'm tired of it.

SLICE: You're too young to be tired of it.

SILKY: I don't know about that. (SILKY *takes out a little pile of jewelry objects*) Look, Slice.

SLICE: More stuff?!

SILKY: Yep !

SLICE: I don't know how you do it.

SILKY: A gift from God that I was born with. I'm lucky.

SLICE: You better believe it.

SILKY (*A pause*): I love you, Slice.

SLICE: What the fuck is going on?!

SILKY: I said I love you, Slice.

SLICE: You told it to me already once before.

SILKY: Well, I'm telling you again, okay?

SLICE: But why? I think you're fucking bananas all of a sudden, that's what I think, Silky!

SILKY: No, no . . .

SLICE: Yes, yes!

SILKY: No, not at all. Something just simply happened to me out there tonight. A miracle of the mind, or something. My mind. Something took place out there with all of them: like my mind was suddenly hit by a flash of lightning, but not dangerous, deadly lightning! No, not at all! But a fast flash of warm, gentle, *telling* lightning, *telling* me to *tell* myself, and then to pass it on, to pass it on to a friend, to *tell* a friend, and that friend is you, Slice, it's you, man!

SLICE: When did this happen to you?! When did this lightning come down on you and then strike you?!

SILKY: I just told you. It happened all of a sudden out there, just like that! Just a few minutes ago. Not more than five minutes ago.

SLICE: What were you doing right before it happened?

SILKY: What's that got to do with it?

SLICE: I need to know, I need to know! I need to know everything! I believe you, Silky, but I need to know everything, so that way I'll believe even more than I do right now, okay, Silky, okay, please, buddy?!

SILKY: Right before it happened? Right before this miracle of agreeable lightning happened to me, I shot my wad for the second time out there tonight . . .

SLICE: Yes, yes, go on, go on, Silky!

SILKY: I shot my wad for the second time. I was fucking Hooker between her tits. About twenty people gathered around us, looking, watching, cheering us both on like a bunch of crazy *inhuman* human beings! I splashed all over Hooker, and she just simply went nuts with sheer ecstacy, just the way I was going nuts with sheer ecstacy, too. The applause was the best. The tops. I felt like I was acting in a play. Hooker felt that way, too. She told me she did, after I told her how I felt, when we were in the bathroom together, wiping each other off . . . it was like Heaven . . . the whole act . . . and then came the flashing, flickering lightning, which nobody saw but me . . . and . . . as you can see, Slice . . . I haven't been the same since. (*A pause*) This might be my last night here, Slice.

SLICE: What?

SILKY: I think I'll be quitting here after tonight.

SLICE: Aw, you can't do that to me, Silky!

SILKY: You can do the same thing, if you want to, Slice.

SLICE: But I can't! There's my wife! Sacrilege! She's here! I love her! I can't quit!

SILKY: Get her to quit with you.

SLICE: It's not that easy.

SILKY: Try it anyway, and see.

SLICE: I don't know. I just don't know anymore.

SILKY: You're the boss now: the boss of your own mind, remember that, Slice.

SLICE: I just can't get rid of that image . . .

SILKY: What image are you talking about? You mean the lightning striking?

SLICE: Hooker's got a great pair of tits . . .

SILKY: What are you talking about?

SLICE: I've always loved her tits . . .

SILKY: What about the lightning striking me?!

SLICE: I've always wanted to fuck her between her tits, just the way you just did tonight, Silky . . .

SILKY: It's all over with now.

SLICE: That's the image I can't get rid of right now: the two of you, Hooker and you, and with an audience besides! You're a very lucky guy, Silky.

SILKY: I'm lucky because of the miracle of the lightning striking me. Not because of Hooker and me, and her tits and my cock.

Source: Glenn Young c/o Applause Theater Books

✦ Cuba and His Teddy Bear

•••••••••••••••••••••••••••REINALDO POVOD

CHARACTERS: TEDDY *(15-17)*, CHE *(30's)*
SETTING: *An apartment in New York City, the present.*

TEDDY *is a bright teenager, with ambitions to write, and to get closer to his drug-dealer father, Cuba, who doesn't know his son is a drug addict.* TEDDY *has introduced his father to* CHE, *a drug dealer who won a Tony Award for Playwriting (modeled after Miguel Pinero, author of* Short Eyes*). Cuba has taken an instant dislike to* CHE *and his cohort Dealer. He has refused to consummate a drug deal with them. Now, Dealer has announced he's going to rip off Cuba's drugs. He has just left.*

TEDDY: You picked him over me? *(Stunned. Jealous. Hurt)* You love him?
CHE: I didn't say that.
TEDDY *(Excited):* I saw it!
CHE: I gave him a rap about your father. You saw what happened, your father fucked up. He was gonna take the pot, blow your father away. I talked him outta that . . . Life is a game of cards to him.
TEDDY: What about you?
CHE: I saved your father's life.
TEDDY *(Sarcastic):* You love him . . . You brought him here.
CHE: Yeah, I brought him here in good faith.
TEDDY: Would you hang out and tell my father that when he asks me what happened to the two pounds?
CHE: You tell him what you want, but I saved his life.
TEDDY: What are you getting for robbing me?
CHE: He wants to give me a couple of ounces, that's the way he is.
TEDDY: But you're accepting it — it's your way. Where's the money *(Excited)* Where's my father's money?!
CHE: Would you have given it to me if I woulda asked you?
TEDDY: No.
CHE: Okay.
TEDDY: 'Cause it's not mine to give.
CHE: That's why I'm accepting only what belongs to me. From his point of view.

TEDDY: Nothing belongs to you.

CHE: That's the way it is. Your father knows how it is.

TEDDY: You're an animal.

CHE: I am an animal.

TEDDY: 'Cause you wanna be.

CHE: 'Cause I have to be.

TEDDY: But I'm your friend.

CHE: So you'll understand.

TEDDY: What about me?

CHE: You're still in one piece.

TEDDY: I'm not in one piece.

CHE: Winter is coming, you want me to sleep in the park, to freeze to death?

TEDDY: What are you talking about?

CHE: You would do it to me if you found yerself sleepin' on the streets.

TEDDY: What about this movie?

CHE: I'm only going up for it. I haven't been okayed for the part.

TEDDY: And if you get the part?

CHE: I get the part, yer father and his partner gets their money.

TEDDY: No, they won't.

CHE: Why?

TEDDY: 'Cause you have no intention to.

CHE: Why?

TEDDY: You don't wanna pay 'em.

CHE: I'll pay them.

TEDDY: No you won't.

CHE: I'll pay 'em.

TEDDY: You won't.

CHE: I won't.

TEDDY: Why?

CHE: I don't wanna pay them.

TEDDY: Why?

CHE: Fuck 'em. — That's the way it is in drugs. I get a bag of rat poison, I shoot it up, somebody says, fuck 'im. Your father rips off another dealer, he says, fuck 'im. I'm sure he's done it. 'Cause that's the way it is in drugs.

TEDDY: Fuck me too, right?

CHE: That's the way it is, yeah.

TEDDY: I don't want a friend who robs me.

CHE: When it comes to drugs —

TEDDY: Our relationship is not about drugs.

CHE: It's not about you and me.

TEDDY: It is about you and me.

CHE: It's only about you baby — you alone.

TEDDY: Where are you?

CHE: I'm in the gutter. Nine years old. No shoes on my feet. I got 'em in the sewer water. My arm is up like this — (*Raises his arm straight about his head*) I'm holding a mango. I'm making believe the bottle cap I'm playing with in the sewer is really a sailboat. I'm playing — living just to play in the street. Hmmmm. I smell fried pork chops. Hmmm. Fried green bananas. I'm playing, playing in the street. Loving it, until this little girl comes behind me and snatches the mango outta my hand. Now, I don't wanna play in the street no more. (*He lowers his arm*)

TEDDY (*After a long pause*):   You robbed me. You fucken robbed me, Che. I never knew you were like this.

CHE: . . . I always wanted to be a junkie. I always wanted to, you know, tread — on blood.

TEDDY: Ah-hah-hah-hah.

CHE: Yeah, to step in it when I saw it on the sidewalk . . . or on the stairs in my building, in my hallway. Man, I'd see it, I couldn't take my eyes offa it. I could hear nothing but the blood throbbing in my ears, and I'd stand, you know, still, lissening to it.

TEDDY: Ah-hah-hah-hah.

CHE: Shut up, man.

TEDDY: I know yer not serious —

CHE: Do you hear?

TEDDY: What, the blood throbbing in your ears?

CHE: I ain't playing with you. I'm tellin' you what I use to say . . . what beast died today?

TEDDY: Yeah.

CHE: What beast died today?

TEDDY: And . . . it was the blood of the beast, and not the blood of a human being?

CHE: You know how I could tell? When I'd see the blood, like say, I'd see it on the stairs in my building, I'd touch it, yeah. I'd stick my finger in it — look at it — and I could tell it was a beast who just died, by rubbing my fingers, like this . . . The blood would be weak, it would disappear like water. And I knew, a junkie died somewhere. A junkie's blood ain't thick, it ain't healthy, like a red-blooded American.

TEDDY: And that's what you wanted to be, a sick junkie?

CHE: The Beast. Alone . . . with my own pitch-black sky, my own black reflection, my own withered flowers growing outta the darkness. I don't gotta share it with nobody — nobody wants it. The Beast.

TEDDY: What is this? Is this outta one of your plays?

CHE (*Angry*):   This is me, man, this is me!

TEDDY: I don't like it.

CHE: Yer weak. I don't need bread and water, a roof on my head. I can live, man, though winter nights. I don't need to know where the fuck I'm going, why the fuck I'm going? Nobody fucks me, 'cause I'm awready dead to them. Yeah, I like that. Being dead. I ain't there, I ain't here.

TEDDY: A junkie.

CHE: The Beast!

TEDDY: Yeah.

CHE: Yeah.

TEDDY: I'm scared. (CHE *smiles broadly*) I'm scared of you.

CHE: Ah-hah-hah-hah.

TEDDY: I'm scared of my father. (CHE *strikes his Pachuco pose, swinging his keychain in a circle*) I'm scared of myself.

CHE: Ah-hah-hah-hah.

TEDDY: I'm scared of people, period.

CHE: I was only teasing you, man.

TEDDY: I am.

CHE: It was all a joke.

TEDDY: But I am, Che.

CHE: Yeah.

TEDDY: I don't want to be.

CHE: Yeah.

TEDDY: I won't be.

CHE: You should be. We were all pushed outta the womb. Nobody crawled out on his own. People are fucken scary.

TEDDY: I tried hitting myself yesterday. I can't do it to myself.

CHE: You wanna be a junkie learn how to hit yerself, become a pincushion.

TEDDY: It hurts, I don't like pain. When you do it for me I never feel the spike going in.

CHE: You want me to show you how to do it, you don't feel the spike going in?

TEDDY: No, I don't wanna learn. Just do it for me. I got three fucking bags. (*He inserts his hand into his pocket, withdraws it. He shows* CHE *he is holding three bags of heroin*)

CHE: Whachu gonna do with that?

TEDDY: I wanna do it.

CHE: Why don't you let me do it?

TEDDY: Some, yeah. You fix the shot and hit me, I'll give you some.

CHE: No, I do it all for myself.

TEDDY: No.

CHE: You can't do it.

TEDDY: I know, but you can do it for me.

CHE: I'm not gonna hit you.

TEDDY: You can do most of it. I jus' wanna little.

CHE: I'll hook it up for you — if you do all three bags.

TEDDY: No, I'll OD.

CHE (*Starts for the door*):   I'm going.

TEDDY: Okay, I'll do all three bags. Lemme get my set of works.
(CHE *doesn't move. He watches* TEDDY *run into his room, lift his mattress and return with the brown paper bag.* TEDDY *drops the contents of the bag onto the coffee table. He goes quickly to the kitchen and returns with a cup of water. He sits on the sofa. He opens one bag of heroin and proceeds to tap out the contents into the bottle cap. He goes to open another bag*)

CHE: Jus' do one bag. Hold on to the other two.

TEDDY (*Puts the two bags of heroin in his pocket*):   This is where I need your help, I dunno how much water to put in. (*He takes the hypodermic and withdraws from the cap*)

CHE: You need brown water.

TEDDY (*Shows* CHE *the hypodermic*):   This much water?

CHE: Brown, like the sewer water in me.

TEDDY: This okay?

CHE: A little more . . .

TEDDY (*Withdraws a little more water from the cup, shows* CHE *the hypodermic again*):   Awright?

CHE (*Nods yes*):   Show the children, I would show the children. Cook it up.

TEDDY (*Squirts the solution into the bottle cap. He lights a match and proceeds to heat the bottle cap*):   Tell me when?

CHE: When. That's enough.

TEDDY (*Blows out the match. Withdraws the solution, screws the needle onto the syringe*):   Here, hit me.
(CHE *takes the hypodermic from* TEDDY. TEDDY *rolls up his sleeve.* CHE *makes a fist and it appears he is going to insert the needle into one of the veins of his own hand*)

CHE: How do you get in touch with somebody's wound?

TEDDY: What are you doing, Che?

CHE: How, huh, without contaminating yerself?

TEDDY: That's for me.

CHE (*Stares down at his fist, searching for a vein*):   How do you get in touch with somebody's wound?
(*As* TEDDY *reaches for the hypodermic, he dramatically pulls back*)
Don't touch the wound.

TEDDY: Stoppit, Che. C'mon.

CHE: How do you get in touch with somebody's wound? Don't touch the wound. But Lazarus had dogs to lick his wounds . . . Commere. Hold yer arm, lemme lick yer wounds.
(TEDDY *holds his bicep, tightly*)
Pump yer hand . . . You'll be like me.

TEDDY: I don't like disliking myself.

CHE: Do something about it.

TEDDY: I am. Why don't you do something about it?!

CHE: I awready have. I'm a junkie. The junkie Christ.
(*He inserts the needle into* TEDDY's *arm.* TEDDY *moans*)
Sometimes little lambs gotta be sacrificed, so God can be revealed.

TEDDY: You robbed me, Che.
(CHE *pulls out the needle. He stares down at* TEDDY *with mingled worry and irritated disapproval.* TEDDY *leans back, nods out.* CHE *takes the brown paper bag from the table and proceeds to put in it the hypodermic, bottle cap, matches and the torn cellophane paper which contained the heroin. He moves through* TEDDY's *room, heading for the bathroom. He returns, sits on the sofa beside* TEDDY. *He inserts his hand underneath* TEDDY's *shirt, rub's* TEDDY's *chest*)

CHE: It feels good . . .

TEDDY: Mmmmm.
(*Silence as* CHE *continues to rub* TEDDY's *chest*)

CHE: I robbed you?

TEDDY: Mmmmm.

CHE: I robbed what? I'm too fucken worthy to rob. Now I lay me down to sleep. I pray the Lord, something, something. God bless, Mommie, God bless, Daddy. If I should die before I wake, — I'm goin' in ya pocket. (*Stops rubbing* TEDDY's *chest and inserts his hand into* TEDDY's *side pocket*) I'm in ya pocket. That's my hand. My fingers.

TEDDY: Mmmmm.

CHE: I'm taking the two bags of dope . . . I'm taking my hand out. In the name of the father, and of the son, and of the Holy Spirit,

Amen . . . Tell yer father I took his pot. (CHE *stands*) He knows how it is. He'll understand.

TEDDY: No, I understand.

(CHE *takes* TEDDY's *hand and smothers it with kisses. He turns and quickly heads for the door*)

I don't wanna see you again, Che.

CHE: No, you shouldn't (*He opens the door*) Bye, bye, Teddy Bear.

Source: Samuel French, Inc.

✥ The Day The Bronx Died

●●●●●●●●●●●●●●●●●●●●●●●●●●MICHAEL HENRY BROWN

CHARACTERS: YOUNG MICKEY (*Black, 14*), ALEXANDER (*Black, 14*)
SETTING: *City street, 1963.*

YOUNG MICKEY *and* ALEXANDER *are black teenagers in the Bronx of 1963.*
They belong to a gang called the Gladiators, whose enemy are the Eagles.
Here, they banter but talk seriously, too, about what's important to them.
YOUNG MICKEY *has a Jewish friend, Billy, and studies piano with a black*
friend, named Daniel.

>   (ALEXANDER's *Tarzan call is heard. Then he's seen swinging across on*
>   *a rope. He lands.* YOUNG MICKEY *goes to the woods where* ALEXANDER
>   *stands*)

ALEXANDER: We gonna war!
YOUNG MICKEY: With who?
ALEXANDER: If you had been at the war party, instead of with those
white boys . . .
YOUNG MICKEY: We had practice.
ALEXANDER: So did we. Are you a Gladiator or what?
YOUNG MICKEY: We're getting too old for this.
ALEXANDER: War is for men.
YOUNG MICKEY: You're fourteen.
ALEXANDER: You gonna war or are you turnin' into a faggot?
YOUNG MICKEY: I ain't no faggot!
ALEXANDER: Is that it? Is that what it is? You got sugar behind your
ears?
YOUNG MICKEY: I ain't no faggot.
ALEXANDER: Mickey is a sweet boy . . . Mickey is a sweet boy.
YOUNG MICKEY: I'm warning you.
ALEXANDER: You got some nuts . . . then you can warn . . . but
you're a sweet boy.
YOUNG MICKEY: Alexander, shut up!
ALEXANDER: I see you going to that faggot's house . . . I see you
going to Daniel's house.
YOUNG MICKEY: He's teaching me piano . . .
ALEXANDER: He's teachin' you how to take it up the booty.
>   (YOUNG MICKEY *takes a step forward*)

ALEXANDER: The li'l sissy is going to try something that even the Prince won't do . . .

YOUNG MICKEY: I'm gonna kick your ass.

ALEXANDER: You're gonna kiss my ass? I knew you were a faggot.
(MICKEY *rushes* ALEXANDER. ALEXANDER *catches* MICKEY *and gives him an expert Judo flip.* MICKEY *gets up and goes after* ALEXANDER *again. This time* ALEXANDER *twists him around and wraps his arm around* MICKEY's *neck.* ALEXANDER *is laughing all through this*)

YOUNG MICKEY: I'm not gonna say uncle . . . I'm not gonna . . .

ALEXANDER: Okay, okay . . . you've got nuts, Mickey.

YOUNG MICKEY (*Still struggling*): That's right, I got big nuts.

ALEXANDER: So don't waste 'em on a fellow Gladiator, save 'em for the Eagles.
(*Pause.* MICKEY *relaxes*)
Hangin' with that Jew-boy hasn't turned you into a chump yet.
(ALEXANDER *lets him go*)

YOUNG MICKEY: He's a good guy.

ALEXANDER: Nah, they're all the same. His old man is just like the Jew my Pops works for . . . They got all the money you know?

YOUNG MICKEY: Who says?

ALEXANDER: My Pops. Rebekoff's filthy rich. You know why he's rich?

YOUNG MICKEY: 'Cause he works hard?

ALEXANDER: Works hard? Are you kiddin' me? My Pops, he works hard supervisin' . . . makin' sure Rebekoff's trucks are loaded. Rebekoff don't do nothin'.

YOUNG MICKEY: He had to do somethin', how else could he get rich?

ALEXANDER: Tha's what I'm tryin' to tell ya. He's rich 'cause he's cheap. They're all cheap. My Moms says they're like squirrels . . . they store away every penny like a squirrel do nuts. It's all a plot man. That's why they don't believe in Christmas . . . so they don't have to buy presents.

YOUNG MICKEY: Get outta here.

ALEXANDER: Square bizness. My Pops says they're real slick because they own all the stores where everybody else shops for Christmas. You know . . . Abraham & Strauss, Klein's, Alexander's, Macy's, man, they're all Jews. Even E.J. Korvettes . . .

YOUNG MICKEY: Korvettes ain't no Jewish name.

ALEXANDER: See, that's how slick they are. My Pops says it's a code.

E.J. Korvettes really stands for Eight Jewish Korean Veterans.

YOUNG MICKEY: How does your Pops know that?

ALEXANDER: He works for a Jew . . . he knows . . .

YOUNG MICKEY: Yeah, well . . . all I know is Billy ain't rich . . .

ALEXANDER: You don't wanna believe me? Fine. We need to talk about the Eagles.

YOUNG MICKEY: There ain't gonna be no rules with those guys. Those project guys really want to hurt us. How we gonna fight 'em?

ALEXANDER: Hand to hand.

YOUNG MICKEY: Whoa!

ALEXANDER: Our Karate and Judo against their boxing.

YOUNG MICKEY: But you're the only Gladiator who really knows martial arts.

ALEXANDER: They don't know that.

YOUNG MICKEY: Yeah, but I'll let you in on a secret . . . don't ask me how . . . but even though they're from the projects, I think they'll figure it out. Those guys get up in the morning fighting.

ALEXANDER: I've been teaching you guys, and we've got time to train.

YOUNG MICKEY: Whew! Good . . . geez, now that makes sense . . .

ALEXANDER: We've got 'til Saturday.

(*Pause*)

YOUNG MICKEY: Saturday . . . as in the day after tomorrow?

ALEXANDER: Well it ain't Saturday next week.

YOUNG MICKEY: Why couldn't it be Saturday next week?

ALEXANDER: Don't go getting faggoty on me again . . .

YOUNG MICKEY: Look Alexander, my Mother's paying an awful lot for these piano lessons . . . and she wouldn't want me to go and break my fingers.

ALEXANDER: She wouldn't want me to break your nappy head either.

YOUNG MICKEY: Alex . . .

ALEXANDER: Weez bloodbrothers since we wuz l'il guys . . . I know we're gettin' older now . . . but my blood is still your blood and your blood is still mine . . . These here Eagles have been snatchin' pocketbooks . . . You know how I hate those project kids . . .

YOUNG MICKEY: I don't hate project kids . . . they're just like us.

ALEXANDER: They ain't just like us . . . They eat welfare peanut butter which they also use for glue. If I lived in the projects, man,

I don't even want to think about it! And stealin' from ladies who live in private houses. They don't give a shit what color you are. This is our honor. We've got to teach those bums. Your mother could be next. (*Pause*) So . . . you a Gladiator . . . or you gonna play Jew-ball with that Jew-boy?

YOUNG MICKEY: Billy's cool.

ALEXANDER: He ain't a Gladiator, he ain't cool. We ain't prejudice, he can join if he can take the initiation.

YOUNG MICKEY: Alex, it's getting late . . .

ALEXANDER: It ain't late . . .

YOUNG MICKEY: I got piano practice. (YOUNG MICKEY *starts to leave*)

ALEXANDER: Don't forget the vaseline.

(ALEXANDER *laughs*. MICKEY *gives him the finger*)

ALEXANDER: You down, huh?

(*Long Pause*)

YOUNG MICKEY: You're my bloodbrother, ain't cha?

Source: Applause Theatre Books

✤ Death in the Pot

•••••••••••••••••••••••MANUEL VAN LOGGEM

CHARACTERS: EWALD (40's), ALBERT (30's)
SETTING: EWALD HAREWOOD's *study, the present.*

EWALD HAREWOOD, *a mild-mannered professor of Mycology (the study of mushrooms), and his wife, Jeanne, live in quiet disharmony. Jeanne is having a non-too-secret affair with* ALBERT, *a handsome young guest in the house.* ALBERT *and Jeanne have begun a plot to murder* EWALD *with his own poison mushrooms in order to collect the insurance money. In this scene,* ALBERT, *a known blackmailer, continues to extort money from the seemingly hapless* EWALD, *all the while playing right into* EWALD's *hands for a later double-cross scheme.*

ALBERT: Ten minutes should be enough.
EWALD: What do you want?
ALBERT: I need money.
EWALD: What? I paid you only yesterday.
ALBERT: Yes, I know but some unexpected debt popped up. Rather urgent I must say. You know how it is, you think you've still got something left, and then it appears that the old wallet is empty. Then you remember that you still have a very good friend who was always willing to help you when you were in need. What does Albert think then? Albert thinks: I'll pay a visit to that dear friend.
   (*Silence*)
EWALD (*With restraint*):   How much?
ALBERT: Oh, I think five hundred would go quite a long way.
EWALD: What?
ALBERT: Was my pronunciation not clear enough? That's because of the wine. Wine blurs the words. But I'm quite willing to repeat it. Five hundred pounds. Five — hundred — pounds — sterling.
EWALD: Impossible.
ALBERT: What a pity. What an awful pity.
EWALD: I gave you two hundred yesterday. You know I'm not rich. I had to borrow it. And you promised it would be the last payment. Now five hundred again. Impossible.
ALBERT: Yet you have to cough it up.

EWALD: How?

ALBERT: That's your problem. Not mine.

EWALD: And yesterday you promised it would be the last time.

ALBERT: Did I really say that?

EWALD (*Tiredly*): Yes.

ALBERT: You must've made a mistake.

EWALD: No, I didn't.

ALBERT: You move me. You're one of those people whom people like me always dream of meeting. One of those soft, simple, unimpeachable human beings who have only once made a misstep. People like you think that words mean what they mean. If I wasn't so hard pressed I'd let you keep the money. I would just make you a present of it.

EWALD: My God. No! I won't give it to you.

ALBERT: Oh, how annoying that would be.

EWALD (*Enraged*): I could kill you.

ALBERT: Who could've thought that so much blood-lust could exist in such a soft man?

EWALD: If he is sufficiently provoked. (*Breathes deeply*) I've made up my mind.

ALBERT: You're a brave fellow.

EWALD: I can't go on like this.

ALBERT: You know what I have in my possession.

EWALD: Yes.

ALBERT: By the way, I've never understood why you left the proof of your mis-step . . . for in my opinion it's only a little mis-step . . . just like that in your desk drawers, where anyone the least bit curious could find it.

EWALD: I could never imagine that a man who came into my house as a friend would search my desk.

ALBERT: Let this be a good lesson to you. Don't trust anybody. Ever. No man is to be trusted. That's what I learned early in my life, and it has done me a lot of good. Of course, you've had bad luck. You couldn't have known that it's my job to rummage in the desks of people who have learned to trust me. I'm a nice guy and people trust me rather quickly. Only after a while do they find out that it costs them money. I make a living from the confidence of my fellow men. (*Threateningly*) And if you don't pay, Ewald, the world will know that your work on the Harabolet, which is so highly praised in scientific circles, was stolen from you late colleague Derksen, and that I have in my possession the original manuscript as a proof of your plagiarism. No, Ewald, that was not nice, to publish another man's scientific study under your own name. It's simply stealing!

EWALD: Stop it.

ALBERT: In God's name how did you ever get the silly idea? I don't understand that. I'm quite a good judge of character and I have always seen you as an honest, simple mushroom freak. And then such a thing pops up. Really, Ewald, you ought to be ashamed.

EWALD (*More to himself than to* ALBERT):   For years I had been working on the subject. I had discovered the development and metamorphosis of the Harabolet. It had always been one of the secrets of mycology. And then I found that Derksen was working along the same lines. He had made even more progress than I. It was a horrible shock. I was already sure to be old Melcher's successor. He had the chair and would retire soon. Derksen let me read his manuscript. I knew that all my work had become useless. Then he died unexpectedly. He had a weak heart. Everybody knew that. He lived in retirement. Only his old housekeeper took care of him. Nobody knew about the manuscript. Till this day I don't understand why I did it, but when things had gone so far I couldn't go back. I've been an awful coward, but I had the justification that I had discovered on my own strength what Derksen had found, too, though I must admit he had advanced further. When he died I somehow had the feeling that I had made his investigations myself. Of course, I should have made a confession at that time, but I lacked the courage. (*Silence*) I will have to retire.

ALBERT: That's rather hasty, isn't it? We can talk about it. I've asked five hundred.

EWALD: I don't have it.

ALBERT: Ah, ah, never tell lies, Ewald. Honesty is the best policy. You should know that by now. You have four hundred in your moneybox. The last installment on your mortgage.

EWALD (*Bitter*):   Why didn't you pinch the money?

ALBERT (*Indignantly*):   I'm no petty thief.

EWALD: It's all I have.

ALBERT: All right. Then you'll get your manuscript for four hundred. I'm not as hard as I look.

EWALD: I don't trust you.

ALBERT: Nice people don't say those things.

EWALD: I know your kind. What assurance can you give me that you won't plague me again?

ALBERT: I'll give you your manuscript.

EWALD: You could've made God knows how many copies.

ALBERT: My word of honor. (*Silence*) And if that doesn't suit you, you can have it as you want. If I don't get that four hundred I'll have you in the pillory tomorrow.

EWALD: This *must* be the last time.

ALBERT: That's a promise.

EWALD: You said that yesterday, too.

ALBERT: But now you have my word of honor. And the manuscript.

EWALD (*Taking the money from the box*):   Here's the money. Where's the manuscript?

ALBERT: Here it is. (*They exchange. He counts the money, superfluously*) In small bills. Just as I like it. I don't even count them. That proves how I trust you.

EWALD: If you bother me again . . . or if it comes out that you have had a copy made . . .

ALBERT: Then what?

EWALD: Then that will be the end. Listen carefully. (*In deep earnest*) I mean it. This must be the last time. Either I'll resign as Professor . . .

ALBERT: Nobody will be the better for that.

EWALD: Or I'll kill you.

(*Long silence*)

ALBERT: I like you, Ewald, really, and that's why I promise you that this is the last time. Really.

(EWALD *goes to the bookcase and gets the bottle of whisky and a glass from behind the books. He fills it and takes a gulp*)

EWALD: I hope you realize how sincerely I meant that.

ALBERT: That's all right. But wouldn't it be polite to offer a touch of the stuff to an old friend? After all we've just done a bit of business.

(EWALD *looks at him, astonished, then shrugs his shoulders. He goes to his cooking corner, takes a glass which he first carefully wipes, and then puts it on a tray. He fills this glass with whisky and offers it, still on the tray, to* ALBERT)

ALBERT (*Drinking*):   Your health.

Source: Broadway Play Publishing, Inc.

✤ Digby

•••••••••••••••••••••••••JOSEPH DOUGHERTY

CHARACTERS: DIGBY (30's), HARRY (30's)
SETTING: DIGBY's office, New York City, the present.

DIGBY *is an intelligent, soft-spoken guy who works as a copywriter for an advertising firm. He is an avid Mets fan. He is also disgusted with everyone's preoccupation with sex. When he meets Faye, a gorgeous woman who already has a string of boyfriends, he merely want a platonic relationship with her. HARRY, DIGBY's aggressive, woman-chasing pal and co-worker, tried to help DIGBY with his "problem".*

> (*Lights come up on* DIGBY's *office, or rather* DIGBY's *cubicle; a boxy little compartment defined by five-and-a-half foot tall partitions. There's a desk with the usual equipment including telephone and water pitcher; a file cabinet and a coat hook or hall tree from which hang* DIGBY's *Mets jacket and cap. There are a sleeping bag and a knapsack on the floor below the jacket and cap. We hear the radio play-by-play of a ballgame through a radio on* DIGBY's *desk. There's a Dwight Gooden poster on the back partition.*
>
> DIGBY *is there, in jeans. He is typing, grim face, as he listens to the game out of the corner of his ear.* DIGBY *finishes his typing and pulls the sheet from the machine. It's a multi-carbon affair which he separates and takes to the file cabinet to file. The progress of the game is making him very nervous*)

RADIO ANNOUNCER: Mets down to their last out this afternoon. Gary Carter on second with the tying run, young Darryl Strawberry the potential winning run on first. One ball, two strikes to George Foster. If Davey Johnson's Mets can stay alive to win this one, they'll be a half-game behind first place St. Louis when the Cards meet the Expos tonight. Here's the pitch. A little wide. Two balls and two strikes. Fred Toliver coming on in relief for the Phillies this afternoon has walked one and given up a single to Strawberry. Up high, ball three. Full count on Foster.

> (DIGBY *is motionless, listening.* HARRY, *dressed for the office, enters* DIGBY's *cube*)

HARRY: You got . . .
DIGBY: Wait a second, wait a second.

(HARRY *waits*)

RADIO ANNOUNCER: Three-two delivery. Line drive to right center. A base-hit by George Foster. Carter around third is coming home with the tying run. Behind him Strawberry. It's Three-Two Mets and the game is over.

(DIGBY *exhales and switches off the radio. He looks exhausted*)

HARRY: That's how you act when they win?

DIGBY: The sons-of-bitches are half-a-game out of first. I don't have a fingernail I can call my own.

HARRY: Congratulation, they really turned it around.

DIGBY: I think I liked it better when they were in the basement.

HARRY: What are you talking about? They're winning!

DIGBY: I know, I know. But I had more fun when they were losing. There wasn't this kind of pressure.

HARRY: I thought you just loved the game.

DIGBY: I still love it. It's just easier to be philosophical when you're twenty-two games out of first place. You *have* to be philosophical when you're twenty-two games out. Do you realize, if the Cardinals lose tonight, the Mets will be tied for first place. (DIGBY *look at the Gooden poster on his wall*) How can you people *do* this to me?

HARRY: You got that Pacific Power stuff for Evert to take to L.A. on Monday?

DIGBY: It's ready, it's ready. (*He hands* HARRY *a set of the carbons he's been working on*)

HARRY: He still wants to see us Monday morning before he leaves.

DIGBY: Yes, I know, I know.

HARRY: Aren't you out of uniform?

DIGBY: What? Oh, I'm getting ready to leave early. Going upstate.

HARRY: By yourself?

DIGBY: With Faye, she has a cabin up there.

HARRY: Sounds cozy.

DIGBY: Sure is. Just me and her and The Three Pep Boys, Manny, Moe and Jack.

HARRY: Uh-oh.

DIGBY (*Suspicious*):   Uh-oh what?

HARRY: Nothing. Just uh-oh.

(DIGBY *lets it slide.* HARRY *adopts what for him passes as a serious expression*)

Digby, can I talk to you like a brother?

DIGBY (*Simple*):   No.

(HARRY *plows on anyway*)

HARRY: You have become a real drudge these last few weeks, the bear of the thirty-first floor. It's the girl, isn't it? It's Faye. Do you want to talk about it?

DIGBY: No.

HARRY: It'll make you feel better.

DIGBY: No, it'll make *you* feel better.

HARRY: Every man goes through it now and then, it just happens. I wouldn't want it to get around, but it even happened to me. Once.

DIGBY: What the hell are you talking about?

(HARRY *leans across the desk*)

HARRY (*Confidentially*): Your "problem".

DIGBY: Problem?

HARRY (*A whisper*): Your . . . "difficulty".

DIGBY: Difficulty?

(*A beat*)

HARRY: Your impotency.

DIGBY: My impotency!

HARRY: Hey, not so loud. Keep it down, I mean . . .

DIGBY: You think I'm impotent?

HARRY: It's nothing to be ashamed of.

DIGBY: I am astonished at the sexual aberrations and dysfunctions a man can be labeled with simply because he chooses to abstain.

(HARRY *is thrown by this*)

HARRY: To what?

DIGBY: To abstain, Mr. Crocker. To put one's hand over the glass; to say thanks but no thanks; to leave one's mighty sword within its sheath . . . just stop me when we come to one you like.

HARRY: You don't have a case of the limps?

DIGBY: To the best of my knowledge, no.

HARRY: And you and this girl don't . . .

DIGBY (*Cutting him off*): That's right, we don't.

(HARRY *finds this unprecedented*)

HARRY: Then what do you do with her?

DIGBY: Oh, golly, all sorts of things. We go to plays and movies then sit in as yet undiscovered restaurants and talk for hours at a stretch. We go to the zoo, we go to museums and ballgames and have intellectual fist fights over each other's favorite books. Last Friday night at my apartment we drank a bottle of Asti and listened to Mahler's Second Symphony and all my Spike Jones records.

HARRY: And after the wine and the music?

(*A beat*)

DIGBY: I took her home. (DIGBY *moves things on his desk, things in no need of moving*)

HARRY: Jesus.

DIGBY: I took her home to her apartment.

HARRY: Jesus Christ.

DIGBY: Where one Alfred Becker awaited, his head thrust into her open refrigerator the way an anteater shoulders into a termite mound.

HARRY: This guy lives in her apartment?

DIGBY: No, he has a key. Everybody's got a key to Faye's apartment.

HARRY: Including you?

DIGBY: I turned mine down.

HARRY: Why?

DIGBY: I didn't want to walk in on anything I didn't want to walk in on.

HARRY: There's a lot of that, is there?

DIGBY: One of them's always there when I bring her home. I think they work in shifts. And they are a swell bunch of guys. Worth has the easy grace of a vivisectionist, Becker has the brain of a Big Mac, and Delehanty just stares at me the way our cat used to stare at everybody from the top of the living room breakfront. What the *hell* does she see in them?

HARRY: Maybe that's what they're asking about you.

DIGBY: What's that supposed to mean?

HARRY: I'm just saying that, maybe, if you looked at it from the other guy's perspective . . .

DIGBY: I see it from the other guy's perspective all the time. Whenever the two of us go out I get up to here with the other guy's perspective. We're on line for a movie and every male eye is drawn to her. Sometimes I get a little look myself, one of those "Atta boy, you got your self a prime one" looks, and I stand there waiting for the line to move so we can get in the theatre and they can turn the lights out. But she's still there in the dark, next to you, making your head vibrate like a tuning fork.

HARRY: Uh-oh.

DIGBY: Harry, you are forbidden to say "uh-oh" in my cubicle. (DIGBY *goes back to putting his desk in Friday afternoon order*)

HARRY: Digby, can I talk to you like a Dutch Uncle?

DIGBY (*Simple*): No.

HARRY: Friend, you are having an unnatural relationship.

DIGBY: Unnatural? What's unnatural about being friends with a woman?

HARRY: For one thing it's having a negative effect on your personality.

DIGBY (*Furious*):   It is not!

HARRY: Is too.

DIGBY: Is not!

HARRY: Then why did you threaten Havemeyer with an electric pencil sharpener?

DIGBY: That's not a problem with *my* personality, that's a problem with *his* personality.

HARRY: It's just not normal.

DIGBY: What isn't?

HARRY: This thing you have with this girl.

DIGBY: What thing?

HARRY: You know what thing.

DIGBY: Say it. Are you afraid your tongue will turn black? She's my friend. What's so abnormal about that? Women are fifty-one percent of the population, Harry. What do you think they're all doing over there? Trading lipsticks and waiting for you to make your move? There are minds and thoughts and loyal, intelligent friendships and perfume and patient understanding and bottomless eyes and fascinating ideas and laughter that sounds like it comes from someplace deeper than her throat and such delicate hands and skin that glows, skin that looks so amazingly soft and glows with a cool light and is as soft as, as a, I think I'd like a glass of water.

(DIGBY *sits down heavily in his chair, shaken.* HARRY *pours a glass of water and hands it to* DIGBY *who drinks deeply*)

HARRY: I guess you're starting to find out you're no Gandhi.

DIGBY: Worth was right, the son-of-a-bitch. I'm turning into lime Jell-o. Lime Jell-o with little marshmallows floating in it. I've shot clean through the looking glass this time. She sleeps with everyone but me and that makes me special which is wonderful except, goddamn it, I want her too!

(*A beat*)

HARRY: So.

DIGBY: So?

HARRY: As in "So, what's the big deal?" As in "So, who cares?" Where is it written sex is supposed to be anything but fun? A way to get off. You know what your problem is? You think too much. You think about things that aren't problems until they *become* problems and then you think about them some more. And what does all that thinking get you? It gets you a strawberry sundae of a girl who everybody is screwing except you. That's what thinking get you: Blue balls *that big!*

DIGBY (*With quiet admiration*): Harry, you are a marvel. You really are and I envy you.

HARRY (*Surprised, but pleased*): Well, Dig, it's like I said, "life experience".

DIGBY: Oh, no, it's more than that. You're like one of those four-story tarantulas from the horror movies. They could shoot bullets and bazookas at you all day and never hit a vital spot. (DIGBY *heads for the coat hook to claim his cap, jacket and bag*)

HARRY: That's a great way to talk to a friend. I'm just trying to show you how easy life can be if you don't take it serious.

DIGBY: Jesus Christ, Harry, if we don't take life seriously, what the hell *should* we take seriously? If you're trying to tell me man was meant to simply stumble across the landscape with an idiot grin, whacking the tops off the flowers with a stick as he goes, then I'm telling you something went wrong and we were never meant to be in charge of this planet. Better it belong to the ferns and the starfish than to the lethal likes of us.

(*A beat*)

HARRY: You know what your problem is?

(DIGBY *drops his hands to his sides*)

DIGBY: No, Harry. I don't know what my problem is. Won't you please tell me?

HARRY: You don't know how to have a good time.

DIGBY: Then my troubles are over. Faye's teaching me to dance. (*He picks up his bag and exits*)

Source: Dramatists Play Service, Inc.

✦ Eastern Standard

RICHARD GREENBERG

CHARACTERS: STEPHEN (30's), DREW (30's)
SETTING: *A Manhattan restaurant, the present.*

STEPHEN, *a successful architect, and his college friend,* DREW, *a gay artist from Greenwich Village, meet for lunch at a fashionable midtown restaurant.* STEPHEN *has just confessed to an abortive suicide attempt the night before, claiming that he is lonely and hates his job ("I* am *urban blight.")* DREW *tries to be supportive but reacts with typically campy sarcasm.*

STEPHEN: Do you think I could whine a little more? I don't think I'm whining quite enough. *(Beat)* She's not usually this late.
DREW: Tell me about her.
STEPHEN: We — well, it's stupid.
DREW: You've seen her every day for three weeks running.
STEPHEN: Almost every day. Almost three weeks.
DREW: And there's something between you?
STEPHEN: We've never spoken, we've . . . Christ, it's ridiculous.
DREW: You've never spoken?
STEPHEN: No.
DREW: Then, Stephen, if I may be so bold — it's not a real relationship.
STEPHEN: Of course, it's not a real relationship! I don't *have* real relationships. I place myself beside emotionally teetering women and wait for them to fall on me. I share jangled nerves with neurotics for short spans of time . . . it's preposterous, I'm a preposterous figure —
DREW: She's beautiful.
STEPHEN: She's all I've been able to think about —
DREW: Stephen —
STEPHEN: It's like I'm nineteen, I'm obsessed, I follow her . . . I follow her places . . . she doesn't know . . . I stare . . . I nod, I smile, I *scrape* . . . Nothing will come of it, nothing will ever come of it, it will just end up making me more miserable than ever. Why can't I control myself? *Where is she?*
DREW: Stephen —

STEPHEN: Shoot me, take that knife and run it through my heart.
  [(*Phoebe enters, sees* STEPHEN's *back, smiles to herself, takes seat at Stage Left table*)]
DREW: Stephen?
STEPHEN: What?
DREW: Is that her?
  (STEPHEN *whips around to look at her, whips back quickly*)
STEPHEN: Oh, Jesus.
DREW: Do you always twist so violently when you see her?
STEPHEN: Yes.
DREW: That may be a flaw in your strategy. My my . . .
STEPHEN: How does she look to you?
DREW: Fiscal.
STEPHEN: Drew!
DREW: No, this is incredible; I have never seen anyone so ambient of Wall Street in my life. She looks as if she breakfasts on ticker tape and the Dow rises with her hemline, she's your Platonic half, oh, Stephen, lunge!
STEPHEN: Would you lower your voice, we're in a restaurant.
DREW: She can't hear me.
  [(*The waitress brings her a drink; they smile, nod: waitress exits*)]
  Oh my God!
STEPHEN: What?
DREW: The waitress just brought her a white wine. She didn't even ask for it, now that's classy — would you relax your back, you look like a porcupine.
STEPHEN: I should never have asked you to come, I can see that.
DREW: I'm just having some fun — I absolutely approve.
STEPHEN: There's nothing to approve of.
DREW: Well, there may be.
  [(*Peter enters, kisses Phoebe on the cheek, sits by her; they begin to talk, all of this inaudible to us*)]
  Oh my God! (*He rises, stares at Peter*)
STEPHEN: What are you talking about?
DREW: It's what the Garden of Eden must have looked like.
STEPHEN: What?
DREW: The two of them together.
STEPHEN: There's a man with her?
DREW: Yes. A beautiful one.
STEPHEN: There's never been before.
  [(*Peter lights a cigarette*)]
DREW: Thank you for asking me here.

STEPHEN: How can there be a man? She always eats alone.
DREW: They're like perfect reflecting pools, God it's —
STEPHEN: I want to die.
DREW: Their children will be *incredible*!
STEPHEN: Children! Oh God — !
DREW: Stephen —
STEPHEN: I'm an idiot!
   (*Beat*)
DREW: Listen, Stephen. In a couple of weeks, it'll be summer. We'll go to your place on the Island. We'll get out of the city, okay? It's just the city. Forget about her. Okay? Forget about her. It's silly. Everything will be fine.

Source: Grove Press

✤ El Salvador

•••••••••••••••••••••••••••••RAFAEL LIMA

CHARACTERS: FULLER (30), FLETCHER (40)
SETTING: *A hotel suite at the El Dorado Americana, El Slavador, January, 1981.*

JOHN FLETCHER *wears glasses and is middle American personified; he is a video newsman.* FULLER *wears jeans, T-shirt, has a no-nonsense face and carries a video camera. Both men are in a hotel room used as an International News Bureau; it is their duty to record what is going on in El Salvador even though they dislike their assignment.*

FULLER: This is here, Larry — this is now — this is different. Do you know what our lives have narrowed down to? Every night it's curfew and every night we're in here drunk. Every morning we get in the van, roll down the street a few blocks and the driver says "There's one. There's one." And we see this, like, crumpled up dead animal on the side of the street. Only the animal has got this bloody rag tangled around it. We get closer to this dead animal and it's not a dead animal OK? We've gotten used to shooting tape of bodies by the side of the road right? We get up every morning and go shoot tape of more bodies by the side of the road. (*Pause*) And for what? For fucking TV. For the beast — for this television beast that gobbles up disasters, eats up tragedy, consumes grief. It lives off this shit, man. We feed this beast, this electronic computerized fucking nightmare that sucks in tears and horror. We feed it. We make it burst with blood. This electronic leach is eating our soul and drinking the blood of every poor motherfucker we get pictures of. We feed this vast . . . this consuming machine. Everyday we shoot another frame of a blood-soaked corpse. Tape, electrical images, scan lines, one pass near a magnetic field and the tape becomes history. The blood, the kid in the street becomes static. We're killing ourselves for ghosts — incandescent crap. I'm gone. I'm outta here.

FLETCHER: Fuller, you just can't walk out on me —

FULLER: I mean after a while your heart pumps shit through your veins and your brain turns to glass, and you realize you've lost your sense of judgement.

FLETCHER: Stay one day. Stay 'til I get another crew.

FULLER: I wish I could, Boss.

FLETCHER: Fuller, if you leave and some shit happens and I don't have a crew, it's my responsibility — they'll have my job, man.

FULLER: Boss, if I don't do it now, tonight, I may never get out of here. I'm gone tomorrow morning. I just don't understand why anyone else is staying. I mean why are we here? Why aren't we back in the States? Because we love Latin America? Or because we don't like mowing the fucking lawn? I mean we have to consider there are easier ways of making money.

FLETCHER: Fuller, I can't get fired —

FULLER: Best thing that could ever happen to you, Fletch, is you get fired and you get sent home.

FLETCHER: Fuller, this may be the asshole of the world, but I need this job.

FULLER: Fletcher you put on an act for our benefit, but you don't want to go home.

FLETCHER: Fuller, this is cocaine talking.

FULLER: Come on, John, you don't want to go home.

FLETCHER: No. Of course not. I enjoy spending my evenings with you bunch of hard-legs.

FULLER: You could quit.

FLETCHER: Of course I could, go back to local TV.

FULLER: If you thought by going back you could save your marriage you'd go — you'd quit. You'd be on the plane with me tomorrow morning.

FLETCHER: Give me a break, Fuller.

FULLER: You don't want to go home. The only thing that's kept that relationship together as long as it has is the fact that you're not there.

FLETCHER: Oh fuck you, Fuller.

FULLER: And you got New York to assign you to El Salvador. You get fucked up every night — it goes with the territory — everybody here gets fucked up every night.

FLETCHER: Hey, asshole, didn't you hear me ask Charlie for a bureau stateside?

FULLER: Very convincing.

FLETCHER: I can stop drinking.

FULLER: Sure you can.

FLETCHER: I can.

FULLER: OK. Here. (FULLER *takes* FLETCHER'*s bottle and begins to pour it out in the nearby sink*)

FLETCHER: Hey, that's enough man, come on . . . hey, Fuller . . . Fuller. Hey come on will ya . . . for Christ's sakes, cut the shit. Quit being an asshole. For fuck's sake, Fuller, what the fuck is wrong with you? (*Takes bottle back*)

Source: Samuel French, Inc.

✦ Eyes of the American

••••••••••••••••••••••••SAMM-ART WILLIAMS

CHARACTERS: JAMES (*West Indian, 40's*), BENNY (*Black, 40's*)
SETTING: JAMES' *shanty on an island in the Independent West Indies,*
  the present.

BENNY *is an American CIA agent assigned to the island to assure that Cheddy, the current leader, remains in power. He discovers that* JAMES, *his best friend for years, is not the simple native taxi driver he appeared to be, but is actually the secret leader of a rebel faction. Now that the rebels have toppled Cheddy's regime,* BENNY *is stunned to learn* JAMES's *real identity. In the past,* BENNY, *posing as a textile industrialist, had always pumped* JAMES *for political information, as witnessed in the flashback within the scene, but it was actually* BENNY *who provided* JAMES *with helpful information. The flashback is in* JAMES's *mind, and it should be performed simply, with all props pantomimed.*

JAMES: I taught you how to fish. How to gather coral, without cutting off your hand.
BENNY: Who is . . . "The Leader"?
JAMES: A man I guess.
BENNY (*Silence, as he looks at* JAMES. *He suspects that* JAMES *is the leader*):   Somebody jammed Cheddy's shortwave. We couldn't get out. The rebels knew Cheddy's every move. Somebody else on this island had a shortwave radio.
JAMES: You still playing undercover agent. Still interrogating. Your children must hate you, man.
BENNY (*Silence*):   Do you know . . . I'd never gone fishing before, in my entire life.
   (*Flashback. Lights change. They are now fishing. They both have fishing poles to be mimed. The sounds of celebration fade out*)
JAMES: Cut the bait, me boy. Chop the damn thing, then put it on the hook. (JAMES *shows* BENNY *how to cut the bait. This entire action is mimed*)
BENNY: Like this?
JAMES: Like that. Now cast. Throw it out. Like this. Damn, you stupid for you age, boy.

BENNY: I grew up in the city, what you expect. Hey Jimmy, I like fishing. I got one! Look! Look!

JAMES: Hold on! Hold on! Pull it in!

BENNY: I lost it. Damn! Hey! You bring the bush rum?

JAMES: Like always. (*He passes the rum to* BENNY)

BENNY: I love bush rum. Taste like moonshine, you know that?

JAMES: So you say.

BENNY: Drink up. Drink, drink. Too bad it's illegal. I'd like to take a ship load back to the States.

(JAMES *begins to drink.* BENNY *and* JAMES *position their fishing poles in the sand Downstage Right and Downstage Left. They move back Upstage*)

JAMES: When you going back to the States? You been here a long time.

BENNY: When my boss tells me to come back, I guess.

JAMES: You do everything your boss tell you to do? Seem like he control you body and soul, man. I don't want no boss like that.

BENNY: I don't like him either, but the pay is good.

JAMES: Pay? That all that matter to you? Pay?

BENNY: I like to live good. What's this? I ask the questions, right?

JAMES: Yeah. Like you always do. Get me drunk . . . so you think . . . and ask me about island politics. Where the rebels, Jimmy? You know the leader, Jimmy? Always the same. Textiles must be a very complicated industry.

BENNY: Too complicated.

JAMES (*Sitting next to* BENNY, *then moving to Stage Left platform*): Sometimes I look at my island and she so beautiful it bring tears to me eyes. Nobody see it like island people. Everybody want it. The Yanks. The Cubans. I climb them mountains. Many, many times. Looking for God, you know. Old Mister Timmons tell me God live on Island Peak. So I climb for a day, hands bloody, knees raw, feet sore, steady going up, up, up to the clouds. It got dark and damp. Rain forest. Darker. Darker. Higher. Higher. All the time I shouting, God! God! It's me man! James Horsford Ottley The Third! Show your face. I get to the top and I wait two days. No God. He don't come. I wanted to ask him . . . ask him why did he make me poor? Why I have to live in Shanty Town? Why I have to take . . . take shit from tourist. Why I have to take shit from British. The Americans. Why? Why?! Among all this warm gentle beauty of forest, mountain and sea. Why, God, did you cast me in poverty? I ask him, man, for three days, I didn't eat or sleep. I just stood on top of that mountain, shouting to him these questions. I must embarrass the man, 'cause he ain't show he face. You good friend, Benny. (*Crosses Stage Left, down from platform*)

BENNY: Yeah . . . yeah, I guess so. I'm on a treadmill, Jimmy. Going so fast I sometimes forget where I am. Forget to look for God. Sometimes I'm ashamed of myself. I . . . wish I could love this place.

JAMES: You growing soft, boy? (*Moves Downstage Right to check his fishing pole*)

BENNY: No. I know what I got to do.

JAMES: Maybe you should give up your mortgage and two cars. Then you could stop and see the . . . beauty.

BENNY: I can't. I . . . wish that I could.

JAMES: How much they paying you?

BENNY: Who?

JAMES: The . . . textile company.

BENNY: A lot. Here. Here. Drink up.

JAMES: I getting drunk, man.

BENNY: So am I. What the hell.

JAMES: I wish you could see me through my eyes, Benny, and not your own.

BENNY: Rum is the answer! Rum is the key! Hey! Tell me about the rebels, which hill do they store their guns? I know you know everything you little raggedy bastard.

JAMES: They're there. And there. There and there. They're everywhere! More rum! More rum man!

BENNY: Here. Here's money. Good old U.S. dollars. You hear anything. Anything . . . you come tell me. It's my job to help this government. Got to keep it stable.

JAMES: The Cubans say the same thing.

BENNY: Fuck the Cubans! The U.S., baby. The U.S.! Feel this green money. Feels good, don't it? I love the feel of money.

JAMES: Cheddy must talk to the U.S. a lot.

BENNY: Yeah. That bastard own the most sophisticated radio system I've ever seen. I could tell you more.

JAMES (*Realizes that* BENNY *has valuable information*):   Here. Drink up. Drink, man.

BENNY: Thanks. Can't get too drunk. Responsibility . . .

JAMES: He ever let you talk on it?

BENNY: Talk on what?

JAMES: The radio, man.

BENNY: Once or twice. He's a tricky S.O.B. He keeps it stored in the living room behind the biggest fucking Picasso known to man. Hey, don't tell anybody about the radio.

JAMES: Oh, no, man. Me lips shut tight. He ah . . . got guns in that house?

BENNY: Naw. He keep the guns at Police Headquarters, along with the rest of the toy army. Three hundred troops. What a joke. What the hell could we want with this island?

JAMES: Textiles!

BENNY: Right. Right!

(*Flashback ends. Lights come back to normal. We are now back in the shanty.* JAMES *and* BENNY *are sitting at the table looking away from each other*)

JAMES: The wedges of friendship. We're victims, Benjamin, you and me. Doesn't matter that you're from Washington and I'm from Shanty Town. We're both disposable pawns, who now think of killing each other, when we should be fishing.

BENNY: Do you want to be King? (*Silence*) You're the Leader, aren't you?

JAMES: I knew there was something strange about you when you stepped out of the airport. You didn't have a camera around your neck. This one, I said is no tourist. The tourist come with their white shoes and out-of-place straw hats and the ugliest cameras ever manufactured by man. I can show them the most gorgeous part of the island. So pretty, it will take the breath of angels. They don't want to photograph that. But they see one child standing naked or ragged in front of a shanty and they click away. Or some poor person begging in the street. They click away with their camera. God, that would make me so mad! But you . . . no camera for you. You had another purpose. You think I didn't know who you were? I say to myself the U.S. send a Chameleon. One the same color as me. And you are the worse, Benny. The worse.

BENNY: You're full of shit, you know that. All that self-righteous, poor poverty stricken, salt of the earth . . . bullshit. You not only hated Cheddy, you envied him. You wanted the large house on the hill. You want the same thing as the rest of us greedy bastards. Power! You want it! Yeah . . . I got you figured Mr. Leader! You're sitting here fighting with your conscience. Do I take the power, or do I remain here in my poverty-laden dignity? You're afraid of power, James. Afraid of what it will turn you into. Well, you've got it. Now let's see you put onto practice all of that idea-

listic shit you're always talking about. Let's see you do it . . .
KING!

JAMES: Don't you want the same thing?! (*Stands and moves Stage Left*)

BENNY: Yes! But I have to say you fooled me for a while. This poor, poor taxi driver. What am I doing to him? His family? Then I said to me, no, this poor ignorant, pitiful taxi driver wants the same thing I want. My conscience is clear, buddy. Clear! Clear! (*Silence*) I loved little George. Everytime I looked at him, I wanted to hold him to me and just hug him. I wouldn't have done anything to hurt that boy or Roberta. When I heard, I screamed, man. I went out on the veranda and I screamed NO! NO! NO Cheddy! Not his family!

(JAMES *crosses to the doorway and looks out*)

You wanted me to prove to you that you were right. To clear your conscience. See world, I tried to befriend the black American. He betrayed me. And more will come in just like this Benjamin Parker . . .

(JAMES *joins in*)

JAMES *and* BENNY: Benjamin Parker. Trying to take our island from us. Only I can stop that. Make me your king. I'll be a just tyrant. Not like Cheddy. I gave my family's life so that you, my people, shall live. I know economics. Make me your king! ME! Me!

Source: Samuel French, Inc.

✤ Goose and Tomtom

●●●●●●●●●●●●●●●●●●●●●●●●●●●●●●●●●●DAVID RABE

CHARACTERS: GOOSE (20's-30's), TOMTOM (40's)
SETTING: *An apartment in the underworld, the recent past.*

GOOSE *and* TOMTOM *are pals and petty crooks. They are hiding out because they believe that the mob, led by Bingo, is gunning for them. Lorraine, their girlfriend and partner in crime, has arrived and discovered that the jewels they have stolen for her have in turn been stolen from the apartment. She also discovers Bingo's sister bound and gagged in the closet.* TOMTOM, *the mastermind of the trio, is convinced that they must pull another heist in order to replace Lorraine's jewels and to prevent her from swinging her allegiance to Bingo.*

TOMTOM: We gotta make a plan! (TOMTOM *runs to the kitchen table and grabs some pens and a huge pad on which to draw his plan*)
GOOSE: How long was I gone?
TOMTOM: What?
GOOSE: When I looked into her eyes and you couldn't see me.
TOMTOM: We gotta make a plan!
GOOSE: I bet it was a long, long time. I bet it was a long, long, long time. I coulda been anywhere. I coulda done anything. Where'd I go? What'd I do? I don't know. You don't know. (*Wandering about, looking for himself, looking for where he might have gone, he ends up again on the floor by* BINGO's *sister*)
TOMTOM: What we gotta do is get money! To go about all over the earth trying to steal some duplicates just like she lost would take forever. We don't have forever. She'd be unhappy forever. So we'll steal money, and with the money we'll go to a store and in the store we'll purchase the gems and jewels. So this is the plan with which we steal the money to buy the jewels and buy the gems to bring back the smile of Lorraine. There's a bank. A bank. A big red bank. Brick-red walls. Full of money. A black safe. A huge hole full of money. So we'll take our guns. We'll take a car. We'll drive the car down a shady street. Past quiet houses. Everybody's busy. Nobody's lookin'.
GOOSE: Where'm I?
TOMTOM: With me.

GOOSE: I'm in the car with you?

TOMTOM: Got it.

GOOSE: Good. You're drivin'. (*He pulls the hassock up beside* TOMTOM *and sits*)

TOMTOM: So what we'll do is park the car just down the street a little from the bank.

GOOSE: Just a little is how far?

TOMTOM: Twenty yards.

GOOSE: What's the name of this bank?

TOMTOM: I don't know. It's red brick.

GOOSE: So we got our car parked twenty yards down the street from this red-brick bank, we don't know its name. So . . . we get out. (GOOSE *rises, steps out of the car*)

TOMTOM: We got our guns.

GOOSE (*Pulling out his gun*):   I got mine.

TOMTOM: We're walkin' up the street. No one notices us.

GOOSE: Who's gonna notice us, 'cause we're dressed up in businessmen's suits. (*From the clothes tree he grabs two hats, putting one on* TOMTOM, *and other on himself*)

TOMTOM: Right.

GOOSE: We go those little suitcases like very important men in business always got 'em. (*Dashing upstage, he grabs two suitcases, putting one on* TOMTOM's *lap, holding the other himself*)

TOMTOM: Briefcases.

GOOSE: We got these briefcases.

TOMTOM: The bank's full of money.

GOOSE: We got these briefcases an' the bank's fulla money, and we're walkin' up the street. (GOOSE *starts to stroll off*) Nobody knows what we're up to. We got 'em all fooled.

TOMTOM: So we come up to this mailbox and at the mailbox we're gonna synchronize our watches.

GOOSE: So we're doin' that, right, I don't know what it is.

TOMTOM: It's we make our watches say the same thing.

GOOSE: So whatta we make 'em say?

TOMTOM: We make 'em say five of three.

GOOSE: What time is it?

TOMTOM: Five of three. Almost closing time.

GOOSE: Good.

TOMTOM: Or do you mean now?

GOOSE: What?

TOMTOM (*Hurrying to* GOOSE *to straighten things out*):   Now? Do you mean now?

GOOSE: What?

TOMTOM: Wait a minute; wait a minute.

GOOSE: No, no. After the thing there and the street and we're by the mailbox there, and we do the thing there by the mailbox, you know with our watches — so what happens next?

TOMTOM: You mean in the plan?

GOOSE: Yeh. I mean, fuckin' A. That's what we're talkin' about. The plan!

TOMTOM: Well, maybe when we're really doin' it! I thought you was askin' what was gonna happen then when we're really doin' it.

GOOSE: Oh.

TOMTOM: You know.

GOOSE: Yeh.

TOMTOM: I don't know that. That's what I'm sayin'. There's no way to know that, so I hope you're not askin' that. I mean, I know you're not — I just, you know — I mean, I know, you know. That's why we're makin' the plan — that's why we're talkin' about the goddamn plan, we can know what's happenin' in the plan. Right?

GOOSE: Right.

TOMTOM: Okay.

GOOSE: You know, I'm gettin' depressed.

TOMTOM: What'sa matter?

GOOSE: I'm just thinkin'.

TOMTOM: 'At's okay.

GOOSE: I mean, they probably got us spotted already; we are not as inconspicuous as we would like in our business suits no matter how hard we're tryin' to look unlike ourselves. They got us spotted. We're out there by the mailbox, you know, and we're doin' this stuff about five of three to our watches, and somebody's probably looked out the window and seen us and said there's two crooks out there pretendin' they're businessmen. So the place is crawlin' with cops. That's what I'm thinkin'.

TOMTOM: You mean, there's cops comin'.

GOOSE: Yeh.

TOMTOM: We gotta fight 'em. (TOMTOM *tries to make the appropriate revision or even a new plan, ripping up sheets*)

GOOSE (*Pointing to the plan*):   There's too many.

TOMTOM (*Revising*):   No.

GOOSE (*Hitting the plan*):   There's too many. We gotta run. We take off runnin'. (*He runs*)

TOMTOM: We stand and fight. We got guns that never miss. We got bullets that knock 'em down like steam rollers! (*Ripping a calendar down from the wall,* TOMTOM *jams his plans onto the hook so it hangs there*)

GOOSE: I'm in a alley trapped, Tomtom. They got me; they're gonna get me.

TOMTOM (*Working on his plan on the wall*):   Don't give up.

GOOSE: They got me. I thought I was tougher.

TOMTOM: I don't feel good. I don't feel good.

GOOSE: I don't feel good.

TOMTOM: I feel sick.

GOOSE: I don't know what's going' on.

TOMTOM: I feel awful. Like I ate some poison.

GOOSE: I bet when I disappeared from lookin' into Lorraine's beautiful eyes, I was gone back to the swamp is where I went, to the swamp, eatin' worms and flies — an' my belly now is full of worms and flies, rotten, makin' me sick.

TOMTOM: I got flu bugs up my nose.

GOOSE: I got worms in my tummy.

Source: Grove Press

✤ A Handful of Stars

•••••••••••••••••••••••••••••••BILLY ROCHE

CHARACTERS: JIMMY (17), TONY (17)
SETTING: *A pool hall in a small town in Ireland, the present.*

JIMMY *and* TONY *have been best pals since childhood. But* TONY *is beginning to grow up.* JIMMY, *on the other hand, has grown wilder with the frustrations of perpetual youth. Specifically, he has just been dumped by a girlfriend — Linda. Now, he has fought in a pub and tried to pull a robbery with a gun. The police are after him and people like the jealous Conway are helping them. Detective Swan, in particular, is his nemesis. As he awaits his fate,* JIMMY *says good-bye to* TONY.

> (*The Club. Lights come up on* JIMMY *who is sitting in a moody half light. He is ruffled-looking and his hand is bleeding. The glass panel behind him is smashed, with 'Jimmy' scrawled in chalk on the door.* TONY *enters through the front door which has been left ajar*)

TONY: Jimmy, Jimmy, where are yeh?

JIMMY: I'm over here. Come in and close the door after yeh.

TONY (*Closing the door gently*): What did yeh leave it open like that for? I could have been anybody. (*The sight of the smashed glass panel stops* TONY *in his tracks*) What happened here? Aw Jaysus Jimmy there was no need to go and do that . . .

JIMMY: Give it a rest will yeh.

> (TONY *looks down at* JIMMY *in disgust*)

What are you lookin' at me like that for? You'd think I was after pissin' on a shrine or somethin' the way you're goin' on. That's only a room in there Tony. It's just a room.

> (TONY *hangs his head, disappointed that* JIMMY *has abused the back room.* JIMMY *eyes his woebegone friend*)

Look if you're worried about gettin' the blame for this don't. I'll tell them you had nothin' to do with it. Okay?

TONY: That doesn't matter.

JIMMY: Yes it does matter. When I get out I expect you to be a staunch member here with your own key and everything. Sure you've already got the ingredients to be a miniature Conway. Money in the Credit Union and a set of bicycle clips now and you'll be away with it.

TONY: There's nothin' wrong with Conway, Jimmy. He's alright.

JIMMY: Oh I know he's alright. You can bet your sweet life on that. The Creep.

TONY: So he's a creep and your a fuckin' ejit. What's the difference?

JIMMY: None I suppose. But if I had a choice I'd prefer to be an ejit than a creep.

TONY: Why?

JIMMY: I don't know. I just would.

TONY (*Sighs*):   Look what do you want to do Jimmy?

JIMMY: What? I don't know.

TONY: Well you'd better make up your mind. I'm gettin' married in the mornin' don't forget.

JIMMY: I don't think so Tony. I think I just got you a reprieve.

TONY: What are you talkin' about?

JIMMY: Listen I want you to do me a favor. I want you to go up to the barracks and tell them where to find me.

TONY (*Flabbergasted*):   Haw? What do you think I am, a squealer or somethin'? I couldn't do that . . .

JIMMY: Look I'm askin' you to go . . . as a favor. I don't want them burstin' in here after me like they were the Sweeney or somethin'.

(TONY *paces up and down nervously, shaking his head*)

TONY: You're landinin' me right in the middle of it all. Supposin' Swan decides to hold on to me for the night too. What if one of those bastards feels like takin' it out on me? They might try and implicate me just because I was with you earlier on tonight . . .

(JIMMY *is sitting there biting his nails, a frightened, hunted look in his eyes.* TONY *sees that* JIMMY *is afraid and stops talking.* TONY *sighs and there is a long silence while* TONY *thinks it over*)

What do you want me to say?

JIMMY: Tell them where I am. Tell them the door will be wide open and the lights full on. And don't forget to say that I'm unarmed.

TONY: The door will be wide open and the lights full on. And he's unarmed.

JIMMY: Yeah. Go to Swan himself.

TONY: Where is the gun anyway?

JIMMY: Tell them you don't know where it is.

TONY: What? Now they're goin' to want to know where that gun is.

JIMMY: That's their hard luck.

TONY: Aw come on Jimmy I'm supposed to be gettin' married in the mornin'. I don't fancy gettin' the ears boxed off me half the night over you. What's the point anyway?

JIMMY: The point is you never know when you might need a gun. You might be glad of it one day to blow your brains out.

TONY: What are you on about? Gettin' me a reprieve. And me blowing me brains out. Anyone would think that it was me who was in trouble or somethin'. Jimmy you're the one that's goin' up the river not me.

JIMMY: Never mind about that. I know well enough where I'm goin'. But you've been shanghai'd in your sleep Tony. You're on a slow boat to China or somewhere boy and yeh don't even realize it.

TONY (*Angry and hurt*): At least I never went berserk over a girl anyway.

JIMMY: This has nothin' to do with her.

TONY: Oh yeah? Pull the other one Jimmy. Linda gave you the shove and you went berserk. Admit it.

JIMMY: She didn't give me the shove. We had a bit of a row that's all.

TONY: Oh yeah? Well then why don't yeh get her to do your dirty work for yeh. Why don't you ask her to go up and see Swan . . . No, you won't do that will yeh? 'Cause yeh have the auld gom here. Well you needn't think now for one minute that I'm goin' up there until know exactly where that gun is 'cause I'm not.

(JIMMY *shakes his head and smiles.* TONY *becomes furious and moves in closer to* JIMMY)

What's so funny Jimmy?

JIMMY: You. You'd give it all up just like that wouldn't yeh? You'd hand it to them on a plate. Well not me. I want to see them runnin' around, like blue arsed flies. And when I'm up in that courtroom and somebody mentions a gun I'll say, 'Gun? What gun? I don't see no gun.'

TONY: And what about the rest of us? What about me?

JIMMY: What about yeh?

TONY: They're goin' to assume that I know where it is. That you told me.

(JIMMY *just shrugs*)

You're a bad bastard you are.

JIMMY: Yeah that's right Tony. I'm a bad bastard. Where has being a good boy ever gotten you?

TONY: The one night I ever asked yeh not to start anythin'. The one night . . .

JIMMY: Yeah alright Tony. So what do you want me to do now? Get down on me knees and kiss somebody's arse or somethin', just because you're afraid to take a couple of clips in the ear? Look if you don't want to do what I asked you to do, get the fuck out of me sight.

TONY (*Desperately*):   I'm supposed to be gettin' married in the mornin'.

JIMMY (*Dismissive*):   Go and fuck off away from me will yeh.

(JIMMY *turns away from him*. TONY *stays where he is*. JIMMY *turns back and shoves* TONY *away from him*)

Go on, get out of me sight before yeh make me vomit.

TONY (*Brushing* JIMMY'*s hand aside*):   Don't push Jimmy.

JIMMY (*Pushing him again*):   Why?

TONY: I'm warnin' yeh Jimmy, don't start.

(JIMMY *shoves* TONY *yet again*. TONY *loses his head and goes for him. There is a brawl with the two boys stumbling over the pool table and onto the floor. They punch one another and wrestle until* JIMMY *gets the better of* TONY. *He stands over the bleeding boy in a defiant stance*)

JIMMY: Nobody's goin' to wrap me up in a nice neat little parcel. I'm not goin' to make it handy for you to forget about me — not you, not me Ma nor me Da, not Swan, nobody.

(JIMMY *picks up a cue and holds it above his head*. TONY *cowers away from it*. JIMMY *turns and storms at the door to the back room and begins kicking it and hunching it with his shoulder. Eventually, as* TONY *gazes on in awe and disgust,* JIMMY *manages to break in, falling into the back room. We hear him wrecking the place in there, pulling down cupboards, kicking over chairs, scattering balls and breaking an out-of-sight window. When* JIMMY *appears in the doorway he has a frenzied look about him*)

Tell them Jimmy Brady done it. The same Jimmy Brady that's scrawled all over this town. Jimmy Brady who bursted that big bully of a bouncer with a headbutt when everyone else was afraid of their livin' lives of him. The same Jimmy Brady who led Detective Garda Swan twice around the houses and back again . . . Yeh see that's the difference between me and Conway. He tiptoes around. I'm screamin'. Me and Stapler are screamin'. So if you want to join the livin' dead then go ahead and do it by all means Tony but don't expect me to wink at your gravediggers. Conway . . . the big he-man with no bell on his bike. I hates him I'm not coddin' yeh I do.

TONY (*Tearful*):   It's not Conway's fault you're up to your ears in shit Jimmy. It's not my fault you fell out with your man in the bar. You can't blame Paddy for . . .

JIMMY: Alright. It's not Conway's fault, it's not your fault, it's not

Paddy's . . . Who's fault is it then Tony? Mine? Tell me who's to blame will yeh til I tear his friggin' head off.

TONY (*Sighs, stalls and comes closer to* JIMMY, *his voice taking on a more tender edge*): I don't know who's to blame. Maybe it's nobody's fault. Maybe that's just the way it is.

JIMMY: Yeah right, it's nobody's fault. (JIMMY *plonks himself down hopelessly on the bench*) It's nobody's fault. Everyone's to blame.

Source: Nick Hern Books

✛ Haut Gout

•••••••••••••••••••••••••••••••ALLAN HAVIS

CHARACTERS: JULES GOLD (40), FURST (60's)
SETTING: *A birthday party for* JULES GOLD *in his home.*

JULES GOLD, *an idealistic physician, supports Third World medical schools
and exchange doctors. He is also devoted to research and charity. In this
scene,* JULES *is asking his superior,* DR. FURST, *for a leave of absence to study
his milk formula in the Caribbean.*

GOLD: I need a favor, Ludwig.
FURST: Not now. Ply me with your best liquor.
GOLD: You know what I'm about to ask.
FURST: Yes, your secretary told me. (*Abrupt switch*) Every society is
    divided into classes. One chooses with care the class which
    makes one happiest. You've chosen yours, Jules, as you've cho-
    sen your sports cars and winter vacations. We're members of the
    privileged class, thank God.
GOLD: And God is pleased?
FURST: God is pleased.
GOLD: I didn't know that God sided with the high tax brackets.
FURST: Where are they now?
GOLD: Touring the garden. Jo Anne has landscaped again.
FURST: What talent she has.
GOLD: She's strip mined the azalea beds, and upset the sewer sys-
    tem. Twenty-seven thousand dollars later, I can't decide whether
    it's a gold course or a sanctuary for Trappist monks. (*Ironic*) It
    keeps her happy.
FURST: Better she stay in the garden. You run your home very
    well.
GOLD: She even converted the oven into a planter.
FURST: Shirley's uncontrollable.
GOLD: Buy her a spade and compost pile. You'll get a miracle.
FURST: She doesn't have the patience for such things.
GOLD: Shirley's . . . spirited.
FURST: Demented.
GOLD: Her sixth sense is more accurate than your scalpel.
FURST: Your diplomacy, I admire. I like your cleverness, Jules. I

covet your beautiful wife, your darling children, your million-dollar practice. (*Holds out glass*) Another shot, if you please. (GOLD *pours*) I toast my young protege. My protean wunderkind.

GOLD: Dr. Feelgood.

FURST: Dr. Spentwell. To Dr. Jules Morris Gold, one hell of a physician, who loves his patients like family, and treats family like patients. Who loves medicine. Who loves life.

GOLD: Don't stop.

FURST: I could rant about your diabolic golf game. Or your once celebrated cocaine habit.

GOLD: That's past.

FURST: Really it's all the same to me. Just because my generation prefers alcohol.

GOLD: Certainly, you've had periods of depression?

FURST: Never. I only appeared depressed. Cynical mudslide smiles. Marital pains erode the jowls of my clay-baked mask. It's said, you know, that every deceased doctor mars the human face. Little scars lining up madly, like ladies at a clearance sale. (*Pause*) Aren't you drinking with me?

GOLD: I'm on call tonight at the hospital.

FURST: Tonight of all nights?

GOLD: A favor to Schyler.

FURST: So responsible of you. How does one paint the portrait of an austere Jewish saint in his Jaguar? Mercy, mercy, mercy . . . if we could grant absolution to our lost patients, Jules. If we could provide the ointment to the dull cancer in the soul, if we could act like priest, rabbi and sage all in one. If we could . . . we could charge that much more.

GOLD: At your rates, you could give out gift premiums.

FURST: A sense of humor matters, like Jo Anne has. Like you have.

GOLD: You dampened it.

FURST: Nonsense.

GOLD: Too many hospital fights.

FURST: I'm a peacemaker. A dove. Holder of the olive branch.

GOLD: You're a carpetbagger.

FURST: Not true.

GOLD: A foreigner, Ludwig.

FURST (*Masking his German accent with a Texas air*):   I am thoroughly American, I can assure you.

GOLD: Why do you treat me like a prodigal son at staff meetings?

FURST: It's how I show favoritism.

GOLD: Like King Lear at probate court?

FURST: I'm building up your mettle, Jules.

GOLD: You make me feel ludicrous.

FURST: When you support Third World medical schools and exchange doctors, yes . . . you're ludicrous. (*Softer*) Oh, pick up your drink, Jules. This was supposed to be a special occasion. Your fortieth birthday? Or fiftieth? Your age is an enigma to me.

GOLD: Aerobic sex and green salad.

FURST: No traces of graft or cynicism anywhere. No naked signs of appetite. Things I do envy. Your vitality, we all admire at the hospital. That you have time for research and charity, you're a rare physician, Jules. (*Ironic*) But really, do you want to see hacks from Pakistan and Costa Rica in our ward?

GOLD: I really couldn't give a damn.

FURST (*Sweetly*):   They're taking over our hospital beds, our parking spaces, our best cabanas at the country club. Do I sound like a bigot?

GOLD (*Understated*):   Yes.

FURST: One must have a correct sense of prejudices. I've no love for quotas. There's a horde of Mickey Mouse interns about to invade our shores. I abhor two things in life: Caribbean doctors and Puerto Rican car mechanics. When we invaded Grenada, we forgot to level the medical school.

GOLD: We invaded Grenada to mask our humiliation in Beirut.

FURST: Patriotism first, Jules.

GOLD: After Reagan leaves office. Just watching him gives me polyps. (*Pause*) Ludwig, about this request.

FURST: Name it.

GOLD: Give me a leave of absence. For my research grant. At the most, four months. This is the most important project in my career. The Health Institute is providing everything I need, no strings attached.

FURST: Four months . . . too long, Jules.

GOLD: Honor this project, Ludwig.

FURST: I'm not here to worship you.

GOLD: I'm not asking for worship. Just four months.

FURST: You're my right hand at the hospital.

GOLD: Schyler can fill in for me.

FURST: I hate Schyler. What a putz! You've a commitment to the hospital.

GOLD: My milk formula must be tested.

FURST: Hire some flunky to test it.

GOLD: They want me to test it. There are too many variables to worry over. (*Pause*) The first step against infant mortality. If I'm this close, does it make sense to deny myself?

FURST: You know, Jules, I've always stressed breast-feeding. (*Perhaps deadpan*) Especially delinquents. It's the tactile thing. I was breast-fed, by a beautiful neighbor in Stuttgart. It was the finest relation of my life. Breasts are exceedingly soothing. Have you reinvented the breast, Jules?

GOLD: I have.

FURST: I salute you.

GOLD: This shouldn't threaten your oral pleasure, Ludwig.

FURST: I think you're self-righteous. (*Pause*) I'm not letting you go, Jules.

GOLD: Of course you are. You're not going to stand in my way. I'm light years ahead of other researchers. Why begrudge me?

FURST: My generous German instinct. *Zugzwang*. You cannot move.

GOLD: I'd sooner quit the hospital. You're jealous, Ludwig.

FURST: Perhaps I am.

GOLD: I'll share the credit when the publicity breaks. A miraculous gift for the underdeveloped world.

FURST: Don't make my life any harder, Jules.

Source: Theatre Communications Group

✣ Hope of the Future

•••••••••••••••••••••SHANNON KEITH KELLEY

CHARACTERS: DENNIS (30), REX (30)
SETTING: *Flushing Meadow Park, Queens, five years ago.*

DENNIS *and* REX *were buddies and roommates in graduate school five years ago. They have remained friends, and here they get together to relax in Flushing Meadow Park.*

(DENNIS *and* REX *are sunning themselves:* DENNIS *is bare chested, wears gym shorts.* REX *has opened the top three buttons on his shirt, rolled his pants to mid-calf and is barefoot like* DENNIS. *Their shoes are under the aluminum and plastic chairs in which they sit. Scuffed jogging shoes tossed under* DENNIS. *Neatly placed wingtips unde*r REX. *Two taped plastic spoons serve as blinders on* DENNIS' *eyes*)

DENNIS: My self-image sucks.

REX: That's why we're drinking twelve year old scotch from paper cups?

DENNIS: I'm telling you, I understand these guys who walk backwards on Broadway babbling their own private pig Latin.

REX: You do? You understand them?

DENNIS: Not what they're *saying*.

REX: Oh.

DENNIS: How they got there —

REX: I don't want to know —

DENNIS: What got them walking backwards and babbling —

REX: Drink your Chivas.

DENNIS: Won't help.

REX: Can't hurt.

DENNIS: Agreed. (*He removes blinders, stirs drink with them*)

REX: Nice cups.

DENNIS: Thanks for the Chivas. (*Drinks*) So how's your life?

REX: Oh, no. Not me. You're not getting me to examine my existence. You're miserable, I'm not. I'm content.

DENNIS: That bad, huh?

REX: Not play*ing*. I'm not play*ing*. The ole switcheroo won't work.

DENNIS: It all started with high school Commencement.

REX: What? Why am I saying "what"? Dennis is going to tell me.
   (*Beat*)

DENNIS: How long's it been since we saw each other?

REX: Who's counting?

DENNIS: That bad, huh?

   (*They smile.* REX *spreads white sunscreen on his nose*)

REX: Your self-image was fine four months ago. I came through here en route to upstate last March.

DENNIS: That party sucked.

REX: Next time I won't take you.

DENNIS: Wasn't your fault.

REX: Damn right. I fixed you up.

DENNIS: Fixed me is right. Fixed me as in neutered.

REX: Ariella is *the* finest looking straight skater in the company.

DENNIS: Has a strong self-image. Very "centered".

REX: She does have this one hang-up.

DENNIS: Spent all night, I repeat, all night telling me how "centered" she was.

REX: Best pair of legs you ever went out with.

DENNIS: I don't want legs.

REX: Then you came to the wrong man. Ice skaters have legs. You want tits, get a buddy connected with Atlantic City. (*Beat*) What do you want?

DENNIS: That's the problem, Rex.

REX: Denny Den, truth and beauty died with grad school.

DENNIS: But *I* didn't.

REX: Pass the bottle.

   (DENNIS *takes the bottle from the cooler, hands it to* REX. REX *pours himself a drink*)

DENNIS: Need a cube?

REX: Please.

   (DENNIS *takes an ice cube from the cooler, where they rest loosely, drops it in* REX's *cup, returns the bottle to the cooler*)

DENNIS: This is serious, Rex.

REX (*Indicating the cup*):   I can tell by the solemnity with which you deposited the cube in my Igloo cup.

DENNIS: I live in *Queens*, for God's sake.

   (*Beat.* REX *takes the bottle from the cooler, takes* DENNIS' *cup, fills it. Places the bottle on the ground. Adds a cube to* DENNIS' *cup, hands it to him.* DENNIS *drinks*)

REX: I used to live in Manhattan.

DENNIS: Sun shines just as bright on scenic Flushing Meadow Park.

   (*A jet roars deafeningly overhead*)

DENNIS (*As if a proper riposte*):   LaGuardia.

REX: I remember a studio apt. at 89th and Riverside. I remember one room with live-in roaches.

DENNIS: I have roaches now. Little rickety ones — look like *New Yorker* cartoons — move like they're ashamed.

REX: I don't want to know.

DENNIS: Now, the roaches on the Upper West Side. Strong. Slick. Hard-shelled. Crawled with a purpose.

REX: Will you listen to yourself?

DENNIS: Rex, they were Manhattanites.

(Beat)

REX: You can't dwell on the past, Den.

DENNIS: You miss the point.

REX: The point being that for months you didn't leave your apartment except for nature calls to the communal toidy down the hall. You were unemployed, lived off a personal loan.

DENNIS: I'll pay you back.

REX: I'm not worried about the one thousand three hundred and fifty.

DENNIS: Really?

REX: Well, I'm worried. I'm not desperate.

DENNIS: You want a check. I'll write a check. It'll bounce but I'll write it.

REX: It's been five years, I can hold out a bit longer.

DENNIS: Thanks. Five years?

REX: Drink your Chivas —

DENNIS: I was happy, Rex. My life had meaning. Now, now I have a job.

REX: And a good one.

DENNIS: Not as good as yours.

REX: True. I mean, if we're talking money.

DENNIS: Money. *(He waves the thought away)* I didn't come to this city to be an editorial assistant at Cat's Eye Classics.

REX: You didn't have to accept the position.

DENNIS: Who has a choice? A weekly wage? Come on. *(Beat)* My future does not lie in editing original paperback mysteries by former high school teachers from Great Falls, Montana. *(Beat)* Did I tell you they want to make me an assistant editor?

REX: I thought that's what you are? I mean, you're an actor — and a good one — a damn good one.

DENNIS: I was an editorial assistant. Now, I'm an assistant editor.

REX: You accepted? — who has a choice.

DENNIS: I used to be an actor. When I lived in Manhattan.

(*A jet roars deafeningly overhead*)
Kennedy.

REX: You're right.

DENNIS: I am?

REX: Your self-image sucks. What are you going to do about it?

DENNIS: Need a cube?

REX: I'm fine.

(DENNIS *adds a cube to his cup. Thinks, adds scotch*)

DENNIS: That's easy for you to say. Your life's in order.

REX: It's easy for me to say what I said to *you*. Because we're friends. Simpatico to the core. So I take what others might call this liberty in being completely up front with you. You're a good actor, Den.

DENNIS: Yeah.

REX: Best Second Woodsman in *As You Like It I* ever saw.

DENNIS: There are no small roles.

Source: Prima Facie

✛ The House of Correction

•••••••••••••••••••••••••••••NORMAN LOCK

CHARACTERS: STEVE (*30's*), CARL (*30's*)
SETTING: CARL *and Marion's home in suburban New Jersey, the present.*

STEVE *is an odd, intelligent man who is obsessed with justice. After his wife was brutally murdered, he went on a rampage, destroyed his apartment, lost his job, and is now homeless. He has talked his way into* CARL *and Marion's home by pretending to be an old friend.* CARL *and Marion, each thinking that the other knows* STEVE, *have been tricked into letting him move in for a few days.*

(*The basement workshop. The following evening. Lights up.* STEVE *is making something. Whatever it is, it's too early to tell. After a moment,* CARL *enters*)

CARL: So here you are.
STEVE: Here I am.
CARL: Marion said you were down here.
STEVE: You've got a nice little shop.
CARL: Yeah, though I'm hopeless when it comes to tools and things.
STEVE: Then why have it?
CARL: I don't know . . . It's one of those things you just have — if you have a basement. Sometimes I like to come down here and just look at all the screwdrivers and saws. I like to drive a nail once in a while. It relaxes me.
STEVE: My old man did home remodeling for a living. I used to help him sometimes. I'm pretty good with my hands.
CARL: What's that you're making?
STEVE: Can't tell yet.
CARL: Just messing around, hunh?
STEVE: That's right. Just messing around. Who knows . . . It may turn into something. (*Pause*) Something on your mind?
CARL: No.
STEVE: Liar.
CARL: What?
STEVE: I said you're a liar.
CARL: Now look . . . Who do you think you are? (*Pause*) As a matter

of fact, there is something I want to talk to you about.

STEVE: See? I was right.

CARL: I don't want you to think me rude or inconsiderate after all you've been through . . .

STEVE: Thank you.

CARL: You're welcome. But my wife and I were wondering . . . We were wondering who you are.

STEVE: A friend of the family, remember?

CARL: No —

STEVE: I'm not a friend of the family?

CARL: The fact is neither of us have ever laid eyes on you before last night.

STEVE: So that's what's bothering you.

CARL: I wouldn't say it was bothering me . . .

STEVE: You wouldn't?

CARL: Not exactly . . .

STEVE: Not exactly, but it is, shall be say, upsetting you?

CARL: Well, yeah, I think that's a fair way of putting it.

STEVE: That you're upset.

CARL: Yes. Both Marion and I are upset. You're a complete stranger for God's sake!

STEVE: Oh, is that all?

CARL: Isn't that enough? You're in our guest room under false pretenses.

STEVE: How do you mean "false pretenses"?

CARL: We — that is Marion and me — each assumed that the other one knew you. That you were a friend . . . of Marion's . . . or mine. You understand?

STEVE: Did I ever say I knew either one of you?

CARL: No, at least not to me, but you were on the sofa together when I got home. She introduced you as . . . as if you were a long lost friend.

STEVE: You jumped to conclusions, didn't you?

CARL: Goddamn it, we both did! And you knew it and said — did nothing to set us straight. And that's upset me.

STEVE: Perhaps she wanted you to think we were old friends.

CARL: Why would she do that?

STEVE: So that you'd invite me to move in.

CARL (*Angrily*):   What are you suggesting?

STEVE: Nothing.

CARL: We are very happy, and you are here only because of my generosity.

STEVE: I said I'm not suggesting anything.

CARL: You better not be. My wife and I are happy!

STEVE: Are you?

CARL: Yes. Very happy. We are in a position now . . . to be . . . happy. After fourteen years. We can be happy. As happy as we want. So we don't want any outside influences spoiling our happiness.

STEVE (*Quietly*):   She needs someone to jump her bones.

CARL: What did you say?

STEVE: Nothing.

(*Pause*)

CARL: You're a very strange man, Steve.

STEVE: She needs a good fucking.

CARL: I heard that! Look, I'm going to have to ask you to leave.

STEVE: Sorry.

CARL: No, really. You can't get away with saying things like that. I can forgive a lot, knowing that your tragedy has probably unhinged you . . .

STEVE: What tragedy?

CARL: Your wife's death.

STEVE: Ah, that.

CARL: Well, yes, of course that! I don't think you're yourself, Steve.

STEVE: You're probably right.

CARL: It's understandable. I mean Marion and me both understand that a man whose wife — let me put it this way . . . When violence — horror suddenly comes out of nowhere into your life — abruptly, like it did yours . . . there's bound to be upset, confusion. You're going to talk and act peculiarly for a while.

STEVE: That's a very compassionate attitude.

CARL: Compassion — yes! That's the great thing in a case like this, and that's why we want you to know . . . we understand and are willing to forgive . . . much and . . .

STEVE: And?

CARL: And — but you know, Steve. we don't know who you are.

STEVE: Yes, I know.

CARL: And even ignoring the fact that you are under our roof under false colors —

STEVE: Colors? what colors are those, Carl?

CARL: Please let me finish! You are here because of a mistake. But it was ours — I'm willing to give you the benefit of the doubt and accept full responsibility for your being here.

STEVE: That interests me very much, Carl. (*He takes out a pocket note-*

book and pencil and begins to take notes)

CARL: What does?

STEVE: That you're willing to accept responsibility.

CARL: For your being here, yes.

STEVE: For my being here — I've been waiting to hear you say that.

CARL *(Surprised)*: You have?

STEVE: Yes. I want you to be and to feel responsible.

CARL: Well, I've always been aware — acutely — of my responsibility to my fellow beings.

STEVE: Even animals?

CARL: I'm a member of the zoo. I wrote letters to the auto companies protesting head injury experiments on live baboons. What are you writing?

STEVE: Just taking a few notes. So you're opposed to suffering?

CARL: That's right. Suffering offends me. It makes me feel sick inside and hurts my sense of . . .

STEVE: Your sense of design?

CARL: No, what a strange thing to say! My sense of what's right.

STEVE: You consider suffering unseemly.

CARL: I didn't say that! Look, I'm having trouble putting this into words.

STEVE: But you're a wordsmith! You won a fucking Clio for your brilliant work in asparagus.

CARL: Advertising, Steve . . . That was advertising. This on the other hand is something else again.

STEVE: This is an area where you cannot lie.

CARL: I told you before I do not lie! Neither in the spoken word or the written word. In my copy I am absolutely truthful.

STEVE: Absolutely?

CARL: One hundred percent. *(Slight pause)* As far as I know.

STEVE: Define as far as you know.

CARL: Well, I'm only a copywriter after all, not a technical person. I take what the technical people give me and dress it up. I make it flow.

STEVE: But suppose they — the technical people — aren't telling you the truth?

CARL: I'm sure they are.

STEVE: How can you be?

CARL: Because I deal with honorable people.

STEVE: How do you know?

CARL: This isn't the nineteenth century! I'm not selling snake oil in the backwoods!

STEVE:　Aren't you?

CARL:　The whole philosophy of business — I'm talking about legitimate business — is different. Business is no longer out to hoodwink the consumer. Instead, we try to educate him to the benefits of the product.

STEVE:　And if the product is bad?

CARL:　There are no bad products anymore.

STEVE:　I see. And you, as a responsible man, make it your business to investigate every product before you dress it up in award-winning words?

CARL:　That's not necessary. Nor is it possible. I take what they tell me on trust.

STEVE:　Trusting in their honorable intentions toward the public?

CARL:　That's right.

STEVE:　That's very interesting, Carl. (*He closes the notebook and returns it to his pocket*) I wondered how it happened.

CARL:　How what happened?

STEVE:　How it works. It's very interesting. I'm glad you told me. Now let me ask you one last question. What — just supposing now — what if, by some unaccountable fluke, a product which you have helped to sell to the consumer — you, Carl, as the advertising copywriter — suppose the product turned out to be bad, even harmful. Are you willing to be responsible?

CARL (*Considering*):　Well, supposing — and it's only a supposition — if people bought a harmful product because of my words . . . I could not be held accountable, no. If the facts were misrepresented by the manufacturer, or not known by them at the time, I could not be held . . . responsible.

STEVE:　But would you feel responsible?

CARL:　Feel?

STEVE:　If, say, someone got sick, seriously ill, or was maimed because of your words. Would you feel responsible for his or her suffering?

CARL:　No. I cannot accept that. I simply take what they tell me and make it lively — that's all I do. Do you understand what I'm saying?

STEVE:　I understand.

CARL:　That's not to say I wouldn't feel sorry . . .

STEVE:　Of course.

CARL:　Now, Steve, what I came down to talk to you about is just how long do you intend to remain here with us? We're perfectly willing to put you up, temporarily; but in all fairness to Marion, I think we should set some sort of time limit — don't you agree?

STEVE: I agree.

CARL: Good. Then shall we say Sunday? Sunday night? That gives you three days to get yourself situated.

STEVE: Sunday night will be fine.

CARL: That's O.K. then. Thank you, Steve, for being so reasonable.

STEVE: Thank you, Carl.

(CARL *turns to go*)

STEVE: Carl, I enjoyed your watercolors.

(*Pause*)

CARL: Oh? When did you see them?

STEVE: This afternoon while you were at work. Marion showed them to me. In the master bedroom. It's a very nice bedroom.

(*Pause*)

CARL: You were in the bedroom with Marion?

STEVE: Yes. It's a lovely bedroom. My wife and I weren't lucky enough to have such a bedroom, with so many lovely things. (*Slight pause*) Such a soft mattress.

CARL: You tried the mattress?

STEVE: I really must compliment you on your watercolors. They're exquisite.

CARL: Where was Marion while you were looking at them?

STEVE: And I really must compliment you on your wife.

CARL: How do you mean?

STEVE: She has such nice skin. Really exquisite.

CARL: What are you trying to say? What happened in the bedroom? (*Slight pause*) Did anything happen in the bedroom between you and Marion?

STEVE: She was so nice to me. Her skin is so clear and pink and pretty.

CARL (*Screams*):   No!

STEVE: Yes, Carl. And she squealed just like a pink little piggy. She was so happy. We both want her to be happy. Marion's happiness is everything.

CARL: You're lying!

STEVE: I'm not the one who lies, Carl.

CARL: You're a fucking liar!

STEVE: What kind of language is that? In this house such language is forbidden. In this house such language is unseemly.

CARL: I'll kill you!

(*He goes for* STEVE, *but is easily subdued.* STEVE *immobilizes him by pushing one arm up behind his back*)

STEVE: The world may shout and stamp its feet, but here in this house we will have peace and decency. We will stay in control of ourselves.

CARL: You're hurting me!

STEVE: Are you suffering, Carl?

CARL: You're breaking my arm!

STEVE: The bedroom paper is very chic. It is indigo with a pattern of tiny roses and green fern . . .

CARL (*Like an animal*): Awww . . . !

STEVE: The bedspread is elegant. A pale green to match the pale green of the ferns.

CARL: Bitch!

STEVE: And the sheets are rose-colored satin. Cool against the skin.

CARL: Whore!

STEVE: Her skin is soft . . . like rose petals, Carl. Like moss . . . damp moss. I buried my face in it, and for a moment I was in heaven. Heaven! For a moment I forgot all my troubles.

(CARL *is quiet, exhausted by his struggle and his emotions.* STEVE *releases his arm, and he slumps onto the floor*)

STEVE: I'm building something, Carl. Something which will make us all feel better. No, I can't tell you what it is yet. You're not ready. But you will be. And when you are, I'll show you. It won't take me long — I'm handy. I'm very good with my hands. Ask Marion, ask your lovely wife. Oh, it's no trouble, Carl, no trouble at all. It will be ready by Sunday night. Sunday night is our deadline. As an ad man you know all about deadlines. No, don't thank me. It's the least I can do for such a good friend.

Source: Broadway Play Publishing, Inc.

✤ Jeffrey

•••••••••••••••••••••••••••••••PAUL   RUDNICK

CHARACTERS: JEFFREY (30's), STEVE (30's)
SETTING: *A street in New York City, the present.*

JEFFREY *is attractive and well put together, an innocent who believes that life should be wonderful. But for a gay man today it is not. So,* JEFFREY *decides to avoid danger by abstaining from sex. But he breaks his resolve with* STEVE, *a very sexual man who knows what he wants and goes after it. They have flirted and kissed. Now, feeling remorse and fear,* JEFFREY *has broken their date. But he runs into* STEVE *on the street.*

> (STEVE *enters from the opposite side of the stage*)
> STEVE: Jeffrey.
> JEFFREY: Steve! Did you — ?
> STEVE: I got your message. That party. You poor guy. But I was all revved up, so I went out anyway. Dancing.
> JEFFREY: Great. I . . . I . . .
> STEVE: I know.
> JEFFREY: No, I really . . .
> STEVE: Jeffrey, it's not the first time this has happened to me. You freaked. Cold feet.
> JEFFREY: That's not true . . .
> STEVE: Stop it. I can understand, about the HIV thing. It's not easy. But I don't like lying about it. I don't like . . . politeness. Not anymore.
> JEFFREY: I'm sorry. I just — couldn't deal with it. Not right now.
> STEVE: Okay. Fine. (*A beat*) There's lots of things we could do. Safe things. Hot things.
> JEFFREY: I know . . .
> STEVE: But you just . . . don't want to.
> JEFFREY: I'm sorry.
> STEVE: You're sorry. I'm sorry. It's the new national anthem. You said that you . . . thought about me. That you . . . fantasized.
> JEFFREY: I know.
> STEVE: Do you? Still?
> JEFFREY (*After a beat*):   Yes.

STEVE: But . . . Jesus Christ. Jesus *Christ.* I can take being sick, I can fucking take dying, but I can't take this.

JEFFREY: You should have told me.

STEVE: I did.

JEFFREY: Sooner! Before . . . things happened!

STEVE: Before I kissed you!

JEFFREY: Yes!

STEVE: Okay! You didn't have all the . . . information. Okay. I've been positive for almost five years. I was sick once, my T-cells are decent, and every once in a while, like fifty times a day — an hour — I get very tired of being a person with AIDS. A red ribbon. So sometimes . . . I forget. Sometimes I choose to forget. Sometimes I choose to be a gay with a dick. Can you understand? At all?

JEFFREY: Yes.

STEVE: Can I . . . forget again?

JEFFREY: No.

STEVE: Can I do something, say something, that will let this happen? I want you, Jeffrey. I may very well even love you. And that means nothing? That should beat anything. That should win!

JEFFREY: I know.

STEVE: Then why are you the one with the problem? Why do I get to be both sick and begging? (*A beat*) Why won't you kiss me? (JEFFREY *moves toward* STEVE. *They are about to kiss.* JEFFREY *pulls away*)

JEFFREY: I'm sorry — no, I'm sorry I said I'm sorry! I'm sorry you're sick! And I'm sorry I lied! I'm sorry it's not ten years ago, and I'm sorry that life is suddenly . . . radioactive!

STEVE (*After a beat, staring at* JEFFREY): Apology accepted.
(STEVE *exits*)

JEFFREY (*Exploding*): I hate sex! I hate love! I hate the world for giving me everything, and then taking it all back!

Source: Plume

✤ Killers

•••••••••••••••••••••••••••••••JOHN OLIVE

CHARACTERS: BLACKWELL (40's), LOU (20's)
SETTING: *A run-down boarding house in a large city, the 1950's.*

CHARLES BLACKWELL, *a famous writer of pulp fiction, furiously tries to bang out the ending of his latest story.* LOU *is a hyperactive and desperate young punk. He is sexually ambivalent and has probably been intimate with* BLACKWELL. LOU, *needing rent money, barges in on* BLACKWELL *with a stolen baseball bat and a plan.*

(BLACKWELL *starts typing*)
LOU: Whaddaya doin', Mister Blackwell?
BLACKWELL: I'm working. Call me Charley.
LOU: Charley. Charley. Jeez, ya don't look like a Charley. (*Beat*) You look like a Blackie. (*Quick beat*) Okay, okay, you tole me not to call you that, and I won't, 'cause I'll tell you, Mister Blackwell, I about love your ass inside out, you know that? Oh, God. Oh, God. I love you so much. You — You — You — You — You know what I owe you?
BLACKWELL (*Typing*):   Your life?
LOU: I owe you my life! You — You — You — You saved my life! Oh, God!
BLACKWELL: I didn't save —
LOU: You did! I stuck my head in that oven 'cause I wanted to die! And you pulled me out, you — !
BLACKWELL: Earl pulled you out.
LOU: Yeah, but you slapped me around, knocked the sense back into me! Oh, Blackie!
BLACKWELL: Lou!
LOU: Me?
BLACKWELL: Don't call me Blackie. And relax.
LOU (*Belligerantly*):   Will you stop that typing!? Christ sake.
   (BLACKWELL *goes on typing*)
LOU (*Lets go a heartrending sigh*):   Ohhhhhhhhhhhhhhhhh . . . Oh, God. I'm back on the rent. (*Beat*) Four walls. That's the thing, more than food, or clothes, or wine even. Ya gotta feel them four walls. I feel like I'm livin' in a fuckin' gymnasium! I can't even

see 'em! (*Beat*) Mister Blackwell. (*Beat*) Hey. Blackie. Mister
Blackiewell — I mean — Black — Mister — (*Shouts*) HEY!!!

BLACKWELL (*Stops typing. Annoyed*):   What.

LOU: You got some money I can have?

(*A moment of genuine menace.* LOU *taps the floor with the bat, softly.*
BLACKWELL *looks at him*)

BLACKWELL: No, Lou. No.

(*Tense beat. Suddenly* LOU *jumps up, grabs the bat, swings it
viciously, slamming into* BLACKWELL*'s mattress*)

LOU: Wham! Wham! Wham!

(LOU *goes to* BLACKWELL, *kneels in front of him, puts his hands on*
BLACKWELL*'s knees.* BLACKWELL *shoves his hands away*)

LOU: Mister Blackwell —

BLACKWELL: Lou!

LOU: Okay, I'll call you Charley!

BLACKWELL: Don't touch me!

LOU: I can't help it! Look, here's the plan.

(*Music: tense edgy sax, percussive and atonal*)

LOU: What's that joint, down on Franklin, you know, with the —
the — the — the — the — the — the — the — the — the —
the — the — the —

BLACKWELL: The strippers?

LOU: Yeah.

BLACKWELL: The Brite Spot.

LOU: Get a fat one.

BLACKWELL: What?

LOU: You know! Talk to him. You're such a good talker. And then
. . . You know what I'm saying.

BLACKWELL: I don't know what you're saying.

LOU: You know! Pimp him! Tell him, here, I know, tell him it's your
cousin. From Iowa. And she's only fifteen. He can bust her. Ten
bucks. Ooh, she wants it.

(*Puts his hands on* BLACKWELL*'s knees.* BLACKWELL *laughs, and
shoves his hands away*)

LOU: She wants it so bad. And then, you bring him back through
the alley, get him all hot, and I'll step out and do a Mickey Man-
tle up alongside his head. (*Smashing the mattress with the bat,
shouting*) Wham! Wham! Wham! Wham!

[EARL (*In the kitchen, shouting*):   Shut up! Shut up! Lousy punk! Shut
up!]

(BLACKWELL *is laughing.* LOU *beams*)

LOU: Great plan, eh? We'll get his wallet, and his watch, and his rings, if we can get 'em off his fat fingers. Get a fat one. Oh, Blackie, ya gotta get a —

BLACKWELL: Why?

LOU: Huh? 'Cause — 'Cause —

BLACKWELL: You'll kill him!

LOU (*Smiles*): Maybe.

BLACKWELL (*Laughing*): Lou . . .

LOU: Good plan, eh?

BLACKWELL: Lou, it's great. It's the finest plan I ever heard.

(BLACKWELL *turns away from* LOU, *looks at the paper in the typewriter, for a quick beat, then types.* LOU *gets teary:*)

LOU: Aw, Blackie, ugly as y'are, and you are, you know, you're uglier'n dogshit in the spring. But I love your ass. I do. I love you. I just . . . Aw.

BLACKWELL (*Not looking at* LOU): Don't start crying.

LOU: I won't. (*Bursts into tears*) Oh! Oh!

(BLACKWELL *types.* LOU *weeps freely. Sits on the bed, picks up a piece of crumpled paper, opens it up, uses it to wipe tears off his face*)

LOU: I'm depressed.

(*Suddenly,* BLACKWELL *stops typing, rips the paper out of the machine*)

BLACKWELL: Damn it!

(LOU *starts reading the piece of paper, with difficulty:*)

LOU (*Reads, with difficulty*): "Some . . . one . . . laughed."

BLACKWELL: Lou.

LOU (*Reading*): "It . . . was . . . me. He . . . laughed . . . again." Jeez, that's real good, Blackie. (*Picks up another page*) "The . . . wind . . . was . . ." Wow. Oh. "Gritty. With . . . dust . . . and . . ."

(BLACKWELL *snatches the paper away*)

LOU: You gonna hit me?

BLACKWELL: Insanity.

LOU: Huh?

BLACKWELL: Dust and insanity.

LOU: Tell me a story. One a your stories. I won't laugh. Please? Ooh, I got the blues so bad.

BLACKWELL: All right.

LOU: All right!

BLACKWELL: Here's the one I'm working on. I'm trying to get the ending. It's about a travelling salesman, who —

LOU (*Laughs*): Oh, that's great! Travelling salesman. Mister Blackwell. Wow. You're somethin'.

BLACKWELL (*Patiently*): He sells door to door. He tries to sell to this old lady and she cheats him, but he catches her. And living with this old lady is this . . . young woman, and —

LOU: Does he fuck her?

BLACKWELL (*After a pause*):   Yes.

LOU (*Laughs again*):   Oh, Mister Blackwell.

BLACKWELL: The salesman and the girl kill the old lady.

LOU: Whoa!

BLACKWELL: The old lady's got thousands of dollars hidden in the basement, money she stole from the girl's family. The two of them split the money. He thinks that's the end of it. But the girl won't let him be. She comes into his life as a constant presence. The guy's wife thinks he's having an affair with the girl.

LOU: Huh?

BLACKWELL: His wife thinks he's having an — She thinks he's fucking the girl.

LOU: He is fucking her.

BLACKWELL: Once, Lou! Once. Okay? Wife throws him out of their house. Guy lives in his car.

LOU: Really?

BLACKWELL: Yeah. Guy gets bizarre. The girl talks to his best friend, his best friend in the world, tells the friend everything. Guy kills his friend. Then his boss knows.

LOU: He kills the guy.

BLACKWELL: Yeah. The girl tells him she wants all the money. He decides to kill her. But she eludes him. He follows her across country.

LOU: Kills her.

BLACKWELL: He buries her body in a train hopper full of coal. That night he watches the train pulling away. (*Beat*) The moon's like a rotted orange on the horizon. (*Laughs*) His business card! It's in her purse, she's had it ever since that first night. He's yelling. Running. "Where's this train going?" A man's on top of the hopper, black against the moon. "Omaha." (*Beat. Laughs again*) Omaha!

(BLACKWELL *goes back to his writing desk, excited, and starts to type.* LOU *goes to him*)

LOU: I got really bad dreams, Blackie.

BLACKWELL: Yeah, I know. You sleepwalk. And if you call me Blackie one more time I might have to kick your ass.

Source: Dramatists Play Service, Inc.

✤ The Lisbon Traviata

•••••••••••••••••••••••••TERRENCE MCNALLY

CHARACTERS: STEPHEN (*30's-40's*), MIKE (*20's-30's*)
SETTING: STEPHEN *and* MIKE's *apartment, New York City, the present.*

A number of pressures have been building up inside STEPHEN *which have contributed to pushing him right to the edge of his sanity. The final shove occurs when* MIKE, *his lover of several years, flagrantly brings a handsome young guy home for the night. During the emotional argument which ensues,* MIKE *packs his bags and declares that he is moving out. It will add to the effectiveness of the scene if the musical selections mentioned in the stage directions are pre-recorded and played back on a tape player.*

STEPHEN: I was a good lover, Michael. I made you happy. We can try. At least try. We owe ourselves that.
MIKE: It's not just about sex.
STEPHEN: Yes it is. Right now it is. Most of the time it is. We were wonderful that way. What happened?
MIKE: I don't know.
STEPHEN: So why are we doing this?
MIKE: I don't know. (MIKE *exits to bedroom*)
STEPHEN: Nice try, Bubbles. The good doctor's got a heart of stone this morning. (*Calling off to* MIKE) What do you want to hear? What about Tebaldi? You always liked her more than Maria. That should have been a tip off! Do you think people like us read too many books about people like us? How about the Lisbon *Traviata*! That seems to be the record of the month. (*He calls off to* MIKE *in the bedroom*) It's on the top shelf in my closet. The blue tote. Behind the tennis balls.
   (*He walks to the door and talks to* MIKE *without going into the bedroom.* MIKE *will continue to cross in and out of the bedroom and the bathroom packing certain items to take with him.* STEPHEN *will seem superfluous to his activities*)
   What about the house anyway? What about Aspen? What do we tell George and Kenneth? That we're not coming? Just like that?
MIKE: This is difficult enough. Let's not make it worse.
STEPHEN: What am I supposed to tell my lawyer? I left everything to you. I'm not changing my will again.

MIKE: Tell him you want to leave everything to build a memorial statue to Maria Callas.

STEPHEN: You know, that's not a bad idea.

MIKE: Why not? She's dead. It's the living you have trouble with.
(*He goes again.* STEPHEN *begins to play* La Traviata *and stands listening to the "Prelude" which begins to fill the room*)

STEPHEN: I'll never forget the night she did this at the old Met. The excitement in the air. Everybody was there. Jackie Kennedy was in a box with Leonard Bernstein. No, that was for the return as Tosca seven years later and she was Jackie Onassis and she was with Adlai Slevenson. I'd been in love with the sound of her voice since the first records. That strange, sad siren song I knew she was singing just for me. I could play those records for hours. I had them memorized. Every nuance, the slightest intake of breath, the fiercest tones, the hushed, still pianissimo. Hers was the only voice who heard what I heard, said what I wanted to hear. This would be the first time I'd seen her. I'd waited on line for days for standing room. The curtain rose. I didn't see her at first. She was to one side. I thought she'd be center. But then she sang those first phrases — "Flora, amici" — and I saw her. She look my breath away. She wasn't just a voice on a record. She was there, she was real. I was on the same planet at the same moment in time as Maria Callas. The rest of the evening passed like a dream, a dream I remember more clearly than the color of my lover's eyes. I miss you, Mme. Callas.
(*He goes to the window and looks out. He stands with his back to us.* MIKE *comes out of the bedroom with a small tote bag and some final articles he will pack in the suitcase*)

MIKE: You have my brother's number?

STEPHEN: Don't go. Please, don't go.

MIKE: Will you be going out to the house this weekend?

STEPHEN: What do you care?

MIKE: I think it will be easier to get my things out if you aren't here.

STEPHEN: So soon? I don't see the hurry.

MIKE: Yes or no?

STEPHEN: If Caballé cancels her recital, yes. If she deigns to put in an appearance, no.

MIKE: When will you know?

STEPHEN: With Caballé it's right down to the wire. Why don't you call her? She's staying at Burger King.
(*The phone begins to ring*)
Aren't you going to get that?

(*The phone machine is set to answer on the fourth ring*)
That could be him. He could be home by now. I'm not going
near it all day. The House of Knopf can think I'm dead. This is
like waiting for water to boil. Don't give up on me, Michael.
(*The machine picks up, interrupting the fourth ring.* MIKE *looks at
phone, anxious to hear who's calling*)

PAUL'S VOICE: Mike? It's Paul. Are you there? Do you want to pick
up?

(MIKE *picks up tht phone*)

MIKE: Paul, where are you? What happened? I think we should,
too. How soon? What did you tell them at work? The whole
day? Great. I'll be there. (*He hangs up*)

STEPHEN: Let me guess. He said "I think we should talk" and you
said "I think we should too." Now he's calling in sick. You see
the effect you have on people?

(MIKE *is dialing another number*)

MIKE: Go to hell.

STEPHEN: Now who are you calling?

MIKE (*Into phone*):   This is Dr. Deller. Number 52. The blue BMW.
Thank you. How soon?

STEPHEN: What did they tell you? Ten minutes? That should be the
name of that garage. It's probably the only English they speak.
"Ten minutes." Please don't go. I don't want him in our car.

MIKE: Fine. I'll take a cab.

STEPHEN: I didn't mean that. You know what I mean. What if we
got a bigger apartment? Two bedrooms.

MIKE: Ten bedrooms wouldn't be big enough.

STEPHEN: Does it have to be this morning?

MIKE: It should have been three years ago. You can't love what
we've become.

STEPHEN: I don't know how to deal with it!

MIKE: Neither do I.

STEPHEN: I was hoping it would go away or one of us would get
used to it or both of us would or a new soprano would come
along, another Callas, but I suppose that was too much to ask
for, or I could see one of your tricks and not be ripped by jealousy.

MIKE: I thought you were the most terrific looking, acting, everything man I'd ever met.

STEPHEN: Shut up. Please, shut up. Just hold me. Or I could not
mind so desperately being stood up by a cute waiter who's too
young for me anyway. But at his age and given half a choice in

this city of a million of them, I wouldn't want to sleep with me either. You can't leave. No one else will want me.

MIKE: That's not true.

STEPHEN: I look in the mirror and see a young, attractive man but no one else does.

MIKE: You are attractive.

STEPHEN: I said young, attractive. Or I could castrate myself or I could castrate you or we could just get heavily into salt peter and just pretend that none of this mattered — none of it, none of — get another dog and gracefully grow old together.

MIKE: I don't know what to say, Stephen.

STEPHEN: Sure you do.

MIKE: I can't anymore.

STEPHEN: Sometimes I think this is the most beautiful music ever written. (*He puts the phonograph needle to the beginning of "Ah, forse lui".*)

MIKE: I do love you, you know.

STEPHEN: Other times it's the Good Friday Music from *Parsifal*. Or *The Magic Flute*, Pamina's aria, or *Fidelio*, the entire second act.

MIKE: Stephen.

STEPHEN: I heard you. You just don't want to hold my hand when I'm afraid of the dark.

MIKE: I just want to be away from you.

STEPHEN: So you can hold someone else's hand when he's afraid of the dark.

MIKE: You'll be fine without me.

STEPHEN: I won't make it without you.

MIKE: You just think you won't.

STEPHEN: Don't tell me what I think. I'll tell you what I think and what I think is this: you're leaving me at a wonderful moment in our long, happy history of queerness to seek a new mate to snuggle up with right at the height of our very own Bubonic Plague.

MIKE: You'll find someone.

STEPHEN: I don't want someone. No, thank you. I'll stay right here. Those are dark, mean and extremely dangerous streets right now. You can say all you want against Maria, no one's ever accused her of causing AIDS. Renata Scotto, yes; Maria, no.

MIKE: Why can't you be serious?

STEPHEN: It hurts too much, okay? Asshole. Self-centered, smug, shit-kicking, all-his-eggs-in-one-basket, stupid asshole. (*He goes to the stereo and moves the needle to Callas singing the recitative leading to "Sempre Libera" beginning with "Follie, follie!"*)

MIKE: That's not going to make it hurt any less.

STEPHEN: Shut up! Shut up and listen to this. The least you can do is sit there and listen to one last "Sempre Libera" with me. "Always free!",that's you, Michael.

MIKE: I don't want to.

STEPHEN: It's from the by-now-almost-legendary Lisbon *Traviata*.

MIKE: I don't care if it's the Hoboken one.

STEPHEN: Mendy would kill to hear Maria sing this.

MIKE: I'm not Mendy! I've spent the past half-hour trying to get through to you; I've spent the past eight years. You live in *Tosca*. You live in *Turandot*. You live in some opera no one's ever heard of. It's hard loving someone like that.

STEPHEN: Maria does this phrase better than anyone.

MIKE: Listen to me! Turn that down and listen to me.

STEPHEN: It's hard loving someone like me!

(*He turns up the volume to a painfully loud level. Callas is all we can hear.* MIKE *tries to move past* STEPHEN *who pushes him back*)

Where are you going?

MIKE: Let me go.

(STEPHEN *pushes* MIKE *again and picks up the pair of scissors* MIKE *had previously used to destroy the Polaroids. He will brandish them to keep* MIKE *from moving*)

STEPHEN: You love him, don't you?

MIKE: I said, let me go.

STEPHEN: You're not getting past me.

MIKE: Come on, Stephen, put those down. I'm not staying here with you.

(*He takes a step forward.* STEPHEN *forces him back with the scissors*)

STEPHEN: You're going to him. You do love him.

MIKE: Yes. I love him.

STEPHEN: Then you don't love me anymore? Then you don't love me anymore?

MIKE: No, I don't love you anymore.

STEPHEN: But I still love you. I adore you.

MIKE: What's the point of this? I have to go.

(*Again he tries to move past* STEPHEN *who again forces him back with a violent lunge with the scissors*)

STEPHEN: I am to lose my life's salvation so that you can run to someone else and laugh at me? You're not going. You're staying here with me.

MIKE: Give way, Stephen.

STEPHEN: I'm not going to warn you again.

MIKE (*Stepping forward, opening his arms wide*):   All right, do it! Do it or let me by.

STEPHEN (*Raising the scissors above his head*):   For the last time, will you stay here?

(MIKE *holds his hand with the ring in front of* STEPHEN's *face*)

MIKE: You gave me this ring. (*He pulls it off*) I don't want it anymore. (*He throws it down*) Now will you let me by?

(MIKE *walks directly past* STEPHEN *who still stands with the scissors raised. Just as* MIKE *passes him,* STEPHEN *grabs him from behind with a cry and pulls* MIKE *towards him.* STEPHEN *stabs* MIKE)

Jesus!

(MIKE *begins to fall.* STEPHEN *drops the scissors and helps him to the floor.* STEPHEN *leans* MIKE *back against him*)

Jesus, Stephen, Jesus!

STEPHEN: This part. Listen. No one does it like Maria.

MIKE: I'm hurt. I'm really hurt.

STEPHEN: Listen to that. Brava la Divina, brava.

MIKE: This is real, Stephen!

STEPHEN: I know.

MIKE: Stephen, please, you've got to call somebody. We can't handle this. You killed me.

STEPHEN: We killed each other. People don't just die from this. They die from what you were doing to me. They die from loss.

Source: Dramatists Play Service, Inc.

✤ Living At Home

•••••••••••••••••••••••••ANTHONY GIARDINA

CHARACTERS: DAVID (20's), JOHN (20's)
SETTING: *The kitchen of the Bogle home in Watertown, Massachusetts, the present.*

DAVID, *the eldest son, is a senior in college and has applied to several medical schools.* JOHN, *his younger brother, has dropped out of college and is floundering. Their father has just gone off to work in the bowling alley, where both boys also work as assistants.*

DAVID: What are you reading? (JOHN *holds up O'Neill*) "Long Day's Journey Into Night".
JOHN: It reads like the story of our lives.
DAVID: Yeah I think I read it.
JOHN: Why do you have to stop by Alice's? I saw you come in with your jacket last night.
DAVID: What, have you been up all night?
JOHN: Yeah.
DAVID: What for?
JOHN: Watching this.
DAVID: Oh yeah? All night long?
JOHN: In a funny sort of way, I cared, during the early part of the night. I wanted to watch the old stuff, over and over again. I wanted to see him running on the beach and playing with John John, stuff like that. Then I started in on Dad's Seagram's 7, and it began to look sort of absurd, them showing that stuff over and over again, like it had something, anything to do with what happened yesterday. I mean, if he had been shot down while running on the beach, or playing with John John, it might actually apply. But by about three this morning, I was laughing at it. At first, just sort of giggling — than actual laughter. I wasn't laughing at *it*. I was laughing at my own serious self, sitting here with a bottle of Seagram's 7, mourning for the American condition, along with David Brinkley and those guys.
DAVID: I don't know. Alice was pretty upset.
JOHN: Upset enough to put out?
DAVID: That's why I've got to see her. Last night — hey, listen, can you keep a secret?

JOHN: Sure.

DAVID: I don't know. Maybe it was the wrong thing to do. But I got in — about an inch last night — and the thing is I got her convinced she's still a virgin. Yeah. She was crying on my shoulder. You know how that gets you hot. She was crying about how beautiful Kennedy looked, and how beautiful Jackie looked, even with blood all over her. And I was getting hotter by the minute. So I got her down, like usual, and I got her bra off, like usual, and she started holding onto me like a crazy woman, like there was no way I could get away, and then she started moving under me, like she really wanted it. But when I put my hand down there, she grabbed it back. But she kept moving. I thought I was gonna come in my pants any minute. So I said to her, Listen, don't do this to me, it's driving me crazy. So she stopped. For about thirty seconds, and then started again. So finally she let me touch her down there. She was saying, "Please don't" the whole time and I promised her, out loud, which is the terrible part, that I wouldn't do anything to change anything. I said, I'll only go in just a little way, so you'll still be a virgin. Which she believed. I went in about half an inch, and she said, "I'm still a virgin, right?" And I said, "Yes, technically I'm not even in you." And that made it just fine. She even let me in a little more and — Pow! I came a flood. It was amazing. She believed it! If I work it right I can lay her every night of the week and twice on Sundays and she'll still believe she's a virgin. Only I've got to go see her before work. I promised her last night and I can't break a promise, not now.

JOHN: Hey, congratulations. Alice finally puts out. Her parents going to give her a putting out party, or what? "Debutante puts out", the papers'll say. "Miss Alice Langtree, daughter of Blondie and Dagwood . . . "

DAVID: Okay, that's enough. No big deal. It's just that it's so much better to come home and not have to finish it off in bed.

JOHN: I thought things were a little quiet up there last night. No rattle of springs, no groans, the ceiling didn't drip like usual. Alice is really performing a service for the future and well being of this old house. Most guys jerk off, they come in a hot little clot, if you're real good with your hands, you can actually catch it. My brother jerks off, the walls pound, the house gets flooded.

DAVID: All right, that's enough of that. We gotta hurry.

JOHN: Right. Before you know it, it'll be 10:01 and there'll be hell to

pay. What does *that* mean? Hey, what if she smartened up over-
night, read a book or something?

DAVID: Don't even think about it. Listen, she can't know you know.

JOHN: David, David, it's no big thing. Girls do it all the time. You
should have gone away to college. You get wised up real quick.

DAVID: Like you?

JOHN: Yes, like me.

DAVID: I suppose you get laid all the time?

JOHN: You know I haven't gotten laid in the last eleven months.

DAVID: At UMass, I suppose you got laid all the time?

JOHN: I got my share.

DAVID: Sure you did.

JOHN: David, it's no big thing. It is now a commonly accepted fact
that girls have sexual appetites. Even at Brandeis.

DAVID: Yeah, yeah, I know. There are girls, the loose ones, everybody knows about them.

JOHN: David, what does "loose" mean? Tell me.

DAVID: You know what "loose" means.

JOHN: No, I don't. I honestly don't.

DAVID: Get out of here.

JOHN: What, is it me? I honestly don't understand anymore what
anybody in this house is talking about. "Loose". What exactly
does that mean, David?

DAVID: All right. You're playing with me, I'll play. "Loose" girls.
Girls who put out just for the hell of it. Without loving a guy.
Girls with animal natures. Girls who just want it. There. There's
your definition, wise guy.

JOHN: Don't you think they have a right to want it?

DAVID: Sure they have a right, but someday some guy might come
along and fall in love with them, and he doesn't want anybody
to have been there before him.

JOHN: But you're missing the point. We've got a right, don't we?

DAVID: To want it? Sure.

JOHN: Why not them?

DAVID: Well, if you love each other, and you both want it, fine.

JOHN: What if you don't love each other? What if you both just
want it?

DAVID: Look, you're a big man. You've been to Amherst, you've
gotten laid, now you're comin' at me with this free love bullshit.
But you couldn't cut it, John. You left, you dropped out. If it was
all so terrific, all that free love, why'd you come back here?

JOHN: It had nothing to do with getting laid.

DAVID: Obviously no. Eleven months is a long time for a stud like you.

JOHN: Okay, let's drop it.

DAVID: What for? Tell me, if that's the answer, two people wanting it, two people doing it, why'd you leave that world to come back to this one? Don't read your book, answer me!

JOHN: Take the goddamn car, I don't want it.

(DAVID *grabs keys, storms out the door. Silence.* DAVID *returns, in the manner of a kid who's just run away from home but forgotten his suitcase*)

DAVID: Listen. Mary wants to go out with you.

JOHN: Who's Mary?

DAVID: Come on, you know who Mary is. Alice's sister. Alice thinks it'd be a good idea for the four of us to double.

JOHN: Why does Mary want to go out with me?

DAVID: How the hell should I know? She just broke up with some guy from Harvard. You want me to tell her no?

JOHN: No. (*Pause*) Let me get this straight. Mary is the one with blonde hair and the face like Greer Garson?

DAVID: No, that's Cynthia. Mary is the one with brown hair you met bowling two weeks ago.

JOHN: She bowls?

DAVID: Yeah.

JOHN: I don't want to go out with her.

DAVID: Are you crazy? She's a peach.

JOHN: A what?

DAVID: A peach.

JOHN: What's that mean?

DAVID: All right, I'm taking the car, Good bye. (*He starts out*)

JOHN: No, wait. You say she's a peach.

DAVID: Yes.

JOHN: When is this famous double date supposed to happen?

DAVID: You doing anything special tonight?

JOHN: You know damn well I'm not doing anything special tonight.

DAVID: All right, then, tonight.

JOHN: Wait, I've gotta find out what's on "Saturday Night at the Moves".

DAVID: Don't be so nervous.

JOHN: Who's nervous. (*He riffles through the paper*) Rio Bravo. Forget it. *Rio Bravo* is on. I refuse to miss Walter Brennan singing

"When You Comin' Home, Cindy Cindy" for the sake of Alice's kid sister.

DAVID: Dummy. There's not going to be any movie on tonight. This stuff is gonna be on til Kennedy's buried, and then there'll be burial commentaries, and commentaries on the burial commentaries.

JOHN: That's right. I understand that movie theaters have never had such record audiences. People, they say, are pouring out of their houses. Now what does *that* mean?

DAVID: Look, it's getting late. Do you want to go or not?

JOHN: Yes, yes, I'll go. I haven't got any money, though.

DAVID: That's okay. I'll stand you. Let's go. We can talk on our way over there.

JOHN: Wait a minute. You mean I have to see her? Now?

DAVID: Yeah. She'll probably be there.

JOHN: Oh, Christ, David, I can't go. You take the car.

DAVID: What's the matter with you?

JOHN: Listen, David, look at me. Why does she want to go out with me?

DAVID: She's heard about your reputation.

JOHN: What reputation?

DAVID: She's got friends at UMass. Look, I don't know why she wants to go out with you. Don't look a gift horse in the mouth. Maybe she just likes you.

JOHN: How can she? She doesn't even know me. What'll we talk about?

(DAVID *goes into the hall and comes back with two jackets*)

DAVID: Kennedy. Talk about Kennedy.

JOHN: There isn't exactly much left to say. You think she just likes me, huh?

DAVID: Here. Put this on.

(JOHN *puts jacket on, goes to a drawer and comes up with funny glasses and mustache*)

JOHN: I'll stay in the car. Introduce me as your friend Bruno from Brandeis.

DAVID: Bruno from Brandeis. What are you so afraid of?

JOHN (*Removing glasses*): Mom says I'm lost. We've got to go upstairs and give her the good news. "I'm goin' out with a girl, Ma, everything's gonna be fine!"

DAVID: Come on, what is this with Ma all of a sudden?

JOHN: She's dying, David.

DAVID: Miggsy's home, isn't she?

JOHN: She had a pajama party to go to last night. She hasn't gotten back yet.

DAVID: With this they didn't cancel it?

JOHN: With what?

DAVID (*Indicating TV*):   With *this*.

JOHN: Did you cancel *your* pajama party?

DAVID: That's different. I don't like leaving Ma alone.

JOHN: She'll be all right. She doesn't need anything.

DAVID: What if she falls?

JOHN: What if?

DAVID: There'll be nobody to pick her up.

JOHN: David, just go out and start the car. I'll be out in a couple of minutes. I'll just go up and explain to her that Miggsy'll be home soon.

DAVID: Yeah, okay. Turn that thing off, too.

(DAVID *exits.* JOHN *waits for a moment, flips up the collar of his jacket, puts his book in his pocket, then goes to the TV, watches it for a few moments. Then he puts his hand on the knob, turns it off. He waits a moment in silence, then turns it quickly back on, switching the channel. When the picture has been realized, he looks up the stairs leading to his mother's room, but turns quickly in the other direction and goes out the door. The lights come down and the television image flickers alone in the dark*)

Source: Dramatists Play Service, Inc.

✤ M. Butterfly

•••••••••••••••••••••••DAVID HENRY HWANG

CHARACTERS: GALLIMARD (65), SONG (30's)
SETTING: *A courthouse in Paris, 1986.*

Diplomat RENE GALLIMARD, *held captive by the French government, recalls the time that he fell in love with his ideal woman, the beautiful diva,* SONG, *who turns out to be a male spy for the Chinese government. As the scene opens,* GALLIMARD *and* SONG *review their love affair.*

SONG: Do you remember? The night you gave your heart?

GALLIMARD: It was a long time ago.

SONG: Not long enough. A night that turned your world upside down.

GALLIMARD: Perhaps.

SONG: Oh, be honest with me. What's another bit of flattery when you've already given me twenty years' worth? It's a wonder my head hasn't swollen to the size of China.

GALLIMARD: Who's to say it hasn't?

SONG: Who's to say? And what's the shame? In pride? You think I could've pulled this off if I wasn't already full of pride when we met? No, not just pride. Arrogance. It takes arrogance, really — to believe you can will, with your eyes and your lips, the destiny of another. (*He dances*) C'mon. Admit it. You still want me. Even in slacks and a button-down collar.

GALLIMARD: I don't see what the point of —

SONG: You don't? Well maybe, Rene, just maybe — I want you.

GALLIMARD: You do?

SONG: Then again, maybe I'm just playing with you. How can you tell? (*Reprising his feminine character, he sidles up to* GALLIMARD) "How I wish there were even a small café to sit in. With men in tuxedos, and cappuccinos, and bad expatriate jazz." Now you want to kiss me, don't you?

GALLIMARD (*Pulling away*): What makes you —?

SONG: — so sure? See? I take the words from your mouth. Then I wait for you to come and retrieve them. (*He reclines on the floor*)

GALLIMARD: Why?! Why do you treat me so cruelly?

SONG: Perhaps I *was* treating you cruelly. But now — I'm being nice. Come here, my little one.

GALLIMARD: I'm not your little one!

SONG: My mistake. It's I who am *your* little one, right?

GALLIMARD: Yes, I —

SONG: So come get your little one. If you like, I may even let you strip me.

GALLIMARD: I mean, you were! Before . . . but not like this!

SONG: I was? Then perhaps I still am. If you look hard enough. (*He starts to remove his clothes*)

GALLIMARD: What — what are you doing?

SONG: Helping you to see through my act.

GALLIMARD: Stop that! I don't want to! I don't —

SONG: Oh, but you asked me to strip, remember?

GALLIMARD: What? That was years ago! And I took it back!

SONG: No. You postponed it. Postponed the inevitable. Today, the inevitable has come calling.

(*From the speakers, cacophony:* Butterfly *mixed in with Chinese gongs*)

GALLIMARD: No! Stop! I don't want to see!

SONG: Then look away.

GALLIMARD: You're only in my mind! All this is in my mind! I order you! To stop!

SONG: To what? To strip? That's just what I'm —

GALLIMARD: No! Stop! I want you — !

SONG: You want me?

GALLIMARD: To stop!

SONG: You know something, Rene? Your mouth says no, but your eyes say yes. Turn them away. I dare you.

GALLIMARD: I don't have to! Every night, you say you're going to strip, but then I beg you and you stop!

SONG: I guess tonight is different.

GALLIMARD: Why? Why should that be?

SONG: Maybe I've become frustrated. Maybe I'm saying "Look at me, you fool!" Or maybe I'm just feeling . . . sexy. (*He is down to his briefs*)

GALLIMARD: Please. This is unnecessary. I know what you are.

SONG: You do? What am I?

GALLIMARD: A — a man.

SONG: You don't really believe that.

GALLIMARD: Yes I do! I knew all the time somewhere that my happiness was temporary, my love a deception. But my mind kept the knowledge at bay. To make the wait bearable.

SONG: Monsieur Gallimard — the wait is over.

(SONG *drops his briefs. He is naked. Sound cue out. Slowly, we and* SONG *come to the realization that what we had thought to be* GAL-LIMARD'*s sobbing is actually his laughter*)

GALLIMARD: Oh god! What an idiot! Of course!

SONG: Rene — what?

GALLIMARD: Look at you! You're a man! (*He bursts into laughter again*)

SONG: I fail to see what's so funny!

GALLIMARD: "You fail to see — !" I mean, you never did have much of a sense of humor, did you? I just think it's ridiculously funny that I've wasted so much time on just a man!

SONG: Wait. I'm not "just a man."

GALLIMARD: No? Isn't that what you've been trying to convince me of?

SONG: Yes, but what I mean —

GALLIMARD: And now, I finally believe you, and you tell me it's not true? I think you must have some kind of identity problem.

SONG: Will you listen to me?

GALLIMARD: Why?! I've been listening to you for twenty years. Don't I deserve a vacation?

SONG: I'm not just any man!

GALLIMARD: Then, what exactly are you?

SONG: Rene, how can you ask — ? Okay, what about this? (*He picks up* BUTTERFLY'*s robes, starts to dance around. No music*)

GALLIMARD: Yes, that's very nice. I have to admit.

(SONG *holds out his arm to* GALLIMARD)

SONG: It's the same skin you've worshipped for years. Touch it.

GALLIMARD: Yes, it does feel the same.

SONG: Now — close your eyes.

(SONG *covers* GALLIMARD'*s eyes with one hand. With the other,* SONG *draws* GALLIMARD'*s hand up to his face.* GALLIMARD, *like a blind man, lets his hands run over* SONG'*s face*)

GALLIMARD: This skin, I remember. The curve of her face, the softness of her cheek, her head against the the back of my hand . . .

SONG: I'm your Butterfly. Under the robes, beneath everything, it was always me. Now, open your eyes and admit it — you adore me. (*He removes his hand from* GALLIMARD'*s eyes*)

GALLIMARD: You, who knew every inch of my desires — how could you, of all people, have made such a mistake?

SONG: What?

GALLIMARD: You showed me your true self. When all I loved was the lie. A perfect lie, which you let fall to the ground — and now, it's old and soiled.

SONG: So — you never really loved me? Only when I was playing a part?

GALLIMARD: I'm a man who loved a woman created by a man. Everything else — simply falls short.

(*Pause*)

SONG: What am I supposed to do now?

GALLIMARD: You were a fine spy, Monsieur Song, with an even finer accomplice. But now I believe you should go. Get out of my life!

SONG: Go where? Rene, you can't live without me. Not after twenty years.

GALLIMARD: I certainly can't live with you — not after twenty years of betrayal.

SONG: Don't be so stubborn! Where will you go?

GALLIMARD: I have a date . . . with my Butterfly.

SONG: So, throw away your pride. And come . . .

GALLIMARD: Get away from me! Tonight, I've finally learned to tell fantasy from reality. And, knowing the difference, I choose fantasy.

SONG: *I'm* your fantasy!

GALLIMARD: You? You're as real as hamburger. Now get out! I have a date with my Butterfly and I don't want your body polluting the room! (*He tosses* SONG's *suit at him*) Look at these — you dress like a pimp.

SONG: Hey! These are Armani slacks and — ! (*He puts on his briefs and slacks*) Let's just say . . . I'm disappointed in you, Rene. In the crush of your adoration, I thought you'd become something more. More like . . . a woman. But no. Men. You're like the rest of them. It's all in the way we dress, and make up our faces, and bat our eyelashes. You really have so little imagination!

GALLIMARD: You, Monsieur Song? Accuse me of too little imagination? You, if anyone, should know — I am pure imagination. And in imagination I will remain. Now get out! (GALLIMARD *bodily removes* SONG *from the stage, taking his kimono*)

SONG: Rene! I'll never put on those robes again! You'll be sorry!

GALLIMARD (*To* SONG): I'm already sorry! (*Looking as the kimono in his hands*) Exactly as sorry . . . as a Butterfly.

Source: New American Library

✦ Man Enough

•••••••••••••••••••••••PATTY GIDEON SLOAN

CHARACTERS: JOEY (*18*), DONAL (*30's*)
SETTING: *The Delaney home, Flatbush, Brooklyn, New York, the present.*

JOEY *is mentally retarded and is about to be sent to a sanitarium because his family can no longer give him the constant attention he requires.* DONAL, JOEY's *older brother, has a witty and charming personality which barely masks his dark, disillusioned side. He has just flown in from out of town to visit* JOEY *before he is sent away.*

JOEY: You take the bed, Donal. I'll take the cot.
DONAL: You sure you want to give up your bed for me, kid?
JOEY: Sure I'm sure.
DONAL: Well, thanks. I appreciate that.
　　　(JOEY *puts suitcase and tube on cot, begins trying to unzip suitcase, ignoring tube*)
　　　Here, let me get that.
　　　(*But* JOEY *elbows* DONAL *back*)
JOEY: I can do it.
DONAL (*Smiling*): You know where everything goes?
JOEY: Sure.
　　　(JOEY *starts throwing clothes out of bag onto cot, paying no attention to them. He appears to be looking for something.* DONAL *watches for a moment, amused*)
DONAL: Looking for something?
JOEY (*Engrossed*): I can do it. (*When bag is empty,* JOEY *picks it up, looks inside, turns it upside down, shakes it*)
DONAL (*Affectionately*): Okay, okay, kid. I think I know what you're looking for. (*Picks up tube, holds it out to* JOEY) Here.
JOEY (*Taking tube*): Oh, boy. (*But it is obvious* JOEY *has no idea what to do with tube*)
DONAL: What is it?
JOEY: I don't know.
DONAL: Try opening it.
　　　(JOEY *tries to figure out how to open tube; starts twisting it*)

(*Soft laugh*) No, no. Here. (*Takes tube; begins unscrewing cap*) Take this off.

JOEY: It turns. It turns. I can do it. (JOEY *works to get cap off, then looks at cap with pleasure of accomplishment, forgetting about tube*)

DONAL: Look inside.

(JOEY *holds up tube as if it were a telescope, looks inside*)

JOEY: It's shiny.

DONAL (*Surprised*):   Even in the tube? (DONAL *takes tube, looks into it*) By golly, you're right. (DONAL *reaches in tube, pulls out rolled sheet, hands tube to* JOEY, *who cuddles it possessively.* DONAL *opens sheet, holds it up to display map of the stars*) Now what is it?

JOEY (*Excited with recognition*):   Stars . . . stars.

DONAL: That's right. It's a map of the stars that are over our house at night. And it glows in the dark.

JOEY: Oh, boy.

DONAL (*Turning to wall*):   And we're going to hang it on your wall so you can see the stars when you go to bed just like you were sleeping outside. How do you like that?

JOEY (*Very impressed*):   I like it.

(DONAL *finds thumbtacks in wall, begins tacking map to wall*)

DONAL (*Singing as he tacks*):   "The stars at night, are big and bright, deep in the heart of Flatbush . . . "

JOEY (*Repeating*):   . . . Flatbush.

DONAL (*Thumping map with knuckles*):   There we are. Pretty impressive, huh?

JOEY: Yeah. (JOEY *climbs up on bed, jabs finger at star where* DONAL *had thumped map*) There we are. That's us.

DONAL (*Laughing*):   No, Joey. I didn't mean, "There *we* are." As a matter of fact, that's Star XJ105, and it's due to explode any minute now.

JOEY (*Stubbornly; throwing tube on floor*):   No! That's us. That's where we live.

DONAL (*Reacting to tube-throwing; angrily*):   Wait a minute!

(JOEY *gets off bed, stalks to chair, sits down, turns his back on* DONAL. DONAL *looks at him a moment, then softens*)

(*Gently*) Wait a minute. (DONAL *leans close to map as if reading.* JOEY *watches out of the corner of his eye. As if reading*) "715 East 39th Street." By golly, Joey, you're right again. I never saw the address on there before.

JOEY (*Stubbornly*):   Yeah, I'm right.

(*Pause;* DONAL *watches* JOEY)

DONAL: Pretty good present, huh?

JOEY (*Mollified*): Yeah. Better than pretty good.

DONAL: All right! Better than pretty good. (*Then businesslike*) Okay, now, enough of that. We gotta get these clothes put away.

JOEY (*Getting up; eagerly*): I can help.

DONAL: Yep. (*Sitting* JOEY *back down*) You can sit right here and watch to see I put everything in the right place, okay?

JOEY: Okay. (JOEY *watches as* DONAL *begins putting clothes in drawer of chest and in closet*)

DONAL (*After a moment*): So — how's it going? How're you feeling?

JOEY: Feeling good. (*Pause; less certain*) Feeling . . . okay.

DONAL: Well, that's good to hear. Yep, I'm certainly glad to hear that.

(*Pause.* DONAL *works.* JOEY *is thinking; his face begins to sadden*)

JOEY: You know why you came this time, Donal?

(DONAL *pauses slightly, his back to* JOEY. *Pain flickers across his face as he perceives* JOEY'S *sadness*)

DONAL (*Lightly*): Sure, kid, I know why I . . .

JOEY: You came to see me off.

DONAL: That's right.

JOEY (*Standing up to reach calendar*): Sunday . . . Sunday's the big day.

DONAL: Yep. Two more days till the big day. (*Pause; gentle*) So — how do you feel about it?

JOEY (*Shrugging; too cheerfully*): S'okay by me.

DONAL: Good.

JOEY (*Looking down; softer*): S'okay by me.

(DONAL *waits but* JOEY *does not look up*)

DONAL: Good. (*Turns back to his work*)

JOEY (*Suddenly blurting out*): I could go with you, Donal.

(*Again pain flickers over* DONAL'S *face*)

DONAL (*Softly*): Well, I wish you could, pal, but . . .

JOEY: Me and Roby . . . we could both go with you.

DONAL: You and Roby . . . ?

JOEY: We could come live with you. And you'd like to have us, too, I bet.

(*Pause.* DONAL *eyes* JOEY)

DONAL: You and Roby been talking about this, have you?

(JOEY *looks away, avoiding* DONAL'S *question*)

'Cause you know . . . you *both* know Roby can't come live with me. He's got to stay with his mom . . . even though I would like it a lot.

(DONAL *touches* JOEY'S *shoulder;* JOEY *jerks away, sits in misery.*

Pause)
(*Gently joking*) C'mon, kid. Whaddaya think you're doing? You wanna get me in big trouble around here? I mean, I run off with you and Roby, and I'm in BIG trouble around here. (*Pause*) Listen . . . you gotta be man enough to meet this new challenge, champ. You gotta be man enough to . . . to stand up . . . (DONAL *stands*) . . . chest out, stomach in, and say . . . "Put up your dukes. I can lick anyone in the house, I tell ya, anyone in the house."
(JOEY *is now smiling, trying not to cry*)
Come on . . . Up!
(DONAL *helps* JOEY *up, and, with a little coaxing,* JOEY *copies his brother's stance*)
(*Coaxing*) 'At's it. Put up your dukes. Now let's hear you say, "I can lick . . . "

JOEY (*Strongly*): Anyone in the house. I can lick anyone in the house.
(*They pretend to box for a moment with carefully choreographed jabs that indicate they've done this many times before. Then* DONAL *cuffs* JOEY *affectionately*)

DONAL: You sure can, Buster. Sonuvagun if you can't.

Source: Samuel French, Inc.

✤ The Medal of Honor Rag

• •TOM COLE

CHARACTERS: DALE JACKSON (24), DOCTOR (40's)
SETTING: *A doctor's office, the present.*

DALE JACKSON, *a black man, has had a history of mental problems due to serving in Vietnam. As the scene opens, the new doctor tries to get* JACKSON *to deal with his depression.*

DOC: Sergeant Jackson? (DALE JACKSON *nods*) Well, they seem to be keeping a pretty close eye on you.

D.J.: Where's the other doctor?

DOC (*Settling back in his chair*): Sit down, please.

D.J.: They keep changing doctors.

DOC: Would you rather see the other doctor?

D.J.: No, man . . . it's just that I have to keep telling the same story over and over again.

DOC: Sometimes that's the only way to set things straight.

D.J.: You're not in the Army, huh?

DOC (*Twinkle*): How can you tell?

D.J.: Your salute is not of the snappiest.

DOC: I came down from New York today. To see you.

D.J.: I must be a really bad case.

DOC: You're a complicated case.

D.J.: Like they say, a special case. I am a special case. Did you know that?

DOC: They keep a pretty close eye on you now.

D.J.: I went AWOL twice. From this hospital.

DOC: Oh?

D.J.: But they'll never do anything to me.

DOC: I understand.

D.J.: You understand, huh?

DOC: I understand your situation.

D.J.: Yeah, well, mind telling me what it is?

DOC: You don't need me to tell you that.

D.J.: So what *do* I need you for?

DOC: I don't know — maybe *I* need *you*.

D.J.: That's a new one. That's one they haven't tried yet.

DOC: Oh?

D.J.:   Every doctor has his own tricks.

DOC: Oh?

D.J.:   That's one of yours.

DOC: Oh? What's that?

D.J.:   When it's your turn to talk, you get this look on your face —
kind of like an old owl who's been constipated for about five
hundred years, you know, and you say (*Imitation of* DOC*'s face*),
"oh?"

(*The* DOCTOR *laughs at this, a little, but he is watching* D.J. *very
closely*)

(*Sudden anger*) Man, this is a *farce*! (D.J. *turns away — as if to "go
AWOL" or to charge to the door . . . but he gets immediate control of
himself. He is depressed*)

DOC (*Calmly*):   What should we do about it?

D.J.:   Who's this "we"?

DOC: Who else is there?

D.J.:   We just going to keep asking each other questions?

DOC: I don't know — What do you think?

D.J.:   What do *you* think, man? *Do* you think?

DOC: I listen.

D.J.:   No, man, I mean, what do you think? You got that folder there.
My life is in there. I'm getting near the end of the line with this
stuff. I mean, sometimes I feel like there's not much time. You
know? (*As* D.J. *talks, he has wandered over to the desk; where he proceeds to thumb through the folders on his case. He does this with a
studied casualness*)

DOC: I'm aware of that.

D.J.:   You some big-time specialist? (*Suddenly suspicious*)

DOC: In a manner of speaking.

D.J.:   What are you a specialist in?

DOC: I do a lot of work with Vietnam veterans and their problems.

D.J.:   Well I can *see* that, man. But what do you *specialize* in?

DOC: I specialize in grief.

D.J. (*Laughs, embarrassed*):   Shit. Come on.

DOC (*As if taking a leap*):   Impacted grief. That's the . . . special area I
work in.

D.J. (*Disgusted*):   I'm going to spend another hour in jive and riddles
and double talk. Only it's not even an hour, right? It's, like,
impacted.

DOC: You know the word "impacted"?

D.J.:   How dumb do you think I am?

DOC: I don't think you're dumb at all. Matter of fact, the reverse . . .
(*While speaking these words, he has opened the dossier to a sheet, from*

which he reads aloud) "Subject is bright. His Army G.T. rating is equivalent of 128 I.Q. In first interviews does not volunteer information —" (*Smiles to* D.J., *who allows himself a small smile of recognition in return; then continues reading*) "He related he grew up in a Detroit ghetto and never knew his natural father. He sort of laughed when he said he was a "good boy" and always did what was expected of him. Was an Explorer Scout and an altar boy. . ."

D.J.: The other doctor talked a lot about depression.

DOC: What did he say about it?

D.J.: He said I had it.

DOC: Oh? And?

D.J.: He thought I oughta get rid of it. You know? (*The* DOCTOR *reacts*) Yeah, well he was the chief doctor here. The chief doctor for all the psychos in Valley Forge Army Hospital! See what I mean?

DOC: Valley Forge.

D.J.: Yeah . . .

DOC: Why *don't* you get rid of it?

D.J. (*Animated*): Sometimes that's just what I want to do! Sometimes I want to throw it in their faces! (*Recollecting himself*) Now ain't that stupid? Like, whose face?

DOC (*He is keenly on the alert, but tries not to show it in the wrong way*): What do you want to throw in their faces?

D.J.: What are we talking about?

DOC: What are you talking about?

(D.J. *stares at him. He won't or can't say anything.* DOC *continues gently, precisely*)

I was talking about depression. You said your doctor said you should try to get rid of it. I asked, simply, why don't you get rid of it?

(D.J. *stares at him, still. He is a man for whom it is painful to lose control. He is held in, impassive*)

You meant the medal, didn't you, when you said, "throw it in their faces"?

D.J.: Well. That's why you're here, right? Because of the medal?

DOC (*Gentle, persistent*): But I didn't bring it up. You did.

D.J.: You asked me why I don't get rid of it.

DOC (*Repeating*): I was talking about depression.

D.J.: No. You meant the medal.

DOC: *You* meant the medal. I never mentioned it . . . Are you glad you have it?

D.J.: The depression?

DOC: No. The medal.

D.J. (*Laughs*): Oh, man . . . Oh, my . . . Suppose I didn't have that medal...You wouldn't be here, right? You wouldn't know me from a hole in the wall. I mean, I would be invisible to you. Like a hundred thousand other dudes that got themselves sent over there to be shot at by a lot of little Chinamen hiding up in the trees. I mean, you're some famous doctor, right? Because, you know, I'm a special case! Well I am, I am one big tidbit. I am what you call a "hot property" in this man's Army. Yes, sir! I am an authentic hero, a showpiece. One look at me, enlistments go up 200% . . . I am a credit to my race. Did you know that? I am an honor to the city of Detroit, to say nothing of the state of Michigan, of which I am the only living Medal of Honor winner! I am a feather in the cap of the Army, a flower in the lapel of the military — I mean, I am *quoting* to you, man! That is what they say at banquets, given in *my* honor! Yes, sir! And look at me! *Look at me*!! (*Pointing to himself in the clothing of a sick man, in an office of an Army hospital*)

Source: Samuel French, Inc.

❖ Meeting The Winter Bike Rider

●●●●●●●●●●●●●●●●●●●●●●●●●●●●●●●JUAN NUNEZ

CHARACTERS: MARK (16), TONY (14)
SETTING: *The attendant's room in an old-fashioned gas station.*

TONY, *a sensitive boy of fourteen, has run away from home after a fight. Passing through a small town late one night, his bike breaks down. He walks it to a secluded gas station which is manned only by* MARK, *a friendly, aggressive, lonely sixteen-year-old. The two begin to strike up an uneasy friendship.*

TONY (*Interested*):   Do you have many girlfriends?
MARK: No. I had one; just broke up with my first a few weeks ago. She was a real letdown. (*Slight pause*) I'll agree with you, in a way, about the demands and hardships of having a girlfriend. Let me tell you, Tony, most girls don't want someone they can talk to; they want a gerbil, something to pet and water and mother. And I'm not saying this because of one experience; I say it because I've looked around and talked to people. When I broke up with my girlfriend, I told her I was doing it because she was boring, and she was. I told her she wasn't giving me anything. She cried and apologized and it was a touchy scene, but we'd still be friends, right? Now whenever we run into each other I whisk myself away to some nether plane and temporarily cease to exist.
TONY: Why did you go out with her?
MARK: I've intellectualized it, and I decided that we went out because I wanted something memorable. And she was pretty too.
TONY: Don't you think she wanted something memorable?
MARK: I suppose.
TONY (*Probing*):   You think you're the most interesting person in the world, don't you. That you should be famous and you're easy-going and one hell of a nice guy, right?
MARK (*Tight*):   You're sure talking a lot now.
   (TONY *shrugs, self-conscious.* MARK *slides down in his seat and his foot touches* TONY's. TONY *moves.* MARK *touches him again;* TONY *moves.* MARK *touches* TONY's *foot a third time, and as* TONY *moves,* MARK *kicks his foot aside*)

MARK: It bothers you that my foot touched yours.

TONY: I don't know.

MARK (*Irritated*):   You do, because it does, and I think it's ridiculous. I remember going to the show with a friend of mine whom I've known for years, and he wanted to sit with a seat between us because he said it looks better. What is that? I'm not going with him so I can yell to him from across the theater. Little kids don't worry about those things. And I've known this guy practically all my life, we slept over each other's houses and hung around and all that; but then I touch a foot and, Oh, my God! Move your foot!

TONY: What can you do. People are like that.

MARK: I suppose they are. (*He tucks his feet behind his stool*) Well, at least we're talking.

(*Silence, then* TONY *is startled by a sudden gust of wind*)

TONY: Listen to that wind. Sounds like it's going to blow the building down.

MARK: Isn't that true. But I doubt it. I've been told that these windows have been up for thirty years.

TONY: Really? (*He walks to the windows*) That's hard to believe. Just think, these windows have been around longer than I have.

MARK (*Stands beside* TONY):   Yeah. You warmer yet?

TONY: Why? Are you getting ready to leave?

MARK: No . . . not yet.

TONY: Good. (*Pause*) I like your selection of gas. (*He points*) Regular and regular.

MARK: So we're not exactly contemporary.

TONY: That's good, though. It gives the place style. (*Distant*) If this window were in my room, it would look great. Of course, I couldn't look out of it — my room's downstairs — but this way it would never get broken. (*Pause*) You know, I always wonder what the parents of killers and murderers think, or what they thought about when their kids were growing up. You think they knew?

MARK: I don't know. Maybe.

TONY: I wonder what my parents think I'll be?

MARK: I hope not a killer.

TONY: I like to draw, and I'm not that bad, but my parents don't think of art as a possible career. There's no money in it.

MARK: You want to be an artist?

TONY: Yeah. Why not.

MARK: Well, it seems to me —

TONY (*Loudly*):   Are you going to tell me to do whatever I feel and who cares what they think?

(MARK *is silent*)

Sorry. (TONY *walks around room*) You know, no one knows I'm here? They know I'm gone, but they don't know where. I wonder what they're doing now?

MARK (*Sitting behind desk*):   Probably calling the police and all the hospitals.

TONY: More likely they're calling friends and relatives. Or they might be checking the stores.

MARK: Have you done this before?

TONY: A couple of times, when I get upset or something. I know it's childish, but what else am I supposed to do? Hop in a car I don't know how to drive, and go somewhere? Move away? The options aren't great. Still, tonight wasn't so bad.

MARK: No. (*Pause*) Tony? Do me a favor and tell me why you're here.

TONY: I — Well, it centers around my getting in a fight, I guess. It was stupid because I hate fights. I always run from them. I don't think I'm afraid, but I always run. Except today. Today I got in a fight, and I've never been in a fight before.

MARK: And you lost.

TONY: No.

MARK: You won?

(TONY *nods*)

Then what's the problem?

TONY: The problem is that I didn't want to fight him.

MARK: And that bothers you? I mean, I guess it should . . . but if this guy was pushing you around, well, what else could you do?

TONY: Probably nothing.

MARK: All right, then. Just relax. Don't let it bother you. You did what you should have, what you had to do, anyway, and it's over.

TONY: Yeah. (*Nods*) But I started it.

MARK: What? Why?

TONY: Oh, how should I know?

MARK: What do you mean "how should I know"? You hit him.

TONY: I hit him but I'm not sure why. (*He begins to explain, then stops himself*) Forget it.

MARK (*Excited*):   No! This is cruel. This is interesting as hell. Don't do this. People always do this to me.

TONY (*He looks at* MARK, *turns away*):   I'm one of those kids that everyone picks on.

MARK (*Struggling to make the connection*):   Yeah.

TONY: My parents know this. Once they saw me getting teased and pushed around in front of our house by some kids. It didn't bother my mother so much as it bothered my father. He wanted me to do something, defend myself, I guess. He wanted to see what I'd do, which was nothing, and then he acted like it never happened. But I knew he was watching.

MARK (*Still struggling*):   Yeah.

TONY: So I let him down! (*Pause*) My brother wasn't average . . . he got a lot of trophies from baseball and ribbons and things from school. There are pictures . . . in my parents' bedroom . . . of him and my father together, and I can see that my father was real proud of him. He still is, you know?

MARK: Yeah. That's — that's weird.

TONY: My father used to spend a lot of time with me when I was younger, trying to get me into sports or something, but I wasn't any good. Now he never bothers with me. I don't think he expects anything from me.

MARK: Have you told him how you feel?

TONY: Yeah.

MARK: And?

TONY: I still feel the same way.

MARK: So tell him again.

TONY: Oh, it won't do any good.

MARK: How do you know?

TONY (*Explosive*):   Because I do! (*Slight pause*) Today after school this fat kid bumped into me and I dropped all of my books and I got upset. I was pretty upset already, so I really bore down on this kid, teasing him about his weight and his mother. And he was really getting hurt but he wouldn't do anything. Then everybody started telling me to beat him up, but I didn't want to, so I kept cutting him down. Then they were saying that I was scared. So I hit him. But I wasn't really mad anymore. And he just stood there and took it, which really pissed me off. Do you follow me? (*Slight pause*) I went home. My parents ask what happened, and my father is very proud of me. Good. Great. What I hate most and he's proud. Wouldn't that — (*He catches himself*) Wouldn't that bother you?

MARK (*Empathic*):   Yeah. I think it would.

TONY (*Protracted sigh*):   Yeah. So I just left. I was so disgusted, I just left. I don't know. God I — (*Laughs*) I feel so old.
(*Silence*)

MARK: So what are you gonna do now?

TONY (*Standing*):   Now? Now I guess I'll probably go home.

MARK: Well . . . yeah. That's about the smartest thing to do.

TONY (*Loud*):   I know, I know. I always do that. Sometimes I wish I'd quit trying to make sense out of things . . . sense! (*On the word "sense" TONY sits down heavily on the stool, tipping it back. He falls*)

MARK (*Amused*):   Are you all right?

TONY (*Shaking head*):   Yeah, yeah. How come you aren't laughing?

MARK (*Laughs*):   I don't know. I guess I didn't think to.

TONY (*A moment, then he laughs*):   God, but you're weird.

MARK: What?

TONY: Don't worry. (*Considering himself*) I'm a jerk who falls off chairs.

MARK: So what? You fell off and big deal.

TONY: Yes, big deal. I've just ruined your movie. I'm not much of an actor, am I?

MARK: No, no. You worked out good. You even unbored me.

TONY (*Standing*):   Yeah, but I bet you'd have liked it better if I had never shown up tonight, huh? Am I right?

MARK: Geez, Tony. Listen to me. I'm telling you —

TONY (*Suddenly playful. With near hysteria; hysterical energy*):   Tell me the truth. I can take it. (*He stands in front of* MARK) Do I get in your hair? (*He runs his hands through* MARK's *hair. A second, then* MARK *reacts to the pun*) Do I irritate you? (TONY *grabs* MARK's *ears*) Sorry. But I need you. (*He knees* MARK) And you're not going anywhere. I got my eye on you.
(*He puts his eye to* MARK's *shoulder.* MARK *grabs* TONY *by the arms*)

MARK (*Firm; unsure*):   That's — that's funny. (*He runs his hand through* TONY's *hair*) You're funny, you know that? You're all right. You're all right.
(*A moment, then* TONY *impulsively tries to embrace* MARK. MARK *starts and pulls back*)

TONY: Hey, what's the matter.
(MARK *is motionless*)
Hey, I didn't mean anything.

MARK: Okay. Calm down. I believe you.

TONY: Oh, brother.

MARK: Wait. I know what was —

TONY: Forget it, Mark. Okay? Hey — hey, listen. I've got to go. It's late. (*He awkwardly shakes* MARK's *hand*) I'm glad we met. (TONY *walks to the door*)

MARK: Tony, wait. Don't leave now and make me feel stupid.

TONY: Forget it, okay?

MARK (*A moment, then he speaks*):   Sure.

(TONY *steps outside. He starts to walk quickly away, pushing his bike*)

TONY (*Stopping momentarily*):   I hope your movie went well. It's as good as most.

MARK (*From doorway*):   You're wearing my shirt.

(TONY *touches the shirt*)

Keep it, you know?

(TONY *nods and continues walking, exiting stage right.* MARK *closes the door and, for a moment, stands in the middle of the room. He picks up the fallen stool. The lights fade. Curtain*)

Source: Dell

✤ Mr. Universe

●●●●●●●●●●●●●●●●●●●●●●●●●●●●●●JIM GRIMSLEY

CHARACTERS: VICK (40's), JUDY (20's)
SETTING: *New Orleans.*

For many years, VICK *has worked as a professional drag queen doing drag shows at a bar on Rampart Street.* JUDY *is the illegitimate son of a New Orleans stripper who was raised by his grandmother in rural Alabama.* JUDY *has only recently moved to New Orleans. For a time,* JUDY *and* VICK *were lovers.*

VICK: Sweetheart what are you trying to do, make this month's rent?

JUDY: You're just jealous because I have better legs than you do. Don't you think you've put on enough lipstick by now?

VICK: Please don't flap your hand in my face. And who do you think you are teaching me about makeup when I have worked on the professional stage. You can't teach me anything about being a woman, I have done it all.

JUDY: I bet you have. All at JuJu's Hideaway.

VICK: Your Mama never worked any better place honey, not even with real tits.

JUDY (*Haughty*):   I do not want to talk about my Mama if you don't mind.

VICK: Are you ready to go? (*Takes a few steps*)

JUDY: I am not interested in one bar up that street, I am tired of old men and chicken.

VICK: Well I am not going to ruin my good gown walking up and down the waterfront to find you a sailor.

JUDY: Why not?

VICK: You are completely out of your mind; the sailor never sailed who would give you the time of day.

JUDY: But you promised.

VICK: Just exactly when did I promise to walk down to the waterfront and get myself killed?

JUDY: You said you thought it would be fun.

VICK: I said I thought it would be fun if we could fool them boys, but we can't.

JUDY: All we ever do is go to the same old bar and drink the same old drink and talk to the old men.

VICK: I am not having this discussion with you again.

JUDY: I want to have some fun Vick, please take me down to the river, please please. I'll be such a good girl you won't even know me. We'll just walk down there and walk back, we don't have to stay.

VICK: And you'll pick up some trash not fit to clean toilets and have him laying up in my apartment till I throw his ass out.

JUDY: You're just jealous.

VICK: Sweetheart, when you get your own apartment you can sleep with every bum from here to Lake Charles.

JUDY: Please don't start at me Vick, you know I can't afford my own place, I still got to pay Maison Blanche for my alligator pumps.

VICK: Shut up whining about them shoes. Here comes a friend of mine.

[(*Enter a man whose large muscles are obvious even through his clothes. He walks tentatively as if he is lost in the city. He stops some distance from the drag queens*)]

JUDY: You never knew anybody like that in your life.

VICK: Did you ever . . . Just look at that!

JUDY: I could peel him like a grape. Do you think he's one of us?

VICK: He's too butch.

JUDY: Well sweetheart, we're not all sissies. Though you'd never know it by the company we keep. (*Laughs at his own joke*)

VICK: Don't cackle like a crow, he isn't paying the least attention to us.

JUDY: You mean he isn't paying any attention to you.

VICK: No he isn't. I didn't say he was.

JUDY: What's the matter honey, you falling in love?

VICK: Stop it, don't talk so loud.

JUDY: It's nothing to be embarrassed about dear, you can't help it. It's the Cinderella Complex, it's a common thing for us girls. When you see a man like that you can't help dreaming he's Mister Right.

VICK: Shut up, I'm not dreaming anything.

JUDY: You really are upset aren't you?

VICK: Let's go.

JUDY: No, I think I just want to stand right here for a little while and check out the street life.

VICK: Don't bet on it sweetheart.

JUDY: You just wait a minute.

VICK: Life's too short dear. I don't have all night, and neither do you. I've seen you after midnight. (*Exit* VICK)

JUDY: You come back here bitch.

VICK (*From offstage*): Why I can almost hear that sweet disco music.

JUDY: Wait a minute. Wait for me, please wait.

Source: William Morris Agency

✥ A Most Secret War

●●●●●●●●●●●●●●●●●●●●●●●●●●●KEVIN PATTERSON

CHARACTERS: ALAN (40's), WILLS (30's-50's)
SETTING: ALAN's flat in Wimslow, England, 1952.

This play dramatizes the true story of ALAN TURING, *the British scientist who became a hero during World War II by breaking a secret German code. He was mistakenly outspoken about his homosexuality and was subsequently imprisoned. In the play,* ALAN's *flat has been robbed by the friend of a young man he had picked up in a park and had taken home. He has called the police, and* DETECTIVE WILLS *has come to investigate the robbery.*

(*There is a knock at the door.* ALAN *opens it, revealing* DETECTIVE WILLS)

WILLS: Mr. Turing?

ALAN: Detective Wills. Please come in.

(WILLS *enters*)

Please excuse appearances. The flat reeks of white powder from having been checked for fingerprints.

WILLS: I hope I'm not disturbing you.

ALAN: Not at all. They told me at the station to expect you. Can I offer you a cup of tea or glass of whiskey? I expect there is a rule about not drinking on the job — !

WILLS (*Interrupting*):   There is a rule. But a little whiskey would be nice.

ALAN: I was going to have some myself, but I hate drinking alone.

(*He hands* WILLS *a glass of whiskey in a chemical beaker.* WILLS *looks at it, apprehensively*)

Nothing to fear. It's been thoroughly washed with detergent.

WILLS: Detergent?

ALAN: I've got pans full of weeds and things trying to see what kind of chemicals I can concoct by natural means. To this day my mother chastises me for testing solutions with my fingers. Cheers!

WILLS (*Suspiciously*):   Cheers.

(*He starts to drink, but pulls away in disgust*)

ALAN: Is anything wrong?

WILLS: A most peculiar smell.

ALAN: Oh, my. I must have given you the wrong glass. Terribly sorry.

WILLS: What is it?

ALAN: A little chloride, that's all. I suppose it could give you a rather bad stomach ache. Nothing serious. Let me fetch you another glass.

WILLS: No, thank you. I seem to have lost my thirst.

ALAN (*Laughing weakly*): Why, someone might think I was trying to poison you!

(WILLS *says nothing and pulls out a note pad*)

WILLS: Mr. Turing, several days ago you reported a robbery. Exactly what is missing?

ALAN: Some money. A pair of trousers. A few books.

WILLS: It seems an odd collection, if you don't mind me saying.

ALAN: The whole matter has had a rather disturbing effect on me. I go about expecting a brick wall to fall on my head.

WILLS: I have your description of the suspect. (*He reads*) "He's about 35 years of age. Five foot ten inches tall with black hair."

ALAN: That's correct.

(WILLS *regards him, evenly*)

WILLS: Mr. Turing, this is difficult for me to say. But we have reason to believe your description is false. Why are you lying?

(ALAN *says nothing*)

Does the name Harry Lancaster mean anything to you?

ALAN: Harry Lancaster?

WILLS: That's right. He's in custody on a similar charge in Manchester. His fingerprints match those found in this flat.

ALAN: Then you've found your man, Detective.

WILLS (*Shaking his head, dubiously*): Your physical description doesn't fit. Lancaster is six feet two inches tall. You said he was five foot ten. He has blond hair, but you said he had black hair.

ALAN: Forgive me. Physical description is not my forte.

WILLS: Oh?

ALAN: Besides, the description was provided by a friend.

WILLS: By any chance would that friend be Tony Nichols?

ALAN: Why?

WILLS: Begging your pardon, Mr. Turing, but Lancaster said Tony Nichols was something more than a friend.

ALAN: I don't understand.

WILLS: Now do you want to tell me all about it?

ALAN (*Quietly*): I don't think there's anything to tell.

WILLS: I beg your pardon?

ALAN: I said I don't think there's anything to tell.

WILLS: You don't think there's anything to tell.

ALAN: Tell me, Detective Wills, what are you trying to do?

WILLS: Do, Mr. Turing? I'm not trying to do anything.

ALAN: You're trying to make me say things I don't want to say.

WILLS: Not at all. Surely you can appreciate my position. It's the truth I'm after.

ALAN: The truth?

WILLS: Yes, sir.

(*Pause*)

ALAN: Very well. I tried to mislead you about my informant.

WILLS: Oh. Why is that?

ALAN: He knew about the robbery and didn't tell me.

WILLS: Why didn't he tell you?

ALAN: Because he has a criminal record and was afraid of being implicated.

WILLS: A criminal record?

ALAN: That's right.

WILLS: Why were you trying to protect him?

ALAN: I was having an affair with the young man.

WILLS: An affair?

ALAN: I picked him up on Oxford Street. He's been to my home many times.

WILLS: This sheds quite a different light on matters.

ALAN: I was certain you'd understand. Naturally I regarded his friend's conduct as a form of blackmail, which is why I didn't report him. I don't know how I could have been so stupid.

(*Pause*)

WILLS: Mr. Turing, are you quite sure of yourself?

ALAN: Absolutely.

WILLS: Because I have to inform you, sir, that a grievous crime has been committed.

ALAN: Not at all, Detective. Some books. A little money. Can't we forget the whole matter?

WILLS: The crime I am referring to is Gross Indecency.

(*Pause*)

ALAN: What?

WILLS: I'm afraid I will have to ask you to accompany me to the station for fingerprinting and booking.

ALAN: There must be some mistake. I've done noting wrong.

(WILLS *reads aloud from his pad*)

WILLS: "I picked him up on Oxford Street. He's been to my home many times."

ALAN: This is ridiculous!

WILLS: You and Tony Nichols are in violation of the Criminal Amendment Act, and I have no choice but to arrest you.

Source: Samuel French, Inc.

✤ Moving Pictures

•••••••••••••••••••••••••••••STEPHEN LOWE

CHARACTERS: JIM (17), PETE (17)
SETTING: *Front room of* JIM's *parents' flat, England, 1963.*

JIM *and* PETE *are best friends. Their parents are frustrated; their fathers drink and gamble; their mothers complain.* JIM *works in a bank. He's describing what has happened when his father, who has been fading physically, loses his job.* JIM *wants to be a writer or a film director. In either case, he wants to emulate the work of DH Lawrence.*

> (*Dora's front room. Cross fade up on* PETE, *in his working suit, staring out.* JIM, *revealed, sits behind him, perched on the edge of his father's armchair. He wears his school blazer*)

PETE (*Distressed*): It was just seein' em both, I suppose. The other side of the glass. It's bad enough when it's folk you don't know, come cap in hand, but when it's me own mam and dad. He thought we were the bookies. He kept scrawling names of horses on the forms, and sliding 'em under the glass. Grinnin' away. He din't know who I was. When I saw her come into the office, draggin' him like a dog on a lead, I just din't know . . .
(*Silence*)

JIM: Coun't she've hung on 'til you got home to tell you the doctor had laid him off for good?

PETE: She din't come to tell me. She'd been round the Panel screamin' blue murder at them stoppin' his money. Then she'd come straight round to us, to see what we had goin'. She saw me as a soft touch. She went up the bloody wall when I told her what the rate was. I mean, I can't work miracles. I wish I could. I should have done someat for him. There's nought I could do. I feel such a failure. He looked so bloody lonely.

JIM: Dad still goes to see 'im.

PETE: Them visits're all that keeps 'im alive. Funny how the war, all that killing, should be the only thing that keeps them goin'.

JIM: It's someat, though.

PETE: I kept catchin' me face in the glass when I looked at 'im. I'll end up like 'im. I know I will.

JIM: No, we won't. Neither of us'll end up like our dads.

PETE: It's all right for you. You'll be off to college come September. It's us who are left here. Wi'out anybody.

(JIM *suddenly stands up and begins to push the chairs back*)

JIM: Come on.

PETE: What?

JIM: You're right. We can't wait for wars to gi' us contacts in our old age. We have to free ourselves now of everything they've ever laid on us.

PETE: I'm not wi' you.

(JIM *begins to take his shirt off*)

(*Nervous*) What you doin'?

JIM: Come on. Take your clothes off.

PETE: What for?

JIM: *Women in Love.*

PETE: Women? What have women got to do with you and me?

JIM: Lawrence. Gerald and Birkin. In *Women in Love.* A nude wrestling match. You and me. Break through the conventions that kill us men. Know each other.

PETE: I don't want to know you. Well, I do, but . . . I don't want to fight you. Why do I want to fight you?

JIM: You don't fight me. You fight *with* me. We struggle for life together. You can't do it on your own. We have to fight to bring each other into life. (JIM *is down to his underpants*)

PETE: Ye', fine, but we don't have to actually . . . fight. I mean, I mean, we. . . not actually . . .

JIM: It's a ritual bond between us. It has to be acted out or we don't recognize it. It'd be just words otherwise.

PETE (*Desperate*):   Look, the last time we did someat like this, I almost bled to death. These games allers hurt me more than they do you.

JIM: That's the pain of living. (*He starts to take his underpants off*)

PETE (*Panicking*):   All right. I'll fight you. But I can fight you just as well wi' our clothes on. Put your clothes back on, please.

(JIM *strips*)

JIM: We can't bare our souls if we won't bare our bodies.

PETE (*Looking away*): In the book, they had a log fire and they were pissed. That's why they did it.

JIM: Well, we've got central heating. Only the externals change. The challenge remains the same.

PETE: This is crazy, Jim.

JIM: Of course it is. Where else can you look for hope in this so-

called sane world? (*Pause*) Do you want to end up like your dad?
It's now or never. (*Silence*) Trust me.

(PETE *begins to strip, slowly*)

PETE: I don't think I want to do this, you know.

JIM: Me neither. But it has to be done.

PETE: Nobody can see in, can they?

JIM: No.

(*He strips and turns to face* JIM. JIM *stretches out his hands to grapple.*
PETE *turns away. He turns but looks away. He holds out his hands.*
They wrestle. PETE *hardly puts up a fight. He clings on to* JIM *as they*
topple over to the floor. They are locked in an embrace. JIM *breaks it*
viciously. PETE *cries out.* JIM *stands, and angrily walks away. He*
begins to get dressed)

(*Furious*) What the hell are you playin' at? You have to fight. You
din't fight.

(PETE *remains on the floor, crying silently*)

I din't hurt you. Come on. It's over. It didn't work for you. It
failed. Let's forget it.

PETE: What was supposed to happen? What was we s'posed to feel?
(*Silence*)

JIM: It's nothing to do with sex. It's above all that. That's what Birkin could never make Ursula understand. It's completely different. Finer.

PETE: What?

(JIM *is dressed*)

JIM: Get your clothes on. Somebody will be coming home soon.
(*He leaves the room.* PETE *stands, and begins to dress*)

Source: Methuen London Ltd.

✤ Nasty Little Secrets

●●●●●●●●●●●●●●●●●●●●●●●●●●●LANIE ROBERTSON

CHARACTERS: ORTON (20's), HALLIWELL (30's)
SETTING: ORTON *and* HALLIWELL's *small apartment in London.*

HALLIWELL *returns from a publisher who has just rejected the novel which he and* ORTON, *his lover, have written together. In this scene,* ORTON *suddenly realizes that he is better off writing on his own.*

ORTON: Well? Well, come on. Tell me! Did you go?
HALLIWELL: Yes. Yes, I went.
ORTON: And? And you saw them?
HALLIWELL: Yes. They saw me. I . . . I don't know if I'd dressed appropriately. The woman there kept looking at my beret. I felt I shouldn't have worn it.
ORTON: To hell with the receptionist. What'd they tell you about the book? You did meet with them?
HALLIWELL: Yes, I met with them. They were quite friendly. More so than the last time we were there. They asked after you. I told them it's our usual custom not to go out together. One of us always liked to stay home, guarding the hearth as it were.
ORTON: But . . . but what did they say.
HALLIWELL: They thought it very quaint. The younger one said he thought it quite charming.
ORTON: About the book!
HALLIWELL: Well. They . . . They didn't like it.
ORTON: *Didn't* like it?
HALLIWELL: Yes.
ORTON: But they said before they *did.* That it was just those few changes.
HALLIWELL: They didn't like it at all. They said we'd taken a wrong tack. They said the novel now lacked the subtlety of the earlier version. Without making it more generally commercial, as we'd cut the humor along with the excessive eroticism.
ORTON: In other words, they told you exactly what I said. Didn't they.
HALLIWELL: It wasn't exactly what you'd said. Generally speaking it was.
ORTON: It was exactly what I said! I *told* you that!

HALLIWELL: Don't take that tone with me.

ORTON: Don't talk to me about "tone". Tone was what's wrong with the rewrites! I told you we were destroying the comedic tone!

HALLIWELL: What did you want it to be? A farce?

ORTON: Perhaps! Yes! What's wrong with it? Firbank wrote farce. Evelyn Waugh writes farce.

HALLIWELL: I hope we're a cut above Evelyn Waugh.

ORTON: Evidently we're not! Not if they're not willing to publish. I told you all that stuff you wrote, all those long, rambling purple passages of political palaver were ruining it! I knew! Taking out the really comic turns! I told you that was wrong!

HALLIWELL: What do you want me to say? That you were right? I can't believe you were right. I don't believe they're right. Seems to me we have a serious novel on our hands. Something important to say.

ORTON: You don't have to be lugubrious in order to be serious! You've made it lugubrious. I knew they wouldn't like it. I KNEW! I shouldn't have listened to you. Six months! Six months laborious work destroying everything that was once GOOD about it. I knew! That's what gauls me!

HALLIWELL: How dare you say that to me! What are you, anyway?

ORTON: What?

HALLIWELL: What did you come to me with? I'm the one who introduced you to Ronald Firbank and Evelyn Waugh. How dare you now throw them up in my face as though I'm not cognizant of their accomplishments. Whitmur and Bridges are not the only publishers in town, you know.

ORTON: Oh, yes. How well I know. Here's the list of publishers. Here's the list! But they are the only ones interested in us! The only ones who've corresponded with us, the only ones who've met with us. Theirs was the first interest, the first nibble, the first chance! And we've tossed it away! Oh, I'm not blaming you! I blame myself. I listened to you! I shouldn't've! I KNEW better. (*Pause*) I knew better than you. Better. For the first time in my life. And they were right. It wasn't funny enough, wasn't vibrant enough. But there were some comic turns, some funny scenes, some bits and pieces of dialogue that we should have honed, should have developed. We shouldn't have slashed out and abandoned. We took exactly the wrong turn: I KNEW it! I can only blame myself, Kenneth. I don't blame you. I really don't.

HALLIWELL: You say that, don't you. But of course you blame me. I was the one who conceived the idea of the rewrites. I was the one who . . . Ah, I'm so tired, tired. This is only your first. It's my fifth. Fifth novel. Four alone. One with you.

ORTON: Yes! This one with me. And it's the first one anyone's been interested in.

HALLIWELL: Oh. What am I to make of that?

ORTON: That's your question. What am I to make of it's the question for me.

HALLIWELL: I see. You no longer wish to collaborate. Is that it?

ORTON: Yes, I think that's it.

HALLIWELL: And what would you do on your own?

ORTON: This.

HALLIWELL: What's this?

ORTON: The manuscript of a novel I'm writing. An out and out comedic novel. And it's totally original with me. I'll not say you're not a character in it. You are. We both are. It's based on our fantasy life here.

HALLIWELL: Our fantasy life?

ORTON: The life of two mad queens living together, reading *The Decline and Fall of the Roman Empire* aloud to one another at night. *The Life of Dr. Johnson*, the complete plays of Shakespeare. All of the wonderful things we do. And the fantasies that sets going for them, so they live Don Quixotically in their day dreams.

HALLIWELL: It sounds perfectly dreadful. I hope you sell it to the pictures so you can move to Hollywood and become a Movie Queen. Then at least you'd stop living with me.

ORTON: You mean that?

HALLIWELL: God no, of course I don't. Oh God! It was so horrible going in that office. So horrible. I should have sent you. You're their favorite, anyway. But no, I always protect you, don't I. I go out and meet strangers! I see people and talk with them. It kills me but I do it! So that you can have free time. So that you can read what the literary traditions are. What they are! That they! THAT THEY EVEN EXIST! I've done everything for you!

ORTON: Do you think I'm not grateful enough?

HALLIWELL: Of course you're grateful enough. It's just that I'm . . . I feel beaten down. I felt so certain . . . this time, this time! Know what I did walking over there?

ORTON: What?

HALLIWELL: I purposely went by that little Men's haberdashery. I went in. I even picked out something for myself! But basically I kept seeing you in all those clothes. Well, actually, what I kept seeing was me purchasing them for you. You were trying them on and the shop keepers all looking at one another with knowing glances and we ignored them. And my calling out, "Yes! We'll take two of those suits, I think, and . . . FIVE of those lovely shirts. The SILK ones! One in each of your colors. He looks SO good in them, don't you think? DEE-lishous." And relishing all the while their thinking me a rich old queen pampering my young, young man. It was a heavenly fantasy. While it lasted.

ORTON: You see, it's that sort of thing I've put in my novel.

HALLIWELL: Damn your novel! Do you think I want to read a novel of my life? Only Shakespeare could do justice to our life. He could write a tragedy of it.

ORTON: Or a comedy. It's not so bad. (ORTON *has put his arms about* HALLIWELL)

HALLIWELL: No. It isn't. It isn't, is it. Maybe you're right! Maybe I should go back to working on something on my own. And you should branch out. You should write something. I shall read it with cucumber relish!

Source: Samuel French, Inc.

✤ On The Open Road

•••••••••••••••••••••••••••••••STEVE TESICH

CHARACTERS: AL *(20's)*, ANGEL *(20's)*
SETTING: *A landscape stripped bare by civil war, in a a time of civil war.*

AL *and* ANGEL *are trying to make their way to the border and freedom. Hiding from marauding armies, they travel the country, gathering great art treasures from crumbling museums. But with the border to freedom in sight, they're captured by forces from the new coalition government. They are about to be hanged when* AL *is freed to do a certain job. There are rumors that Jesus Christ has appeared in a rally at a soccer stadium. Here,* AL *explains what the job is.*

> (ANGEL *is on the stool, with the noose around his neck. Looking around. Enter* AL, *pulling the cart, but the cart is empty)*

ANGEL: Al. What's going on?

> (AL *comes over to him. Takes out a knife. Cuts his legs free. Then cuts his hands.* ANGEL *is suspicious and hesitant, but he does remove the noose from his neck)*

ANGEL: Is this deja-vu or what?

AL: Maybe now you won't think I'm such a bad negotiator.

ANGEL: I don't know what to think, Al. I'm afraid to think. I mean, I thought I was gonna die. I'd hate to think I'm not, if I still am. I mean, am I free?

AL: We're both free. With conditions.

ANGEL: Real free?

AL: Real free with real conditions.

ANGEL: I don't mind any conditions as long as I'm free.

AL: Then you're free.

ANGEL: What are the conditions?

AL: I got us a job.

ANGEL: A job?

AL: That's right.

ANGEL: What kind of job?

AL: It's only a part-time job.

ANGEL: So is life, it seems.

AL: My point exactly.

ANGEL: Meaning what?

AL: The two go hand in hand. Quid pro quo, if you know what I mean.

ANGEL: I'm not sure I do.

AL: No job: No life.

ANGEL: Is that how it was put to you?

AL: In so many words.

ANGEL: We accept this job, we live. We don't accept, we die?

AL: Exactly.

ANGEL: What's the job?

AL: It's a part-time job.

ANGEL: I already know that part. What's the other part?

AL: What other part?

ANGEL: The 'do' part. What do we have to do?

AL: Render a service.

ANGEL: It's a service industry we're working for?

AL: In a manner of speaking, yes. Public service.

ANGEL: The government, we're working for the government?

AL: Part-time.

ANGEL: I didn't know there was a government.

AL: There is now.

ANGEL: Then the Civil War is over.

AL: For the time being.

ANGEL: Who won?

AL: The government we're working for. It's a coalition, I think, of all the former implacable foes. A brand new flag was waving outside the ministry of the interior.

ANGEL: What do we have to do?

AL: Kill a man.

ANGEL: One man?

AL: Just one.

ANGEL: What man?

AL: Part-time man.

ANGEL: Part-time man?

AL: Yes. Part-time man. Part-time Messiah.

ANGEL: Jesus?

AL: Yes.

ANGEL: Jesus Christ?

AL: Yes, Jesus Christ.

ANGEL: We have to kill Jesus Christ!

AL: We don't have to.

ANGEL: To live, I mean.

AL: Yes. If we want to live, we have to kill Him.

ANGEL: I thought they already killed Him.

AL: So did I. But they didn't. They took Him prisoner and took Him to this place outside the city. (*He takes out a map. Unfolds it*) Here. They gave me a map. How to get there. It's right here, see? (*He points to a spot on the map.* ANGEL *looks*)

ANGEL: I don't get it.

AL: What now?

ANGEL: Why didn't they kill Him?

AL: They who?

ANGEL: They they. The government.

AL: The government is a concept. Concepts can't do anything. The government doesn't kill people. People kill people.

ANGEL: Why do we have to kill him? I mean, I know why. To save our ass. But why did they choose us? Why didn't they choose somebody else?

AL: To them, we are somebody else.

ANGEL: But why not some other somebody else? Why us?

AL: What difference does it make? Had they chosen some other somebody else they'd be standing here just like we're doing and asking themselves the same question: Why did they choose us instead of somebody else? You can still choose death if you want.

ANGEL: What about you?

AL: After much agony, I've decided to choose death for Jesus Christ instead. Are you in or are you out?

ANGEL: I'm in, but I'd like a couple of minutes to agonize over it.

AL: Fine.

ANGEL: The way I see it, somebody's gonna kill Jesus, if not us, then somebody else, right?

AL: Right.

ANGEL: And who's to say who that other somebody else might be. For all we know he might be a family man. Whose wife loves him. Whose children adore him. Whose neighbors respect him. Knock! Knock! There's a knock on his door. Hello, you have been chosen to kill Jesus Christ. Somebody else was chosen, but he refused and because he refused you have been picked to do the job. Oh, Al! The poor guy! He can't win. If he refuses, they'll kill him and who'll feed his family. If he accepts he becomes a murderer. His kids don't adore him anymore. His wife leaves him. It's very tempting, Al, to worry about my own scruples at a

time like this, but I just don't know if I can plunge that poor gu
into the jaws of this dilemma.

AL: It would be pretty cruel of you if you did.

ANGEL: You're right. So the responsible thing to do, the
humanitarian thing to do, the Christian thing to do is to kill
Christ.

AL: Talk about brilliant agony. That was magnificent. Top drawer.

ANGEL: It made me feel so good I could agonize some more.

AL: Better save some for after we kill Him.

ANGEL: You're right. (*Takes a look at the empty cart*) What happened
to your art collection?

AL: It's been confiscated by the state. When we bring back the body
of Christ, they promised to return it. Not only that, we get exit
visas. We bring back the body, get our stuff and our visas and
across the border we go.

ANGEL: To the Land of the Free, right?

AL: Right.

ANGEL: Alright.

(ANGEL *pulls the cart*. AL *leads. They exit*)

Source: Applause Theatre Books

✤ Other People's Money

•••••••••••••••••••••••••••••••JERRY STERNER

CHARACTERS: COLES (40's), GARFINKLE (40's)
SETTING: *The New York office of* GARFINKLE.

WILLIAM COLES *is the President of New England Wire And Cable. The chairman of his company, Jorgenson, is sixty-eight and plans to retire at seventy. In this scene,* COLES *is talking to* GARFINKLE, *an elegant and cunning New York "take-over artist."* COLES *is asking for time before* GARFINKLE *takes over the company;* COLES *wants the needed time for Jorgensen to retire so that he can run the company.*

COLES: That's an impressive office you have out there.
GARFINKLE: No big deal. Only lawyers. What can I do for you?
COLES: Thanks for seeing me on such short notice. I'm not really here on business. My wife and I came down to spend the evening with Bill, Jr. He's attending Columbia. Got two more after him. Both girls. Claire's out shopping now. It's always a treat to come to this city.
GARFINKLE: Great.
COLES: We're from small towns in Florida. Met at Florida State.
GARFINKLE: What'd you come here for — to give me your biography?
COLES: I didn't know I was boring you.
GARFINKLE: Now you know.
COLES (*Trying to control himself*): . . . I'll get to the point. I see by the latest 13-D you hold just over four hundred thousand shares. That's ten per cent.
GARFINKLE: Four hundred and twenty-five thousand. Bought some this morning.
COLES: The filing says they were purchased for "investment purposes only".
GARFINKLE: I never read filings.
COLES: What does "investment purposes only" mean?
GARFINKLE: Means I bought them to make money.
COLES: How much more do you intend on buying?
GARFINKLE: That's none of your business.
COLES: Can we speak frankly?

GARFINKLE: No. Lie to me. Tell me how thrilled you are to know me. Tell me how gorgeous I am.

COLES: You don't want to speak frankly?

GARFINKLE: I always speak frankly. I don't like people who say "Can we speak frankly?" Means they're bullshitting me the rest of the time.

COLES: I'm sorry. I won't use that phrase anymore.

GARFINKLE: What do you want?

COLES: Two years. I want two years.

GARFINKLE: For what?

COLES: Jorgenson is sixty-eight. In two years he'll be seventy. He steps down at seventy.

GARFINKLE: Says who?

COLES: It's an agreement he has with the Board. His employment contract expires at seventy.

GARFINKLE: The Board are his cronies. He is the Board. What he wants done gets done.

COLES: He gave me his word. He's a man of his word.

GARFINKLE: Stop playing with yourself.

COLES: Twelve years ago he told me if I did the job it'd be my company to run when he steps down. That's why I came to that God-forsaken place. It's the same reason I'm here. I don't want the rug pulled out from under me so close to the finish line.

GARFINKLE: You're wasting your time. I don't have two years.

COLES: Listen, Mr. Garfinkle. I said we could grow our other businesses by fifteen per cent. I was being conservative. We'll grow them in excess of twenty. I can manage. I can manage the hell out of a company. In two years we'll be worth considerably more.

GARFINKLE: Billy boy, look at me. I weigh a ton. I smoke three packs a day. I walk from here to there I'm out of breath. I can't even steal life insurance. Two years for me is forever. Do what you have to do now. I'm not a long term player.

COLES: I can't do it now. I can't do it till he leaves. If I try I'm out on my ear.

GARFINKLE (*Handing* COLES *his briefcase*):   That's the problem with working for a living.

COLES: Two years is not a long time. I have waited a lifetime for the opportunity.

GARFINKLE (*Puts his arm around* COLES's *shoulder*):   You got stock, don't you?

COLES: Yes.

GARFINKLE: Fifty, seventy-five thousand, right?

COLES: Sixty.

GARFINKLE: Well, shit, look — want to feel better? (GARFINKLE *taps out stock on his quote machine*) Before you heard my name your stock was ten. Now it's fourteen and a half. In two months I made you a quarter of a million dollars. Billy boy, the least you can do is smile. Ossie at the bank sends me flowers. All I'm asking from you is a smile.

Source: Applause Theatre Books

✤ Perestroika

•••••••••••••••••••••••••••••••TONY KUSHNER

CHARACTERS: ROY COHN (50's-60's), BELIZE (30's)
SETTING: *Hospital room, the present.*

ROY COHN, *powerful lawyer and political fixer, lies in his hospital bed, fighting his fear of dying of AIDS, which he denies he has. He is tended to by a black registered nurse.* BELIZE *is a former drag queen whose real name is Norman Arriaga but his stage name has stuck.* COHN, *who prides himself on knowing everything about everyone important, is about to be taught how to die.*

> (ROY *in his hospital bed, sick and very scared.* BELIZE *enters with the IV drip)*

ROY: Get outta here you, I got nothing to say to you . . .

BELIZE: Just doing my . . .

ROY: I want a white nurse. My constitutional right.

BELIZE: You're in a hospital, you don't have any constitutional rights.
> *(He begins preparing* ROY's *right arm for the IV drip, palpating the vein, disinfecting the skin, etc.)*

ROY *(Getting nervous about the needle)*: Find the vein, you moron, don't start jabbing that goddamned spigot in my arm till you find the fucking vein or I'll sue you so bad they'll repossess your teeth you dim black motherf . . .

BELIZE *(Had enough; very fierce)*: Watch. Yourself. You don't talk that way to me when I'm holding something this sharp. Or I might slip and stick it in your heart. If you have a heart.

ROY: Oh I do. Tough little muscle. Never bleeds.

BELIZE: I'll bet. Now I've been doing drips a long time. I can slip this in so easy you'll think you were born with it. Or I can make it feel like I just hooked you up to a bag of Liquid Drano. So you be nice to me or you're going to be one sorry asshole come morning.

ROY: Nice.

BELIZE: Nice and quiet. *(He puts the drip needle in* ROY's *arm)* There.

ROY *(Fierce)*: I hurt.

BELIZE: I'll get you a painkiller.

ROY: Will it knock me out?

BELIZE: I sure hope so.

ROY: Then shove it. Pain's . . . nothing, pain's life.

BELIZE: Sing it, baby.

ROY: When they did my facelifts, I made the anesthesiologist use a local. They lifted up my whole face like a dinner napkin and I was wide awake to see it.

BELIZE: Bullshit. No doctor would agree to do that.

ROY: I can get anyone to do anything I want. For instance: Let's be friends. (*Sings*) "We shall overcome. . . " Jews and coloreds, historical liberal coalition, right? My people being the first to sell retail to your people, your people being the first people my people could afford to hire to sweep out the store Saturday mornings, and then we all held hands and rode the bus to Selma. Not me of course, I don't ride buses, I take cabs. But the thing about the American Negro is, he never went Communist. Loser Jews did. But you people had Jesus so the reds never got to you. I admire that.

BELIZE: Your chart didn't mention that you're delusional.

ROY: Barking mad. Sit. Talk.

BELIZE: Mr. Cohn. I'd rather suck the pus out of an abscess. I'd rather drink a subway toilet. I'd rather chew off my tongue and spit it in your leathery face. So thanks for the offer of conversation, but I'd rather not. (BELIZE *starts to exit, turning off the light as he does*)

ROY: Oh forchristsake. Whatta I gotta do? Beg? I don't want to be alone.

(BELIZE *stops*)

ROY: Oh how I fucking *hate* hospitals, *nurses*, this waste of time and . . . *wasting* and weakness, I want to kill the . . . Course they can't kill this, can they?

(*Pause.* BELIZE *says nothing*)

ROY: No. It's too simple. It knows itself. It's harder to kill something if it knows what it is. Like pubic lice. You ever had pubic lice?

BELIZE: That is none of your . . .

ROY: I got some kind of super crabs from some kid once, it took twenty drenchings of Kwell and finally shaving to get rid of the little bastards. *Nothing* could kill them. And every time I had to itch I'd smile, because I learned to respect them, these unkillable crabs, because . . . I learned to identify. You know? Determined lowlife. Like me. You've seen lots of guys with this . . .

BELIZE (*Little pause, then*):   Lots.

ROY: How do I look, comparatively?

BELIZE: I'd say you're in trouble.

ROY: I'm going to die. Soon. That was a question.

BELIZE: Probably. Probably so.

ROY: Hah. I appreciate the . . . the honesty, or whatever . . . If I live I could sue you for emotional distress, the whole hospital, but . . . I'm not prejudiced, I'm not a prejudiced man.

(*Pause.* BELIZE *just looks at him*)

ROY: These racist guys, simpletons, I never had any use for them — too rigid. You want to keep your eye on where the most powerful enemy really is. I save my hate for what counts.

BELIZE: Well. And I think that's a good idea, a good thing to do, probably. (*Little pause; with great effort and distaste*) This didn't come from me and I *don't* like you but let me tell you a thing or two: They have you down for radiation tomorrow for the sarcoma lesions, and you don't want to let them do that, because radiation will kill the T-cells and you don't have any you can afford to lose. So tell the doctor no thanks for the radiation. He won't want to listen. Persuade him. Or he'll kill you.

ROY: You're just a fucking nurse. Why should I listen to you over my very qualified, very expensive WASP doctor?

BELIZE: He's not queer. I am. (*He winks at* ROY)

ROY: Don't wink at me. You said a thing or two. So that's one.

BELIZE: I don't know what strings you pulled to get in on the azidothymidine trials.

ROY: I have my little ways.

BELIZE: Uh-huh. Watch out for the double blind. They'll want you to sign something that says they can give you M&M's instead of the real drug. You'll die, but they'll get the kind of statistics they can publish in the *New England Journal of Medicine*. And you can't sue 'cause you signed. And if you don't sign, no pills. So if you have any strings left, pull them, because everyone's put through the double blind and with this, time's against you, you can't fuck around with placebos.

ROY: You hate me.

BELIZE: Yes.

ROY: Why are you telling me this?

BELIZE: I wish I knew.

(*Pause*)

ROY (*Very nasty*):   You're a butterfingers spook faggot nurse. I think . . . you have little reason to want to help me.

BELIZE: Consider it solidarity. One faggot to another.
(BELIZE *snaps his fingers, turns, exits.* ROY *calls after him*)
ROY: Any more of your lip, boy, and you'll be flipping Big Macs in East Hell before tomorrow night!

Source: Theatre Communications Group

✥ A Perfect Relationship

●●●●●●●●●●●●●●●●●●●●●●●●●●●●●DORIC WILSON

CHARACTERS: WARD (30's), GREG (30's)
SETTING: *The living room of a Greenwich Village apartment, the present.*

WARD *and* GREG *are two gay men who are subletting an apartment from Muriel, a friend of theirs. As the play begins, the author sets the scene:*

> (WARD *and* GREG *are only roommates, have never been lovers. They are both in their late thirties, attractive, athletic, in a word,* butch. *Their "masculinity" is unstudied, almost inadvertent. Their interplay is leisurely locker-room, they counter what could be called bickering with a carefully measured virility. It is after five o'clock on a snowy Friday evening in January.* WARD *enters from the hall, keys and briefcase in hand. Conservatively dressed in a three-piece suit and tie,* WARD *is returning from work)*

WARD (*As he enters*):   Greg, good buddy, you home yet?
GREG (*In his bedroom*):   Is that you, Ace?
WARD (*Crossing to the kitchen*):   Sure is.
GREG (*In his bedroom*):   You're late.
WARD: Sure am. (*At the icebox*) You want a beer?
> (GREG *enters from his bedroom, wrapped in a khaki quilt. He has also just returned from work, is in the process of changing his clothes. He carries a can of Budweiser)*

GREG (*As he enters*):   Got one.
WARD (*Coming to the counter, opening his beer*):   It's snowing.
GREG (*Bitterly*):   It's been snowing all day.
WARD: You shouldn't take weather so personally.
GREG: I ran into the landlord in the hall.
WARD (*Worried*):   Did he say anything?
GREG (*Sipping his beer*):   I think he thought I was a tenant.
WARD: You are a tenant.
GREG: He doesn't know that.
WARD: Did you happen to mention to him that our garbage hasn't been collected for two weeks?
GREG: He knows.
WARD: How do you know he knows?
GREG: He was digging through it.

WARD: Did you tell him we prefer heat every day, instead of only on alternate Tuesdays and Thursdays?

GREG: And have him figure me for some sort of a crank?

WARD: Did you at least report the broken window in your bedroom?

GREG: Muriel said she did.

WARD: When?

GREG: Last month.

WARD: Maybe he needs a reminder.

GREG: You remind him.

WARD: He doesn't know I live here.

GREG: He doesn't know *I* live here.

WARD: You just said you thought he thought you were a tenant.

GREG: I wouldn't want to prove it.

WARD: We had another crisis meeting of the faculty after school today.

GREG: They announced further cutbacks and you no longer have a job?

WARD: No such luck. No, Mrs. Randolph discovered another queer.

GREG: Naw.

WARD: Yep.

GREG: The principal?

WARD: Not yet.

GREG: The gym teacher!

WARD: She was on to him first semester. She happened to observe him hanging around the gymnasium.

GREG: Wouldn't that be considered part of his job?

WARD: Not any longer. She had him fired.

GREG: Who'd she nail this time?

WARD: Henry somebody. Henry teaches math. (*Significantly*) Last Saturday, Mrs. Randolph caught Henry at the K-Mart.

GREG: What was "Henry" doing?

WARD: Wearing Adidas.

GREG: "Adidas"?

WARD: Mrs. Randolph read in *Time* magazine we wear Adidas.

GREG: They can fire him based on that?

WARD: They're keeping him under observation.

GREG: Why aren't you under observation?

WARD: I smoke a pipe.

GREG: Since when?

WARD: Also, I have a cleft chin.

GREG: You do not.

WARD: At school I do. (*Exits to his bedroom to change clothes. As he exits*) You taking a shower?

GREG: Not if you want to.

WARD (*In his bedroom*):   Not if you want to.

GREG: You go ahead.

WARD (*In his bedroom*):   You go ahead.

GREG: I can wait.

WARD (*In his bedroom*):   Doesn't matter to me, good buddy.

GREG: You sure, Ace?

WARD (*In his bedroom*):   Sure am.

GREG: Doesn't matter to me.

WARD (*In his bedroom*):   O.K.

GREG: O.K.

(*Pause.* WARD *comes to the door of his bedroom, half-dressed*)

WARD: O.K., which?

GREG: Which what?

WARD: Which of us is taking a shower?

GREG: I thought you were.

WARD: I thought you were.

GREG: Not if you want to.

WARD (*As he exits back to his bedroom*):   Not if you want to.

GREG: It's too cold in here. I'll take mine later.

WARD (*In his bedroom*):   Maybe I'll take mine later.

(GREG *begins selecting his wardrobe from the litter of laundry. He starts with a pair of faded Levi's, strategically torn to display a wide range of erogenous zones. When dressed,* GREG *will project an understated cowboy image taken directly from the pages of* Mandate *magazine*)

GREG (*Piqued*):   The first flake of snow and they take to the air like a herd of geese. I resent . . . I truly resent loud, rude, smug, greedy, obnoxious people who can afford to travel south for the winter.

WARD (*In his bedroom*):   If it bothers you so much to see people travel, maybe you should get out of the travel business.

GREG: You hate the students you teach.

WARD (*In his bedroom*):   That's essential to the educational process. Anyway, you travel.

GREG: Not this winter. Not after what I spent on Christmas.

WARD (*In his bedroom*):   You shouldn't be so generous.

GREG: I shouldn't be so selfish. If I weren't so selfish, I wouldn't need to be so generous at Christmas.

WARD (*In his bedroom*):   Maybe if you dressed more warmly.

GREG: Be practical. (*An idea*) Ward?

WARD (*In his bedroom*):   No.

GREG: You don't even know what I'm going to ask.

(WARD *comes to the door of his bedroom, half-dressed*)

WARD: No, you may not have back the Tiffany cuff links you gave me for Christmas to sell to raise money to take a trip south.

GREG: You never wear them.

WARD (*As he exits back to his bedroom*):   Pawn the present I gave you.

GREG: Great, that should get me as far south as Newark. (*With resigned contempt*) They all bought tickets for Bermuda. Except for the "piss-elegant queens", who all bought tickets for Key West. Except for the "chicken hawks", who all bought tickets for Puerto Rico. I made 'em pay for their fun in the sun. I fucked up their connecting flights.

WARD (*In his bedroom*):   Are we eating in tonight?

GREG: What's in the icebox?

WARD (*In his bedroom*):   Didn't you look when you got your beer?

GREG: Did you look when you got yours?

WARD (*As he enters from his bedroom, dressed as Colt Studio's concept of a construction worker*):   You're much better at that stuff than I am.

GREG (*On guard*):   What "stuff"?

WARD: You're much more "domestic" than I am.

GREG (*Sneering*):   Says who?

WARD (*Snidely*):   You can cook.

GREG: No better than you can.

WARD: I only heat things up. You read recipes.

GREG: You sew.

WARD: As of when?!

GREG: I caught you, remember? All hunched over in the moonlight, needle and thread in hand.

WARD: There were extenuating circumstances.

GREG: So you said at the time.

WARD: You're still the better homemaker.

GREG: Your whites are whiter.

WARD: Your dishes are cleaner.

GREG: Your floors never have yellow waxy build-up.

WARD: You can make a souffle — don't deny it!

GREG: An omelet.

WARD: Ha!

GREG: Lots of men make omelets.

WARD: With strawberries?

GREG: My masculinity is inherent.

WARD: Meaning?

GREG: You pad your crotch.

WARD: I do not!

GREG: You do when you wear your leather pants.

WARD (*The most devastating accusation of all*):   You have hidden away in a suitcase under your bed seven Judy Garland albums.

GREG: What were you doing under my bed? (*Covering*) And I have no knowledge of the records of which you speak. And sneaking through personal possessions is against the rules.

WARD: I don't recall any such rule.

GREG: Only because you never play by them.

WARD: Only because you make them up as we go along.

GREG: Are we eating in?

WARD: You have to do the dishes first.

GREG: They're your dishes.

WARD: They're *our* dishes.

GREG: Mostly yours. (*Crossing to the counter*) This one bowl I dirtied, but this pot and those pans are yours. And as I always use the same glass, all these other glasses belong to you.

WARD: You expect me to take your word for that?

GREG: Starting the day before yesterday, the bowl, the one cup, the one plate, the one pan, the three utensils and the one glass I use, I initialed with a china marker.

WARD: You didn't. (*Checking the bottom of the glass*) You did.

GREG: You gonna look in the icebox?

WARD: You look in the icebox.

(*An amused* GREG *crosses to the kitchen*)

(*Less amused*) You initialed the dirty dishes?

GREG (*In the kitchen*):   The longer I live with you, the more I come to think like you.

WARD: You realize, do you not, your unilateral action can be construed as hostile. That it could . . . that it *will* ultimately lead to a deterioration of the balance of power in this apartment.

GREG (*In the kitchen*):   We have a package of frozen corn niblets . . . a bottle of ketchup . . . four cans of Bud . . . and an empty ice cube tray.

WARD: I'll go out and shop if you cook.

GREG (*Coming to the counter*):   If you wash up.

WARD: If you do the laundry.

GREG: If you vacuum.

WARD: Let's eat out.

GREG: Let's.

WARD (*Naming a restaurant*): Fedora's?

GREG (*Ditto*): Trilogy.

WARD: Your Master Charge?

GREG: Yours.

WARD: Yours — and you can pick the restaurant.

GREG: If you bring me the laundry bag.

WARD (*As he exits to the bathroom for the laundry bag*): If you change the sheets on my bed.

GREG (*Calling after him*): If you walk the dog.

WARD (*In the bathroom*): We don't have a dog.

GREG: We should get a dog.

WARD (*In the bathroom*): A German shepherd.

GREG: A Doberman pinscher.

WARD (*As he enters from the bathroom, laundry bag in hand*): He sleeps in my room.

GREG: He sleeps at the foot of my bed.

WARD: Buster would never be that disloyal.

GREG: Buster?

WARD: That's the name of our dog.

GREG: Our dog is called Spike.

WARD (*Giving the laundry bag to* GREG): When you do the laundry, this time could you please remember to use a separate machine for your jockstraps?

Source: Seahorse Press

✠ Power Failure

•••••••••••••••••••••••••••••LARRY GELBART

CHARACTERS: WORTH (40's), BILLINGS (40's)
SETTING: *Doctor's office, the present.*

WORTH *is a businessman, whose wife is a high powered journalist.* BILL-INGS *is your worst nightmare of a doctor.*

> (WORTH *dressed in a Saville Row suit, waits anxiously. He checks his watch. He fidgets nervously with the seat of his pants, apparently ill at ease in them.* BILLINGS *enters, in a doctor's white jacket and a stethoscope around his neck, carrying a thick medical file.* WORTH *immediately takes his hand from his bottom, as though he has been caught at something)*

BILLINGS: Sorry to have taken so long.

WORTH: Quite all right.

BILLINGS: I wanted to double check everything.

WORTH: I understand.

BILLINGS: Each report. Very carefully.

WORTH: Of course. And?

BILLINGS: Perhaps you'd like to sit down?

WORTH: I'm fine.

BILLINGS: After running the most extensive, the most exhausting tests imaginable — (*Placing several x-rays on display*) Cardiovascular, respiratory, digestive system, neurological. The works. Every part of your body. I must tell you there is not a thing wrong with you, Mr. Worth.

WORTH: You're certain?

BILLINGS: You are totally sound. Remarkably so. I have patients who would die to be as healthy as you are, sir.

WORTH (*Staring at the x-rays*):   Absolutely nothing? I am perfectly fit?

BILLINGS: You could get a second opinion, of course. I think you'd find it largely a waste of time.

WORTH: Not my favorite word at the moment. Time.

BILLINGS: I assure you you have a good deal of it ahead you, sir, from a medical point of view.

WORTH: From a criminal point of view, I'm afraid I have even more.

BILLINGS: I won't be coy with you, Mr. Worth. I read the papers.

WORTH: I find it ironic, to say the least, that this country, which purports to be such a bastion of freedom should be so preoccupied with depriving me of my own. My lawyers have informed me that if I'm found guilty on only half the counts the government has charged me with, the minimum I can expect is five hundred years. Five hundred years, Doctor Billings. Half a millennium in a federal penitentiary.

BILLINGS: With no time off for — ?

WORTH: For good behavior? Yes, they tell me that could knock a century or so off my time. The fines, of course, will come to several hundred million. Conceivably a billion. It all depends on where the judge decides to put the comma.

BILLNGS: Well, trite as it may seem, you do still have your health.

WORTH: In truth, doctor, I find that a bit of a handicap right now.

BILLINGS: Oh?

WORTH: I won't be coy with you either. Doctor Billings, I would like you to do for me what you have on certain occasions done for others.

BILLINGS: My prescription pad is not for hire.

WORTH: I'm not interested in a prescription, sir. I want you to give me an illness. I want you to induce a disorder in me; create a designer disease that will make it difficult, if not impossible for me to appear in a court of law, but one that is, with proper treatment, reversible and, in any case, not in any way life threatening.

BILLINGS: And you're just assuming that I can, or would go, along with such a scheme?

WORTH: Doctors may not talk about their patients, doctor, but let me assure you that patients do a good deal of talking about their doctors.

BILLINGS: And do patients also talk about what the cost of such a procedure would come to?

WORTH: I know that it's seven figures, and that almost all of them are zeros.

BILLINGS: Mr. Worth, were such a treatment even remotely possible, I imagine it would be necessary to engage the assistance of a number of other people. In addition to having to perform certain — how to put it? — unique applications of medicine — they would need a considerable amount of coaching. They would be required to say what they were told to say at the appropriate time.

WORTH: Of course.

BILLINGS: There are others who would be required to say nothing at all. That kind of silence could be golden and a half.

WORTH: Going to eight figures would be no problem at all. If you could see the world as I have seen it, you would know that outrageous has no meaning for me.

BILLINGS (*Into his intercom*):   Helen, please hold all calls. (*An added thought*) Oh, if it's an emergency, say I'm out of town. (*To* WORTH) Please sit down.

WORTH: I prefer to stand.

BILLINGS: Given your requirements, sir, there are several options I believe are possible, each of which I can guarantee will diminish your health in varying degrees.

WORTH: You *can* make me ill?

BILLINGS: I can.

WORTH: You're certain?

BILLINGS: I'd stake my reputation as a doctor on it, sir. The possibilities available cover a range of severity.

WORTH: Not too severe, I would hope.

BILLINGS: The choice has a good deal to do with the PR factor. During the course of the illness, the public would be treated to a steady stream of pictures and footage of you in a variety of telegenically sympathetic situations. You, on a stretcher. Or in an ambulance. Or seen on various life-support systems. Medical teams rushing from choppers to vans with organ transplants, if that is the route we decide to go.

WORTH: There is a history of phlebitis in my family, if that helps me at all.

BILLINGS: Phlebitis.

WORTH: Isn't that what you gave to Nixon?

BILLINGS: It was a rather obvious choice. By the time I saw him, the man literally didn't have a leg to stand on. I, more or less, made the metaphor medical. But I'm not sure it's a good idea to repeat myself. Are you familiar with endocarditis? (WORTH *is not*) It's an inflammation of the membrane that lines the heart. Sounds like passion, actually it's pus. I could give it to you quite simply by causing a bacterial infection.

WORTH: Sounds a bit drastic.

BILLINGS: It happens routinely in hospitals. Only here, I'm admitting it.

WORTH: What precisely would I be letting myself in for?

BILLINGS: You would display certain symptoms: fever, changes in heart rhythm that would be medically convincing to whichever doctors might be acting for the prosecution. Any damage to your heart valves, which I would hope to keep to a minimum, could be corrected by surgery later.

WORTH: You're certain?

BILLINGS: I had great success with that with Ferdinand Marcos.

WORTH: But he died, didn't he?

BILLINGS: An unfortunate side effect, to be sure. Perhaps there is a *cluster* of disorders we could whip together rather quickly. I could, with luck, give you all the symptoms of acrosyanosis, sometimes known as Raynaud's sign. It's an abnormal condition that is brought about by exposure to cold or emotional stress, both of which we could easily expose you to. You would take on a bluish coloration, which would, of course, photograph very well. I could implement this by giving you a condition known as dacryocystitus, inflaming your lacrimal or tear ducts which would cause continuous crying. As a last touch, you could be coached rather quickly to appear to be a victim of coprolalia. The La Tourette Syndrome? (WORTH *doesn't know it*) It manifests itself in a constant stream of uncontrollable grimaces, tics, grunts, in addition to compulsive outbursts of obscene and offensive remarks of the foulest nature. I think between the blue face and the blue language, with the tears thrown in for the sympathy factor, we'd have ourselves a very attractive package. I might just want to play around with a little anemia, too.

WORTH: You're the doctor. I'll take whatever you give me. With the exception of — I made a note of it — (*Checking a note in his pocket*) Tay-Sachs Disease. I'm advised that that's the only sickness I must positively stay clear of.

BILLINGS (*Taking the note from him*):   Have you been talking to someone about Tay-Sachs? You haven't been shopping around for other scenarios?

WORTH: No, no, it's just that my lawyers tell me that it is a disease that occurs almost exclusively among those of the Jewish faith.

BILLINGS: In young children, yes.

WORTH: You will appreciate that I do a great deal of business with Arab interests. While I'm sure they would quite enjoy the prospect of any Jew being unwell, especially a young one, I wouldn't want them to think that I'd been two-faced about my anti- Semitism.

BILLINGS: I understand.

WORTH: Well, then. When do we begin?

BILLINGS: Whatever we decide you're going to get, I think the sooner you see me, the better. Monday morning, if that's all right.

WORTH: Monday morning, I'm in Brussels. Perhaps you can join me on my plane? Could you do your work there?

BILLINGS: I might come along for the ride, just to talk further perhaps. I'd really rather infect you in the office, where everything's more sterile. If I start treating you, say, the following Monday, I think, with any luck, I can have you on your back within a week.

WORTH: It's essential that I attend my daughter's wedding on the twentieth.

BILLINGS: We'll get you there somehow. I read that Father Little will be performing the ceremony?

WORTH: It can't hurt at this particular time for me to be seen standing beside a man of his stature on the six o'clock news.

BILLINGS: Quite.

WORTH: Before I go, perhaps we should nail down the precise fee?

BILLINGS: I always prefer to do it on the first visit. Shall we say, ten million plus any out-of-pocket expenses?

WORTH: And what sort of payment do you prefer?

BILLINGS: I'm rather neutral about it. Switzerland will be fine.

WORTH: I took the liberty of opening a bank account in Zurich that would supply the funds for your services in this matter. All that remains is for you and I to agree upon a password so that you may draw your fee from the amount on deposit immediately. This is the bank book.

BILLINGS: Thank you.

WORTH: And I believe I have the ideal password, if you agree.

BILLINGS (*Helping him into his topcoat*): Yes?

WORTH: May I suggest "Hippocrates"?

BILLINGS (*Smiles*): Perfect.

(*As* BILLINGS *opens the door for him,* WORTH *once more tugs at the back of his trousers. Then, using the same hand to shake* BILLINGS')

WORTH: Good day, sir.

BILLINGS: Good day to you.

(*And* WORTH *is out the door. Blackout*)

Source: Applause Theatre Books

✤ Precious Sons

•••••••••••••••••••••••••••••••GEORGE FURTH

CHARACTERS: FRED (30's), FREDDY (13)
SETTING: *The Small family living room, the South Side of Chicago,*
1949.

*The Smalls are a boisterous, loving, middle-class family, but problems are
beneath all the roughhousing and horseplay.* FREDDY, *a precocious child
actor, has just been cast in a well-paying tour, but he opts to make his father
happy by turning down the part and going to school. Bea, the mother, has
just thrown a wild tantrum in response to* FRED's *stubbornness and his
often brutal treatment of* FREDDY. FRED *has vowed to divorce Bea. The following evening, father and son meet for their first real talk.*

> (FREDDY *is alone on stage, seated at the dining room table, working on
> a manual project and listening to "Inner Sanctum". As he works on the
> project* FRED *appears on the front porch. He is coming from work and is
> carrying a large gift-wrapped box of some size and weight and a large
> bottle of Scotch. He stand outside the window, taking in the living
> room for a long second, then enters)*

FRED: Is this a private party or can any slob join?

FREDDY: It's not much of a party, just me.

FRED (*Crosses to radio. Goes to turn it off. Stops*):   Mind?
   (FREDDY *shakes his head and* FRED *shuts off radio*)
   Where's the old battle-ax?

FREDDY: Well, she cleaned the house, got all dressed up and
   moseyed on out after lunch, and I haven't seen hide nor hair of
   her since.

FRED: Let's hope she got hit by a car.

FREDDY: Unlikely.

FRED: That broad'd dent the car. Here. (*Puts gift box down on table*)

FREDDY: What?

FRED: Open it.

FREDDY: You gave me the watch.

FRED: I only forked over for it.

FREDDY (*Opening gift*):   Did you go to work?

FRED: A corset. (*"Of course"*) Kennerly give me a bottle of Scotch.

(*Puts it on table*) Son of a bitch can't wait to get rid of me. Let's do some fast living.

(*Takes bottle crossing to highboy for glasses. Stops. Sighs and exits in kitchen Down Left. Sounds offstage of opening cabinets and getting glasses and filling them with ice*)

FREDDY: I haven't acquired that taste yet.

FRED (*Offstage, Down Left, calling*):   Have you ever tried alcohol?

FREDDY: Certainly. I'm in show business.

FRED (*Offstage*):   Well, the way I sees it, a guy should have his first real drink with his old man so you just get you ready. You can sip it. They say you should sip it. I'm not much one for sipping. (*Enters. Puts ice-filled glasses and bottle on table*) I'm going to have a hair of the dog myself. Haven't had a drink from my operation till yesterday. Never did appreciate how it works on me. Beer suits me fine. How's it suit you?

FREDDY: Fine.

FRED: Pay your fine on the way out. (*Opens bottle and pours*) Stayed at Sandra's folks last night and Jesus does her old man put the booze away.

FREDDY: You hardly know them.

FRED: Like hell. He was a Demolay as a kid like me and we're Lodge brothers. Plus, like I told them, I knew they had a spare bed with their daughter out shacking up with my son.

FREDDY: Are they still passed out on the floor?

FRED: Well, I didn't use those exact words.

FREDDY (*Gets package open. Stunned*):   A typewriter.

FRED: Remington. They're supposed to be good. That's what they say anyway.

FREDDY: It's beautiful.

FRED: It's portable. So you can bring it when you come home on trips from school.

FREDDY (*Puts his arms around* FRED's *neck while* FRED *is holding the two glasses*):   I never thought I would have my own.

FRED (*Withdrawing immediately. Self-conscious and uncomfortable but behaving as if* FREDDY *is spilling the drinks*):   Hey, hey, hey, hey, look what the hell you're doing, will ya'? Heads up here. Your mother will murdalize us both.

(*A self-conscious pause.* FREDDY *takes typewriter exiting into Down Right bedroom.* FRED *calls*)

Well, are you joining me or what?

(FREDDY *re-enters. Crosses to table and sits*)

That Sandra's got to have *the* most dry ball folks. Jesus Christ.

They sit and watch their new TV all goddamn night. You never seen anything like it. Wrestling and these old cartoons and some silent movie and then these bull-shit artists all sitting around talking to each other. I couldn't fucking believe it. If you excuse the expression. "When are you getting yours?" the mother asked me. "After looking at this goddamn mindless thing all night I don't give a rat's-ass if I never get mine" I wanted to tell her. But I just said my wife didn't feel they were really perfected yet. And then the old man, who was shit-face by this time from all the hootch he kept slugging down there, I mean really knocking them away bam, bam, bam. Anyway, then he took this fit of laughing at Betty Boop. Pathetic.

FREDDY: Did they think it was weird you coming over there?

FRED: Who the hell knows what those drips think?

FREDDY: You tell them you and Ma had a fight?

FRED: A "domestic difference", I said. (*Hands him drink, fills his own glass*) Finish that and I'll pour you another. And to me that wasn't a fight. Takes two to fight. Me, I walk the hell away. (*Indicating the drink*) Finish it.

FREDDY: I hate it.

FRED: You hate everything. Didn't your mother ever tell you it's not nice to hate. Here.
(*Lifts* FREDDY's *hand, holding the glass, to* FREDDY's *mouth and* FREDDY *finishes it*)
Good boy. Now that was a man's drink. That'll put hair on your chest. That'll put hair on your hair. See how nice to talk? What the hell are you making? I never saw you make anything in your life.

FREDDY: I was putting my diploma in a frame. To hang it. I have two left hands.

FRED: Which could be good if you were only left-handed. Here. Let me help you out. (*Pulls it all to him with one hand while pouring two drinks with the other hand*) Hang this on a *big* wall because it's going to have a lot of company, right?
(FREDDY *lifts glass to drink and* FRED, *not looking up from his task, reaches out and stops his hand from reaching his mouth.* FREDDY *stops and* FRED's *hand goes away.* FREDDY *lifts the glass again and* FRED's *hand stops him again.* FREDDY *stops and as* FRED's *hand goes away* FREDDY *switches hands, turns away quickly and drinks.* FRED *laughs*)

FREDDY: I'm going to get tanked.

FRED (*Pouring him another*):   So what? Sew buttons on your overcoat.

FREDDY: How many times do I graduate from eighth grade anyhow?

(FRED *downs his drink and pours himself another while he puts the diploma in the frame, fastens it and connects wires in back*)

FRED: Who hit Annie in the fanny with a flounder?

FREDDY: Who hit Nelly in the belly with the jelly?

FRED: Who hit Bea in the knee with the tea?

FREDDY (*Seriously*):   Know what?

FRED: What?

FREDDY: That's what.

(FREDDY *points at* FRED *and they laugh.* FRED *holds up arms in surrender*)

FRED: I fell. You got me. Christ, do you remember how Arf drove me nuts with that?

FREDDY: *You* nuts?

FRED: *Us* nuts.

FREDDY: I thought Ma went to meet you, maybe.

FRED: Oh, Christ knows what that mad-woman's up to. I'm telling you right now I'm going to make a few things clear to her when she gets back. Mark my words. Get a few things straight around here once and for all. Just a little too goddamn much interference the way I sees it.

FREDDY: Ma has a lot of nervous energy.

FRED: Got a lot of nerve is what *she's* got. Did you call them to turn down the play?

FREDDY: Ma said she'd take care of it.

FRED: Just so it's taken care of.

FREDDY: It's a wonderful play.

FRED: Good, we'll all go see it. Subject's closed. Think I'll let them know the first of the week it's Cincinnati. Here. (*Gives him framed diploma and pours him a drink*)

FREDDY: Thanks.

FRED: How does it look?

FREDDY: Professional.

FRED (*Nods*):   Think you might get used to Cincinnati?

FREDDY: How did Cincinnati win?

FRED (*Pours himself a drink. A big one. Drinks steadily and heavily*):   Three smart reasons. It's still the mid-west so old-lady-breakdown won't feel so removed. Two, it's close if she wants to come back and visit her asshole friends. And the biggest reason is because we get a full month and a half to pack and sell the goddamn house and not have everybody running around here like a chicken with its head cut off.

FREDDY: The play goes to Cincinnati.

FRED: Closed subject. Did I ever tell you I have my will in my top drawer of my chifferobe?

FREDDY: The one Ma says she'll never touch?

FRED: Anyway, it's in the top drawer of my chifferobe. Pay no attention to her unless you're doing a study on severe mental illness. It's on the left side behind my Masonic books. I divided everything equal between you and your brother. Even though you got all the savings. I'd never want you to some day entertain any notion I played favorites. So everything's divided equal. Fifty-fifty. Right down the line.

FREDDY: In Ireland the oldest son gets it automatically. It's called "Primogeniture".

FRED: Not here. Not in this house. Here everything's divided equal. Same way I should have been dividing my time between you two. But half the time I'd be coming home from work just as you'd be going out to work. And see, that wasn't right because I wasn't really there for you. I acknowledge that. I regret that. I say it to your face. I deeply regret that.

FREDDY: You feel I shouldn't have been acting?

FRED: Yes, I do. Even though I know we never pushed you. You chose it.

FREDDY: But see I really didn't choose it. It's more like it chose me. I wanted to act before I even knew what it was. If it didn't exist I bet I would have invented it. When Ma would come pick me up in your car every night after the play I used to get her to drive past the Ellwyn and the Harris and the Erlanger so I could get to watch the other actors coming out of their theatres before we'd drive home. The only hard thing for me doing a play ever was not to turn around and laugh with the audience when they laughed. And the best part of all was if it was a Wednesday or a Saturday, because then I got to do it two times. Every play I was in I knew everybody's lines in the script. And I bet I could still do all their parts, do them word perfect almost, even today, I bet. I have everything, everything ever written about every show that ever came to Chicago in my boxes in the basement. I got boxes and boxes. Because I think, out of all the things there are or ever will be, a stage play is, far and beyond, the most wonderful, wonderful of things.

FRED: Hard to figure. It's just hard to figure. So now how come you want to stop and go on to the Lab School then?

FREDDY: You'll laugh.

FRED: I think I'm too looped to laugh.

FREDDY (*Thinks. Then*):   Because if you know more you can communicate more. (*Pause*) Do you understand?

FRED: Yes.

FREDDY: Really?

FRED: I'm not a dumb as I look.

FREDDY: The more I know the more I can be. The less I know the less I'll be.

FRED: At fourteen you know this? How?

FREDDY: I don't know how. Maybe when you don't talk much you think more.

FRED: You'll never believe this but when I was a kid I was just like you. Well, very similar. See, I had those rickets so I didn't really walk till I was five.

FREDDY: I always forget that.

FRED: Sure. And I was always quiet and reading just like you. When my father started me working at the factory when I was fourteen is really when I changed. I soon picked up the lingo there and I hung around the guys more and I got on their baseball team and I became accepted — started to fit in. It's why you gotta admire Artie. Right from the beginning he knew how to fit in. I admire that.

(FREDDY *has an elbow on the table and* FRED *lifts the arm and brings it down on the table hard*)

FREDDY: Owww.

FRED (*Quickly*):   Sh, sh, sh. I hope you just might be coming out of yourself. Look. In your whole life you never talked as much as tonight.

FREDDY: In my whole life I never drank as much as tonight.

(FRED *pulls* FREDDY *toward him and affectionately and playfully rubs his knuckles into his head*)

(*Pulling away, struggling*) Owwww.

Source: Samuel French, Inc.

✤ Pvt. Wars

•••••••••••••••••••••••••••••JAMES MCCLURE

CHARACTERS: SILVIO (20's-30's), GATELY (20's-30's)
SETTING: *An Army hospital, 1979.*

SILVIO *and* GATELY *have become friends while recuperating from injuries, both physical and mental, sustained during service in Vietnam.* SILVIO, *a tough, street-wise Italian-American, has had his genitals destroyed by shrapnel and delights in opening his robe and ""flashing" the nursing staff.* GATELY, *a Southerner who has completely lost his confidence and is mentally slow, spends days tinkering with an old radio which he feels he must fix before he can leave the hospital. They meet near the table where* GATELY *is fixing his radio.*

(GATELY *fixing radio. Off-stage we hear* SILVIO's *voice*)
SILVIO: Hey, gorgeous. turn around. Ta-dah! Woo! (*Entering*) Did you ever ask yourself the secret of my incredible sexual power over women?
GATELY: No.
SILVIO: Why the nurses can't resist me?
GATELY: The nurses hate you, Silvio.
SILVIO: Ah. That's what they would have you believe.
GATELY: They got me believin' it.
SILVIO: You wanna hear a great line for picking girls up?
GATELY: Sure.
SILVIO: Now this works best for Catholic girls.
GATELY: Okay.
SILVIO: You tell 'em you're a priest.
GATELY: A priest.
SILVIO: Okay. Look we'll set the scene. This is what they call settin' the scene. Now, you're sitting there. At the table. What can this table be?
GATELY: A table.
SILVIO: Okay. We'll make it a table. We're in a night club.
GATELY: Can it be a singles joint?
SILVIO: Gately, you been to a single joint?
GATELY: No.

SILVIO: Okay, I tell you what. In settin' the scene we'll make this a singles joint.

GATELY (*Awed*): Where'd you learn all this?

SILVIO: Once I hung around a USO group that was rehearsing. A Bob Hope thing. I tell you something', Gately . . .

GATELY: Yeah?

SILVIO: Never be afraid to mingle in the arts.

GATELY: All right!

SILVIO: Okay, so we're in a singles joint. And you're a broad. Everybody's being hustled. It's a fucking meat market!

GATELY: What's a nice girl like me doing in a place like this?

SILVIO: That's it! That's it! That's what's called gettin' into character!

GATELY: Am I lonely?

SILVIO: Are you lonely? A face like that. What do you think.

GATELY: I'm lonely, huh?

SILVIO: That's right. You're like ugly Catholic girls all over the world. You're like a different breed. You sit there being ugly, ruining life for everybody else.

GATELY: Are you lonely?

SILVIO: Gately! I'm a priest! Of course I'm lonely. I'm one of the loneliest, horniest guys on the face of the earth. OK, you're sitting there by yourself. So I come in. And I'm very depressed. So I come in and I look around. No, you don't see me yet, Gately. I see you. I come over and I say, "Pardon me, miss, is this seat taken?"

GATELY: Yes, it is.

SILVIO: What?

GATELY: Buzz off.

SILVIO: No. You don't say nothing.

GATELY: You want me to call the management?

SILVIO: That's not the way it goes.

GATELY: Male chauvinist pig.

SILVIO: Gately.

GATELY: What?

SILVIO: Don't give me such a hard time, OK?

GATELY: I just wanted to make it realistic.

SILVIO: Okay. But you're making it too realistic. We'll do it again. So I come in very depressed and — you don't see me yet, Gately — I see you and I come over and I say, "Pardon me, miss, but is this seat taken?"

GATELY: Well, why not.

SILVIO: Mind if I sit down?

GATELY: Well, why not.

SILVIO: May I order you another drink?

GATELY: Well, sure.

SILVIO: Bartender. Two more of the same. Do you mind if I smoke?

GATELY: Well, why not.

(SILVIO *takes out two cigarettes, puts them in his mouth, lights them both. He offers her one*)

I don't want it.

SILVIO: Why not?

GATELY: You've slobbered all over it.

SILVIO: No I haven't.

GATELY: You've had it in your mouth.

SILVIO: Gately, take the fuckin' cigarette.

(GATELY *takes the cigarette*)

I hope you won't think I'm being too personal but . . . what's your name.

GATELY: Woodruff Gately.

SILVIO: Woodruff?

GATELY: Woodruff.

SILVIO: I've never known a girl named Woodruff before.

GATELY: You've never known a girl like me.

SILVIO: If I seem a little nervous, it's because I don't usually come to this kind of place. Have you ever come to this kind of place?

GATELY: I'm a Baptist.

SILVIO: You must be very lonely.

GATELY: Why, because I'm a Baptist?

SILVIO (*Putting his hand on* GATELY's *leg*):   Can I tell you something very personal.

GATELY: Okay. But don't get smutty.

SILVIO: I just wanted to tell you that I don't get a chance to meet beautiful women. You see, actually, I'm a priest.

GATELY: Well, I don't get a chance to meet men. You see, actually, I'm a lesbian.

SILVIO (*Gets up angrily*):   That's it! Forget it, Gately.

GATELY: I'm sorry!

SILVIO: No! No! Let's just forget it. I try to teach you something! Give you the benefit of my experience, my life! You know what you are. I'll tell you what you are. A fucking ingrate, that's what you are. Why'd you make her a lesbian?

GATELY: I don't know.

SILVIO: Not even a priest could pick up a lesbian. Nobody could pick up a lesbian.

GATELY: A lesbian could!

SILVIO: Who cares! That does me no good. I can't become a lesbian every time I wanna get laid.

GATELY: No.

SILVIO: You see my point.

GATELY: You could become a transvestite.

SILVIO: What?

GATELY: Wear women's clothes.

SILVIO: But I don't want to wear women's clothes.

GATELY: I know you don't.

SILVIO: I know I don't, too.

GATELY: You want to wear a kilt.

SILVIO: That's right.

GATELY: Which is nearly women's clothes.

SILVIO (*Pause*):   You know something, Gately? At the rate you're going, you may never get laid.

Source: Dramatists Play Service, Inc.

✣ Safe Sex

•••••••••••••••••••••••••••HARVEY FIERSTEIN

CHARACTERS: GHEE (30's), MEAD (20's-30's)
SETTING: *A house by the beach, the present.*

GHEE *and* MEAD *are gay lovers who have a problem.* MEAD *has accused* GHEE *of becoming so obsessed with the AIDS issue that he can no longer enjoy having sex. As the scene begins, their lovemaking has erupted into a wrestling match because* MEAD *wanted to do something which is not on* GHEE's *list of safe sex practices. In the Broadway production, Harvey Fierstein played* GHEE *and John Wesley Shipp played* MEAD. *As originally staged, this scene was played in a large, abstract seesaw, as referred to in the stage directions. The scene can easily be played in a more realistic setting.*

GHEE (*Slow and definite*): Don't touch me. (MEAD *does not move or react*) Did you hear what I said? (*No reaction*) I'll get the list.

MEAD: Don't bother.

GHEE: I'm sure it wasn't safe.

MEAD: Sure.

GHEE: I'll show you right on the list. (*Pause*) You want to see it on the list?

MEAD: Forget it.

GHEE: 'Cause you know I'm right and you know that if I show it to you right on the list in black and white then you'll have to admit that I'm right. Right?

MEAD: Right.

GHEE: You don't believe me. I'll get the list.

MEAD (*Covering his face with his hands*): Forget it. Just forget it. It doesn't matter. It's over.
(*Silence between them*)

GHEE: There aren't many things that I know a lot about, but on "Safe Sex" I happen to be an expert. (*Another silence*) Did you say something?

MEAD: No.

GHEE: I hate when you get like this. Now you're mad at me when all I was trying to do was protect us both. (*No response*) Why can't you stop when I ask you to? Huh? (*No response*) Why does it always have to come to hurt feelings? (GHEE *sits up straight. He sees that* MEAD *is withdrawn. He drops his head*) I'm scared, alright? What's so hard to understand? I'm scared! (*No response*) Being scared is smart. You have to be scared. You're supposed to be scared. You're not normal if you're not scared. Everyone's scared. (*No response*) And I suppose you're not scared?

MEAD: I'm concerned.

GHEE: You're scared.

MEAD: I'm tired.

GHEE: You're angry.

MEAD: Don't tell me what I am.

GHEE: Don't yell at me.

MEAD: Don't tell me what to do.

GHEE: Don't touch me!

(*They turn their backs to each other, their legs hanging off the ends of the board. Balanced*)

The honeymoon is over. (*Pause*) Would you say that was a safe assessment? (*No response*) Lovers for five and a half years, separated for nearly two years, back together for less than a week and already the honeymoon is over.

MEAD (*Under his breath*): Jerk.

GHEE: Fine. It's all my fault. Dump the blame on me. Like I don't feel guilty enough as is.

MEAD: I said you were a jerk. I wasn't blaming you for being a jerk. I didn't say that being a jerk was your fault. Nor was I attempting to make you feel guilty for being a jerk. I made a simple observation. You're a jerk. Now just drop it.

GHEE: I'm a jerk because in the face of this devastating epidemic I insist we take a few precautions?

MEAD: No. You're just a jerk.

GHEE: Well, that's obvious. Who else but a jerk would want you back? Who else but a jerk would *take* you back? Who else but a jerk would fall in love with you in the first place?

MEAD: Want to see a list?

(GHEE *spins around and bounces on his end of the seesaw, throwing* MEAD *up into the air*)

Damn!

(GHEE, *enjoying the advantage of having* MEAD *at his mercy, bounces the board for emphasis as he speaks*)

GHEE: Well, come on. I'm waiting. Let's hear the list. How many?

MEAD: You know.

GHEE: No, you see, I only know about your little Larry. But you said that there's whole list. And much as you cared for him, I'd hardly call little Larry a list.

MEAD: You want to stop?

GHEE: I want to know how many. Larry and who else?

MEAD: Someone else.

GHEE: Who?

MEAD: You wouldn't know them.

GHEE: Them? How many of "them", Casanova?

MEAD: A few. Alright?

GHEE: Fine with me, but I wonder how little Larry felt about your "thems".

MEAD: Once I met Larry there was no one.

GHEE: No one?

MEAD: No one!

(MEAD *bounces hard on the board, tossing* GHEE *off the ground, restoring the balance*)

He left me. I didn't leave him.

GHEE: And you came crawling back to me.

MEAD: You begged me to come back.

GHEE: I never begged!

MEAD: I never crawled!

(*They face off, staring each other down.* MEAD *breaks it*)

I hate when you do this! You're not happy unless you've got me bashing your head into a wall.

(GHEE *lies back glamorously*)

GHEE: I'm horny. (*No response*) There's definitely something wrong with me. All I have to do is think about you with someone else and I get crazy. What's that: love?

MEAD: Jealousy.

GHEE: No. You think? No! Well . . . Yeah. Maybe. But if that's jealousy why does everyone put it down?

MEAD: It's an immature emotion. As irrational as it is insulting. It puts an object value on pure emotion and reduces what should be a free partnership into possessor and possessed.

GHEE: I love it. (*Pause*) Whenever I remember your first telling me that you had slept with someone else, all I can think about is the incredible sex we had that night. (*Giggles*) I don't remember pain, though I know there was. I don't remember anger, though there certainly was some of that. Just this overwhelming burning that flamed into the most intense passion I had ever felt. (*Pause*) Remember?

MEAD: I remember waiting for you to scream. Guilt. I remember waiting to be punished. Hurt. I remember lying next to you after you'd fallen asleep and thinking about the sex we had just had.

GHEE: It was great, wasn't it?

MEAD: Could have been. That wasn't important. All I remember is that that was the first time you had touched me, let alone made love to me, in over three months.

GHEE (*Angry*):   That's a lie.

MEAD: True.

GHEE (*Bolting up to look at him*):   It wasn't three months.

(MEAD *stares* GHEE *down*)

Maybe three days. Or maybe three weeks.

(MEAD *just stares.* GHEE *submits. They both lie back once again. Silence. Balance*)

I was scared. (*Pause*) It was a bad time for me. All you read about, every headline, the only thing on TV, was AIDS. Joey had already died. Tommy was in the hospital. And how many other friends did we have who had it? How many others did we think might?

MEAD: So, I got locked out.

GHEE: I was scared.

MEAD: Of what? We'd been together for five years. We'd already done everything they said you shouldn't. If one of us did have it, if one of us was going to infect the other, it was already done.

GHEE: I was in a panic. I wasn't thinking.

MEAD: You were thinking. About yourself.

GHEE: And you. Before we met I was pretty wild. You talk about your lists? Boy if I had to, I don't think I could ever remember all the guys I had sex with.

MEAD: You didn't have sex with anyone. Trust me, I laid next to you all those years. Sex is something you don't have. Oh, you fiddle and diddle, but sex? Real sex?

GHEE: I don't remember getting any complaints.

MEAD: You never hung around long enough to hear them.

GHEE: That's bull.

MEAD: Think so?

GHEE: What about us our first year? We never got out of bed.

MEAD: I don't remember.

GHEE: You couldn't keep your hands off me.

MEAD: That so?

GHEE: I used to have to beg for dinner breaks.

MEAD: That was years ago.

GHEE: Years before AIDS.

MEAD: Our problems started years before AIDS. AIDS was your salvation.

GHEE: That's sick.

MEAD: You ran right out, got your list of Do's and Don'ts and embraced it like a priest takes his vows. Safe Sex, there in black and white you finally had what you always wanted: a concrete, board-certified, actual, purposeful excuse to avoid intimacy. God, you were in your glory! You waved it in my face with one hand and shoved me across the bed with the other. You took your list and nailed it to the headboard like the goddamned sexual commandments: "Thou shalt not . . . Thou shalt not . . . Thou shalt not . . . " You're not scared of AIDS, you're scared of sex.

GHEE: Me?

MEAD: Or me.

GHEE: You're scared of sex?

MEAD: You're scared of me.

GHEE: Me scared of you? Don't flatter yourself.

MEAD: When I first started fooling around I reasoned that I was justified. I certainly wasn't getting anything at home. I had a right to look elsewhere. But my lies were so blatant, my excuses so lame . . . I wanted you to catch me. I wanted you to know that you could lose, actually lose, me. I did it right under your nose, right in your bed . . . I left phone numbers around, and clothes . . . And nothing!

GHEE: I suspected.

MEAD: You hoped. Wished even. One more excuse to push me away.

GHEE: And what were you dong? Your fooling around was supposed to make me feel safer? What are you, out of your mind?

MEAD: Didn't it? You just said that the best sex we ever had was after you found out about Larry. When there actually was danger. When I actually could have been infected.

GHEE: That was different. We had Safe Sex.

MEAD: We had Safe Distance, and that's all you've ever wanted.
(*Silence. Both consider what has been said.* GHEE *sits up, cross-legged, and looks at* MEAD)

GHEE: So what're you saying; that I'm a lousy lay?
(MEAD *covers his head in frustration*)

Source: Atheneum/Macmillan

✤ Saxophone Music

•••••••••••••••••••••••••••••BILL BOZZONE

CHARACTERS: HECTOR (20's-30's), EMIL (30's)
SETTING: *A room in a New York City boarding hotel, the present.*

EMIL *is a simple, trusting, unkempt, slightly retarded man who plays a mean saxophone. His pal,* HECTOR, *is a sharp operator who takes care of* EMIL. *They escaped together from a mental hospital and are now sharing a room.* HECTOR, *the smarter of the two, is depressed over losing his job. And now, the roles are reversing because it is* EMIL *who is supporting them both by playing his saxophone on a streetcorner, managed by a street person named Silky.*

(EMIL *enters from the hall. He now wears a brightly colored scarf around his neck. He closes the door and fumbles in the dark*)
HECTOR (*Dark*):   Turn it on.
EMIL (*Dark*):   Hector?
HECTOR (*Dark*):   Turn it on.
(EMIL, *at the wall switch, turns on the lamp. He is carrying his saxophone case.* HECTOR, *barefooted, is seated in the chair and turned three-quarters looking out the window. His socks are hanging over the lampshade.* EMIL *carries two paper bags: one from Dunkin Donuts and the other from Woolworth*)
EMIL: I was trying to be quiet. I thought you'd be asleep.
HECTOR: Do I look asleep? (*No response. Pause*) I like to sit in the dark and look out, okay?
EMIL: For two days?
HECTOR: Yeah, for two days. What are you? A fuckin' cop?
(EMIL *moves toward the bed*)
(*After a moment*) What the hell's on your neck?
EMIL (*Approaching, taking the scarf off*):   Silky gave it to me.
HECTOR: Silky . . .
EMIL: It's warm. Try it.
HECTOR: Get the fuckin' thing away from me.
(EMIL *puts the scarf on the bed*)
EMIL: I wanted to drop these off. Silky's waiting for me in the coffee shop across the street.
HECTOR: Well we don't want to keep Silky waiting, do we?

EMIL: I just saw the landlady on the steps. I asked her if I could see the new room. (*Pause*) It's in the cellar, Hector. (*Pause*) I gave her ten bucks to hold this room for another week.
HECTOR: You did what?!
EMIL: I gave her ten bucks to —
HECTOR: I set that up!
EMIL: I figured we'd be better up here.
HECTOR: You figured. (*Beat*) Well you stay up here. You don't tell me what to do.
(*Pause*)
EMIL: I got some Dunkin Donuts.
HECTOR: If I wanted Dunkin Donuts, I'd get my own Dunkin Donuts.
(EMIL *opens the Woolworth bag, takes out a cheap transistor radio, turns it on, sets it on top of the dresser. A jazz station, with less than perfect reception, plays.* EMIL *smiles, looks over at* HECTOR *for approval. No response from* HECTOR)
EMIL: The man in the store showed me how it works. (*Short pause*) You can listen to it anytime you want. (EMIL *goes back to the Woolworth bag*) And I got something else. Two for nine dollars. One for me, one for you. (EMIL *takes out two different-colored flannel shirts*) Flannel. Very warm.
(*Pause.* HECTOR *reaches out, takes one of the shirts, studies it, tosses it on the bed*)
HECTOR: I can't wear this.
EMIL: Wrong size?
HECTOR: Is a cowboy shirt! I look like a cowboy?!
EMIL: Lotta people wear these shirts. You don't have to be a cowboy.
HECTOR: I hate the shirt, Emil, okay?! What can I say?! You my mother now?! You pick out my clothes?!
(*Pause.* EMIL *rises, goes toward the dresser with both shirts*)
EMIL: I'll put them away.
HECTOR: You do that.
(EMIL *puts one shirt in top drawer, one in drawer underneath*)
(*Sarcastically*) You "play" tonight?
(EMIL *ignores the sarcasm, faces* HECTOR, *smiles*)
EMIL: Almost nine hours. (*He goes to the bed, picks up the saxophone case*) I had over $90 in here when I got done. Made a hundred-and-thirty-something. Silky took $45, I got the rest. (*He sits on the bed with the saxophone case on his lap. He opens it, takes out some bills, counts them*)

HECTOR (*After a moment*): Well I hope you enjoy it, I really do. (*Pause*) Because it's all gonna come down around your ears very soon, Emil. People get very tired of the same old saxophone music. Couple days, you can't make a fuckin' dime.

(EMIL *has taken out a few bills. He extends them toward* HECTOR)

EMIL: Here.

HECTOR: What.

EMIL: Money.

HECTOR: I know it's money. I've seen money.

(*Pause.* EMIL *puts the cash back in the saxophone case, leaves the case open on the bed*)

EMIL: Eat today?

HECTOR: None of your business.

EMIL: Doughnut?

HECTOR: No!

(*Pause*)

EMIL: Just trying to help.

HECTOR: You wanna help, leave me alone.

EMIL: You always helped me. (*Pause*) We always shared the money when we got out of the crazy house.

HECTOR: Was different.

EMIL: How come?

HECTOR: Because it was mine! I came up with the plan! I got you to take the money! You wouldn't've listened to nobody else! (*Pause*) I worked for that money, Emil! I didn't do nothing to get (*Indicates* EMIL'*s money*) this shit! (*Pause. He stares out the window*) (*Mock laugh*) Look at me. Hector Diaz. No job. No dignity. (*Beat*) One pair of socks every morning still wet from the night before
. . .

(*Long pause*)

EMIL: You need some new socks?

(*Pause.* HECTOR *rises, approaches* EMIL)

HECTOR: Lemme explain something to you. (*Pause*) You take something from somebody, you know what that means? (*Beat*) Means you his. (*Short pause*) Is okay if it's your boss or your wife or something, that's okay. (*Short pause*) But for *me* to take from *you*
. . . (*He stares at* EMIL. *Pause. He returns to the chair, looks out*)

EMIL (*After a moment*): I could give you a job.

(*Pause.* HECTOR *faces* EMIL)

HECTOR (*Mock laugh*): What?

EMIL: Partners. We split fifty/fifty.

HECTOR: I work for you?

EMIL: You could keep the people back. (*Short pause*) Sometimes the coins land on the sidewalk and other people pick them up.

HECTOR (*Rises*): I could dress up like a monkey . . . (*He mimics an organ grinder's monkey*) . . . dance around while you play.

EMIL (*Short pause*): We could try it.

(*Pause*)

HECTOR: Okay, Emil. You want to give me something? Lemme give you something. Lesson in life. (*He opens the window. Some night noise — a typical Saturday night at midnight*) I want you to watch very close. (*He moves to the bed, quickly snatches the saxophone from the case*)

EMIL: Hey!

(HECTOR *quickly moves to the window holding the saxophone. He holds the instrument, by the mouthpiece, out the window.* EMIL *quickly rushes over*)

HECTOR: Any closer and I let it go, Emil. I'm not kiddin'.

(EMIL *freezes*)

You see? This is the difference between you and me. I let go of this and it's over for you, man. No more saxophone, no more Emil. (*Pause*) Hey, well sure, you could buy a new one, but it wouldn't change nothing. Somebody could still take it away from you easy. Bang. Out the window. (*Pause*) But I have ability, Emil. A brain. I can think. Nobody can take that away. (*Pause*) You want your saxophone?

EMIL (*Still frozen*): Gimme my saxophone.

HECTOR: Please?

(*Pause*)

EMIL: Please.

(*Pause.* HECTOR *brings the instrument back inside, extends it toward* EMIL. EMIL *hesitates a moment before clutching the saxophone. Without putting the instrument back in the case, he closes the case, picks it up, starts for the door*)

EMIL (*Stops*): Don't you ever do that again, Hector.

HECTOR: So what if I do? What are gonna do? Kill me?

EMIL (*At the door, facing* HECTOR): No. (*Pause*) But I won't come back, either.

(EMIL *exits.* HECTOR *stares at the closed door for a moment*)

HECTOR (*To himself*): So don't.

(*Pause.* HECTOR *shivers, rubs his arms. He looks toward the open window, approaches it, attempts to pull it shut. It's stuck. He curses, bangs on the window, gives up. Pause. He goes to the dresser and roughly turns off the transistor. He starts back, sees the doughnut bag, stops.*

He picks it up. He sits, stares out the open window, takes a doughnut from the bag, takes a bite. He stops. Pause. A moment of realization. He sticks what's left of the doughnut back in the bag, throws the bag across the room, wipes his mouth. He sits back. Pause. He rises, slowly climbs out on the window ledge. After a moment or two, reenter EMIL. EMIL *quickly snatches the scarf he'd left on the bed, starts for the door. He stops, studies the room, looks toward the window)*

EMIL: Hector? (EMIL *puts his saxophone case on the bed and cautiously approaches the window)*

HECTOR (*Outside*): Get away from me, Emil!

(EMIL *stops by the window)*

I'm serious! I'm not kidding with you! (*Short pause*) GET OUTTA HERE, MAN!

EMIL: It's all right, Hector.

HECTOR (*Outside*): Get outta here, man.

EMIL: Give me your hand.

HECTOR (*Outside. Frozen*): I don't need you.

EMIL: Come on.

(*Long pause*)

HECTOR (*Outside. Nervous laugh*): I can't move.

EMIL: It's okay, Hector.

HECTOR (*Outside. Nervous, almost frantic laugh*): I can't fuckin' move.

EMIL: Hector?

HECTOR (*Outside*): Help me, Emil.

EMIL: Come on.

HECTOR (*Outside*): Help me.

EMIL: Give me your hand.

(HECTOR *does*)

Swing your leg in.

(HECTOR *does*)

Watch your head. Watch your head!

(*After a moment,* HECTOR *is inside.* EMIL, *with an arm around him, supports* HECTOR's *weight. They pause together)*

HECTOR (*With relief*): Whuu. (*Pause. Slight laugh*) Some scary shit out there, man.

EMIL: It's okay.

HECTOR (*Laughs*): Little tiny people and cars and shit.

(EMIL *has led him to the edge of the bed. Both sit.* EMIL's *arm still supporting* HECTOR)

EMIL: You all right?

HECTOR: Yeah. Sure. (*Pause*) Whuu. (*He laughs. Pause*) So listen. I was thinking. Maybe the weekends, I got nothing to do. I could help you out. "Strong-arm" for you. You know, keep an eye on things while you busy playing.

EMIL: All right.

HECTOR: Is not a bad room downstairs, man. Just takes a little getting used to, right?

EMIL: Right.

(*Pause*)

HECTOR: Thanks, Emil.

EMIL: It's okay.

HECTOR: Thanks.

EMIL: It's okay.

(*Pause.* EMIL *goes to the window, closes it.* HECTOR *stands. Pause*)

HECTOR: You wanna know something else?

(EMIL *looks toward* HECTOR)

The fuckin' doughnuts were stale.

Source: *Ensemble Studio Theatre Marathon (84),*
Broadway Play Publishing, Inc.

✤ The Speed of Darkness

•••••••••••••••••••••••••••••STEVE TESICH

CHARACTERS: JOE (40's), EDDIE (18)
SETTING: JOE's home in South Dakota, the present.

JOE *is a troubled Vietnam veteran who works as a building contractor. He lives with his wife and his teenage daughter, Mary.* EDDIE, *Mary's boyfriend, is a nice, regular guy who looks up to* JOE *to the point of hero worship.* JOE *is slowly cracking under the pressure of secrets he is keeping, his disillusionment with the American Dream, and the fact that Lou, his old army buddy, has just shot himself in* JOE's *living room. The baby in this scene is Mary's imagined infant, which is actually a sack of soil wrapped in a blanket.*

> (EDDIE *is sitting center stage, facing the audience, holding the baby in his arms. Maybe he's rocking it slowly, but maybe he's doing it to calm himself. He's very stiff and anxious. Enter* JOE. *He's coming home. Absorbed in his own thoughts. Suit and tie, but he's loosening the tie as he walks on. He sees* EDDIE, *just as* EDDIE *becomes aware of him and instantly stands up.* JOE *looks at him for a beat*)

JOE: What're you doing here?
EDDIE: Nothing. I mean I'm just waiting for Mary to come back. Your wife said I could wait for her.
JOE: What's wrong with waiting at your own home?
EDDIE: Everything's wrong there that's usually wrong there.
> (JOE *makes himself a drink. He's in a kind of daze*)
My Dad's at home. He's go the flu. My Mom . . . well . . . Easter's just around the corner and I believe I've already pointed out to you once before the rather catastrophic side effects religious holidays, or the mere threat of religious holidays looming on the horizon, have on my Mother's nervous system. She was dismantling my Dad's life when I left her, comparing it to those T.V. pilots that don't get picked up by the networks. "No new episodes, for you. No guest starts. No spin-offs . . . "
JOE: You talk too much.
EDDIE: I certainly do. Yes. Nerves.
JOE: What're you nervous about?

EDDIE: It's a kind of generic nervousness. Something to do with my life, I think.

(JOE *looks at his watch. He hardly seems to be listening to* EDDIE)

JOE: I guess the funeral service should be starting right about now.

(*He kind of toasts Lou's spirit and drinks up the drink in one shot*)

EDDIE: I understand.

JOE: You what?

(*It almost sounds like a threat.* EDDIE *backs off*)

EDDIE: Nothing.

(JOE *starts fixing another drink*)

I was going to go to the funeral myself, but Mary didn't think we should take the baby to the funeral and since somebody had to look after him . . .

JOE: That's my grandson. Lou Junior. Right?

(EDDIE's *not sure how to reply. Should he smile. Should he be serious. He settles for some nervous middle ground*)

EDDIE: I suppose.

JOE: And you're the father!

EDDIE: So I'm told.

JOE: You don't sound very sure to me. And stop staring at me like that.

(EDDIE *looks away.* JOE *chugs his drink*)

EDDIE: It's too bad you don't like me, Sir.

JOE: Yeah, it's a crying shame.

EDDIE: Not that I blame you. If I were a man like you, of your stature, I'd want a more manly figure for my daughter myself. If it's any consolation to you, I'm strictly temporary. Mary's going to college and I'm not. My wishes to the contrary, this is not going to be one of those relationships that survives a separation.

(JOE's *making another drink*)

As things stand now, I'll be following in my Dad's footsteps and seeking a career for myself in the world of real estate.

(*He stops.* JOE *is just standing there, with his drink, absorbed in his thoughts. He seems even to have forgotten he has a drink in his hand.* EDDIE *looks at him. Takes a small step toward him. Stops*)

I'm so very sorry.

JOE: What?

EDDIE: I feel the loss and I hardly knew him. It must be terrible for you.

(JOE *becomes aware of the drink*)

JOE: What's that? (*Drinks it*)

EDDIE: Lou doing that in your own home. It probably brought back the whole nightmare for you.

JOE: What're you talking about, Eddie. What nightmare?

EDDIE: The war.

JOE: I don't have nightmares about the war. The war was a piece of cake.

EDDIE: I find that hard to believe, Sir.

JOE: Piece of cake.

EDDIE: I don't really know much about it myself, but . . .

JOE: Sure you do.

EDDIE: I've seen a few movies.

JOE: Then you know all about it.

EDDIE: I'm sure there's more to it than that.

JOE: Not much.

EDDIE: Were you ever wounded in battle?

JOE: Once.

EDDIE: It must have hurt a lot.

JOE: Still does.

EDDIE: Really?

JOE: Yes.

EDDIE: You mean you're in pain now?

JOE: Yes.

EDDIE: Is it real bad?

JOE: Yes. Anything else you'd like to know?
    (*A beat*)

EDDIE: Did . . . did you ever have to kill somebody?

JOE: I don't know if I had to . . . but I did. (JOE's *making another drink*)

EDDIE: Really.

JOE: Yes.

EDDIE: It wasn't one of those atrocities, I hope.

JOE: No. Merely killing.

EDDIE: And how . . . how did it make you feel . . . to actually . . .

JOE: Kill somebody?

EDDIE: Yes.

JOE: Piece of cake.

EDDIE: I find that hard to believe.

JOE: Me too. I find it amazing.

EDDIE: The worst part, I hear, from the little I know, was not knowing who the enemy was.

JOE: No. The worst part was finding out. See. For all you know, I'm the enemy.

EDDIE: Is that what it was like over there?
  (JOE *drinks up*)
JOE: Do you really wanna know what it was like?
EDDIE: Yes.
JOE: Come here.
  (EDDIE *takes a few cautious steps and stops*)
  Closer.
  (EDDIE's *becoming anxious and worried, but obeys. Stops*)
  Closer.
  (EDDIE *obeys again and stops next to* JOE)
  Tell me, Eddie, man to man, what's it like to fuck my daughter?
  (EDDIE *can't believe he heard the question*)
EDDIE: Sir?
JOE: You heard me. What's it like?
  (EDDIE *starts to move away, but* JOE *grabs him by the collar and pulls him back*)
  What's it like to fuck her, Eddie?
EDDIE: You can't really . . . Please, Sir. Let me go.
JOE: What's the matter, Eddie? You can't tell me, is that it?
EDDIE: No.
JOE: Why not? It's personal. Is that what it is? It's personal.
EDDIE: Yes.
JOE: It's more personal that what happened to me in the war? Is that what you're telling me?
EDDIE: I'm very sorry, Sir. Please.
JOE: I'm public property. Is that what I am. A library book.
EDDIE: I didn't mean to . . .
JOE: Take off your pants, Eddie. Let's see your balls. Let's see 'em, Eddie.
  (*He lets go his shirt collar and, as* EDDIE *tries to move away,* JOE *grabs him violently by the balls.* EDDIE *screams in pain. Almost drops the baby but holds on. He's made helpless by it*)
  That's what it was like. You're asking me to take mine off and show them to you.
  (*He seems to squeeze harder.* EDDIE *lets out a terrible scream.* JOE *pulls his hands away and let him go.* EDDIE, *out of breath and bent over, but clutching the baby in his arms, exits slowly, groaning and fighting for air.* JOE *looks away from him. Walks to a chair, taking the bottle and glass with him. Sits down where* EDDIE *sat*)

Source: Samuel French, Inc.

✤ Speed-The-Plow

•••••••••••••••••••••••••••••••DAVID MAMET

CHARACTERS: GOULD *(40's)*, FOX *(40's)*
SETTING: GOULD's *office, morning.*

GOULD, *a high powered Hollywood producer, recently promoted, and his assistant, FOX, wax euphoric over their prospects of power and fortune in connection with a new movie deal they're about to close.*

GOULD: The question, your crass question: how much money could we stand to make . . . ?
FOX: Yes.
GOULD: I think the operative concept here is "lots and lots . . . "
FOX: Oh, maan . . .
GOULD: Great big jolly *shitloads* of it.
FOX: Oh, maan . . .
GOULD: But money . . .
FOX: Yeah.
GOULD: Money, Charl . . .
FOX: Yeah . . .
GOULD: Money is not the important thing.
FOX: No.
GOULD: Money is not Gold.
FOX: No.
GOULD: What can you do with Money?
FOX: Nothing.
GOULD: Nary a goddamn thing.
FOX: . . . I'm gonna be rich.
GOULD: "Buy" things with it.
FOX: Where would I *keep* them?
GOULD: What would you *do* with them?
FOX: Yeah.
GOULD: Take them out and *dust* them, time to time.
FOX: Oh yeah.
GOULD: I piss on money.
FOX: I know that you do. I'll help you.
GOULD: *Fuck* money.
FOX: Fuck it. Fuck "things" too . . .

GOULD: Uh huh. But don't fuck "people".

FOX: No.

GOULD: 'Cause, people, Charlie . . .

FOX: People . . . yes.

GOULD: Are what it's All About.

FOX: I know.

GOULD: And it's a People Business.

FOX: That it is.

GOULD: It's *full* of fucken' people . . .

FOX: And we're gonna kick some ass, Bob.

GOULD: That we are.

FOX: We're gonna kick the ass of a lot of them fucken' people.

GOULD: That's right.

FOX: We get rolling, Bob. It's "up the ass with gun and camera".

GOULD: Yup.

FOX: 'Cause when you spend twenty years in the barrel . . .

GOULD: . . . I know . . .

FOX: No, you *don't* know, you've forgotten. Due respect.

GOULD: . . . may be . . .

FOX: But, but . . . oh maan . . . I'm gonna settle some fucken' scores.

GOULD: Better things to do . . .

FOX: If there are, *show* them to me, man . . . A bunch of cocksuckers out there. Gimme' a cigarette. Oh, Man, I can't come down . . .

GOULD: No need to. Huh . . . ?

FOX: Ross, Ross, Ross isn't going to fuck me out of this . . . ?

GOULD: No. Absolutely not. You have my word.

FOX: I don't need your word, Bob. I know you . . . Drives right to my house. I need a cup of coffee.

GOULD (*Into phone*): Could we get a cup . . . well, where did you try? Why not try the *coffee mach* . . . well, it's right down at the . . . down the, no, it's unmarked, just go . . . that's right. (*Hangs up*)

FOX: What, you got a new broad, go with the new job . . .

GOULD: No. Cathy's just out sick.

FOX: Cute broad, the new broad.

GOULD: What? She's cute? The broad out there is cute? Baby, she's nothing. You wait 'til we make this film.

FOX: She's nothing?

GOULD: Playing in this league? I'm saying, it's Boy's Choice: Skate in One Direction Only.

(*Pause*)

FOX: Oh, man, what am I going to do today?

GOULD: Go to a movie, get your hair done.

FOX: I'm jumping like a leaf.

GOULD: It's a done deal. We walked in *tomorrow* . . .

FOX (*Picks up the book*):   What's this, what's the thing you're reading I come in?

GOULD: This thing?

FOX: Uh huh . . .

GOULD: From the East. An Eastern Sissy Writer. (*Passes the book to* FOX)

FOX (*Reads*):   "The Bridge: or, Radiation and the Half-Life of Society. A Study of Decay".

GOULD: A Novel.

FOX: Great.

GOULD: A cover note from Richard Ross: "Give this a Courtesy Read."

FOX (*Reads*):   "The wind against the Plains, but not a wind of change . . . a wind like that one which he'd been foretold, the rubbish of the world — swirling, swirling . . . two thousand years . . . " Hey I wouldn't just give it a *courtesy* read, I'd *make* this sucker.

GOULD: Good idea.

FOX: Drop a dime on western civilization.

GOULD: . . . 'Bout time.

FOX: Why don't you do that? *Make* it.

GOULD: I think that I will.

FOX: Yeah. Instead of our Doug, Doug Brown's *Buddy* film.

GOULD: Yeah. *I* could do that. You know why? Because my job, my new job is one thing: the capacity to make decisions.

FOX: I know that it is.

GOULD: Decide, decide, decide . . .

FOX: It's lonely at the top.

GOULD: But it ain't crowded.

Source: Grove Press

✢ A Walk in the Woods

●●●●●●●●●●●●●●●●●●●●●●●●●●●●●●●●LEE BLESSING

CHARACTERS: HONEYMAN (45), BOTVINNIK (57)
SETTING: *A pleasant woods on the outskirts of Geneva.*

World peace flutters in the wind as the American and Soviet negotiations take a walk in the woods. The imminent U.S. election heats up HONEYMAN's *desire for a breakthrough, but* BOTVINNIK *remains cool and philosophical.*

HONEYMAN: . . . and believe me, the State Department is not going to be patient with this. We made this proposal months ago. Since then you've done nothing but argue over details.

BOTVINNIK: We are making a careful examination —

HONEYMAN: You're stalling! You're using a tiny point to hold up a major agreement.

BOTVINNIK: Tiny to you —

HONEYMAN: Tiny. To anyone. Do you want to know what the President thinks?

(BOTVINNIK *shrugs acquiescently*)

He's called me twice this week. He flew me home last week. "What's wrong with Botvinnik," he asks. "Has he said no so many times he's forgotten how to say yes?"

(BOTVINNIK *laughs*)

Well? Have you?

BOTVINNIK: You have an amusing president. I hope he does well in the election.

HONEYMAN: Whether he wins or loses will have no effect on our proposal.

BOTVINNIK (*Brushing leaves off the bench*):   Perhaps. Come, sit down. Relax.

HONEYMAN: You're purposely holding off, aren't you?

BOTVINNIK: Well . . .

HONEYMAN: The more time you waste trying for a slight advantage from our elections, the colder this proposal gets.

BOTVINNIK: So don't have so many elections. Look how bright the leaves are! I'm glad you asked me to take this walk. You said we would never do it again, but here we are.

HONEYMAN: You're not going to exploit our political process.

BOTVINNIK: Your political process exploits itself. So does our. How does your side act when our leaders are old and sick? Do you rush into negotiations? No, you wait. You *should* wait.

HONEYMAN: So when do we negotiate agreements? When there isn't a president up for election? When there isn't a Soviet leader in bad health? How often is that?

BOTVINNIK: Now and then.

HONEYMAN: Now and then? You want to discuss the life or death of this planet *now and then*?

BOTVINNIK: You think it should be more often?

HONEYMAN: Andrey, this is our best proposal to date. The President's dedicated himself to the image of peacemaker. He wants to do some lasting work. You should take advantage of that.

BOTVINNIK: I'm as sorry for the delay as you. But you must understand. Our leaders are naturally careful. The experience of the war for us was —

HONEYMAN: That was forty years ago!

EOTVINNIK: But still —

HONEYMAN: But nothing. It's a dead issue. Your country has made a state religion out of what's essentially smugness. "No one suffered the way we suffered. Twenty million died."

BOTVINNIK: Twenty million did die.

HONEYMAN: Eighty million died. All over the world. Everybody suffered. The Soviet government has no more right than anyone else to preach absolutes because of it.

BOTVINNIK: This is marvelous. I was pleased when you suggested a walk, but to find such emotion. This is very wonderful. Thank you.

HONEYMAN: Don't digress.

BOTVINNIK: I'm sorry.

HONEYMAN: My point is, any past horror, any breakdown of civilization can be used for decades thereafter by an unscrupulous government to frighten a population into impotence and obedience.

BOTVINNIK: And that is what we have done?

HONEYMAN: Yes. It is.

(BOTVINNIK *smiles, not insulted*)

Aren't you going to disagree?

BOTVINNIK: Maybe later. Go on — please.

HONEYMAN: So . . . anyway, I feel the excuse that your leaders are overcautious because of the experience of World War II is a cynical, self-serving, and manipulative . . . lie. An outdated lie at that.

(His tone has grown softer before BOTVINNIK's *open, unoffended gaze)* And I wish you wouldn't do it anymore.

BOTVINNIK: Very well. In our private conversation, I will not speak of it again.

HONEYMAN: Well . . . fine. Thank you.

BOTVINNIK: Don't mention it.

HONEYMAN: You know, I don't think your government appreciates the —

BOTVINNIK *(Holding up a bright yellow leaf):* Tell me, what kind of leaf is this?

HONEYMAN: Andrey . . .

BOTVINNIK: Just what kind? Please.

HONEYMAN: That's a linden.

BOTVINNIK: Linden. Very nice. Botany — that's your hobby. I remember from our reports on you. *(Twirling the leaf)* Yellow as sunlight, eh? Do you have these in Wisconsin?

HONEYMAN *(Sighing):* Yes. We call it basswood.

BOTVINNIK: Basswood? Like the fish?

HONEYMAN: I don't know. Andrey, I may have been a little harsh just now, but —

BOTVINNIK: It is my great regret I have never visited your country.

HONEYMAN: Thank you. All I was trying to say was —

BOTVINNIK: Your home city. What is it — Wausau? *(This he pronounces poorly — something like: Vah-sow)*

HONEYMAN: Wausau.

BOTVINNIK *(Nodding, as though their pronunciations match):* Vah-sow.

HONEYMAN: No. No, Wau-sau. Wausau, Wisconsin. Andrey, if I was harsh, it's only because —

BOTVINNIK *(Practicing it, but no better):* Vah-sow.

HONEYMAN: Andrey —

BOTVINNIK: I think I have it now: Vah-sow.

HONEYMAN *(Angrily):* Wausau! It's Wausau! You can say it, you speak English perfectly!

BOTVINNIK: I'm only trying to —

HONEYMAN: You're only trying to irritate me! I can see that! But why?! Do you feel it gives you the upper hand? It doesn't. If these talks fail, we both look bad. You realize that, don't you?

BOTVINNIK: I have failed before.

HONEYMAN: I haven't. *(A beat)* What about this tiny point? When can we expect movement from your side?

BOTVINNIK: After your election.

HONEYMAN: That's five weeks from now.

BOTVINNIK: We can only go so fast. We have hawks and doves, just like you. Sometimes the hawks eat a few doves.

HONEYMAN: This is ludicrous. The President won't accept this.

BOTVINNIK: He'll have no choice.

HONEYMAN: What if we force the matter?

BOTVINNIK: You could lose the whole proposal.

HONEYMAN: Of course you have to say that.

BOTVINNIK (*With a tone of complete frankness*):   You'll lose the proposal.

(HONEYMAN *walks away from* BOTVINNIK, *kicks at the ground angrily*)

A frustrating business, yes?

HONEYMAN: Quiet, please.

BOTVINNIK: You're upset. Perhaps you would like to be alone. I can go back now. Excuse me. (BOTVINNIK *starts out*)

HONEYMAN: Andrey.

BOTVINNIK: Yes?

HONEYMAN: If we go back so soon the reporters might think we're in trouble on this.

BOTVINNIK: We are in trouble on this.

HONEYMAN: There's no reason for *them* to think so.

BOTVINNIK: I thought you believed in freedom of the press.

HONEYMAN: Don't be cute. Come back and sit down.

BOTVINNIK (*Returning to the bench*):   What shall we talk about?

HONEYMAN: We don't have to talk about anything. We just have to wait here a decent amount of time.

BOTVINNIK: Ah.

(HONEYMAN *sits beside him. The two men stare out in different directions for a long moment*)

How are we doing?

HONEYMAN: You cold use your influence, you know. They listen to you about these things.

BOTVINNIK: Not always.

HONEYMAN: Sometimes. So why not talk to them?

BOTVINNIK: It can be risky. It could put me out of fashion with the leadership.

HONEYMAN: Out of fashion?

BOTVINNIK: It's not an insignificant risk.

(*A beat*)

HONEYMAN: Could anything induce you to take that risk?

BOTVINNIK (*His face lighting up expectantly*):   Is this a bribe?

HONEYMAN: No.

BOTVINNIK: Too bad. I never accept bribes, but I love to know what's being offered.

HONEYMAN: I mean, is there anything we can do to convince you to help. That's all I mean.

BOTVINNIK: What can the Americans do? To make me want to take chances with my career?

HONEYMAN: Yes.

BOTVINNIK: Absolutely nothing.

(HONEYMAN *gives a short sigh of frustration*)
Now ask me what you can do.

HONEYMAN: You just said. We can't —

BOTVINNIK: No, no — you. John Honeyman. What can you do to get me to help. Ask me that.

HONEYMAN (*Eyes him distrustfully*):   What . . . um, what is there I can do?

BOTVINNIK: Are you sure you want to know?

HONEYMAN: Yes, I want to know.

BOTVINNIK: Are you completely sure?

HONEYMAN: *Tell me.* What can I do?

BOTVINNIK (*Almost conspiratorial*):   Be frivolous with me.

HONEYMAN: Frivolous?

BOTVINNIK: Yes. Frivolous.

Source: New American Library

✤ Yankee Dawg You Die

●●●●●●●●●●●●●●●●●●●●●●PHILLIP KAN GOTANDA

CHARACTERS: BRADLEY (20's), VINCENT (60's)
SETTING: Santa Monica, the present.

Two Japanese-American actors debate the political and social roles their dramatic personas play in the evolution of a stereotype-free society.

BRADLEY: You seem to think that every time you do one of those demeaning roles, all that is lost is *your* dignity. That the only person who has to pay is you. You selfish son-of-a-bitch. Don't you realize that every time you do a portrayal like that millions of people in their homes, in movie theaters across the country will see it. Be influenced by it. *Believe* it. Every time you do any old stereotypic role just to pay the bills, you kill the right of some Asian American child to be treated as a human being. To walk through the school yard and not be called a "chinaman gook" by some taunting kids who just saw the last Rambo film. You kill the right of that child to be seen as he or she truly is. You? What about the rest of us. Not you. You older actors. You asked to be understood, forgiven, but you refuse to change. You have no sense of social responsibility. Only me . . . (*Continue*)
VINCENT (*Overlapping*): No . . .
BRADLEY (*Continuing*): . . . me, me. *Shame on you.* I'd never play a role like that stupid waiter in that musical. And . . . (*Continue*)
VINCENT (*Overlapping*): You don't know . . .
BRADLEY (*Continuing*): . . . I'd never let them put so much make-up on my face that I look like some goddam chimpanzee on the screen. (*Continue*)
VINCENT (*Overlapping*): You don't know . . .
BRADLEY (*Continuing*): I don't care if they paid me a million dollars what good is it to lose your dignity. I'm not going to prostitute my soul just to . . . (*Continue*)
VINCENT (*Overlapping*): There's that word. I was wondering when we'd get around to *that* word. I hate that word! I HATE THAT WORD!
BRADLEY (*Continuing*): . . . see myself on screen if I have to go grunting around like some slant-eyed animal. I'm only going to

do roles that are dignified. You probably wouldn't know a good role if it grabbed you by the balls!

VINCENT: I have played many good roles.

BRADLEY: Sure, waiters, viet cong killers, chimpanzees, drug dealers, hookers, sexless houseboys . . .

VINCENT (*Interrupts*): I was the first to be nominated for an academy award.

BRADLEY: Oh, it's pull-out-the-old-credits time. But what about some of the TV stuff you've been doing lately. Jesus, TV! At least in the movies we're still dangerous. But TV? They fucking cut off our balls and made us all house boys on the evening soaps. What is this, some new kind of fad? (*Calling out*) 'Get your very own neutered, oriental houseboy!'

VINCENT: I got the woman once.

(BRADLEY *doesn't understand*)

In a movie. I got the woman.

BRADLEY: Sure.

VINCENT: And she was white.

BRADLEY: 'Missy Collins, here's ya champagne. Don't mind me. You and massa go on screwing in the bubble bath. I'm a eunech.'

VINCENT: And I kissed her!

BRADLEY: You're so full of it.

VINCENT: ON THE LIPS! ON THE LIPS!

BRADLEY: What, a little peck on the cheek?

VINCENT: *I GOT THE WOMAN.*

BRADLEY: Nah.

VINCENT: Yes.

BRADLEY: Nah?

VINCENT: YES. (*Pause.* VINCENT *moving to seat himself at a table*)

BRADLEY (*Pondering*): When was this? In the 30's. Before the war? (*Continue*)

VINCENT (*Overlapping*): No.

BRADLEY (*Continuing*): Because accidents like that happened back then. After the war forget it. Mr. Moto even disappeared and he wasn't even played by a Japanese. It was Peter Lorre.

VINCENT: No, no. This was the 50's.

BRADLEY: Come on, you're kidding.

VINCENT: 1959. A cop movie. (*Correcting himself*) Film. "The Scarlet Kimono". Directed by Sam Fuller. Set in L.A. 2 police detectives, one Japanese American and one caucasian. A white woman, they both love. And a murder.

BRADLEY: Yeah . . . I remember. And there's this violent kendo fight between you two guys because you both want the woman. (*Realizing*) And you get the woman.

VINCENT: See, I told you.

(*Pause.* BRADLEY *seating himself*)

BRADLEY: Except when I saw it you didn't kiss her. I mean I would have remembered something like that. An Asian man and a white woman. You didn't kiss her.

VINCENT: TV?

(BRADLEY *nods.* VINCENT *making the realization*)

They edited it out.

Source: Dramatists Play Service, Inc.

✥ Zero Positive

HARRY KONDOLEON

CHARACTERS: HIMMER (20's-30's), PATRICK (20's-30's)
SETTING: HIMMER's *father's Upper West Side apartment, New York, August, 1987.*

HIMMER *is an acerbic, pampered young man who works for* Life *magazine. He lives with his father, and they have just suffered the loss of* HIMMER's *mother, who was estranged from her husband.* HIMMER *is a well-adjusted homosexual, but he has recently received the unsettling news that a close female friend of his has tested positive for the AIDS virus.*

(HIMMER *is sitting on the couch. He is having lunch with his friend* PATRICK. *The air conditioner is still on.* PATRICK *is an actor, good-looking but banal, one of a million. As he will go mad in this scene, it is important he start with a place to build, gradually becoming furious, making little peaks and valleys of emotional outburst before falling off the top*)

HIMMER: More salad, Patrick?
PATRICK: It's delicious! Oh, I've dirtied another plate.
HIMMER: That's okay, there are lots.
PATRICK: Which is my glass? I'm drinking out of every glass.
HIMMER: It doesn't matter, they're all yours. I'm just chewing gum, I'm not hungry. Tell me about your new film.
PATRICK: I'm not in it, I'm just up for it.
HIMMER: You're up for it. That means you're auditioning and hope to get it, right?
PATRICK: I'm perfect for it, but you know the casting people are very narrow. Very narrow. So, how are you doin'?
HIMMER: I'm not very well.
PATRICK: You're sick?
HIMMER: No, I'm not sick.

(PATRICK *is suddenly singing, lots of energy, musical-comedy style. The song wavers between furiously happy and stagy shyness. Who is he singing to? His eyes are focused on everything and nothing*)

PATRICK: Hey! Aren't you the one I've been looking for?
Hey girl! I think it's you, yeah.
Woke up in the morning

Had no warning
Took a shower
Picked a flower
Said howdy-do to the people I met
My life I figured was all set.

Walked on, yeah, I walked on
What was I looking for?
What was I looking for?
Hey, nothing! Nothing till I found you.
You girl, yeah you girl.
Popped into my life!
Took me by surprise!
Just about my size —
Took you for my wife!
Took a second to realize, girl
You're the one I'd been looking for
Without knowing what I'd been looking for.

Oh, now I feel twice as good
Kinda knew I would
Drifting around like wood
You threw me in the fire
Hmmm, that warm desire
Now when I take a shower
Or I pick of flower
Hmmm, it's for you girl
Hmmm, I think it's you girl.

HIMMER (*After a slight pause*):   My goodness, what's that?

PATRICK: It's my song. What do you think, fantastic, right? My voice teacher can't believe how far along I've come. I'm one of those people who never thought they could sing who really can. It's important to have an audition song at your fingertips you can just leap up and do whenever you have an opportunity. (*Singing suddenly again, peppy*) Took me by surprise! (*Winking*) Just about my size! (*Stopping*) What do you think?

HIMMER: Well, it's very moon and spoon.

PATRICK (*Happily, uncomprehending*):   Yeah, it is, right. I wrote it myself. I figured I didn't want to screw around with copyright and all, you know, if something takes off.

HIMMER: How are your children?

PATRICK: Why did you ask me that?

HIMMER: I wondered how they were.

PATRICK: They're fine. It's a very small part, but that's all I go up for these days is very small parts. I'm between age groups. I'm too old to play a teenager and too young to play an old man. And in TV, film and theatre they're very narrow. They admit it, they say they're very narrow. I go to an audition and I'm brilliant, I mean it, *drop-dead brilliant*. I know it, it's not an opinion. My cues are superb. I'm incapable of uttering a false word. I'm tops in emotional guns! A relative of Stella Adler told me she'd never seen physical work like mine. I'm a natural that way. My childhood was very athletic. I fence. I dive. I ski. I can climb ropes. I can shoot a pistol. I can do modern dance. I have an appreciation for the ballet. *Why won't my career take off*?!

HIMMER: Patrick, I really don't know the answer to that question. Would you like a cookie? Actually one of the reasons I thought it might be fun to have lunch together today was that I accidentally unearthed these little sliver of plays I guess my mother wrote at school and then forgot about and you're the only person I know in theatre and all so I thought I might show one to you and get your opinion, find out if it's possible to maybe put it on somewhere in some way.

PATRICK: Your mom just passed away, right?

HIMMER: That's right, recently.

PATRICK: And here I am going on about my career. I must make you sick to your stomach.

HIMMER: Not at all, I'm interested in all that stuff, it's like a foreign country to me. You know in my job all I do is paste pieces of paper together.

PATRICK: Oh, I know what you do, you're great! I just have to get a foothold, you know, just a foothold! They have you hanging on my your teeth, from a ledge, for years. What do they want, blood? My balls? What do they want? Do you know?!

HIMMER: No, no, I don't know.

PATRICK: No. How was the funeral? Was there a funeral?

HIMMER: Oh, yeah, it was okay, nothing special.

PATRICK: Right. I've got a good face, the camera likes my face, *a lot*. There was this book written by a big wheel in Hollywood, he said there was a day you could throw a stick and hit ten Robert Redfords on the beach in Malibu. Ten of them, a hundred, and then *Butch Cassidy* came out and he's on the cover of *Life* — your magazine.

HIMMER: It's not my magazine, I just —

PATRICK: One hundred Robert Redfords standing around Malibu, you just had to throw a stick! And I haven't even been to Malibu.

HIMMER: It's nothing.

PATRICK: I haven't been anywhere! And why because every nickel goes to my two children and don't get me wrong — I love my boy and girl — I mean two girls — I love them, but the truth is I don't even know them. I had my divorce in the maternity ward. I wouldn't recognize them if the two of them flew into the room this second!

HIMMER: Patrick, I seem to have a little headache, maybe it would be better if we another time —

PATRICK (*Suddenly this is an audition for him, this event, imbued with all life-and-death terror*):   No, no! No! Show me your mother's thing. Where is it, her play, what's it called?

HIMMER (*Handing it to him with reservations*):   Here. That's the best of the bunch.

PATRICK: *The Ruins of Athens*.That's not a good title. It's not commercial. I have to be straight with you, Himmy, the first thing you'll have to do is come up with something else. I work with these people so I know. I walk up and down Times Square all day so I know. The titles defy your eyes. *My Pussy Is on Fire* — that's new, a huge hit. Maybe I should do porn. I've got the body. I have an excellent body and a nice penis. I can keep an erection for hours. I shock my girlfriends. And I don't have to come until I'm told to, I just say tell me when you want me to come and then I come. I swim. I box. I do situps while I'm waiting for my tub to fill. (*Frightened suddenly by the trains, which are still*) What are all these toys in here?

HIMMER: They're my father's.

PATRICK: Is he senile? That's my big fear.

HIMMER: He has sort of lost his mind a bit. He's sort of skipped to another place in time, with my mother apparently. But that's so long ago I don't remember them together. Although he thinks I'm a little boy. It's weird, everything juggled up. I find him more lovable now, though, more tender. I never cared for his poems. I'm reading them all again. I like them.

PATRICK: I can do backflips, cartwheels, somersaults. (*Suddenly PATRICK's attempting one or more of these feats; if he can do them, fine, if not, the attempt will do. Either way he may collapse with exhaustion and/or frustration*)

HIMMER: Patrick! Patrick, take it easy. What are you doing. Take it easy now.

PATRICK (*Out of breath*):   I used to walk on a rope. I was so balanced. Help me, help me somehow.

HIMMER: How can I help you, Patrick, I called you up for your help.

PATRICK: That's right, that's right, and I can give it to you. You want to put your mom's play on, that makes sense. You miss her, you were very close.

HIMMER: Actually no, she lived alone in the woods and drank a lot.

PATRICK: That's my big fear. (PATRICK *quickly drinks — downs — whatever is left in the glasses on the table — iced tea, water, vermouth, whatever is there, like a man in the desert at a mirage*)

HIMMER: She lived with two gay guys who got depressed and drowned themselves.

PATRICK: She liked gay guys, then why didn't she like you?

HIMMER: She did like me, a lot, she just drank and we lost touch with each other. Why do you say that?

PATRICK: Nothing. I came from a strict family. A strict religious household where nothing was permitted, nothing. We had to sit still and wait, for everything. I'm tired of waiting! I don't want to wait anymore! What am I waiting for! I went up for *The Big Knife* — I'm perfect for it — I could've written the part! I get the call, you're not right for it. (*Between his teeth*) I'm telling you if there's a human being right for it I'm right for it! I'd kill the fuckin' bastards if I could just see them! (*He twirls around in place in one frantic sweep to see no one is around him, and then suddenly speaks more calmly*) I'm up for *The Screens*. That's hardly ever done. Lots of Algerians. Jean Genet, you know. What do you think? Do you think I have a chance at it?

HIMMER: Patrick, you should go home now. I recently got some very bad news and I misjudged my ability to have company, okay?

PATRICK (*Distracted, talking to no one*):   No, no, let me stay just a little bit longer. Please, I'll stay. You're upset about your mom. How did her friends drown themselves, the two fellows?

HIMMER (*Uncomfortable cooperating*):   In a pond.

PATRICK (*Logical*):   Now, what we have to do is think of the name of this gal I know who just came into a large fortune from some brouhaha with her family's estate. She's a millionairess, a frustrated something-or-other, art lover, just have to think of her name and then you call her. She'll go for it, yeah. She'll put on your mom's show. When I think of her name I'll tell you.

HIMMER: Patrick, I really have to go to sleep now. I want to take a nap.

PATRICK (*Deaf*):   I come from a strict household religious.

HIMMER: Strict what? What religion? Catholic? Protestant? Jewish? Buddhist? Strict what?

PATRICK: Strict nothing. You don't understand. My father disapproves of me and I take money from him to feed my children. I take money from an old man! I'm a failure!

HIMMER: No, you're not.

PATRICK (*Picking up a penknife from a table*):   What's this?

HIMMER: A penknife. It was my mother's, in with her things.

(PATRICK *uses the penknife to point, to become deliberately pedantic and lend, he thinks, some dignity to the points he makes*)

PATRICK: They are the devils. The evil devils. I swear on your mother's grave, devils walk the earth and they pray to their greedy god called Personal Gain and everything is sacrificed to its big fat mouth. Now, I'm an actor so I don't know your career but you can make an analogy to your experience at *Life*, everything is cutthroat, I know that, I'm not getting special bad treatment. But there are certain arenas where one is led to suspect beauty of spirit will rule the day and if not why then do the devils that tread there pick such a puny arena to pitch their tents? *What a bright nice fire!* I'll say when I watch them burn. And I will. I'll come back from the dead if I have to and chew on the devils' throats . . . I cannot get a job, I cannot get a job.

HIMMER: Patrick.

(*The shock of hearing his own name jolts to mind the name* PATRICK *has been trying to remember. With every utterance of her name he jabs the penknife into his left wrist, up and down quickly and violently as if to accomplish a task and switching hands quickly to accomplish the right wrist with one quick stroke before dropping the implement and staring wildly up, crying out horrified as if an entirely different soul committed the violence, crying and shaking*)

PATRICK: Deborah Fine! Deborah Fine! Deborah Fine!

HIMMER: What are you doing?

(*Blood pouring out of* PATRICK's *wrists gets all over* HIMMER's *white shirt.* PATRICK *staggers about hysterical, going into shock*)

PATRICK: Call Deborah Fine. Call Deborah Fine.

HIMMER (*Running out of the room*):   I'm calling an ambulance.

PATRICK (*Before collapsing to the floor*):   Someone call Deborah Fine. Call Debbie Fine. One good nude scene and I could make it. Make a name for myself. One. Nude. Scene.

Source: Dramatists Play Service, Inc.

ACKNOWLEDGEMENTS

Caution: The use of excerpts contained in this volume must be confined to study and reference. They are fully protected under the copyright laws of the United States of America, the British Empire, the Dominion of Canada, and of all countries covered by the International Copyright Union, the Pan-American Copyright Convention and the Universal Copyright Convention, and of all countries with which the United States has reciprocal copyright relations. All rights, including professional, amateur, motion picture, recitation, lecturing, public reading, radio broadcasting, television, video, or sound taping, all other forms of mechanical reproduction, such as information storage and retrieval systems and photocopying, and the rights of translation into foreign languages, are strictly reserved. Particular emphasis is laid upon the question of readings, permission for which must be secured from the authors' agents in writing. If no agent is listed, inquiry should be sent to the publisher or directly to the author.

Grateful acknowledgement is made for permission to reprint excerpts from copyrighted material:

AMERICAN NOTES by Len Jenkin. Copyright © 1988 by Len Jenkin. Reprinted by permission of the author and Dramatists Play Service, Inc. No stock or amateur performances of the play may be given without obtaining in advance the written permission of the Dramatists Play Service, Inc., and paying the requisite fee. All inquiries should be addressed to Dramatists Play Service, Inc., 440 Park Avenue South, New York, NY 10016.

APOCALYPTIC BUTTERFLIES by Wendy MacLeod. Copyright © 1989 by Wendy MacLeod. Reprinted by permission of the author's agent, Helen Merrill, 435 West 23rd Street, #1A, New York, NY 10011.

AWAY by Michael Gow. Copyright © 1986 by Michael Gow. Reprinted by permission of the author's agent, Nellie Flannery, The Robyn Gardiner Agency, P.O. Box 128, Surry Hill, 2010, Australia.

BEIRUT by Alan Bowne. Copyright © 1994 by Alan Bowne. Reprinted by permission of the William Morris Agency, Inc. on behalf of the author. Originally produced on the off-Broadway stage by Barbara Darwall and Peter von Mayrhauser. Inquiries concerning rights should be addressed to William Morris Agency, Inc., 1350 Avenue of the Americas, New York, NY 10019, Attn: Peter Franklin.

A BETROTHAL by Lanford Wilson. Copyright © 1986 by Lanford Wilson. Reprinted by permission of the author's agent, Bridget Aschenberg, International Creative Management, Inc., 40 West 57th Street, New York, NY 10019. The amateur production rights in A BETROTHAL are controlled by the Dramatists Play Service, Inc., 440 Park Avenue South, New York, NY 10016. No amateur performance of the play may be given without obtaining in advance the written permission of the Dramatists Play Service, Inc., and paying the requisite fee.

BEYOND YOUR COMMAND by Ralph Pape. Copyright © 1994 by Ralph Pape. Reprinted by permission of the William Morris Agency, Inc. on behalf of the author. Inquiries concerning rights should be addressed to William Morris Agency, Inc., 1350 Avenue of the Americas, New York, NY 10019, Attn: Peter Franklin.

BIG TIME by Keith Reddin. Copyright © 1988 by Keith Reddin. Reprinted by permission of the author.

BORDERLINE by John Bishop. Copyright © 1989 by John Bishop, Inc. Reprinted by permission of the author and Dramatists Play Service, Inc. No stock or amateur performances of the play may be given without obtaining in advance the written permission of the Dramatists Play Service, Inc., and paying the requisite fee. All inquiries should be addressed to Dramatists Play Service, Inc., 440 Park Avenue South, New York, NY 10016.

THE BOYS NEXT DOOR by Tom Griffin. Copyright ©1988 by Tom Griffin. Copyright © 1983 by Tom Griffin under the title "Damaged Hearts, Broken Flowers". Reprinted by permission of the author. The stage performance rights in THE BOYS NEXT DOOR (other than first class rights) are controlled exclusively by Dramatists Play Service, Inc., 440 Park Avenue South, New York, NY 10016. No professional or non-professional performance of the play (excluding first class professional performance) may be given without obtaining in advance the written permission of the Dramatists Play Service, Inc., and paying the requisite fee. Inquiries concerning all other rights should be addressed to Gilbert Parker, c/o William Morris Agency, Inc., 1350 Avenue of the Americas, New York, NY 10019.

BRILLIANT TRACES by Cindy Lou Johnson. Copyright © 1986, 1988 by Cindy Lou Johnson. Reprinted by permission of the author's agent, Jeannine Edmunds, The Artist Agency, 230 West 55th Street, Suite 29D, New York, NY 10019.

BURN THIS by Lanford Wilson. Copyright © 1987, 1988 by Lanford Wilson. Reprinted by permission of Hill and Wang, a division of Farrar, Straus and Giroux, Inc., 19 Union Square West, New York, NY 10003, and by permission of the author's agent, Bridget Aschenberg, International Creative Management, Inc., 40 West 57th Street, New York, NY 10019.

THE COCKTAIL HOUR by A.R.Gurney. Copyright © 1989 by A.R.Gurney. Reprinted by permission of the author. The play was first produced in New York by Roger L. Stevens, Thomas Viertel, Steven Baruch, and Richard Frankel. The world premiere at The Old Globe Theatre, San Diego, California (Artistic Director Jack O'Brien; Managing Director Thomas Hall. All inquiries concerning English language stock and amateur performing rights should be directed to the Dramatists Play Service, Inc., 440 Park Avenue South, New York, NY 10016. Inquiries concerning all other rights should be addressed to the William Morris Agency, Inc., 1350 Avenue of the Americas, New York, NY 10019, Attn: Gilbert Parker.

COYOTE UGLY by Lynn Siefert. Copyright © 1986 by Lynn Siefert. Reprinted by permission of the author's agent, David S. Singer, 1560 Broadway, Suite 800, New York, NY 10036.

A CRITIC AND HIS WIFE by John Ford Noonan. Copyright © 1994 by John Ford Noonan. Reprinted by permission of the author. Inquiries should be directed to 484 West 43rd Street, #46-G, New York, NY 10036.

DRIVING MISS DAISY by Alfred Uhry. Copyright © 1986, 1987 by Alfred Uhry. Reprinted by permission of the author and Dramatists Play Service, Inc. No stock or amateur performances of the play may be given without obtaining in advance the written permission of the Dramatists Play Service, Inc., and paying the requisite fee. All inquiries should be addressed to Dramatists Play Service, Inc., 440 Park Avenue South, New York, NY 10016.

EMERALD CITY by David Williamson. Copyright © 1987 by David Williamson. Reprinted by permission of Currency Press Pty. Ltd., P.O. Box 452, Paddington N.S.W. 2121, Australia, and by permission of Applause Theatre Book Publishers, 211 West 71st Street, New York, NY 10023.

526

John Horvath, a native of Wallingford Connecticut, received his Master's Degree in Directing from Emerson College and his Bachelor of Arts degree in Theatre from Southern Connecticut State College. He has studied acting and directing at Rider College in Lawrenceville, New Jersey, where he also taught two musical theatre courses. As an actor and director, Mr. Horvath has served with various regional, stock and university theatre companies, including the New Amsterdam Theatre Company on Broadway. Many singers, actors and periodicals continue to consult him for his knowledge of musical theatre technique. Mr. Horvath would like to thank his parents for their continued support and encouragement.

Lavonne Mueller is the Director of the Playwright's Workshop at the University of Iowa. She has also served as an instructor at Columbia University and at other universities through the Woodrow Wilson Visiting Scholar Award. Her plays include *Letters to a Daughter from Prison*, which was first produced at the First International Festival of the Arts in New York City and then in India. *Violent Peace* was produced in London in 1992 and was named *Time Out* magazine's Critic's Choice. Ms. Mueller, a Woodrow Wilson Scholar and Lila Wallace Reader's Digest Writing fellow, received the John F. Kennedy Playwriting Award in 1992. She has been awarded grants from The National Endowment for the Arts, Guggenheim and Rockefeller Foundations. Fulbright Fellowships have enabled her to work abroad in Argentina and Jordan; the Asia Culture Council and U.S. Friendship concerns have supported her work in India and Japan. Ms. Mueller is also the author of the text-book *Creative Writing*, which continues to be used by students around the world.

Jack Temchin produced *El Grande de Coca-Cola* which ran for 1500 performances in New York City. He also produced the film *Home Movies*, which was directed by Brian DePalma. He was Associate Artistic Director of the Manhattan Theatre Club and is now an Artistic Consultant there. Mr. Temchin has written for both television and films. His most recent book, *One on One: Best Monologues for the 90's* was published by Applause Books in 1993.

ONE ON ONE

BEST MONOLOGUES
FOR THE 90'S
Edited by Jack Temchin

You have finally met your match in Jack Temchin's new collection, *One on One*. Somewhere among the 150 monologues Temchin has recruited, a voice may beckon to you—strange and alluring—waiting for your own voice to give it presence on stage.

"The sad truth about most monologue books," says Temchin, "is that they don't give actors enough credit. I've compiled my book for serious actors with a passionate appetite for the unknown."

Among the selections:

David Mamer OLEANNA
Richard Greenberg THE AMERICAN PLAN
Brian Friel DANCING AT LUGHNASA
John Patrick Shanley THE BIG FUNK
Terrence McNally LIPS TOGETHER, TEETH APART
Neil Simon LOST IN YONKERS
David Hirson LA BETE
Herb Gardner CONVERSATIONS
WITH MY FATHER
Ariel Dorfman DEATH AND THE MAIDEN
Alan Ayckborn A SMALL FAMILY BUSINESS

MEN: ISBN: 1-55783-151-3
WOMEN: ISBN: 1-55783-152-1

SOLILOQUY!

The Shakespeare Monologues
Edited by Michael Earley and Philippa Keil

At last, over 175 of Shakespeare's finest and most performable monologues taken from all 37 plays are here in two easy-to-use volumes (MEN and WOMEN). Selections travel the entire spectrum of the great dramatist's vision, from comedies and romances to tragedies, pathos and histories.

"Soliloquy is an excellent and comprehensive collection of Shakespeare's speeches. Not only are the monologues wide-ranging and varied, but they are superbly annotated. Each volume is prefaced by an informative and reassuring introduction, which explains the signals and signposts by which Shakespeare helps an actor on his journey through the text. It includes a very good explanation of blank verse, with excellent examples of irregularities which are specifically related to character and acting intentions. These two books are a must for any actor in search of a 'classical' audition piece."

ELIZABETH SMITH
Head of Voice & Speech
The Juilliard School

paper•MEN: ISBN 0-936839-78-3
WOMEN: ISBN 0936839-79-1

APPLAUSE

SHAKESCENES: SHAKESPEARE FOR TWO

The Shakespeare Scenebook

EDITED AND WITH AN INTRODUCTION BY JOHN RUSSELL BROWN

Thirty-five scenes are presented in newly edited texts, with notes which clarify meanings, topical references, puns, ambiguities, etc.

Each scene has been chosen for its independent life requiring only the simplest of stage properties and the barest of spaces.

A brief description of characters and situation prefaces each scene and is followed by a commentary which discusses its major acting challenges and opportunities.

paper ∎ ISBN 1-55783-049-5

APPLAUSE

MONOLOGUE WORKSHOP

From Search to Discovery
in Audition and Performance

by Jack Poggi

To those for whom the monologue has always been synonymous with terror, *The Monologue Workshop* will prove an indispensable ally. Jack Poggi's new book answers the long-felt need among actors for top-notch guidance in finding, rehearsing and performing monologues. For those who find themselves groping for speech just hours before their "big break," this book is their guide to salvation.

The Monologue Workshop supplies the tools to discover new pieces before they become over-familiar, excavate older material that has been neglected, and adapt material from non-dramatic sources (novels, short stories, letters, diaries, autobiographies, even newspaper columns). There are also chapters on writing original monologues and creating solo performances in the style of Lily Tomlin and Eric Bogosian.

Besides the wealth of practical advice he offers, Poggi transforms the monologue experience from a terrifying ordeal into an exhilarating opportunity. Jack Poggi, as many working actors will attest, is the actor's partner in a process they had always thought was without one.

paper•ISBN 1-55783-031-2 • $12.95

APPLAUSE